Complete England

RED GUIDE

Complete England

Edited by Reginald J. W. Hammond F.R.G.S.

WARD LOCK LIMITED

116 Baker Street, London W1M 2BB

Town plans reproduced by kind permission of Map Productions Limited.
Based upon the Ordnance Survey map with the sanction of the Controller of
H.M. Stationery Office.

Text filmset by Typesetting Services Limited, Glasgow.

Printed and bound by Editorial Fher SA, Bilbao, Spain.

Contents

CONTENTS

CONTENTS

Town Plans

THE RED GUIDES

Edited by Reginald J. W. Hammond

Barmouth and
   District

Bournemouth,
   New Forest

Channel Islands

Cornwall : North

Cornwall : South

Cornwall : West

Cotswolds

Dorset Coast

Isle of Man

Isle of Wight

Lake District

Llandudno,
   Colwyn Bay

London

Norfolk & the Broads

Peak District

South Devon

South Wales

Wales N.
   (Northn. Section)

Wales N.
   (Southn. Section)

Wye Valley

Northern Ireland

SCOTLAND

Edinburgh and
   District

Highlands of
   Scotland

Northern Scotland

Western Scotland

RED TOURIST GUIDES

Complete England

Complete Scotland

Complete Ireland

Complete Wales

Lake District
   (Baddeley)

Complete Devon

Complete West
   Country

Complete South-East
   Coast

Complete Yorkshire

Complete Scottish
   Lowlands

Complete Cotswolds
   and Shakespeare
   Country

WARD LOCK LIMITED

Introduction

This is a Guide to all England in that all the territory has been considered for reportage. However, since a quart cannot be contained within a pint pot, the editor has been obliged to make his choice not so much as to what should be included, but rather what, without prejudice, should be omitted. An honest endeavour nonetheless has been made to include everything of note and of interest to the visitor.

The acknowledged tourist regions and visitor movements have been taken into consideration and the Guide has been arranged with these in mind. Thus a visitor to any chosen centre will have on hand references to all the principal places and items of interest within the compass of a walk or drive from that centre.

Accommodation in England ranges from luxury hotels to modest bed and breakfast facilities in private houses. The names of some of the principal establishments in various grades, and known to give good service, are noted in the Guide. There are of course very many more and the omission of a name in the lists carries no inference concerning that establishment. Most local authorities issue comprehensive lists of accommodation within their areas and these may be obtained from the Town Clerks or Information Offices concerned. Both the Royal Automobile Club and the Automobile Association issue lists of recommended establishments to their motorist members. During the holiday season accommodation in the main centres and holiday resorts is at a premium and advance reservation is advisable if at all possible.

YOUR HELP IS REQUESTED

A GREAT part of the success of this series is due, as we gratefully acknowledge, to the enthusiastic co-operation of readers. Changes take place, both in town and country, with such rapidity that it is difficult, even for the most alert and painstaking staff, to keep pace with them all, and the correspondents who so kindly take the trouble to inform us of alterations that come under their notice in using the books, render a real service not only to us but to their fellow-readers. We confidently appeal for further help of this kind.

THE EDITOR

WARD LOCK LIMITED
116, BAKER STREET,
LONDON, W.1

London

The area defined by the Registrar-General for census purposes as Greater London covers 720 square miles and has a population of slightly under eight millions. The principal and larger part lies to the north of the river *Thames*. Fortunately for the visitor the major sights are confined to a relatively small central area consisting of the so-called West End and of the ancient City.

Royal London

Banqueting House (Whitehall, S.W.1). One of few remaining parts of old Whitehall Palace, and outstanding example of work of Inigo Jones. Cromwell held his parliaments here. The painted ceiling by Rubens is notable. Weekdays 10–5, Suns in summer.

Buckingham Palace (The Mall, S.W.1). The London residence of the British Sovereign. Rebuilt by Nash in 1825 and refaced in 1913 in Portland Stone from designs by Sir Aston Webb. The Royal Mews are open Weds 2–5 and additionally Thurs in summer, 2–4. The Queen's Gallery is in reconstructed private chapel as art gallery, daily except Mons 11–5, Suns 2–5.

Clarence House (Stable Yard, St. Jame's, S.W.1). London residence of Queen Elizabeth, the Queen Mother, built 1825 for William IV, the Duke of Clarence.

Hampton Court Palace (Hampton Court). Stately palace built by Cardinal Wolsey and given to Henry VIII. There are about 1,000 rooms, most of which are occupied by royal pensioners. State Apartments with pictures, furniture, tapestries; Great Vine, Maze, Great Hall, Great Kitchen and Cellars, Orangery, open throughout the year from 9.30. Tudor Tennis Court and Banqueting House, Apr.–Sept. only. Gardens daily.

Houses of Parliament (Parliament Square, S.W.1). The building, completed in 1857, is in rich Gothic style and occupies an area of eight acres. The designs of Sir Charles Barry were accepted after the destruction by fire of St. Stephens Chapel, the former meeting place of the House of Commons for over 300 years. The Clock Tower is 316 feet high. Big Ben, the hour bell, weighs 13½ tons. The great Victoria Tower is 323 feet high and 75 feet square. In the House of Lords Chamber is the Sovereign's throne and facing it the Woolsack, on which the Lord Chancellor sits. The House of Commons chamber was designed after bomb damage by Sir Giles Gilbert Scott. The Palace of Westminster is open on Sats, Easter Mon. and Tues, Spring and Summer Bank Hols and Tues, all Mons, Tues and Thurs in Aug., and Thurs in Sept. (when House is not sitting), 10–4.30. For debates in House of Lords from 2.40, Tues and Weds and from 3.10 on Thurs—in House of Commons from 4.15 (Fri. 11.30).

Jewel Tower (Westminster, S.W.1). Restored fragment of the Old Palace of Westminster dating from 14*c*. Moat. Open throughout the year 10–4.30 or 6.30.

Kensington Palace (Kensington Gardens, W.8). William III house reconstructed by Wren and Kent. Birthplace of both Queen Victoria and Queen Mary. Now "Grace and Favour Residences" and occupied in part by the London Museum.

Lambeth Palace (Lambeth Palace Road, S.E.1). For over 700 years the London residence of the Archbishops of Canterbury. Gatehouse built in 1490, Lollards Tower in 1436. Ancient chapel restored after war damage. Great Hall open daily, except Suns 10–5.

Marlborough House (Pall Mall, S.W.1). Built by Wren in 1709 for the Duke of Marlborough and later a Royal residence. Now a Commonwealth centre. Easter–Oct., conducted tours at 12.30, 1.30 and 3.30. Weekends and Bank Hols, 2–6. The Queen's chapel is always open.

Palace of Westminster. See Houses of Parliament.

St. James's Palace (St. James's Street, S.W.1). "Our Court of St. James's" to which foreign ambassadors and ministers are still accredited. No longer the sovereign's official residence though part (York House) often used by members of Royal Family. Services in Chapel Royal on Sunday mornings in winter open to public.

Tower of London (Tower Hill, E.C.3). The fortress, including the Moat, now drained, occupies an irregular pentagon of 18 acres, the circuit of the outer walls being nearly two-thirds of a mile. The central Keep or White Tower dates from 1078. Overlooking river is St. Thomas's Tower, with Traitors Gate beneath it. The chapel of St. John is one of the most perfect specimens of Norman architecture extant. Armouries, Crown Jewels, Gun Wharf. The picturesque State Dress uniform of the Yeoman Warders has remained unchanged since the reign of Henry VII. Weekdays from 10; Suns (May–Oct. only) from 2.

Westminster Hall (Parliament Square, S.W.1). From 1224 until 1882 the Law Courts were held here. The scene of the trial of Charles I and of the proclamation of Cromwell as Lord Protector. Hall begun by William Rufus in 1097 and rebuilt by Richard II in 1397. Notable oak roof. Weekdays 10–4. When House sitting closes one hour before House meets.

Pageantry

Military. Troops usually stationed in London are the Household Cavalry at Knightsbridge Barracks; the King's Troop, Royal Horse Artillery at Regent's Park Barracks; and battalions of the Guards at Wellington Barracks (St. James's Park) and Chelsea Barracks. In summer the Guards full dress is scarlet tunic and blue trousers, and the various regiments may be distinguished from the plumes in the bearskin caps and by tunic button spacing. The Grenadier Guards wear a white plume; the Coldstream Guards, red; the Irish Guards, blue; the Welsh Guards, white with strip of green; the Scots Guards, none. The Foot Guards furnish the Queen's Guard (Palace sentries). Mounted escorts are provided by the Household Cavalry of Life Guards (red tunics and white plumes) and the Royal Horse Guards (blue tunics and red plumes).

Changing of the Guard. Buckingham Palace. Daily at 11.30. Horse Guards. Weekdays at 11, Suns 10.

Trooping the Colour (Horse Guards Parade, S.W.1) Annual ceremony on Sovereign's birthday in June.

Ceremony of the Keys (Tower of London). Ancient ceremony that has taken place nightly (9.40–10) for over 700 years. Written application necessary to Constable's Office.

MAJOR SIGHTS

Bank of England (Threadneedle Street, E.C.2). Fortress-like building between Threadneedle Street, Princes Street, Lothbury and Bartholomew Lane. A military guard is mounted nightly. Entrance Hall only open to public.

Chelsea Royal Hospital (Royal Hospital Road, S.W.3). Wren-designed buildings occupied by the Chelsea Pensioners. Great Hall with interesting portraits, museum, grounds. Weekdays 10–12, 2–6, Suns 2–6. Chapel service, Suns 10.50.

County Hall (Westminster Bridge, S.E.1). English Renaissance-style building, headquarters of the Greater London Council.

Dickens House (48 Doughty Street, W.C.1). Dickens lived here from 1837–39 writing final parts of "Pickwick Papers", "Nicholas Nickleby" and "Oliver Twist". Museum of relics. Weekdays 10–12.30, 2–5.

Discovery (Victoria Embankment, W.C.2). Jointly with nearby HMS *Crysanthemum*, headquarters of the London Division of the R.N.V.R. The ship was used by Captain Scott as a research vessel during the National Antarctic Expedition in 1901. Daily 1–4.45.

Dr. Johnson's House (17 Gough Square, Fleet Street, E.C.4). Dr. Johnson lived here from 1748–1759 and toiled over his great Dictionary. Manuscripts, autographs, first editions, etc. Weekdays, 10.30–5.

Guildhall (King Street, Cheapside, E.C.4). Civic Hall of the Corporation of London. The Great Hall, restored after war damage, is used for the annual election of the Lord Mayor and Sheriffs and for many civic and political gatherings. Library, museum, art gallery. Weekdays 10–5.

Keats House and Museum (Wentworth Place, Keats Grove, N.W.3). Keats wrote the ode "To a Nightingale" in the garden here. Weekdays 10–6. Keats Memorial Library in adjoining library.

Kenwood (Hampstead, N.W.3). The mansion is fine example of work of Robert Adam. Iveagh Bequest of furniture and pictures. Extensive gardens, concerts. Weekdays from 10, Suns from 2. To north-east are the beautiful Highgate woods. To south-west is Hampstead Heath (320 acres) with extensive views.

Lancaster House (St. James's, S.W.1). Presented to the nation by late Lord Leverhulme for housing the London Museum and for provision of a centre for Government hospitality. The main museum collections have been moved to Kensington Palace, and Lancaster House is now used for International conferences and by visiting Government guests. Open Easter–Dec. on Sats, Suns and Bank Hols, 2–6.

Law Courts (Strand, W.C.2). Monastic Gothic-style building of the Royal Courts of Justice. Central Hall with fine rose window in the gable. The public galleries of the courts are open Mon.–Fri., 10–4. In roadway is Temple Bar, marking an ancient portal to the City of London.

Madame Tussaud's (Maryleborne Road, N.W.1). Famous waxwork exhibition of famous and infamous people. 10–5.30 (6.30 Apr.–Sept.). Adjoining is the Planetarium.

Mansion House (Bank, E.C.3). The official residence of the Lord Mayor with fine Corinthian portico. Fine Egyptian Hall. Alternate Sat. afternoons on written application.

Old Bailey (Newgate Street, E.C.4). Central Criminal Court on site of old Newgate Prison. Public gallery, weekdays 10.15 and 1.45. Conducted parties on days when courts not sitting at 11 and 3.

Planetarium (Marylebone Road, N.W.1) A projector throws a realistic reproduction of the ever-changing night sky as seen from any point on the

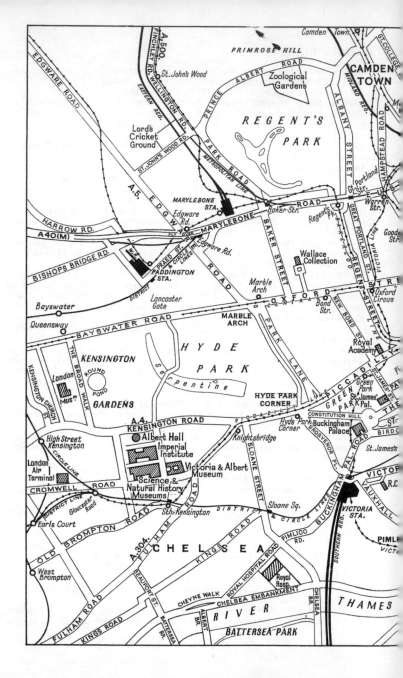

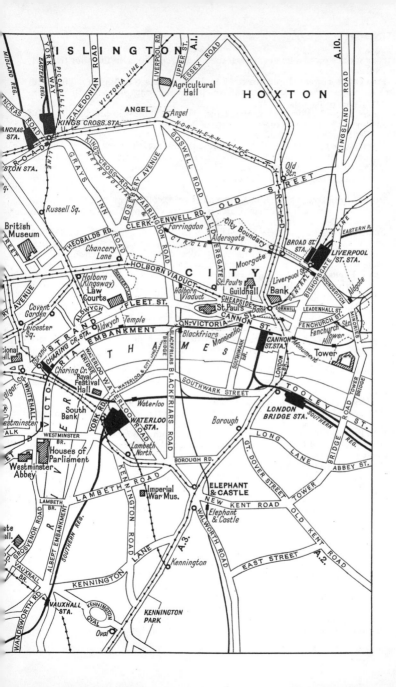

earth's surface on to a hemispherical ceiling. Presentations on the hour from 11, Suns from 1.

Post Office Tower (Maple Street, W.1). Britain's tallest building (580 feet with 40-foot mast). At top is restaurant which revolves once in every 20 minutes. Viewing platforms, lifts. Daily.

Public Record Office (Chancery Lane, W.C.2). Fine Gothic building and repository of National records since time of Norman Conquest. Museum, Mon.–Fri., 1–4. Search rooms, 9.30–5.

Royal Exchange (Bank, E.C.3). The present building, the third on the site, was designed by Tite and opened in 1844. A gilded grasshopper, crest of Sir Thomas Gresham who founded the Exchange in 1568, surmounts the clock tower. Interior court, daily from 10. The Guildhall Museum is temporarily housed here, 10–5.

Royal Mint (Tower Hill, E.C.3). Produces coins, official medals and seals for U.K., Commonwealth and many foreign countries. Applications to see coining processes to Deputy Master at least six weeks in advance.

Somerset House (Strand, W.C.2). Head office of Inland Revenue, the Probate Registry where Wills are kept and may be inspected, and office of the Registrar General of Births, Deaths and Marriages. Weekdays, 9.30–4.30. The East Wing is occupied by King's College, University of London.

Stock Exchange (Throgmorton Street, E.C.2). Visitors' Gallery from which floor of House may be observed, Mon.–Fri., 10–3.15. Films are shown at regular intervals describing activities of the Stock Exchange.

Syon House (London Road, Brentford). Home of His Grace the Duke of Northumberland, noted for its magnificent Adam interior. Portraits and furniture. Apr.–Oct., Mons–Fris only 11–1, 2–4.30.

Tower Bridge (E.C.3). Famous two-tier bridge with raised footway (142 feet, now closed) and twin bascules or leaves which are raised to allow passage of large vessels.

Trinity House (Trinity Square, E.C.3). Rebuilt 1953, and headquarters of Corporation of Trinity House, the General Lighthouse Authority for England and Wales.

University of London (Woburn Square, W.C.1). Buildings designed by Charles Holden include the Senate House; the Tower (210 ft); and various schools and institutes.

U.S. Embassy (Grosvenor Square, W.1). Mammoth new embassy completed in 1960 on west side of Grosvenor Square, one of London's finest squares. On north side is Franklin D. Roosevelt Memorial.

Wallace Collection (Manchester Square, W.1). Collection of treasures and works of art bequeathed to the nation by Lady Wallace. Lord Hertford resided in Paris where he assembled most of the French works of art of 17/18c. which give the Collection its special character. Weekdays, 10–5, Suns, 2–5.

Zoological Gardens (Regent's Park, N.W.1). The London Zoo occupies an area of about 31 acres in the northern part of Regent's Park. Summer from 9, winter from 10.

Inns of Court and Chancery

The four great inns of court were originally founded for the education and lodging of law students, to one or other of which all barristers are "admitted".

Inner and Middle Temple (Fleet Street, E.C.4). The Inner Temple Hall was rebuilt after war damage and dates from 1955. The Middle Temple Hall similarly damaged has been restored to its ancient 16c. splendour. In the courtyard is the fountain immortalized by Charles Dickens in "Martin Chuzzlewit".

Lincoln's Inn (Chancery Lane, W.C.2). Another great Inn of Court with powers of "calling to the bar". The Old Hall dates from 1506. The New Hall and library were built in 1845. The library is largest law library in London.

Gray's Inn (Gray's Inn Road, W.C.1). Occupies large area from Holborn to Theobald's Road. The Hall, chapel and library have been rebuilt after war damage.

Staple Inn (Holborn, E.C.1). Though long connected with the law, it owes its name to an earlier use, when it served as a custom house where wool was weighed and dues collected.

LONDON'S GREEN HEART

No other city possesses so many parks and open spaces as does London. Besides the great parks under the control of the Crown, like Hyde Park, Kensington Gardens, St. James's, and Regent's Park, there are many under the management of the G.L.C. and the total area amounts to over 7,000 acres. It is possible by just crossing the road at Hyde Park Corner to walk from the Westminster corner of St. James's Park in an almost direct line for nearly three miles through parks and gardens abounding in magnificent trees and wild bird life.

Parks and Gardens

Alexandra Park (Wood Green, N.22). The grounds of Alexandra Palace with lake. Fair, roller skating, racecourse.

Battersea Park (Queens Road, S.W.11). One of the largest of South London's pleasure grounds, adjoining south bank of the *Thames*. Old English Flower Garden. Festival Gardens section with funfair. Open-air concerts and music.

Bushy Park (Teddington). A royal demesne of 1,099 acres noted for its deer. Famous Chestnut Avenue is magnificent in May. Diana fountain.

Green Park (Westminster, S.W.1). Triangular space of 53 acres between Constitution Hill and Piccadilly. The Queens Walk on eastern side was named after Queen Caroline, wife of George II. The iron gateway on Piccadilly side is memento of the old Devonshire House, town residence of Duke of Devonshire.

Hampstead Heath (Hampstead, N.W.3). With its broken heights, grassy glades, lakes and furze-covered expanses, one of the most natural and bracing of London's open spaces. Far-reaching views. To south-east is Parliament Hill. To north-east is Kenwood and, beyond, the beautiful Highgate Woods.

Holland Park (Kensington, W.8). Former grounds of the Jacobean mansion. Woodland area. Dutch garden, Iris gardens, open-air concerts. Yucca garden with Scottish country dancing.

Hyde Park. With an area of 340 acres and joined on the west by Kensington Gardens (275 acres) this is London's finest lung. The Serpentine is artificial sheet of water (41 acres) with boating and swimming lido. Rotten Row is reserved for horse riding. Bandstand. Teahouse and restaurant.

Kensington Gardens. Appropriated from the old Hyde Park by Queen Caroline. The Serpentine is crossed by pretty five-arched bridge with picturesque views. The Round Pond is a paradise for juvenile yachtsmen and proud owners of model craft. The Broad Walk leads to Kensington Palace on west side. The statue of Peter Pan beside the Long Water is by Sir George Frampton, R.A.

Kew Gardens (Kew). Three hundred acres of lordly park with every species of tree, shrub and flower labelled for the visitor's interest. The prime function of the Royal Botanic Gardens is the correct identification of plants, but for most people the gardens are a delight of verdant lawns, flower displays, lake and ponds, palm house and conservatories, museums and classic temples. Gardens, daily from 10. Hot-houses from 1, museums from 10.

Parliament Hill (N.W.3). Wide expanse (270 acres) with extensive views southward over London. Highgate Ponds are in north-east portions. There is lido, athletics track, swimming, entertainment.

Regent's Park (N.W.1). One of the largest of London's parks having with Primrose Hill to the north an area of 670 acres. Laid out by John Nash for the Prince Regent. Around the park runs the two-mile Outer Circle road. The Inner Circle road encloses the Queen Mary's Gardens with beautiful floral displays. Open-air theatre. Ornamental lake with boating. To north is the London Zoo.

Richmond Park (Richmond). First enclosed by Charles I, extends to 2,358 acres and between 10 and 11 miles in circumference. Large herds of deer roam the park. Woodland garden. Golf course. Pen Ponds (18 acres) are favourite with skaters when conditions permit. The White Lodge is used by the Lower School of the Royal Ballet. Pembroke Lodge is now restaurant; it has fine gardens. Polo near Roehampton Gate on Tues and Thurs evenings and Sat. afternoons in season.

St. James's Park (S.W.1). One of the oldest and most beautiful of London's parks. The lake extends nearly the entire length and is haunt of many varieties of wild fowl, including white pelicans. Lunch-time and evening band concerts.

Shopping Centres

Regent Street, W.1. Laid out by architect Nash in 1813, but his buildings have been replaced by marble and concrete palaces that make the street the finest shopping thoroughfare in the world. Many famous companies have premises here, stores, shops and agencies, i.e. Liberty's, Dickens & Jones, Hamley's, Waring and Gillows, Fifth Avenue, Austin Reed, Swan & Edgar.

Oxford Street, W.1. Busy thoroughfare extending from Marble Arch to Tottenham Court Road thronged throughout the day by shoppers to the great stores, including Selfridge's, John Lewis's, Marks & Spencers, Marshall & Snelgrove, Bourne & Hollingsworth, D. H. Evans, Gamages, and many others.

Bond Street, W.1. Running between Oxford Street and Piccadilly both portions, Old and New, make up London's most fashionable shopping street. Many famous shops, notably jewellers, milliners and art galleries.

Piccadilly, W.1. One of London's most attractive thoroughfares said to derive its name from the pickadils, or ruffs, worn in the early Stuart period. Extends westward from Piccadilly Circus for nearly a mile to Hyde Park Corner. The eastern portion only is occupied by shops including Simpson's, Fortnum & Mason, Hatchards.

Knightsbridge, S.W.1. Fashionable shopping quarter for furniture dealers, jewellers, antique shops and the famous store of Harrods.

Kensington High Street, W.8. Favourite shopping quarter of many small but specialist shops and the larger stores of Barkers and Pontings.

Markets

Billingsgate Market (Lower Thames Street, E.C.3). Principal fish market of London. Best visited from 8 a.m.

Covent Garden (W.C.2). Chief wholesale market in London for fruit, vegetables and flowers. On west is St. Paul's Church, built by Inigo Jones in 1633. On east side is Royal Opera House.

Leadenhall Market (Gracechurch Street, E.C.3). For vegetables and poultry, etc. Stands on site of ancient Roman basilica or town hall of Londinium. Weekdays 9–5.

London Silver Vaults (Chancery Lane, W.C.2). The largest collection of silver in the world, displayed by many individual merchants. Mon.–Fri., 9–5.30, Sats, 9.30–12.30.

New Caledonian Market (Bermondsey Square, S.E.1). Open Fri., 8–1.

Petticoat Lane (Middlesex Street, E.1). Famous open-air market, Sun mornings 9–12.

Portobello Road Market (W.11). Vegetables, fruit, flowers daily except Suns. Antiques Sats, 9–6.

Smithfield Market (E.C.1). Ancient jousting ground outside City walls, now Central Meat Market and poultry, fish and vegetable markets. Weekdays.

Spitalfields Market (E.1). Fruit, vegetables and flowers, among the largest and most modern markets of its kind in the world. Weekdays.

Museums

British Museum (Great Russell Street, W.C.1). Vast National storehouse famous for its collections of sculpture, prints, drawings and books. Notable Greek and Roman antiquities. Elgin Marbles. The famous Reading Room (ticket-holders only) accommodates 500 readers. The library has statutory right to a copy of every book published in the U.K. Weekdays 10–5, Suns 2.30–6.

Commonwealth Institute (Kensington High Street, W.8). Modern building with tent-like roof sheathed in copper. The galleries house colourful display devoted to countries and peoples of the Commonwealth. Films, temporary exhibitions. Weekdays.10–5.30, Suns 2.30–6.

Geffrye Museum (Kingsland Road, E.2). Small but interesting collection of furniture and domestic objects from Elizabethan times to present day. Reading room. Tues to Sats, 10–5, Suns 2–5.

Geological Museum (Exhibition Road, S.W.7). Regional geology of Great Britain is demonstrated by exhibits including rocks, fossils and minerals, relief models, photographs. Exhibits of useful rocks and minerals of the world. Daily 10–6, Suns 2.30–6.

Guildhall Museum (Royal Exchange, E.C.3). Extensive collections of articles of archaeological and civic interest bearing on the history of the City. Many Roman relics. Weekdays, 10–5.

Horniman Museum (Forest Hill, S.E.23). Ethnographical collections from all parts of the world, musical instruments, natural history collection, reference library. Concerts and lectures in winter months. Daily 10.30–6, Suns 2–6.

Imperial War Museum (Lambeth Road, S.E.1). Commemorates the effort and sacrifice of men and women of British Commonwealth in two World Wars. The galleries contain naval, military and air service relics and souvenirs of all campaigns in which British Forces have been engaged since August 1914. Reference library. Photographic library. Film library. Daily 10–6, Suns 2–6.

London Museum (Kensington Palace, W.8). Originally at Lancaster House but since removed to Kensington Palace pending new premises to be built. Collections illustrate the history, social and domestic life of London in all periods. Daily from 10, Suns from 2.

National Maritime Museum (Greenwich S.E.10). Illustrates sea affairs from Tudor times to the present day. The Queen's House is the oldest Italianate house in England (1618–35). In west wing is notable marble rotunda. Library; medal and seal rooms. Navigation room. Weekdays, 10–6, Suns 2.30–6. To south is Greenwich Park. Nearer the river is Royal Naval College where the Chapel and Wren's Painted Hall are open daily, 2.30–5 except Thurs and in winter, Suns. In dry dock near Greenwich Pier is the *Cutty Sark,* the last survivor of the famous tea-clippers. Weekdays, 11–5, Suns 2.30–5.

Natural History Museum (Cromwell Road, S.W.7). Part of British Museum and principal centre in British Commonwealth for general study of natural history. National collections of recent and fossil forms of animal and plant life, rocks and minerals, and meteorites from outer space. The elaborate sculptural ornamentations are of interest. Daily, 10–6, Suns, 2.30–6.

Science Museum (Exhibition Road, S.W.7). National Museum of Science and Industry, illustrating their development through the years. Many working models. Daily, 10–6, Suns 2.30–6. Lectures, films. Library in Imperial Institute Road.

Soane Museum (Lincoln's Inn Fields, W.C.2). The private house built in 1812 by Sir John Soane, architect. Collections of architectural significance, including 26,000 drawings from 16–19c. Egyptian and Roman antiquities. Tues to Sats, 10–5. Closed in Aug. and Bank Hols.

Victoria and Albert Museum (South Kensington, S.W.7). Museum of Fine and Applied Art of all countries, styles and periods. It includes Architectural Details, Arms and Armour. Art of the Book, Carpets, Costumes, Drawings, Embroideries, Furniture, Glass, Gold and Silversmiths' Work, Ironwork, Ivories, Jewellery, Lace Lithographs, Miniatures, Musical Instruments, Oil Paintings, Pottery and Porcelain, Tapestries and Woodwork. Weekdays, 10–6, Suns, 2.30–6.

Wellington Museum (Apsley House, Hyde Park Corner, W.1). Town residence of Duke of Wellington built 1771–78. Museum contains Spanish, Dutch and Flemish paintings together with many personal relics of the First Duke of Wellington. Weekdays 10–6, Suns 2.30–6.

Art Galleries

Courtauld Institute (Woburn Square, W.C.1). University of London's galleries containing pictures bequeathed to the University. Works by Botticelli, Bellini, Veronese. Collection of 19c French paintings. Mons–Sats, 10–5, Suns, 2–5.

National Gallery (Trafalgar Square, W.C.2). Unequalled as a representative collection of the various schools of painting with over 2,000 paintings. Especially rich in Italian and Dutch schools. Weekdays, 10–6, Suns, 2–6.

National Portrait Gallery (St. Martin's Place, W.C.2). Over 5,000 portraits of famous British men and women of the past. Paintings, drawings, busts and miniatures. Weekdays from 10, Suns from 2.

Royal Academy of Arts (Piccadilly, W.1). Founded in 1768, its members are elected from among the most distinguished artists practising in Britain. The Summer Exhibition has been held each year since 1769. Daily (May–Aug.) 10–6, Suns 2–6.

Tate Gallery (Millbank, S.W.1). Contains the National Collections of British Painting, Modern Foreign Paintings, and Modern Sculpture. Especially notable for examples of Blake, Turner, Stevens, Sargent and the Pre-Raphaelites. Weekdays 10–6, Suns 2–6.

Concert Halls

Albert Hall (Kensington Gore, S.W.7). One of the largest concert halls in the world with seating capacity of nearly 7,000. The magnificent organ comprises some 10,000 pipes.

Central Hall (Storey's Gate, S.W.1). Imposing square block in Renaissance style. The dome is third largest in London.

Royal Festival Hall (Waterloo Bridge, S.E.1). Built in 1951 as outstanding example of contemporary architecture and acknowledged among finest concert halls in the world. Smaller theatres and music rooms have since been added.

Churches

All Hallows by the Tower (Byward Street, E.C.3). Founded in 675 by the first abbess of Barking Abbey. The Guild Church of Toc H.

All Souls (Langham Place, W.1). Built in 1824 by John Nash to complete his design for Regent Street. Unusual spire.

Brompton Oratory (Brompton Road, S.W.). Italian Renaissance style, opened by Cardinal Manning in 1884. Has great tradition in sacred music. Fashionable wedding church.

St. Andrew Undershaft (St. Mary Axe, E.C.3). Deriving its name from a long shaft or Maypole which used to be set up opposite the south door, and which the Puritans declared an idol, and caused to be burnt. In north side is alabaster monument to Stow (d. 1605) chronicler of London, with quill pen in hand.

St. Bartholomew the Great (Smithfield, E.C.1). The oldest church in London next to the chapel in the Tower. Fine Norman building founded by Rahere in 1123.

St. Bride's (Fleet Street, E.C.4). Rebuilt by Wren, after Great Fire, in 1680. Museum with Roman relics. The church has close associations with the Press.

St. Clement Danes (Strand, W.C.2). Wren church built 1681. Restored and reconstructed 1958 as central church of the Royal Air Force. The annual service at which oranges and lemons are distributed to children is held at end of March. The bells ring out the tune of the nursery rhyme every third hour.

St. George (Hanover Square, W.1). Small but attractive church by John James, a pupil of Wren, completed in 1725. Fashionable wedding church.

St. George's Cathedral (Lambeth Road, S.E.1). Roman Catholic cathedral rebuilt 1953–58 but to designs of the original church by Pugin.

St. James (Piccadilly, W1). Built by Wren 1680–84 with fine interior, restored after war damage. In Garden of Remembrance is impressive figure of "Peace" by Alfred Hardiman, R.A.

St. Margaret's (Westminster, S.W.1). Mother church of the City of Westminster and parish church of the House of Commons. Fashionable wedding church.

St. Martin-in-the-Fields (Trafalgar Square, W.C.2). The Royal Parish Church, Buckingham Palace being within the parish. George I was at one time a church-warden. Nell Gwynne buried here.

St. Paul's Cathedral (Ludgate Hill, E.C.4). Wren's masterpiece, begun in 1675 and completed 1710, built in Portland stone. Length 515 feet; width 250 feet; height to top of cross 365 feet; diameter of inner dome 112 feet. The golden ball is 6 feet in diameter.

Savoy Chapel (Savoy Street, W.C.2). Queen's Chapel of the Savoy originally part of the old palace erected in the Manor of Peter of Savoy in 1241 and now disappeared. Private chapel of her Majesty the Queen by right of her Duchy of Lancaster.

Southwark Cathedral (London Bridge, S.E.1). Recently restored but one of London's oldest buildings. Portions of Norman nave incorporated. The Choir and Lady Chapel built about 1207.

Temple (The Temple, Fleet Street, E.C.4). Joint property of the Inner and Middle Temple. The Round Church, built by the Knights Templars, contains remains of the effigies of nine knights. Norman porch.

Westminster Abbey (Parliament Square, S.W.1). Edward the Confessor is usually regarded as the founder. William the Conqueror was crowned here as have almost all monarchs since. The burial place of kings and queens. Length 513 feet; breadth 200 feet; western towers 225 feet.

Westminster Cathedral (Ashley Place, S.W.1). Roman Catholic Cathedral. Vast structure of brick and stone in Early Byzantine style. Campanile, 273 feet (to cross 284 feet); length 360 feet; width 156 feet.

Memorials

Albert Memorial (Kensington Gardens, S.W.7). Designed by Sir Gilbert Scott on model of Eleanor cross. Memorial to Prince Regent after Great Exhibition of 1851.

Cenotaph (Whitehall, S.W.1). Designed by Sir Edward Lutyens, R.A. and commemorating those who died in the two World Wars. Scene of annual Armistice Day ceremony (Nov.).

Charles I (Whitehall). Equestrian statue cast in 1633. All mileage distances from London are calculated from this spot.

Cleopatra's Needle (Victoria Embankment, W.C.2). Towed here by sea from the great temple of Heliopolis. Of red granite with inscriptions, the obelisk weighs 180 tons and is $68\frac{1}{2}$ feet high.

Duke of York Column (Carlton House Terrace). Granite pillar 124 feet high commemorating second son of George III.

Eros (Piccadilly Circus, W.1). At London's hub, graceful aluminium statue, part of memorial fountain to Lord Shaftesbury.

Monument (King William Street, E.C.4). Fluted Doric column of Portland stone (202 feet) by Wren commemorating the Great Fire of 1666. 311 steps to caged balcony. Weekdays, from 9. Suns in summer from 2.

Nelson Column (Trafalgar Square, W.C.2). Granite corinthian column surmounted by statue of Nelson. Total height 170 feet 2 inches. Four colossal lions by Landseer crouched around the base.

Nurse Cavell (St. Martins Place, W.C.2). Work of the late Sir George Frampton, R.A. It bears her fateful words: "Patriotism is not enough; I must have no hatred or bitterness for anyone".

Richard I (Old Palace Yard, S.W.1). Marochetti's fine statue of Richard Coeur de Lion.

Roosevelt Memorial (Grosvenor Square, W.1). Statue of Franklin D. Roosevelt, unveiled by Mrs. Roosevelt in 1944.

The South-East

LONDON TO ROCHESTER

The A2 road runs from the southern end of Vauxhall Bridge through built-up urban streets of New Cross, Deptford and Blackheath to reach Dartford in 16 miles from London.

Dartford (Pop.: 45,670. Hotel: *Royal Victoria and Bull*) is a busy industrious town on the river *Darent* with engineering, paper-making and other light industry interests. One or two timbered houses and the galleried *Bull Inn* only remain from former days. The Parish Church, restored, has a Norman tower and some old brasses, and the tomb of Sir John Spielman (*d.* 1626) who built one of the first paper-mills in England. To the north-east two-and-a-half miles is the modern Dartford–Purfleet road tunnel *(toll booth on south side)* under the *Thames*.

Gravesend (Pop.: 54,050. Hotels: *Tollgate Motel, Clarendon Royal*) on the south bank of the *Thames* is well-known as the headquarters port of the Thames Pilotage Service. From the open Gordon Promenade there is a fine prospect of shipping activity on the river which has a width of over half-a-mile at this point. A passenger ferry plies to Tilbury on the Essex bank. A few old buildings remain in the narrow High Street, but considerable residential development has taken place in recent years particularly to the south and east of the old town. There are good sports facilities with golf course, swimming pool, various parks and recreation grounds, and a theatre and entertainments complex. In the church, St. George's, are memorial windows to Pocahontas, the Indian princess who saved the life of Captain John Smith, colonizer of the State of Virginia. She is buried in the chancel. A statue has been erected in the gardens nearby.

East of Gravesend extends the peninsula between the *Thames* and the *Medway*, with, at its tip, the **Isle of Grain** dominated by its immense oil refinery. At **Cooling,** seven miles north-east of Gravesend, are the remnants of an old castle with its 14th-century gatehouse.

The A2 continues to Rochester just before which the modern M2 motorway diverges to the right to by-pass the town.

Rochester

Distances.—Canterbury, 27; Dartford, 13; Gravesend, 7; London, 30; Margate, 43.
Early Closing.—Wednesday.
Entertainment.—*Medway Little Theatre,* High Street.
Hotels.—*Royal Victoria and Bull, King's Head.*
Population.—55,460.
Post Office.—High Street.

Rochester is a considerable town of great historical interest on the *Medway*, three bridges connecting with its suburb Strood on the west bank of the river. Once the *Durobrivæ* of the Romans it still shows fragments of its old city wall, of both Roman and medieval date. Most of the present industrial and maritime activity is based at Strood and along the riverside, but within the old city boundaries there are many old buildings of both literary and historic interest.

The **Castle.** From the Esplanade (swimming pool) steps lead up to the neat grounds. The original castle was built by Bishop Gundulf in 1087 but only curtain walls and towers remain of his work. The huge Keep *(daily, fee)* was built in the late 1120s under the direction of William de Corbeuil, Archbishop of Canterbury. With walls 12 feet thick and reaching to a height of 120 feet, the keep is a fine example of Norman defensive architecture.

The **Cathedral,** one of the smallest of English cathedrals and dating mainly from the 12th–14th centuries, has a fine west front noted for its splendid Norman doorway. The central tower and spire (156 feet), a replacement, dates from 1904. The nave is Norman. The choir, unusual in that it has no aisle-arcades, is Early English. In plan the Cathedral is similar to Canterbury having double transepts, raised choir and a spacious crypt. The latter is one of the finest of its kind in the country. Opposite the Bishop's throne is part of a 14th-century wall painting. The Cathedral has a number of tombs of early bishops and is famous for its library.

South of the cathedral precincts are *King's School* and *The Vines,* an area of pleasant avenues. Beyond on the Maidstone Road is **Restoration House** *(by appointment)* an Elizabethan house with Charles II associations. **Eastgate House,** a little north, is now a museum. This house was described in "Edwin Drood" by Charles Dickens whose Swiss Chalet is preserved in the grounds. In and around the High Street are several old buildings of interest including the gabled house known as *Watts' Charity* founded in 1579 for "six poor travellers", the old *Corn Exchange* of 1706, the *George Inn* with 14th-century undercroft, and the 17th-century *Guildhall* with a fine collection of paintings and a "ship" vane on its roof.

Upnor Castle *(daily, fee)* 2 miles north-east of Strood on the west side of the *Medway* served as a blockhouse for the defense of the river. Built 1560–63 and altered later it comprises a large pointed bastion and gatetower.

A mile south of Rochester is *Borstal,* the original reformatory from which other similar corrective establishments take their name.

Chatham (Pop.: 56,921) contiguous with Rochester on the east is a busy engineering centre long famous in naval history for its Royal Naval Dockyard *(guided tours).* Opposite St. Mary's Church is a statue of Lord Kitchenor *(d.* 1916) brought from Khartoum in 1958. Considerable residential development has taken place at Chatham with modern shopping centres and high tower blocks of flats. Charles Dickens spent his early school years in the town but little remains that he would recognize today.

Gillingham (Pop.: 86,700. Hotel: *Park*) linked to Chatham on the east and largest of the three Medway towns, has a fine church in the Perpendicular style, with good windows and a Norman font. Opposite the Brompton Barracks is an unusual statue of General Gordon *(d.* 1885) on camel-back.

From Gillingham the A2 runs almost straight for Canterbury, but in 5 miles the A249 cuts across and runs north-eastward for Sheerness, Minster and the Isle of Sheppey.

Sheerness (Hotel: *Royal Fountain*) is a busy port and the principal town of the Isle of Sheppey. At one time an important naval dockyard, much of the place has been redeveloped. On the main front are pleasant gardens, swimming pool and facilities for various sports.

Farther along the A2 are **Sittingbourne** busy with cement and paper making, and **Faversham** an ancient town and one-time seaport on an inlet of the river *Swale.* The town lies in a rich fruit and hop growing area and is busy with marketing and canning this produce.

Round the South-East Coast

Along this coast are some of England's largest and most famous holiday resorts. Some are sizeable towns attracting thousands of visitors, but also having a considerable residential population. The whole area is one of the sunniest and healthiest regions in the country.

WHITSTABLE TO DUNGENESS

Whitstable

Distances.—Canterbury, 7; Herne Bay, 5; Margate, 17; London, 56.
Early Closing.—Wednesday.
Golf.—Seasalter (9 holes), and Chestfield (18 holes).

Hotels.—*Tankerton, Royal, Wheatsheaf, Marine, Duke of Cumberland.*
Population.—23,780.
Post Office.—High Street.
Sports.—Bathing, boating, bowls, tennis, golf.

Modern Whitstable has developed from the ancient port of Whitstable, together with the neighbouring village of **Church Street** clustered about the parish church. Its western suburb **Seasalter** carries in its name a reminder of its former salt-pans. To the east **Tankerton** has developed as a summer and residential suburb.

The older parts of Whitstable still retain many picturesque corners. The oyster industry here has been renowned from the days of the Roman occupation, and still provides a good deal of employment. Shipbuilding has dwindled, but yachts are still built; and there is a considerable coasting trade. A little east of the Harbour a long causeway known as *The Street* stretches out to sea, and is almost entirely uncovered at low tide. The Parish **Church of All Saints,** in Church Street, dates mainly from the 15th century, with traces of Saxon work. The tower originally served as a watch-tower and place of defence, and the mussel gatherers supported a special light called the Muskyll Taper. At the western end of the main street is an old Toll House and near by is *Barn House,* a 15th-century manor. The **Castle,** originally called Tankerton Tower, is a castellated mansion of which the octagonal tower is probably 15th century. The Castle now houses municipal offices, and the grounds form a public park.

Between Tankerton and the sea the fine Marine Parade extends for more than a mile. Instead of cliffs there are grassy slopes descending to the Promenade.

Herne Bay

Bathing.—Good from shingle beach. At low tide shallow water over sand.
Distances.—Birchington, 12; Canterbury, 9; London, 60; Margate, 16; Reculver (road), 5.
Early Closing.—Thursday.
Entertainment.—King's Hall, Pier Pavilion, Central Bandstand.

Hotels.—*Beauvalle, St. George, Queen's, Pier, Dolphin,* and many others.
Population.—24,000.
Post Office.—Cavendish Road.
Sports.—Bowls, tennis, putting. Golf (18 holes) at Eddington.

Herne Bay has grown in favour for residential purposes, and enjoys a delightful and bracing climate. The town is symmetrically laid out, the principal roads running parallel with the sea, with shorter connecting streets. There is a total sea-front of about seven miles with rising ground at the eastern end; inland is well-wooded and slightly hilly country. Bathing, fishing and boating are good; regattas and a carnival are held in August. There are also ample facilities for golf, tennis and cricket. The *Pier* has had a chequered history. The first pier of 1832 was designed by Telford, and extended for 3,500 feet. This was replaced in 1873 by a much shorter structure. The Pier Pavilion was destroyed by fire in 1928, and its successor burnt down in 1969. Eastward from the Pier is the Central Parade, separated by lawns and flower beds from the shingly shore with its many groynes. Farther to the east is the grassy slope known as the Downs, a popular part where the cliffs in places reach a considerable height. The *Clock Tower,* on the front, is classical in style and rises in four stages to a height of 85 feet. The principal thoroughfares are William Street, running inland from Central Parade, and Mortimer Street and High Street crossing it at right angles. Near the south end of William Street is the *Memorial Park* of 16 acres, with boating lake, bowling greens, tennis courts and cricket ground.

Herne village lies about a mile inland. The church has a massive flintstone tower. The early 15th-century font bears the arms of Henry IV.

To Reculver. The sister towers of Reculver are a familiar landmark between London and Margate. In ancient times Reculver, under its Roman name of Regulbium, guarded the north entrance to the channel of the Wantsume as did Richborough the south.

The Saxon church and Roman fortress are in the care of the Department of the Environment. The church is open daily, *fee.* The walls of the fort may be seen at all times, *free.*

The **castrum,** when entire, occupied about eight acres, and at one time was garrisoned by the first cohort of Vetasii from Brabant. Considerable portions of the south and east walls still remain, and below ground many valuable relics have been found. The north wall has long since disappeared under the sea, and but for the protecting sea-wall and groynes the rest would not be long in following. In Leland's time Reculver stood "wythin a quarter of a myle or little more of the se syde". The footpath eastward and a turn right leads to the still massive **Roman Walls.**

The modern parish church of St. Mary the Virgin at **Hillborough** serves a growing population, and is largely built of the materials of old Reculver Church.

To Blean Woods. A mile or two south-west of Herne are the extensive **Blean Woods.** Only here and there is it possible to penetrate these leafy recesses, but several public roads lead through parts of the woods, and a fair idea of their beauty and extent is gained by motorists.

To Chislet, Upstreet and Grove Ferry. Leave the town by Mickleburgh Hill and the Margate road. Cross the railway by Blacksole Bridge and bear left to **Hunter's Forstal,** a pleasant little village said to owe its name to the fact that it was long the rallying-place of the huntsmen in the district. Then turn right to **Broomfield,** with a large pond in which tradition declares that many a voluble scold has been soundly ducked. At the pond the road bends right-ward, presently dropping somewhat steeply to **Ford,** a picturesque one-street hamlet with a modern interest as the site of the Herne Bay waterworks, and a more alluring old appeal as the site of Archbishop Cranmer's manor house, the scanty remains of which can be seen to the rear of the farmhouse on the left-hand side of the road.

Ascending the hill, continue by the straight road through picturesque **Maypole** to four cross-roads. The road on the left climbs up to **Hoath,** another delightful village, its little church— formerly a chapelry to Reculver—with its small shingled tower and spire containing several ancient brasses and a fine modern oak reredos. The winding road continues eastward for another mile-and-a-half to **Chislet.**

The Church is of far greater interest than the ugly wooden excrescence that caps its massive Norman tower would lead one to suppose. There is a fine Norman chancel arch, and the square, carved and panelled font, canopied sedilia and stone carvings in the chancel are of great beauty. Close to the church is the farm house of Chislet Court, a fine Queen Anne building.

From Chislet the southerly road leads in less than a mile up to the Canterbury and Margate and Ramsgate road. The village bordering the road is **Upstreet,** where are some fine old Georgian and Queen Anne mansions. **Grove Ferry** is a noted fishing centre and a popular place for picnics, with a pleasant riverside hotel *(Grove Ferry)* with tea and beer garden.

To Sturry and Fordwich. From eastern end of Central parade turn inland by East Cliff Hill, which becomes the Canterbury road. Pass under railway to Eddington and Herne (1¾ miles).

At Church bear right and pass the leafy Strode Park. **Sturry,** derives its name from the river *Stour,* on which it is prettily situated. It is the site of the Junior King's School of Canterbury which is installed in Milner Court, formerly the home of Viscount Milner. Additional buildings have been erected between the new work and the old. The Church, set among giant chestnut-trees, has a fine embattled tower, beautiful timbered porch and 15th-century font. Under the tower is buried the last abbot of St. Augustine's Abbey, Canterbury.

Fordwich, a quaint old village was once the port of Canterbury, a tidal estuary of the sea finding its way right up to it. The diminutive **Town Hall** *(fee)* is a gem, the overhanging upper portion half-timbered, the ground floor of brick and stone. It is believed to date from the earliest years of the 15th century. The **Church** is a building of great antiquity, containing traces of Saxon work in the tower, Norman windows and font, a rare "heart shrine," and enclosed pews. A beautifully carved Early Norman tomb is said to be part of St. Augustine's, whose monastery of St. Peter and St. Paul was established at Fordwich and re-established at Canterbury.

Birchington and Westgate-on-Sea

Both of these places are now incorporated with Margate, and have similar excellent sands and safe bathing. **Birchington** *(Bungalow, Court Mount),* four miles west of Margate, has three bays. **Minnis Bay,** the most westerly has a promenade that serves as a sea-wall to protect the low-lying land in this area. A cliff path skirts the coast and marshland to Reculver. **Grenham Bay** is quiet and secluded, and **Epple Bay**—the easternmost—provides an invigorating cliff-top promenade with wide sea views. Inland is the Square, through which runs the Margate—Canterbury high road. At the south-west corner stands the ancient and interesting *Parish Church of All Saints,* in the churchyard of which Rossetti was buried. Half-a-mile to the south is the old manor house *Quex Park,* and near this is the fascinating *Powell-Cotton Museum* of African and Asian wild life and the arts and crafts of primitive races.

Westgate-on-Sea *(Ingleton, Kimberley, Bridge),* two miles to the east, is a well laid-out town with excellent facilities for bathing and sport. The small bays, St. Mildred's Bay and West Bay, are girdled by substantial sea-walls and promenades. Pleasant Gardens overlook the sea, and on the Green is the Pavilion used for entertainments. From here one has a good view of Margate in one direction and Reculver's twin towers in the other.

Margate

Beach.—Broad expanse of flat sand.

Distances.—Birchington, 4; Broadstairs, 5; Canterbury, 16; Deal, 15; Dover, 27; London, 71; Whitstable, 20.

Early Closing.—Thursday.

Entertainment.—Daily at Winter Gardens, Theatre Royal and the Oval. Dreamland Amusement Park. The Lido, Cliftonville and Queen's Entertainment Centre.

Hotels.—*Nayland Rock, Endcliffe, Walpole Bay, Grosvenor Court, Bicken Hall, Hereward, Holland House, Palm Bay, Roxburgh, Norman, Royal Crescent, Berkeley Court,* and many others.

Population.—49,080.

Post Office.—Cecil Square.

Sport.—Full facilities for all sports. Fine greens for putting and bowls. Tennis (many courts). Golf at Kingsgate. Boating and sailing.

Margate has been popular with Londoners and others as a family holiday resort, by virtue of its bracing air, its extensive tide-washed sands, and its safe bathing. Liberal provision is made for the amusement of all classes of visitors. The town is also an excellent centre for excursions to places of interest in east Kent. Sea trips of all kinds are available.

The older part of Margate has lost most of its 19th-century staid charm, and now caters specially for the amusement of the day tripper and short-term holiday maker. But eastward from the Harbour one rises to the quieter and more open area of Cliftonville, with modern hotels and residences and less congested beaches. The Harbour, once a busy port of call for shipping, is now mainly used by yachts and other pleasure craft. The carved stone protecting breakwater dates from 1815 and is known as the Harbour Pier. Near by is a 1,240-feet long structure which would elsewhere be called a pier, but at Margate is termed the Jetty. A miniature railway runs from end to end, and at one time the hexagonal jetty extension handled a busy steamer traffic. St. John's Church, at the inland end of High Street, was founded about 1050, and restored 1875–79, being given a new roof and a spire that is visible for many miles around. In the interior there are many old brasses. Westward from the Harbour, the Marine Parade extends past the Clock Tower and Marine Pool to *Dreamland,* with a 20-acre Amusement Park and also a Safari Park, and on to Westbrook and Westgate.

Eastward from the Jetty, one ascends to the heights of **Cliftonville** either by Fort Road or by the promenade at the cliff foot that leads to steps in the neighbourhood of the Fort; this is a pleasant promenade with a fine sea-wall surrounding the *Winter Gardens* with its concert halls and gardens.

Continuing eastwards, Queen's Promenade leads to the Cliftonville *Lido,* and a footbridge crosses the Newgate Gap, the first of several deep cuttings in the chalk cliff that afford convenient access to the sands and beach chalets. The coast promenade continues to the *Flagstaff,* and beyond this is a fine walk to the North Foreland and Broadstairs. About half-a-mile from the sea is *Dane Park,* and near it is a once-popular curiosity known as the *Grotto,* vaults in the chalk lavishly decorated with shells. The Grotto was discovered in 1835 and was then mistakenly thought to be of extreme antiquity.

Broadstairs

Bathing.—Excellent from sands. Tents and chalets for hire.
Boating.—Rowing, sailing and motorboat trips.
Early Closing.—Wednesday.
Entertainment.—Garden-on-the-Sands Pavilion, cinema.
Golf.—North Foreland Golf links.
Hotels.—*Royal Albion, Curzon, Castlemere, Beechfield, Merriland,* and others.
Population.—20,450.
Post Office.—High Street.
Sport.—Bowls, tennis, fishing, riding.

Broadstairs is renowned for its healthy situation in the heart of the Thanet holiday area. As a holiday resort for children it is ideal. There is a splendid sandy beach and a high level of sunshine. The greater part of the town stands 100–200 feet above sea level. High Street—extending almost to the sea front—and its adjacent roads form the principal shopping quarter. The pretty semi-circular Viking Bay is bounded on one side by steep chalk cliffs, and on the other by what Dickens described as the "Quaint old Pier", a much-tarred structure dating mainly from 1808. Broadstairs cherishes its old-world charm and in particular its many associations with Charles Dickens. The novelist wrote much of "David Copperfield" at **Bleak House**—then known as Fort House, and previously occupied by Wilkie Collins. A later owner converted it into the present castellated residence occupying a commanding position on the north cliff. Harbour Street, a narrow lane winding upward from the pier to Albion Street, contains an interesting relic in the shape of *York Gate,* a flint arch originally built 1540. The coastline of Broadstairs comprises four miles along the edge of the cliffs and skirts seven attractive bays. Another pleasant feature of the sea-front is the mile-long stretch of wide lawns. The seascapes are delightful, and on clear days the coast of France is visible.

To **North Foreland** (1½ miles), **Kingsgate** (2 miles). At Holy Trinity Church either turn right to Eastern Esplanade, or follow Stone Road northward. Continue to the extensive plantation surrounding **Stone House,** long the seaside residence of Archbishop Tait, and now a private school. Farther along the North Foreland road the lighthouse can be seen immediately ahead.

North Foreland Lighthouse *(daily, except Suns, from 1 p.m.)*. The tower is 85 feet high and is ascended by steps round the inside of its walls. The 175,000 candlepower light is 188 feet above high-water mark, and visible for 20 miles. The light is eclipsed five times in seven seconds every twenty seconds.

Kingsgate. The road from the lighthouse skirts the grounds of Kingsgate Castle, a picturesque building in a unique situation and now converted into residential flats. In the grounds adjoining (originally belonging to the Castle), on **Hackemdown Point,** is the *Castle Keep Hotel,* built in the Italian style. Steps opposite the white houses give access to the sands, where there is good bathing. At low tide there are interesting walks beneath the cliffs in either direction, with fine arched rocks and caves and several acres of seaweed-covered rock.

On the northern side of the bay is the battlemented *Captain Digby Inn* with car park adjoining. This is a favourite walk out from either Broadstairs or Margate.

Ramsgate

Bathing. — Fine sandy beach. Marina Bathing Pool.
Distances. — Broadstairs, 2; Canterbury, 18; Dover, 20; London, 74; Margate, 5; Pegwell Bay, 2; Herne Bay, 15.
Early Closing. — Thursday.
Entertainment. — Granville Theatre, cinema. Amusement Park. Olympia Hall.
Hotels. — *Court Stairs, Beverley, San Clu, Regency,* *Sycamore, Savoy, Moorings, Westbourne, Four Winds,* and many others.
Population. — 39,200.
Post Office. — High Street.
Sports. — Bowls, tennis, fishing, golf (St. Augustine at Ebbsfleet), greyhound track (Dumpton Park). Boating and sailing.

Ramsgate is built on and between two lofty chalk cliffs. The opening is said to have given the place its name, the *Gate of Ruim,* the British name for Thanet. The town has sunny terraces, gay gardens, and wonderful facilities for pleasure, sport and entertainment. Despite modern developments the town retains much of its old-time picturesqueness, a quaint grouping of houses one above the other, with the piers and the shipping in the foreground. Ramsgate was for centuries a "limb" of its Cinque Port neighbour Sandwich.

The fine Harbour, formerly the centre of a flourishing fishing industry, now handles the import and export of cars, spares, and mixed cargoes. The non-tidal inner harbour forms a marina for small craft. The harbour is enclosed by the East and West Piers; at the end of the West Pier is a stone Lighthouse. Both piers form popular promenades. From them one obtains a good view of the town, with the elegant frontages of Nelson Crescent and Wellington Crescent on either side of the harbour. From the East Pier a Lift, or alternatively the winding Madeira Walk, ascends to the East Cliff Promenade, with a lower promenade and the sands 90 feet below. From the western end of the harbour the Royal Parade rises gradually to the West Cliff. Below the cliff is the long West Undercliff Promenade, a delightful sun-trap sheltered from the wind.

The ancient *Church of St. Laurence,* once the parish church, stands at the inland end of the High Street. It was from *c.* 1062 a chapel-of-ease to Minster Abbey, and attained its present form about 1200. It has a massive square tower, and contains much Norman work of interest. *St. Augustine's Abbey Church* (Roman Catholic) stands in St. Augustine's Road, which runs parallel with the West Cliff Promenade, and was the work of A. W. Pugin, the famous Gothic Revival architect (1812–52).

MANSTON–MINSTER–THE GOODWINS

Manston lies two miles from Ramsgate by way of St. Lawrence. Manston Aerodrome, for many years a famous military air base, is now used jointly as a civil terminal for air services to and from the Continent and by the R.A.F. The Royal Air Force Station was famous in both World Wars.

Pegwell Bay, a mile west of Ramsgate Harbour, is finely shaped, but the flatness of the coast and the expanse of sand exposed at low water, rather spoil it. The mouth of the river *Stour* can be seen across the bay. Pegwell is renowned for its shrimps, which may be bought fresh, or potted and pasted.

A modern development is the **International Hoverport** on the shore from which daily flights operate to Calais. There are spectator and refreshment facilities.

At **Cliffsend** *(Sportsman Inn)* the cliffs that guard the coast of Thanet end abruptly.

Two Historic Landings. It was with the landing of Hengist and his war-band at **Ebbsfleet** (449) that English history began. To commemorate the 1,500th anniversary of this historic occasion a stone was unveiled in the vicinity by H.H. Prince Georg of Denmark on 29th July, 1949. Also at this spot is the Viking Ship *Hugin,* an exact replica of the vessel in which Hengist sailed to Britain.

It is curious that yet another famous landing should have taken place on this very spot. It was in August, 597, that Augustine and his forty monks arrived on that mission to the Saxon Ethelbert which was to be fraught with such momentous consequences. Although Queen Bertha was a Christian, and was attended at court by a French bishop, the King knew so little of the new religion that he stipulated that Augustine's first interview with him should on no account be held under a roof, but in the open air, as he feared the charms and spells of the strangers. The traditional spot where the meeting took place is by some lavender gardens on the Minster road, where it is crossed by the railway line near the Golf House, and is marked by a **Cross,** erected by the late Lord Granville in 1884.

Close to the Cross are the St. Augustine's Golf-Links, three miles distant from either Ramsgate or Sandwich. *St. Augustine's Well,* a natural spring said to have appeared when St. Augustine asked for water, lies on the golf-course, but permission to visit it is readily granted by the Secretary.

Minster, five miles from Ramsgate is much visited on account of its famous church, and has some lovely orchards and lanes. It has a few picturesque old houses and cottages, the oldest being an admirably preserved 16th-century cottage, now in use as a restaurant. The **Church** consists of a Late Norman nave, two side aisles, and Early English chancel and transepts. The tower has a fine Norman doorway. Parts of the existing building and the adjoining abbey ruins date from the 11th century. At the south-east corner of the tower is a Saxon stair-turret.

Minster Abbey *(weekdays)* lies a few yards north-east of the churchyard. It was built on the site of St. Edburga's monastery, established in the 7th century. The Abbey was given by Canute to St. Augustine's Abbey in Canterbury in A.D. 1027. Later the Manor House was built as a residence for the monks. In 1937 the Abbey was transferred from private ownership to nuns of the Benedictine Order.

Monkton, about midway between Minster and Sarre, has some beautiful farms and old houses, and an interesting church, with a plain square tower and long nave, outside which may be seen the old parish stocks. In the church are a fine brass in memory of a priest, dated 1460, and a good Jacobean pulpit.

The Goodwin Sands are about seven miles from Ramsgate in the direction of Deal, and extend parallel with the coast for about 10 miles from north to south, with an average breadth of two miles. In fine weather motor-boats put off almost daily from Ramsgate and Broadstairs for trips to the Goodwins; landings are occasionally made at low water.

The Goodwins are at once a safeguard and a danger to shipping. The great sandbank acts as a natural breakwater, protecting from north and east winds a deep channel known as **The Downs.** This is open to the south, but is sheltered by the land from the most prevalent winds, except when they are of extraordinary velocity. Tradition ascribes the name of the sands to the fact that they once formed part of an island belonging to Earl Godwin, the father of Harold. A remarkable fact concerning the sands is that they are steadily moving landward and, some authorities believe, will eventually join, or rejoin, the mainland.

The Cinque Ports. The original Cinque Ports were Hastings, Sandwich, Dover, Romney, and Hythe, hence the application to them of the word "cinque," the old French equivalent of five. Later, the "Ancient Towns" of Winchelsea and Rye were added, making seven, but the old French name was retained. To each of the head Ports were attached a number of "limbs"—not always coast towns—some of which were corporate, others non-corporate. Several of the smaller "limbs" have entirely disappeared, and of the head Ports Dover is now the only one of maritime importance. The jurisdiction of the Ports extended from Birchington to Seaford in Sussex.

From the time of the Romans there was a defensive system along the exposed south-east coast, under the leadership of the Count of the Saxon Shore. William the Conqueror changed that title to Lord Warden of the Cinque Ports, but retained the function of the Confederacy. In the 13th century the fleet of the Cinque Ports was powerful enough to vie with the whole French navy. In 1229 Henry III prescribed that the Ports should provide 57 ships, to serve the King at their own expense for 15 days each year. The number of ships to be furnished by each Port gives a good idea of the relative importance of the towns at the time. Dover had to send 21, Winchelsea 10, Hastings six, and Sandwich, Hythe, Romney and Rye five each.

Sandwich (Pop.: 4,620. Hotels: *Bell, Guildford, Fleur-de-Lis, Haven*), is a lovely mellow old town with narrow streets and timbered houses. At one time it was the chief of the Cinque Ports, but its importance gradually declined as the estuary silted up, and the sea is now one-and-a-half miles away. Sweyn and Canute landed here in 1013, and in medieval days Sandwich was a busy port. In the 15th and 16th centuries the declining fortunes of the town were to some extent restored by an influx of Flemish and Huguenot refugees, who established a flourishing weaving industry. The Guildhall dates from 1579. Perhaps the best known feature of the town is the picturesque chequered *Barbican* and toll house, by the swing bridge at the north end of High Street. A short way eastward along the river bank is the ancient *Fisher Gate* (14th century), the only one remaining of the original five.

The former importance of Sandwich is attested by its three great churches. Of these *St. Clement's Church*, with its five arcaded Norman tower, was designated the parish church in 1948. The other medieval churches are *St. Mary's Church* and *St. Peter's Church;* in each of these the tower collapsed in the 17th century and has not been replaced. In St. Mary's the ancient Peter's Pence box is worth noting. In the street called Moat Sole, off the Market Place, is St. Thomas's Hospital, an ancient institution housed in comparatively modern buildings. Near the railway station is another old almshouse foundation, *St. Bartholomew's Hospital*.

Richborough Castle *(daily, fee)*, lies on the *Stour* one-and-a-half miles north of Sandwich. The length and even height of the massive walls, which crown the old island and overlook rich river pasture lands, make them appear low when seen from the road. It is only when they loom close that their forbidding bulk is fully appreciated. They are one of the most remarkable relics of the Roman occupation of Britain and of intense interest both to archaeologists and laymen, who in the carefully exposed and preserved foundations can read the story of the might and far-reaching power of the early Roman Empire. Many of the objects found in the course of excavations are exhibited in **The Museum** near the entrance.

Richborough and Reculver, known to the Romans as *Rutupiae* and *Regulbium,* guarded respectively the south and the north entrances to the mile-wide channel of the *Wantsume,* which at that time separated the Isle of Thanet from the mainland. Rutupiae was the principal landing place and base for the legions crossing from the opposite coast of Boulogne under the Emperor Claudius in A.D. 43. From that time it was inhabited continuously through the whole period of the Roman occupation, and served as one of the principal ports for continental traffic, from which the great Roman road, later known as Watling Street ran to Canterbury, London and the north.

CANTERBURY

Canterbury

Distances.—Deal, 19; Dover, 16; Herne Bay, 9; Hythe, 17; London, 56; Margate, 16; Ramsgate, 18; Sandwich, 13; Whitstable, 7.
Early Closing.—Thursday.
Hotels.—*Abbots Barton, County, Chaucer, Falstaff,*

Queen's Head, Slatter's, Barcroft.
Population.—33,140.
Post Office.—High Street.
Theatre.—*Marlowe Theatre,* St. Margaret's Street.

Canterbury, the chief cathedral city of the Kingdom (its Archbishop bears the title Primate of All England), is the goal of thousands of pilgrims and visitors throughout the year. In addition to possessing a beautiful Cathedral and many ancient buildings, it is a flourishing country town with busy cattle and general markets.

There has been a settlement on this site since the Iron Age, later occupied by Britons, Romans, Saxons, occasional Danish marauders, and finally Normans. Here was Ethelbert's capital at the time of his conversion to Christianity in 597 A.D. Augustine founded the Abbey that still bears his name, as well as the church that became the Cathedral. For many years the Abbey was of the greater importance, being the burial place of the Kings of Kent, of St. Augustine himself, and of various succeeding archbishops.

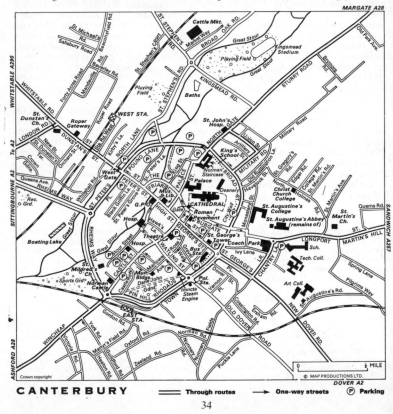

CANTERBURY ═══ Through routes → One-way streets Ⓟ Parking

34

Entering the city from the London road, on the corner one sees the church of *St. Dunstan-without-the-Westgate*. At the eastern end of the south aisle are monuments to the Roper family, and in the family vault below is the severed head of Sir Thomas More. A short distance farther on, past the 15th-century *Falstaff Inn*, St. Dunstan's Street crosses a branch of the river *Stour* to the massive **West Gate.** This replaces an earlier gate and dates from 1380. It was long used as the city gaol, and now houses a small but interesting museum. To the right of the West Gate is the **Church of Holy Cross,** rebuilt at the same time as the West Gate. Behind the church are the pretty Westgate Gardens, which follow in part the line of the old Roman city-wall.

From the West Gate the road continues as St. Peter's Street until it reaches King's Bridge over the main branch of the *Stour*. Flanking the river are the picturesque half-timbered houses of the *Canterbury Weavers,* originally Huguenot and Flemish refugees. In High Street is the **Royal Museum** and **Public Library** with its ornate façade.

Along Stour Street on the right is the entrance to the remains of *Grey Friars,* a Franciscan friary built about 1267. An even older foundation, the Poor Priests Hospital, is now shared by the city health department and the *Museum of the Buffs* (East Kent Regiment). At the end of Stour Street, Church Lane leads to **St. Mildred's Church,** perhaps the most interesting of Canterbury churches. In a by-road off Wincheap is the *Martyr's Memorial* to the Kentish Martyrs (30 men and 11 women) who suffered under Queen Mary I.

Near at hand is the Norman **Castle,** of which only the shell of the Keep remains. Following the line of the old city walls one comes to Dane John Gardens, a pleasant recreation ground in which is the *Dane John* (Donjon) *Mound,* thought to have been a Roman-British burial site. In the Gardens is a monument to Christopher Marlowe, who was born at Canterbury in 1564; and at the Watling Street entrance is Stephenson's locomotive *Invicta,* second only in interest to the "Rocket".

From here one may return to the Cathedral via Bridge Street and St. George's Street. The eastern part of Canterbury suffered heavily during the air-raids of World War II. Excavations during reconstruction led to many archaeological discoveries: in Butchery Lane a Roman mosaic pavement was found, part of a large building erected about 100 A.D. a little farther along the Parade, Mercery Lane leads to the Cathedral. On the corner, incorporated with modern shops, is the stone arcade of the famous *Chequers of the Hope,* a celebrated hostelry that sheltered countless pilgrims, including Geoffrey Chaucer.

The Cathedral

Both Cathedral and Abbey were founded by St. Augustine about 600 A.D., the former on the site of Ethelbert's palace. After the Norman Conquest, the Cathedral was completed by Lanfranc and his successor Anselm. Towards the end of the 14th century Lanfranc's Norman nave was replaced by the present Perpendicular one.

Christ Church Gate, giving access to the precincts, bears the date 1517. A beautiful specimen of Perpendicular work, it was restored in 1935–37. The turrets, which in the last century were lowered to provide a local resident with a clear view of the Cathedral clock, have been re-erected, the stonework faced, and the painted heraldry revived.

The great Central Tower, or Bell Harry, is 235 feet in height, and of magnificent proportions and harmonious design. It was built at the end of the 15th century. Bell Harry, the great bell at its summit, is rung every evening as a curfew and tolled on the death of a sovereign or archbishop.

The South-west Porch, the principal entrance to the Cathedral, was completed about 1420. In the centre is a defaced representation of the "Altar of the Sword's Point".

The **Nave** was built in the latter half of the 14th century, in Perpendicular style, and resembles that of Winchester built at the same time. The series of clustered pillars have been aptly called a forest of stone. The aisles are narrow and very lofty.

North Aisle. Note the Font (1639) the oak Pulpit, and the memorial to men of H.M.S. *Kent* lost at the Falkland Isles battle in 1914.

The **Choir Screen,** adorned with six figures of Kings is 15th-century work.

The **Choir,** most important example of Early Gothic architecture in the country, was built 1174–84. The pointed and rounded arch are used almost indiscriminately. The Decorated screen that surrounds the choir was constructed by the Prior of Eastry (1284–1331); the north doorway is remarkably fine.

The **South-west Transept** was built in the 15th century. Leading out of this is **St. Michael's Chapel;** this is longer than when first built in the 11th century, the newer east wall passing across the tomb of Stephen Langton, the leader of the barons who wrung Magna Carta from King John. **St. Anselm's Chapel,** farther to the east, is set obliquely. Above the chapel is a small watching chamber, in which a guard was stationed at night to protect the treasures of Becket's shrine. The *Pilgrims' Steps,* the deep indentations of which tell of countless pilgrimages, lead up to:

Trinity Chapel, built to receive the Shrine of Thomas Becket. The site of the shrine, despoiled by Thomas Cromwell, is shown by the marks worn in the stone by generations of pilgrims. Near by is the tomb of *Edward the Black Prince (d.* 1376). The figure is clad in full armour, and above hang replicas of the warrior's brazen gauntlets, casque, shield, and emblazoned surcoat; the originals are in a glass case at the foot of the Pilgrims' Steps. Opposite the Black Prince's tomb is that of Henry IV, the only monarch buried in the Cathedral.

At the extreme east end is the circular chapel known as the *Corona,* or Becket's crown. On the left side is the tomb of Cardinal Pole, the last Archbishop to acknowledge the supremacy of Rome. In the centre stands the so-called Chair of Augustine; it is of Purbeck marble and dates from the beginning of the 13th century. The chair is still used at the ceremonial enthronement of an Archbishop. From the Corona one sees the full length (514 feet) of the nave. The windows of Trinity Chapel are filled with glass dating from the 13th century onwards, and portraying cures wrought at Becket's tomb.

The **Chantry of Henry IV,** dedicated in 1440, is one of the gems of the Cathedral. Down the steps on the right is *St. Andrew's Chapel,* corresponding to St. Anselm's on the other side of the choir, and forming an approach to the Norman Treasury.

The **North-east Transept** shows the skilful adaptation of earlier work made by William of Sens to harmonise with his own Choir. In the north-east corner is the *Chapel of St. Martin of Tours,* disused since the Reformation, and restored in memory of Viscount Milner (1854–1925).

The **North-west Transept** is known also as *The Martyrdom,* and was the scene of the tragedy that established the fame of Canterbury throughout Christendom. It was almost completely rebuilt in the 15th century, and the doorway leading into the Cloister replaces the one by which Becket and the Knights entered the Cathedral. In the south-east part the Murder Stone marks the spot where Becket fell.

The Murder of Becket. The quarrel between Henry II and Becket centred on the question of whether priests should, or should not, be subject to civil laws. The banished prelate ventured to return to England in 1170 and acted in a high-handed manner which incurred the wrath of Henry, then in France. The King's thoughtless remark "Will no man rid me of this turbulent priest?" was taken up by four of his knights, Fitzurse, de Moreville, de Tracy and le Bret, who went to Canterbury and threatened Becket in his Palace. Monks insisted that Becket should take refuge in the Cathedral, but he was followed and slaughtered in the north-west transept. Later Henry II did penance and allowed himself to be scourged by monks in the crypt of the Cathedral.

From the Martyrdom one can descend to the **Crypt,** the whole of which was dedicated to the Virgin, "Our Lady of the Undercroft". The westward portion was built by Prior Ernulf in Anselm's time, and is a fine specimen of Norman groin-vaulting. Note especially the quaint devices on the capitals of the pillars. The eastern Crypt was the work of William the English-man (1180–84). It is much loftier and lighter than the other portion. Here Becket's body was placed for 50 years before its removal into the magnificent Shrine above.

The Monastic Buildings. The **Cloisters** are reached from the Martyrdom. Portions of the earlier cloister of Lanfranc's time may still be traced, and the north wall—part of the frater or dining-hall—shows some beautiful Early English arcading. Among those buried in the

Cloisters are Dean Farrar, Archbishop Temple, Dean Wace, and "Dick" Sheppard (Dean 1929–31). From the east side of the Cloisters one enters the **Chapter House,** originally built by Lanfranc, rebuilt in 1304, and restored 1897. The adjoining **Library** is a rebuilding after war damage. There are some 30,000 printed books and many old manuscripts. Farther east are the remains of the Infirmary and the Water-tower. Library Passage leads from the Infirmary to *Green Court,* a most delightful and picturesque part of the precincts. Around the court were once grouped the brewery, the bakehouse, and other menial offices of the monastery.

Across the court is the Norman Porch and Staircase, now forming a part of **King's School.** This famous school received its present name when refounded by Henry VIII, but claims to have been in existence from the days of Ethelbert and Augustine. The few remains of the Archbishop's Palace, in Palace Street, have been incorporated into the present Palace.

St. Augustine's Abbey and College *(Abbey ruins daily, fee. College between 2 and 4 p.m., Weds and Thurs).* The Abbey, outside the city walls, was founded at the same time as the Cathedral. It is the burial place of King Ethelbert and his Queen, of St. Augustine himself, and of a number of the early Archbishops. After the Conquest, the Abbey Church was completely rebuilt in the Norman style, and lasted until the Dissolution in Henry VIII's time, when it was pulled down and the materials sold for building purposes. By the early 19th century everything had fallen into decay, and the land and ancillary buildings were being used for a variety of purposes. In 1844 a benefactor bought up all that was still available, and donated the site for a College to train missionaries; this was opened in 1948.

The **College** stands a short distance to the south-east of the Cathedral, and is entered from Monastery Street, through the fine Abbey Gateway built in 1309. Adjoining this on the west side of the court is the 14th-century Guest House that now serves as the College dining hall. The Library opposite stands on the foundations of the Abbot's Banqueting Hall. Since 1969 the College has been occupied by theological students of Kings' College of the University of London.

The **Abbey Ruins** lie beyond the College. Traces can be seen of the monks' dormitory, kitchen, refectory and cloisters. The great Abbey Church was once about the size of the cathedrals of Gloucester or Norwich, but little now remains. The most striking part of the ruins is the Crypt. A short distance eastward is the ruined Church of St. Pancras, built of Roman brick.

From St. Augustine's turn left along Monastery Street, and then left again into Longport, when after a short distance one sees on the left *St. Martin's Church.* Though largely rebuilt this can claim to be oldest church in this country that has been in continuous use. Queen Bertha was already using it as a Christian oratory before St. Augustine ever set foot in England.

One can return to the city by way of Longport, Church Street and Burgate, where is the *Roman Catholic Church of St. Thomas,* containing a relic of the Saint. At the end of Burgate is the site of the old Butter Market.

About a mile from the city, in a fine commanding position on St. Thomas's Hill, are the buildings of the **University of Kent.**

Harbledown (1 mile), on the Chatham road—the old Watling Street—is the "little town" of Chaucer, where the pilgrims obtained their first sight of the Cathedral. Here is the Black Prince's Well. The ancient *St. Nicholas' Church,* on the left of the road, should be seen. It was built in 1085 as part of a hospital for lepers, and was such for 100 years. The parish church of St. Michael, much restored, is on the right of the road.

The road from Watling Street to Chartham Hatch traverses **Bigbury Wood,** where is an extensive earthwork hill-fort of the Early Iron Age.

At **Hackington,** a mile north of Canterbury, are an ancient Church and Sir Roger Manwood's Almshouses.

On the Maidstone road, just outside Canterbury, is **Thanington,** an ancient manor mentioned in Domesday Book.

DEAL–BETTESHANGER

Deal

Angling.—The long stretch of coast here is popular with deep-sea anglers. There are cabins at the pier-head. Boat and shore fishing.
Beach.—Shingle in steep terraces. Sand at low water at north end.

Early Closing.—Thursday.
Hotels.—*Queen's, Black Horse, Royal, The Gables.*
Population.—27,130.
Post Office.—Stanhope Road.

Deal, amalgamated with Walmer since 1935, can be recommended to those who like bracing air and the bustle of the sea. The sea-front is somewhat austere. The low coast line runs north–south in a straight line from Sandown Castle to Walmer Castle, with a shingle beach that rises in steep terraces. Upper Deal, the oldest part of the town, lies back from the sea. From the railway station it is some three-quarter-mile along the London Road to the old parish *Church of St. Leonard.* This dates in part from the 12th century, and the curious cupola crowning the tower was once a landmark for shipping. From the station the shortest way to the beach is by Queen Street; this is crossed at right angles by High Street, which continues its southward course as Victoria Road and then the Strand.

On the Front is the square *Signal Tower,* with a time-ball at its summit. In 1957 a new Pier was opened, from which Channel cruises and trips to France run in summer. Fronting the Pier is South Parade, southward of which is Victoria Parade, leading to **Deal Castle** *(fee).* The castle was erected by Henry VIII as part of a great scheme of coast defence—at the same time as Walmer and Sandown castles. It is circular in form with a double row of stone bastions. Entrance is from the landward side, across a drawbridge. A plaque in Marine Road, near the castle, records the landing of Julius Caesar in 54 B.C. somewhere near this spot. Inland from the Strand is the *Royal Marine Depot.* About one mile farther south along the coast is **Walmer Castle** *(fee).* Since the the early 18th century, this has been the official residence of the Lord Warden of the Cinque Ports, and its character has gradually changed from a castle to a dwelling-house. The apartment known as the Duke of Wellington's Room is preserved exactly as when the Duke (*d.* 1852) occupied it. Northward from the Pier a series of promenades run for a mile to **Sandown Castle,** of which little now remains but the arched foundation-walls. The site now forms an attractive rock garden.

To Kingsdown and Ringwould. Kingsdown is two miles from Dene Castle and can be gained along the shore. Old Kingsdown is one of the quaintest and prettiest places imaginable; its cottages all at right angles to the beach. At the back of the village is the pretty church while south of the old village is the clubhouse of the *Walmer and Kingsdown Golf Club.* From the top of the cliffs there are good views over the Downs. **Ringwould** is a mile inland on a lofty site with a fine seaward prospect. The 12th-century church of flint and 17th-century tower with heavy brick buttresses, and two wonderful old yew trees in the churchyard are set on a hill.

To Betteshanger, Eastry, etc. (Bus services). From the railway station follow the Upper Deal Road to the Church, there turning right, along the Sandwich road, to Sholden, where turn left to **Great Mongeham,** two miles west-south-west of Deal. The Church, with its massive embattled tower, is mainly of the Norman and Early English periods. The road turns to right just south of the Church and descends steeply and ascends more steeply to **Northbourne,** where there is a fine little church originally built by monks from St. Augustine's, Canterbury. A mile or more westward of Northbourne is **Betteshanger House,** at one time the seat of Lord Northbourne, and now a school. In the park is a pretty little modern Church built of flint in Norman style and retaining an original Norman window and doorway from the old church.

Eastry lies a mile-and-a-half northward on the old Roman road from Dover. It is a place whose name figures largely in early Kentish annals. Many remains of the British, Roman and Saxon periods have been found in the locality. The Church contains Norman features, notably the tower and west doorway, but is for the most part Early English with a fine high clerestoried nave.

38

Woodnesborough, midway between Eastry and Sandwich, was another important Saxon station. The name is said to be derived, like our Wednesday, from the god Woden. The Church, with a curious little bell tower, probably of Flemish influence, contains a beautifully carved piscina and sedilia and three brasses.

About two-and-a-half miles north-west of Eastry on the Wingham road is the farming village of **Staple.** The Church has traces of Saxon work and a Norman south wall, but is chiefly of the 14th and 15th centuries.

To Knowlton, Goodnestone and Adisham. A good walk of about 12 miles can be taken between Eastry and Wingham (both of which are in touch with Deal by bus). From Eastry go south-westward and by Mill Lane reach **Heronden.** At the top of the hill take footpath on left to the tiny old village of **Knowlton.** The little church has a fine Jacobean three-decker pulpit.

From Knowlton either continue west for a mile to **Chillenden,** where there is a windmill and a church with Norman doorway, some ancient glass, and a Jacobean pulpit; or go through Knowlton Park and Nonington Park (near St. Alban's Court) north-west to **Goodnestone.** This stands in the midst of a beautiful park, the 13th-century church raised high above the village street, and containing many brasses.

Adisham (station on the Canterbury–Dover line) is reached via the hamlet of Raling. It was on the ground formerly occupied by Adisham Mill that, in 54 B.C., Caesar's legions attacked and defeated the Celts. The large Church is beautifully situated near the crossroads at the north end of the straggling village street. The nave still has, running round the interior of its walls, the medieval "bench-table". The slope of the floor is from west to east. The 13th-century *Chancel* contains fine carved stalls and book rests. A few fragments of the medieval screen are inserted in the present chancel screen, and there are many medieval encaustic tiles in the floor.

St. Margaret's Bay *(Granville)* lies due south of Deal. The bay has good bathing, boating and fishing facilities and is famous for its prawns. The village, **St. Margaret's-at-Cliffe,** is a little inland. The church, a very fine Norman building, has an interior of Caen stone. Leathercote Point is the highest point on the coast hereabouts. On the point is the *Dover Patrol Memorial.*

The **South Foreland Lighthouse** *(not open)* where Marconi carried out some of his experiments has existed in one form or another since 1634 when the light was a coal fire.

Dover

Angling.—Excellent from piers, beach and boats.
Distances.—Deal, 8; Folkestone, 7; Canterbury, 16; Hythe, 12; London, 72; Ashford, 24; Ramsgate, 19.
Early Closing.—Thursday.
Hotels.—*Dover Stage, White Cliffs, Central, White House, East Cliff, Webb's, Mildmay* and others.
Population.—35,810.
Post Office.—Biggin Street.
Sports.—Bathing, boating, bowls and tennis, putting. Golf at Kingsdown.

Dover, a busy port and commercial centre, is situated between two high cliffs at the mouth of the river *Dour,* which in Roman times was navigable and formed the haven. The modern Port has one of the largest artificial harbours in the world. The most prominent feature of the town is the ancient Castle that dominates the East Cliff. The **harbour** is enclosed by the Eastern Arm (2,800 feet) and on the west the Admiralty Pier (4,000 feet). Cross-Channel services operate from the latter, adjacent to which is the Marine Station. The upper promenade of the Admiralty Pier affords unsurpassed views of the Channel. Beyond the two arms of the harbour, and unconnected with land, is the massive Southern Breakwater. The sea-front promenade, with its gardens and fountains, provides a pleasant walk from one side of the harbour to the other.

From the harbour the town extends along the Dour Valley. King Street leads to the Market Place, passing Castle Street on the right, and continuing to Cannon Street and the Parish *Church of St. Mary* with its fine tower. A little farther on the Folkestone Road branches off left, and Biggin Street continues past the Town Hall to High Street and the London Road. The Town Hall incorporates the **Maison Dieu Hall** *(fee)*, originally a "hospital" founded by Hubert de Burgh in 1203. Opposite the Town Hall a road leads to Dover College which includes portions of the ancient St. Martin's Priory.

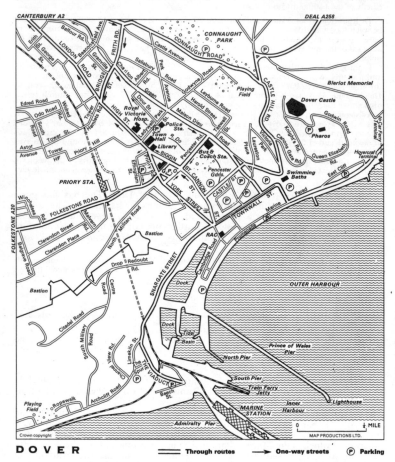

D O V E R　　━━━ **Through routes**　　→ **One-way streets**　　Ⓟ **Parking**

In 1970–71 the construction of a new road led to important archaeological discoveries near the harbour of Roman forts, confirming that Dover was the headquarters of the Roman fleet.

The **Castle** *(daily, fee)* is reached from the Market Place by way of Castle Street and the Constable's Tower, defended by drawbridge and portcullis. The massive Keep lies within the circular fortifications of the Inner and Outer Baileys. It was built by Henry II about 1180–86, and is of three storeys. The oldest buildings within the Castle are the **Church of St. Mary-in-Castro,** dating from the early 11th century, and beside it the stump of the Roman *Pharos* or Lighthouse, which together with a companion light on the Western Heights once marked the entrance to the haven. From medieval times onwards the defence system of the Castle has developed underground passages cut in the cliffs.

To Shakespeare Cliff. The first object for which a Channel voyager approaching Dover looks is the sharply-pointed peak, a little westward of the Admiralty Pier, known as **Shakespeare Cliff.** The railway from Dover to Folkestone runs along the shore until it reaches the foot of the slope, when it tunnels right through the Cliff. A footway along the edge of the cliff leads to a footpath which ascends steeply to the summit. A bus may be taken as far as Ropewalk.

To Buckland, River, Ewell, St. Radigund's Abbey. Go through the town to Buckland and River. Just before the bridge over the *Dour* is crossed at Buckland an asphalted footpath will be seen on the left, running between a large paper mill and **Buckland Church** (St. Andrew's), which can be seen well from the railway. It has a lofty nave with Norman pillars and an Early English archway. Continue by the road, and pass under the railway to the Athletic Ground at Crabble. Here is the County Cricket Ground. The road bends right for a few yards and then left at a mill, and runs side by side with the shady, picturesque *Dour* to the village of **River.** The prettily situated Recreation Ground at River has public tennis courts and bowling greens. River Church (St. Peter's), a flint and brick building, contains a font consecrated in the year 1010 by Archbishop Alphege, which was brought from an old church at Canterbury.

Of **St. Radigund's Abbey** the only parts remaining are the massive tower, portions of the chapel and refectory. The moat may be traced in the fields beyond. The Abbey was founded in 1190 and covered at one time an extensive circular area.

To Ewell Minnis and Alkham. The deep lateral depression of the Alkham Valley, served by buses from Dover and Folkestone, is extremely picturesque. The hills on the right of the road may be climbed to **Ewell Minnis,** a breezy upland village surrounded by a wealth of wild flowers, out from whence a pleasant woodland footpath leads down to **Alkham** *(Marquis of Granby),* two-and-a-half miles from Kearnsey along the valley road (B2060). This old village, sentinelled by lofty elms, lies in the deepest recess of the valley. The Early English church, standing high above the road, is of flint, with a square tower capped by a tiled, pyramidical roof.

Beyond Alkham is the Drellingore Spring, the source of one of the most important intermittent streams in the district; its river joining the *Dour* near Dover. The road climbs to the head of the valley and joins the Canterbury–Folkestone road about two miles north of Folkestone.

To Waldershare Park and Barfreston. Waldershare Park is most easily visited from Dover by bus from Pencester Road. Motorists take the main Canterbury road, turning to the right along A256 just before Ewell and left at the roundabout at the top of Whitfield Hill. At **Church Whitfield,** a mile to the east of the road (turn off at either end of Whitfield), there is a beautiful little church with Saxon windows, arch and masonry, as well as Norman and Early English work. The pleasant red-brick village of **East Langdon,** has an ancient flint church of some interest. Its particular treasure is a 15th-century red velvet cope-hood.

Waldershare Park is a seat of the Earl of Guildford. The mansion was built after a design of Inigo Jones in the reign of William III. The church is not visible from the road. It is reached from the Dover road by a lane having a letter-box at the corner, about a quarter-of-a-mile south of the signpost "to Eythorne". The church contains a number of curious monuments to members of the Monyngs and Furnese families.

Eythorne is a curious mixture of rural seclusion and industrial activities. On one side of it are the wooded acres of Waldershare, and on the other the *Tilmanstone Colliery.* At Upper Eythorne is the oldest Baptist Chapel in this part of Kent. It was built in the days of the Stuart persecution, in order that the worshippers might avoid the penalties of the "Five Mile Act", but there was a meeting-house here as early as the reign of Queen Mary.

Barfreston. Barson, as the place is commonly called, although its official name is Barfreston or Barfreystone, lies in the middle of open, breezy down country interspersed with parks and beech woods. A huge yew of great age in the churchyard contains the belfry. The lovely little Norman Church is dedicated to St. Nicholas and is as beautiful inside as out. The length

41

is only about 43 feet 4 inches. Built of flint and stone, it is said to have been erected about 1170. Both inside and out it is richly decorated with grotesque carvings. Just beyond Barfreston is the beautiful **Fredville Park.**

Along the Dover–Canterbury Road. The road follows the railway through Buckland and Ewell beyond which it veers away to **Lydden,** past which the road climbs the long and steep Lydden Hill (455 feet).

At six-and-a-half miles from Dover, a road goes off leftward to the pretty villages of Wootton (1¼ miles) and Denton (¾ mile farther). Wootton church dates mainly from the 13th century but the base of the tower is Norman. **Denton** is a peaceful place. Its church stands in a fine park surrounding *Denton Court,* with magnificent topiary. At eight miles from Dover the road from Folkestone (A260) joins the Dover Road (A2), having passed through Denton, about a mile-and-a-half south. The junction of the two roads is on the eastern side of **Broome Park,** a beautiful estate owned and loved by the first Earl Kitchener. The house was built in the reign of Charles I. A quarter-of-a-mile north of Broome Park a left-hand road leads to **Barham,** with a fine church surrounded by beautiful beeches. It has an unusual green copper spire, a fine roof, a 14th-century font with Jacobean cover, and several brasses. Eleven miles from Dover, a narrow road to the left leads in half-a-mile to **Bishopsbourne,** of interest through its association with *Richard Hooker,* the English Church theologian of the 16th century. He held the living from 1595 until his death in 1600. The large and stately **Church** with high tower has a wealth of glass, some of the 14th and 17th centuries, and the rest modern, including a west window by Burne-Jones and William Morris. In the chancel is a monument to Hooker. Skirting Bourne Park the main road drops to the village of **Bridge,** from the vicinity of which fine views are obtained. Bridge is ecclesiastically united with Bekesbourne and **Patrixbourne,** a pleasant little village of Tudor and Carolian houses, which clusters upon the north bank of the *Nailbourne,* about a mile eastward of the Canterbury road.

Folkestone

Distances.—Ashford, 17; Canterbury, 17; Deal, 15; Dover, 8; Hastings, 38; London, 71; Margate, 27; Ramsgate, 26.
Early Closing.—Wednesday.
Entertainment.—*Leas Pavilion* (repertory), *Marine Pavilion,* *Leas Cliff Hall* (concerts), cinemas, dancing. Bandstand on the Leas.
Hotels.—*Burlington, Continental Wampach, Grand,* *Lyndhurst, Garden House, Esplanade, Princes, Barrelle* and many others.
Population.—45,270.
Post Office.—Bouverie Place.
Sports.—Bowls, tennis, squash, putting, croquet, bathing, boating, sailing. Angling from pier, boats and beach.

The growth of Folkestone from a small but ancient fishing village began in 1843 when the South-Eastern Railway Company cleared the harbour, and inaugurated the Folkestone–Boulogne cross-Channel ferry service. Since then Folkestone has expanded as a residential and holiday resort and has fine hotels, public gardens, and entertainment facilities. Folkestone is best approached from the Dover road, from which one can look down on the town and harbour, and to the coast beyond.

The best known feature of Folkestone is the magnificent marine promenade called *The Leas,* one-and-a-half miles in length, with gardens and lawns high above sea level. Below is the *Undercliff,* with shady paths to the beach. At the foot of the cliffs is the Lower Sandgate Road *(toll for vehicles),* a favourite walk or drive. The Harbour Pier, 1,480 feet long, has a raised promenade that is open to the public. East of the Fish Market are the East Cliff Sands—the only non-pebbly stretch of sand. From North Street steps lead up to St. Peter's Church and the East Cliff; from here a broad promenade extends as far as the Warren. The oldest part of the town is that near the harbour. From Harbour Street one can ascend to the Town Hall by the quaint and narrow High Street (now for pedestrian use only). From the Town Hall, Church Street leads to the parish church of St. Mary and St. Eanswythe, whose chancel dates from about 1217. Westward from the Town Hall runs the long Sandgate Road.

FOLKESTONE ═══ Through routes → One-way streets ℗ Parking

Sandgate, about one mile from the centre of Folkestone, is a pleasant little place at the foot of the Shorncliffe heights. The Lower Sandgate Toll Road ends at the Riviera and Castle Road, near which are the remains of **Sandgate Castle** on the shore. Little remains but the circular keep of this castle, which like that at Deal was built in the reign of Henry VIII.

To the Warren. The Warren, the coastal area north-east from Folkestone, is as wildly beautiful as the famous Landslip between Shanklin and Ventnor in the Isle of Wight. Motorists can follow Wear Bay Road at the back of the East Cliff. Pedestrians can go along the East Cliff or take the bus up the Dover Road as far as the *Valiant Sailor Inn,* at a height of 546 feet above sea level. Here a footpath leads along the cliff to the end of a zigzag path cut in the cliff and leading down to the Warren. At low tide it is possible to go along the sands and boulders at the foot of the Wear Bay Cliffs.

To Caesar's Camp and Paddlesworth. Caesar's Camp (400 feet), the conical knoll immediately north of the by-pass, is the most prominent and the best known of the chain of hills girdling the town. It is generally considered that the hill has no real title to the name it bears; that the great earthworks and entrenchments, which can still be clearly traced, were

43

constructed between 1000 and 1150. At the base of the hill, on the western side, is the series of three Reservoirs, from which Folkestone is supplied with water.

From the northern slope of Caesar's Camp, a straight road following the municipal boundary leads eastward to the Canterbury road, near the Holy Well, and westward by Cheriton Hill, presently dropping down to Newington. From this road two roads lead northward over the hills to Paddlesworth, the highest village in East Kent (611 feet). The better road branches off about half-a-mile east of the Camp, and passes **Hawkinge Airfield,** the one-time famous Battle of Britain R.A.F. station. The tiny church at **Paddlesworth** has Saxon and Norman features and includes a small nave and smaller chancel, separated by a Norman arch.

To Shorncliffe Camp. Shorncliffe Camp occupies an extensive area on the ridge above Sandgate, about two miles west of the centre of Folkestone. Its name signifies the bare or shorn rock. Sir John Moore, the hero of Corunna, trained his troops at Shorncliffe in 1794; it remained a military station until 1815, and after a period of disuse was re-established during the Crimean War. The Camp is now the Headquarters of 2nd Infantry Brigade and of the Dover/Shorncliffe Garrison.

To Lyminge and Elham. These historic spots can be reached by the road through Cheriton, Newington and Beachborough. The Canterbury via Elham buses will aid walkers, while motorists can have a pleasant run outward by the Elham Valley. **Lyminge,** seven miles north-west of Folkestone, was the *Villa Limenoea* of the Romans. The Church is built of flint. It contains tiles, probably taken from early Roman buildings, and traces of Saxon masonry. Northward the road for several miles keeps company with the *Nailbourne,* a tributary of the *Little Stour.* After one mile there is a turning to the right for Acrise, where the Church, mentioned in the Domesday Book, is of Saxon origin, and was extended in Norman times. Note the carved Royal Arms of William and Mary with escutcheon to the effect that they were placed there after the death of Mary. *Acrise Place,* is of Tudor origin, the north front being mainly Elizabethan. In two miles road and river arrive at **Elham** (pronounced Eelham), a one-time market village, picturesque and interesting alike for its ancient church and its quaint old dwelling-houses. The wonderful Tudor house in the High Street contains magnificent carving both inside and in the oak brackets unholding the eaves.

Hythe (Pop.: 11,700. Hotels: *Imperial, Stade Court, Leabrook, White Hart*) about five miles west of Folkestone, was once an important Cinque Port, but its harbour has long silted up and the sea receded. The newer part of the town is on reclaimed land; the older part is on the hillside, dominated by the Parish *Church of St. Leonard* with its square pinnacled tower. The Crypt dates from 1225, and contains a vast collection of skulls, probably from a medieval ossuary.

An attractive feature is the **Royal Military Canal,** which starts at Eastbrook on the eastern limit of Hythe, and extends through the town to Rye and beyond. The Canal was constructed during the Napoleonic era, at the same time as the Martello Towers that dot the south-east coast. Between the canal and the sea are numerous public gardens and recreation grounds, and a long Sea Wall and Promenade.

The **Romney, Hythe and Dymchurch Railway** is a miniature railway of 15-inch gauge that is much appreciated by holiday makers. It was developed by a railway enthusiast, Captain Howey, and opened in 1927 between Hythe and New Romney. Soon after it was extended to Dungeness Lighthouse, making a total track length of 13¾ miles.

Saltwood Castle *(Weds, July–Aug., fee)* two miles north-west. Most of the Norman castle is in ruins but the hall now restored is used as a library. The two towers of the gateway are early Perpendicular work.

Stutfall Castle on the bank of the Royal Military Canal was a Roman fortress covering about 10 acres. Huge masses of masonry lie at the foot of the cliffs.

Lympne, two-and-a-half miles west of Hythe, stands on a lofty cliff above Romney Marsh. The church with massive central tower is of Norman origin. The **Castle** *(June–Sept., daily. Also Weds, Suns, Bank Hols, Apr., May, Oct.)* is a medieval building built on site of an earlier castle. To the west is Ashford airport.

Romney Marsh. The Royal Military Canal, in its wide semicircular sweep from Hythe to Rye, roughly follows the former coastline. The thinly populated tract of alluvium and shingle between c. nal and sea is known as Romney Marsh; though this is sometimes sub-divided into Romney Marsh proper, Walland Marsh, and Denge (or Dunge) Marsh that adjoins Dungeness. The sea erosion is kept back by the ancient and massive Dymchurch Wall, four miles in length and over 20 feet in height. In the shelter of this sea-wall, and well below the level of high tide, is the village of **Dymchurch** with its little Norman church. One of the attractions to the holiday-campers in this area is the five-mile stretch of firm sand, in contrast to the usual shingle or pebbles.

New Romney (contemporary with neighbouring Old Romney) was once a Cinque Port, but now lies one mile inland. In 1086 it possessed three churches, of which one of great interest still remains. Lydd, some four miles to the southwest, is of pre-Saxon origin. It is a small town with interesting old buildings, and a great medieval Church that is sometimes termed "the Cathedral of Romney Marsh". At one period of his life Cardinal Wolsey was the Rector of this parish.

Dungeness. The Ness, the most southerly point of Kent, is a steep-sided promontory formed of shingle. The modern lighthouse was built 1960. The Dungeness "A" Power Station is the fifth nuclear power station in England.

Into Sussex

Rye (Pop.: 4,430. Hotels: *Mermaid, George, Hope Anchor, Ship Inn*) is a busy and picturesque small town that delights all visitors. It lies about three miles within the borders of Sussex. If approached from Romney Marsh, Rye will be seen to stand on a hill, with the Parish Church of St. Mary at the summit. The church dates from 1120; it is one of the largest in Sussex and has a notable Tower Clock of which the long pendulum swings within the church. Rye was once an important port but the sea has receded for two miles, exposing a broad stretch of marshland across which the *Rother* winds its way to the coast. Adjoining the Church is the 18th-century Town Hall, and nearby is the Ypres Tower, a venerable watch-tower that now houses the Rye Museum. West of the church, Mermaid Street descends to the Strand and the site of the former Strand Gate, where a portion of the old wall still remains. From the Strand one may ascend via the Mint, High Street and East Cliff to the Landgate (*c.* 1360), the only survivor of the three portals that guarded the town.

From Rye the road runs south to Winchelsea, passing on the left the ruins of **Camber Castle,** another of Henry VIII's coast defences, once by the sea but now left high and dry.

Winchelsea *(New Inn)* was once considerably more important than its near neighbour Rye. But this was when it was a port, some three miles south-east of its present position. So severe was erosion by the sea that at the end of the 13th century the whole town was rebuilt farther inland. The new and well-planned town suffered repeatedly from attacks by French raiders, notably in 1380, and all that now remains of Winchelsea is a quiet and picturesque village though with many traces of its former glories. The Church is but the easternmost portion of the great church erected 1288–92 and dedicated to St. Thomas the Martyr. Among its monuments is the richly decorated tomb of Gervase Alard, Admiral and Warden of the Cinque Ports in the reign of Edward I. Three of the gateways in the old town wall still survive—the Pipewell (or Land) Gate, the Strand Gate which is the best-preserved, and the New Gate to the south.

Hastings and St. Leonards

Beach.—Shingle, but wide expanse of sand at low tide. Swimming at White Rock Baths.
Early Closing.—Wednesday.
Entertainment.—*White Rock Pavilion, Pier Pavilion,* cinema, dancing. Warrior Square and Alexandra Park (bands). Dancing.

Hotels.—*Queens, Royal Victoria, Warrior, Yelton, Fairlight Cove, Chatsworth* and many others.
Population.—69,110.
Post Office.—Cambridge Road.
Sports.—Bathing, boating, bowls, tennis, putting. Regatta in June.

Hastings was one of the original Cinque Ports established by Edward the Confessor. St. Leonards, now continuous with it, was founded and built by James Burton (father of the more famous Decimus) from 1828 onward. The two towns are now merged and form one of the largest resorts on the south coast, combining historical associations and modern amenities with beautiful surroundings.

The beach is of sand and shingle, and the sea-front has a splendid Parade three miles in length, the busiest section being White Rock immediately west of the Pier. Here is the *White Rock Pavilion* for concerts and conferences; it also houses the Hastings Embroidery (even longer than the Bayeux Tapestry) which was commissioned from the Royal School of Needlework to mark the 900th anniversary of the Battle of Hastings. Behind the Pavilion are White Rock Gardens and near these is the *Hastings Museum.* From the east end of White Rock, Robertson Street leads to the Clock Tower Memorial, from which six roads radiate. Close by is the Town Hall. Wellington Street leads to the elegant Pelham Crescent and the *Church of St. Mary-in-the-Castle.* A little farther on, a sloping Lift rises 228 feet to West Hill.

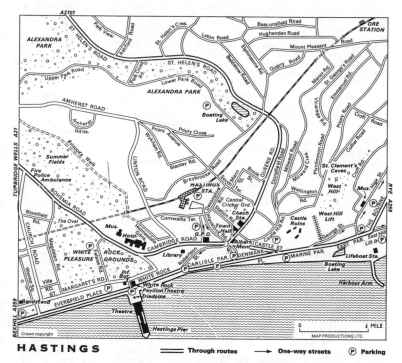

HASTINGS ════ **Through routes** ⟶ **One-way streets** ℗ **Parking**

The **Castle** *(daily, fee)* stands high on the cliffs. The "Battle of Hastings" actually occurred six miles away, but William the Conqueror's first priority after the victory was to start the construction of a strong castle at Hastings. Fragments of this remain among the present ruins. Beyond Castle Hill is a small lighthouse, and beyond this are **St. Clement's Caves,** a series of mainly artificial passages cut in the cliff, and developed during the 19th century as a tourist attraction. From West Hill steps near the lighthouse lead to the ancient **St. Clement's Church** (1380) and the Old Town. High Street (in which is the Old Town Hall Museum), and All Saints' Street to the east of it are representative of by-gone Hastings. *All Saints'*

47

Church (1430) is at the top of All Saints' Street; the lower end leads to the eastern limit of the Parade and to the Fishermen's Quarter. The Stade, or beach, is dotted with wooden "net-shops" for drying and storing the nets, and nearby is the old Fishermen's Church now a museum. The original haven was somewhat farther to the west, and silted up about 600 years ago. Efforts were made at the end of the last century to construct a harbour, but resulted in failure, and only the western arm remains. From the road called Rock-a-Nore, by the Fishmarket, a hydraulic lift (or alternatively 272 steps) brings one up to the wide expanse of East Hill.

Westward from the Pier is the "double-decker" Parade—Eversfield Place above, and a covered promenade below. This extends to Warrior Square, which roughly indicates the point where St. Leonards linked up with Hastings. Grand Parade and Marina lead farther west; past St. Leonard's Gardens and its portentious archway. St. Leonard's Parish Church was destroyed in 1944 and rebuilt in 1956. Its modern pulpit is shaped to resemble the prow of a boat.

To East Hill and Ecclesbourne. East Hill can be ascended by the lift or by All Saints' Street, Crown Lane and Tackleway. The summit of East Hill is a wide expanse of heath and greensward. The highest point of the cliff is 342 feet above the sea and the prospect is quite magnificent. **Ecclesbourne Glen** derives its name from "eagle's bourne". Picturesque, indeed, is the dainty gorge with its winding path, its crags, its tiny rivulet, and its miniature forest.

To Fairlight. By far the most interesting route is over East Hill, crossing the bridge over the mouth of Ecclesbourne Glen and ascending the eastern slope. A path then leads in a mile or more to the sister ravine. **Fairlight Glen** is even more beautiful than Ecclesbourne. There are few spots in the south of England where rock, foliage and water combine so well.

In the vicinity is Mallydams Wood, Fairlight, an extensive area maintained by the R.S.P.C.A. as a wildlife sanctuary.

Fairlight Down is the highest hill on this part of the coast, having an altitude of 575 feet. The church, a mile farther eastward, on the road to Pett Level, is a modern building in the Early English style erected in 1845.

To Westfield and Brede. Westfield is reached in five miles from Hastings by the A21, turning on the A28 shortly beyond Baldslow. The church includes much Norman work including a low chancel arch with squints on either side. Beyond the struggling village the road descends to the Brede Valley. At **Brede** the embattled church tower has a good peal of bells one of which is of pre-Reformation date. Notable features are a sundial in the south wall and, within the south chancel, a handsome effigy of Sir Goddard Oxenbridge dated 1537. Southward the churchyard commands a magnificent view.

To Sedlescombe. Just off the A21 seven miles north of Hastings, Sedlescombe is an attractive village with pretty 16th- and 17th-century half-timbered houses of mellow red brick and gay gardens. By the village green the *Queen's Head* displays a signboard representing Queen Bess. On the steep hill the churchyard is lined with some fine ancient chestnut trees.

Battle *(Beauport Park, George)*, seven miles from Hastings has developed on the site of the great battle of 1066. The main street runs through the heart of the old battlefield, and is bordered on its south side by the Abbey wall. In the Market Place the old Bull Ring is still preserved. **Battle Abbey** *(weekdays, Sats till 12.45. Also Sats p.m. and Suns in Aug., fee)* was erected by William the Conqueror in fulfilment of a vow made on the eve of the battle. The fine 14th-century Gateway stands overlooking the green. The Terrace covers the site of the old Guest House, and from here one has a good view of the battlefield, sloping down to the valley of the *Santlache* (or *Senlac*). Most of the great Abbey is now in ruins, but one part has been incorporated into a school for girls. Opposite the Abbey is the Parish **Church of St. Mary,** with its embattled tower; it was founded 1107–24 and still includes much Norman and Early English work.

Five miles to the north of Battle is the straggling village of **Robertsbridge,** and just beyond it the river *Rother* flows eastward, passing Bodiam to join the Sussex–Kent border for some miles and then curling back to Rye and the sea. The *Rother* is popular with anglers.

Bodiam can be reached by a right-hand turning half way between Robertsbridge and Hurst Green, but from Hastings the shortest route is via Sedlescombe. **Bodiam Castle** (N.T., *Weekdays, Suns, Apr.–Sept., fee*), moated and curtain-walled, was built in 1386 as a protection against French raids; only the walls and towers remain standing.

Northiam is easily reached from Bodiam via Ewhurst. The village possesses many ancient timbered houses, and the Church shows Saxon and Norman work. **Great Dixter** *(Apr.–mid-Oct., daily except Mons, fee)*, a mile from the village, was built about 1460 on the site of an earlier manor. The house and gardens were extensively restored by Lutyens in 1911.

Bexhill

Beach.—Fine shingle with sand at low tide.
Early Closing.—Wednesday.
Golf.—At Cooden and Highwoods.
Hotels.—*Annadale, Granville, L'Avenir, Southlands Court, Victoria.*

Population.—33,500.
Post Office.—Devonshire Square.
Sports.—Boating and sailing, bowls and tennis, putting. Fishing from boats.

Less than 100 years ago Bexhill was a small village, lying slightly back from the sea. Modern Bexhill is a popular and compact holiday and residential town. The dominant feature of the long sea-front is the *De la Warr Pavilion*, a striking glass-fronted modern building, with theatre, concert hall, restaurant and bars. Behind the Pavilion is the spacious roadway known as Marina. From here the West Parade extends towards Cooden, and the De la Warr Parade runs eastward towards the green slopes of Galley Hill.

Bexhill is well supplied with open spaces for recreation. Immediately to the north of the Clock Tower on West Parade is *Egerton Park* with lake, swimming pool and museum; adjoining is *Polegrove* Recreation Ground. A little to the west lies *Collington Wood*, an unspoilt tract of 12 acres. Farther inland is Bexhill Down, 44 acres of breezy common. From the eastern end of Marina, Sea Road runs inland for just over half-a-mile to the Old Town. This represents the site of the old village, clustered round the fine old *Church of St. Peter*, set on a hill. The building is mainly modern, but its history extends back to Saxon times.

Cooden lies two-and-a-half miles west of Bexhill and the intervening space has been completely developed with modern and attractive property. The beach, however, remains popular for bathing. Inland are the links of the Cooden Beach Golf Club extending almost to **Pevensey Sluice** now also known as Norman's Bay. The Sluice is a good spot for coarse fishing. The Martello towers that girdle the coast here were erected in Napoleonic times.

Crowhurst, four miles north-east of Bexhill, is famous for its old yew tree which stands propped up to the south of the church. It is believed over fourteen hundred years old.

Pevensey, once on the coast and an important port, lies some seven miles west from Bexhill. It is now a mere village, and its chief items of interest are the 13th-century *Church of St. Nicholas*, the old *Court House* (with museum), and the *Mint House (daily)*. This last dates from the 14th century and was so named because it was built on the site of a Norman mint.

Pevensey Castle *(daily, fee)*. Between Pevensey and its twin village Westham the road makes a loop to conform with the Roman walls of the fortress of *Anderida*, built 250–300 A.D., one of nine such fortresses guarding the southern shore. When William of Normandy landed in Pevensey Bay in 1066 he apparently had no trouble from this ancient strong point, and shortly after the Conquest the strong Pevensey Castle was constructed within the Roman walls. The castle was largely rebuilt in the 13th century, and substantial portions remain. The Roman walls are of flint rubble, of 10–12 feet thick and, in places 20–30 feet high.

Westham has a notable church, *St. Mary's,* with many additions since its Norman foundation. There is a fine view from its 15th-century tower.

Three miles north of Pevensey is **Wartling** *(Lamb Inn),* with its quaint old church. A farther half-mile north is **Herstmonceux Castle** *(Grounds only Apr.– Oct., Mons, Weds, Thurs)* a fine example of a medieval moated brick mansion. The castle is occupied by the Royal Greenwich Observatory and part used as residence of the Astronomer Royal. In the grounds is the Isaac Newton Telescope *(daily).* Herstmonceux church has a number of notable monuments and brasses. The village lies some way to the north.

Eastbourne

Beach.—Shingle, with flat sands at low tide. Bathing from shore and at Devonshire Baths.

Distances.—Bexhill, 12; Brighton, 22; Hastings, 17; Lewes, 17; London, 64; Newhaven, 13; Tunbridge Wells, 31.

Early Closing.—Wednesday.

Entertainment.—*Devonshire Park Theatre, Royal Hippodrome, Congress Theatre,* Dancing at *Floral Hall, Winter Gardens.* Band area. *Pier Theatre.*

Golf.—Royal Eastbourne Golf Club.

Hotels.—*Alexandra, Burlington, Cavendish, Clifton, Cumberland, Grand, Imperial, Lansdowne, Lawns, Mansion, Norfolk, Princes, Queen's, Sandhurst, Sussex, Verne House* and many others.

Population.—70,000.

Post Office.—Upperton Road.

Sports.—Bathing, boating, bowls, tennis (Devonshire Park), croquet, putting.

Eastbourne lies at the eastern foot of the South Downs, between the heights of Beachy Head and the low-lying shore of Pevensey. A model seaside resort, laid out on a generous scale, it owes its initial development (from about 1850) to the 7th Duke of Devonshire. The terraced Sea-Front is unsurpassed, and extends five miles with not a shop from end to end. The beach is shingle and sand, and there is a good Pier with a theatre at its end. Eastward from the pier runs Marine Parade, continued as Royal Parade past the *Redoubt,* a circular fort built in 1806, to end at Princes Park. Westward from the pier is the fine Grand Parade, carpeted with flower-beds. Opposite the Band Stand (with seats for an audience of 3,000) is the wide avenue of Devonshire Place.

From the western end of Grand Parade, the long Carlisle Road runs inland, and a short distance along this is *Devonshire Park,* the *Congress Theatre* and *Winter Gardens*—forming an entertainment centre catering for all tastes. Grand Parade is continued as King Edward's Parade, on the seaward side of which is the *Wish Tower,* a Martello tower that now houses a museum. The Western Lawns form a popular resort. Continuing in the direction of Beachy Head, the parade comprises four thoroughfares at different heights above sea level, the slopes between being clothed with shrubs and flowers. The lowest promenade terminates in the picturesque dell known as *Holywell,* a sheltered retreat for rest and refreshment.

From near the pier, Terminus Road runs inland to the Station. Beyond this one comes by way of the Goffs and High Street to the Old Town, the original East Bourne. At the top of the High Street, overlooking the churchyard, is the *Lamb Inn,* one of the oldest in the country. The *Parish Church,* dedicated to St. Mary the Virgin, dates from the 12th century. It has some fine oak screens and interesting old brasses. Just north of the Church are pretty *Motcombe Gardens,* with an ancient flint dovecot, and a pond that marks the source of the *Bourne.* On the seaward side of the church are more of Eastbourne's open spaces; first Manor Gardens (with the *Towner Art Gallery*), then Gildredge Park (with bowling greens), and a little south of this the Saffrons cricket and football ground. To the west of these lies the Royal Eastbourne Golf Course. Some two-and-a-half miles from the sea, near Willingdon, is *Hampden Park,* a fine wooded tract of 82 acres, with facilities for tennis, bowls and cricket; also a putting green and a cafeteria.

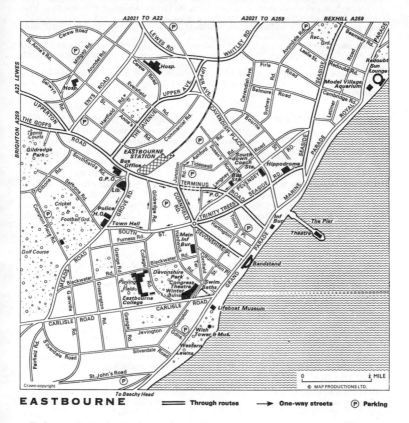

EASTBOURNE ═══ **Through routes** ➝ **One-way streets** Ⓟ **Parking**

To Beachy Head. The Head, one of the boldest, most romantic, and highest points of the South Downs, lies three miles south-west of Eastbourne. The route is via the Duke's Drive. The summit is 536 feet above sea level and provides far reaching views. The Lighthouse below was completed in 1902 and replaced the Belle Tout lighthouse now a residence, two miles west. Farther west is **Birling Gap** a remarkable dip between the lofty cliffs, and beyond again rise the famous **Seven Sisters,** high undulating grass-topped chalk cliffs.

Eastdean is a pretty, secluded South Down village three miles west from Eastbourne along the Seaford road, and rather more than a mile inland from Birling Gap. **Friston**, half-a-mile west, commands fine views.

Jevington is a small village on the Friston–Polegate road. The cottages are set amid rolling downland that stretches away on all sides—on the east to Combe Hill (636 feet) and Willingdon Hill (659 feet). Northward is **Wannock** with an old windmill and a beautiful sylvan glen.

Litlington is 10 miles north-west of Eastbourne with good fishing in the *Cuckmere* river.
Lullington, a mile north, claims the smallest church in England, 16 feet square.
Wilmington, eight miles north-west of Eastbourne, has an ancient Priory *(daily except Fris,*

51

fee). The adjoining church retains much 12th-century work. The famous **Wilmington Giant,** or Long Man, is a figure 80 yards in height, cut in the face of Windover Hill (600 feet). This is the largest representation of the human figure in the world.

Polegate has a fine red-brick windmill built in 1817 one of the few remaining tower mills in Sussex still turned by the wind.

Hailsham *(George)*, seven miles from Eastbourne, is a busy market town with a well-known cattle market on Wednesdays. The church has a fine embattled and pinnacled chequer-work tower.

Mitchelham Priory *(Easter–mid-Oct., daily)*, two-and-a-half miles west of Hailsham, is owned by the Sussex Archaeological Society. There is a restaurant and concerts and exhibitions take place in season.

Seaford (Pop.: 15,600. Hotels: *Seaford Head, Seven Sisters, Watersplash, Newhaven Mercury Motel*) is a quiet resort that offers a pleasing blend of sea-shore and Downland, and possesses two notable golf courses. It is comparatively sheltered from east winds by Seaford Head and the high ground above Cuckmere Valley. The long Esplanade is protected by a high sea wall. Towards the eastern end is a Martello tower, the last of a chain of 74 lining the coast from Folkestone. Sheltering behind the sea wall is the Salts Recreation Ground, offering facilities for various sports. The *Church* (St. Leonard's), near the railway station, has been much rebuilt, but retains some medieval work of interest. Adjoining Seaford on the north is **East Blatchington,** a suburb noted for its old church, its trim church-yard, and its picturesque houses.

To Seaford Head. The Head is the site of a prehistoric Camp, probably constructed about 300 B.C. but mostly destroyed by the action of the sea. The magnificent view is sufficient attraction, however, the hill-top being nearly 300 feet above sea level. The walk to the Head can be extended by continuing over the hill and descending to **Cuckmere Haven,** two miles from Seaford Church.

To Bishopstone. About two miles to the west of Seaford, at the head of a valley open to the sea, is the pretty village of Bishopstone. It may be reached by following the Esplanade westward and turning inland through the railway arch from which point the church is clearly seen ahead. To the right on entering the village is the former *Manor House,* a charming old building, since converted into maisonettes. On the front is a small stone slab with the Pelham buckle and the date 1688. The **Church** is remarkable for its ancient architecture, which includes Saxon, Norman, and Early English work. The oldest portion is the Saxon south porch, over which is a decorated Saxon sundial.

To Hindover. Hindover, or High-and-Over, two miles north-east of Seaford, is a favourite spot for picnics, with free car-parking facilities. It is nearly 300 feet high and commands a beautiful view over the valley of the *Cuckmere* and over Seaford Bay.

To Alfriston. The direct road leaves the town at Sutton Corner, and passing High-and-Over descends and runs almost parallel with the west bank of the *Cuckmere.* **Alfriston** is a picturesque old-world village just over four miles from Seaford on the west bank of the *Cuckmere.* It is a charming place amid quiet meadows between the river and the Downs. The fine old cruciform church stands in an open space a little east of the main road, with the river behind. The whole building dates from the second part of the 14th century. Close to the church is the Old Clergy House (N.T., *daily*), one of the few remaining pre-Reformation clergy houses. It dates from about 1350. Another great attraction of the village is the *Star Inn,* which dates from the early 15th century. It is adorned both inside and out with curious old contemporary wood carvings. At the corner is a large red wooden lion supposed to have been the figurehead of a vessel wrecked on the neighbouring coast in the 17th century. The carving just above this, of a bear and another beast with a staff between them, is thought to represent the supporters of the Dudley arms—a bear and ragged staff. Another interesting relic of by-gone days is the *Market Cross House,* an old inn taking its sign from the Market Cross opposite. The *George Inn,* opposite the *Star Inn,* is late-15th century and has a splendid stone fireplace.

To Firle Beacon and Glynde. The Beacon lies five miles south of Seaford and is a favourite objective for a tramp on the Downs via the Bletchington road and the golf links. The summit is 718 feet above sea level. At the top is a small cairn. The return is via **Glynde** which lies just below the Beacon and is reached by a path which descends by a plantation a little west of the summit. At West Firle is **Firle Place,** the seat of Lord Gage and home of the family since the 15th century. The Tudor mansion has a long panelled gallery and contains an outstanding collection of paintings, porcelain and furniture. *(Easter, then June–Sept., Weds, Thurs, Suns and Bank Hols, fee.)* Close to Glynde village is **Mount Caburn** (490 feet) the site of a hill-city occupied by Celtic people in the Early Iron Age. **Glynde Place** *(Easter, then May–Sept., Thurs, Sats, Suns and Bank Hols, fee)* is a fine example of early Elizabethan architecture with collections of bronzes, needlework and pottery. There is a small aviary.

Newhaven, now a busy cross-Channel port, was originally the village of Meeching on the west bank of the *Ouse.* Its name was changed in the 16th century when the course of the river changed, and this became the new port of Lewes. From the river the High Street leads up to the ancient Parish Church of St. Michael on Church Hill. The church is unusual in that the chancel is in the lower stage of the tower. The Harbour entrance is dominated by a high chalk cliff, and is protected on the western side by a long Breakwater and lighthouse. On the other side is the East Pier, also with lighthouse. The busy Newhaven–Dieppe services operate daily. There is also some import and coastal trade, and in summer the harbour is popular with yachtsmen.

North of Newhaven the A275 runs to **Piddinghoe** and two miles on, **Southease** with a little 12th-century church famous for its round tower. Next comes **Rodmell** at one time busy with silk manufacture.

Lewes (Pop.: 14,160. Hotels. *White Hart, Downside, Tatler*), administrative centre of East Sussex, is an ancient and attractive town set on a hill beside the river *Ouse.* The Eastbourne–Brighton road approaches the river by Cliffe High Street, in which the 15th-century *Church of St. Thomas à Becket-at-Cliffe,* Beyond the bridge the road continues straight on to pass through the centre of the town—up School Hill to High Street, and the farther rise of St. Anne's Hill.

The **Castle** *(daily, fee)* is reached by a short turning north of High Street. At the corner is Barbican House, and the entrance to the castle grounds is opposite this, just short of the 14th-century Barbican that spans the road. Lewes Castle, now a ruin, was at its prime one of the strongest castles in the country. From the Keep on its artificial mound, there is a fine view. The castle is now held in trust by the Sussex Archaeological Society, whose headquarters at *Barbican House* has an interesting Museum (the Society has another museum at *Anne of Cleves House* in Southover High Street). A little beyond the castle is *St. Michael's Church* with its circular tower and shingled spire.

If on foot, one can descend the steep and ancient Keere Street from near the church, passing on the left Southover Grange, to Southover High Street and *St. John's Church.* In the south-east corner of the church the Gundrada Chapel houses the remains of Earl de Warenne, and his wife Gundrada, daughter of William the Conqueror. They were originally buried in the great Priory of St. Pancras, which was totally destroyed at the Dissolution of the Monasteries by Henry VIII. Its scattered ruins lie to the south-east of the church. At the top of the hill, on the left is *St. Anne's Church,* one of the most interesting of the old churches of Lewes.

BRIGHTON AND DISTRICT

Brighton and Hove

Bathing.—The beach is of terraced pebble with sand at low tide. Swimming baths at North Road, King Alfred, Black Rock, Rottingdean and Saltdean.

Distances.—Arundel, 21; Bognor Regis, 28; Chichester, 31; Devil's Dyke, 5½; Eastbourne, 22; London, 53; Lewes, 8; Peacehaven, 7; Worthing, 11.

Early Closing.—Wednesday/Thursday, or Saturday.

Entertainment.—*Theatre Royal, Palace Pier Theatre,* Concerts at *Dome, Western Bandstand, Western Lawns.* Music Festival *(Mar.).* Brighton Festival *(May).* Casino, Cinemas, Dancing.

Hotels.—*Bidford, Brighton* Touring, Clarges, Cook's, Courtland's, Crest, Curzon, Dudley, Grand, Imperial Centre, Langford, Lawns, Metropole, Norfolk Continental, Old Ship* and many others of all grades.

Population.—Brighton: 164,700. Hove: 72,100.

Post Office.—Ship Street and 107 Church Road, Hove.

Sports.—Angling from piers and boats; bowls, tennis, putting, croquet, golf (6 courses); ice-skating rink, greyhound stadium; racecourse.

Brighton and Hove have so merged that it is usual to consider them as one unit. The development of this area dates from the end of the 18th century, and the interest of the Prince Regent (later George IV) in the small resort and fishing village Brighthelmstone. The twin towns now form a world-famous resort. The elegance of the Regency and Victorian town planning, the proximity of Downland, and the invigorating air, have attracted vast numbers of holiday visitors. Add to this the easy access from London, and one can see why Brighton has to some extent suffered from over-popularity. The Sea-Front extends for five miles from West Hove to Black Rock. The beach is pebbly, with sand at low tide, and there are two piers; from midway between them West Street leads to the railway station.

The *West Pier* was built in 1886, and emerges from that part of the promenade called King's Road. Immediately to the west, the foreshore is laid out with boating lake and putting greens, beyond which the King Edward Memorial marks the boundary between Brighton and Hove. Westward from here is a long stretch of wide lawns between Kingsway and the esplanade. Inland are the well-planned avenues and drives of Hove. Midway along Kingsway and on the seaward side is the *King Alfred Sports and Social Centre,* with two swimming pools, sauna bath, and restaurant. A stout sea wall continues westward, sheltering a stretch of reclaimed land that has been made into tennis courts, bowling greens, and a large lagoon for boating.

The *Palace Pier,* opened in 1901, is equipped with all amenities, including a Theatre. Between the foot of the pier and the opening to Old Steine (pronounced "Steen", and once the fashionable centre of Brighton), the road divides into Marine Parade on the high ground and Madeira Drive below. In the angle between these roads is the *Aquarium,* which now includes a dolphinarium. At the eastern end of Madeira Drive is a new Marina. Along the beach from Palace Pier to Black Rock (1½ miles) runs *Volks Electric Railway,* with an intermediate stop at the Children's Playground.

The best known of Brighton's public buildings is the fantastic but beautiful **Royal Pavilion,** built for the Prince Regent. The style is vaguely Oriental, with cupolas and minarets. Notable among the State Apartments are the Banqueting Room and Music Room, both added by Nash in 1815. The *Dome,* an outbuilding of the Pavilion, was constructed as the royal stable. It has now been converted to a concert hall, and the neighbouring Riding School to an exhibition hall. The *Library, Museum and Art Gallery,* in Church Street, adjoin the Dome. Other museums include the *Booth Museum of British Birds,* in Duke Road, and the *Thomas-Stanford Museum,* of 18th-century furniture and silver, in Preston Park. Brighton Town Hall and the Post Office both lie within the limits of the original

Brighthelmstone, as indicated by West Street, North Street, East Street, and the sea. Within this area, too, are the picturesque old *Lanes,* now given over to the selling of antiques.

BRIGHTON ═══ Through routes ⟶ One-way streets Ⓟ Parking

The *Parish Church* of Brighton (St. Peter's) is at the junction of the London and Lewes roads. The *Church of St. Nicholas,* in Dyke Road, though often rebuilt still shows Norman and medieval work. In the churchyard is the headstone to Phoebe Hessel, who served as a soldier and was wounded at Fontenoy; she died at the age of 108. Other churches include *St. Paul's,* with paintings by Burne-Jones and William Morris; *St. Andrew's,* the old parish church of Hove; and *All Saints,* Hove's fine modern parish church.

Brighton and Hove are rich in parks and gardens. In the central area the main floral display is concentrated at the Victoria Gardens, Old Steine, the Pavilion Grounds, and the sunken gardens along the sea front. *Stanmer Park* lies off the Lewes road, on the outskirts of the town. Here are the grounds and buildings of the **University of Sussex.** *Preston Park* is the largest of the central parks, and has many sports facilities. *Withdean Park* lies rather farther along the London Road, and opposite—reached by Tongdean Lane—is the *Sports Arena*. Other Brighton parks include *Queen's Park,* a quarter-mile inland from Marine Parade; and *Hollingbury Park* adjoining the Ditchling road, including both the municipal golf course and a prehistoric hill fort. In Hove are *Hove Park,* on Old Shoreham Road; the beautifully wooded *St. Ann's Well Gardens,* near the top of Brunswick Square; and the small formal garden of *Palmeira Lawn,* with its two-dialled Floral Clock.

To Patcham and the Downs. Patcham lies to the east of the London road and, away from the modern settlement, has attractive low-roofed cottages and a medieval tithe barn and dovecote. In the church is a "Doom" painting dating from 1170. The *Chattri* on the Downs commemorates Indian soldiers killed in the 1914–1918 War. Two miles north-east is **Ditchling Beacon** with fine views.

To the Devil's Dyke (5½ miles). Reached via Hangleton and the Brighton and Hove Golf Club. Strictly the name applies to a large earthen rampart thrown up in early times, but today is more generally applied to a great V-shaped cleft in the downs. The view from the top is magnificent.

To Rottingdean. Rottingdean is situated in a dene or valley four miles east of Brighton. From Black Rock an Undercliff Walk extends beyond Rottingdean to Saltdean. On the cliff-top road is the famous *Roedean School* for Girls. Rottingdean has developed as a popular resort in recent years but still retains much of its old-world flavour. **Saltdean** is a rising township with facilities for tennis, putting and a popular lido. **Peacehaven** is a popular residential area. On the cliff here a concrete monument marks the point where the prime meridian of Greenwich crosses the coast.

Shoreham-by-Sea, seven miles west of Brighton, stands at the mouth of the *Adur*. Old Shoreham lies on the east bank of the river a mile or so from the coast. It has an old church showing Saxon and Norman work and some notable carving. Old Shoreham Bridge, a timber structure that was the delight of artists, is now a mere footbridge, the A27 now using the new bridge lower down the river. As the *Adur* became less navigable, the port moved to "New" Shoreham, which also has a Norman church, St. Mary de Havra (i.e. of the Harbour), with a stately tower, and a 13th-century chancel that now serves as nave. Nearby is an interesting old building known as *Marlipins (museum),* which dates from the 12th century.

The mouth of the *Adur* widens out into a shallow harbour, protected by a long peninsula of sand and shingle with a good bathing beach on the seaward side. The river is spanned by a bridge which forms part of the road to Worthing and Chichester. Of late years the harbour has been greatly enlarged, and there is a brisk sea trade with the Continent. Many vessels entering Shoreham harbour turn east into the Canal, which extends for two miles towards Hove. Two new locks were opened in 1933 and 1958 respectively. Immediately to the west of the *Adur* is *Shoreham Airport*.

Lancing College *(Chapel daily)* stands on the slopes of the Downs overlooking the *Adur,* and is a conspicuous landmark. Founded in 1848 the buildings stand in grounds of over 550 acres. The Chapel was designed on exceptionally magnificent lines.

Bramber (from the Saxon Brymmburh—fortified hill) is a pretty unspoilt village six miles north of Worthing. The **Castle** (N.T., *daily, fee*) stands a ruin on a tree-clothed mound. The church is only a fragment of the original Norman building. In High Street is the *Potter Museum (weekdays, fee)* a kind of animal Madame Tussaud's. **St. Mary's House** *(Easter– Oct., daily except Mons, fee)* is a fascinating museum of English social history.

Steyning has a population six times that of Bramber but it is almost as quiet and reposeful in aspect, consisting of a long main street, with several old inns, a Grammar School founded in 1614 and some picturesque half-timbered houses. The quaint little Market Hall is almost extinguished by its clock tower. From Steyning it is an easy ascent to **Chanctonbury Ring** (783 feet) a fine viewpoint.

WORTHING TO CHICHESTER

Worthing

Beach.—The upper part is shingle but extensive sands are exposed shortly after high tide. Pool at Aquarina, and Lido west of pier.

Early Closing.—Wednesday.

Entertainment.—*Connaught Theatre* (repertory). *Pavilion* (music and shows); cinema, dancing.

Hotels.—*Beach, Berkeley, Burlington, Chatsworth,* *Cumberland, Eastley, George, Kingsway* and others.

Population.—83,080.

Post Office.—Chapel Road.

Sports.—Angling from pier and boats, bowls, tennis, riding, putting, golf (3 courses).

Although Worthing is a favourite quiet resort for many holiday makers, its rapid growth has been mainly due to an appreciation of its residential advantages by retired people and commuters. The town includes Broadwater to the north, and Goring to the west, and now has a population of about 88,000. The Sea Front extends for two miles. There is a sloping beach of shingle with sand at low tide. From the Pier the longer part of the Parade extends to the Marina Gardens and West Worthing. Eastward from the pier Marine Parade runs to Denton Gardens, adjoining Beach House and the *Aquarina* with swimming pools and café. Across the Brighton Road is Beach House Park, and beyond this the 17 acres of Homefield Park. From opposite the Pier, South Street leads inland to the suburb of Broadwater, and at the junction with Richmond Road are the *Town Hall* and the *Library, Museum and Art Gallery.*

    Broadwater Church is a mile north of the Town Hall. A cruciform stone building it has a massive central embattled tower and some fine old brasses.

    Sompting stands at the base of the Downs two miles north-east of Worthing. Here the church has a remarkable late-Saxon tower (10th century).

    High Salvington reached from the Findon by-pass by way of Bost Hill has a notable *Windmill.* This is a good starting point for the elevated walk along the Downs towards Long Furlong.

    Goring-by-Sea, the western flank of Worthing, is a prosperous township and **Ferring-on-Sea** also is another resort popular for holidays. *Highdown Hill* (N.T.), a mile north of the latter is crowned by an ancient earthwork and, on its western slope, is an excavated bath-house of Roman date.

    Lancing is two-and-a-half miles east of Worthing. There is a good sand and shingle beach and various recreational activities. To the north is the imposing Lancing College.

    To Findon and Washington. Findon is a picturesque little place regaining its old charm now that the by-pass takes most of the London–Worthing traffic. The church, on a Saxon foundation, retains some interesting features including an old sanctus bell above the pulpit. Findon has long been famous in connection with racehorse training and several stables provide hacks and hunters.

    Cissbury Ring (N.T.) is the largest and most impressive of the South Downs earthworks, a great oval series of embankments well preserved in spite of 2,000 years of exposure. Six hundred feet above the sea and with over a mile of ditch and ramparts enclosing its 80 acres, it is still a wonderfully imposing relic.

    Washington, two-and-a-half miles north of Findon is an attractive centre for Downland walks. The church was rebuilt in 1866.

    Chanctonbury Ring, 783 feet, is an ancient camp more or less oval within which remains of Roman buildings were disclosed in 1909.

    Storrington is a beautiful secluded village in Downland country. **Parham House** *(Easter–Sept., Weds, Thurs, Suns, Bank Hols),* two miles west, was built in 1577, with a fine Great Hall and panelled Long Gallery and rooms of beautiful furniture and paintings. The park contains deer and a heronry.

LITTLEHAMPTON–ARUNDEL

Littlehampton (Pop.: 18,200. Hotels: *Beach, Burbridge, Clarewood, Dolphin, New Inn*) is situated at the mouth of the *Adur* and displays a charming combination of sea, river and wooded downland. The river is navigable for small boats, and motor-launches run daily to Arundel and Amberley. At the mouth of the harbour is a lighthouse and a small pier. The river is crossed by a ferry to the golf links, and higher up by a swing-bridge to the Bognor road. A feature of this end of the sea front is the Green. Here is the *Western Pavilion* and a large Amusement Park —a never failing attraction for the children. The beach has a good expanse of sand at low tide.

From the Green, Fitzalan Road runs inland to join Maltravers Road near the *Library and Museum*. Off Maltravers Drive are the Pleasure Gardens, and a short distance to the north-east is the Sports Field. From here Berry Lane leads to the *Mewsbrook Pleasure Grounds* and boating-lake, near to the eastern end of the sea front.

Rustington, two miles east of Littlehampton, is a pleasant suburb with a sand and shingle beach. **East Preston** adjoins.

Toddington is a small village north of the town amid orchards and market gardens. Of interest is the Saxon chimney on Toddington House. Beyond **Wick** is **Lyminster** dating from Saxon times. The church was originally the chapel of a small nunnery probably founded about 925. The view from the churchyard towards Arundel is very fine.

Angmering is an old-world village about four miles north-east of Littlehampton. The church has a fine chequered stone and flintwork tower. Golf links lie a little north of the railway. About half-a-mile west is the site of a Roman villa, finds at which are to be seen in Littlehampton Museum. **Angmering-on-Sea** has a quiet shingle and sand beach.

Climping, on the west side of the *Arun* appears in Domesday Book as Clepinges. It was part of the extensive possessions of Earl Godwin, father of Harold, the "last of the Saxons". The church is notable for its design, the tower occupying an unusual position at the end of the south transept. The font and pulpit are 14th century. Beyond **Ford,** a small village which owes its name to its position on the disused Chichester and Arundel Canal, is **Tortington** where a barn at Priory Farm incorporates remains of the old priory. At **Yapton** the inn displays the remarkable sign *The Shoulder of Mutton and Cucumbers*.

Arundel (Pop.: 2,380. Hotels: *Norfolk Arms, Bridge, Camellia*) nestling below the castle of England's premier Duke, is an idyllic spot. From the Bridge over the *Arun*, the High Street rises to the crown of the hill, and castle and cathedral church tower grandly above the town. After crossing the bridge, one may turn right into Mill Road, in which is Lower Lodge the only entrance for visitors wishing to see the Castle buildings and apartments.

The Castle *(fee, and stated times)*. A Keep existed here at the Conquest, and was enlarged into a strong castle by later owners, notably Fitzalans and Howards. The Castle withstood two sieges in the 12th century, but during the Civil War it was laid in ruins by the Roundheads. The present buildings are mainly 18th and 19th century, but the circular Keep is original Saxon and Norman work. It stands on a mound 70 feet high. The Fitzalan Chapel, founded 1380, is actually part of the same building as the Parish Church. The great **Park** of 1,100 acres is freely open to the public, and can be entered either from Mill Road or from the London road at the top of High Street. Within the Park is the beautiful Swanbourne Lake.

The Parish Church of Arundel is dedicated to St. Nicholas and dates from 1380. The eastern portion—the Fitzalan Chapel—can now be seen from within the church. Nearby is the vast and imposing Roman Catholic Cathedral Church, built at the expense of the 15th Duke of Norfolk and opened in 1873.

Burpham is pleasantly situated near the *Arun* with fine views across to the castle and park. In a creek nearby was found in 1885 an ancient canoe formed from a single oak hollowed out by some ancient Briton. It is now in the Lewes Museum. The church is mainly of late Norman and Early English style. There is a so-called "leper-window" containing fragments of old glass.

Poling, south of the A27, is in pleasant surroundings. The church, which has associations with the Knights Templars is 12th century partly rebuilt 300 years later.

To Amberley, Bury and Bignor. The road route is through the woodland to Whiteways Lodge with a steep drop to **Houghton** where at Houghton Bridge boats can be hired *(teas)*. **Amberley** is five miles north of Arundel, a peaceful village attractive to artists and on a ridge with a precipitous drop on the northern side. The Castle *(not open)* was once a residence of the Bishops of Chichester. **Bury** is a prettily-placed little village near the main road and where John Galsworthy resided at Bury House.

Bignor is two miles from the main road at Bury on high ground. Bignor is the *Ad-Decimum* of the Roman itineraries—that is to say, "at the tenth milestone" from *Regnum* (Chichester) and lies on the old Roman Stane Street running across the Downs. The **Roman Villa** *(Tues, Suns, Bank Hols, Mar.–Oct., and Mons in Aug., fee)* was discovered in 1811. Part has been roofed over and in the subdued light mosaic work on the floors looks like a rich carpet.

Bognor Regis

Bathing.—Good from extensive firm sands.
Early Closing.—Wednesday.
Entertainment.—Cinema, theatres, shows, Music Marquee.
Hotels.—*Black Mill House, Clarehaven, Marl-borough, Royal, Royal Norfolk, Sussex, Victoria* and others.

Population.—31,220.
Post Office.—High Street.
Sports.—Boating, bowls, tennis, putting, golf at Felpham, riding. Fishing in *Arun* or from pier.

Bognor Regis has been known as a health resort for over a century, but still retains a quiet individuality. It has become a residential as well as a holiday area. The Sea Front has an expanse of hard sand and affords good bathing. The one-and-a-quarter mile Esplanade is raised a few feet above the groined beach, and stretches eastward as far as Felpham, which now forms part of Bognor. The Pier projects from near the western end of the Esplanade, and opposite is the seaward end of Waterloo Square, the hub of Bognor for holiday makers. Here are rock gardens and bowling greens. High Street runs to the north-east, and London Road, on the left leads past the Parish Church of St. John, whose spire is visible for many miles around. Inland from the Esplanade, by Gloucester Road and the east end of High Street, is the Upper Bognor Road, tree-shaded and with many fine mansions. Hotham Park, now owned by the town, was once the estate of Sir Richard Hotham, who towards the end of the 18th century made the first efforts to develop Bognor as a resort. Westward from the Pier, the Esplanade soon turns inland—at the Esplanade Theatre—to become Aldwick Road, which crosses Victoria Drive and Nyewood Lane. This last leads northward to the Sports Ground, and southward to the pleasant Marine Park Gardens.

Felpham, the eastern part of Bognor, is delightfully unconventional and has fine tide-washed sands. **Middleton-on-Sea** farther east has been developed on garden city lines.

To Aldwick, Nyetimber and Pagham. Reached by road or along the sands. Aldwick comprises, apart from modern residences, the *Ship Inn*, the post office, and a few thatched cottages. **Nyetimber,** two miles west, is a growing residential area and has a large holiday club. The shore at **Pagham** consists of a wide bank of shingle sloping one side to the sea and the other to low-lying land flooded at high tide.

CHICHESTER AND DISTRICT

Chichester

Distances.—Arundel, 11; Bognor Regis, 7; Bosham, 3; Brighton, 31; London, 64; Selsey, 8; Worthing, 22.
Early Closing.—Thursday.

Hotels.—*Bedford, Chichester Motel, Dolphin and Anchor, Ship.*
Population.—20,740.
Post Office.—West Street.
Theatre.—*Festival Theatre* in Oaklands Park.

Chichester is one of the earliest sites of the Roman occupation, when it was known as *Regnum*. It is now the county town of West Sussex. The Roman plan persists: from the Market Cross four streets radiate in the direction of the cardinal points, and once terminated at Gates into the town. The old defensive Walls that linked up these gates are for the most part still clearly marked. In the angle formed by South Street and East Street is a miniature replica of the same plan. North, South, East and West Pallants, an area once under the jurisdiction of the Archbishops of Canterbury.

The Cathedral was originally consecrated in 1108 but was destroyed by fire and rebuilt towards the end of the same century. In 1861 the spire collapsed, but was rebuilt within five years. The *Campanile*, or Bell Tower, is detached from the main building and adjoins West Street.

The *West Front* presents much of its original appearance. On entering by the West Door one's attention is arrested by the massive Norman architecture of the piers and arches.

In the *South Transept* is the beautiful tracery of the great South Window, 14th-century work but with 19th-century glass. The *South Choir Aisle* is notable for two magnificent 12th-century stone carvings depicting the story of Lazarus. The South Door gives access to the *Cloisters;* from here a walled passage leads into Canon Lane, extending from West Street to the Bishop's Palace.

The octagonal *Market Cross,* at the junction of the four main streets, was erected in 1500 as a shelter for traders. Near it is an old coaching inn, the *Dolphin and Anchor*. North Street has many attractive Georgian houses, and a fine old pillared Council House, built 1731. From beside the Council House, Lion Street gives access to the ancient *St. Mary's Hospital,* an infirmary and chapel built in the 13th century. Since the 17th century the infirmary portion has become eight model flatlets for old people.

Priory Park, within the north-east portion of the city walls, was once a monastery of Grey Friars; a portion of the church survives in the Park, and now houses some of the city's historic relics. The main Museum is in Little London, just south of the park. Outside the walls, beyond the site of Northgate, is Oaklands Park with its modern *Festival Theatre*.

East Street has some fine old houses. From Eastgate Square, St. Pancras Road runs north-east, and marks the start of the Roman Stane Street from Chichester to London.

Fishbourne Roman Palace and Museum *(May–Oct., daily, fee)* lies one-and-a-quarter miles west. The palace is the longest Roman residence found in Britain. The buildings covered five-and-a-half acres. Fine mosaic floors are to be seen. The museum illustrates the history of the site.

Bosham stands at the head of a creek of Chichester harbour. The historic Quay Meadows (N.T.) are best seen at high tide. This quaint and charming place is an ideal yachting centre.

Goodwood House *(certain days, May–Sept., see notices)* the fine ancestral home of the Duke of Richmond and Gordon, is three-and-a-half miles by road from Chichester. The house stands in a park with a circumference of over six miles. The building is of Sussex flint work by James Wyatt. There is a fine art collection. The Goodwood racecourse is very beautiful—the races were established in 1802. The traditional meeting commences on the last Tuesday in July, with two-day meetings in August and September.

The Selsey Peninsula. The tongue of land providing the southernmost point in Sussex lies directly south of Chichester, the distance from the city to Selsey Bill being nine miles. The west and north of the peninsula are bounded by the Channel from Chichester Harbour, that runs almost to Fishbourne on the western outskirts of Chichester.

The Chichester–Selsey road runs through **Sidlesham** and passes close to **Pagham Harbour.** **Selsey** is a small resort at the extreme south. Its Church is a reconstruction, using most of the materials from the ancient church at Church Norton in the north of the parish. Here the chancel of the earlier church still exists, and adjoining the churchyard is a Mound which in Roman times served as a defence point for Pagham Harbour.

Selsey Bill once ran much farther out to sea, and a Beacon warns shipping of the dangerous shoals. From the Bill the fine sands of Bracklesham Bay stretch westward to the resorts of *East and West Wittering*. The "Bracklesham Beds" that lie off the coast, and are uncovered at certain seasons, are rich in fossils and of great interest to geologists. The westwardmost part of the Peninsula is the narrow spit of land, East Head—so called because it is at the east side of the entrance to Chichester Harbour. The village of **West Itchenor,** opposite the mouth of Bosham Creek, is a boating centre. Two miles to the east is **Birdham,** a well-known yachting centre with a new Marina. The village lies one mile inland.

Along the Pilgrim's Way

WINCHESTER TO CANTERBURY

A pleasant route that begins in the woodlands and rolling hills of Hampshire, passes through the commons and heaths of Surrey and ends in the chalky downs of Kent. The route skirts the southernmost suburbs of the London conurbation. Many of the towns have retained their original character due to the absence of pronounced industrial development in the region. The route generally follows the Pilgrim's Way along the southern slopes of the Downs. The Way is an ancient track dating from prehistoric times. However it is traditionally associated with the medieval journeys to Canterbury Cathedral where the pilgrims paid homage at the tomb of the martyr St. Thomas a Becket. The pilgrimage was immortalised in *The Canterbury Tales* by Geoffrey Chaucer (1340–1400).

Winchester to Alton and Farnham

The road (A31) passes beautiful National Trust lands comprising parks and forests on the south. Just before **New Alresford** take the road on the left to **Itchen Abbas** and thence to **Avington Park** *(weekends, May–Oct.)* seat of a fine mansion dating from the 16th century. The house has a fine painted hall and red drawing room. The ballroom has a magnificent ceiling.

Farther along the A31 and one mile before Alton is **Chawton** where the novelist Jane Austen (1775–1817) spent the last years of her life and wrote *Emma* and *Persuasion*. Jane Austen died in Winchester but her mother and sister are buried in Chawton churchyard. The writer's house is now a museum.

Alton (Pop.: 12,700. Hotels: *Swan, Alton House*) 16 miles from Winchester, derives its main income from brewing beer. The church on the north side of the town has four Norman arches under the tower but the rest of the building dates from the 15th century. The south door is scarred by bullets fired in a skirmish between Royalists and Parliamentary troops in 1643. Do not miss the enormous yew tree in the churchyard. The *Curtis Museum* has objects of local historical interest including ancient farming implements. "The Wakes," a house opposite the church, has a library and museum with relics of Lawrence Edward Oates (1880–1912) the explorer who reached the south pole with Scott and died a hero's death in the icy wastes.

Farnham (9 miles from Alton) lies just over the Surrey border. Potteries and brickworks are its chief industries. Farnham is a very pleasant town on the river *Wey* and has many attractive Georgian houses. The Castle on the hill dates from 1662. It was once the seat of the Bishops of Winchester and is now a college. The ruins of *Waverley Abbey*, the first Cistercian community in England (1128), are two-and-a-half miles outside Farnham. William Cobbett, reformer and author of the great chronicle *Rural Rides* (1762–1835) was born in Farnham in what is now *The Jolly Farmer* and lies buried in Farnham churchyard.

Haslemere (10 miles south of Farnham) nestles among wooded hills. The town is famous for its annual July Musical Festival founded in 1925 by Arnold Dolmetsch. The festival features medieval music played on recorders and other old instruments. The *Educational Museum* is a pioneer in its field having opened in 1888. At nearby **Aldworth** is the home built by the poet Alfred Lord Tennyson who died there in 1892. Close by is **Hindhead,** a modern town near a huge depression known as *The Devil's Punchbowl.*

Farnham to Guildford

Leave Farnham by the A31 and about five miles toward Guildford there rises the *Hog's Back*. This is a long narrow chalk ridge, its sides sloping to north and south. The ridge rises to about 500 feet and forms part of the North Downs which extend to Kent in the east.

Guildford (Pop.: 57,000. Hotels: *White Horse, Angel*) 10 miles from Farnham is the county town of Surrey and has a cathedral and a university both of recent date. The steep, bustling High Street is full of picturesque buildings. The Royal Grammar School at the top of the hill dates from the 1600s. Its library has 80 chained books. The school also has the original *History of the World* written by Sir Walter Raleigh when Queen Elizabeth I imprisoned him in the Tower of London. The timber-faced Guildhall has a 17th-century clock that juts out over the street. Well worth a visit is the colourful *Angel Hotel*. The **Cathedral,** consecrated in 1961, stands on Stag Hill outside the town. It was designed by Sir Edward Maufe and built in pink brick in the modern Gothic style. A statue of St. John the Baptist by Eric Gill stands in the transept. C. L. Dodgson (1832–1898), better known as Lewis Carroll, the author of *Alice in Wonderland,* is buried in Guildford Cemetery. His house in Quarry Street is marked with a plaque. The *Yvonne Arnaud Theatre,* a circular building on the banks of the *Wey,* was inaugurated in 1965. Guildford dates from the times of Alfred the Great (900). Its name in Saxon meant *the ford of the golden flowers.* There are remains of Saxon walls on the hills rising on either side of the *Wey*.

Godalming lies four miles to the south of Guildford along the A3100 and was once Surrey's chief wool town. It has narrow streets and quaint houses. James Oglethorpe (1696–1785), founder of the state of Georgia, was born here. Charterhouse School was moved from Clerkenwell in London to Godalming in 1872. Distinguished former pupils include Lord Baden-Powell (1857–1941) founder of the Scout movement and Ralph Vaughan Williams (1872–1958), the composer. **The Winkworth Arboretum,** three miles south-east of Godalming along the road to **Dunsfold** has rare trees and shrubs and presents a splendid spectacle in autumn. Many wild birds live around the two lakes set in 99 acres of National Trust property.

Guildford to Reigate and Redhill

The road (A25) goes east through National Trust land. Some five miles along turn right toward Albury for **Albury Park,** the seat of the Duchess of Northumberland, where the house and gardens are open to the public *(May–Sept., Weds, Thurs)*. Continuing on toward Dorking we come to **Shere** regarded as the prettiest village in Surrey.

Dorking (12 miles from Guildford) is an excellent centre for visits to nearby beauty spots such as *Box Hill* which rises to 590 feet and *Leith Hill* the highest point in south-east England at 965 feet. There is a tower from the top of which 13 counties can be seen. The *White Horse* in Dorking High Street has an 18th-century front and parts of the building are 400 years old. Well worth a visit is **Polesden Lacey** *(Mar.–Nov., Tues, Weds and weekends)*, a Regency mansion built in 1824. The property of the National Trust the house stands in 900 acres of grounds near **Great Bookham,** three miles north-west of Dorking. On view are paintings, furniture and the gardens.

Reigate (6 miles from Dorking) is pleasantly situated at the foot of the chalk downs. Visit the church of St. Mary Magdalen, dating from the 1200s but famous for its wealth of 17th-century statuary. The most important monument is the tomb of Lord Howard of Effingham (1536–1624) conqueror of the Spanish Armada in 1588. **Redhill,** to the east of Reigate, is a modern suburb with a station on the main line railway to Brighton.

From Reigate and Redhill, roads run southward. Eight miles south on the A23 is **Gatwick Airport,** London's second airport. Just over the border into Sussex is **Crawley,** one of the "new towns" built after World War II.

From Crawley the A264 runs south-west for seven miles to **Horsham,** a busy market town with old buildings at the Causeway next to West Street. The town museum in Causeway House displays ironware and old instruments of punishment such as stocks and a whipping post. Two miles south-west of the town are situated the redbrick buildings of **Christ's Hospital,** founded in 1552 by Edward VI to educate poor children, and moved to Horsham in 1902. The scholars still wear the Tudor costume of blue cassocks, white collars and yellow stockings. The essayist Charles Lamb (1775–1834) and the poet Samuel Taylor Coleridge (1772–1834) were old boys of the famous Bluecoat School.

Reigate to Sevenoaks

The road (A25) passes through residential Surrey towns such as **Godstone** and **Oxted.** At **Limpsfield** the composer Frederick Delius (1863–1934) who died in France is buried in the churchyard. Just over the border into Kent is **Westerham,** a pleasant town to stop and have tea and visit its antique shops. This is the birthplace of General James Wolfe (1727–1759) who died while leading the capture of Quebec. There is a statue of Wolfe on the Green and **Quebec House** (N.T., *Tues, Weds, Suns, Bank Hols, Mar.–Oct.)* is where he spent his early years. Westerham Hill which overlooks the town is the highest spot in Kent at 809 feet.

Squerryes Court *(Mar.–Oct., Weds, Sats, Suns, Bank Hols, fee)* on the western outskirts of Westerham dates from the reign of William and Mary. It was here Wolfe received his first commission. The house contains period furniture and pictures and there is an attractive garden.

A diversion two miles south of Westerham leads to **Chartwell** (N.T., *Mar.–Nov.*), home of the statesman Sir Winston Churchill for 43 years until his death in 1965. The house, rich in Churchilliana including a brick wall built by the great man himself, is Tudor and enjoys a fine view of gardens and lake.

Sevenoaks (Pop.: 18,250. Hotels: *Crown Crest, Bligh's*) is a large and prosperous country town. Though overbuilt it has several attractive quarters such as the High Street with the 16th-century *Chequers Inn.* The top of the hill is crowned by a group of excellent 18th-century houses, Sevenoaks Grammar School and the Almshouses. The school was founded in 1432 but the buildings are Georgian. Sevenoaks has England's reputedly oldest cricket ground, the Vine, which dates from about 1775. Other older buildings in the town include the old Post Office and the *Royal Oak Hotel.*

Knole (N.T., *Weds, Thurs, Fris, Sats, Bank Hols, except Jan.–Feb., fee*) a magnificent baronial palace, is situated in the south-eastern fringes of Sevenoaks. The seat of the Sackville family it is set in 1,000 acres of fine parkland and presents one of the noblest structures in England mingling Tudor, Jacobean, Gothic and Renaissance styles with domes, battlements and courtyards. The complex of buildings occupies three acres and was begun in 1456. The building is much as it was in the reign of Charles I. On view are the state apartments, the Venetian ambassador's room, the King's Room, the Reynolds room, together with fine paintings and furniture. Herds of fallow deer wander in the spacious park.

Sevenoaks to Tunbridge Wells

The road (A21) goes by River Hill which with its gradient of 1 in 10 affords fine views of the Weald of Sussex and Kent.

Tonbridge (7 miles from Sevenoaks) a small but prosperous market town, is set amid charming scenery of orchards and hop fields. On a mound on the west bank of the river *Medway* stand the ruins of a **Castle** first built in Norman times. The remains comprise a 13th-century gatehouse consisting of two massive towers with a hall on an upper level. Tonbridge School was founded in 1553 but the oldest existing buildings date from 1760. Though overbuilt and plagued with traffic Tonbridge has managed to retain some of its old character, seen in such inns as the *Chequers*, the *Rose and Crown* and the *Elephant and Castle*.

Penshurst Place *(Easter–mid-Sept.)*, about three-and-a-half miles west of Tonbridge, is an imposing mansion begun in the 14th century and extended in Tudor and later times. The seat of the de Lisle and Dudley family, it has associations with the Black Prince, Henry VIII, Queen Elizabeth I and Sir Philip Sidney, author of *Arcadia*, who was born here in 1559. The house contains many of his relics.

A little farther west and well worth a visit is **Hever Castle** *(Easter–mid-Oct.)*, birthplace of the ill-fated Anne Boleyn. The castle began as a fortified farmhouse in the 1200s and became a manor in Tudor times. Tradition has it that Henry VIII first met Anne Boleyn here and he certainly became a frequent visitor during his courtship days. The castle has been much modernised by its present owners, the Astor family. It has a moat, a working drawbridge and fine gardens with a lake.

Tunbridge Wells (Pop.: 44,500. Hotels: *Spa, Calverley, Beacon, Royal Wells Inn, Swan, Marlborough*) lies five miles south of Tonbridge on the A26. It is officially known as Royal Tunbridge Wells after being patronised by delicate members of the Royal Family during the 19th century. Other distinguished patrons include Macaulay, Thackeray and Meredith. The town is 400 feet above sea level and won renown for its "chalybeate spring" discovered in 1606. The main attraction is the Pantiles, an old covered parade named after the flat Dutch tiles that were originally used to pave it. The Pantiles has many antique shops, a colonnade and across the road there is a beautiful row of limes. Mineral water is still sold there. The church of King Charles the Martyr, completed in 1696, is just across from the Pantiles and worth seeing for its fine ceiling. Toad Rock on Rusthall Common and the High Rocks a mile south-west of the town are curiously eroded pieces of sandstone that attract many visitors.

Tunbridge Wells to Ashford

The road (A21 and A262 after Lamberhurst Quarter) is an attractive route through fine Wealden landscapes. It passes through a region once famed for its iron industry and many of the villages along the way had their specialised forges and furnaces. **Pembury** is the first village after Tunbridge Wells and is better known for Pembury Woods nearby, a beauty spot much favoured by walkers. At **Lamberhurst Quarter** one can continue along the A21 which finally leads to Hastings and come to **Lamberhurst** (6 miles from Tunbridge Wells). It was here that the massive black iron railings of St. Paul's Cathedral in London were made. Lamberhurst has a street of pretty houses with white weatherboard and tiled fronts.

From here one can visit the neo-Gothic **Scotney Castle** and its gardens (N.T., *Apr.–Oct. except Mons and Tues*). The **Owl House,** home of the Marchioness of Dufferin and Ava also has gardens *(Mons, Weds, Fris, Suns and Bank Hols, fee)*. Close by is *Bayham Abbey* with ruins of a house dating from 1208.

On the A262 to Ashford we come to *Goudhurst,* another of the old iron villages. It stands on a ridge and commands fine views. There are several monuments to the Culpepper family in the church. The Culpeppers came from Bedgebury about two miles south, now the site of the **National Pinetum** occupying 50 acres.

At **Sissinghurst** (12 miles from Tunbridge Wells) **Sissinghurst Castle** is a castellated mansion built in the 16th century which later fell into ruin. It was purchased by the writer Sir Harold Nicolson who with his poetess wife Vita Sackville-West rescued it by transforming its courtyard area into enchanting and highly individual gardens and the ruins into a romantic home. Well worth seeing, the gardens are particularly beautiful in the spring (N.T., *Apr.–mid-Oct.*).

Biddenden some five miles along the A262 was also the site of a busy iron industry. It is remembered also for its "Maids": Siamese twin girls born about 1500. The girls, believed to have been great benefactresses to the town are still remembered every Easter Monday with a distribution of cakes decorated with their figures.

After Arcadia the road joins the A28 to **Ashford** (32 miles from Tunbridge Wells). This is a busy market town specialising in cattle. Much of Ashford was re-developed during the expansion of the railways in the 19th century but there is a large parish church dating from 1350 with a fine steeple in the Perpendicular style. Two miles west of Ashford is **Godinton Park,** a Jacobean mansion worth visiting for its panelling and wood-carvings. There is also a large collection of pictures and furniture *(Jun.–Sept., Suns and Bank Hols)*.

Sevenoaks to Maidstone and the North Downs

The road (A25 and later the A20) passes through Kent's most important hop-growing region. At **Ightham** (5 miles from Sevenoaks) a short detour leads to **Ightham Mote** *(Fris, fee)* which is just to the south of the village. This was probably a *moot,* a Saxon meeting place, though the building dates from the 14th century. There is a gateway, a moat, a tower, a hall and a chapel.

Some two miles to the east of the Mote is the hilltop village of **Plaxtol. Old Soar Manor,** situated at the top of a steep lane, is a fine example of a 13th-century residence and is now the property of the National Trust *(daily, Apr.–Sept., fee)*.

Beyond Ightham there extends a busy complex of roads with the A20 and the M20 in the north. **Wrotham** (8 miles from Sevenoaks) is a peaceful retreat from the traffic and Wrotham Hill just before the village gives splendid views of the surrounding countryside. Wrotham has a charming village square and a spacious old church. The A228 leads to Mereworth Castle about three miles south. This is a mansion based on Palladio's Villa Capra at Vicenza in Italy. It presents a handsome sight with its 60-foot dome set amid gracious parkland. The Earl of Westmoreland had it built in 1723 and with a somewhat arrogant decision had an entire hamlet cleared to provide the site.

West Malling (3 miles from Wrotham on the A20) has the ruins of a Benedictine abbey founded in 1080.

Maidstone (Pop.: 71,000. Hotels: *Royal Star, Bull, Veglios*), 17 miles from Sevenoaks, is the county town of Kent and a busy shopping and market centre. It has associations in history with the rebellions of Wat Tyler in 1381 and Jack Cade in 1450. The town's industries include brewing and paper-making. The 14th-century All Saints Church near the bridge is flanked by the Archbishop's

Palace. This contains old stables turned into a *museum of carriages*. The palace also has a banqueting hall with fine panelling. **Chiddingstone Manor** in St. Faith's Street is a municipal museum with a collection of good paintings and interesting archaeological exhibits. There are also relics of the writer William Hazlitt (1778–1830) who was born in Maidstone.

Aylesford (4 miles north-west of Maidstone) has a 14th-century bridge over the *Medway*. The Friary, first founded in 1240, is still used as a religious institution. At nearby **Eccles** there is a large Roman villa built in the early stages of the Roman occupation of Britain.

Allington Castle, two miles from Maidstone, is a late 13th-century building. Sir Thomas Wyatt executed in 1554 for rebellion against Queen Mary ("Bloody Mary"), lived here. It is now a Carmelite institution and can be visited by arrangement.

Boughton Monchelsea Place, four miles south of Maidstone, is an Elizabethan Manor *(May–Sept., Sats, Suns, Bank Hols, Weds in Aug.).*

Stoneacre at **Otham** (3 miles south-east of Maidstone) is a yeoman's house built in about 1480. It has been carefully preserved and skilfully restored with a wealth of timber in the interior.

From the A20, beyond Maidstone, **Leeds Castle** can be seen through the trees on the right. It is situated in the middle of a lake and was formerly the home of Lord Colepepper whose grandson Lord Fairfax took the young George Washington under his wing. **Lenham** has a fine village square and an unusual war memorial cut into the grass of the downs. **Charing** (13 miles from Maidstone) has a steep High Street with 18th-century timbered houses and a charming square in front of the church that was mainly rebuilt in 1590. At **Charing** the A252 leads to Canterbury and rises to 627 feet at the summit of Charing Hill with fine views over the North Downs.

At **Chilham** (8 miles from Charing) stands **Chilham Castle** built in 1616 by Inigo Jones. It has a Norman keep on Roman foundations and is the home of Viscount Massereene and Ferrard *(The falconry and gardens are open Easter–Oct., daily except Mons and Fris).*

For **Canterbury,** *see* Index.

Hants and Wilts

CHICHESTER TO PORTSMOUTH

The coastline between Selsey Bill and Portsmouth is broken by two harbours—Langstone Harbour and Chichester Harbour separated only by a narrow strait south of Havant to isolate Hayling Island. Their creeks were used by the Romans and the remains of their occupation can be seen at the *Roman Palace* at **Fishbourne,** less than two miles west of Chichester *(daily, Mar.–Oct., Nov. at weekends only)*.

The Chichester–Portsmouth road skirts the creeks at **Bosham, Southbourne, Hermitage** and **Emsworth,** all havens for yachtsmen. Bosham was the port from which Harold set sail on that fateful voyage to Normandy and this is the scene which begins the pictorial history of events on the famous Bayeux tapestry.

At Havant a road runs south to **Hayling Island** which widens in the south to a four-mile stretch of the Channel shore with fine golf links at Sinah Common, sandy beaches with pony riding for children, and extensive views of the Channel. Between St. Mary's Church and the beach is *The Hayling Billy,* a licenced house named after the engine which once ran on the island's narrow gauge railway. It now stands in the forecourt.

Portsmouth and Southsea

Distances.—Brighton, 48; Chichester, 17; Fareham, 8; Petersfield, 17.

Entertainments.—Cinemas—*Classic,* 151 Commercial Road; *Essoldo,* 42 Albert Road, Southsea and High Street, Cosham; *Gaumont,* London Road; *Odeon,* 94 London Road; *Palace,* Commercial Road; *Rex,* Fratton Road; *Tatler,* Kingston Road; *Troxy,* Fratton Road.

Dancing.—Locarno Ballroom, Arundel Street; Savoy Ballroom and Restaurant, South Parade, Southsea.

Early Closing.—Wednesday. Osborne and Palmerston Roads, Southsea close on Saturdays.

Hotels.—*Centre,* Pembroke Road; *Keppel's Head,* The Hard; *Ocean,* St. Helen's Parade; *Pendragon,* Clarence Parade; *Queen's,* Osborne Road; *Royal Beach,* South Parade; *Solent,* South Parade.

Library.—Central Library, The Square, Portsmouth.

Population.—227,000.

Post Office.—Commercial Road.

Sports.—Bowls: Greens at Pembroke Gardens, Southsea Common, near Canoe Lake, and in Alexandra, Cosham, College and Milton Parks. Cricket: The Hampshire C.C. plays matches on the United Services Officers Ground, Park Road. Fishing: From the shore and boats is permissible at all times and from South Parade Pier in winter. Golf: *Portsmouth City Golf Course* (18 holes). There is an "approach and putt course" (9 holes) between South Parade Pier and Eastney. Putting greens on Southsea Common. Tennis: Southsea Common (opposite Southsea Castle), in Pembroke Gardens, and near the Canoe Lake. There are also courts in the Portsmouth Public Parks.

Portsmouth city centre is dominated by the **Guildhall** planned in the classic style, the east front approached by a fine flight of steps leading to a portico of six columns. The building was badly damaged by enemy action in 1941 but was reconstructed and re-opened by the Queen in 1959.

Commercial Road runs north from the Guildhall to No. 393, the house where Charles Dickens was born in 1812. It is now a museum of Dickens relics with first editions of his works *(daily, free)*.

The **Dockyard** is approached from the Guildhall by way of Park Row and the Hard. Here lies **H.M.S. Victory** the flagship from which Nelson signalled to the

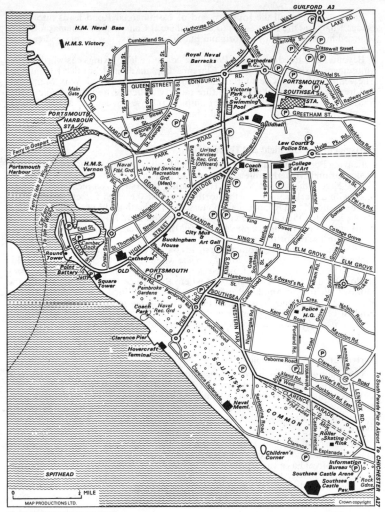

PORTSMOUTH ═══ **Through routes** → **One-way streets** Ⓟ **Parking**

men of his fleet before the Battle of Trafalgar. Visitors are taken over the ship. The tour includes the poop from which the famous signal "England Expects . . ." was hoisted, the quarters where Nelson planned the campaigns and the gun decks where the crew worked and slept, the quarter-deck where Nelson was wounded and the cockpit where he died. Just across the dockside is the *H.M.S. Victory Museum.*

FAREHAM–GOSPORT

From the Guildhall the southern end of Commercial Road leads into Cambridge Road and the High Street to the **Cathedral Church of St. Thomas à Becket** founded in 1180. Little of the original building remains; it was enlarged early in the 18th century.

Beyond the Cathedral is **Sally Port.** The coastline here swings eastwards to the amusement park at Southsea, the Clarence Esplanade and Southsea Common. The seafront bus service to Eastney passes the Royal Naval War Memorial, children's paddling pool and miniature railway, roller skating rink, Ladies Mile, Southsea Castle and Rock Gardens, Lumps Fort Rose Garden and Model Village, the miniature golf course and Royal Marine Barracks.

Portsmouth to Petersfield and Haslemere

Leaving Portsmouth the road to Petersfield skirts the eastern end of **Portsdown,** passes through **Waterlooville** and **Horndean** and then climbs the slope of Butser Hill (888 feet), the highest point in Hampshire. **Petersfield** is a pleasant Georgian town with a market square at the northern end of the High Street. Opposite the southern end, Heath Road leads to Petersfield's "Heath and Lake", an ideal place for a picnic over the close turf covers well-drained sandy soil. There are rowing boats and canoes for hire, a playground for the children, ducks for the youngsters to feed, and seats for the onlookers.

The road north-east from Petersfield passes through wooded country to **Liphook.** Here is the famous *Royal Anchor* where Samuel Pepys stayed with his wife in 1688, where Admiral Lord Nelson drank tea by candlelight on his journey to Portsmouth before Trafalgar, and where the Prince Regent lunched with the Duke of Wellington and his Prussian ally, Marshall Blücher, after the victory at Waterloo. Three miles beyond Liphook is the market town of **Haslemere** with a High Street of attractive red brick buildings. The Haslemere Educational Museum *(daily, Sun. afternoons in summer)* caters particularly for children.

Portsmouth to Southampton

The Southampton road from Portsmouth hugs the coast as far as **Portchester** where a turning to the left leads through the old village to the Castle, a large square fortress of flint walls built by the Romans, the only one of its kind remaining in Europe. Within these walls the Normans built a great square tower or keep. The ancient priory church of St. Mary, Portchester, also within the walls, is still in use today.

Fareham (Pop.: 80,300. Hotels: *Red Lion, Heathfield Manor, Kintyre*) is a busy town at the head of a creek at the north-west extremity of Portsmouth Harbour. The High Street has a variety of Georgian building and there are many old houses in the town mostly built of "Fareham reds", the bricks produced locally and exported from the tidal water at Lower Quay. From Fareham it is possible to approach Gosport, five miles to the south. (It can also be reached by ferry from Portsmouth.)

Gosport *(Anglesey)* is complementary to Portsmouth as a naval centre for it has the Royal Clarence Victuallery Yard for stores and supplies and has been called "the larder of the Navy". There are several Naval training centres. Gosport is also a holiday resort. There are parks and playgrounds, an open-air swimming bath, the *Gosport and Stokes Bay Golf Club* (18 holes), and good facilities for yachtsmen. Similar facilities are also found at **Lee-on-the-Solent** two miles to the west.

Beyond Fareham the Southampton Road passes near **Titchfield** with a fine church and the remains of Titchfield Abbey *(daily, fee)*. The road then crosses the River *Hamble* at **Bursledon,** noted for the building of small boats. Turn left half a mile beyond the bridge to visit the beautiful ruins of **Netley Abbey,** a Cistercian foundation established in 1239.

Southampton

Distances.—Bournemouth, 30; Chichester, 31; Salisbury, 23; Winchester, 12.

Entertainments.—Cinemas: *ABC*, Above Bar; *Gaumont*, Commercial Road. Dancing: Dances are held at the Guildhall, Royal Pier Pavilion and the Polygon Hotel. Theatre: Productions are staged from time to time at the Guildhall and the Nuffield Theatre at the University.

Early Closing.—Wednesday/Thursday.

Hotels.—*Berkeley House*, Cumberland Terrace; *Cotswold*, Highfield Lane; *Dolphin*, High Street; *Langholm,* Regents Park Road; *Polygon*, Cumberland Place; *Royal*, Cumberland Place; *Skyway*, Herbert Walker Avenue.

Information Bureau.—London Road.

Library.—Civic Centre, Commercial Road.

Population.—₂15,000.

Post Office.—Chief Post Office, High Street (just below Bernards Street).

Sports.—Cricket: The *Hampshire County Cricket Ground* is at Northlands Road. Fishing is possible from the piers and quays of Southampton Water, and from boats. Golf: *Municipal Courses,* Bassett Road (18 hole and 9 hole); *The Stoneham Golf Course* (18 hole). There are public putting greens in East Park, the Sports Centre, and at the Municipal Golf Course. Swimming: Lido and Central Baths, Western Esplanade. Tennis: Public Courts at East Park and the Sports Centre; also at Portswood and Shirley Recreation Grounds, and Weston Lane, Scholing.

The river *Test* flows into Southampton Water to be joined some four miles downstream by the river *Itchen;* the town of Southampton is built on the spear-shaped peninsula between them. Farther south the waters are divided by the Isle of Wight into the Solent and Spithead providing Southampton with a double tide —first from the Solent and two hours later from Spithead. Moreover these tides scour the channels so that the port is able to handle the world's largest vessels.

The **Town Quay** is a good starting point for the visitor to Southampton. Not far from the Royal Pier stands the *Pilgrim Fathers' Memorial* erected in 1912 to commemorate the fact that it was from here that the Mayflower set out in 1620 on her voyage to North America carrying the Pilgrim Fathers who founded the New England States. From this point the old **Town Wall** can be seen flanking the Western Promenade. The line of the old wall can readily be followed. The northern part runs east and west along Bargate Street and the Bargate itself forms the principal entrance to the old town. The eastern boundary was along the lane known as Back-of-the-Walls. Within these walls lie many of the most interesting old buildings.

The medieval **Bargate** in the High Street houses the Guildhall Museum *(weekdays 10–12; 1–5. Sundays 2.30–4.30)* reflecting the town's history. Near the seaward end of the High Street is God's House Gate and **God's House Tower** on the Town Quay, now a museum of archaeology *(weekdays 10–5. Suns 2.30–4.30)*. **Maison Dieu** was founded in the 12th century as a hospice for pilgrims bound for France or pilgrims from Europe visiting English shrines. Bugle Street which runs parallel with the West Wall has several old buildings. On the corner by the Quay is the **Wool House,** a 14th-century warehouse used by the Abbot of Beaulieu to store wool. In the 18th century it was used to confine prisoners-of-war and is now a *maritime museum (weekdays 10–5; Suns 2.30–4.30)*. Farther up Bugle Street on the right is **The Duke of Wellington,** a 12th-century stone house which was rebuilt and became an inn known as Bere House in the 15th century. The name was changed soon after the Battle of Waterloo. The present timber-framed building, was restored in 1962–3. Farther along Bugle Street is St. Michael's Square with the **Tudor House Museum** *(daily, free)* a large 16th-century timber-framed house which has been carefully restored.

Southampton **High Street** has always been the main approach to the harbour and the old inns that served the travellers to the ships still survive on the eastern side. *The Star* is a Georgian coaching inn and by the yard entrance the old "Coach to London" notice can still be seen. The *Dolphin* dates back to the 15th century. In 1648, John Taylor, "The Water Poet", refers to the inn as a resting place on the three-day journey from London to Carisbrooke in the Isle of Wight where Charles I was imprisoned. He wrote of the horses

71

SOUTHAMPTON

> With firey speed the foaming bit they champt on
> And brought us to the Dolphin at Southampton.

Queen Victoria stayed at the *Dolphin* on her way to Osborne House and during World War I Field Marshall Earl Haig used the Hotel as his headquarters when preparing for the embarkation of the British Expeditionary Force to France. Farther down the street is *The Red Lion* with an unimpressive exterior, but inside is a half-timbered hall with a gallery which is known as Henry V's Court Room. It was here that a hastily arranged treason trial was held in 1415 when the King was preparing for Harfleur and Agincourt. As a result Richard, Earl of Cambridge, Lord Scrope of Masham and Sir Thomas Grey of Heton were condemned to death and executed outside the Bargate.

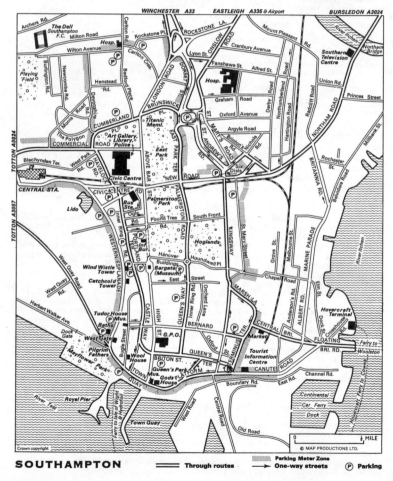

SOUTHAMPTON

━━━ Through routes · ➝ One-way streets · Ⓟ Parking

▓ Parking Meter Zone

© MAP PRODUCTIONS LTD.

Crown copyright

Before leaving the old part of Southampton it is well worth while exploring the dock area. The best overall impression is obtained from a launch cruise from the **Royal Pier** though this can only be taken in summer. Otherwise, it is usually possible to get a permit from the Office of the British Transport Docks Board in Canute Road to use the balcony on the **Ocean Terminal** where the great ocean liners berth.

North of old Southampton, beyond the Bargate, is **Above Bar Street** where many of the large shopping stores are found. Here the **Civic Centre** comes into view, an impressive range of buildings which include the *Municipal Offices* and *Council Chamber*, the *Law Courts and Police Offices*, the *Guildhall* and the *Central Public Library and Art Gallery*. Around this block are gardens with flower beds and trees.

Above Bar continues as London Road and The Avenue leading through to the **Common**, a large area of open woodland where there are opportunities for playing football or cricket, for sailing model yachts on ponds, or for exercising the dog. On the eastern side of the Common at Highfield is the **University of Southampton** which obtained its Charter in 1952. There are many modern buildings planned by Sir Basil Spence and the *Nuffield Theatre* which serves as a cultural centre not only for the students but also for the townspeople.

Winchester

Distances.—Andover, 14; Basingstoke, 18; Bournemouth, 40; Salisbury, 24; Southampton, 12.
Entertainments.—Cinemas: *Studios 1, 2 and 3*, North Walls, *Theatre Royal*, Jewry Street.
Early Closing.—Thursday.
Hotels.—*Royal*, St. Peter Street; *Southgate*, Southgate Street; *Stanmore*, Stanmore Lane; *Wessex*, Paternoster Row; *Winchester*, St. Cross Road; *Winton Court Hotel*, 49 Southgate Street.
Libraries.—Winchester Public Library, Jewry Street; Hampshire County Library, 81 North Walls.

Population.—31,000.
Post Office.—Central Post Office, Middle Brook Street.
Sports.—Bowls: North Walls Recreation Ground; Fishing is available in the Weirs (licence from 11 Upper Brook Street) but elsewhere the *Itchen* is strictly preserved. Golf: *Royal Winchester Golf Club* (18 holes) on Teg Down and the *Hockley Golf Club* (18 holes) one mile south of the city. Swimming: The Lido, Worthy Lane (open air).

Winchester, the *Venta Belgarum* of the Romans, became the capital of Wessex in Saxon times and there is a statue of King Alfred close to the Guildhall and the City Bridge over the *Itchen*. From this point a main road comprising the Broadway and the High Street runs through the city but the lower part of the High Street which includes the colonnaded Pentice has been closed to traffic to form a pedestrian precinct. At the northern end of the High Street is the **Westgate,** one of the surviving gatehouses of the medieval city. This houses a small *museum* illustrating the civic history *(daily, 5p (free on Thurs); children 3p. Suns 2–4.30)*.

Two hundred yards south of the Westgate is **Castle Hall,** completed in 1235 in the Early English style with clustered columns of Purbeck marble and stone window seats. After Westminster Hall it is the finest medieval hall in Britain and fortunately survived when the old castle was demolished after the Civil War. On the wall hangs the famous Round Table at which King Alfred sat with his 24 knights. It was in this hall that Sir Walter Raleigh was tried in 1603 and that the notorious Judge Jeffreys condemned Dame Alice Lisle to be burned for sheltering two of Monmouth's men after Sedgmoor.

Winchester High Street descends steeply between a fascinating variety of old buildings including the **House of Godbegot** to the 15th-century **City Cross** or Butter Cross. Here a narrow passage leads to The Square past the parish Church of St. Lawrence built on the site of William the Conqueror's Palace. A timbered 14th-century building which backs on the Church was for some time the rectory; it is now *The Eclipse*, a licensed house named after the famous Derby winner of that name born during the eclipse of 1763.

From Great Minster Street an avenue of limes leads across the green to the Cathedral. To the right is the tombstone of Thomas Thetcher, a Grenadier of the Hampshire Militia who died in 1764.

> Here sleeps in peace a Hampshire Grenadier
> Who caught his death by drinking cold small beer.
> Soldiers be wise from his unseemly end
> And when ye're hot drink strong or none at all.

The Cathedral. The original Saxon monastery at Winchester was replaced in the 11th century by a Norman building erected by Bishop Walkelyn. Extensions were made in the 12th century, but the ground was found to be marshy and tree trunks were laid in the wet peat to provide a firm foundation. In the 14th century the Cathedral was rebuilt again with a nave in the Perpendicular style. This work was started by Bishop Edington and completed by Bishop William of Wykeham who founded Winchester College and whose tomb is in the Chantry Chapel half-way along the south aisle. A walk around the Cathedral reveals the grace of the Perpendicular in the nave, its transepts and choir, with gradations from the pure Norman. Note particularly the magnificently carved stone reredos, the tombs of William Rufus, Isaak Walton and Jane Austen, and the headless figure of a woman in the retrochoir. The fact that these treasures may still be seen is due to the work of one man, William Walker. In the 19th century the Cathedral started slowly to sink. The tree-trunk foundations which had held for 700 years were no longer sufficient. In 1906 Walker went into the murky waters around the foundation in a diving suit and patiently worked in the darkness for six

WINCHESTER   Through routes   One-way streets   (P) Parking

years underpinning the walls with bags and blocks of cement. There is a little bronze statue of William Walker to the right of the Lady Chapel with the inscription: "The Diver who saved this Cathedral with his two hands" 1906–1912.

A door in the south nave aisle leads into the **Cathedral Close.** On the east side is the ruined Norman *Chapter House* and beyond this the old Prior's House, now the *Deanery* with tall 15th-century windows. On the far side of the Close is **Kingsgate,** one of the old city gates above which is the little 14th-century **St. Swithin's Church.** It was probably used as a chapel for Priory servants.

The archway leads into College Street where on the right is the little house in which Jane Austen died. Beyond this is the entrance to **Winchester College,** founded by William of Wykeham in 1382. *Visitors are shown round by a guide (except Weds and Sun. mornings).* Small charge. Lower down College Street on the left are the ruins of **Wolvesey Castle,** a Norman building destroyed by Cromwell. From this point a left turn leads to the Weirs and the City Bridge. Here the waters of the *Itchen* worked the City Mill (rebuilt 1744) which is now National Trust property, used as a Youth Hostel.

Some visitors may prefer to take the route opposite Wolvesey Castle gateway which, via College Walk and the river bank, leads to the

Hospital of St. Cross, the finest medieval almshouse in the country. The Hospital was founded by Bishop Henry de Blois in 1136. It was built to house "thirteen poor men" but in 1445 Cardinal Beaufort added a second foundation for men of "noble poverty". Entering the courtyard, the brew house lies to the west, the kitchen and offices to the east, and the fine Beaufort tower ahead. At the hatchway to the gatehouse visitors are still offered the "Wayfarer's Dole", of bread and beer served in cups of horn. *(There are guided tours on weekdays 9–12, 2–3.30 (summer to 5), fee.)* Admission to the Chapel of St. Cross, a superb example of Transitional Norman work, is free.

Winchester is a good centre for exploring the county for roads, many of them of Roman origin, radiate from the city in every direction—to Romsey, Stockbridge, Andover, Whitchurch, Basingstoke, Alresford and Alton.

Romsey (Pop.: 10,000. Hotels: *White Horse, Dolphin, Abbey, Phoenix*) is an old market town which grew up around a Benedictine nunnery founded in the 10th century.

The present **Abbey Church** includes two Saxon carvings—a stone crucifix over the altar in the Chapel of St. Anne in the south choir aisle, and a larger crucifix or Rood on an outside wall of the south transept. The Abbey building, however, dates from the 12th century. The choir and nave have Norman work as good as any in Britain, and in the nave Transitional work appears and the last three bays, Early English in style, fuse with the Norman stonework. Still later Gothic work is seen in the north aisle.

When the monastic community was dissolved in the 16th century the parishioners bought the church for £100. Look for the 13th-century wall paintings in the small chapel behind the high altar; the 16th-century painted wooden reredos in the Chapel of St. Laurence (north transept) and the Cromwellian monument to the St. Barbes who once owned Broadlands, later to become the home of Lord Palmerston and then of Earl Mountbatten of Burma. Recent furnishings include the beautiful bas-relief of the Blessed Virgin and Child above the high altar, and the curtains over the Abbess's doorway finely embroidered by students of Southampton College of Art.

Near the Abbey is **King John's House,** a 13th-century hunting lodge given to the Abbey by Henry III. The *White Horse Hotel* in Cornmarket started as the guest house for the Abbey. After the Dissolution, this hospice was demolished and a new inn was built. Some years ago Tudor wall painting was revealed. In the 18th century the inn became a galleried coaching house with stabling for 50 horses. The old gallery has now been enclosed and forms a corridor to the bedrooms.

ANDOVER–BASINGSTOKE

NORTHERN HAMPSHIRE

The road from Romsey to Stockbridge follows the east bank of the river *Test*, the most famous chalk stream for—dry fly trout fishing in the world. Just beyond the *Bear and Ragged Staff* there is a turning leading to **Mottisfont Abbey** *(Weds, Sats. Grounds Tues–Sats, fee)*, on the river bank, originally a 12th-century Augustinian Priory, now N.T. property. It has an 18th-century south front and there is a drawing room designed by Whistler.

Stockbridge *(Grosvenor)* can be approached from either side of the river, by way of **Houghton** on the west or **King's Somborne** on the east. *The Grosvenor* in the main street is a resort of fishermen and the headquarters of the exclusive Houghton Club.

From Stockbridge the road to Andover follows the valley of the *Anton*.

Andover (Pop.: 25,500. Hotels: *Star and Garter, White Hart*) has grown rapidly in recent years and has large housing estates and a new shopping precinct, but the old Guildhall, built in 1825, still stands sentinel in the High Street. The town was once a flourishing coaching centre with many inns. *The Angel* near the shopping precinct dates from Tudor times and has some fine old timbers, the *Star and Garter* was a half-way house for George III on his way from London to Weymouth and the *White Hart* once had stabling for 75 horses.

The Basingstoke road leads eastward through **Whitchurch, Laverstoke** (where the paper for bank notes is made), and **Overton.**

Basingstoke (Pop.: 52,500. Hotels: *Red Lion, Golden Lion*) has also expanded rapidly under a Town Development Scheme designed to cater for overspill from Greater London. The character of the town has changed. Industrial estates, new roads, housing estates and new shopping areas now predominate. On the fringe, however, there are reminders of the past. Two miles to the east are the ruins of *Old Basing House* besieged during the Civil War and four miles to the north at **Sherborne St. John** is **The Vyne** (N.T., *Apr.–Sept., Weds, Thurs, Suns and Bank Hols, fee*), a 16th-century house of diaper brickwork with classic portico, left to the National Trust in 1956 by Sir Charles Chute, Bt.

The road south to **Alton** skirts some of Hampshire's finest parkland. The town itself has some attractive Georgian houses and a 15th-century parish church where the doors still show the holes made by bullets fired during the Civil War. At **Chawton** is *Jane Austen's House*, a red brick Georgian building with hipped roof. While she lived here her books began to appear —*Sense and Sensibility, Pride and Prejudice, Mansfield Park* and *Emma*. Visitors can still see the dining parlour where she wrote *(daily, closed Mons and Fris, Nov.–Mar., fee)*. **Selborne** is no more than three miles from Chawton and "The Wakes" where Gilbert White wrote *The Natural History of Selborne* is now a museum *(daily, except Fris, fee)*.

Return to Winchester through **Alresford**, another little Georgian town. The birthplace of Mary Russell Mitford who wrote *Our Village* can be seen in Broad Street. It was to *The Swan* in West Street that Arthur Orton, the impostor who laid claim to the Tichborne estate, first came in 1866, a claim which led to a criminal trial in 1873 and a prison sentence. West of Alresford is **Itchen Abbas**, the road passing **Avington Park** *(May–Sept., weekends and Bank Hols, fee)* which Cobbett described as "one of the prettiest places in the county". The red brick house is in the Wren tradition but perhaps the most interesting feature is the perfect little Georgian church in the grounds with box pews of Spanish mahogany taken from an Armada galleon, and a rare church barrel organ.

76

The New Forest

The New Forest is a large tract of open heathland and tall forest in the south-west of Hampshire. It touches the shores of Southampton Water and the Solent in the east and extends westward to within less than two miles of Ringwood and Fordingbridge. The total area is about 144 square miles of which nearly three-quarters is under public ownership. The Forest has been a Crown possession since Norman times and came under the control of the Forestry Commission in 1924. Happily, the Commissioners encourage the public to enjoy the woods and heath-lands though this freedom implies an obligation to observe the bye-laws and particularly to remember the risk of fire and avoid leaving matches, cigarette ends or camp fires to smoulder on the ground. The area has a very special interest for naturalists who come to study the trees and plants, the birds and wild animals which include deer.

For many people one of the main attractions of the Forest is provided by the Commoners' animals, particularly the hardy Forest ponies which give birth to their foals in the open country and are later rounded up for the foals to be claimed and marked. Visitors will see the mares and foals everywhere in spring and summer but are asked to refrain from feeding them. The ponies are readily attracted to the roadside by people offering food from cars but over a period this can create a real danger to drivers and animals. The full beauty of the area can only be fully enjoyed away from the main roads, on horseback or on foot. People are remarkably free to roam; even some of the areas enclosed by fences to protect young trees can be crossed by riders and ramblers.

Lyndhurst

Distances.—Bournemouth, 20; Lymington, 9; Ringwood, 12; Salisbury, 19; Southampton, 9; Winchester, 19; London, 84.
Early Closing.—Wednesday.
Hotels.—*Crown, Evergreens, Forest Lodge, Lynd-hurst Park, Ormonde House, Parkhill, Whitemoor.*
Library.—Branch of the County Library at Community Centre.
Population.—3,000.

Post Office.—Near bottom of Main Street, opposite *Lyndhurst Park Hotel.*
Sports.—Golf (14 holes) at east end of village, by the Southampton Road. Fishing permits for the small streams in the New Forest should be applied for at Queen's House. Shooting licences are granted annually by the Deputy Surveyor and entitle the holder to shoot game (excluding deer) over the Open Forest for three days a week during winter. Apply at Queen's House.

Lyndhurst stands at the intersection of the roads from Southampton to Bournemouth, and Cadman to Lymington, and forms the natural centre of the New Forest. It is also the centre from which the Forest has long been controlled for it is here that the Verderer Court is held four or five times a year at **Queen's House,** a late 17th-century building, once the residence of the Forest Lord Warden, now used for the offices of the Deputy Surveyor. The Court consists of one official appointed by the Queen, five elective Commoners and four appointed Representatives. When the Court meets the senior Agister stands and calls "all manner of persons who have any presentment or matter or thing to do at this Court of Swainmote let him come forward and he shall be heard". The *Verderer's Hall* where the Court is held has many old Forest relics *(daily 10–5; Sats 9–1, free)*.

Roads radiate through the Forest from Lyndhurst in every direction like spokes from the hub of a wheel. Following them in a clockwise direction they provide a complete picture of the area.

Lyndhurst to Burley and Ringwood. The A35 south-west from Lyndhurst runs for some four miles through Crown woodland and then crosses common land to Wilverley Post where the road turns right across Burley golf course to **Burley,** a typical Forest village which attracts many visitors. The road to the west swings round Castle Hill, an ancient defensive camp, and leaves the true Forest before reaching **Ringwood** an ancient little market town on the east bank of the *Avon.* Close to the bridge is a row of thatched cottages, near which stands **Monmouth's House,** so called because it is said to have been the temporary residence of the Duke of Monmouth after his capture. At the *White Hart,* Monmouth wrote to his uncle, James II, the memorable appeal for mercy which Macauley justly describes as "the letter of a man whom craven fear had made insensible to shame". The Church, dedicated to SS Peter and Paul, was rebuilt in 1854 in the Early English style. It is a large cruciform building with square tower, clock and eight bells.

Lyndhurst to Bolderwood. The fine trees which abound in the New Forest are best seen west of Lyndhurst. Take the Bournemouth road and fork right to Emery Down. Then turn left through the woodlands for about three miles. Where the trees end on the left, a track runs to a gate and a cattle grid. This entrance leads to *Bolderwood Arboretum.* It is possible to park a car and to walk along the track to a cottage. Continue by car along the forest road past great beeches into *Knightwood Enclosure* where a signpost directs visitors to the enormous *Knightwood Oak* with a girth of 22 feet. A little farther on cross the main road and continue along the Ornamental Drive lined with rhododendrons, where the more unusual trees are labelled. After travelling about a-mile-and-a-half through the forest the road crosses open heathland to Brockenhurst, less than four miles south of Lyndhurst by direct road.

Lyndhurst to the Rufus Stone, Breamore and Fordingbridge. The road north from Lyndhurst runs in a direct line to **Cadnum** on the edge of the Forest, an important road junction but still an attractive village with the long thatched and cream-washed inn, the *Sir John Barleycorn.* The Rufus Stone can be approached from the Lyndhurst–Cadnum road to Minstead where *The Trusty Servant* stands by the village green. The sign is a copy of a painting in Winchester College. It shows a creature with the head of an ass, its pig's snout closed with a padlock, stags feet and human hands. The sign bears the same words as the picture which begin

> A Trusty Servant's portrait would you see,
> This emblematic figure well survey;
> The porker's snouth, not nice in diet, shows
> The padlock shut, no secrets he'll disclose.
> The patient ass, his master's wrath will bear
> Swiftness in errand, the stag's feet declare

The road through Minstead soon reaches the Ringwood road. Turn left and almost immediately right, descend the hill and on the left is the **Rufus Stone.**

When William the Conqueror died in 1087 he was succeeded by his second son, Rufus, usually known as "William the Red", a cruel monarch. In the summer of 1100 people were already talking about his death. Some monks dreamt that he had been shot by an arrow and rumours spread that he had been killed. Soon after, however, he did meet a sudden death while hunting in the New Forest. The Rufus Stone marks the site. The original inscription on the stone was defaced by vandals over a hundred years ago. They are now recorded on a cast-iron casing:

'Here stood the oak tree on which an arrow shot by Sir Walter Tyrell at a stag, glanced and struck King William the Second, surnamed Rufus, on the breast, of which stroke he instantly died on the 2nd August 1100.'

The inscription tells us that he was laid in a cart 'belonging to one Purkis, and drawn thence to Winchester, and buried in the Cathedral Church of that City'.

Continue beyond the Rufus Stone and turn left at the main Salisbury Road. Just beyond the edge of the Forest take the left turning to **Hale Park** *(Weds, Thurs and Bank Hols, fee)*, a Georgian country house built in 1715 by Thomas Archer and overlooking the *Avon.* It contains fine pictures and Aubusson tapestries. The road leads on to Breamore where is **Breamore House** *(Apr.–Sept., daily except Mons and Fris, fee)* an Elizabethan building of red brick and stone-mullioned windows. In plan it is the shape of an E, a gesture of courtesy to the Queen, with two outer gables and a smaller central gable, and high chimneys rising above the roof. Early in the 18th century Breamore House was purchased by Sir Edward Hulse and it is still the family home, beautifully furnished with Jacobean oak, Dutch marquetry and Regency furniture.

Fordingbridge lies three miles south of Breamore and is noted for the local fishing. The church has a fine early 15th-century "hammer-beam" roof. Nearby, at **Burgate,** was the last home of Augustus John, the artist.

Beaulieu and Buckler's Hand

(Abbey ruins, Palace House and Motor Museum, daily fee, Cafeteria and Restaurant)

The Beaulieu road runs south-east from Lyndhurst mainly across open heathland. **Beaulieu** is a village which attracts for here is the ancestral home of Lord Montagu of Beaulieu and the Motor Museum he founded in 1952.

In the grounds lie the ruins of **Beaulieu Abbey,** a Cistercian monastery founded by King John in 1204. Although relatively little remains, the foundations and walls are labelled so that visitors can visualise the original layout and see what relation each part bore to the whole. Close to the abbey is the old gatehouse which was made into a private house in 1538, now known as Palace House. It is the home of the Montagu family. It has some fine 13th-century stone vaulting but much dates from late Victorian times when many alterations were made. There are fine portraits, early oak and yew furniture, and a number of water-colours and photographs which show how the house has changed over the years. Also in the grounds is the **National Motor Museum,** one of the most comprehensive museums of its type in the world.

The *Beaulieu* river is a quiet stretch of water used for mooring yachts and can be used at any state of the tide by craft drawing up to five feet.

Three miles down river is **Bucklers' Hard** *(The Master Builders' House)* where *Agamemnon* (64 guns) and many other naval vessels were launched. Relics of ship-building days are to be seen in the *Maritime Museum,* housed in the former New Inn. The little church here is interesting.

Lyndhurst to Brockenhurst and Lymington. South of Lyndhurst the road takes a straight course through woodland to Brockenhurst with the open green of the *Balmer Lawn Hotel* on the left as the village is approached. This becomes a cricket ground in summer with ponies grazing around. **Brockenhurst** (Pop.: 2,800. Hotels: *Forest Park, Brockenhurst, Watersplash, Balmer Lawn, Rose and Crown*) is a growing residential village with banks, church, library, shops and garages. It has advantage over Lyndhurst in that it lies on the main London–Southampton–Weymouth railway and is a junction for Lymington. Crossing Setley Common the road winds towards Lymington on the west of the *Lymington* river.

Lymington

Distances.—Bournemouth, 17; London, 93; Lyndhurst, 9; Ringwood, 15; Southampton, 18.

Entertainments.—Cinema—Waverley; New Milton.

Early Closing.—Wednesday or Saturday.

Ferry.—Across the Solent to Yarmouth, Isle of Wight.

Hotels.—*Angel, Londesbrough, Mayflower, Passford House, Stanwell House.*

Population.—Old town 7,000.

Post Office.—High Street.

Sports.—Billiards, bowls, fishing, riding, tennis, swimming (Corporation sea water Baths), yachting (Annual Regatta).

Lymington, situated close to the mouth of the *Lymington* (or *Boldre*) river, is best known for its yachting facilities and as the starting point of British Rail's car-ferry service to Yarmouth in the Isle of Wight. It has a large open-air sea-water swimming pool whilst model yacht pond, sports grounds, beautiful gardens and park and good sea fishing are among its attractions. The church, parts of which date from Norman times, has a square tower surmounted by an unusual lantern-like cupola.

LYMINGTON TO BOURNEMOUTH

Milford-on-Sea lies south-west of Lymington on Christchurch Bay. It is a pleasant resort with good bathing and a long row of beach huts available to rent. To the east the shingle shore curves away to the spit on which stands **Hurst Castle** *(May–Sept., daily, fee)* and a white lighthouse. The castle formed part of Henry VIII's coast defences. Further east is **Keyhaven** a little yachting creek with moorings and the H.Q. of two important yacht clubs.

The main road to Bournemouth runs west a little inland from Christchurch Bay skirting Barton-on-Sea, New Milton and Highcliffe. **Barton-on-Sea** is served by the railway station at New Milton. It is a developing resort and residential area with bowling and putting greens, bathing facilities and fishing. **Highcliffe-on-Sea** is similar in many ways to Bournemouth with its houses laid out among pine trees and with its wooded glen or chine known as "Chewton Bunny" leading down to the sea. *Highcliffe Castle,* an early 19th-century building, erected for the third Earl of Bute, Prime Minister in the reign of George III, is set in beautiful grounds, some parts of which are open to the public. Highcliffe is served by a railway station at Hinton Admiral on its northern outskirts and nearby on the Brockenhurst road is the *Cat and Fiddle,* an old thatched inn with lattice windows and walls of whitewashed cob. **Mudeford,** at the west end of Christchurch Bay, overlooks the narrow channel by which the combined waters of the *Stour* and *Avon* escape from Christchurch Harbour. Although part of Christchurch, it retains many of the characteristics of an old fishing village with boating and fishing though in summer the sandy beaches are crowded with bathers and holidaymakers.

Christchurch (Pop.: 31,000. Hotels: *King's Arms, Dolphin, Hengistbury House*) has a fine harbour formed where the waters of the *Stour* (from Dorset) and the *Avon* (from Hampshire) meet. Of the Norman castle on an artificial mound, only a few remnants remain. In Quay Road is the Red House Museum *(daily)* of regional interest.

The Priory Church stands on the neck of land between the two rivers. Designed by Bishop Roger Flambard, chosen friend of King Rufus, it displays fine Norman work particularly in the exterior walls of the north transept. Inside, the nave has massive Norman arches of great height. There is Early English work in the north porch and in the windows of the north aisle; and windows in the south aisle are Decorated. A fine carved 14th-century screen divides the church in two. To the east lies the Choir, the Lady Chapel and the Miraculous Beam. The choir stalls, misericords and 14th-century stone reredos are superbly carved.

Christchurch Quay is an attractive resort with tea gardens, bandstand, putting green and car park, a place for boating parties.

On the south side of Christchurch Bay is **Hengistbury Head** readily approached from Christchurch by way of Southbourne, though it lies within the Borough of Bournemouth. There are car parks where the roads give way to footpaths for the highest point of the headland can only be reached on foot. The views are among the finest on the coast.

Bournemouth

Distances.—Blandford, 18; Dorchester, 28; Romsey, 31; Salisbury, 31; Southampton, 29; Weymouth, 32.

Entertainments.—Cinemas: *Gaumont,* Westover Road; *A.B.C. 1 and 2,* Westover Road; *Premier,* Albert Road. Dances are held in many hotels and at the Pavilion and the Royal Ballroom, Boscombe. Concerts by the Bournemouth Symphony Orchestra are given at the Winter Gardens and there are Military Bands in Pine Walk and Fisherman's Walk. Theatrical performances are given in the *Pavilion,* the *Playhouse Theatre,* Westover Road, and light summer shows are given in the *Pier Theatre.*

Early Closing.—Some shops in the centre of the town close on Saturday; others and those in the suburbs and Commercial Road on Wednesday.

Hotels.—*Carlton,* East Cliff; *Royal Bath,* Bath Road; *East Cliffe Court,* East Cliff; *Highcliff,* West Cliff; *Marsham Court,* East Cliff; *Norfolk,* Richmond Hill; *Palace Court,* Westover Road, and many others.

Library.—Central Public Library, Lansdowns.

Population.—153,500.

Post Office.—The Head Post Office is in Post Office Road, running between Old Christchurch Road and Gervis Place, about a minute's walk from The Square.

Sports.—Bathing is excellent along the six-mile stretch of sand with little difference between high and low tide. Bathing bungalows bordering the Undercliffe Drive can be rented from the Corporation. Corporation Baths at Pier Approach. Bowls in Meyrick Park, King's Park, Argyll Gardens, Redhill Park, Knyveton Gardens and Malvern Road. Cricket pitches can be hired in Meyrick Park, King's Park and the Weston Recreation Ground. County matches are played at Dean Park and there are cricket Festivals in June, July and August. Sea Fishing for bass, plaice, grey mullet, mackerel and sea bream can be had along the coast. Annual Fishing Festival in the autumn and competitions from pier and boats. Golf on first class public courses at Meyrick Park (18 holes) and Queen's Park (18 holes). Ice Rink in Westover Road. Squash at Meyrick Park. Tennis in the Upper Gardens, Boscombe Gardens, Meyrick Park, King's Park, Knyveton Gardens, Winton Recreation Ground, Redhill Park, Swanmore Gardens, Seafield Gardens and Malvern Road.

Bournemouth established itself as a major resort in the reign of Queen Victoria and there are many reminders of this fact in its layout and its buildings. The sandy soil is suitable for the growth of pines and heather and many roads are bordered by conifers. The sandy shore encourages bathing and the Bourne valley and chines are laid out as public gardens for the equable climate is excellent for many unusual plants. Not only is Bournemouth a favourite resort but there are large residential areas where retired business and professional people can make a new home. The Bourne valley divides the town into two parts—the East Cliff and the West Cliff. Its Upper, Central and Lower Gardens form a long and beautiful park some two miles in extent from the northern town boundary to the Square.

The **Square** is the great traffic centre, separated from Bournemouth Pier by the Lower Gardens. The **Pier** has a fine theatre seating about 900 people and a modern café with a semi-circular sweep of windows giving extensive sea views. During the summer there are motor-vessel excursions to the Isle of Wight and Swanage. Close by is the **Pavilion** with a large theatre and a ballroom as well as restaurants and licensed lounges. Alongside the Pavilion is Westover Road one of the most important shopping and amusement centres in the town. The **Winter Gardens** in Exeter Road, west of the Lower Gardens, is the home of the Bournemouth Symphony Orchestra *(concerts weekly).*

East of Bournemouth Pier the *Undercliff Drive* and Promenade extend for about a-mile-and-a-half to **Boscombe Pier.** Zigzag paths lead to the East Overcliff Drive and opposite Meyrick Park there is an electric lift. Near the western end of the Overcliff Drive is the **Russell-Cotes Art Gallery and Museum,** with paintings by Turner, Rossetti, Cooper, Frith, Etty and Landseer. One room is devoted to relics associated with Sir Henry Irving. A few yards away is the **Rothesay Museum** with a fine marine collection.

West of Bournemouth Pier there are promenades at the foot of cliffs and along the top with frequent steps to join them and the West Cliff lift. The *West Overcliff Drive* takes a winding course around the heads of the little valleys or chines. These include, from east to west, Water Chine, Little Durley Chine, Durley Chine with its pine clad banks and seats among the heather, Middle Chine and Alum Chine separated by the Argyll Gardens. Behind the coastal strip are many attractive roads which radiate from the Square. To the east Bath Road divides to become Christchurch Road which leads to Boscombe, and

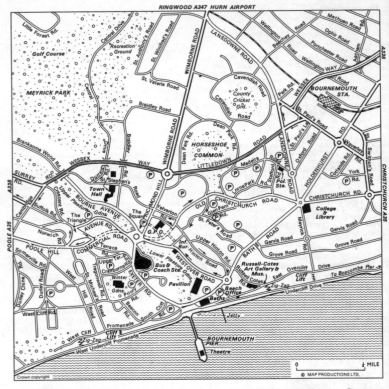

BOURNEMOUTH ═══ Through routes ⟶ One-way streets ℗ Parking

Holdenhurst Road to the Station and Queen's Park. The Lansdowns is reached by turning left off the Holdenhurst Road along St. Paul's Road. Here is the **Central Public Library** and the **Colleges of Art and Technology.** *The Round House Hotel* built in a circular plan makes a striking architectural feature. To the west the Poole Road sweeps inland to join the roads which skirt Poole Harbour.

Poole (Pop.: 106,500. Hotels: *Antelope, Riviera, Dolphin, Sea Witch*) lies immediately west of Bournemouth but few visitors realise where one ends and the other begins. The four-mile sea frontage, which includes Branksome Chine, Canford Cliffs and Sandbanks continues the West Cliff stretch of the Bournemouth front. At Canford Cliffs are the famous **Compton Acres** gardens. But Poole is a much older town, a seaport with a very long history. Poole Harbour covers a large area seven miles long and half as broad with many little bays and creeks and a number of islands. Almost closing the harbour is **Sandbanks** a mile-long spit now built over with houses and hotels and with a highly popular beach *(Ferry, cars carried, every few minutes to Studland).*

Brownsea Island covers about 500 acres. Much of it is wooded and on the south side the unspoiled heathland is a paradise for the botanist. In 1907 Colonel Baden-Powell used the island for his first experimental Scout Camp. It is now National Trust Property *(landing fee, motor boat services from Sandbanks Ferry and Poole Quay)*.

The old town of Poole is on the northern side of Poole Harbour and here is the **Quay** with its warehouses, mills and shipping. Among them are a number of attractive buildings including the **Custom House** with its double flight of curving steps leading to a pillared portico. **Poole Pottery** at the eastern end of the Quay displays its wares in a showroom *(daily, 9 to 5)*.

High Street running from the Quay to the Station is a main shopping centre with an enclosed precinct, the Central Library and an indoor Sports Centre. At the southern end is the **Old Town House** (Scaplen's Court), Poole's first "Guildhall" but now a museum of local history. The **Guildhall** with a stone staircase to Market Street (west of the High Street) is a fine example of Georgian architecture. Within is the *Poole Museum (daily, fee)*.

At the northern end of the High Street three roads diverge. The Wimborne Road leads to Broadstone and the *Dorset Golf Club;* Longfleet Road leads to the Ringwood Road and past the *Northbourne Golf Course.* The Parkstone Road leads to Park Gates East with the Municipal Buildings, and thence via Commercial Road to Bournemouth. Immediately south of Parkstone Road lies *Poole Park,* some 50 acres in extent.

Salisbury

Distances.—Bournemouth, 30; Lyndhurst, 19; Romsey, 16; Southampton, 23; Winchester, 24.

Entertainments.—Cinema: *Odeon,* New Canal. Concerts: Band concerts in Guildhall Square in summer. Theatre: *The Playhouse,* Fisherton Street. Dancing: occasionally at City Hall.

Early Closing.—Wednesday.

Hotels.—*Cathedral,* Milford Street; *County,* Bridge Street; *King's Arms,* St. John Street; *Red Lion,* Milford Street; *White Hart,* St. John Street.

Library.—Public Library and Picture Gallery, Chipper Lane.

Population.—35,550.

Post Office.—Castle Street.

Sports.—Boating on the *Avon.* Bowls in Victoria Park. Golf on the *South Wilts Club Course* (18 holes) at Netherhampton (2½ miles) and the *High Post Golf Course* (18 holes) on the Amesbury Road (3 miles). Racing four times a year at Race Plain, three miles west of the city. Swimming in open-air heated baths near Castle Street. Tennis in Victoria Park.

Salisbury is a clean, bright and attractive city with ancient houses, good hotels and shops, and the magnificent Cathedral.

The Market Place is a focal point. Here stands the **Guildhall,** a heavy classical building dating from 1795. Open-air markets are held Tuesdays and Saturdays. Queen Street, next to the Guildhall, is the *House of John A'Port,* built in 1425. Queen Street leads into Catherine Street and then St. John Street dominated by the *White Hart Hotel* with its impressive Georgian frontage. *The King's Arms* beyond is timber-framed with overhanging storeys. In St. Ann's Street is the **Salisbury and South Wiltshire Museum.** St. Ann's Gate, opposite St. Anne's Street, leads into the Cathedral Close. On the west side is the Old Deanery, a 13th-century domestic building. On the north side of Chorister's Square is **Mompesson House** (N.T., *May–Sept., Weds, Sats*) a Queen Anne merchant's house built in 1701.

Salisbury Cathedral was consecrated in 1092 and enlarged in the early part of the 12th century. The completed building was consecrated in 1258. A century later the great tower and spire were added in the Decorated style. The history of the Cathedral ever since has been the problem of keeping these extra 6,400 tons of stone in position. Wren surveyed it and added an iron band. James Wyatt advised in the late 18th century and so did Gilbert Scott a hundred years later, adding more ties. From the top of the battlemented tower, at a height of 212 feet from the ground, the graceful spire, profusely ornamented with crockets and sculptured bands of stone, tapers for nearly 200 feet more, so that it is the loftiest in all England.

The West Front is chiefly noted for its many niches fitted with figures representing the Te Deum. In spite of the coldness of the interior, arising partly from the lack of stained glass windows, the effect of austere beauty is made even more impressive by the uniformity of the architecture. The vaulting is plainly and boldly executed, rising to a height of 81 feet from the pavement, and the nave arches are adorned with an effective series of deep mouldings, beneath which the slender columns of dark Purbeck marble look still more elegant from their division into many separate shafts. The ribs of the roof are of the same material as the walls—a freestone cut from the Chilmark quarries, about 12 miles west of the City. The Nave is divided into 10 arches, with an extremely striking triforium, or open gallery, between them and the clerestory windows above. The Cloisters, on the south side, show good late 13th-century work, seen also in the Chapter House, a masterpiece of Early Decorated style. Its graceful doorway is particularly noteworthy.

SALISBURY ══ Through routes → One-way streets Ⓟ Parking

SALISBURY PLAIN

Salisbury Plain is not really a plain but an undulating plateau ranging from about 120 feet to as much as 900 feet above sea level. It is formed largely of porous chalk through which the water percolates leaving a dry surface soil. Several valleys drain the area and it is in these valleys that the Wiltshire villages are mainly found. They straggle close to the rivers *Avon, Wylye, Nadder* and *Bourne*.

The Avon Valley

The *Avon* winds from **Pewsey** in the north to Salisbury in the south through a number of delightful villages and hamlets. Pewsey was once a flourishing market town but with the disappearance of canal traffic and the diversion of other traffic to the major roads, it has declined somewhat in importance. As an old Saxon town it is appropriate that there should be a statue of King Arthur in the town centre.

Manningford Bruce is a typical chalkland village with an early Norman church surrounded by thatched houses and farms. Another branch of the *Avon* flows through Charlton to **Rushall. Charlton** boasts an interesting public house—*The Charlton Cat* with associations with one Stephen Duck who in 1740 rose from farm labourer to librarian at Richmond Park.

Upavon, a mile below Rushall was also once a market town. Parts of the church of St. Mary date from the 13th century. Then comes **East Chisenbury, Enford, Fittleton, Netheravon, Figheldean** and **Durrington. Netheravon** has an interesting church with a lofty tower. The west doorway is a fine example of Norman work and there is a piscina in the chancel and another in the north aisle. At Durrington is *Woodhenge* an ancient circle marked by posts.

The villages of this part of Wiltshire are quiet except overhead where aircraft from Boscombe Down are constantly in the sky. This is a part of the Plain used by the services. There are large military camps at Larkhill, Bulford and Tidworth, famous for its annual tattoo.

Amesbury is a focus for these camps. An abbey was built here over a thousand years ago, but the present Amesbury Abbey dates from about 1840 and is on the site of an earlier house where the third Duchess of Queensbury entertained John Gay, one of her protégés. He is said to have written *The Beggar's Opera* at Amesbury. The pilgrim hospice for the original abbey became Crown property at the Dissolution and took the name of The George and Dragon, now *The George Inn.*

Two miles west of Amesbury is Stonehenge.

Stonehenge *(daily, fee)* is a most remarkable circle of huge stones which has puzzled archaeologists for centuries and even today presents many problems. However, evidence to date suggests that it is not a uniform structure of one period, but several structures of widely separated dates. The visitor will find the official pamphlet available on the site but the essential parts of the monument can be described under two main headings.

1. *The Circular Ditch* is crossed by the visitor soon after he has passed through the entrance. This together with a half-circle of holes now marked by patches of chalk and known, from the name of their discoverer as *Aubrey Holes,* represent a circle 288 feet in diameter. Excavations revealed that the bottom of the ditch contained deer antlers, and towards the top were potsherds of the earliest part of the Bronze Age, about 2000 B.C. It is thought that the Aubrey Holes contained a series of wooden posts and it is noteworthy that the Aubrey circle had the same centrepoint as the ditch.

2. *The Stones.* The complex structures of stones are centred on axes drawn from the north-west and south-east stones, the south barrow and the north barrow (no longer visible), all of which are generally known as "Station points". A line joining the Heel or Friar's Heel Stone, near the road, the Slaughter Stone, and the Altar Stone, also passes through this centre which is aligned on the position of the sun at sunrise on the summer solstice.

The present grouping of the stones gives little idea of the original layout of the monument. It then consisted of an outer circle of massive sarsen stones capped by lintels with carefully made toggle joints; and a second circle of upright foreign stones, usually called "Blue Stones" which enclosed finally a horizontal slab known as the Altar Stone.

The "horseshoes" open to the north-east and it is a notable fact that standing in the middle of the opening and looking across the Altar Stone and the centre of the trilithon behind it, the Friar's Heel is seen cutting the horizon at the precise point of sunrise at the summer solstice.

It is of particular interest to note that the "Blue Stones" came from the Prescelly Hills in Pembrokeshire, 150 miles away, a fantastic feat of transport in prehistoric times. The stone complex is dated at between 1800 and 1500 B.C.

The Wylye Valley

The main Wylye Valley runs from Warminster to join the *Nadder* at Wilton. **Warminster** is at the western extremity of Salisbury Plain and is mentioned in Domesday Book. It is at the junction of roads from Bath, Frome, Salisbury and Shaftesbury and consists essentially of one long street. Unfortunately, many of the old buildings are now gone. One of the oldest to survive is Lord Weymouth's 18th-century Grammar School where Dr. Arnold of Rugby was educated. For many years the town had a particularly large corn market which is mentioned by Daniel Defoe and by William Cobbett. There are two attractive inns—*The Bath Arms* and *The Old Bell*.

Four miles down the valley is **Heytesbury,** once a Saxon borough and a place of some importance. In 1723, however, a serious fire destroyed over 60 houses and it never regained its former significance. Then come the villages of **Wylye, Steeple Langford** (where Cobbett lived for a time as a boy), **Stapleford** and **Great Wishford,** noted for its Oak Apple celebrations.

Wilton, on the Exeter road lies only two-and-a-half miles from Salisbury. It has a famous carpet industry which was established in the days of Queen Elizabeth I. **Wilton House** *(Apr.–Sept., daily except Mons, fee)*, the work of Inigo Jones and later of James Wyatt, is one of the most beautiful houses in England.

The **Nadder Valley** runs from west to east some four or five miles south of the *Wylye,* from Tisbury, through Dinton and Barford St. Martin to Wilton. At **Dinton** is **Phillip's House** (N.T., *Weds, fee)*.

The **Bourne Valley** runs south from Savernake Forest along the eastern border of Salisbury Plain winding through Collingbourne Kingston and Collingbourne Ducis to Tidworth, Shipton Bellenger, Cholderton and three Winterbournes (Gunner, Dauntsey and Earls) to Salisbury. Except for **Tidworth,** these are quiet places which have known man since prehistoric times, for Salisbury Plain is scattered everywhere with ancient camps and burial places, and with celtic fields. North-west of Tidworth is the prehistoric earthwork of *Sidbury Hill.*

Along the Bath Road

From Reading the Bath road skirts the attractive open spaces of Prospect Park and the Calcot Golf Course and passes through **Theale** and **Woolhampton** to **Newbury** *(Chequers, Bacon Arms)*, once noted for the clothing trade with a regular wool market, and also as a coaching centre. The fine old Jacobean Cloth Hall in Wharf Street, near the Market Place, has been recently restored and houses *Newbury Museum.* A narrow balustered bridge crosses the *Kennet and Avon Canal* in the middle of the town. South of the bridge is the new shopping precinct, the bus station and car parks.

The Bath road next passes through **Hungerford** *(Bear)* though, to reach the main part of the town with its wide High Street involves a left turn at *The Bear,* a 16th-century inn where on 8 December, 1688, William of Orange received three emissaries led by Lord Halifax with a message from his father-in-law, James II. Beyond Hungerford the road passes through the northern edge of **Savernake Forest** and descends into **Marlborough** *(Castle and Ball, Ailesbury Arms, Bear)* with its wide main street. Originally there were two narrow streets but two disastrous fires in 1654 burnt the houses between them. There are buildings of many periods in the High Street, mainly Georgian and on the north side a colonnade extends over the pavement described by Samuel Pepys as "Penthouses supported by pillars". This extends on either side of the *Castle and Ball* which catered for the fashionable coaching traffic between London and Bath. The Marlborough Coach reached the inn from London in twelve hours, a distance of 74 miles, and passengers stayed to rest. At the west end of the High Street is *Marlborough College,* established in 1843.

To the west of Marlborough the road crosses chalk downland to **Beckhampton** and the turning to **Avebury** noted for its fine stone circle and also for Avebury Manor *(daily except Tues, fee)* a delightful Elizabethan house with fine gardens.

At **Calne** the road swings past a large brick-built bacon factory on the right and the *Lansdowne Arms* on the left which occupies most of one side of the old Market Square, close to the Town Hall. Note the huge barometer set into the wall of the inn.

Chippenham (Pop.: 18,700. Hotel: *Angel*) is a flourishing town with some fine old buildings and modern industries. It lies in a valley on the south side of the river *Avon*. The old bridge across the river was recently rebuilt to carry the increasing traffic. The *Angel* in the Market Place is a Georgian coaching inn of three storeys surmounted by a balustrade.

The Isle of Wight

Crossing to the Island.—By Ship.—The Isle of Wight is connected with the mainland by regular services at three points: Portsmouth–Ryde, Southampton–Cowes; Lymington–Yarmouth.

Car-Ferry Services operate at frequent intervals (but reservations essential in summer) Portsmouth–Fishbourne, Lymington–Yarmouth, and Southampton–Cowes.

Hovercraft Services.—(Passengers only) Southampton–Cowes; Southsea–Ryde.

Hydrofoil Service.—Southampton–Cowes.

Exploring the Island.—Excellent bus services link up all areas; coach tours to chief centres of interest. A railway line runs from Ryde, through Brading and Sandown to Shanklin with connecting bus services. Roads are good and adequately sign-posted. Cyclists and ramblers have a wide choice of by-roads, paths and cliff-walks.

Accommodation.—Most centres have a wide range of establishments from good class hotels to simple boarding houses.

The Isle of Wight (population 109,000) has a total area of 147 square miles, circumference 60 miles, length 23 miles and width 13 miles. A range of chalk hills and downs stretches across the middle of the island from the Culver Cliff at the northern end of Sandown Bay, to the Needles, at the extreme west. Another range of hills runs along the south coast from St. Catherine's to near Shanklin, and shuts in "the Madeira of England", the lush district of the Undercliff. The coastline is deeply indented by fine sandy bays and there are several clefts, or "chines", in the cliffs, the most noted of these being at Blackgang and Shanklin. The principal river—the *Medina*—rises at the foot of St. Catherine's Down, flows north to traverse the width of the Island to Cowes. The *Western Yar* has its origin at Freshwater Bay, within a few yards of the English Channel, and in its short course northward to Yarmouth attains a fair width. The *Eastern Yar* is a narrow winding stream, rising near Niton, within a mile of the coast, and emptying itself in the sea near Bembridge. *Wootton River*, after a short course of two miles, falls into the Solent at Fishbourne, where it forms a wide creek, navigable at high water. Besides these, there are the *Newtown River*, a curious and irregular creek, which admits vessels of some size; the *Lukeley*, a tributary of the *Medina*, which it joins at Newport; and a number of other small streams.

Many centuries ago, Wight formed part of the mainland of south-east England. The river *Solent* gradually developed and became a navigational ocean channel —now five miles wide. The Island is famous for its unusual geological stratification, and a fine geological collection in the branch county library at Sandown is of great interest. Botanists and nature lovers are attracted by the luxuriant sub-tropical vegetation and the many varieties of wild flowers. Many relics mark the presence of man from the Early Stone Age onward—flint, bronze and iron age implements; pottery and tumuli. About A.D. 44 the Island was occupied by Romans who knew it as *Vectis*. Six Roman villas have been uncovered. After 449, the Island was occupied by Jutes then Saxons—many island place names are of Saxon origin. The Danes followed and then Norman invaders who appointed Norman lords as rulers. The island became part of the realm of England when it was repurchased by the Crown in 1293 and later ruled by a succession of Captains and Governors. The present Governor, Lord Mountbatten of Burma, was installed in July, 1965. For long administered as a part of Hampshire, the Island is now a county in its own right. Interesting events in history are the imprisonment of King Charles I in Carisbrooke Castle in 1647 and the purchase of the Osborne Estate by Queen Victoria in 1849.

This lovely island is popular for its mild climate, beautiful and varied scenery and pleasant coastal resorts. The sandy bays are safe for children and there are abundant facilities for sports and entertainments. The Island is famous as a yachting centre. Regattas are held and excursions by boat are numerous.

Ryde

Amusements.—*Pavilion*, Eastern Esplanade. Concerts in Esplanade Gardens. Carnival first week in September. Cinemas.
Bathing.—Good sandy beaches.
Dancing.—At Town Hall and local ballrooms.
Distances.—Bembridge, 6; Brading, 4; Carisbrooke, 8; Cowes, 8; Freshwater Bay, 18; Newport, 7; Shanklin, 8; Ventnor, 13.

Early Closing.—Thursday.
Golf.—*Ryde Golf Club* (9 holes) on west side of town.
Population.—22,700.
Post Office.—Union Street.
Sports.—Bowling greens. Tennis clubs open to visitors. Putting.

Ryde overlooks the Solent and has good hotels, shops and excellent bathing and fishing facilities. The main streets rise steeply from the front. At the junction of West Street with Queen's Road is the **Parish Church of All Saints,** built 1869–77 and notable for a rich alabaster pulpit, reredos and font. From the top of the tower, which has a fine 180-foot spire, are extensive views. The **Roman Catholic Church of St. Mary,** in the High Street, was designed by Hansom the originator of Hansom Cabs.

Ryde Pier, nearly half-a-mile in length, has three separate sections; for pedestrians, for the railway, and the now disused tramway. The pier head, 636 feet wide, is the starting point for races and regattas. At the shore end is the **Esplanade Station** and the **Hovercraft Terminal.** West of the Pier are gardens, shelters, an Information Bureau, and steps leading to the Children's Corner of the sands. East of the pier are extensive sands and an attractive **Esplanade,** with gardens and a Pavilion where a theatrical company entertains nightly. Beyond is a bandstand where orchestral concerts are given; there are bowls, tennis, miniature golf and other facilities. An extensive **Canoe Lake** provides good boating and there is a modern swimming pool. Beyond to the south are **Sandringham Gardens** where is a putting green, and **Appley Park,** with gardens, lawns, woods and a fine 18-hole pitch and putt course. A sea-wall walk connects Appley with **Puckpool Park,** a pleasure garden equipped for many sports. There are also beach huts for hire, children's swings, cafés, an aviary and an aquarium. Adjoining is a large holiday camp.

Seaview, two-and-a-half miles to the east, is an attractive yachting village reached by road or on foot by the seawall and a path. The firm sands here, good bathing, beach sports and fishing have made the place popular for family holidays.

Binstead, a suburb of Ryde lies one mile west. The ancient Church of the Holy Cross near the shore retains some Norman features but was mostly rebuilt in 1844.

Quarr Abbey, two miles west, is built of stone from the local quarries. In 1132 it was the most important abbey on the Island. At the Dissolution of the Monasteries it was destroyed and the stones used for defences at Cowes and Yarmouth. The enclosure wall and a few ruins are all that remain. In 1907, Benedictine monks repurchased the estate, and by 1914, had built a new abbey a mile away from the Norman ruins. This magnificent Abbey Church, vaulted and arched, with a massive tower and soaring campanile was designed by one of the monks. (It is always open to the public.)

Westward of Quarr Abbey is **Fishbourne,** attractively situated on *Wootton Creek.* Once a small fishing hamlet it is now a busy terminus of the Car Ferry service to Portsmouth. The *Creek* is a pretty tidal inlet favoured by yachtsmen. In **Wootton** (Wood Town) village is the church of St. Edmund (**c**. 1087) with a Norman doorway and a Jacobean pulpit. **Wootton Bridge** is a modern village with an inn and a small quay on the main Ryde–Cowes road.

St. Helens, four miles south-east of Ryde, is a scattered little village above Brading Harbour. Around the village green are 18th-century cottages, once well known to smugglers. The Church (1717) is north of the village. Of the ancient church built on the shore, only the square tower remains. It is now useful as a sea-mark. The "Holystones" taken from the ruins, were used as pumice for scouring ships' decks. St. Helen's is connected with Bembridge by ferry and by a road along the harbour embankment. Offshore are **St. Helen's Roads**—a famous anchorage, mentioned in Nelson's dispatches. Occupying nine-and-a-half acres inland, is **St. Helen's Common,** now National Trust property.

Bembridge is a yachting resort at the mouth of Brading Harbour and connected by ferry with St. Helen's. There are good sea views, fine sands, bathing and fishing. The *Ruskin Gallery* at Bembridge School has a large collection of pictures and MSS *(admission by appointment)*. In the village are modern villas, hotels, antique shops and a few ancient cottages. At the end of the High Street is **Bembridge Windmill** (National Trust, *May–Oct.*), a stone tower mill built about 1700 and the last remaining mill in the Island. From Bembridge the coast may be followed past the Foreland to secluded **Whitecliff Bay** and **Culver Cliff.** The obelisk on Bembridge Down is to Lord Yarborough the first commodore of the Royal Yacht Squadron.

Brading, situated three miles inland on the direct route between Ryde and Sandown was once a "King's Towne" with royal charters, a harbour and a navigable inlet. In 1878, many acres of land were reclaimed from the sea; and are now used for farming and market gardening purposes. The ancient town has much of interest—Town Hall, with stocks and whipping post; a bull-ring once used for baiting and a fine church (1150–1250). The Oglander chapel within the church has memorials and effigies of the famous Oglander family. In the Sanctuary, an incised slab of 1441 depicts Sir John Cherowen. Opposite the church is a 16th-century building, housing a **Wax Museum** *(daily, fee)*.

A mile to the south-west, near Yarbridge, is a **Roman Villa** *(daily in summer, fee)*. From coins found on the site this villa must have been in occupation towards the end of the 5th century. There are various items to be seen including well-preserved mosaics, remains of the baths and a wall.

West again is **Nunwell Manor,** the family seat of the Oglanders. Henry VIII and Charles I each visited here *(open certain days)*.

Sandown

Angling.—From pier and boats for bass, whiting, grey mullet and conger.

Beach.—Sand. Excellent bathing and boating.

Distances.—Bembridge, 5; Brading, 2; Carisbrooke, 10; Freshwater Bay, 20; Godshill, 5; Newport, 10; Shanklin, 2; Ventnor, 6.

Early Closing.—Wednesday.

Entertainment.—Pier Pavilion (summer show), Town Hall (concerts), Eastern Gardens (bands), cinema, dancing, etc.

Golf.—*Shanklin and Sandown Golf Club* on Lake and Blackpan Common.

Museum.—Geological Museum, High Street.

Population.—7,000.

Post Office.—Beachfield Road.

Sports.—Bowls, putting, tennis, etc.

Sandown is a popular resort situated at a break in the cliffs of a beautiful bay amid fine scenery. The prosperous modern town has comfortable hotels, good entertainment, shops and cafés. The extensive sandy beach is quite flat and there is excellent bathing and boating. A broad Esplanade runs for a mile in front of hotels, cafés, shops and amusements. At the southern end a path continues by the Battery Gardens and over the cliffs to Shanklin. The Pier juts out to sea for nearly a thousand feet. At the shore end is a large entertainment Pavilion; at the head a swimming club and a theatre. North of the Pier the Esplanade leads to *Sandham Castle Pleasure Centre* with tennis courts, putting and bowls. In the town is a branch of the County Library and a Geological Museum. The Parish Church dates from 1845.

To Shanklin (2 miles). Reached by cliff path, a fine walk. At low tide, an alternative is by the sands. The road route is via Lake.

To Culver Cliff (2½ miles). From the northern end of the Esplanade the Yaverland road bends inland beyond the Zoo. A steep cliff path leads to the summit of Culver. The return can be varied by descending to **Yaverland** village where is a tiny 12th-century church, cottages and a Jacobean manor house.

To Alverstone Mill (2¼ miles west). A pretty inland village with picturesque cottages, a water-mill and a wealth of wild flowers. The return can be via the hamlet of Queen's Bower and Borthwood Copse, or the excursion can be extended to **Newchurch.** This pleasant village was once a very large parish. The church was founded in 1087 and though rather plain still has its original lancet windows and other features of interest. A-mile-and-a-half west, reached by field paths or road *(bus)* is **Arreton**, on the Sandown–Newport road. The church, Manor House and farm make a charming group among trees. The 12th–16th-century church has a beautiful chapel and many interesting features. **Arreton Manor** *(in summer)* is a well-proportioned Jacobean mansion with period furniture, and a museum of toys and bygones. Above the village is **Arreton Down**—a fine viewpoint.

Shanklin

Angling.—Angling Club. From pier or boat for bass, whiting, mullet, conger, codling, plaice.
Beach.—Sand, extensive at low tide. Good bathing and boating.
Early Closing.—Wednesday.
Entertainment.—Concert parties at Pier. Theatre.

Rylstone Gardens (bands). Bingo. Cinema. Amusement arcade.
Golf.—*See* Sandown.
Population.—6,000.
Post Office.—High Street.
Sports.—Bowls, tennis, putting, cricket, etc.

Shanklin shares its beautiful bay with its twin town, Sandown, two miles to the north. The two towns are amalgamated for local government purposes. Shanklin is a highly popular resort with a narrow sea-level promenade and roadway running in front of a line of hotels and gardens, behind which cliffs rise sheer to a height of 150 feet and on which the main town is built. Steep slopes at each end and a lift in the centre of the Esplanade, give connection between the two parts. The tide recedes a good distance and exposes a great expanse of flat sand with ample space for beach games. Bathing is safe and boating ideal. The Pier has a Casino, a Dance Pavilion and amusements. In the Second World War the "Pluto" pipe-line through which petrol was pumped to Cherbourg, started from the pier head. On the cliff-top is **Keats Green** recalling that the poet lived here in 1819. The beautiful **chine** (Anglo Saxon *cine,* a fissure) winds down to the sea. After rain tumbling cascades add to the beauty of the scene. Adjoining are the picturesque **Rylstone Gardens.** Chine Road leads to **Shanklin Old Village,** most attractive with its thatched cottages and flowers. The Old Church, dedicated to St. Blasius, although much restored is quaint and picturesque and has remnants of 14th-century work. Parts of the Rectory date from the 16th century.

To Sandown (2 miles) via cliffs or by the sands.

To Luccombe Chine and Landslip. Luccombe Road climbs steeply, with fine backward views over the bay, to a path over Luccombe Common. The chine lies seaward and is reached by any of several paths. The Landslip is a wild area of gnarled oaks and tangled hazel thickets.

To Wroxall, 3½ miles. Lies in a hollow of the Downs and can be reached by bus or a climb over the hills. Nearby is the ruined mansion of **Appuldurcombe** *(daily)* built *c.* 1710 and for long the seat of the Worsley family.

To Godshill, 3½ m. 'es, on the main Shanklin–Newport road *(bus)*. The scene of church, thatched cottages and pretty gardens is one of the most attractive in the Island. The church, dating from the 14th century, has much of interest including a nave mural—the *Lily Cross*.

Ventnor

Angling.—Good sea angling from pier and boats. Angling club.
Beach.—Sand and fine shingle.
Distances.—Shanklin, 4; Sandown, 7; Newport, 12; Fishbourne, 15; Cowes, 16; Ryde, 13.
Early Closing.—Wednesday.
Entertainments.—Winter Gardens and Royal

Victoria Pier. Carnival is mid-August. Cinema in summer. Dancing.
Golf.—On Rew and Week Downs (9 holes).
Population.—7,314.
Post Office.—Church Street.
Sports.—Bowls, tennis, putting, cricket.

Ventnor is built on a series of terraces on the cliff face. Facing due south almost every house is drenched in sun and enjoys a seaview. The beach of sand and shingle is reached by steps and zigzag lanes. There is a modern pier, built 1955, and a short Esplanade with canoe lake and paddling pool. Above is the **Winter Gardens Pavilion,** with sun terraces, lounges, and a concert hall which has an excellent dance floor. To the west is **Ventnor Park,** with cascades, flower beds and a putting green.

A mile eastward is **Bonchurch,** an old village now much modernised with good houses, hotels and shops. The famous *Pond* is a picturesque sheet of shallow water presented by H. de Vere Stacpoole, the novelist, who lived here. The village has two churches dedicated to St. Boniface. The **Old Church** (*c.* 1170) is a tiny building of early Norman design. The new Church, 1847–8, has a memorial to Earl Jellicoe, whilst in the graveyard lie Swinburne and other notables.

St. Boniface Down (N.T.) rises high behind Bonchurch. The unspoiled downland covers 221 acres and commands magnificent views. The summit, at 785 feet above sea level, is the highest point in the Island topping the next highest point, St. Catherine's Down, by 4 feet.

Inland two-and-three-quarter miles from Ventnor is the village of **Whitwell** with an interesting church. West of Ventnor, the main coast road and a fine cliff walk lead via the Undercliff to **St. Lawrence,** a village of modern houses and some very old cottages. The "Old Church" is a very tiny Norman building *(open all day)*. **Niton,** two miles west on the main road, is a pleasant village with a 13th-century church and a coastal radio station. It is a good centre for excursions. To the south is **St. Catherine's Lighthouse** *(weekday afternoons)*, 136 feet above the sea on St. Catherine's Point. On **St. Catherine's Down** (781 feet) are the ruins of an ancient beacon and a 72-foot column put up in 1814 to the Czar of Russia and known as the *Alexandrian Pillar*. It also serves as a Crimean War Memorial.

The "back of the Island" lies between St. Catherine's Point and the Needles. Below St. Catherine's Hill is **Blackgang Chine,** once a base for a "black gang" of smugglers. It is now a *Disneyland* with a model village, a maze, water garden, souvenir bazaar, etc. A 400-foot high *Observation Peak* gives extensive views.

From **Chale** a fine switch-back road runs for 10 miles along the coast to **Freshwater.**

An alternative route is via the inland villages of **Chale Green, Kingston,** of manor house, farm and church, and **Shorwell,** with its thatched cottages and 15th-century church. **Brighstone** is a charming stone-built village with ancient church. **Mottistone** has a 16th-century manor house and a church founded in the 12th century which has many interesting features. Adjoining are woods (N.T.) and the *Long Stone,* a 13-foot high pillar believed to be part of a long barrow of 2,500 B.C. At **Brook** the inner road joins the coastal road to the Freshwater Peninsula.

Between Brook and Freshwater Bay the coast road rounds **Compton Bay** where the sands provide excellent bathing.

Freshwater is a scattered inland parish with good hotels and modern shops. The ancient church has Norman windows and doorways, and memorials to the Tennyson family who lived at nearby *Farringford.* **Freshwater Bay** on the coast is a later development with hotels, marine terraces, etc. Golf, fishing, bathing and boat excursions available.

High Down, or better known as **Tennyson's Down,** stretches away to the west and provides the finest of all the fine walks on the Island. In 1927 Lord Tennyson presented the Downs to the National Trust in memory of his father, the Poet Laureate. The *Tennyson Cross* dates from 1897. At the western extremity of the Bay are the jagged chalk spires known as **The Needles.** On one of the three still visible, is the famous lighthouse 80 feet above high water.

Alum Bay is famed for its coloured cliffs. Twelve distinct colours have been counted. Souvenirs filled with the sand are sold locally, but many people are invariably to be seen scraping away at the cliffs and collecting their own. There is a gentle descent to the bay through the grounds of the *Royal Needles Hotel* passing the Marconi monument. A modern innovation however, is a chair lift giving access to the beach.

Totland Bay is a restful resort with firm sands. There is an esplanade, a short pier and a shopping centre.

Colwell Bay, two miles north, is a popular family resort with comfortable hotels, safe bathing from a sandy beach, and putting.

Yarmouth

Access.—Car ferry from Lymington. Bus connection with Newport, Shanklin, Ventnor, etc.
Beach.—Sand at Norton, west of Yarbridge.
Distances.—Alum Bay, 4½; Freshwater Bay, 3; Totland Bay, 3; Newport, 10; Cowes, 12; Ventnor, 22.
Early Closing.—Wednesday.
Population.—1,000.
Post Office.—Quay Street.

Yarmouth is a small ancient town mentioned in Domesday Book as "Ermud". In 1206 it was the headquarters of King John and many years later the seat of the Governor or Captain of the Island. **The Castle** *(daily),* built in 1543 as a coastal defence, was garrisoned until 1885. The **Town Hall,** rebuilt in 1763, is on the site of a 13th-century market. The church (17th century) contains a fine statue of Sir Robert Holmes a hero and governor. Yarmouth is a yachting centre with a quay, pier and harbour and a fine old tide mill.

Cowes (Population 18,900) is the chief entrance to the Island from Southampton. It has a port, a fine harbour and is internationally famous as a yacht racing centre. Regattas are held frequently in summer, the peak being *Cowes Week* at the beginning of August. The town is divided into East and West Cowes by the river *Medina.* West Cowes has tortuous hilly streets with bow-fronted shops and balconied houses. The High Street leads into **Victoria Parade**—a good viewpoint.

Cowes Castle, originally a fort built by Henry VIII to defend the Solent, is now the headquarters of the *Royal Yacht Squadron*. During the Second World War, the main operations of "D" Day were controlled from the Castle. The Esplanade extends to **Egypt Point** and **Gurnard,** a popular resort on the site of a Roman town. A Floating Bridge *(toll)* connects West with East Cowes, where there are shipyards, aircraft and hovercraft works. The Esplanade extends three-quarters of a mile to the grounds of *Norris Castle* built for Lord Seymour in 1790. Queen Victoria spent holidays here in her youth, and it is still privately owned. The park adjoins the Osborne Estate.

Osborne House *(Mons–Fris, Apr.–Oct.)* was built between 1845–48 as a seaside retreat for Queen Victoria. It was presented to the nation by King Edward VII after his mother's death there in 1901. The south wing is used as a convalescent home for officers. The **Swiss Cottage** in the grounds was the playhouse of the Royal children. In the nearby museum built 1862 are various curios and mementoes.

Whippingham Church a little to the south was used by the Royal Family. It is a mixture of Early English and foreign architecture. Across the river is **Northwood Church** with a Norman doorway and Jacobean pulpit.

The road southward leads to **Parkhurst Prison** to the west of which is the **Camp Hill Prison. Parkhurst Forest** extends to 1,100 acres, the largest woodland tract on the Island.

Newport (Population 22,300) is the capital town, the commercial and bus centre of the Island. Ships traverse the *Medina* estuary to the busy docks. Newport is an ancient town. The first charter dates from 1180, when it became the "New Port" for Carisbrooke. The **Church of St. Thomas,** 1854, retains relics of an older church—pulpit, 1636, font, 1633, and a monument to Princess Elizabeth, the second daughter of Charles I. In 1648 the King lodged in the old **Grammar School** in St. James's Street; the building is now used by a Youth Club. Other houses of interest are *God's Providence House* (1701) and *Chantry House* (1612) in Pyle Street, and *Castle Inn* (1684) in High Street. The *Guildhall* (1814–16) designed by John Nash, replaced the old Town Hall in which Charles I held negotiations with Parliamentary Commissioners in 1648. The **Roman Villa** in Avondale Road, has mosaic floors and a complete bath system. The *County Library,* in Upper James's Street, has a collection of Island literature.

Carisbrooke, one mile south-west of Newport *(bus service)* formerly for centuries the capital of the Island, has remained an unspoilt village, in spite of the great attractions of its castle and church.

The **Castle** *(daily, car park, café)* stands on the plateau summit of a wooded hill, at a height of 150 feet. Built in the 12th century by Normans on the site of a Roman fort, there were constant additions in medieval and Elizabethan times. Charles I sought refuge here in 1647. He was imprisoned and made several unsuccessful attempts to escape. In 1648 the King was transferred to Hurst Castle. Carisbrooke Castle has an imposing *Gatehouse* with massive inner gates, dating from 1470. The *Ramparts* and the lofty *Keep* were built in the 12th century. The domestic buildings which have remained are the *Great Hall* with a chimney-piece of 1390, parts of a 13th-century *chapel* and the *Great Chamber (no admission)*. The *Museum* has an interesting collection of relics, manuscripts, curios, antiquities and portraits. The *Well House* is popular with children. This is a restored 16th-century building, in which water is drawn up 160 feet by a donkey treading inside a large wheel. Near the Gatehouse is the modern chapel of *St. Nicholas in Castro,* now the Isle of Wight Memorial. It is on the site of a Norman Chapel founded in 1070. The present building is a reproduction of the sanctuary at the time of Charles I's imprisonment.

Carisbrooke Church *(always open)* is reputedly the finest in the Isle of Wight. A Christian church has stood on this site since 700. The nave was built in 1070, replacing a Saxon building. There are 14th- and 16th-century windows, Transition arches, interesting effigies and memorials. The crowning glory of the church is the fine 14th-century tower with five stages. On the north wall outside are graffiti, scratched about 1440.

Carisbrooke and Newport make capital centres for downland walks and bus excursions.

Gatcombe, four miles south-west, is an unspoiled village of thatched cottages, trees, a stream and a beautifully tended *church* mainly 13th-century.

Calbourne, four miles west, on the main Freshwater Road has a water mill, a pleasing church and rectory and the much photographed **Winkle Street.**

Shalfleet is six miles on the Newport–Yarmouth road. The church founded about 1070 has a Norman tower, old roofs, pleasant box pews and a Jacobean pulpit.

Newtown, half a mile north of Shalfleet, is the most ancient town on the Island. It was originally called *Francheville* and noted for its salt industry and oyster cultivation. Francheville was destroyed in 1377 by French raiders and Newtown was built. It is now a decayed port with a silted-up harbour and a Town Hall dating from 1699. In the estuary is a nature reserve and an oyster fishery (N.T.).

Newbridge, one mile from Calbourne on the road to Yarmouth, is a straggling village of stone and brick cottages. On the south-east outskirts of Yarmouth is **Thorley** an inland parish of good farming land. The church has an unusual bell-tower.

Blackwater, two miles south of Newport on the main road, is a good starting point for the walk over St. George's Down (363 feet) on the eastern side of the Medina valley. There are fine views of the river and of the Yar valley. The road along the summit leads north-west over Pan Down to **Shide** ($1\frac{1}{4}$ miles) and Newport (2 miles). Eastward the road can be followed to Arreton ($1\frac{1}{2}$ miles) and **Horringford.**

Dorset and the Coast

SWANAGE AND DISTRICT

The coast of Dorset extending from Poole Harbour to the Devon border by Lyme Regis is varied, beautiful and spectacular, with curious rock formations, caverns, cliffs, harbours and miles of golden sands. A striking feature is the Chesil Beach, a great shingle bank connecting the Isle of Portland with the mainland and acting as a breakwater to protect lovely Weymouth Bay. Inland ancient towns and villages, historic castles, churches, manor houses and other buildings, contrast happily with the modern coastal resorts. The hinterland is ideal for walking or motoring.

Swanage

Distances.—Bournemouth, 12; Dorchester, 27; London, 115; Wareham, 10; Corfe, 6; Studland, 4; Wool, 15.
Early Closing.—Thursday.
Entertainment.—Mowlem Theatre (summer shows).
Hotels.—*Grosvenor, Ship, Wolfeton, Saxmundham,* *Chatsworth, Suncliffe, York, Pines, Westbury.*
Population.—8,550.
Post Office.—Station Road.
Sports.—Angling, bathing, boating, bowls, putting, tennis.

The small village of old Swanage with its quaint winding High Street, charming inns and cottages, tiny stone lock-up and 13th-century church tower, has expanded into a delightful holiday resort. The beautiful bay with fine steep coast giving glorious views is of great charm and variety. The Parade and Shore Road extend for nearly a mile. The pier or jetty (fishing) has landing stage for small vessels (trips to Bournemouth, Isle of Wight). The Town Hall has an elaborate Wren facade (1670) imported from the Mercers' Hall, London. Nearby is the Old Lock-up dating from 1803. St. Mary's Church has a square tower of 13th-century date. Behind the shore road is a Recreation Ground with tennis, bowls and a bandstand. Nearby are the Beach Lawn Tennis Courts.

Peveril Point is a low headland forming the southern horn of Swanage Bay. On the northern side is the Lifeboat House. The prominent Clock Tower once stood at the south end of London Bridge.

To Durlston Head, Tilly Whim Caves, Great Globe and Anvil Point *(bus service)*. The Head lies one mile south. The modern Durlston Castle is now a restaurant. Paths lead down to the **Great Globe** of Portland stone weighing 40 tons. From the Globe a bird-haunted cliff path 102 feet above sea level continues south-west to the **Tilly Whim Caves,** remains of an old quarry and once a smuggler's haunt. In the West Country "whim" is the name of any mechanical contrivance for raising or lowering the produce of mines. A short distance along the cliff is **Anvil Point** with its Lighthouse *(weekday afternoons)*.

To St. Aldhelm's Head. St. Aldhelm's (or St. Alban's) Head lies five miles west of Anvil Point and can be reached from the latter by cliff path. The Head, most prominent feature of the coast between Swanage and Weymouth, stands nearly 400 feet high. The views on every side are magnificent. On the summit stands a little Norman chapel and a coastguard station. On the west side is **Chapman's Pool.** The beach is strewn with shaly rocks and boulders and hundreds of cormorants nest in the rocks.

To Langton Matravers, Worth Matravers and Kingston. The route is via **Herston,** once a tiny village of quarry workers. To the long street (Saxon "long-tun") of stone cottages at **Langton Matravers** has been added several modern housing estates. The church was built in 1876. Westward is **Worth Matravers** a stone-quarrying village where the church is said to have been begun in the year 700, and much added in Norman times. The chief inn bears the sign of the *Square and Compass.* The pretty village of **Kingston** screened in woods stands at a height over 400 feet. The elaborate church was designed by Street.

To Ballard Down and Old Harry Rocks. An easy round route of six miles northward past "Rest and be Thankful" a stone seat set on the crest of the ridge beyond which is Ballard Point, a bold chalky promontory with vertical walls (382 feet) forming the northern extremity of Swanage Bay. A mile north-east is the Foreland or Handfast Point below which are **Old Harry Rocks,** pillars of chalk forming well-known landmarks.

Studland, three miles north of Swanage, can be reached by footpath over the downs (2¾ miles), or by car via the Ulwell road (3½ miles) *(bus service).* The charming unspoilt village lies in a perfect setting of woodland, sea and downland. There are safe, warm sands and good anchorage for boats. The dunes and Shell Bay are popular with picnic parties. The heathland includes a National Nature Reserve and the *Agglestone* (i.e. Holy Stone) a curiously eroded mass of ironstone. The church, probably dating from 1180, is a singularly perfect and unaltered specimen of Norman architecture. A ferry connects Studland Bay with Sandbanks.

Corfe *(Bankes Arms, Greyhound)* four-and-a-half miles north-west of Swanage is a picturesque village of stone-built houses. The apex of the tiny place, with a steep approach from the Wareham side, is the little Square, flanked on one side by the church, and on the other by old inns and houses, gay with flowers, while the castle on its hill behind dominates the whole. With the exception of the tower, which dates from the end of the 14th century the church was rebuilt in 1859. The **Castle** *(daily, fee)* which King John used as a residence, has towers leaning at all angles and a ruined keep on the hill summit.

A mile-and-a-half to the west is **Church Knowle** with an inn, some pretty, flower-covered cottages and a 13th-century church.

Kimmeridge is five miles by road from Corfe and stands a mile inland at a height of over 300 feet. The small stone church in Norman and Decorated styles has an ancient font and a small bell turret. **Kimmeridge Bay** is similar to Chapman's Pool. A mile south-east is **Smedmore** *(mid-June–mid-Sept., Weds)* an 18th-century manor house with Dutch marquetry furniture and some antique dolls.

The **Blue Pool** just off the Corfe–Wareham road is the largest of many lakes scattered over Wareham Heath.

Wareham *(Red Lion, Black Bear, Antelope)* near heathland, sea, river and harbour, is an interesting town with broad streets, fine churches and picturesque old inns among the latter being the *Black Bear* and the *Red Lion.* The town "walls" are grassy ramparts. The old church, St. Martins, on the walls, is part Saxon and has Norman wall-paintings. It contains an effigy of T. E. Lawrence of Arabia. Near the bridge is St. Mary's Church with a unique lead font and the empty coffin of King Edward the Martyr. Wareham Priory (now private) was founded by St. Aldhelm and is one of the oldest in the country.

Bere Regis, six-and-a-half miles north-west, is a pretty village of some historic interest. The church is the burial place of the Turbeville family from whom Thomas Hardy based his *Tess of the D'Urbervilles.*

Wool is five miles west of Wareham. Here is the red-brick *Wool Manor House* now a farm, once the residence of the Turbevilles. Across the railway is ruined **Bindon Abbey** *(daily, fee)* founded 1172 by Robert de Newburgh for Cistercian monks. The gatehouse and a few walls have survived.

Bovington lies amid a large area of heathland to the north-west of Wool. At Bovington Camp is the Royal Armoured Corps' **Tank Museum** *(daily, free)*. A mile north, on Bere Regis road, is **Cloud's Hill Cottage** (N.T., *Weds, Thurs, Suns, fee)* where T. E. Lawrence lived his later years.

Wareham to Poole. The drive is of extreme interest, and seems to give an epitome of the town's history and industry. The road leaves Wareham by the level crossing at the station, fine views of the heath being obtained. Several potteries, both for machine-made and hand-made work, and the golf links are passed. Four miles out of Wareham the inn of *St. Peter's Finger* (probably a corrupt form of St. Peter ad Vincula) stands at a junction of roads, and from Lytchett Minster onwards the way becomes increasingly urbanised.

Wareham to the Arne Promontory. A turning to the left at Stoborough on the Corfe road leads over wild and lonely heathland to **Arne.** Cars cannot be taken right down to the shore, but must be left in the tiny village. Walkers have the advantage of an infinite number of by-ways and no parking difficulties, but, whether walking or driving, the views, especially over the Harbour at sunset, are varied and magnificent. The little church of St. Nicholas at Arne, attached as a Chapel of Ease to Wareham Parish, dates from the 13th century.

Lulworth Cove, a little oyster-shaped inlet 17 miles west of Swanage, lies almost hidden by frowning cliffs whose contorted strata bear witness to rock-folding on a grand scale in the far-distant past. There is bathing from pebble and sand beaches, boating and there are several cafés, lobster teas being a specialty.

The pleasantest way to see the cliffs and coves is to take a boat. Rounding **Nelson Fort,** several fine caves are reached at **Stair Hole.** Their structure is unique. In one, great pillars of rock rise from the water and support the gigantic superstructure, quite meriting the name **Cathedral Cavern.** A fine bay, with sandy beach, follows, then come the charming **St. Oswald's Bay** and **Man o'War Bay,** where the bathing is excellent. Beyond, at about a mile from the Cove, is the **Durdle Door,** a large natural arch some 40 feet high and wide. To reach the Durdle Door by the cliffs is not more than an hour's walk. Go through the car park, up the well-defined white track up the hill, and follow the cliff path until the Door is reached. A mile farther, where a perpendicular white cliff rises from the beach, there is another arch tunnelled out by the waves. Provision has been made for camping near Durdle Door on reserved ground, with water supply, modern sanitation and general store. At low tide it is possible to return to Lulworth Cove by way of the sands via **Man o' War Bay** and **St. Oswald's Bay.**

Sloping to the sea on the *east* side of the Cove is a wonderful **Fossil Forest.** Among the marvels are fossilised stumps of trees, with the whole inside gone, standing as they have stood for ages. They are large enough to hold several people.

Almost overlooking the Cove are the remains of **Little Bindon Abbey,** associated with the great Cistercian house near Wool.

Two miles east of the Cove is **Worbarrow Bay,** where the stratified cliff scenery is considered by many even finer than that displayed at Lulworth Cove.

At East Lulworth is **Lulworth Castle** in a beautiful park. A fine Jacobean mansion of 16th-century date, it was partly destroyed by fire in 1929. In the restored Stable block is the Weld family's art collection removed here from Ince Blundell Hall, Lancashire *(see announcements)*.

Wimborne (Pop.: 5,000. Hotels: *Crown, King's Head, Griffin, Compton's*) lies seven miles north of Poole. Over a thousand years ago it was a town of repute, the object of many a saintly pilgrimage, the home of kings and the chosen burial-place of one of the most famous of the early Saxon rulers. Now it is a small but pleasant market town serving a large agricultural area.

Wimborne Minster *(small fee for chained library)*. The present church was built soon after the Conquest though there have been many additions and alterations since. Cruciform in shape the church has both a western and central tower. High up on the western tower is the wooden Quarter Jack dressed as a British Grenadier in the time of Napoleon. Among much else to be noted within are an Astronomical Clock constructed by a monk about 1325 and the famous Chained Library with about 240 volumes. This library is the third largest in the country.

Wimborne is a convenient centre from which to visit the quiet but interesting country of the Dorset Uplands and **Cranborne Chase.** A pleasant excursion is via the Hintons to Cranborne, over the Dorset–Hants border to **Damerham,** then north-westward up the Allen Valley and across Bokerley Dyke to the main road, where turn left to Blandford with a choice of two roads back to Wimborne. **Blandford Forum** *(Crown),* a market town, stands on the *Stour.* It has several fine mid-18th-century buildings.

Shaftesbury *(Grosvenor, Royal Chase)* is a hill-top town on the edge of the plateau which extends north-west from Cranborne Chase and overlooks the Blackmoor Vale. Behind the Town Hall is the well-known Gold Hill with its wall. It once had a Benedictine Abbey founded by Alfred the Great which was a great resort for pilgrims, but little now remains but the Abbey Ruins **Museum** in Park Place where are objects retrieved from excavations on the site. In the lounge of the *Grosvenor Hotel* is the famous Chevy Chase sideboard which tells the story in carved oak of the battle of Chevy Chase at Otterburn in 1388.

WEYMOUTH AND DISTRICT

Weymouth

Distances.—Abbotsbury, 9; Bournemouth, 31; Cerne Abbas, 16; Corfe, 22; Dorchester, 8; Poole, 30; Swanage, 27; Wareham, 19; London, 132.

Early Closing.—Wednesday.

Entertainment.—Cinema, Clubs, Pavilion (summer shows), dancing at Pavilion Ballroom, Dog Racing.

Fishing.—Excellent from pier and boats. Mackerel trips.

Hotels.—*Gloucester, Kingswood, Ingleton, Oxford, Royal Crown, Lupins, Trelawney, Clifton, Grand* and many others.

Information.—Esplanade.

Library.—Westwey Road.

Population.—42,330.

Post Office.—St. Thomas Street.

Sports.—Bowls (Greenhill Gardens, Melcombe Regis Gardens), golf (Weymouth Links, 18 holes), dog racing (Wessex Stadium), tennis (in parks).

Weymouth is a popular resort on both banks of the *Wey* which here runs to the sea via Radipole Lake and the narrow harbour. Across the inner harbour the Town Bridge connects Old Weymouth on the south with Melcombe Regis, the more modern portion with its hotels and shops strung out along the bay. The extended frontage faces east with wonderful sands and a magnificent seascape view. The shopping centres of the town are St. Thomas Street and St. Mary Street, between Harbour and the King's Statue (George III). The Esplanade which they join curves round to the Pier, the triangular space between being filled with quaint wedges of houses and narrow little cross alleys. St. Mary's Church dates from 1817. Holy Trinity, a finer building, was erected in 1836. Weymouth harbour is the terminal of British Rail passenger and car ferry service to the Channel Islands. To the south of the harbour is the Nothe promontory with views over the extensive Portland Harbour. Southward from the Nothe, road and paths lead past Newtons Cove, and **Bincleaves** to Castle Cove. Of *Sandsfoot Castle* there are but scant remains. From Bincleaves runs the huge breakwater forming the northern arm of Portland Harbour. Its length is a little over two miles broken by an entrance gap in the centre.

The village of **Radipole,** about two miles from Weymouth, is situated at the northern end of the once navigable Radipole Lake. The church has an unusual bell turret with openings for three bells. At **Nottington** a mile to the north is a curious octagonal Well House built about 1830 and now a private house. In the time of George I Nottington was a renowned spa.

On the Dorchester road is **Broadwey** with a little church built in Decorated style with Norman doorways and Elizabethan oak pulpit. **Upwey** lies in a pretty wooded valley. Its famous *Wishing Well* stands near the church. Its water was often sampled by George III whose gold cup was kept for Royal use in a nearby house. This cup later became the original gold cup presented by his successors for the Ascot races. The little church dates from 1267.

Preston is a pretty village, though now much built over, four miles west of Weymouth. In a small hut is preserved a Roman tessellated pavement discovered in 1852. Along the cliffs is **Bowleaze Cove** with its striking holiday centre. Close to Preston is **Sutton Poyntz** a Dorset village with old thatched cottages. On the downs to the north-east is the **White Horse** with its rider, a huge figure cut into the hillside to expose the chalky subsoil. The figure measures 323 feet high by 280 feet long.

A mile beyond Preston, along the hilly main road is **Osmington,** and a little farther a narrow road leads off seaward to **Osmington Mills.** Crossing the hills this road descends to the coast ending abruptly in a group of cottages one of which is signed *The Picnic Inn.* Beyond Osmington Mills is **Ringstead Bay** with the fine White Nothe cliff.

Portland is a rocky peninsula joined to the mainland by the great Chesil Beach. It consists practically of one solid mass of rock or freestone and contains nine or ten villages or hamlets. The names of the villages are pure Anglo-Saxon and illustrate the importance once paid to wells of water. On an isolated rock like this wells of pure water would have been an absolute necessity of life—hence Fortuneswell, Maidenwell, Southwell and Chiswell. The island is covered with quarries and Portland stone is known all over the world.

Portland Castle was built by Henry VIII. When its military value ceased it remained in use as living quarters and is still well-preserved.

Fortuneswell is the main shopping area. Across Verne Common is an H.M. Prison Training Centre. Near Easton is *Borstal* once a convict prison but now a detention centre for young men between 16–21 years of age. Near the coast is *Avice's Cottage* now a Hardy and Portland museum. Above Church Ope Cove are the ruins of Rufus Castle originally built by William II. At Portland Bill stands the modern Lighthouse *(weekday afternoons)* replacing the old lighthouse built in 1789 and still standing half a mile north.

The Chesil Beach is a remarkable ridge of pebble extending from Portland to Bridport—about 18 miles. The average height is from 50–60 feet above sea level and its breadth about 200 yards. The stones, largest in size at the Portland end, gradually diminish in size as strong currents drive them farther into the bay. Bathing from the beach is dangerous.

Abbotsbury *(Ilchester Arms)* nine miles west of Weymouth is a large attractive village with 17th-century houses, a 16th-century church, a 15th-century tithe barn, and ruins of a Benedictine abbey. The **Sub-Tropical Gardens** *(daily, Apr.–Sept., fee)* are beautiful and extensive. The **Swannery** *(same times)* maintains over 500 swans. **Portisham,** two miles east, is cradled in trees with a stream rippling down its main street. Overlooking the village is **Blackdown** (or Blagdon) **Hill,** over 800 feet high. Two miles from the village is the *Hardy Monument* to Admiral Hardy, Nelson's flag-captain.

Dorchester (Pop.: 13,700. Hotels: *King's Arms, Antelope, Junction, Victoria, George*) is a charming, old, really English, county town on the river *Frome.* Its weekly market is one of the biggest in the West of England. The Romans named the site *Durnovaria* and built strong defence walls, fragments of which and some tessellated pavements still survive. The Town Hall is an ornate modern building. Opposite, **St. Peter's Church** is a venerable foundation though the present building is nearly all 15th-century work. Adjoining is the **County Museum** *(weekdays, fee).* Opposite the Chief Post Office are *Napier's Almshouses* of 1616 now used as business premises. In High West Street is the Roman Catholic Church of Our Lady Queen of Martyrs and St. Michael, built in the Early English style. In the Bridport road is the **Dorset Military Museum** with collections of the Devonshire and Dorset Regiments and other military works.

The **Walks** are fine avenues of limes, chestnuts and sycamores which surround the town on three sides and follow the lines of the old Roman walls. Dorchester has associations with the Puritan emigration to America, the Rev. John White, Rector of St. Peter's Church, having been largely instrumental in planning the colony of Massachusetts.

Maumbury Ring is a short distance along the Weymouth road. The rampart dates back to Neolithic times. **Poundbury** half a mile north-west of the town is of Early Iron Age date.

Maiden Castle, two miles south-west, dates from the 1st century B.C., and is the finest known example of a prehistoric fortress in this country, with enormous earthworks and complicated entrances. The remains of a 4th-century Roman temple have been discovered within the fortifications.

To Milton Abbas. Along the A35 to **Puddletown** where the church has a carved ceiling of Spanish chestnut, turning left on to A354 for Milborne St. Andrews. Here a left turn leads in four miles to **Milton Abbas** standing amidst lovely scenery. The thatched cottages of the village were built by the first Earl of Dorchester in the mid-18th century. **Milton Abbey,** a stately structure, was begun in 1322 and was restored by Sir Gilbert Scott in 1865. The adjoining mansion, now a school, incorporates a portion of the former abbey.

The Hardy Country

So close was the connection between Thomas Hardy and the corner of the country where his ancestors had lived for generations and which he himself loved so well, that it is possible, in a short walk of two or three miles, to see his birthplace, school, home, and the spot in old Stinsford Church where his heart is buried.

Thomas Hardy was born on June 2, 1840, in an old house in the hamlet of Higher Bockhampton, on the edge of the wild and primitive moorland he called "Egdon Heath". He went to the little village school at Lower Bockhampton (the "Melstock" of *Under the Greenwood Tree*). His father was a builder, and he himself, intending to become an architect, was articled in Dorchester and later removed to London. His literary genius, however, would not be denied, and he published his first book, *Desperate Remedies*, in 1871. Many novels and poems followed: *The Dynasts*, an epic, the finest of the latter, and *Tess*, probably the best known of the former.

Hardy built himself a secluded house, Max Gate, just off the Wareham road about a mile from Dorchester. He died there on January 11, 1928.

First go along the Wareham road out of Dorchester, passing on the left, nearly a mile from the town, *Max Gate* at the corner of a side road leading to the left. Keep straight on along the main road for about 200 yards, and then take the left fork. This crosses the railway after about half a mile, and then, bearing round to the left (leaving the West Stafford road on the right), descends into the green "Vale of Great Dairies", where the *Frome,* with countless little daughter channels, meanders through its wide flood-plain.

Lower Bockhampton is a long grey village, where Hardy's little school (now private residence) may be seen, on the hilly road just beyond the river. The Greenwood Tree was considered unsafe and cut down. At King George V's Silver Jubilee another was planted and rails were put round to protect it.

Continue straight up through the village, past cross-roads with a signpost pointing to Tincleton on the right and Dorchester on the left, till a small road is reached leading off to the right at a post box. Go along this between farm buildings until a tiny hamlet, **Higher Bockhampton,** is reached. At the very end of this, and on the edge of **Puddletown Heath** (Hardy's "Egdon"), is an old thatched house with crossbeams and lattice windows, his birthplace. Opposite it and on the edge of the wild moor country is a granite obelisk, "Erected by a few American admirers in 1931".

To get to Stinsford, either return to the cross-roads mentioned above and turn to the right, reaching the church in about a mile, or else take a footpath nearly opposite the little Higher Bockhampton road through *Kingston Park* (the "Knapwater House" of the Wessex novels).

This leads on to the **Stinsford** ("Mellstock") road. The church, dedicated to St. Michael, lies back a little from the road, but a side road leads to it and cars may be turned round a tiny green. It is a little quiet grey building with plain tower and grotesque gargoyles. Inside there is a window on the south erected by public subscription, and also an organ presented by Miss Hardy in memory of her parents, brothers and sister. Oak panelling from Kingston Manor lines part of the Church, and another point of interest is the Norman font, restored in 1920. In the churchyard, shadowed by an old yew-tree, Hardy's heart—his ashes lie in Westminster Abbey—is buried beside the grave of his first wife and close to generations of his ancestors.

Dorchester to Sherborne

The road follows the *Frome* for a mile and after passing Wolfeton House a right turn (A352) enters the valley of the *Cerne* and passes through **Charminster** and **Godmaston** where the *Smith's Arms* is one of England's smallest inns.

Cerne Abbas is a beautiful village with some overhung Tudor cottages and a church with high tower ornamented with grotesque gargoyles. The ruins of Cerne Abbey lie beyond the fine Abbey House (Pamela, Lady Digby). All that remains is a handsome gateway and a 14th-century "guest house".

The **Cerne Giant.** Well seen from the Sherborne road is the giant figure, 180 feet long, with club in right hand, cut in the turf of Giant Hill (700 feet). The figure is of Romano-British work and about 1,500 years old.

Sherborne (Pop.: 7,250. Hotels: *Half Moon, Eastbury, Post House*) is an ancient warm-tinted stone town set among green hills on the northern border of Dorset on the *Scir Burn* which gives it its name. It is famous for its Abbey Church and its School. Other buildings of note include almshouses, castle, conduit and many old houses. The **Abbey Church** is chiefly Perpendicular but tower and transepts exhibit their Norman origin. The porch is also Norman. The roof of both nave and choir show magnificent fan vaulting. At the west end is the Saxon doorway the only remaining part of the former Saxon church.

Sherborne School is a large public school of some 600 boys. It was endowed by Edward VI in 1550. Some of the old buildings have been incorporated into modern additions. The **Conduit** in Cheap Street originally stood in the Cloisters. The picturesque ruins of the **Old Castle** stand in a fine park on the eastern side of the town.

Bridport

Distances.—Dorchester, 15; Exeter, 38; Lyme Regis, 10; London, 139; Weymouth, 20.
Early Closing.—Thursday.
Golf.—*Bridport and West Dorset Golf Links,* East Cliff, West Bay.

Hotels.—*Bridport Arms, Greyhound, Bull, Eype's Mouth, West Mead.*
Population.—6,400.
Post Office.—West Street.
Sport.—Angling at West Bay from shore and boats, boating, bowls, golf, swimming, tennis.

The town of Bridport lies two miles inland from the sea and its off-shoot, West Bay. The red-brick buildings and the generally warm colour of the place have a pleasing effect, enhanced by its wide main streets and a picturesque, wooded background. Bridport is the chief centre in Britain for the production of fishing nets, lines, twines and cordage. At one time the town enjoyed almost a monopoly in the manufacture of ropes and cordage for the navy, whilst gallows ropes were also made here, hence the grim retort often heard in "Wessex": "You'll live to be stabbed with a Bridport dagger!" Most great industries leave their mark on the architecture of a town and influence its planning. To this general rule Bridport is no exception, the great width of the streets being for the purpose of allowing each house to have a "rope-walk".

The church is a fine Perpendicular building with Early English transepts and a good central tower capped with pinnacles and containing eight bells. Opposite are some picturesque almshouses. The Town Hall is a pleasing brick building of Georgian design. The **Museum and Art Gallery** *(mornings, fee)* in South Street have collections of local interest.

The quaint harbour and holiday resort of **West Bay** is popular with campers and caravanners, there being a well-organised municipal camping ground. There is good bathing from a pebble beach, fishing, boating and sailing. From the Esplanade there are good sea views. The harbour with wide quays and a jumble of boats and nets is situated at the mouth of the *Brit* which is tidal for about a mile but not now navigable for ships.

To Eype and Chideock. Westward in a break in the cliffs is **Eype** where the beach and an extensive common provide opportunities to laze in quiet. In the next break over Thorncombe Beacon is **Seatown** *(Anchor Inn)* a little settlement and offshoot of **Chideock** a mile inland on the Lyme Regis road. Chideock is an attractive village with picturesque cottages built in local sandstone. In the church is the black marble tomb and effigy in complete plate armour of Sir John Arundell *(d. 1515).* **Symondsbury** lies to the north; the *Ilchester Arms* here is an interesting thatched inn.

To Whitchurch Canonicorum. The delightful village of Whitchurch Canonicorum in Marshwood Vale is one of the largest parishes in the county. It is reached by a right turn at Morecombelake on the Lyme Regis road. The 13th-century church incorporates part of an earlier Norman building.

To Beaminster and Broadwindsor. The Beaminster road runs north from Bridport. In a mile a right turn at the *Kings Head Inn* leads to **Bradpole** a pleasant little village where the Memorial Hall commemorates W. E. Forster the statesman mainly responsible for the Elementary Education Act of 1870 which made education accessible to all children. Eastward, housing development connects with **Loders** an attractive village where the *Farmers' Arms* is overlooked by several tor-like hills crowned with firs. **Uploders** forms the eastern end. **Beaminster** *(White Hart)* lies six miles north of Bridport in the midst of rich agricultural land. It is a typical country town with streets radiating from the market square. The tower of the church is built of warm-coloured Ham Hill stone and dates from the early 16th century. Highly ornamental, it is adorned with 38 crocketed pinnacles. **Broadwindsor**, three miles west, is the third largest parish in the diocese of Salisbury. It was to this village that Charles II made his way after the "miraculous divergence", staying at the then George Inn. The church was rebuilt in 1868 and contains one of the best Jacobean pulpits remaining in Dorset. In the neighbourhood **Pilsdon Pen** (909 feet) and **Lewesdon Hill** (894 feet) are prominent landmarks. On the north-west slope of Pilsdon is *Racedown Lodge* for two years the home of Wordsworth and his sister. The village of **Pilsdon** was the birthplace of Sir John Hody, Chief Justice of the King's Bench in 1440.

Burton Bradstock *(Anchor Inn, Three Horseshoes)* close to the mouth of the river *Bride* (or Bredy), three miles south-east of Bridport, is a very pretty village. There is good bathing and fishing from a beach of fine shingle. Its neighbour **Burton Freshwater,** half a mile west, has a caravan site. At **Bothenhampton,** near West Bay, the ancient church has an 800-year-old font.

Charmouth (Pop.: 900. Hotels: *Coach and Horses, Queen's Arms, Sea Horse*) lies astride the main Bridport–Axminster road about half a mile from the sea. The surrounding scenery is splendid and from the summit of the coastal hills all viewpoints offer a superb panorama. The river *Char* is spanned by two stone bridges: the one at the eastern end of the main street bears an old metal plaque threatening transportation for life to any person who damages the bridge. Nearby is a toll house, a relic of the days of private turnpike roads. The *Queen's Arms* is an interesting old building in which it is said Charles II spent a night on his unsuccessful attempt to leave the country by way of Charmouth. Another old hostelry is the *George* with a quaint projecting window over the porch.

A short distance northward are two very ancient earthworks, **Coney's Castle** and **Lambert's Castle**; the former said to have been the camp of Egbert when he fought the Danes. Lambert's Castle a mile northward and 842 feet above sea level was an important British earthwork having triple mounds and ditches. The camp is D-shaped and covers 12 acres.

Charmouth to Golden Cap. Golden Cap is a high cliff to the east of Charmouth crowned with a stratum of sandy gravel which when viewed from the sea glows with reflected sunlight. It can be reached from the beach at Charmouth then climbing the cliff and following the coast *(avoid crumbling cliff edge)*.

Lyme Regis

Distances.—Axminster, 6; Bridport, 10; Crewkerne, 17; Dorchester, 24; Exeter, 28; London, 152; Seaton, 8; Sidmouth, 17; Taunton, 28.

Early Closing.—Thursday.

Entertainment.—Cinemas, aquarium, dancing, Marine Theatre.

Golf.—*Lyme Regis Golf Club,* Timber Hill.

Hotels.—*Royal Lion, Alexandra, Three Cups, Victoria, Bay, St. Michael's, Buena Vista, Stile House,* and others.

Museum.—Bridge Street, Fossil collection.

Population.—3,500.

Post Office.—Broad Street.

Sports.—Bathing (shingle but sand at low tide), boating and sailing, bowls, fishing from Cobb or boat, putting, tennis.

Facing south and sheltered from northerly winds by a protecting background of hills, Lyme Regis is beautifully set in a steep opening on to a wide bay. The view seaward is magnificent, enclosing miles of lovely coastline including Golden Cap, Chesil Beach and Portland Bill. Good bathing may be enjoyed from a shingle beach. At low tide the shingle is edged by a fine stretch of sand dotted with many pools. There is boating in the bay, tennis courts in the valley and golf links high on a cliff overlooking the town. The streets slope sharply from the cliff top to the beach and promenade.

The **Cobb** is an old stone pier forming an extensive harbour and believed to date from the time of Edward I. With a curving length of 870 feet it forms a fine promenade. On the Cobb are headquarters of sailing and powerboat clubs and the Marine Aquarium *(daily)*. The Parish Church stands close to the seafront. Due to the steep slope of the hillside the floor is on three different levels. Erected in 1500 it shows parts of the earlier Norman structure. Its old lectern serves as a display case for several antiquities including an old chained "Breeches" bible. The Museum contains items of local interest, the old stocks, a man-trap, and relics of Monmouth's Rebellion and the Siege of Lyme. Close to the Langmoor Gardens in Pound Street is the **Peck Memorial Chapel** once a stable.

The Landing of Monmouth. On June 11, 1685, James, Duke of Monmouth, a natural son of Charles II, landed at Lyme, on the beach at the back of the Cobb, and within a few days some 5,000 recruits had flocked to his standard. After his defeat at Sedgmoor 12 local men in the Rebellion were hanged on the landing place, Judge Jeffreys having refused all pleas for clemency.

The **Landslip** extends westward from Lyme Regis practically all the way to Seaton—a walking distance of eight miles. The Landslip took place on Christmas Day 1839 and left a chasm about three-quarters of a mile long by 400 feet wide and varying from 100 to 150 feet in depth. The whole area presents a wild and rugged appearance all covered with creeper-hung trees and bracken.

Bristol and District

Bristol

Airport.—At Lulsgate, 8 miles south-west.
Art Gallery and Museum.—Queens Road.
Distances.—Bath, 13; Bridgwater, 33; Chepstow, 17; Clevedon, 13; Gloucester, 35; London, 116; Malmesbury, 26; Salisbury, 52; Taunton, 43; Wells, 21.
Early Closing.—Wednesday/Saturday.
Entertainment.—*Colston Hall* (concerts), *Theatre*

Royal (drama), *Hippodrome* (shows), *Little Theatre* (repertory), *cinemas.*
Hotels.—*Grand, Grand Spa, Unicorn, Bright's, Royal, College Close, Hawthorn, St. Vincent's Rocks, Greyhound* and others.
Information Bureau.—City Centre.
Population.—425,300.
Post Office.—Smale Street.

The city of Bristol is situated at the confluence of the *Avon* and the *Frome*, six miles from the Bristol Channel at Avonmouth. Bristol has always been famous for its bold and enterprising seamen. From the 12th to 15th centuries its imports were mainly wine and cloth; later it turned to trade with the Americas. Bristol is still a famous port, importing oil, grain, timber, tobacco and foodstuffs, etc. But larger vessels now dock at Avonmouth. It has also become an important manufacturing centre, with many industries—from tobacco manufacture to aircraft and aero-engines. Much of the city, including some of its oldest and finest areas, has had to be rebuilt following extensive air raid damage in 1940–41.

St. Mary Redcliffe Church described by Queen Elizabeth I as "the fairest, goodliest" of all English parish churches is sometimes mistaken for the Cathedral. Little remains of the original 13th-century church except the inner North Porch and the lower stage of the tower. The present magnificent church was built in the 14th century. The massive tower is richly decorated and surmounted by a spire rising to 290 feet. The interior is 240 feet long. The north and south transepts are unusual with their double aisles. Many of the 1,200 roof-bosses are of great beauty. There are many interesting brasses and in the chapel below the tower are displayed various curios of note.

The *North Porch* has inner and outer sections; the treasury house above is where Chatterton (the "boy-poet" 1752–70) pretended to have discovered the Rowley M.S. in an old chest. Under the great window of the south transept is the huge "four-poster" tomb of Wm. Canynges the younger and his wife. North of the pews in this transept is the black tomb slab of Admiral Sir Wm. Penn, whose son founded Pennsylvania (see also his monument and armour at the west end of the nave). In the north choir-aisle are the canopied monuments of the 15th-century Mede family. Southey and Coleridge were married in this church in 1795 to the sisters Fricker.

Redcliffe Way leads across the Redcliffe Bridge, spanning part of the Floating Harbour, to the open and grassy Queen Square. The statue in the centre is of William III, a bronze by Rysbrack. On the east side is the building of the Port of Bristol Authority. Leading out of the Prince Street Roundabout at the north-west corner is King Street. On the left is the old **Theatre Royal** with its Victorian frontage. Founded in 1766, this theatre is the oldest playhouse in the country and the home of the Bristol Old Vic Company. The building next door, recently restored, is *Coopers Hall,* built for the Coopers Company in 1744. Next, at the corner of King Street and Queen Charlotte Street are the *St. Nicholas Almshouses* (*c.* 1656). During restoration in 1960–61 a bastion of Bristol's medieval wall was revealed. Opposite, on the corner, is the 17th-century half-timbered seafarers' inn, known as the *Llandoger Trow* (trow = barge). King Street leads to Welsh Back, running beside the Floating Harbour to **Bristol Bridge.** The present bridge was erected in 1768 though since widened.

Northward of the bridge is High Street in an area which was the oldest part of the city, almost completely destroyed in 1940–44. On the right are the remains of the Church of St. Mary-le-Port. To the left are the walls of St. Nicholas Church, with its restored tower and 14th-century crypt. The top of High Street meets Broad Street, Corn Street and Wine Street at a crossing that was a central point of importance in earlier times. Wine Street to the right has been completely rebuilt, the Grecian and Italianate buildings of Corn Street to the left have remained unscathed. Here is the **Exchange,** designed by John Wood of Bath and erected in 1740–43. A corn market is held here each Thursday. Behind the Exchange is the Market. Outside the Exchange, on the pavement, are the four famous Brass Nails, used by merchants for making money payments; thus the phrase "Pay down on the Nail". In Small Street, leading off Corn Street, is the General Post Office.

At the eastern end of Corn Street, opposite the Old Council House, is **All Saints Church,** partly Norman and partly 15th century. The famous Bristol philanthropist, Edward Colston, who died in 1721, is buried in the church.

At the corner of Broad Street opposite is **Christ Church** rebuilt by William Patty in 1789–90. Above the entrance is a small gallery with clock and two quaint quarter-jacks, carved by James Paty in 1728. Close by the church is the *Grand Hotel,* largest of Bristol's hotels. On the other side is the Gothic-fronted *Guildhall,* erected in 1843. In Taylor's Court, off Broad Street, is the former *Merchant Taylors' Hall,* still showing its coat of arms over the doorway. At the bottom of Broad Street is **St. John's Gateway,** the last of the nine main gates of the city. On the outer arch may be seen the grooves which carried the portcullis. The carved figures over the gateway are of Brennus and Belinus, mythical founders of Bristol in the 4th century B.C. Surmounting the gateway is **St. John the Baptist Church,** well worth a visit (key from 23 Broad Street).

Through the arch and turning right in Nelson Street, one comes to **Broadmead,** now a very modern shopping centre. Standing a little back is **John Wesley's Chapel** *(daily, except Suns, and Weds),* where John and Charles Wesley preached for 40 years. South-east, off Merchant Street, is *Quakers' Friars* a quiet square with the remains of a Dominican Friary and a former Friends' Meeting House.

Lower Castle Street leads to Old Market Street, where once the old fairs were held. Here is the *Stag and Hounds,* beneath an open colonnade of which was held the "Pie Poudre Court", at which market thieves and debtors were summarily dealt with. This court is declared open at 10 a.m. on September 30 each year, and then immediately adjourned to the Tolzey Court. Also in Old Market Street is the **Methodist Central Hall.**

Reached by Whitson Street is the **Priory Church of St. James,** Haymarket. Only the nave remains of the original 12th-century building. Above three round-headed Norman windows is a unique wheel window. The south aisle dates from 1698. There are many monuments. North of the church is the bus and coach station. Westward are the **Bristol Royal Infirmary,** the **Eye Hospital** and the **Dental Hospital.**

From the hospitals, Upper Maudlin Street leads to Colston Street where on the left is the interesting 17th-century relic known as **Christmas Steps,** leading steeply down to Colston Avenue. Here are recessed stone seats, six on either side, and the ancient **Chapel of the Three Kings of Cologne** (1504). *Key at adjoining almshouses.* The **John Foster Almshouses** were founded in 1483, before the chapel, but the present galleried buildings around an attractive courtway were rebuilt 1861–83.

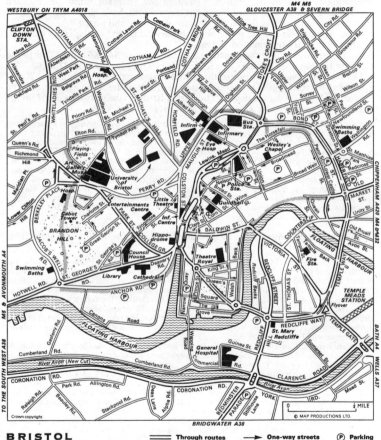

BRISTOL ══════ **Through routes** ➝ **One-way streets** Ⓟ **Parking**

Farther down Colston Street is **Colston Hall,** one of the finest concert halls in the country. Adjoining is the **Little Theatre** where repertory is presented.

The City Centre. From Colston Street it is but a few steps to St. Augustine's Parade, which with Broad Quay opposite and Colston Avenue to the north, bound the large open space now serving as Bristol's modern Centre. In the middle are lawns and flower-beds and low brick walls. Originally part of the course of the

Frome, this section was finally filled in in 1938 and forms a great hub from which roads and traffic radiate in all directions.

Colston Avenue was formed earlier in 1893, also by filling in part of the Floating Harbour. Here is the war memorial and statues of Edmund Burke, statesman, and Edward Colston, philanthropist. On the east side is **St. Stephen's Church** with a lofty 15th-century tower. The south porch is lavishly decorated. There are several interesting features in the church, including the "blanket tomb" of Edward Blanket and his wife, a wool-merchant reputed to have given his name to blankets. St. Stephen's is the parish church of the city and port.

In St. Augustine's Parade is the **Hippodrome,** the largest of the city's theatres. Near by is the **City Information Bureau.**

At the southern end of the Centre stands the *Neptune Statue.* It backs on to the Floating Harbour, on the east of which Narrow Quay leads to the Docks.

The **Port of Bristol** comprises of three dock systems: the City Docks, the Royal Edward and Avonmouth Docks on the northern side of the Avon estuary, and the Portishead Dock on the south side. The port of Bristol is the only major port in the kingdom administered by a municipal authority.

A short walk from the Centre along Narrow Quay brings one to the vicinity of **Prince Street Bridge,** a good vantage point from which a number of berths can be seen, including those at Prince's Wharf, where vessels discharge timber and other wood products from Scandinavia and Finland. Looking towards the great spire of St. Mary Redcliffe, Bathurst Wharf lies on the right. The City Docks are mainly concerned with the coastal and short sea trades and regular liner services are operated to and from the Continent, the Mediterranean, the Baltic and Ireland. On the east end of the transit shed at Prince's Wharf there is a tablet commemorating the building in 1838 of Brunel's *Great Western,* the pioneer ship of transatlantic steam navigation. In the Wapping Dry Dock Brunel's even more revolutionary iron screw-steamer *Great Britain* was built, and is now on exhibition. Her maiden voyage to New York was made in 1845.

The Cathedral stands on the south side of College Green but a few steps from the Centre.

Architecturally Bristol Cathedral is one of the most interesting of English Cathedrals. The Gatehouse and the Chapter House are splendid late Norman work, but the glory of the church is the Choir. Bristol is unique amongst the greater churches of England in being a "Hall-church", for the aisles go up to the same height as the centre vault: the first major church to adopt this plan in Europe. There is no clerestory, and the thrust of the centre vault is therefore not carried over the aisle roofs by flying buttresses, but by unique stone bridges inside the church from which spring the transverse vaults of the aisles. The result is a new kind of church, a great room where the eye is no longer directed upward and eastward, but can range over the whole space which is filled with light.

Entrance to the Cathedral is normally by the north-west porch, leading to the nave. At the west end are 17th-century monuments brought here from elsewhere in the church—to Dame Joan and Sir John Young (much restored) and, much finer, to Sir Charles Vaughan. The screen at the entrance to the choir is, like the reredos, the work of J. L. Pearson, the architect of Truro Cathedral.

The **North Transept,** late 15th-century, has a rich vault with bosses of great variety and interest to which colour has now been restored. On the north wall is the memorial to Bristol's greatest bishop, Joseph Butler (1738–50), the inscription by Robert Southey.

The **South Transept** has the only Norman round-headed window left in the church. On the east wall is a Saxon coffin-lid, (*c.* A.D. 1000) found under the Chapter House floor.

The **Eastern Lady Chapel** is one of the glories of the Cathedral, its colour restored. The tombs are those of 15th-century abbots. Note the stellar recesses which continue in the choir aisles with the splendid carved heads and crests. The parapet to the reredos is the gift of Abbot Burton (1520). Much glass—the Madonna and child and the shields of the east window, and the martyrdom of St. Edmund in the southwest window—is contemporary with the building.

The **Choir** has been restored to its medieval dimensions. The misericords are most interesting—scenes from scripture, everyday life, and the legend of Reynard the Fox. The theme of the reredos is the Te Deum: the figures in the screens are those of the saints to whom the churches of the city are dedicated.

From the south transept the 15th-century cloister is reached, the windows of which contain valuable fragments of medieval glass. To the east of it is the **Chapter House** (1160), one of the finest Norman rooms in England. Farther south is the slype, the monastic passage to the infirmary and burial ground of the monastery.

To the west of the Cathedral is **St. Augustine's Gateway,** a finely-moulded Norman arch which served as the principal entrance to the Monastery.

The **Central Library** *(weekdays)* adjoins the Cathedral in College Green. Its history dates back to the 15th century when the Guild of Kalendars maintained a library at the Church of All Saints, and this was accessible to any citizen who could read or write. The present building dates from 1906. Its museum-piece is the Bristol Room, a replica of the King Street Library as it was in the 18th century, with the original book presses and the oak fireplace carved by Grinling Gibbons.

Dominating the west side of College Green is the **Council House** a vast modern building serving as headquarters for the Bristol Corporation and depository for the City's archives.

The Lord Mayor's Chapel *(daily, except Fris)*, stands on the eastern side of College Green. It is a small but beautiful building, granted at the Reformation to the Mayor and burgesses as a civic church and is thus the only church in the kingdom administered by a Corporation, and the exclusive property of citizens. The chapel is all that remains of the medieval Hospital of the Gaunts which formerly occupied a considerable area to the north and east.

Park Street ascends steeply and we get a glimpse of Bristol's famous vista, up to the tower of the University. In Frogmore Street, a turning to the right, is the *Hatchet Inn,* a 17th-century timber-framed building. At 7, Great George Street, left out of Park Street, is the **Georgian House** *(free, weekdays 11–5),* a period house administered by the City Art Gallery. Built for a Bristol merchant, in 1789, the house contains some elegant 18th-century furniture. From the left-hand side of Park Street, both Great George Street and Charlotte Street lead to Brandon Hill Park. Here paths wind among greensward and attractive rock gardens. There is a bowling green. Crowning the hill is the **Cabot Tower,** erected in 1897 to commemorate the fourth centenary of the discovery of Newfoundland. There is a grand view over the city from the balcony.

The University of Bristol owes its original foundation to a University College established in Bristol in 1876. In 1908, Henry Overton Wills offered funds for establishing a University, a Royal Charter was granted and the new University opened for its first session in October 1909. The main building (1925), consisting of the tower (215 feet), with its famous bell, Great George, the magnificent Entrance Hall with its two staircases and fan-vaulted roof and the Great Hall, together with rooms housing the Arts and Law Faculties, the Library and Administrative Offices was the gift of George Alfred Wills and Henry Herbert Wills.

The University provides courses leading to first and higher degrees in the Arts, Sciences, Medicine, Law and Engineering together with certificates or diplomas in certain subjects, including Education, Social Studies and Public Health. There are in the region of 6,000 full-time students.

In Queen's Road, adjoining the University, are the **City Art Gallery** and **City Museum** *(weekdays).*

The Museum also controls a **Folk Museum** at **Blaise Castle House,** Henbury, to the north-west of Bristol. Here are shown collections of everyday objects, costume and equipment used in the area from the 16th to 19th centuries. Near by, in the extensive parkland, are a thatched dairy and an 18th-century corn-grinding water mill.

The City Museum also maintains the foundations of two Roman buildings at **Lawrence Weston** and **Sea Mills,** which are available for inspection by the public. **Chatterton House** on Redcliffe Way, the birthplace of the boy poet Thomas Chatterton, is a small museum of Chatterton "personalia".

Farther up on the same side of Queen's Road is the building of the **Royal West of England Academy.** It is a handsome classical building. A marble entrance hall gives access to five excellent galleries in which Artist Members of the Academy hold their annual exhibition in November. At the junction of Queen's Road with Whiteladies Road is the classic building known as the **Victoria Rooms** with its impressive portico. It is now used to house the Students' Union of the University.

Whiteladies Road is a broad thoroughfare lined with numerous attractive shops and buildings of classical architecture. On the right is Broadcasting House, West Country headquarters of the B.B.C.

It is a long, though not unattractive, walk up Whiteladies Road past Clifton Down Station to the Downs.

The Downs. Clifton Down and Durdham Down are magnificent open spaces of 230 and 212 acres respectively. They are crossed by roads, but there is ample space for cricket, football and riding, while facilities also exist for tennis and golf. To the west is **Sea Walls,** a vantage point overlooking the *Avon* with fine views extending along the Gorge from Avonmouth to the Suspension Bridge. Access to the Portway below can be made by the *Gully,* a somewhat hazardous descent. Adjoining Clifton Down are **The Zoological Gardens** *(daily from 9 a.m.; Suns, 11 a.m., fee).*

In Guthrie Road, on the south side of the Zoological Gardens is **Clifton College** founded in 1862 and since risen to a leading place among public schools. Old boys include Haig, Quiller-Couch, and Newbolt.

The **Clifton Suspension Bridge,** designed by Isambard Brunel and crossing the steep Avon Gorge was opened in 1864. It has a total length (anchorage to anchorage) of 1,352 feet and total span (pier to pier) of 702 feet 3 inches. The height of the roadway above high water is 245 feet.

Observatory Hill, overlooking the suspension bridge and 338 feet above high water, affords a fine prospect. In the so-called observatory is a camera obscura and access to a tunnel which emerges at *Giants' Cave,* 90 feet below.

The River—to Avonmouth Docks. From the Cathedral, St. George's Road and the Hotwell Road lead westward to the *Avon* and pass under the suspension bridge to **Portway,** a splendid road built in 1927, which follows the bank of the river. A short distance along is **Sea Mills,** the site of the Roman port of Abona, where the third wet dock in England was built in 1712. On the left bank farther along is the village of **Pill,** traditional home of the Bristol pilots.

Avonmouth Docks (8 miles from Bristol). The first dock was built in 1877. A junction cut leads into the Royal Edward Dock, begun in 1908; the final extension scheme was completed in 1941. This dock is equipped for handling general cargo at almost all the berths, but a number of specialised cargoes are also provided for. There are cold stores, grain silos, and aerial ropeways to convey zinc ores to the smelting works. The Oil Basin handles imports and exports of petroleum products.

Near **Filton,** four miles north of Bristol, are the works of the Bristol Aeroplane Company, with a runway nearly two miles in length.

Portishead is a pleasant resort with a wide outlook 10 miles from Bristol. There is a small pebble beach close to the pier. A shady drive makes a circuit of the steep wooded knoll that stands between the old part of the town and the sea-front. Footpaths lead up through the woods to an old camp site and down to **Battery Point** (fine views). Behind the promenade fronting Woodhill Bay is a fine Marine Lake. The church dates from the 14th century. In the churchyard is a fine old preaching cross.

Clevedon (Pop.: 14,300. Hotels: *Walton Park, Cliffe* and others) is an attractive resort 13 miles from Bristol. The broken coast-line of the bay, with rugged rocks or vegetation growing down to the water's edge; the tree-bowered town itself—part in the valley and part on the undulating slopes of Dial Hill—makes up a pretty picture. There is a large residential population, and the town is only affected to a limited extent by the coming and going of visitors, though it enjoys some popularity as a winter resort. The town offers the usual amenities of a seaside resort. The beach is of rock and shingle and bathing and boating is popular. Many of the roads are tree-lined; and scattered about the place are shady enclosures known as "copses", the natural beauty of which has, to a great extent, been preserved. Clevedon Old Church nestles in a hollow and has a fine Norman arch providing a frame for the chancel.

Clevedon Court (N.T., *Apr.–Sept., Weds, Thurs, Suns, Bank Hols, fee*) home of the Eltons since 1709, lies just north of the Bristol road about a mile east of Clevedon. Formerly a fortified manor house dating from the 12th century various additions have been made from time to time. The chapel, once a boudoir, is 14th century. There is a terraced garden.

Gordano. The district of moor and hill lying directly behind Clevedon is known as Gordano. Starting from the Avon gorge at Clifton the hills run westward to Clevedon, but then turn back north-eastward to rampart the Bristol Channel. Gordano lies in the space between.

To Walton-in-Gordano. A circular walk of about four miles. The direct route is by the main Portishead Road, Walton Road, from Old Street, but a more attractive way is along the coast by Ladye Bay and Margaret's Bay, or over the crest of Castle Hill and following its base to the Look Out, by paths leading through gorse, bracken, or grove. A path runs between the golf club house and Castle Farm to near the Castle ruins. The castle was built in the reign of James I and is an unusual example of ornamental planning.

To Weston-in-Gordano. A short run on the bus, or a pleasant walk of three and a half miles along "the Swiss Valley", leads to Weston-in-Gordano. The very interesting 14th-century Church is built on the site of an older Norman building, the font of which remains. There are two pulpits—a 13th-century stone one in a recess of the wall, and a later oak pulpit. In the north wall is the tomb of Rycharde Persyvale (*d.* 1482). The stalls have misericordes quaintly carved and in the stairs which lead to the rood-loft there is also a curious carving. There is a curious chorister's gallery above the south porch, and in the gable at the east end of the nave hangs the sanctus bell. Outside the church, close to the south porch, is a much-defaced altar tomb in memory of Richard Percival, a Crusader who died in 1190.

To Clapton-in-Gordano four-and-a-half miles north-east. The route lies under Court Hill, where the rhododendrons make a fine show in early summer, and onwards along the foot of the ridge, a very pleasant, quiet road. All the way on the right are hanging woods traversed by paths along which one may wander for miles. But for Clapton-in-Gordano keep to the roads. The village takes its name from the Clapton family, who owned the manor from 1140 to 1615. The Manor house is near the church. The Church standing on high ground, is in the Early English style, with a low tower.

To Kenn. A walk of under two miles southward via Kenn Road leads to the little village of Kenn. The church is chiefly 15th century, but underwent extensive restoration in 1861. The interior walls are of red limestone. There is a tablet in memory of Sir Nicholas Staling (*d.* 1605), "Gentleman Usher and Dayly Waiter" to Queen Elizabeth and King James I. The monument dated 1593, on the wall above the tower has an inscription to Christopher Ken, Esq., of Ken Court, who is depicted kneeling with his two daughters, while below is his wife recumbent with infant. All are in Elizabethan dress. The Kenn family, held the Manor from 1150 for many generations.

To Kingston Seymour. This pretty village, with its rich pasture-lands, is about two miles beyond Kenn. There is an interesting 15th-century Gothic church with a fine tower and spire.

To Tickenham and Cadbury Camp. A walk or bus ride of some three-and-a-half miles along the Bristol road, which goes past Clevedon Court, brings one to the village of Tickenham, with a 15th-century manor house, now a farm, and an interesting church, dedicated to Saints Julietta and Quiricus. The story of their martyrdom is sculptured in relief on the four sides of the beautiful tower.

Walkers should leave the main road just before Tickenham by a rough and narrow lane on the left. It leads up to the crest of the ridge, where is **Cadbury Camp** a stronghold of the Ancient Britons covering an area of seven acres. Double dry walls of limestone and two trenches surround an inner fort. The Camp is 391 feet above sea-level and overlooks the whole of Gordano.

To Backwell, a large village about seven miles east of Clevedon. The church, dedicated to St. Andrew, is Early English in character; the lofty tower has unusual richly ornamented pinnacles. The church contains part of the old rood screen, a Norman font and a chantry chapel endowed in 1537 with a flock of sheep. A beautiful view is obtained from Backwell Hill.

To Brockley Combe, Congresbury and Yatton. This is a popular trip: the neighbourhood can show no finer sight than this rugged, tree-clothed glen. The Combe can be reached either from Yatton or Nailsea station, the latter being two and a half miles from it, the former four miles. It can also be reached easily by bus. **Brockley Combe** is one of the most picturesque nooks of the Mendips. On one side of the road steep rocks crowned with trees tower to a height of 300 feet. On the other hand is shelving woodland. It is a fairly easy scramble to the top of the cliffs from which there is a rewarding view. Turning towards Congresbury for a mile, we come to a lane on the left leading through Cleeve Combe, a wooded ravine of similar character to that of Brockley. Goblin Coombe, farther east, is also well worth a visit. At **Congresbury** the *Yeo* runs for a short distance side by side with the road. The roads to Clevedon and Bristol diverge near the church, St. Andrew, noted for its unusual clerestory and fine spire. In the centre of the village is an ancient and interesting cross. **Yatton** church is a handsome cruciform building with a fine tower crowned with the base of a spire which fell many years ago. The manor house resembles Clevedon Court, but is on a smaller scale.

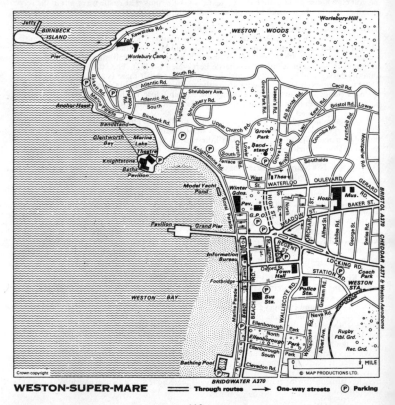

WESTON-SUPER-MARE ═══ **Through routes** ⟶ **One-way streets** Ⓟ **Parking**

To **Wrington and Burrington.** The delightful Avon village of **Wrington** with its famous church tower, and associations with John Locke and Hannah More, is easily accessible from Clevedon by road. The magnificent tower of the church rises to a height of 140 feet and is crowned by four turrets, each supporting four lofty pinnacles. In the churchyard, beneath a yew tree on the south side, is the grave of Hannah More and her four sisters. This writer and philanthropist died in 1833; above the south porch of the church a marble tablet records her virtues. Wrington was the birthplace of John Locke, the 17th-century philosopher. A memorial stone marks the site of the little thatched cottage in which he was born in 1632. **Burrington Combe** is a fine ravine on the northern slope of the Mendips. The Rev. A. Toplady composed the well-known hymn "Rock of Ages" in this Combe whilst sheltering from a thunderstorm. The whole valley is a very popular picnic resort. From the top of the Combe it is only a short climb to **Black Down** (1,068 feet), the highest point of the Mendips.

To the east of **Blagdon** is the Yeo Reservoir, or **Blagdon Lake**, an artificial sheet of water about two miles long. It is noted for its fishing and sizeable trout are to be caught.

Weston-super-Mare

Bathing.—Extensive sands. Open-air pool, South Beach. Uphill Sands. Indoor pool at Knightstone.
Distances.—Axbridge, 10; Bath, 32; Bristol, 21; Cheddar, 13; Kewstoke, 2; London, 136; Portishead, 22; Wrington, 12; Yatton, 12.
Early Closing.—Thursday.
Entertainment.—Winter Garden Pavilion (concerts, dancing), Knightstone Theatre, Playhouse, Cinemas, Pier, Rozel, Madeira Cove.
Hotels.—*Grand Atlantic, Royal, Royal Pier, Cabot,*

Albert. Commodore, Salisbury, Smith's, Grosvenor, Dauncey's, and a great many others of all grades.
Museum and Art Gallery.—The Boulevard.
Piers.—Grand Pier and Pavilion. Birnbeck Pier.
Population.—50,800.
Post Office.—Off High Street.
Sport.—Boating, bowls, tennis, cricket (festival), golf (18 holes. Uphill). Putting, riding, squash.

Weston is situated on a spur of the Mendips forming the northern horn of a spacious and finely curved bay at the point where the estuary of the *Severn* broadens into the Bristol Channel. This popular resort is justifiably famous for its mild climate, firm sands and the variety of its entertainment and sports facilities. Weston's Marine Parades extend for a distance of two-and-a-half miles. They flank Weston Bay, which is hemmed in between the whale-like mass of Brean Down on the south, and the promontory forming the seaward end of the Worlebury Ridge on the north. Beyond the promontory is Weston's second bay, Sand Bay, with Sand Point enclosing the northern end. This horn and Brean Down are five miles apart. Offshore are the two islands, **Steep Holme** and **Flat Holme.**

Kewstoke and Worle. The tree-sheltered Kewstoke road continues the promenade northward to round the Worle promontory. The woods on Worlebury Hill offer beautiful walks and views. On the hill evidence of an ancient British encampment can still be clearly traced. **Kewstoke** is a village which appears at one time to have had the sea as a much nearer neighbour than at present. The Pass of St. Kew (locally "St. Kew's Steps" or the "Old Monks' Steps"), a long flight of 200 steps (N.T.) opposite the church and leading up the hill towards Milton, was originally connected with a landing place serving the camp on Worlebury. Kewstoke church, parts of which date from between 1130 and 1150, has a fine Norman porch. The tower above the trees two miles north is the tower of the ruined *Woodspring Priory* (not open). **Worle,** which a century ago was a much more important place than Weston, is now a pleasant residential suburb embracing the old, attractive village, and stands at the eastern end of the Worle ridge. It is dominated by the little Perpendicular Church of St. Martin with its crooked spire.

Brean Down is the great humpbacked, whale-like treeless promontory that forms the southern horn of Weston Bay. In spite of being so close to Weston, the Down has a remarkable air of remoteness, due largely to the fact that the river *Axe* prevents direct access even to Uphill, except by boat; and the one road to the Down is a coastal lane which starts several miles south of the headland. The Down rises 321 feet and with the exception of Bleadon Hill to the east, Worle and Brent Knoll, is the only high point in otherwise flat country. There are traces of Celtic fields, an Iron Age Fort, and in 1956–58 a Romano-British Temple, of the 4th century A.D. was excavated. The remains are to be seen in the

Weston-super-Mare Museum. The Down has a length of about a mile and a half and a width of about a quarter of a mile. A path leading to the summit will be found near the farmhouse at the base of the ivy-clad landward cliff. In places, the limestone cliffs rise sheer from the sea, and it is well not to venture too near the edge. Beyond the point are the Howe Rocks, sharp and deadly.

Weston to Burnham-on-Sea

The road (A370) runs south from Weston through **Uphill** now part of the larger town and spread out along the northern bank of the *Axe*. At low water the steep mudbanks look forlorn but the river is really quite considerable having its source at Wookey Hole. It is navigable as far as Bleadon. Uphill Old Church stands on a hill but is now a ruin, the modern replacement being situated on the main road. At **Bleadon** the church consists of nave and chancel and a fine 15th-century tower. In the chancel are two stone effigies locally referred to as Adam and Eve. They lay in the churchyard for about 200 years and were brought into the church in 1899. There is a picturesque old cross near the church. Bleadon Hill is the westernmost spur of the Mendip range. The highest point is but a mile north-west of the church.

Southward from Bleadon the main Bridgwater road passes about half a mile east of **Lympsham,** a very pretty tree-shaded village with many cottages built in the Gothic style. The Church, dedicated to St. Christopher, has a curious aspect because the tower, though heavily buttressed, leans from the perpendicular. From the Lympsham turning the main road continues directly southward for a couple of miles and then begins a wide sweep round the base of **Brent Knoll**—the main road passing along the eastern side of the hill, and the prettier by-road following the western edge and passing through the village of the same name.

Brent Knoll is a steep-sided and well-wooded hill of 457 feet rising abruptly from the surrounding plain. From its summit the view is magnificent. There are traces of Roman entrenchments on the summit. A track leads down to Brent Knoll Church, remarkable for its grotesque bench-ends, with geese, foxes, monkeys.

Burnham-on-Sea (Pop.: 12,300. Hotels: *Richmond, Queen's*) with seven miles of sands, highly favoured golf-links and a mild and invigorating climate, has a popular following of visitors. In some respects it resembles some of the smaller east coast resorts—flat, sandy and quiet, but possessing a subtle charm that grows on acquaintance. For children no place could be better: the sands are firm and extensive, and there is no danger from rapidly rising tides. There is good bathing and boating, but the majority of visitors are lured to Burnham by the excellence of its golf. The *Burnham and Berrow Golf Club* has fine sporting links among the sand-hills, and an excellent clubhouse. The principal feature at the southern end of the Esplanade is a marina lake. Built out over the sands towards the northern end is a small Pavilion (entertainments). Farther north is a lighthouse, a wooden structure on piles. The other lighthouse is inland on the Berrow road. Sand dunes, or "totts", are a marked feature of the coast between Burham and Brean stretching in an unbroken line for seven miles.

The fact that the river *Parrett* and the smaller river *Brue* find their outlet to the sea near Burnham ensures always a deep channel of water in the midst of the Flats. It is curious to watch the tugs and small trading vessels making for Bridgwater, apparently floating on an ocean of sand. There is a good deal of traffic—timber, coal, flour, etc. A mile or so up the *Brue* and on the main Bridgwater road is **Highbridge** forming the industrial part of Burnham. A cattle market has been held here for nearly a hundred years.

Along the Mendips

TO CHEDDAR AND WELLS

The Mendip Hills, which slant across the north of Somerset, have a length of about 20 miles. The highest point is Black Down (1,068 feet), about three miles north of Cheddar. The range is of carboniferous limestone, resting on old red sandstone, and is honeycombed throughout by caverns, of which some of the most spectacular are open to the public at Cheddar, Wookey and elsewhere. The possibilities of "caving" attracts many devotees of that sport to the Mendips. The area was in Saxon and Norman times called the *Forest of Mendip*. Doubtless there were extensive woodlands, but the term "forest" as then used implied Royal hunting rights rather than abundance of trees.

An ancient industry was the mining of lead ore, practised by the Britons, and then on a greater scale by the invading Romans. One Roman lead-mining settlement was at Charterhouse, three miles north-east from Cheddar. There are still traces of a Roman road just north of Charterhouse, and this may once have continued to Uphill at the mouth of the *Axe*, from which ore could be shipped. Records of lead mining during the "Dark Ages" have vanished, but plenty remain from the 12th century onwards, by which time lead had become a rich source of income to the Church, which owned extensive lands in Mendip. The lead mines were usually surface excavations (*gruffs* or *grooves*), and land pitted with traces of such former excavations is still termed "gruffy ground".

In medieval times the Mendips—like the Cotswolds—was wool country, and large flocks of sheep were maintained by monks of the religious houses. At the isolated village of Priddy, three miles north-west of Wells, one can see not only the underground passages of Roman lead mines, but also a 600-year old Sheep Fair that is still held (on a reduced scale) every August. By the end of the 18th century much of the more fertile land had become enclosed for crops and cattle. Lead mining died out by the early 19th century, but by then it had become replaced by calamine mining. Calamine is a zinc ore, which when heated with copper (or better, the zinc extracted and melted with copper) produces the alloy brass. (The earlier known alloy, bronze, is composed of *tin* and copper.) A ready market for calamine was provided by the many brass works in and around Bristol.

On the A371 is **Banwell** a village of considerable antiquarian interest. The village derives its name from the deep well that used to fill a large pond, now a bowling green, in its centre. A monastery was founded here in Saxon times, and destroyed by the Danes. It was re-established later, and on the site a Bishop's Palace, stood for centuries. It was succeeded by *The Manor Court House,* for many years a residence of the Bishops of Bath and Wells; this has been rebuilt several times. The Church, chiefly 15th century, is one of the finest. The tower is 105 feet in height. The richly carved and gilded oak rood screen, the octagonal stone pulpit and the roof are worthy of note.

On Banwell Hill, the lofty half-mile ridge beneath which the village lies, are some large caves, one known as the *Bone Cave*. An enormous quantity of bones of animals, many of which are now extinct in England, were found here. The best specimens are in the museum at Taunton. On the hill are traces of an ancient British camp, remains of a Roman villa and on the summit the *Bishop's Tower*, 60 feet high.

CHEDDAR

A road from Banwell church leads in two miles to **Winscombe,** a secluded village on the road to Cheddar. The manor was given, a hundred years before the Conquest, to the monastery of Glastonbury, and passed later to the Dean and Chapter of Wells. In the village is the co-educational Sidcot School, under the patronage of the Society of Friends. The Church has some fine carved roof bosses and carved stonework in the aisles and some of the best medieval stained glass in the country. Taking the path through the churchyard, one may ascend **Crook Peak,** (628 feet), from which there is a magnificent view of the surrounding country.

South of Winscombe the road passes through a deep gorge between **Wavering Down** (690 feet) and **Shute Shelve,** or Callow Hill (850 feet) to **Axbridge,** at one time a place of considerable importance. The Town Hall houses a remarkably interesting collection of town records and documents dating from Henry III's reign. The church is a large Perpendicular structure containing several interesting monuments and brasses. The road hugs the foot of the hills and in two miles reaches Cheddar.

Cheddar *(Cliff)* is one of the most justly popular sights of the west. The village nestles under the southern flank of the Mendips. The church built 1350–1450 is a beautiful example of the Perpendicular-style Somerset parish church. The tower is a landmark in the valley. In the centre of the village is the 15th-century Cheese Cross (market cross). The roof and six arches were later additions.

The sides of **Cheddar Gorge** are sheer escarpments in places over 480 feet. The ledges and interstices are green with ferns and mosses, and in the fissures trees find a precarious foothold. The crag immediately above the entrance to the pass has some resemblance to a lion couchant, and is popularly known as the Lion Rock. At the entrance to the Gorge is Jacob's Ladder, a climb of some 277 steps to the top of the Gorge. There are fine views of the surrounding country, the best being from the Pulpit Rock, which overlooks the upper village and lake. Also at the top is a watch-tower with camera obscura.

The caves have been traced much farther into the hills than the public are permitted to go; and there is no doubt that the whole range is honeycombed in a similar manner.

Cox's Cave was accidentally discovered in 1837. There are now seven chambers open to the public. Much has been done to make its beauties accessible, and electric light has been installed. An interesting feature, in these and similar caves, is the development of mosses and ferns (from wind-borne spores) that has followed the installation of artificial lighting. Here, in these subterranean chambers, Nature has been at work for countless ages. It is not merely the strange shapes of the formations—but their delicacy and beauty of colouring that appeal. Here and there the stalactites pendent from the roof have met the stalagmites rising from the floor, forming slender pillars; but the process is unbelievably slow.

Gough's Caves, the first of which was discovered in 1877, have been opened one by one, the most notable "discovery" being in 1898 when the enormous chamber known as the *Diamond Chamber* was penetrated. The gorgeous colouring varies according to the position of the light. At the entrance to the Caves is a *Museum* housing, among other objects, the *Cheddar Man,* a skeleton of a young man about 23 years of age, who lived roughly 12,000 years ago. It was discovered in 1903 in Gough's Caves.

Cheddar Gorge was at one time thought to be the result of an earthquake or other mighty convulsion of Nature, but later scientific opinion regards it as only an enormous cave, the roof of which has fallen in. The cavern was doubtless excavated in the first place by an underground river; for water charged with carbonic acid has the property of dissolving limestone.

Nearly 10 miles south-east of Cheddar is the **Ebbor Gorge,** less known but ranking with Cheddar in impressiveness. The Gorge is reached by the lane between the village of **Easton** and Wookey Hole, the last part of the journey being by a field path beginning opposite the farm at the top of the hill. Walkers bound for Wookey or Wells should continue through the Ebbor Gorge, climbing the steep ascent between the rocks. At the top bear to the right: a narrow lane about a mile south-east of the Gorge is the best way down to Wookey Hole; for Wells continue to the main road at Rookham Hill, a magnificent viewpoint.

116

Wells

Distances.—Bath, 20; Bridgwater, 21; Bristol, 21; Burnham, 18; Cheddar, 8; Glastonbury, 6; London, 122; Taunton, 28.
Early Closing.—Wednesday.

Hotels.—*Star, Swan, Crown, White Hart, Red Lion, King's Head.*
Market Day.—Saturday.
Population.—8,600.
Post Office.—Market Place.

Very lovely is this city by the Mendips, with its Cathedral encircled by buildings almost as ancient as itself, and still used for the purposes for which they were erected. It would be difficult to find another spot so alluring, the religious centre of a beautiful county. There are ancient gateways; a street of 14th-century houses; a 15th-century Deanery with walls built for defence; and a Bishop's Palace, also with defensive walls, and surrounded by a moat crossed by a drawbridge leading to a castle-like entrance. All adjoin the Cathedral and combine to form a picture of medieval interest unsurpassed even by Canterbury or Chester.

The Cathedral *(generally free, but charges to Central Tower and clock in North Transept).*

The bishopric of Wells was founded, in 909, by Edward the elder, son of Alfred the Great, who chose for its centre a church already standing by "the great fountain of St. Andrew". This older church is thought to have been founded about A.D. 700 by King Ina of the West Saxons. Later the church was pulled down and Bath became the cathedral city of the diocese. In 1206 a compromise was reached, and succeeding bishops have held the title of "Bath and Wells", though the bishops henceforth lived at Wells. The first builder of the present church was Reginald de Bohun, consecrated Bishop in 1174. Jocelyn, who became Bishop of Bath in 1206 and held the diocese for over 36 years, built the exquisite West Front, and completed the nave.

The best point to get a first view of the Cathedral is by way of the **Dean's Eye,** a 15th-century gateway in Sadler Street leading from the Market Place.

The **West Front,** majestic and graceful with tier upon tier of fine statuery ranks as the finest existing example of Early English work.

The **North Porch** is one of the oldest parts and a good example of the Transitional Norman period. The statues on the east capital of the outer doorway represent the martyrdom of King Edmund. To the left of the porch is a Clock Dial with two bells, and two "quarter jacks" in 15th-century armour, that strike the quarters with their battle-axes. To the left is the famous bridge, known as the Chain Gate, connecting the Cathedral with the Vicar's Close; chains were once drawn across it at night to close the road.

The **Nave,** 192 feet long, 82 feet wide and 67 feet high, is Early English, with distinct traces of the Norman style. The oldest work is seen in the four eastern bays, which, with the ritual choir and transepts, formed Bishop Reginald's church; and Bishop Jocelyn, in completing the nave, contented himself with following the architectural style of his predecessors. The result is a stately unity in style. The **Inverted Arches,** a bold, original and effective device for supporting the weight of the Central Tower, are a characteristic feature of the architecture of Wells Cathedral. They strike the attention instantly, and remain as an abiding impression of the interior, particularly as seen from the west end.

The **Transepts** are older than the nave, and plainer in style, but the capitals of the piers are particularly interesting for their varied sculpture.

In addition to the grotesque capitals, there is much of interest in the North Transept, notably the curious **Clock,** made about 1325 by a monk of Glastonbury, and showing not only the time of day, but the phases of the moon and the position of the planets. Upon the dial plate is a representation of the moon, with the motto *Sic peragrat Phoebe* "Thus Phoebe (the moon) wends her way". Above the clock are figures of four mounted horsemen, who, at the striking of the hours, revolve several times in tournament fashion. New works have replaced the old, which are preserved in the Science Museum, London. In the north-west angle of the transept is a large figure of a man who strikes the quarters by kicking backwards at two bells with his heels. A charge is made to see the clock.

The **Choir,** extended in the 14th century, and restored in 1848–54, contains an altar screen so unusually low that it gives an exceptionally fine view eastward. The three arches at the east end are surmounted by a window representing the Tree of Jesse, with some of the best 14th-century glass in England.

In the Choir Aisles are many tombs and monuments.

The **Chapter House,** approached from the North Transept by a beautiful flight of deep-worn steps, is a marvellous piece of Decorated work, exquisitely light and graceful. It is a high octagonal building; a marble pillar rises from the centre, splays out high up and joins the vaulting of the wall pillars which divide the wonderfully fretted windows.

On the same side of the Cathedral—the north—is the **Deanery,** a heavily-buttressed 15th-century house. On the north side of Cathedral Green is the **Museum.**

An interesting institution at Wells is the College of the Vicars Choral. The Hall in *Vicar's Close* was built in 1348, and contains the foundation documents by Edward III. Vicars' Close is said to be the most ancient complete street in Europe. At the top is an exquisite tiny chapel.

South of the Cathedral, beyond the Cloisters, is the **Bishop's Palace,** reached from the city by the gateway known as the Bishop's Eye, on the east side of the market place. Within the grounds are the ruins of the *Banqueting Hall.* The Palace is best known for its moat and swans which have learned to pull a bellrope when hungry. Standing over the moat is the 15th-century **Bishop's Barn.**

St. Cuthbert's Church is the largest Parish Church in Somerset and dates back to the 13th century. Of special interest is the Treasury (the Choir Vestry) which is a 13th-century building, the fine 15th-century roof, the Sacristy, the old Parish chest (1640), and the Pulpit (1636). Near the church in Chamberlain Street are some of Wells's ancient almshouses, among them Stills' Almshouses, Bubwith's Almshouses, and the Archibald Harper Almshouses.

Wookey Hole, two miles north-west of Wells, hides itself discreetly in a charming valley which holds the *Great Cave* and the *Hyena Den.* The mouth of the former is in the cliff face. At one time the *Axe* issued from the cave but has worn itself a lower exit. The *museum* contains many relics of the occupation of the cave including bones of many animals, Roman and British pottery and Roman coins ranging from 76 B.C. to A.D. 375.

Glastonbury (Pop.: 6,600. Hotels: *George and Pilgrims, Copper Beech, Crown),* six miles south-west of Wells, is a market town famous for its abbey and association with the Avalon of romance. From whatever direction one approaches, Glastonbury Tor stands up like a beacon.

Tradition says that St. Joseph of Arimathea, sent by St. Philip the Apostle, came with a band of missionaries to preach the Gospel in Britain. They sailed up the Bristol Channel until they came in sight of a hill "most like to Tabor's holy mount", for which St. Joseph in a dream had been instructed to look. This hill—Glastonbury Tor—rose steeply up out of the surrounding marshes.

Close to Glastonbury, on the road to Bridgwater, is **Weary-all-Hill,** or Wirrall, the spot where St. Joseph and his companions, "weary-all" with their journey, are said to have landed. Here St. Joseph planted his pilgrim's staff, which are once took root and sent forth branches, and would burst into flower every Christmas Day.

It is certain that for many centuries there grew here a tree famed through Christendom 'as the Glastonbury Thorn. On the hill may be found the cracked paving-stone marking the place where the original tree flourished, and roughly inscribed "I.A." (Joseph of Arimathea) "Ann. D. xxxi". A cutting was set near the stone in 1951. Several of the ancestral parks of Somerset have trees said to have been grown from slips taken from the original Glastonbury Thorn. There is one in the Abbey grounds. They flower about Christmas-time, and are of Eastern origin.

The Abbey Ruins *(daily, fee).* The entrance is by way of the Abbots' Gateway in Magdalen Street.

The early pilgrims, having landed on the Tor, built a church of osiers wattled together—the first Christian Church in our land. A stone oratory was afterwards erected here; and in 443 St. Patrick, returning from his great mission in Ireland, visited the holy spot, and taught the recluses in the vicinity to dwell together in common, with himself as their abbot. Early in the 7th century the wattled church was covered with boards and lead for its preservation as a sacred relic.

In the 8th century a monastery was founded to the east of the original building. This was plundered by the Danes and restored by the great St. Dunstan, a native of Glastonbury, appointed Abbot in 940. The monastery was damaged by fire in 1184; and more than a century elasped before it was completed in one magnificent building, nearly 600 feet in length, of which the present ruins are a fragment.

. **St. Mary's Chapel** is the oldest and most interesting portion of the ruins. Built in late Norman style it stands on the site of the first wattled church. East is the "galilee" or extension and a solitary fragment of wall that once bounded the nave of the **Great Church.** Of the latter only parts of the tower piers, parts of a north transept chapel and the greater portion of the wall of the south choir aisle remain. The church was begun in 1184 and dedicated in 1303. The nave is six feet higher than the east end of the chapel, and the choir is several feet higher than the nave. The differences in height are plainly shown in the level of the turf which now carpets the interior, and in the stone benches still remaining in the ruins of nave and choir.

On the south side of St. Mary's Chapel (or St. Joseph's) is the **Monk's Cemetery,** a grass-plot held in special reverence as the burial place of many famous personages. Tradition states that this is the burial place of King Arthur and his queen, St. Joseph of Arimathea, St. Patrick, and St. Dunstan.

Connected with the Abbey is the **Abbot's Kitchen,** a square building with an octagonal roof. In it are four fireplaces each large enough to roast an ox, and between the chimneys rises an octagonal pyramid crowned by a double lantern. It is one of the most interesting specimens in England of 14th-century domestic architecture.

Nearly opposite the Market Cross, and just within the High Street, is the **Pilgrims' Inn** (the *George*), built in the 15th century for the accommodation of pilgrims for whom no room could be found in the Abbey. A little beyond, on the same side of the street, is another Perpendicular structure, the **Tribunal,** once the courthouse for the trial of cases over which the Abbot had jurisdiction.

In the Town Hall is the **Museum** of the Glastonbury Antiquarian Society chiefly notable for relics of the dim past rescued from the Lake Villages in the neighbourhood. Close at hand is **St. Benignus's Church,** now usually referred to as St. Benedict's. St. Benignus was an early disciple of St. Patrick who lived and worked in Ireland about A.D. 460. In old age he came to Avalon, built a hermit's cell, and died there. In the High Street is **St. John the Baptist's Church,** the tower of which ranks with the noblest of these structures in Somerset. The church is mainly Perpendicular in feature and was rebuilt by Abbot Selwood in 1485.

By turning to the right at the top of the High Street into Chilkwell Street, we reach the **Abbey Barn,** a very fine cruciform structure of the 14th century *(entrance free)*. Farther along Chilkwell Street, on the left, is Wellhouse Lane, at the corner of which is the Glaston Tor School. Here, in the grounds is the *Chalice Well (fee),* beneath whose waters legend says the Holy Grail was hidden. The stonework of the well is believed to be of pre-Roman origin.

Glastonbury Tor (N.T.) rises to 520 feet above sea-level. On the summit is the tower of St. Michael's Church, built in the late 13th century. The view from the top is very extensive.

In 1892 a **British Lake Village** was discovered near Glastonbury, and the various mounds have since been completely excavated, providing a rich store of domestic and war-like implements. In 1908 another much larger group of lake dwellings was discovered at **Meare,** about three miles north-west of Glastonbury. Since then the site has been systematically examined. At Meare is a 14th-century structure known as the *Fish House,* probably once the residence of the official in charge of the lakes once existing here, from which fish were taken for the supply of the Abbot of Glastonbury's tables.

South-Westward from Glastonbury

Glastonbury is a good starting place for an exploration of the extensive and almost unknown area of low-lying ground between the Mendips and the Quantocks, and relieved by the Polden Hills, Glastonbury Tor and a few lesser heights. It is a district with many historic associations. Southwest of Glastonbury is Sedgemoor, the site of the tragic encounter between Monmouth and James II in 1685; a little farther south-west is Athelney, associated with Alfred the Great; while due west of Wells is Wedmore, where Alfred negotiated with the Danes and drew up the Treaty which, for a time at any rate, rid the country of the peril and fear of Danish raids. The interest of the district is more than historical, for it has a strange beauty of its own. The place-names, too, of this part of Somerset are interesting—Bawdrip, Lyng, Huish Episcopi, Muchelney ("Muckley-Eye"), Hornblotton, Stogursey.

There are few traces today of the **Battle of Sedgemoor,** fought on July 5th 1685, the actual field lying just outside the village of Weston Zoyland, some three or four miles east from Bridgwater. **Chedzoy,** north-west of the battlefield, has definite memories of the battle. The buttresses of the south transept of Chedzoy Church have been much photographed, for they still bear marks said to have been made by the rebels as they sharpened their swords in preparation for the fight. **Weston Zoyland** church is 15th century with a very fine tower and excellent modern restoration. It has a 14th-century octagonal font with unusual moulding. An effigy of a recumbent priest in the north transept dates from *c.* 1290. During the Battle of Sedgemoor the church was filled with some 500 captured Royalists, many wounded and dying. Those killed on the battlefield were interred in a huge, common grave in a field about a quarter of a mile beyond the hamlet of Bussex.

The **Island of Athelney,** an island before the marshes were drained, has little to indicate its past, except a modern monument erected to commemorate Alfred's deliverance from his enemies. A mile or so to the north-east, just above **Burrow Bridge,** is a prominent knoll crowned by the ruins of a church. It is thought that Alfred had a palace on this hill.

Bridgwater (Pop.: 26,600. Hotels: *New Market, Bristol, White Hart, Royal Clarence*) is an ancient town on the *Parrett,* a river-post, a manufacturing centre, and a market for the produce of the rich alluvial plain lying round it. The first element in the name comes from the original manor, and to the Saxon word *Bridge* the Domesday lord, Walter de Douai, added his own name. Hence came Brugge-Walteri and Briggewater. In the Middle Ages, Bridgwater was engaged in the manufacture of cloth. The industrial Revolution drew this lucrative pursuit from Somerset to the northern coalfields, but even now, Somerset teasels are gathered and sent to Yorkshire for the finishing of the cloth. Today Bridgwater's chief industries are brick and tile-making, shirt-making and the manufacture of cellulose, electrical equipment and furniture. "Bath brick", made only at Bridgwater, is compressed clay and sand from the river deposits.

On the Cornhill, where a small octagonal market cross once stood, is Pomeroy's statue of Admiral Blake. The house reputed to be his birthplace is now the town **Museum** *(daily).* It contains a fascinating collection of historical relics. It was on the Cornhill that James, Duke of Monmouth, was proclaimed king before marching out to Sedgemoor. The parish church is a fine example of the Perpendicular style.

Bath and District

Bath

Distances.—Bristol, 13; Cheddar, 24; Devizes, 19; Gloucester, 38; London, 106; Salisbury, 39; Swindon, 32; Wells, 20.
Early Closing.—Mons, Thurs or Sats.
Entertainment.—*Theatre Royal*, cinemas, music at Pump Room. Festival in May–June.
Hotels.—*Francis, Fernley, Lansdowne Grove, Royal York, Pratts, Berni Royal, Southbourne, Old Mill*, and others.
Population.—84,540.
Post Office.—New Bond Street.
Sport.—Boating, angling, bowls, tennis. Golf at Sham Castle and Lansdown. Racing at Lansdown. Swimming Baths.

The city of Bath is beautifully situated, surrounded by hills and in a loop of the river *Avon*. During the earliest days of the Roman occupation a camp was made here, and the hot springs were so appreciated that a thriving spa developed as *Aquae Sulis*. The re-discovered Roman Baths are one of the principal sights of Bath.

During the "Dark Ages" Britons and Saxons destroyed most of the Roman splendour; but the town developed an ecclesiastical importance, and King Edgar was crowned here in 973 A.D. After a further slump in importance, Bath and its Abbey Church were both rebuilt in the Norman period by John de Villula, who became the first Bishop of Bath and Wells.

Early in the 18th century, Bath developed architecturally and became a fashionable watering place. Credit for this is due to Bath's wealthy benefactor Ralph Allen; to the architects John Wood, father and son; and to Beau Nash, arbiter of fashion. Bath remained popular, though slightly less fashionable, throughout the 19th century by virtue of its charm and the alleged healing properties of its waters. It also extended its boundaries as a residential city. Fewer now come to "take the waters", but Bath continues to attract tourists and those in search of a quiet holiday.

The Abbey Church. The paved area known as *Abbey Churchyard* is approximately the site of the Roman forum, and is still a central point for visitors and residents. The Abbey Church developed from the Benedictine monastery at which Edgar was crowned in A.D. 973. The Saxon church was rebuilt in Norman times, and again when the present structure was founded in 1499 by Bishop King. There have been later restorations, notably in James I's time to repair the damage done during the suppression of the monasteries; in 1864–74 when restoration was undertaken by Sir Gilbert Scott; and more recently to repair the damage of World War II. Much of the fine glass was lost, and the former window at the east end of the north aisle has been replaced by one showing the Coronation of Edgar by Archbishop Dunstan. The building is a fine example of the Perpendicular period of English Gothic, with pinnacled tower and an imposing West Front. The latter has side turrets showing ladders on which angels are ascending and descending. This records a dream of the founder-bishop, and to indicate which are the descending angels the sculptor has depicted these head downwards.

The interior shows fine roof vaulting, especially in the transepts, but is overcrowded with monuments and memorials. In the south arcade of the choir is the beautiful *Prior Birde's Chantry*, with its fan-vaulted roof. This was begun in 1515 and is one of the Abbey's gems.

Pump Room and Roman Baths. The attractive 18th-century Pump Room is situated at the south-west corner of the Abbey Churchyard, and is a popular morning rendezvous for coffee and music. In the evenings it is used for various social functions. On the east side of the Pump Room is the Roman Promenade and various ancillary rooms—concert hall, reading rooms, and terrace restaurant. A modern staircase descends to the *Roman Baths;* these were undiscovered until 1827, and only properly explored a hundred years ago, at the time when the Abbey Church was being restored. Further archaeological discoveries have been made since.

The three hot springs of Bath are the only ones in Britain. They pour out about half-a-million gallons daily, at a temperature of 45–49°C. (114–120°F.). The three main baths are the *Great Bath* 80 feet by 40 feet, with a surrounding stone platform 14 feet wide; the *King's Bath* (59 feet by 40 feet), whose fountain is visible from the Pump Room windows; and a smaller *Circular Bath*.

A temple dedicated to Sulis-Minerva existed on the site, and the *Museum* contains many relics from this, including a beautiful bronze head of Minerva, and a sculptured Gorgon's head.

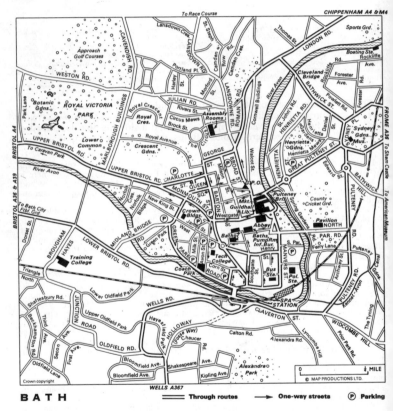

B A T H

═══ **Through routes**   ──▶ **One-way streets**   Ⓟ **Parking**

Northward from the Abbey Church runs High Street; on the right are the Guildhall, New Municipal Buildings, Public Library and Victoria Art Gallery. The 18th-century **Guildhall** has on the first floor a fine Banqueting Hall and some interesting portraits. The *Victoria Art Gallery* contains paintings, furniture, costumes and objets d'art, especially those associated with the city. From High

Street turn left into Borough Walls, which brings one to the foot of Milsom Street, a wide and fashionable thoroughfare. A short way along, on the east side, is the *Octagon,* originally a chapel but now used for concerts and exhibitions. Half-right from the top of Milsom Street, the narrow Bartlett Street ascends steeply from York Buildings to the *Assembly Rooms.* These are not the ones associated with Beau Nash, which stood in North Parade. The Assembly Rooms on the present site were opened in 1771, and after falling into decay were restored to their former glory in 1938. Four years later the rooms were completely burnt out by enemy bombing, but were eventually restored and re-opened in 1963. The rooms now house a *Museum of Costume* (from Elizabethan times to the present day). A short distance westward is the Circus, a monument to the architectural genius of John Wood the elder, as was also the once fashionable Queen Square to which it is linked by Gay Street. Still farther west is Royal Crescent, a masterpiece of John Wood junior; no. 1, Royal Crescent, restored and redecorated, is now open to the public. From the Crescent there is a fine view across the city to *Beechen Cliff.* Adjoining Royal Crescent is the *Royal Victoria Park,* which covers 50 acres and includes a Botanic Garden.

Eastward from the Abbey Church is *Orange Grove,* named in honour of the Prince of Orange, who drank the waters in 1734. Between here and the *Avon* are the delightful Parade Gardens, and across the river is the County Cricket Ground. To the north of the gardens is *Pulteney Bridge,* designed by Robert Adam, and notable for the shops on either side, after the manner of old London Bridge. Across the bridge and past Laura Place is Great Pulteney Street with its handsome terraced houses. At the end is the entrance to *Sydney Gardens,* and here stands the handsome classical building of the *Holbourne of Menstrie Museum,* housing a magnificent collection of porcelain, silver ware, paintings, etc. Running due south from the Museum, Darlington Street becomes Pulteney Road, and a turning right leads back across the *Avon* to North Parade. The original Assembly Rooms stood at the junction of North Parade and Terrace Walk (which leads back to Orange Grove). In Old Lilliput Alley—the lane leading to Abbey Green—is the original bow-windowed shop of *Sally Lunn,* whose buns have become a household word. In South Parade is the *Church of St. John the Evangelist,* with lofty spire and fine interior.

From the Pump Room, Stall Street runs south, past the colonnaded Bath Street and Lower Borough Walls, and continuing as Southgate Street to the Old Bridge. From here one can walk up the steep road called Holloway to **Beechen Cliff,** the most prominent natural feature seen from Bath, and that affording the best view of the city. A gentler, though longer ascent is by the Wells road (to the right) which re-joins Holloway at the *Bear Inn.* Half-way up Holloway is the small *Chapel of St. Mary Magdalen,* which during the Middle Ages was a private chapel of the Priors of Bath.

Beechen Cliff is a precipitous mass 400 feet high, with the city spread below. One sees the winding *Avon,* the Abbey Church, Royal Crescent, Lansdown and Solsbury Hill and many other landmarks. A plan fixed to the terrace assists identification.

BATH TO CASTLE COMBE

The route from Bath leaves the London road about one mile from the Abbey, and climbs to **Swainswick,** leaving on the right Solsbury Hill, whose summit affords a fine view. At Swainswick the church has a fine Norman doorway. The road continues north, crossing the county boundary into Gloucestershire, to the cross-roads at Cold Ashton. A diversion may be made here by continuing northward to **Dyrham Park** (N.T., *daily except Mons and Tues. Closed Dec.–Jan., fee*), a fine 17th-century mansion built by Talman with panelled rooms containing interesting furniture, tapestry and paintings.

Eastward from the Cold Ashton cross-roads is **Marshfield,** an elevated large village at the southern extremity of the Cotswolds. Four miles farther on a road to the left leads to **Castle Combe,** a small village long celebrated for its picturesque appearance. It has stone-built cottages, a fine church tower, and a 13th-century Market Cross. The adjacent wooded hill has been successively fortified by Britons, Saxons, and Normans, thus accounting for the name of the village.

BATH TO BOX, CORSHAM AND LACOCK

Box is on the London road, about six miles from Bath. Before reaching Box one sees on the left the classic frontage of *Shockerwick House,* built by the elder Wood. Box is famous for its underground quarries of Bath stone (which sheltered many museum treasures during the Second World War), and for Brunel's long railway tunnel built in 1837. In the church, which dates from the 13th century, is buried Mrs. Bowdler, who "bowdlerised" Shakespeare.

A short way to the north-west of Box is **Ditteridge** with a Norman church. Still farther north-west is *Three Shire Stone,* on the Roman Fosse Way, marking the junction of Gloucestershire, Wiltshire and Somerset. Two miles south-east of Box is the restored *Chapel Plaster,* once a wayside chapel for pilgrims from Malmesbury to Glastonbury.

About four miles beyond Box is **Corsham,** whose fine old church stands in the park surrounding **Corsham Court,** an Elizabethan mansion now open to the public. It has a notable picture gallery, and part of the house is used by the Bath Academy of Art. The Park was designed by "Capability" Brown. The main road (A4) continues to Chippenham, but by forking right at Corsham one comes to the picturesque village of **Lacock,** with a 14th-century church, and the remains of an Abbey for Augustine nuns. **Lacock Abbey** (N.T., *Apr.–Oct., daily except Mons and Tues, fee*), with 13th-century cloisters, sacristry, chapter house and nuns' parlour was adapted after the Reformation into a Tudor mansion. It was here that Fox-Talbot in 1839–41 carried out his pioneer experiments in photography.

BATH TO TROWBRIDGE AND DEVIZES

The road from Bath, leaving the London road to turn south at **Bathford,** affords some fine views. About six miles from Bathford is the picturesque town of **Bradford-on-Avon** *(Swan),* built on a steep slope and once an important centre of woollen manufacture. It has an old Bridge of nine arches, with a domed building at one end which has often served as a lock-up. The town's greatest treasure is the tiny old Saxon *Church of St. Lawrence,* built early in the 8th century. The building was later used as a charnel house, a charity school, and finally as a residence, and was only re-discovered in the last century. On the south side of the river there is a 14th-century Tithe Barn.

Three miles to the south-east is the old town of **Trowbridge,** where the making of woollen cloth is still practised, together with various other industries. This is now the administrative centre for Wiltshire, and the County Hall was built in 1937. There are some good 18th-century merchants' houses, and stenographers will be interested to learn that Isaac Pitman was born here.

Devizes *(Bear)* lies 11 miles east of Trowbridge, and was once a centre for cloth-making. The churches of St. John and of St. Mary were both founded about 1150, and both enlarged later. There is a decorative Market Cross, and some fine old houses and inns. The Castle is modern, but is on the site of its Norman predecessor. The Museum, in Long Street, is rich in archaeological exhibits. **Westbury** is about five miles south of Trowbridge. On Bratton Down, to the east of Westbury is the famous *White Horse* carved into the chalk hillside. Like the horse at Uffington, this probably dates back to the Iron Age. The Westbury horse, however, was re-carved in 1788 and is the handsomer animal.

BATH TO LONGLEAT

Freshford, six miles south of Bath, is a pretty village, and a centre for some interesting walks. Near by are the ruins of *Hinton Abbey,* founded in 1232 by Ela, Countess of Salisbury, who also founded Lacock Abbey. The Abbey has been thoroughly restored. A mile beyond the Abbey is the village of **Hinton Charterhouse,** with restored medieval church. From here the Frome road leads southward for two miles to **Norton St. Philip,** whose famous *George Inn* was originally the guest-house and grange for Hinton Abbey. On the top floor is a vast 15th-century wool store. The Church, also 15th century, has a tower of extraordinary design. About two-and-a half miles to the north-east is **Farleigh Hungerford.** On a steep hillside overlooking the village are the ruins of *Farleigh Castle (daily, fee),* attractively displayed; the Castle Chapel has been well restored, and contains fascinating relics and memorials of medieval wars. Five miles south is **Beckington,** a village mentioned in the Domesday Book. Its church has a fine tower and shows Saxon and Norman work. The former castle has been converted into a Tudor house. A few miles farther south is **Frome,** a market town long famous for woollens. In the churchyard of the parish church is the grave of Bishop Ken, and near the church a bridge spans the river *Frome.*

About four-and-a half miles south-east of Frome is **Longleat** *(daily, fee),* the seat of the Marquess of Bath. The Park has an area of 2,000 acres and was landscaped by "Capability" Brown. One of the park's entrances is in Somerset, but the mansion is in Wiltshire. Longleat House was begun in 1568 and is a magnificent example of Elizabethan architecture. The grounds include a Safari Park, restaurants, and various novel displays to attract tourists.

BATH TO SHEPTON MALLET AND STOURHEAD

Nine miles south-west of Bath, by the road (A367) that follows the line of the Roman Fosse Way, is the industrialised area of **Radstock.** This small town, together with its near neighbour **Midsomer Norton** is a centre of the Somerset coal industry. A few miles farther on, near Stratton-on-the-Fosse is **Downside Abbey,** founded in 1814 by an English Benedictine community which migrated to Douai in the 16th century and did not return until after the French Revolution. The fine Abbey Church was consecrated in 1935. There is also a monastery, and the community staffs a well known school for boys.

Shepton Mallet *(Red Lion, Shrubbery),* a picturesque small town in beautiful surroundings, has a fine old church, a famous market-cross, and a medieval "shambles". To the south is **Castle Cary,** a village with an interesting small lock-up, but only the foundations of its former castle. A short way north-east is **Bruton,** from whose pack-horse bridge may be seen the 15th-century church, and the "hospital" and school endowed by Hugh Sexey in the 17th century. South-east of Castle Cary is the small town **Wincanton** *(Dolphin, White Horse),* at the northern end of the Blackmore Vale. In the porch of the church is a medieval stone carving depicting St. Eligius, the patron saint of blacksmiths. Some eight miles north-east is **Mere,** a village with two old inns, the *Ship* and the *George.* At the latter Charles II, disguised, rested after the battle of Worcester. The church has a lofty tower and a Tudor chantry.

Near Mere is **Stourton,** a small village (N.T.) that is part of the Stourhead estate. Opposite the church stands the old Bristol High Cross, transferred here in 1763. **Stourhead House** is early 18th century, and contains paintings, sculpture and furniture of interest. The grounds are landscaped round a lake.

TOWARDS BRISTOL

From Bath there are two routes to Bristol. The *Lower Bristol Road,* south of the *Avon,* starts by the Old Bridge and passes through a populous area to **Twerton,** the starting point of a pleasant river trip to Saltford. The road continues past **Newton St. Loe,** on the summit of a hill. The church here is of great interest, with an old gargoyled tower and a 14th-century doorway. In the churchyard is an ancient cross. In Newton Park stands the fine Norman gateway, and other remains, of a castle once occupied by King John for a time as a refuge from the barons. At *Corston Manor* the poet Southey spent his earliest schooldays. **Saltford,** prettily situated in the Avon Valley, is a favourite reach for boating and fishing. Two miles farther on is **Keynsham,** a small town just outside Bristol. The Church has a handsome 17th-century tower. replacing one which collapsed and damaged the fine screen now at the end of an aisle. It was at Keynsham that the first encounter took place between Monmouth's rebel troops and the royal army.

The alternative route by the *Upper Bristol Road* passes through **Kelston,** once a manor belonging to Shaftesbury Abbey and later owned by Sir John Harington, who entertained his godmother Elizabeth I here. Kelston Church, rebuilt in 1860, contains Saxon and Norman work and an Elizabethan font. Beyond Kelston is **Bitton,** a pretty village situated by a small lake that supplies water to some paper-mills, with an interesting old church.

From the Royal Victoria Park the Weston Road follows the line of the Roman Via Julia. In **Weston** two miles to the north-west of Bath, was born in 954 Alphege, first Abbot of Bath, who was murdered by the Danes in 1012 for refusing to allow his diocese to be taxed to supply his ransom. The Church retains its old tower and contains some interesting memorials. From the farther end of Weston, the Via Julia may be followed to Prospect Stile, on Stoke Brow. From here there are extensive views in all directions, and one can survey both Bristol and Bath. A mile to the north-west is the pretty village of **North Stoke;** both village and church are on high ground and command good views.

To Lansdown and Wick

Lansdown to the north-west of Bath, is reached by Lansdown Road. A diversion to the right leads to the attractive village of **Charlcombe,** in a secluded vale; the Norman Church shows many interesting features. Continuing by the Lansdown road one sees *Beckford's Tower* 150 feet high, and situated 813 feet above sea-level. The road continues across breezy **Lansdown,** with the Racecourse on the left, to reach *Grenville's Monument,* an obelisk in memory of Sir Bevil Grenville, who was killed commanding a Royalist force at the Battle of Lansdown in 1643. On Lansdown are many ancient earthworks, the road close to the monument passing through a Roman camp.

Two miles to the north-west is **Wick,** near which are the *Rocks,* a wooded cleavage in a mass of limestone, notable for its geology, botany and scenery.

EASTWARD FROM BATH

From Sydney Gardens it is little over a mile to **Bathampton,** with old houses, attractive cottages and stone bridge. The Church has many interesting memorials including one to Admiral Phillip, first Governor of New South Wales. In the churchyard is buried the Viscount du Barre, killed in a duel on Claverton Down in 1778. If instead of taking the left fork to Bathampton one takes the right, **Claverton** is soon reached. This is one of the prettiest spots in the Avon Valley. In the churchyard is buried Ralph Allen, the creator of Bath's fame. The *Manor House,* on the hill, now contains the *American Museum (May–Oct., daily except Mons, fee),* featuring early American domestic life. A road climbing westward from the village leads through woods to Bathwick Hill on which is *Sham Castle,* an artificial castle that is only a battlemented stone wall. It was built in

1760 by Ralph Allen as a viewpoint, and to be seen from his city house. When flood-lit its appearance from Bath is striking.

The London road from Bath follows the line of the Fosse Way for two-and-a-half miles to **Batheaston,** where there is an old church, enlarged in 1884; near the south porch are the old village stocks. A short distance beyond the church is Eagle House, once the residence of John Wood, the architect who did so much for Bath. About one-and-a-half miles north of Batheaston is **St. Catherine,** a hamlet in the valley of St. Catherine's Brook. The setting is incomparable and the Church was founded about 1490 by Prior Cantlow, who is commemorated in the east window. The church contains a particularly fine Norman font. The manor house known as St. Catherine's Court was built by Prior Cantlow, but altered in Elizabethan times and after.

Little more than one mile east of Batheaston, and just off the London road is **Bathford,** on the slope of Farleigh Down. The church has Norman doorway and font, and a Jacobean oak pulpit. The road forks at the entrance to the village, that to the left rising gradually to the breezy height of King's Down, and that on the right leading to Bradford-on-Avon. About one-and-a-half miles along the latter road, a turning on the left leads to **Monkton Farleigh,** on the borders of Avon and Wiltshire. The Manor-house here stands on the site of an old Cluniac priory. A fine avenue leads to **South Wraxall,** with its fine 15th-century manor-house, and two miles to the south-east of this is yet another manor-house of the same period at **Great Chalfield** (N.T., *Apr.–Oct., Weds, fee*), a notable example of medieval domestic architecture. The manorial buildings are surrounded by a moat. In the small church are 15th-century wall paintings.

SOUTH OF BATH

About one mile south-east of Bath is *Prior Park,* the mansion built by the elder Wood in 1742 for Ralph Allen, mayor of Bath. Many famous people visited Allen here, among them Alexander Pope. The mansion has a Corinthian portico of six columns, and is now used as a Catholic boarding school. In the grounds are lakes and a Palladian-style bridge. To the west of Prior Park is *Combe Down,* honeycombed with caverns from which freestone has been excavated. **Widcombe,** between Combe Down and Bath, has an old church, built about 1500 to replace an earlier structure; in the porch are some interesting Roman fragments. The fine Widcombe Manor, by the church, has associations with Fielding, W. S. Landor, and more recently H. A. Vachell. To the south-east of Combe Down is *Monkton Combe,* and still farther south-east is the beautifully situated village of **Limpley Stoke,** which gives its name to the picturesque Limpley Stoke Valley extending some three miles northward along the course of the *Avon.* **Englishcombe** is an attractive village lying to the south-west of Bath, and was once a residence of Saxon Kings. Later the manor belonged to Thomas de Gournay, who was executed for his part in the murder of Edward II. His castle was levelled and only traces of it remain. Today Englishcombe is a centre for the cultivation of flowers and vegetables. The church retains some Norman features, and south of the church is a monastic Tithe Barn. In a field to the west one can see traces of the *Wansdyke,* an extensive prehistoric defence dyke; other traces south of Bath can be located with the aid of an Ordnance map.

A little farther out from Bath are Combe Hay and Wellow. **Combe Hay** was once a manor of Bishop Odo, half-brother to the Conqueror. The modern church retains its 15th-century tower. About one-and-a-half miles from Combe Hay is **Wellow.** The church here is of great interest; it was rebuilt in 1372, and faithfully restored during the last century. The Lady Chapel contains the tomb of Sir Walter Hungerford.

West Country

BRIDGWATER TO LYNTON AND LYNMOUTH

Westward from Bridgwater the road winds its way towards the Quantock Hills to pass through Cannington to **Nether Stowey.** Once of some importance as a wool market, it began to decay in the 19th century, although the dignity of its fine St. Mary's Street with handsome inns either side and pillared Georgian houses, preserved its air of importance. Near the centre is the quaint old lock-up, and up Lime Street, the house now National Trust property, which was Coleridge's home from 1797–1800—the "Coleridge" room at the cottage is open daily. The fine church is of pink stone with tower and turret.

From Nether Stowey, a road leads north to **Stogursey** from which there is a beautiful, 18-mile route over to Minehead, with views of sea, hills and unspoilt villages. The Saxo-Norman church is a priory church of cathedral-like proportions with a sloping floor and includes the 11th-century church with its 12th-century Norman enlargement.

The Quantock Hills. This "island" of ancient rock rises from the flat Somerset plain and extends almost from Watchet to Taunton. It is a region full of historic associations, interesting earthworks, with peaceful little villages and ancient churches, and grand old manor-houses. The wild red deer abound in the leafy combes, and the Quantock Staghounds hunt here, a favourite meeting-place being **Triscombe Stone,** above the village of Crowcombe set at the Western foot of the Quantocks.

Holford village and church lie in a delightful combe. At Alfoxton House, Wordsworth and his sister lived for a time. Two miles farther on is the hamlet of **Kilve** with a church and the nearby ruins of Kilve Chantry, founded in 1329. **East Quantoxhead** village lies some distance to the right near the sea. The fine Elizabethan manor-house called *Court House* has been owned for nearly 800 years, by the Luttrell family. At **St. Audries Bay** is a popular holiday camp. **Williton** is a long straggling agricultural village with a population of about 2,000. Many of its cottages are thatched and white-washed.

Watchet is a busy little seaport town with a harbour and paper mills. The shingle beach has sandy stretches and rock pools. Bathing, boating, fishing and sports facilities are available. The 15th-century church has some excellent brasses, a Jacobean pulpit and canopy.

Cleeve Abbey, south of the main road at Washford was founded in 1198. The present 13th-century convent buildings are remarkably complete. There is a fine medieval hall.

Carhampton is the home of West Somerset Foxhounds. It has an ancient history and was the site of a Danish victory in the year 833. The church, restored in 1850, possesses a magnificent printed 15th-century screen.

From Carhampton, a lane turns off on the right to **Withycombe,** a picturesque little village situated under the extreme end of the hill running out of Dunster

Park, which is known as *Withycombe Beacon*. Withycombe Church is a small building, with a rood screen and a low tower.

Blue Anchor is a small hamlet on the edge of the sea. Of interest are the alabaster rocks and the fossils found along the beach. Good bathing and excellent facilities for camping are available.

Dunster *(Luttrell Arms, Foresters' Arms)* is a beautiful unspoiled village. Its broad main street, 17th-century yarn market, ancient inn and warm pink stone church are overlooked by the well-preserved castle.

The **Castle** *(Tues, Weds, Thurs in summer, and see notices)*, for centuries the home of the Luttrell family, contains a wealth of beautiful and interesting exhibits. There are fine oak-panelled halls with magnificent ceilings, attractive and interesting portraits and a unique leather gallery. The elegant furniture includes suites made by Chippendale and Hepplewhite, with their original needlework covers in excellent condition.

Minehead

Early Closing.—Wednesday.
Entertainment.—Cinema, dancing, Gaiety Theatre (concert party), fetes, gymkhanas.
Hotels.—*Beach, Wellington, Minehead Bay, Bacton-leigh,* and many others.

Population.—7,500.
Post Office.—The Parks.
Sports.—Bathing (sand), boating, bowls, tennis, golf.

Minehead is a pleasant West Country resort on the Somerset coast, 60 miles from Bristol and 169 from London. The delightful situation, the natural beauty of its surrounding, and its mild climate have brought it much to the front of late years as a health and holiday resort. The **Esplanade** commands a wide sweep of bay, with good sands, affording safe bathing. The town stretches back towards the hills, the prominent feature of these high grounds being **North Hill,** which overlooks the quaint little harbour some hundreds of feet below.

Alcombe, once a part of Dunster parish, is now a township with hotels and guest houses, and numerous shops and churches. One or two old cottages with thatched gable ends still exist, bearing dates of 1665 to 1745. Alcombe is said to take its name from *Auld Combe,* the beautiful combe which may be reached by way of Church Street and Manor Road. The parish church dates from 1902.

Dunkery Beacon. A good road runs to within three-quarters of a mile of the summit of Dunkery Beacon, 1,707 feet, the highest point of Exmoor. The summit is crowned by a cairn and the remains of the hearths in which beacons were piled. From the summit the view is magnificent. A pleasant return can be made by Cloutsham, Stoke Pero with its quaint little church and the beautiful Horner Valley. Horner Hamlet still has an old mill and just before West Luccombe and the main road (bus) is an old packhorse bridge.

To Bossington, Allerford and Selworthy. These lie off the Lynmouth road but can be reached by strong walkers via North Hill, Selworthy Beacon and Bury Castle. **Bossington** is a beautiful hamlet with old-world cottages and enormous walnut trees. On the coast at Hurtstone Point is the Gull Hole, a large natural arch. Between Bossington and Allerford, standing in a farmyard, is the pretty little chapel of **Lynch.** **Allerford** is very picturesque with quaint cottages, remains of a manor house and a much-photographed pack-horse bridge. **Selworthy Green** has been called an artists' paradise. It is an enchanting scene of peace, beauty and harmony. Seven old cottages with thatched roofs, latticed windows, gabled porches and all bright with luxuriant foliage and flowers are grouped round a green, shaded by magnificent walnut trees. At one side a stream lilts and meanders and all around are sheltering woods. The church is a handsome Perpendicular structure with a square battlemented tower.

The route from Minehead to Lynton is one of the most striking in Britain. As far as Porlock the way is through the pretty Selworthy Valley. There is a steep one-way road down to the little village of Porlock.

Porlock *(Castle, Ship, Lorna Doone).* The name signifies a land-locked port, but port it is no longer, as the receding sea has left in front of the village more than a mile of flat country. In the well-known *Ship Inn* is a chimney-corner sacred to the memory of Southey. A footpath, Sparkhayes Lane, leads off from the village to the sea. **Porlock Bay** has a graceful sweep, nearly five miles across; Hurtstone, or Bossington Point, forming its eastern horn, and Gore Point the western horn. **Porlock Church,** dedicated to St. Dubricius, a Welsh saint, is said to have been built on the site of a Saxon church in the early 13th century. It was altered and enlarged in the 15th century and restored in 1890.

Culbone. West of Porlock Weir is **Ashley Combe,** formerly a summer seat of the Countess of Lovelace. Its first mistress was Byron's daughter, Ada, who married the Earl of Lovelace. Through the woods is **Culbone Church,** the smallest complete parish church in England, measuring only 35 feet long by 12 feet 4 inches wide. It contains a 14th-century carved oak chancel screen and a Norman font.

Exmoor was one of the five ancient and royal forests of Britain and remained under the Crown until after the execution of Charles I. It is a vast expanse of wild moorland, combe, and heather-clad waste. But the sweep of the hills, the play of light and shadow over the ground, the glorious purple when the heather is in bloom contrasting with the deep green of the combes, combine to invest Exmoor with majestic dignity and beauty. It measures 35 miles from east to west and 20 miles from north to south, and the moor proper is mostly in Somerset. Dunkery Beacon has been presented to the nation, and many thousands of acres are leased in perpetuity by the National Trust. Over this expanse the red deer roam wild as they did when Saxon monarchs hunted them from their palace at Porlock. The Exmoor pony also has the liberty of the moors, and thousands of sheep browse on the sedgy grass.

All over Exmoor vestiges of a prehistoric age are to be found in the shape of great tumuli, barrows, earthworks, and monuments; a stone circle is to be seen on Withypool Common, and the remains of another on Porlock Common at the top of Porlock Hill. In the Devonshire part of Exmoor, there are the remains of stone rows, triangles, parallelograms, etc. Two Romano-British inscribed stones have been found on Exmoor. The best known, which is protected by a stone structure built round it, stands on Winsford Hill. Its rude inscription has been deciphered to read "CARATACI NEPUS", and is supposed to commemorate some Exmoor chieftain, perhaps, who was a kinsman of Caratacus.

Simonsbath stands at an important junction of roads in the centre of Exmoor. The village is seated in a deep wooded ravine. The fishing in the *Barle* is good *(tickets from Exmoor Forest Hotel).*

South Molton *(Goose & Gander, George),* 10 miles south of Simonsbath on the A361 Barnstaple road, is an ancient market town with three churches.

Exford is four-and-a-half miles east of Simonsbath, and is a great stag-hunting centre. The kennels and stables of the Devon and Somerset hounds are in the village. It is noted, too, for its annual Horse Show, generally held on the second Wednesday in August.

Withypool, two miles south of Exford, is a favourite angling place, some excellent fishing being held by the *Royal Oak* where day tickets are sometimes available.

Winsford, four miles from Withypool is a picturesque village, with a rambling inn and village green; and overlooked by the fine tower of the Parish Church. There are seven bridges, one of which is a pack-horse bridge scheduled as an ancient monument.

Dulverton *(Caernarvon Arms, Lamb, Lion, Tarr Steps)* is a quiet little country town. Its situation on the borders of Exmoor, with the proximity of two packs of staghounds, has made the town one of the most important centres for the red deer hunts. There is excellent fishing in the numerous streams (the fishing rights are owned by the *Lamb Hotel*). Rough and cover shooting will be arranged by the proprietor of the *Lion Hotel.*

A favourite walk or drive from Dulverton is to **Tarr Steps** (10 miles). Tarr Steps consist of 20 loose piles or piers of large blocks of stone, apparently taken from the river bed, and raised 2 or 3 feet above water level over the *Barle,* with large flat slabs laid across as a footway.

Lynton and Lynmouth

Early Closing.—Thursday.

Fishing.—Good sea and river fishing. The *East Lyn* is good for trout and for salmon from June onwards.

Hotels.—*Royal Castle, Valley of Rocks, Seaweed,* *Crown, Hoe, Chough's Nest, Tors, Bath, Rising Sun.*

Post Office.—Lee Road, Lynton. Lynmouth Street, Lynmouth.

Lynton and Lynmouth owe their charm partly to their picturesque site and natural beauty of surroundings and partly to the almost dramatic contrast between modern Lynton above, and ancient Lynmouth tucked away at the water's edge. **Lynton** crowns a steep and lofty hill, overlooking Lynmouth with its picturesque harbour at the mouth of the *East* and *West Lyn* rivers. The two villages are united by a cliff railway and steep roads.

Lynton Parish Church (St. Mary's). Scarcely anything remains of the original structure except part of the tower; this is mainly 13th century. The reredos is of carved Caen stone, and the Norman font has also been replaced by one of Caen stone. The registers date from 1569. In a glass case is the Bishops' Bible issued by Anglican bishops in the 16th century. The tower contains a beautiful peal of six bells, two of which are medieval. In the south porch are the old Village Stocks, in a fair state of preservation.

The Town Hall in Lee Road houses the local authority offices, a branch library, and an assembly hall where films, dancing and shows are presented. Behind rises **Hollerday Hill** with open heath country, springy turf and foxgloves and penny-wort on the banks. From the top glorious views embrace the coastline and much of Exmoor.

Lynmouth has a small tidal harbour, sheltered on the west by a stone Jetty on which is the modern replica of the Rhenish tower, originally built a hundred years ago. It was destroyed in the disastrous flood of 1952 but has been rebuilt. The iron cradle at the top contains a powerful electric lamp showing a white light visible for 10 miles.

Westward from the tower the Esplanade runs along the foot of the cliff, with a public *Car Park* at the western end, and the *Old Bathing Pool* which refills at each high tide. The lovely glen down which the rivers rattle is steeply banked by wooded hillsides. Among the trees are charmingly situated houses and hotels. The narrow strip of level ground between the foot of the cliff and the river is filled with hotels, garages, restaurants and shops. The tide-fed *New Bathing Pool* stands on the Eastern Beach facing the Manor Grounds. The Manor House now serves as a Holiday Fellowship centre during the summer months. **Mars Hill** is the most picturesque of the steep little streets of Lynmouth, a glorious medley of colour-washed cottages, fuchsias and roses.

Three bridges cross the stream; the most important being just above the point where the *West Lyn* comes in: this is the bridge by which all road traffic crosses; it is one of the busiest corners in Lynmouth.

The ravine down which the *West Lyn* roars in a succession of falls before joining its sister river and the open sea is known as **Glen Lyn.** It is extremely beautiful and may be visited on payment of a small charge.

To Summerhouse Hill (850 feet). This rises between the *East* and *West Lyn* rivers. It is approached by the zigzag paths from Lynbridge or from the East Lyn Valley. From the latter the path starts opposite Lynmouth Church and winds up the hill through lovely **Glen Lyn Wood.** Half-way up, the woods cease, and the path is broad and safe to the topmost crag, from which is obtained an uninterrupted view of sea, mountain, valley, wood and moorland.

To the Valley of Rocks. By the North Walk, a mile-long terrace cut in the face of the cliff. The **Castle Rock** with its rough stone stairway is nearly 800 feet high and the seaward views are magnificent. The **Devil's Cheesewring** is another fantastic pile of rocks seen almost opposite. Duty Point is a lofty conical height.

To Watersmeet. The wooded gorge of the *East Lyn,* lying between the Tors Hill and Summerhouse Hill, can be entered in two ways but the most popular route for walkers is to cross the bridge from Lynmouth's main street turning right up Tors Road on the north side of the river. Take the riverside path and at the fork keep right to cross the bridge at Black Pool. For motorists, the Watersmeet road (A39) follows the south bank of the *East Lyn* from the bottom of Lynmouth Hill.

Watersmeet is a miracle of varied beauty where the *Combe Park* (or *Hoaroak*) *Water* plunges down a succession of falls, between two high woods, to meet the *East Lyn,* flowing in more peacefully.

To Countisbury Foreland. The distance from Lynmouth is two-and-a-half miles— a magnificent walk, though as the road rises over 800 feet in little more than a mile, many visitors prefer to drive up and reserve their energies for an exploration of the Foreland. Those who walk should either take the main road or follow for the greater part of the way the old **Pack-horse Path.** Take the wide grassy path on the right up the slope, starting from the entrance to Beacon Guest House. Following this the earthwork, an ancient camp 900 feet above sea-level, which crowns Countisbury Hill, is passed. North, south and west the ground slopes precipitously to sea and river, while the east, where the approach is level, is defended by an enormous earthen rampart 40 feet in height. Soon afterwards the main road is reached. *The cliff path above Sillery Sands is unsafe.*

To Oare and the Doone Valley. There is no road up the Doone Valley, but cars can be left at Malmsmead. The lane down to Oare leaves the main Lynmouth–Porlock road quarter-mile east of County Gate and a narrow but charming road follows the East Lyn valley from Oare to Brendon and Hillsford Bridge, whence the way back to Lynmouth is by Watersmeet or up to the left and over Lyn Down.

The road from County Gate runs southward down the long slope to the valley of the *East Lyn,* now become the *Oare Water.* With glimpses of the beautiful gorge winding away to Watersmeet on the right, of the long break in the moors which marks the channel of the *Badgworthy Water* southward, and of other combes at right angles to this, **Oare** parish is entered. Oare Church is a small plain stone building with a low square tower. Near the church is Oare Manor, long the residence of the late Nicholas Snow, whose family held property in the parish for 1,000 years.

At **Malmsmead,** a mile west of Oare, the *Lyn* is joined by the *Badgworthy Water.* The route lies through Badgworthy Wood to Lankcombe near the famous Waterslide. Continuing up the valley for another 50 yards, the remains of a hunting gate is reached, referred to as "The Doone Gate". The generally accepted **"Doone Valley"** lies about 500 yards beyond this and can be recognized by the few traces of ruins.

To Woody Bay, Martinhoe and Heddon's Mouth. The coast road leaves Lynton by Lee Road; the Ilfracombe road, which runs parallel to the coast and about a mile inland, leaves by way of Lynbridge. *All the roads on the Woody Bay estate are private property over which the public have footpath rights only.* It may be added that many others in this direction are steep and narrow. There is a toll charge on the Lee Abbey road.

Woody Bay is a charming glen with a rushing torrent. The cliff drive round to Combe Martin is one of the finest in Britain. At **Martinhoe** the church tower and part of the nave and chancel are over 700 years old, and there is a richly carved font. **Heddon's Mouth** is reached via *Hunter's Inn,* a picturesque building beloved by artists and anglers.

LYNMOUTH TO ILFRACOMBE

From Lynmouth the road climbs beside the river, swings to the right and continues to climb. A mile beyond the Woody Bay crossroad, the main road on the left avoids the steep and awkward descent and ascent through the village of **Parracombe,** but passes close to the ancient Church of St. Petrock, dating from the 10th century. A little over a mile farther on the important crossroads at **Blackmoor Gate** is reached and at which the righthand turn is taken for Combe Martin and Ilfracombe.

Combe Martin *(Delve's, London Inn, Pack of Cards)* nestles in a fertile valley amid delightful scenery. The village consists principally of a single long, straggling street, with some good shops. Strawberry-growing is largely practised, and many tons of fruit are dispatched to large centres every summer. The Church, the chancel of which is vaguely dated at about the 12th century, has a fine tower, 99 feet high.

Close at hand are two hills, **Great Hangman** (1,044 feet) and **Little Hangman** (716 feet).

To **Kentisbury** Church, three miles south-eastward from Combe Martin, is a delightful walk of woodland and rural scenery. Another mile or so leads to Blackmoor Gate.

A mile west of Combe Martin and south of the Ilfracombe road is **Berrynarbor.** The church is of Norman origin and has a fine tower and an interesting interior.

Three miles from Combe Martin is the pretty castellated **Watermouth Castle,** part of which is now a holiday bungalow centre. On the opposite side of the road a gate leads to the *Watermouth Caves.*

Ilfracombe

Early Closing.—Thursday.

Fishing.—Sea fishing for bass, pollack, rock whiting, grey mullet.

Hotels.—*Mount, Imperial, Dilkhusa Grand, Cliffe Hydro, Grosvenor,* and many others.

Population.—8,900.

Post Office.—High Street.

Sports.—Bowls, boating, tennis. Golf at Hele Bay.

Ilfracombe lies deep in the shelter of surrounding hills facing the Bristol Channel. At its seaward end is the Arcade and then Fore Street descends steeply down to the harbour, where is the main car park of the town. The inner harbour, often crammed with small craft, is lined on three sides with picturesque terraces of shops, cafés and the houses of boatmen. On the seaward side, is the old pier, protecting the inner harbour. To the west of the pier is the conical *Lantern Hill* which owes its name to the use made of the small building which crowns it. The structure dates back about 700 years. Opposite the pier is *Larkstone Beach* and a little farther east, the romantically named *Rapparee Cove* with popular bathing beach of rock-free sand. Towering above Rapparee Cove is **Hillsborough Hill.** A much-frequented pleasure ground of the town, it is one of the few spots in England from which the sun can be seen to rise out of and set behind a sea horizon. As the hill is 447 feet high, its summit commands a magnificent view. North-westward of the harbour is the *Capstone,* a huge rock 156 feet high. Almost precipitous on the seaward side, and dizzily sheer on the west, it has a steep grassy slope on the town side.

Around the seaward side of the hill is the Capstone Parade, from which steep steps lead on to the rocks below. Wilder Road, with Market Street and the Market on the left, runs from the Parade parallel to and between the front and High Street. On the seaward side are the attractive Runnymede Gardens and near by by *Holiday Inn* with licensed bars and cafes and the Municipal Offices. Near by in Southern Slope Gardens is the Museum with collections illustrating the geology, flora and fauna of Devon. Beyond on the Promenade are the Municipal Baths. In Wilder Road, where several roads converge, can be seen the entrance to the Tunnels, passages which pierce the cliff and provide easy access to a very popular bathing beach.

Torrs Park Road and Granville Road lead to the entrance to the *Torrs Walks,* a famous beauty spot at the western end of the town. The hills rise to 500 feet above the sea. Upon them is a succession of zigzag paths.

South of the town is **Cairn Top,** a 511-feet high hill, which is a favourite spot for a picnic. Bicclescombe Park, a fine ornamental park, has sports facilities and a children's boating lake.

To the Chambercombe Valley. The historic old manor house *(teas)*, was formerly the manor house of Ilfracombe. The date of the earliest record of it was 1162. Lady Jane Grey is said to have slept in the room above the hall. At *Comyn Farm*, nearby, is the entrance to the Valley and Woods, which are private property but open to visitors.

To West Down. Out via Mullacott Cross and back via Two Pots, a round of 10 miles (bus service). Follow St. Brannock's Road to beyond the Bicclescombe Park and turn on the left. West Down is a typical Devon village with a church dating from the 14th century and a late 16th-century manor house. The return can be made via Hore Downs, Warmscombe Woods, Trayne Farm and Chambercombe Woods.

To Lee and Bull Point. By bus and boat. The road route is via Slade and Lincombe. Walkers can take the coast road across the Downs, or by the Torrs Park Road to Lee Downs and Lee village. Of interest is a small church, the thatched cottage of the Old Maids of Lee (1653) and Chapel Cottage on the site of a Norman chapel (1100). Refreshments available at the Old Mill which dates from 1560 and at tea gardens. **Bull Point Lighthouse** *(weekday afternoons)*, is about two miles west of Lee. From the lighthouse there is a gated road, with right of way for walkers only to Mortehoe, one-and-a-half miles. About half-mile to the west of this road is **Morte Point**, National Trust ground with extensive walks.

To Mortehoe and Woolacombe. By coast five miles via Lee. By road (6 miles). **Mortehoe** church dates from the 13th century. From it there is a steep descent to the coast where is a pleasant sandy beach. **Woolacombe** *(Woolacombe Bay, Watersmeet, Beach, Sands* and others) has a two-mile golden stretch of sand occupying most of Morte Bay between Baggy Point and Morte Point. The sands make a magnificent playground with bathing and surfing. At the northern end is **Barricane Beach** a narrow little rocky cove noted for its shells. The road climbing the hill from the Marine Drive leads over Pickwell Down to the village of **Georgeham**.

ILFRACOMBE TO BARNSTAPLE AND BIDEFORD

The leisurely coast route is by Lee, Mortehoe and Woolacombe. There are three direct routes inland. The first, the New Barnstaple Road, begins with a very stiff hill (Two Pots), rising to a height of over 800 feet, followed by a gentle decline for nearly all the way. The scenery is beautiful. The road continues slightly downhill, with lovely wooded hills on each side. From **Muddiford** (8 miles, *New Inn*), prettily situated amid woods and hills, a stream noted for salmon and trout runs beside the road. The road goes sharply downhill into **Pilton,** and thence over Pilton Bridge into Barnstaple.

The second inland route, known as the Old Barnstaple Road, goes by way of Chambercombe, Marwood and Pilton.

The third but longest route is via Mullacott Cross, Knowle and Braunton.

Barnstaple (Pop. 16,000. Hotels: *Royal and Fortescue, Imperial, North Devon Motel, Barnstaple Motel, Wray Arms,* etc.), is a thriving market town and excellent touring centre for North Devon. Social activities and facilities for sport are excellent. The town stands on the *Taw* with the fine old Long Bridge built about 1350 but since many times repaired and widened. Facing the Square with its clock-tower and a busy junction of ways is the **North Devon Athenaeum** with a good collection of local records, a museum and a branch of the county library. Taw Vale Parade runs by the river to **Rock Park** pleasant with greenery, lawns and a sports centre and swimming pool. By the pool is the *Millenary Stone* - 930–1930, beneath which are buried contemporary coins and town records. Barnstaple is famous for its "Barum Ware" examples of which may be seen in the potteries in Litchdon Street. Back beyond the Square is **Queen Anne's Walk** a colonnade surmounted by a statue of the queen. Near at hand is the busy cattle market and a little farther the modern civic centre. Off the narrow High Street is **St. Peter's Church** (1318) with its twisted steeple. **St. Ann's Chapel** in the churchyard, and part believed to date from 1456, served as a grammar school for 300 years, Bishop

Jewell and John Gay, the poet, having been pupils. The old Guildhall is in High Street with an entrance to the Pannier Market. Alongside is the quaint Butchers' Row. **Pilton** lies north of the little river *Yeo*. The church here once formed part of a priory traditionally said to have been founded by King Athelstan.

To Tawstock. The village three miles south is approached by Seven Brethren Bank on the west side of the river. There is also a pleasant walk through Lake from the bottom of Sticklepath Hill. The little church is famous for the costly 16th- and 17th-century altar tombs of the Bouchiers, Earls of Bath, of whom Tawstock Park was the seat from 1136 to 1654. On the opposite side of the river is Bishops Tawton. To the right of it rises Coddon Hill, with its plainly defined footpath.

To Bishops Tawton and Coddon Hill. Bishops Tawton is on the Exeter road, about two-and-a-half miles from Barnstaple (bus service). The church, St. John the Baptist, in the centre of the village is of interest. Immediately to the south is a farmhouse with two small towers, remnant of one of the palaces of the Bishop of Exeter. Coddon Hill (630 feet), the highest point in the district, is southward of the village. The view from the top repays the climb.

To Umberleigh and Chittlehampton. Umberleigh lies on the main Exeter road eight miles south of Barnstaple. Chittlehampton is situated two-and-a-half miles to the east but can also be reached from Barnstaple via Bishops Tawton, a good road. Umberleigh is a pretty village on the *Taw*. There is good fishing for salmon and trout. Chittlehampton has a spacious village square fronting the church whose tower is unsurpassed in grace and strength, and remarkable for the number of pinnacles. At the eastern end of the village is the old St. Teara's Well.

To Swimbridge. Swimbridge is on the South Molton road five miles south-east of Barnstaple (bus service). About two miles from Barnstaple the road makes a detour to the left at Landkey. Motorists should keep to the main road on the left above the village, but walkers may well use the right-hand one passing Landkey Church. Swimbridge is an attractive village with a church of extreme beauty and interest. Its peculiar name is said to be a corruption of Sawin of Birige, the name of a priest who founded a chapel here in the time of Edward the Confessor. The tower of the church was probably erected about 1310. Three miles beyond Swimbridge towards South Molton is the village of **Filleigh** noted for the fine Castle Hill, a Fortescue residence.

To Braunton, a small town six miles north-west on the Ilfracombe road. The upper part, set back on hilly slopes, is a quaint little place with narrow streets and old inns and cottages. Two miles west are **Braunton Burrows,** a large sandy tract, now a Nature Reserve, abounding in wild flowers and a wealth of sea and marsh birds.

To Saunton and Croyde. Saunton Sands *(hotel)* is a popular resort on the coast three miles west of Braunton. A magnificent stretch of firm sand is backed by sand-hills. Excellent bathing and surfing is available, and golf (18 holes) nearby. Croyde is round the curve of Saunton Down. The village has a stream running down the main street. Croyde Bay is ideal for surfing.

To Arlington Court (N.T., *Apr.–Oct., daily, fee*), a Regency house built in 1821, seven miles north-east of Barnstaple on the Lynton road. It contains relics of Miss Rosalie Chichester.

From Barnstaple bridge the road climbs south-west via **Bickington** and **Fremington** and then down to **Instow** which has a splendid stretch of sands with good bathing, bass fishing and yachting (club). From the quay a ferry crosses to Appledore. In three miles the fine old Bideford bridge crosses the *Torridge* for Bideford.

Bideford (Pop.: 11,760. Hotels: *Royal, Tanton's, New Inn, Ring o' Bells, Duart,* etc.), is a market town and port on the river *Torridge* with trout and salmon fishing. The picturesque stone bridge of 24 irregular arches superseded a 16th-century one of wood. Facing the bridge are the Bridge Hall and the Municipal Buildings, the latter including the library and museum. The rebuilt parish church retains parts of an earlier Norman building. These include the tower, the font and the tomb of Sir Thomas Grenville (*d.* 1513). The tree-lined Quay is a fine promenade with a car park and a starting point for buses and coaches. At the north end is a statue of Charles Kingsley the famous author who lived at Bideford. Backing on to Victoria Park is the Burton Art Gallery. High Street is a busy shopping centre while at the end of Bridge Street is the Market House which has a pannier market and butchers' shops alongside it on each side of a covered way.

On the other side of the river is **East-the-Water**. On the hill is Chudleigh Fort now a war memorial.

To Northam and Appledore. Northam is reached by the Kingsley Road from the north end of the Quay. The little town has a few quaint old houses and a fine church restored in 1865. The river bank is followed for two miles to Appledore a delightful unspoiled place facing the combined estuaries of the *Taw* and *Torridge*. It has narrow streets with many picturesque old houses and cottages, some dating from Elizabethan times and some retaining their old sail lofts. Salmon fishing has been carried on in the estuary since Saxon days and provides continuing interest. Bass fishing is also good. Appledore Regatta takes place in early August.

To Westward Ho! Westward Ho! *(Atlanta, Belle Vue,* etc.), was named after Charles Kingsley's famous novel in 1863! It is a popular bathing resort with magnificent sands, golf links and camping facilities and a large holiday centre with ample space for tennis, putting and children's playgrounds, dance hall and indoor amusements. A great pebble ridge two miles long runs between the sands and the low lying ground behind.

To Abbotsham. One-and-a-half miles south-west from Westward Ho! The village was the ham or homestead of the Abbot of Tavistock in 1086. The fine cliffs present good sea views.

To Littleham and Buckland Brewer. Three miles from Bideford amid fine scenery. Littleham church has an embattled tower and old carved bench-ends. Buckland Brewer is two miles south. The church has a fine Norman doorway. Two miles south again is *Hembury Camp*, one of the first Saxon settlements in the district.

To Great Torrington *(Globe, Newmarket, Black Horse)*, an old market town of great antiquity set on a high hill slope.

BIDEFORD TO BUDE

A good road giving extensive views runs south-westward from Bideford via Ford and Clovelly Cross then turning southward for Kilkhampton, Stratton and Bude. In seven miles is reached Bucks Cross where a right turn leads to **Bucks Mills**, a collection of white houses seemingly perched precariously on the cliffs. In a farther two-and-a-half miles is Clovelly Cross and the turn for Clovelly. Mid-way on the right, is the entrance to the famous *Hobby Drive,* forming an alternative approach.

Clovelly *(New Inn, Red Lion)*, is a quaint cliff-edge village of one steep-stepped and cobbled street descending to a stone quay and pebble beach. Flowers bloom everywhere, covering the fronts of the tiny white-washed cottages, no two of which are on the same level. At the cliff top is the church, with a picturesque lych gate, a rebuilt Norman porch and low embattled west tower. The ancient Saxon font and several brasses are of interest.

Hartland is three-and-a-half miles from Clovelly. At **Hartland Town** the town clock is one of the earliest pendulum clocks in the country. **Hartland Abbey** *(see notices),* incorporates the cloisters of an abbey founded in the reign of Henry II. A mile west is **Hartland Quay** where road and path descend steeply to rocks and a small beach. At **Stoke**, St. Nectan's Church has a striking 15th-century rood screen, font and roof. **Hartland Point** is a fine bold headland, 325 feet high, forming the north-western extremity of the county and the finest coast view—both ways—in North Devon. On the headland are a coastguard station and a lighthouse, both of which may be visited.

From the Hartland road at Clovelly Cross, or farther on at Baxworthy corner, the A39 road heads southward and two miles after crossing the Devon–Cornwall county boundary reaches **Kilkhampton** an attractive village nearly 600 feet above sea level. The church has a conspicuous tall tower and every bench-end is carved in oak black with age. About four miles farther south, a right branch is taken at Stratton and in a further two miles, Bude is reached.

Bude

Distances.—Boscastle, 16; Hartland, 17; Holsworthy, 10; Camelford, 19; Poughill, 2; Widemouth Sands, 2; Combe Valley, 5; Tintagel, 20; Clovelly, 16½; Stratton, 2.

Early Closing.—Thursday.

Hotels.—*Grenville, Falcon, Florida, Maer Lodge, St. Margaret's, Penarvor, Penwethers House, Hawarden, Burn Court, Bay View, Hartland, Ceres, Maer Lake, Westcliff, Grosvenor, Choughs, The Tree Inn.*

Population.—5,200.

Post Office.—Belle Vue.

Sports.—Bathing, surfing, bowls, tennis, golf, riding.

Bude is a popular Atlantic coast resort with fine sands and magnificent coast scenery. Bathing and surfing, tennis, golf, bowls, cricket, rowing, riding, hunting—practically every sport is followed with zest, and the wide grass-covered expanse, known as Summerleaze Downs, with the glorious sands, form an ideal playground for children. With a strong wind the sea at spring flood is a marvellous sight, and the pounding of the waves can be heard many miles inland. Overlooking the Breakwater is Compass Point, a fine viewpoint. Southward to Widemouth extend the delightful **Efford Downs** with Efford Beacon the highest point. The broad Strand runs beside the river towards the business part of the town, continued by Belle Vue, near the top of which is the Post Office. Across the river is Shalder Hill with the War Memorial and beyond, the Recreation Ground.

The Bude and Holsworthy Canal built in 1826 and now only navigable for little more than a mile connects with the sea by means of a lock, the gates of which serve as a footbridge leading to Compass Hill and the Downs. Bude Haven is a small bay protected by a breakwater terminating in the Chapel Rock.

To Stratton and Launcells. Stratton is a quiet little town, two miles by road from Bude, set in a hollow among hills. Apart from many lovely old houses a feature is the finely placed church containing some good examples of Norman work, fine carvings and a timber roof. The interior has good brasses, old stocks, and effigies. The *Tree Inn* was formerly the manor house of the Grenvilles. On a wall is a tablet recalling the Battle of Stamford which took place in 1643 a mile north-west of Stratton. Launcells church a mile or so farther east has notable 15th-century tiles and woodwork.

To Morwenstow. A secluded village in which the poet the Rev. Stephen Hawker lived for 40 years. The Church has rich Norman work, carved bench ends and a font nearly 1,000 years old.

To Marhamchurch. Reached by road or by the canal path to Hele Bridge, then straight up hill. It is a fascinating village, the church standing beyond a wide square flanked by thatched cottages.

To Widemouth and Millook. A good motor road leaves Bude beside the *Falcon Hotel,* passes through Widemouth and continues to Wanson Mouth and Millook. Widemouth sands are enclosed by fine cliffs (good bathing). Millook is at the opening of the Trebarfoote Combe, a beautifully-wooded glen and a favourite spot for picnics.

To Poundstock and Penfound Manor. Reached by the A39 main road to Bangor's Cross where turn right. Poundstock is a scattered village, its church has a notable Norman holy-water stoup and a square Transition–Norman font. The Guildhouse just below the church is a beautiful 14th-century building. On the opposite, east, side of the A39 is **Penfound Manor** an Elizabethan house with older parts and interesting furniture *(weekdays, Easter to Sept., fee).*

To Holsworthy. A pleasant old market town, in Devon, 10 miles east of Bude. The church with tall pinnacled towers has traces of Saxon and Norman work.

BUDE TO WADEBRIDGE

The direct route is by the main A39 road but a more interesting route is to turn off right in 10 miles at Wainhouse Corner and journey by the coast roads visiting Crackington Haven, Boscastle and Tintagel, before rejoining the main road at Camelford.

Crackington Haven is reached from Wainhouse Corner or alternatively from Tresparrett Posts by a steep and winding descent (1 in 6) at the foot of which a bridge is crossed beside the car park. The haven is at the mouth of an extremely picturesque valley. From the haven a path leads upwards to the top of Penkenna (Pencannow) Point, 400 feet, with a wonderful view of the rocky coastline.

Boscastle is a secluded old world village with a narrow rocky harbour (N.T.) winding inland between rugged cliffs. Sea-fishing is excellent but best bathing is at Bossiney (2 miles).

Tintagel *(Wharncliffe Arms, Tintagel, Atlantic View,* etc.), some 300 feet above the sea has an invigorating air whilst the cliff walks disclose some of the finest coast scenery.

In the village is the **Old Post Office** (N.T.), an interesting old building built originally as a medieval manor house and dating from the 14th century. **King Arthur's Hall** was built as headquarters of the Fellowship of the Round Table and is constructed entirely of Cornish stone. The **Church of St. Materiana** on the cliffs overlooking the island has several Saxon and Norman features and a well-preserved stone altar.

Tintagel Castle *(daily, fee).* The earliest remains of this great Norman stronghold are those of the Celtic monastery dating between the 5th and 9th centuries and already in ruins when the castle was built. The Great Hall and Chapel were erected in the mid-12th century. By the mid-16th century it was all in complete ruin. However fragmentary, these ancient remains, so romantically situated, are truly awe-inspiring.

Trebarwith Strand is a charming spot one-and-a-half miles south of Tintagel reached by footpath or via Treknow. The strand provides good bathing.

Camelford *(Sunnyside, Highermead),* the "Camelot" of Tennyson, lies four miles inland from the coast, on the banks of the river *Camel.* It is a small and ancient town, quaint and quiet—except for the traffic. At **Slaughter Bridge,** a good mile above the town, legend says the armies of King Arthur and his nephew, Mordred the Usurper, met in 542. Mordred was killed, and the King mortally wounded. The Bridge should be seen from the low ground by the stream, when its antiquity will be apparent.

To Rough Tor and Brown Willy. A distance of five miles. **Brown Willy,** 1,375 feet (the highest point in Cornwall), and its near neighbour, **Rough Tor** (pronounced like bough), 1,312 feet, are the two principal heights of Bodmin Moor. The scenery is wildly grand, rugged and bleak. At the top of Rough Tor (N.T.) are some magnificently piled rocks.

Launceston (Pop.: 4,700. Hotels: *White Hart, Eagle House*), a pleasant town near the Devon border is well placed high among fine moorland scenery. Formerly the capital of the county and the Norman "Dunheved" (hill-head), the remains of the Norman Castle *(daily)* on the summit of the hill command splendid views. Fragments of a Priory, completed in 1140, are still to be seen, notably in the Norman doorway of the *White Hart.* **St. Mary Magdalene Church,** consecrated in 1524, has a 14th-century tower and exterior walls decorated with elaborate carvings. The Early English South Gate of the town remains. The rooms in the upper storey were once used as the town "lock-up". The **Windmill,** a fine open space, stands 585 feet above sea-level and commands magnificent views. Tennis, golf, swimming pool, bowls and fishing in the river *Tamar* are available.

Wadebridge (Pop.: 3,000. Hotels: *Molesworth Arms, Swan, Rock*), stands at the head of the Camel estuary, about eight miles from the sea. It is a clean and bright town with beautiful river scenery, and a 500-year old bridge, still in daily use. Good boating, fishing, tennis and bowls are available. Two ancient churches are *St. Breock Church,* one mile west, and *Egloshayle Church* across the bridge and about half-mile to the right.

Bodmin (Pop.: 7,950. Hotels: *Queen's Head, Westberry*), the county town of Cornwall, and a touring centre, is on the fringe of Bodmin Moor. St. Petroc's Church contains notable fan-vaulting, a font of *c.* 1200, piscina (1495) and fine 15th-century carving. At the west end of the churchyard is *St. Guron's Well.*

In the neighbourhood are remains of several ancient earthworks, including Castle Canyke, Dunmere camp and a Roman camp at Tregear. Near **Nanstallon,** coins of Vespasian (A.D. 69) and Trajan (A.D. 98–117) were found as well as rings, spearheads and fragments of Roman pottery.

Two-and-a-half miles south-east of Bodmin is **Lanhydrock.** The church contains several monuments. **Lanhydrock House** (N.T., *Apr.–mid-Oct., daily except Suns and Mons*), a mansion of the late Jacobean period, has a remarkable Long Gallery, a battlemented barbican, and fine gardens.

WADEBRIDGE TO NEWQUAY

From Wadebridge to Newquay is about 16 miles, following the A39 to Whitecross and St. Jidgey to **St. Columb Major.** Here the right turn is taken towards the coast and Newquay. The coast route may be taken a mile after Whitecross for Padstow and then by the cliff road via Bedruthan, Trevarrian, entering Newquay from St. Columb Porth. Half way between Whitecross and Padstow is **Little Petherick** where a stop is recommended to see the church.

Padstow

Bathing Beaches.—Down river at Chapel Bar, at Ship-my-Pumps, below Chapel Stile (town beach), St. George's Cove and Harbour Cove (Tregirls Beach).
Buses.—Buses connect Padstow with St. Columb and Newquay, and with various outlying villages and porths.
Distances.—London, 246; Plymouth, 44; Wadebridge, 8; Bodmin, 15; St. Columb, 9; Tintagel, 21; Stepper Point (by cliff path), 2½; St. Merryn, 2½; Trevose Lighthouse, 5; Harlyn Bay, 2½;.

Newquay, 15.
Ferry.—(no cars) across the Camel estuary to Rock (for the golf links), runs from North Quay.
Fishing.—Fairly good fishing for bass, etc., from boats. Fine area for mackerel.
Golf.—Across the estuary at Rock (St. Enodoc) and at Trevose.
Hotels.—*Metropole, Dinas, Old Ship, North Quay.*
Population.—2,560 (inc. Trevone).
Post Office.—Close to Harbour quay.

Ancient Padstow once with ship-building interests is a popular harbour resort at the mouth of the *Camel,* and a residential and shopping centre. There are excellent sands, sailing, golf and bays popular for surfing. **St. Petroc's Church** has been extensively restored. The 13th-century tower is much older than the rest of the church, which was rebuilt 200 years later. There are several old memorials and the old stocks are in the south porch. Padstow possesses many quaint corners, narrow and crooked by-ways and picturesque buildings. **Abbey House** is believed to have been the old Guild House of the Padstow merchants and dates from the 15th century. **Raleigh's Court House,** on the South quayside dates back to the 16th century. Here Raleigh held his Court and collected his legal dues as Warden of Cornwall. At the top of the hill is the imposing Prideaux Place (private). Its castellated façade is of great length and very beautiful. A quaint custom at Padstow is the "Hobby Horse" dance held on May Day.

The Camel estuary averages three-quarter-mile in width and is over six miles long. The entrance is guarded by **Pentire Point** (Rock side) and **Stepper Point** (Padstow side). From Padstow, the Rock Ferry crosses to the north side of the estuary to the parish of **St. Minver** with several places of note. **Rock** is a popular sailing and golfing centre. A mile north is the ancient Church of St. Enodoc. **Polzeath,** 2 miles north of Rock, has fine sands and excellent surfing. On the other side of Pentire Point is **Portquin Bay** with village of Portquin.

Port Isaac *(Castle Rock, Lawns, Slipway House),* lies two miles east, an attractive fishing village. Bathing and boating are from **Port Gaverne** a sheltered cove nearby.

From Padstow the B3276 is taken for St. Merryn. The main road after St. Merryn reaches the coast at **Porthcothan Bay,** and in another two-and-a-half miles a car park is reached, from which a short walk enables one to view from the cliffs the huge detached masses known as **Bedruthan Steps.** The road now continues to **Trenance** descending to **Mawgan Porth** and later to **Watergate Bay.**

Newquay

Bathing.—Excellent at all states of the tide. Extensive sands, clean and firm, but bathers should be cautioned against approaching rocks, especially in Fistral Bay. Bathing at low water on any beach is very unwise.

Early Closing.—Wednesday.

Entertainments.—The *Newquay Theatre,* St. Michael's Road (Olde Tyme Music Hall); the *Cosy Nook Theatre* on Towan Promenade; Cinemas: *Astor,* Narrowcliff, *Victoria,* Chapel Hill, and the *Camelot,* The Crescent.

Golf.—18-hole links at Fistral Bay.

Hotels.—*Atlantic,* Dane Road; *Victoria; Bristol,* Narrowcliff; *Beachcroft,* Cliff Road; *Bay,* Esplanade, Pentire; *Grantham; St. Rumon's,* Fristral Bay; *Glendorgal; Headland; Great* *Western,* Cliff Road; *Penolver,* Narrowcliff; *Edgcumbe,* Narrowcliff; *St. Michael's,* Mount Wise; *Barrowfield,* Hilgrove Road; *Kilbirnie,* Narrowcliff; *Highbury,* Island Crescent; *Trebarwith,* Island Estate; *Beresford,* Narrowcliff; *Savoia,* Lusty Glaze Road; *Pentire; Crescent,* Island Crescent; *Fistral Bay,* Pentire; *Highbury,* Island Crescent; *Beachview,* Island Crescent; *Mount Wise; Min-y-Don,* Island Crescent; *Pentrevah,* Tower Road; *Penruddock,* Tower Road; *Tremont,* Pentire; *Runnymede,* Narrowcliff; *Cotswold;* and many others.

Population.—12,500 (approx.).

Post Office.—East Street.

Sports.—Bathing, boating, fishing, bowls and tennis.

Newquay is the largest and most popular holiday resort on the north coast of Cornwall. It lies midway between Bude and Land's End, 281 miles by rail from London, 254 by road, and 14 miles north of Truro. At this point of the coast Towan Head projects north-westward and with Pentire Headland and Trevelgue Head forms two spacious sandy bays. Newquay's eastern bay is lined with a series of smaller bays with firm sand ideal for bathing. Immediately east of the Harbour is **Towan Beach.** North-eastward of Towan Beach is the **Great Western,** or **Bothwicks Beach,** which can be reached at low tide by going round the **Island. Tolcarne Beach** is reached from the others at low tide, by steps from Narrowcliff at high water and by a cliff path at Crigga Head. **Crigga** and **Lusty Glaze Beaches** are still farther on, and can easily be reached at low water. From the latter there is a path to the top, coming out on the road to Glendorgal and Porth. Beyond Lusty Glaze are **Porth, Whipsiderry** and **Watergate Beaches.** Westward of the Headland is **Fistral Bay** with a splendid stretch of sands and fine surf.

The Harbour is guarded by two very solid stone piers. Access is by a long flight of stone steps or by a rather steep road. This rocky inlet, with its sandy floor at low water, is charming, and is increasingly popular with children. There are occasional fishing boats but principally yachts, and motor and rowing boats, the majority of which are available for hire.

To Porth and St. Columb Minor. Porth lies a mile along the coast. The extreme point of Porth Island is called Trevelgue Head. For the Porth Caves steps have been cut in the rock and lead to the little beach. From Porth on to Watergate, one-and-a-half miles, is a line of sheer perpendicular cliff. **St. Columb Minor** is on the St. Columb Major road. The church has a notable tower and inside is 13th- and 14th-century work.

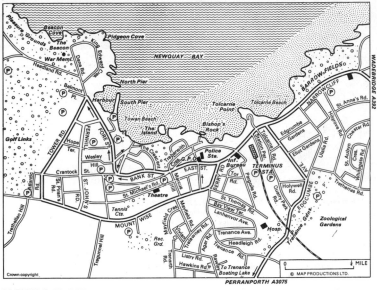

Crown copyright. © MAP PRODUCTIONS LTD.

PERRANPORTH A3075

NEWQUAY ▭▭▭ **Through routes** ➤ **One-way streets** Ⓟ **Parking**

To the Gannel and Crantock. The river *Gannel* can be crossed by a small plank bridge at half ebb-tide, and the passage continues open until two-and-a-half hours before high water. The boatmen will generally put people across for a small fee; otherwise Trevemper Bridge (1¾ miles inland) must be used.

On the opposite side of the estuary is the pretty, wooded **Penpol Creek.**

A war-time boat, moored in the *Gannel,* has been converted into a museum and is open to the public. **Crantock** has an interesting church, and from Crantock Bay, the views are magnificent.

To Trerice Manor and St. Newlyn East. The road route is via St. Columb Minor to Quintrel Downs and in a mile turning off right at Kestle Mill. **Trerice Manor** *(daily in summer except Fris and Sats, fee),* is a 16th-century manor house with notable plasterwork on the ceilings. St. Newlyn East, two miles beyond Trerice, has a good example of one of the larger Cornish parish churches. This 15th-century building, has an interesting Norman font, carved oak bench ends, a well-preserved Royal Arms of Charles I, and handsome screen and choir stalls added in the restoration of 1883.

To St. Mawgan, Carnanton Woods. Five miles northward along the coast is Mawgan Porth, with its high rocky cliffs. Its breakers provide fine sport for surfing. Here the luxuriant Vale of Lanherne opens to the sea and a glorious stretch of sand is available at low tide. **St. Mawgan** *(Falcon Inn)* is charmingly set among trees. The *Menalhyl* runs down the valley, and with the church makes a delightful picture. The entrance to Carnanton Woods is 100 yards up the hill from the *Falcon Inn*; a new road leads through the woods to First Lodge on the St. Columb Major road.

To Cubert and Holywell. Route via Trevemper Bridge beyond which there is a right-hand turn in two miles. Cubert is a pretty little village, the spire of its church forming a landmark for a great distance. The Holy Well is about two miles from the church, in a north-westerly

141

direction, in a cave, access to which is possible at low water. On the coast, half a mile north of the Holy Well, is **Porth,** or Polly Joke, a picturesque V-shaped beach between the cliffs, fed by a stream. Close to Porth Joke is the hamlet of **West Pentire.** Proceeding inland by a good road from here, Crantock is soon reached.

To St. Columb Major. Five miles from the coast, overlooking some very attractive country. The ancient Cornish hurling game is played here twice a year (Shrove Tuesday and Saturday week following).

About two-and-a-quarter miles east by south of St. Columb Major, but a mile farther by road, is **Castle-an-Dinas,** important remains of an early British encampment. The hill itself is called Castle Downs and rises 703 feet. There are two tumuli within the enclosure.

Nearly three miles on the Wadebridge road are the **Nine Maidens,** a group of upright stones said to date from 1500 B.C.

NEWQUAY TO LAND'S END

The A3075 runs from the coast to join the A30 Land's End road about seven miles short of Redruth. Opportunity should not be missed however to make a diversion to visit Perranporth and St. Agnes. Leaving Newquay via Trevemper Bridge, Goonhavern is reached in eight miles where a right turn is taken for Perranporth.

Perranporth (Pop.: 3,600. Hotels: *Boscawen, Sally's, Droskyn House,* etc.) lies at the point where two lovely valleys open to a broad expanse of sand—a children's paradise. The business quarter is pleasantly situated overlooking the well-stocked, colourful Boscawen Public Gardens, the model yacht pond and boating lake for children. The magnificent beach of firm, clean sand, extends nearly three miles between Droskyn Point and Ligger Point. Perranporth is a popular surfing centre with facilities for bathing, tennis, golf, entertainments, and camping. Cliff walks are various—that from Droskyn Point to the south has grand rock scenery, archways, caves and pools.

About one-and-a-half miles north are the remains of the 7th-century **Oratory of St. Piran** which was buried in the sand for over 700 years. **St. Piran's Round,** scheduled as an ancient monument, is a more or less natural amphitheatre capable of holding 2,000 persons; in it the ancient Cornish miracle plays were performed.

St. Agnes *(Driftwood Spars, Pentlands, Peterville Inn),* is a healthy little town with infinite variety and beauty in its immediate surroundings. The town is built high up on the slopes of a hill. Its seaside portion. **Trevaunance Cove,** is one of the most lovely rocky inlets to be found anywhere around this coast. Bathing and surfing are excellent. The town is flanked on the south-west by **St. Agnes' Beacon** (N.T., 630 feet), the ascent of which is quite easy.

Chapel Porth, a miniature rocky cove about two miles south-westward, is a favourite walk over the cliffs, or may be reached by car in a little over a mile from the Goonvrea side of Beacon Drive. At low tide there is an excellent sandy beach and there are many fine caves. It is National Trust property and an ideal spot for a quiet rest.

From St. Agnes the road passes **Porthtowan** with its lofty cliffs and broad sands, then, the small resort of **Portreath,** with a sandy beach and fine surfing. Beyond, a steep climb (keep to the right at the top of the hill) leads out on to the heather-clad cliffs bordering the road almost all the way to **Gwithian.** The road passes Deadman's Cove and Hell's Mouth and fine views are obtained of jagged rocks with the waves creaming at their feet. After sandhills at Gwithian the road turns inland. The right-hand turning opposite the inn in Gwithian meets the Land's End road as it enters **Hayle,** a straggling place with huge towans along the shore. About a mile beyond, the A30 is left on the right by A. 3047 for Lelant, Carbis Bay and St. Ives.

Back on the A30 main road and reached from Portreath by the B3300 are the twin towns of **Redruth** and **Camborne**.

Redruth (Pop.: with Camborne, 38,300. Hotels: *Druids, London, Red Lion*) is both an important commercial shopping centre and an excellent base for touring. Friday is the local market day. At one time Redruth was the old mining capital of Cornwall and had associations with John Wesley and George Fox, the founder of the Society of Friends. William Murdock, a Scottish engineer, invented gas lighting and the cottage and shop where he made experiments leading to the discovery is still to be seen in Cross Street, where a tablet records the event of 1792.

On the left of the road when leaving Redruth in the direction of Camborne is the wild, rugged hill known as **Carn Brea.** The hill is chiefly granite, 750 feet high, and was probably a military station in Neolithic times. It presents some magnificent views.

Camborne *(Vyvyan Arms, White Hart)*, one of the few big industrial centres near the north coast of the Duchy, is a busy and pleasant town and the shopping centre for the scattered rural districts. One of the most important buildings is the School of Mines. Richard Trevithick who invented the high-pressure steam engine was born close by at Pool. His statue fronts the Passmore Edwards Library.

St. Ives

Bathing.—Beaches of firm, golden sand. There is a beautiful stretch of sand from Lelant to Carrack Dhu. Surf-riding from Porthmeor Beach.

Boating and Fishing.—The St. Ives boatmen are expert fishermen, and there will be no difficulty in arranging a day's sport. Pollock and mackerel abound.

Distances.—Camborne, 13; Cape Cornwall, 17½; Carbis Bay, 1½; Falmouth, 25; Godrevy Point, 10½; Gurnard's Head, 7½; Gwithian, 9; Land's End, 22; Lizard, 26; London, 279; Marazion, 9; Newquay, 35; Penzance, 9; Perranporth, 20; Truro, 23.

Early Closing.—Thursday.

Entertainments, etc.—Plays, musical recitals, concerts and ballet are presented at the Municipal Concert Hall and Ballroom, the Guildhall, which is one of the most modern Concert Halls in the West. Dances are also held at the Municipal Ballroom.

Hotels.—*Tregenna Castle, St. Ives Bay, Porthminster, Garrack, Chy-on-Albany, Pedn Olva, Chy-an-Dour, Western, Dunmar*, and many others. *See also* Carbis Bay.

Population.—8,780.

Post Office.—At the foot of Tregenna Place.

Sport.—Bowls and tennis. Golf at Lelant.

Miles of beautiful sands and safe bathing beaches, abundant fishing facilities, a fascinating harbour, fine coast and wooded slopes, make St. Ives a paradise for young and old. It has long been the mecca of artists and of those who appreciate beauty of colour and form. The main road runs steeply into the town. The old town, with its winding streets, its church, public buildings and ancient houses, clusters round the harbour and behind it, and on either side rise hills which are being covered with houses favoured by visitors. These houses command sweeping views of the harbour, and of the great bay. The Church dates from 1410 to 1426. The lofty tower, 119 feet, is the chief architectural feature in any general view of the town. Of interest is the wagon roof and the many fine carvings, some of which date from the fifteenth century. There are some good windows. Outside is a fine fifteenth-century cross, 12 feet high.

Near the church is the Lifeboat House and between the two harbour arms, the Fisherman's Chapel. Westward of the Harbour is the oldest and quaintest part of the town and **Porthmeor Beach,** a fine sandy bay, splendid for surf-bathing. Beyond it are putting greens. To the left, at the extremity of the bay, is the headland of **Carrack Dhu.**

Carbis Bay *(Carbis Bay, Gwel Marten, Karenza, St. Uny,* etc.), is part of the great bay of St. Ives. There is good bathing on excellent sands, boating and fishing and fine golf links.

Zennor Village, four miles south-west of St. Ives, is dominated by its church with a square pinnacled tower. It has a 14th-century font, an Early English window and a carved bench-end. Opposite is the *Tinners' Arms Inn*, a reminder that tin mining once flourished here. On the seaward side of the Church is the Giant's Rock, or Logan Stone. There is a *Wayside Museum*, of great interest to archaeologists, in the village. *Zennor Quoit* is also worth seeing. This cromlech is unique for containing two sepulchres covered by one great stone. The slab, 18 feet by 9½ feet, was formerly supported by seven upright stones. The cromlech is a mile eastward of the village, on the inland side of the main road.

A short distance out of Zennor, a path to the right leads to the Gurnard's Head, one of the wildest and grandest headlands in the country, once the site of one of Cornwall's famous cliff castles. On the isthmus there are still remains of the fortifications. Westward of the Head is Porthmeor where a fortified village of the Iron Age has been excavated.

The road from Zennor towards Land's End leads through delightful country, passing the villages of Morvah and Pendeen (where tin mining is still active) to the small town of St. Just, 14 miles from St. Ives. St. Just *(Wellington, Star Inn, Kings Arms)*, is worth a visit for its church, a 14th-century building with a fine old granite tower. In the town square, adjoining the War Memorial, will be seen a circular enclosure called the *Plane an Gwarry*, the scene in former days of old Cornish miracle plays, wrestling and other sports. Due west of St. Just is Cape Cornwall.

The Land's End road follows the line of the beautiful Whitesand Bay. There are fine cliff walks and coast views are delightful. Five miles from St. Just and a mile inland from the coast is Sennen, or "Churchtown" as it is called, the westernmost village in England. The place is said to have been the scene of the great defeat of the Danes by Cornish forces under King Arthur. Parts of the present church date from the 13th century. Beyond the village and down a very steep incline on the left is the hamlet of Sennen Cove, from which there is a bracing cliff-walk to Land's End.

Land's End *(Land's End, Penrith)*. There are many parts of the coast of Cornwall grander and more beautiful; but visitors as a rule feel a certain pleasure in visiting "the last inn in England" and in sitting on the westernmost rocks. The best time for exploring the peninsula is at low tide, as then it is possible under the charge of a guide, to visit the large cavern called the Land's End Hole.

Within sight of the Land's End on a clear day are the Isles of Scilly, 28 miles distant; while nearer, less than two miles west from Land's End, the *Longship's Lighthouse* rises from its rocky base. Seven-and-a-half miles to the south is the *Wolf Rock*. Both lights are visible for 16 miles. The fog siren on the Longships gives a blast of one-and-a-half seconds in every 15 seconds.

A beautiful cliff walk extends about six miles with extensive views of cliffs and islands eastwards from Land's End to the Logan Rock. Points of interest include *Carn Creis*, the rocky island resembling an Armed Knight and *Gwelas* the sea-birds' rock. The island of *Enys Dodman* has an archway 40 feet in height. *Pordenack Point* is a magnificent granite headland with gigantic columns. Beyond are picturesque coves—*Zawn Rudh* the "red cavern", *Nanjizal* with its brook and *Pendower*, with curious flat boulders and a Logan stone.

The headland *Tol-Pedn-Penwith* forms the extreme western boundary of Mount's Bay. It gains its distinctive name from a great funnel-shaped chasm in a grass-covered neck that joins another mass of rock to the mainland, a few yards to the south-west of the head. The cliffs on either hand are magnificent, especially at the *Chair Ladder* of the headland, where cubes upon cubes of granite rise sheer as though built by Titans. Beyond is the fishing cove of Porthgwarra, famed for lobsters and for two curious tunnels through the cliff on the east connecting the hamlet with the sands. The cove is paved with large stones and has remained unspoilt.

The cliff path continues in half a mile to **Porth Chapel,** so named from a baptistery of St. Levan, the scanty ruins of which stand at the head of an ancient stairway down to Porth Chapel beach. An oratory stands nearby on the cliff just before crossing the brook that comes down from **St. Levan Churchtown,** quarter-mile up the valley.

Three-quarters of a mile to the east is **Treen Castle** (N.T.), a once fortified headland. The castle consists of a huge pile of rocks, grotesquely shaped and rising to a great height. On the western side, near the top, is the **Logan Rock,** said to weigh over 65 tons. Another stone nearby is called the *Logging Lady*.

Penzance

Bathing.—The upper parts of the beaches are shingly, but sand is revealed as the tide recedes. Most popular places are Lariggen and Western Beaches. Open-air pool adjoining Battery docks.

Distances.—Bodmin, 46; Camborne, 13; Falmouth, 23; Helston, 13; Lamorna, 6½; Land's End, 10; Lizard, 24; London, 280; Mousehole, 3; Newquay, 33; St. Ives, 9; Truro, 26.

Early Closing.—Wednesdays.

Entertainments.—St. John's Hall, in the Public Buildings, is used for concerts and dancing.

On the Promenade, near the foot of Alexandra Road, is a *Dance Hall*. There is a cinema, and bands play in the season in Morrab Gardens.

Heliport.—Eastern Green.

Hotels.—*Queens, Mount's Bay, Western, Mount Prospect, Alexandra, Union, Royale, Regent, Star, Yacht Inn, Carlton, Marine, Estoril, Stanmore,* and many others.

Population.—19,000.

Post Office.—Market Jew Street.

Penzance *(pen-sans,* the holy head) is the chief business and pleasure centre of the toe of England. The town is built on the side of a hill on the shore of lovely Mount's Bay. The A30 Land's End Road runs through the town and includes Market Jew Street where are the town's main shops, post office and the *Market House,* a domed granite building part occupied by a bank. In front of its classical façade stands a statue of Sir Humphrey Davy, who was born at Penzance in a house almost opposite where the monument now stands. Nearby is the **Guildhall** with a museum and library of the Royal Geological Society of Cornwall. Near the Market House is a road leading to the northern entrance of the **Morrab Gardens,** of which the lower end is only two minutes from the sea front. There is a fine show of sub-tropical and tender plants all the year round. Nearby is the **Penzance Library** *(daily)* to which members subscribe. Near the upper end of Morrab Road, west of the Gardens, are the *School of Art,* and the **Public Library.**

To the west of Morrab Gardens is the **Penlee Memorial Park** with sports facilities, an attractive *Open-air Theatre* and the **Penlee Museum.**

The sea-front commands an extensive and magnificent view of Penlee Point. Between the road and the beach are the **Bolitho Gardens,** luxuriant with palm trees. Here, too, are tennis courts, a bowling green, putting green, shelters and seats. Eastward from Alexandra Road are the **Alexandra Grounds** with a fine bowling rink, putting green and tennis courts. Farther east are the terraced **St. Anthony Gardens** and the **Jubilee Bathing Pool.** Nearby are the **Battery Rocks,** a popular open-air bathing-place.

The Harbour is tidal and though not large is a busy and interesting place. Boat excursions to the bay and St. Michael's Mount start from here. Overlooking the harbour is **St. Mary's Church.**

Newlyn *(Old Bridge, Antoine, Chypons),* lies a mile west along the shore from Penzance. For long a quiet village with great attraction for artists it has grown to be a busy fishing town. The harbour presents a colourful picture. From the quay twist up the steep and narrow cobbled streets with here and there a quaint old building worthy of note. The tiny original quay and the magnificent views add further to the interest. The **Passmore Edwards Art Gallery** lies beside the main coastal road. There are exhibitions here of traditional and modern painting, pottery, and sculpture, by living Cornish artists.

145

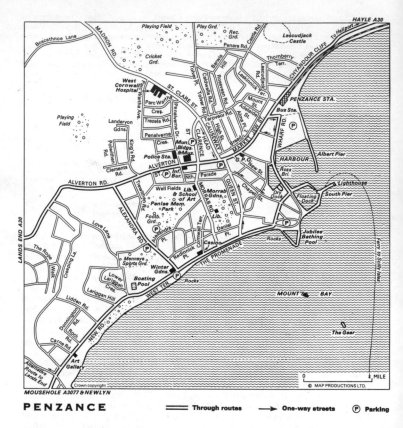

PENZANCE　　　⟱ **Through routes**　⟶ **One-way streets**　Ⓟ **Parking**

Mousehole *(Old Coastguards, Lobster Pot),* two miles from Newlyn, is a quaint fishing village with twisting little streets and a popular harbour. The oldest building is known as the Keigwin Arms.

To Paul. The most direct way from Penzance is by the road facing one at the cross-roads just beyond Newlyn Art Gallery. The church contains one scarred arch of an earlier building burnt by the Spaniards in 1595.

To Lamorna. As above but disregard turnings to Paul and beyond Sheffield keep to right. The turning for Lamorna is on left just beyond a succession of sharp bends and a sudden descent to a stream. The flowery valley of Lamorna with its trout-stream, cascades and rocky cove is popular with artists. There are natural pools for bathing and a sandy beach is exposed at low-tide. Near to the hamlet of **Boleigh** are the standing stones known as the *Pipers* and the stone circle of the *Merry Maidens.*

146

To Gulval, Castle-an-Dinas and Chysauster. Leave Penzance by the Marazion road for Chyandour; quarter-mile farther and to the left is Gulval. The wide lane opposite the north side of Gulval Church climbs steeply and in about a mile reaches *Badger's Cross*, where the right-hand road leads to **Castle-an-Dinas** (765 feet) interesting as the site of a hill-fort, but with more general appeal as a viewpoint. It is a pleasant walk of about a mile from the top of Castle-an-Dinas, following round the south-side of the huge dump of quarry-waste, to **Chysauster,** a prehistoric village inhabited between 100 B.C. and A.D. 100. Pottery and other finds during excavations can now be seen in the Penlee Museum in Penzance.

To Madron, Lanyon Quoit, Nine Maidens-Mulfra Quoit. Madron Church, two-and-a-half miles north-west of Penzance, dates from the 14th century and has several interesting monuments. Nearby are the remains of a Baptistery and an ancient wishing well traditionally visited by hopeful maidens on May Day. **Lanyon Quoit,** on the same route, two miles farther north-west, and a few yards from the main road, is a very fine cromlech dating from 1500 B.C. A mile to the north-east are the remains of a stone circle called the **Nine Maidens.** Eastward from Nine Maidens is Mulfra Hill on the side of which is another cromlech, **Mulfra Quoit.**

To Castle Hornech and Trereife (Treeve). From Penzance the Alverton Road runs westward to Alverton Bridge, where a branch road on the right leads to Castle Hornech, about one mile from Penzance. It is now a Youth Hostel. Near Trereife cross-roads on the main road is Trereife House, a fine 17th-century mansion.

To Sancreed and Boscawen-Un. The main Land's End road leads to **Drift** where a branch road on the right leads to **Sancreed** with a fine 15th-century church. Near the main road to the south is a fine menhir, *Tregonebris Stone* or the *Blind Fiddler.* Half a mile south of Tregonebris Stone and across the main road is an interesting Bronze Age circle of stones— **Boscawen-Un.**

To St. Buryan. Take the Land's End Road to Catchall where the road forks. The left branch road leads in two-and-a-half miles to St. Buryan. The village is noticeable for its Church, the greater part of which dates from the 15th century.

PENZANCE TO FALMOUTH

The Penzance to Falmouth road is the A394 running through Marazion and Helston. **Marazion** is a pleasant place with good boating and bathing, enjoying a very mild climate.

St. Michael's Mount (N.T.), is a lofty isolated mass of rock, some 21 acres in extent, separated from Marazion at high water by about 500 yards of sea, but at low water connected with the mainland by a stone causeway. The Mount rises to a height of over 230 feet and is crowned by the picturesque castellated mansion of the St. Aubyns *(Mons, Weds, Fris)*; along the northern base are several houses and cottages.

About a mile east of Marazion a road goes southward from the Helston road to the village of **Perranuthnoe** *(Victoria Inn)*, picturesquely set above a low cliff. The church, with a good 15th-century tower, is interesting for its carved woodwork and Norman font. The eastern boundary of Mount's Bay is Cudden Point, on which are **Pixies' Cove, Bessie's Cove** and **Prussia Cove. Praa Sands** lie eastward of Mount's Bay and extend from Keneggy Beach to Rinsey Head. It is a popular resort, particularly with caravanners; there are well-equipped refreshment rooms.

Helston (Pop.: 9,620. Hotels: *Angel, Alpha*), is one of Cornwall's important market towns. It appears to have existed in the time of King Alfred and was long a walled city, with a castle. It is a good centre for touring and is famous for its **Flora** or **Furry Day** (May 8), when the Furry Dance takes place through the streets. From Helston runs the fine road (A3083) connecting with the Lizard.

THE LIZARD PENINSULA

The Lizard Peninsula is a tableland over 300 feet above sea level. In 1962 a micro-wave satellite tracking station was installed in the central section, known as Goonhilly Downs, Lizard Point is the southern extremity of England. **Gunwalloe** overlooks Mount's Bay. The village stands some way inland but the church is romantically situated and sheltered behind a cliff. Caves serve as bell tower and one of the bells dates from 1480.

Mullion *(Poldhu, Mullion Cove, New Inn)*, is a good centre with a popular golf course. **Mullion Cove,** with its miniature harbour, is about a mile distant from the village. Above rise lichen-covered cliffs, rocks piled on rocks, vaulted, tunnelled, ribbed and groined, like the ruins of some vast cathedral. At low tide a stretch of sand affords enjoyable bathing. Northward is the pretty little **Polurrian Cove,** and, still farther north, **Poldhu Cove.**

Kynance Cove is less than a mile north of Lizard Town. From the main Helston Road (A3083), a by-road leads in one-and-a-quarter miles to the top of the cove. Kynance is entrancing with brilliant serpentine rocks, firm sands at low tide, fine cliff scenery and interesting caves. The view seawards embraces Asparagus Island, Gull Rock and the huge Steeple Rock.

Lizard Town *(Housel Bay, Lizard)*, is a straggling village having a few hotels and boarding houses. Here the local beautifully coloured and mottled serpentine rock is cut, polished and made into ornamental articles. The "town" is half a mile inland from Lizard Head, east of which is the **Lizard Lighthouse** *(weekday afternoons)*.

East of Lizard Point is the inlet of **Housel Bay,** protected on its far side by **Penolver Point,** a grandly piled rocky headland. **Landewednack** Church is about half a mile east of Lizard Town. A Norman doorway, a hagioscope and a font dating from 1414 are of interest.

Although one of the lesser-known Cornish coves by reason of its inaccessibility, **Cadgwith Cove** is amongst the most picturesque to be found anywhere in the Duchy. The approach, after leaving Ruan Minor, is down a winding, very steep and narrow lane which brings the visitor quite suddenly to the miniature cove, with its thatched-roof, stone-built cottages. A mile north is the hamlet of **Poltesco,** in a wooded, rocky valley, down which a stream flows on its way to Carleon Cove. Beyond this are the very pleasantly situated **Kennack Sands** providing good bathing. **Coverack** is a typical fishing village, with a miniature harbour and a lifeboat station. **St. Keverne** has a large and stately church. The tower with spire makes it a prominent landmark. From St. Keverne take the road to **Manaccan,** a village built high on a hill. It has an interesting church containing Norman work. "Manaccanite", a mineral from which titanium is derived, was first found here.

Helford. The village straddles the creek, an ideal spot in a beautifully-wooded combe. A *Pedestrian Ferry* runs on request daily to the *Ferry Boat Inn* at **Helford Passage** across the estuary, from whence it is but six miles from **Trebah,** at top of hill, to Falmouth (bus service).

Mawgan, west of Manaccan, has a 13th-century church, with 15th-century wagon roofs, other interesting features and memorials. From Mawgan it is but a mile or so of delightfully-wooded road to **Gweek,** a fishing village at the head of a creek of the Helford River. From Gweek to Helston is about four miles.

Falmouth

Bathing.—*Gyllyngvase Beach,* at the western end of cliff road. At the Pendennis end of Cliff Road is the *Castle Beach,* and there are also highly popular beaches at Swanpool and at Maenporth.

Distances.—Helston, 13; Land's End, 36; Lizard via Gweek, 19; Newquay, 26; Penjerrick, 4; Penzance, 26; Redruth, 11; St. Ives, 25; Truro, 11.

Early Closing.—Wednesday.

Entertainments.—Band performances in Gyllyngdune Gardens; cinema; variety shows, concerts and dancing at the Princess Pavilion. Dramatic performances at Falmouth Arts Theatre.

Hotels.—*Falmouth,* Cliff Road; *Green Bank,* Harbour; *Bay,* Seafront; *Royal Duchy,* Cliff Road; *Palm Court,* Melvill Road; *Gyllyngdune,* Seafront; *St. Michaels; Melvill,* Sea View Road; *Madeira,* Cliff Road; *Cheriton,* Stracey Road; *Carthion,* Cliff Road; *Rosslyn,* Kimberley Park Road; *Southcliffe,* Cliff Road; *Gwendra,* Seafront; *Pons-a-Verran,* Port Navas; *King's,* Harbour; *Morvah,* Melvill Road; *Suncourt,* Seafront; *Maenheere,* Harbour; *Membly Hall,* Seafront; and many others. Full lists from Resort Manager, Gyllyngvase Beach.

Population.—17,330.

Post Office.—The Moor.

Sports.—Fishing, bowls, tennis, golf.

Falmouth, the largest town in Cornwall, is beautifully situated on the estuary of the river *Fal,* with a safe harbourage called Carrick Roads. Its equable climate makes it a popular resort in both summer and winter. The hilly nature of the promontory provides two entirely different outlooks—to the north the busy harbour with its quays and dockyards, backed by the tree-fringed *Fal;* on the south a magnificent prospect of sea and cliffs.

Gyllyngvase Beach is the most popular of the beaches. At the rear is a car park, and adjoining this **Queen Mary Gardens,** with miniature golf and other facilities. The nearby **Gyllyngdune Gardens** contain luxuriant subtropical vegetation. **Kimberley Park** farther inland is a fine seven-acre expanse of open grass and parkland. The little beach at **Swanpool** farther round the bay is popular. The traffic centre of Falmouth is the large open space known as **The Moor,** formerly a marsh. Here is the terminus of most of the bus and coach routes, and a handy Car Park. At the foot of The Moor is a large block housing the Municipal Offices and Council Chamber and the Public Library. Near at hand is the **Prince of Wales Pier** from which most of the excursion boats and several of the ferries start. **Pendennis Castle** *(daily, fee),* stands on Pendennis Point at a height of 200 feet above the sea. The castle formed part of Henry VIII's coastal defences. From it there are fine views.

To Swanpool and Maenporth. From Gyllyngvase Beach go westward by Spernan Wyn Road and keep straight on at cross-roads, shortly descending past the cemetery to Swanpool lake and beach. For Maenporth continue past Swanpool and turn left at Golden Bank cross-roads beyond Golf Links. A path on the left strikes off across Pennance Point and runs within sight of the sea all the way to Maenporth, a pretty little sandy cove with cliffs worn into caves and arches. Two-and-three-quarter miles south-west is **Helford Passage** *(Ferry Boat Inn),* the estuary of the lovely Helford River.

To Flushing, Trefusis and Mylor. Reached by ferry from Prince of Wales Pier. Flushing is a warm and sunny little village with fine views across the harbour. From Flushing quay the road leads pleasantly round, past a few private houses, to the woods of Trefusis, **Mylor** with a boat repair yard and yacht harbour is a most peaceful hamlet. Beside the south door of Mylor Church is the largest and tallest Cornish cross extant, said originally to have marked the grave of St. Mylor himself.

To St. Budock Church. About two miles in a westerly direction. The church has an ancient screen. The brass of John Killigrew, of Arwenack, *ob.* 1567, is good and the church has Georgian box pews.

Penjerrick *(Suns, Weds, free),* three miles, has beautiful grounds with rhododendrons, azaleas and camellias brilliant in spring.

To Penryn *(King's Arms, Anchor, Penrynian).* The town, long famous for its granite, stands at the head of the river on which Falmouth old town is built, and although the quays are still generally busy with shipping, there was a time when Penryn was the predominant port in these parts. The few remains of **Glasney Collegiate Church** erected at

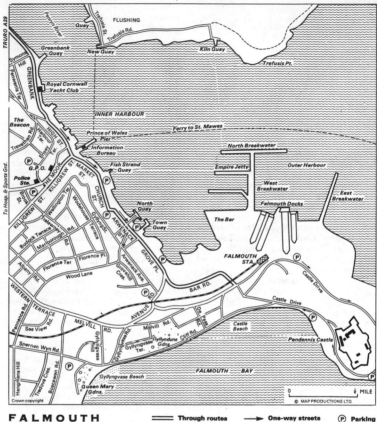

FALMOUTH ═══ **Through routes** ⟶ **One-way streets** Ⓟ **Parking**

Penryn in the 13th century and **St. Gluvias Church** with a 15th-century granite tower are of interest.

Roseland

Roseland is the name given to the charming country bordering the eastern side of Carrick Roads, bounded roughly on the north by the river *Fal* from Ruan and extending southwards to the tip of the peninsula at Zoze Point. The name Roseland has no origin in roses but is a later form of "Rosinis" meaning "moorland isle" and Roseland very nearly is an island.

The narrow promontory facing St. Mawes and terminating in Zoze Point is well worth exploration. Boats from Falmouth call at St. Mawes and cross to the little landing-place opposite *Place Manor Hotel*.

The Church of **St. Anthony-in-Roseland** contains some fine examples of Early English architecture. The south door has a pre-Norman arch, and the nave is mainly Norman. The Lighthouse (¾-mile) may be visited on weekday afternoons.

The cliffs above the Lighthouse are within the care of the National Trust (car park), and can be followed eastwards to Porthscatho. The road joins the road up from Percuil a little short of **Garrans** *(Royal Standard Inn)*, a pleasant village with good views over Gull Rock and Nare Head.

St. Mawes *(Ship and Castle, St. Mawes, Tresanton, Idle Rocks, Victory Inn, Rising Sun)*, on the western shore of the promontory, with a ferry service to Falmouth, is a port and a holiday resort. It is a grand place for sailing and boating with the small *Percuil* river inviting excursions. **St. Mawes Castle** *(daily, fee)*, is contemporary with Pendennis Castle across the water, having been built by Henry VIII in 1543 as part of the coastal defences. It was designed purely as an artillery fort.

Porthscatho is a small, bracing, unpretentious resort.

St. Just-in-Roseland, two miles north of St. Mawes on the western shore, is reached from Falmouth via the King Harry Ferry. It is a pretty village but its chief attraction is the famous churchyard and church.

Veryan *(New Inn)* on the B3078 from St. Mawes is noted for its "round houses". Two stand at each end of the village and one in the centre, each surmounted by a cross.

Mevagissey *(Ship, Fountain, Kings Arms)*, a hilly old-world fishing village and popular resort for summer visitors, has narrow streets and devious alleyways, with cottages perched at crazy angles. On the wharf-side is an attractive aquarium. The Church stands on ground which has been consecrated for over 1,400 years. The first church was erected about 950. This Saxon building was rebuilt about 1100 and again rebuilt in 1259. A north aisle was added about 1450. The final restoration was in 1887. **Polstreath Beach**, beyond the coastguard station, is a favourite spot for safe bathing and picnics.

Inland from Mevagissey are several small but attractive villages, all of them quite unspoilt. The largest is **St. Ewe** *(Crown Inn)* with a church approached through an avenue of palms. From **Pentewan** a very steep road (gradient 1 in 4½) climbs towards **Black Head**, on the northern side of which is **Trenarren,** a delightful little village almost lost among the trees of its lovely narrow valley. Two miles beyond Black Head and hardly more than a mile from the outskirts of St. Austell is **Porthpean.**

FALMOUTH TO ST AUSTELL

There are alternative routes for the motorist. The most enjoyable is the route by St. Mawes to Veryan, and then the by-roads to the coastal villages Pentewan and Porthpean to St. Austell. Those wishing to see Truro and its cathedral, travel via the direct route by the A39 then straight on by the A390 through Probus and Grampound to St. Austell.

Truro (Pop.: 14,590. Hotels: *Royal, Brookdale, St. Georges, Carlton)*, is the county headquarters, a Cathedral City and small port at the head of *Truro* river. It is the main shopping centre for the rural districts. Golf, tennis and bowls and river excursions through delightful scenery to Falmouth are available. There is a quiet dignity about the main thoroughfares such as Boscawen Street, Lemon Street and the less-known backwater of Walsingham Place, each with Georgian buildings.

Truro Cathedral built of Cornish granite was consecrated in 1887. The Central or Victoria tower, 250 feet high, forms a Cornish Memorial of Queen Victoria. The cathedral was built on the site of the old parish church of St. Mary, the south aisle of which was retained to form the south aisle of the cathedral. The Baptistry is a memorial to Henry Martyn, the great Truro missionary. The stones and marbles form a harmony of gorgeous tints. The reredos of Bath stone is of great beauty.

St. Clement, a village one-and-a-half miles south-east of Truro, prettily situated on the banks of the *Tresillian* river has a 13th-century church of note. Near the porch is the famous *Ignioc Stone* which has been a national monument since 1932. From St. Clement, a mile by field-path, is **Malpas** *(Heron Hotel)*, a very ancient little port. Passengers from Falmouth land at Malpas when the tide does not serve for Truro. Across the water from Malpas is **Woodbury,** a noted spot for river picnics.

Beyond Truro the St. Austell road passes through **Probus.** The church was made collegiate by King Athelstan A.D. 926. The richly-carved tower dates from the time of Henry VIII. There are some fine houses in the neighbourhood, notably **Trewithen** with its fine garden *(Garden only: Mons, Tues, Weds, Fris, Mar.–June; Sept. and Oct. House and Garden: Thurs, May–Sept., fee)*. Three miles on is **Grampound,** on the main stream of the *Fal*, where in the small market place is a very old but mutilated Cornish monument originally a kind of cross.

St. Austell (Pop.: 8,500. Hotels: *Carlyon Bay, White Hart, Cliff Head*), chief centre of the local China Clay industry and an important business, shopping centre and residential town, makes a convenient head-quarters for various places of interest. Holy Trinity Church rebuilt in the 15th century has a fine 100-foot tower ornamented with statues in niches, and contains many interesting memorials.

Charlestown *(Rashleigh Arms, Pendennis, Pier House)*, is a tiny port handling a considerable part of the shipping business of the Clay Country. Due south is **Duporth Beach,** a delightfully quiet spot. There is a popular holiday camp in the vicinity and other accommodation. Eastward is **Carlyon Bay,** an attractive modern suburb with hotels *(Carlyon Bay, Cliff Head)*, golf links, excellent sands and facilities for sports and games of all kinds.

ST. AUSTELL TO PLYMOUTH

From St. Austell the A390 works inland to Lostwithiel and in nine miles joins up with the A38 passing through Liskeard before turning south-eastward for Saltash and the fine toll bridge across the *Tamar* to St. Budeaux and Plymouth. A branch off the A390 shortly after Holmbush leads to Par and Fowey.

Par Sands *(Ship Inn:* at Par—*Royal, Haven)*, soon open out with a grand marine view. At low water there is a very extensive flat beach of good sand. The Harbour is small, but has a flourishing and busy trade. Coal is brought and China Clay, stone and granite shipped in large quantities. **Spit Beach,** west of the Harbour, is a popular place for picnics. Not far from Par is **St. Blazey** on the A390 with a 14th-century church. East of Par Sands is the well-wooded, crescent-shaped cove of **Polkerris** *(Rashleigh Inn)*, where a diminutive stone pier shelters a good sandy beach.

Fowey *(Fowey, Greenbank, Safe Harbour, Ship Inn,* etc.*)*, is an ancient seaport, with narrow streets and houses attractively jumbled together. The harbour is a charming inlet between imposing headlands, extending inland for six miles to Lostwithiel, and provides a safe and picturesque anchorage for hundreds of yachts during the summer months. The most popular spot is the Town Quay. To its left the steep hillside at Bodinnick is covered from summit to water's edge in rich, dark green foliage. Opposite is the lovely wooded creek of **Pont Pill** while to the right lies picturesque **Polruan.** The Parish Church, beautifully proportioned, was rebuilt in 1336. The lofty 15th-century wagon roof of the nave has still much of the original carved timber. Nearby **Readymoney Cove** is a pretty spot with good bathing. *St. Catherine's Castle* (1540) a former defence of the harbour is now in ruins. Polridmouth Cove is beyond, and a little distance farther is **Gribbin Head,** with its Beacon, commanding a magnificent view.

Lostwithiel (Pop.: 1,910. Hotels: *Royal Talbot, King's Arms, Monmouth*), is a picturesque old town, much visited for the salmon and trout fishing on the *Fowey* over which runs a fine old medieval bridge. The old *Duchy Palace* was the ancient Exchequer, Shire Hall and Stannary Prison. It dates from about 1280. **St. Bartholomew's Church** has a graceful octagonal spire dating from the 13th century. In the south porch are preserved the parish stocks. The Guildhall was erected in 1740.

Restormel Castle *(daily, fee),* one-and-a-half miles due north of Lostwithiel, reached by the road next to the *Talbot Hotel.* The 13th-century Stone Keep was built on an earlier motte and bailey earthwork.

Lanhydrock House *(daily Apr.–Oct., fee. The park and woodlands are always open),* is three-and-a-half miles north of Lostwithiel. Part of the house is of the Tudor period and stands in a park of 366 acres. The barbican, or principal entrance, is a fine battlemented structure bearing date 1651. The **Church of St. Hydrock** is behind the mansion.

Boconnoc lies in the charming valley of the Lerryn, four miles eastward from Lostwithiel. Boconnoc Church was renewed and dedicated in 1321, but the present fabric dates from the 15th century. **Braddock Down** was the scene of a Civil War battle in 1643.

The **Fowey Valley,** north of Lostwithiel, boasts some glorious scenery. The superb Valley Drive between Bodmin Road and Doublebois may be combined with a visit to Lanhydrock or Boconnoc.

Polperro is a charming old village south-west of Looe and set on the lower slopes of a narrow and precipitous gorge between 400-foot high cliffs. The houses are huddled around the harbour, a little basin dry at low tide and protected by a double quay-head. Outside the narrow inlet leads obliquely to the open sea, between serrated crags only 50 yards apart. At the side of the old bridge is the curious *House on the Props.* Close to the harbour is an interesting *Smugglers' Museum.*

Looe (Pop.: 4,010. Hotels: *Hannafore Point, Bodrigan, Westor,* etc.). The ancient towns of East and West Looe are built on opposite sides of a deep river valley. Inland the waterway widens to lake-like proportions and in two streams wanders between high hills for nearly three miles. A picturesque granite Bridge crosses the harbour and connects the two towns.

At Church End, the seaward extremity of East Looe, is Looe Parish Church, standing upon the site of a chapel dedicated to St. Mary in the year 1259. Beyond the Church is the Promenade, overlooking a sandy beach, the most popular bathing-place. To the right the stone Pier, known from its shape as "The Banjo", forms the eastern arm of the Harbour entrance. Near the Church is the *Old Guildhall* now a museum and reading-room. High up under the porch roof is the pillory, one of the few examples remaining in the country. Between the Old Guildhall and the Bridge is the modern Guildhall, with clock tower. At Quay Head there is a marine aquarium of some interest. In West Looe the most interesting building is the curious little quayside Church of St. Nicholas. The exact date of erection is unknown, but its endowment was confirmed in 1336. From the Church a picturesque cliff road, affording charming views, runs around the hill to **Hannafore,** a pleasant residential area facing the open sea. A ferry from Church End connects with East Looe.

To Duloe. At Sandplace turn left over the bridge to climb the hill. In three-quarter-mile on the left is **St. Cuby's Well.** A right turn at the top of the hill leads to Duloe. St. Cuby's

Church is a spacious Early English building noteworthy for its massive 13th-century tower of a type unusual in Cornwall, with buttresses and a pyramidal roof added when the Church was restored in 1860. In the north transept, aisle and chancel is a notable old oak screen.

Liskeard (Pop.: 4,890. Hotels: *Fountain, Pencubitt*) lies nine miles north of Looe. It is an ancient municipal borough and market town noteworthy for its cattle fairs, held on the second Monday in each month. The great annual Fair of St. Matthew takes place on October 2. The large Church is very fine and has a granite tower, 85 feet in height. Adjoining the Library is *Stuart House,* where in 1644 Charles I once stayed. In Well Lane is the old *Pipe Well,* an interesting and unusual specimen.

To St. Cleer and the Cheesewring. St. Cleer, two-and-a-half miles due north of Liskeard, has a prominent church tower, 97 feet high, in three stages. Not far from the church stands the famous St. Cleer's Well. The special merit of St. Cleer water was its potency to cure madness. To the north-east are the *Trethevy Stones,* or cromlech. Six large upright stones support a huge table-stone. Continuing, the road soon crosses the old rail track and becomes steeper round Caradoc Hill (1,213 feet); I.T.A. transmitter, wide views of Dartmoor. The scenery is wild in the extreme, with huge boulders of granite. All round are deserted mines with decayed and falling chimney shafts and buildings. About two-and-a-half miles from the Trethevy Stone is *Minions Mound,* said to be the burial-place of a king *(Cheesewring Hotel).* Nearby are *The Hurlers,* remains of three large Bronze Age circles. The *Cheesewring* is a remarkable pile of granite slabs—each weighing many tons.

To St. Ive and Callington. St. Ive has a fine church of the Decorated period. Note the unusually fine old wagon-roof, the hagioscope and sedilia; and the sundial over the south porch. Best of all is the fine east window with its beautifully wrought stained glass and graceful niches on its sides. **Callington** *(Blue Cap, Bull's Head),* is a small market town with an imposing Church, rebuilt 1438. According to tradition King Arthur kept his Court at Callington.

To St. Neot. Reached via Doublebois on the Bodmin road St. Neot's Church has a magnificent series of 15th- and early 16th-century stained glass windows. They are quite beyond compare with any others in Cornwall.

To Seaton, Downderry, Port Wrinkle and Sheviock. Leaving Looe by the cliff path, a walk of about two-and-a-half miles over the seaside downs brings one to **Seaton,** where the *Seaton* river winds to a sandy beach. Adjoining Seaton is **Downderry,** a pleasant little place very popular during the holidays. Over the downs is **Port Wrinkle** with a small harbour and two well-sheltered beaches. The old pilchard cellar dating back to the 15th century should be visited. **Crafthole** is a straggling village on the Downderry–Torpoint road. It was a borough in the reign of Edward II. There are two ancient crosses nearby, and a pleasant old inn *The Finnygook*.

To Whitsand Bay, Rame Head and Antony. The Torpoint road is taken (bus service) to the branch road near Tregantle Fort. From the summit of the ridge a splendid prospect is spread out. The four-mile stretch of coast to Rame is now a favourite resort of "week-enders" from Plymouth.

East of Portwrinkle, Whitsand Bay becomes a *death-trap to bathers*; a year rarely passes without at least one fatality. **Rame's** curious little church was reconsecrated in 1259, and contains Norman work.

Rame Head is a promontory from which the cliffs descend sharply on either side. The little chapel here has walls almost a yard thick. It has a vaulted stone roof and looks most antique. To the east is **Penlee Point. Cawsand** and **Kingsand** are twin villages offering beautiful views seaward.

Antony is a quiet old-world village. **Antony House** (N.T., *Tues, Weds, Thurs, Bank Hols, Apr.–Sept, fee*), is a fine early Georgian house. The church at **St. Germans** exhibits much Norman work.

Plymouth

Distances.—Bodmin, 30; Dartmouth, 30; Exeter, 42; Kingsbridge, 21; Looe, 19; Torquay, 32; London, 211.
Ealy Closing Day.—Wednesday.
Fishing.—Excellent sea fishing both from the shore and from boats readily available for hire, the deep-water marks of Eddystone and Hand Deeps being famous. Sea Anglers Club. Open Fishing Festival in August.

Permits for brown trout angling in Burrator Reservoir from Water Department, Municipal Offices.
Hotels.—*Continental, Mayflower Post House, Duke of Cornwall, Grand, Holiday Inn, San Remo,* and many others of all grades.
Information Centre.— Municipal Offices.
Museum—Art Gallery—Library.—Drake Circus.
Post Office.—St. Andrew's Cross.

Plymouth lies at the mouth of the River *Tamar* which here forms the boundary between Devon and Cornwall. It faces on to Plymouth Sound, a great expanse of water almost three miles square. The city incorporates the formerly separate townships of Devonport, Stonehouse and old Plymouth and with a population of 214,000 is the largest centre in the West Country. The foreshore extends for a distance of seven miles from the point where the river *Plym* becomes the *Cattewater,* the old commercial harbour, round the shore of Plymouth Sound and

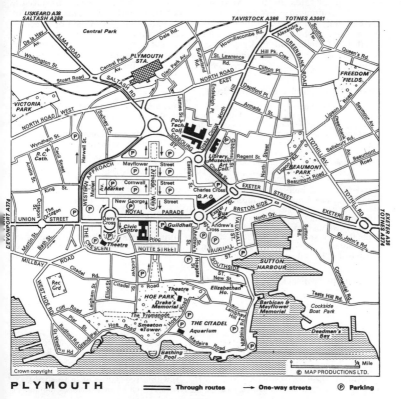

Crown copyright   ¼ Mile
© MAP PRODUCTIONS LTD.

PLYMOUTH   ▬▬ **Through routes**   → **One-way streets**   ⓟ **Parking**

up the *Hamoaze,* the great naval anchorage to beyond the fine road bridge across the *Tamar*.

The **Hoe** is a broad plateau 120 feet above sea-level. On the seaward side it slopes down to the rocks which form the barrier of the waters of the Sound, while townwards it drops gently through gardens fringed with trees. The Sound is a constant theatre of maritime activity. It was on the Hoe that Drake finished his game of bowls despite the approach of the Spanish Armada. **Smeatons Lighthouse** stands boldly on the grassy slopes. It first stood on the Eddystone rock for a 120 years before being replaced. Eastward in a railed enclosure is a beautifully kept little garden and nearby the *Hoe Theatre*. The **Citadel** *(open certain times)*, is a picturesque fortification built in the time of Charles II. In front is the **Aquarium** *(weekdays, fee),* of the Marine Biological Association. **Sutton Pool** is the ancient harbour of Plymouth, lined with quays and stores. Beyond Phoenix Wharf is the old **Barbican,** and near by on the West Pier is the famous **Mayflower Stone** commemorating the departure from this spot of the Pilgrim Fathers in 1620. **St. Andrew's Church,** the parish church, was entirely rebuilt in 1957.

Of great moment to Plymouth has been the rebuilding of the city centre wiped out by the air raids of 1941. An ambitious and farseeing plan has produced a shopping community surrounded by an inner ring road, well landscaped with gardens and with a direct pedestrian route, Armada Way, from the rail centre to the sea. Several traffic-free precincts have been included.

The fine **Guildhall** was badly damaged but a new complex has been built within the old walls. Opposite rises the new **Civic Centre,** a mammoth modern building from the roof of which *(daily, fee),* there is a wonderful prospect.

Plymouth to Ivybridge and South Brent

The A38 Ashburton road runs eastward from Plymouth via Plympton, Ivybridge and South Brent, skirting the southern borders of Dartmoor.

To the south of the road two miles out of the city is—

Saltram House (N.T., *Apr.–mid Oct., daily fee*), standing in a splendidly well-landscaped park with views extending over Plymouth Sound. The Classical façades added in the middle of the 18th century hide the remains of a large Tudor house.

Plympton, once a village, and now contiguous with the city, is famous as the birthplace of Sir Joshua Reynolds. The old church is mainly Perpendicular but shows some traces of Early English work and has a fine lofty tower.

Ivybridge lies six miles to the west in a beautiful situation and is a good centre from which to make various excursions on to southern Dartmoor. The little River *Erme* provides some fishing for trout.

Seventeen miles from Plymouth, on the banks of the river *Avon,* which flows picturesquely over a rocky bed in its short course to the sea in Bigbury Bay is **South Brent,** a typical moorland town, though its Spring Fair and pony market are of much less importance than formerly. The old weather-beaten church is in the Perpendicular and Decorated styles, with a low Norman tower.

Plymouth to Tavistock and Okehampton

The A386 Tavistock road leaves Plymouth on the north from its suburb Crownhill, running past Roborough, the Plymouth airfield, and Bickleigh. In 10 miles from the city is **Yelverton** where the moorland road strikes north-eastward across to Princetown and Two Bridges.

Two miles to the west of Yelverton is **Buckland Abbey** (N.T., *Easter to Sept., daily; in winter on Weds, Sats, and Suns, fee*), a 13th-century monastic foundation subsequently given by Henry VIII to Sir Richard Grenville, grandfather of Richard Grenville of the "Revenge" and later bought by Sir Francis Drake. It is now a naval and Devon folk museum.

From Yelverton it is five-and-a-half miles along the A386 to Tavistock.

Tavistock *(Bedford, Newmarket, Queen's Head),* with a population of just under 7,000 people, is an ancient market town set astride the river *Tavy.* Of its ancient abbey founded in the late 10th century there are few remains. In the town centre buildings of interest include the pinnacled Town Hall, 1860, with some interesting portraits, and the Church, dating mostly from the 15th century. Behind the Town Hall is the market, busy on a Friday. Tavistock's ancient Goose Fair, held on the second Wednesday of October, attracts visitors from many miles around.

North of Tavistock on a by-road is the village of **Peter Tavy,** picturesque with a Perpendicular church surrounded by lime trees and with weather-worn embattled western tower. Back on the main road is the sister village of **Mary Tavy** with a similar church with 15th-century wagon roof.

Lydford, to the west of the Okehampton road, is well known for its castle, gorge and waterfall, while it also possesses a church of some interest. The castle, of which only the keep remains on an artificial mound, was built about 1150 and as a prison had an unsavoury reputation. The church close by, mainly Perpendicular with traces of Early English work, has a Saxon granite font and a beautiful piscina.

Lydford Gorge (N.T.), a mile west of the main road, lies in a beautifully wooded ravine where the *Lyd* frets and fumes among great black boulders. The White Lady waterfall has a drop of some 90 feet.

Okehampton *(Plume of Feathers, White Hart, Okehampton Motel),* is situated between the *East* and *West Ockment* rivers which unite just below the town. The **Castle** *(daily, fee),* stands on a high rock near the Launceston road with a wide view of the valley.

South of Okehampton are **Yes Tor,** 2,027 feet, and **High Willhays,** 2,038 feet, the latter the highest peak on Dartmoor.

PLYMOUTH TO TORQUAY

From Plymouth, Torquay can be reached by several routes. The most direct road is through Ivybridge (10 miles), Bittaford (3 miles), Totnes (11 miles) and Torquay (8 miles), total 32 miles. Another route is over Dartmoor through Yelverton, Two Bridges, Moretonhampstead, Bovey and Newton Abbot (total 45 miles). Yet another is Laira Bridge, Brixton, Yealmpton, Modbury, Aveton Gifford, Kingsbridge and Totnes (total 42 miles) or even Yealmpton, Ermington, Avonwick and Totnes (total 32 miles).

Taking the Kingsbridge route provides opportunity to visit the South Hams and coast resorts to the south-west of Torquay. For convenience these places are dealt with as excursions from Salcombe and Kingsbridge.

Salcombe (Pop.: 2,420. Hotels: *Bolt Head, Marine, St. Elmo, Grafton Towers,* etc.), is built under the lee of a hill clothed in foliage on the west shore of the large Salcombe Inlet. Originally a fishing village, Salcombe later achieved fame for its fruit clippers and its shipbuilding yards. Now it is a quiet fishing and yachting centre. The **Harbour,** the glory of Salcombe, is safe, but the bar and the sunken rocks at its mouth make it somewhat dangerous and difficult to enter at night. Just beyond the *Salcombe Hotel* is the **Jetty,** the starting-point of the ferries to Portlemouth and Kingsbridge.

Kingsbridge (Pop.: 3,300. Hotels: *Buckland Tout Saints, Kingsbridge, King's Arms),* sits at the head of the Salcombe estuary within four miles of the open sea and amid magnificent scenery. A very ancient market town it retains many of its old customs and still possesses a town-crier. The town is built on a hill rising steeply from the water's edge, with the tower and spire of its Church overtopping all other buildings. Near the Church, is a short arcade known as the **Shambles,** or Butterwalk, built about 1586. The supporting granite pillars are undoubtedly of earlier date, while the upper storey was altered in 1796. The **Town Hall** is in the main street (note four-sided clock), and the Cattle Market just outside the town. There is a pleasant Promenade on the quay. **Dodbrooke,** Kingsbridge's twin town, stands on the other side of the valley. It has a venerable Perpendicular church, dedicated to St. Thomas à Becket.

KINGSBRIDGE TO DARTMOUTH

To Bolt Head, three miles south of Salcombe. The road skirts the cliff for most of the way, giving a view of the ruins of *Salcombe Castle* on an island rock, and passing *North Sands,* a little bay with an open front to the sea, then *South Sands,* a favourite picnicking and bathing spot. **Bolt Head** rises 420 feet above the sea and gives far-reaching views.

From the cliff pathway a rough road (signpost) leads to **Sharpitor.** The way winds through a wood on the hillside above South Sands past **Overbecks Museum** and **Botanical Garden** *(Apr.–Sept., Weds, Fris, Suns, fee)*. Part of the house is a youth hostel.

To Aveton Gifford, Modbury, Bigbury. It is a steep ascent from Kingsbridge to Churchstow, with its conspicuous church tower; then it is a drop to **Aveton Gifford** at the head of the estuary of the *Avon.* After a hilly walk of three-and-a-half miles, **Modbury** is reached, formerly one of the smaller centres of the Devon woollen industry. The church has a medieval spire which makes a permanent landmark.

South of Modbury is the village of **Bigbury** *(golf),* set well back from the coast, and **Bigbury-on-Sea,** on Bigbury Bay. There is a car park on the low cliffs and a fine sandy shore. Just offshore is **Burgh Island** connected by a causeway at low tide. There is a large hotel here while the *Pilchards* is an interesting old inn.

To Malborough, Hope, Thurlestone. Malborough is on the Salcombe–Kingsbridge road. The village has an old Perpendicular church with a tower and broach spire. Three miles west—passing through the hamlet of **Galmpton**—is the little village of **Hope,** famous for crabs. There are some hotels *(Cottage, Hope Cove, Grand View, Lobster Pot),* and other accommodation. Thurlestone has a good sandy beach and in the village above, the Thurlestone Golf Club and facilities for bowls and tennis.

To Portlemouth, Prawle Point, The Start. East Portlemouth is Salcombe's *vis-à-vis* on the banks of the *Salcombe* inlet and is reached by ferry. The tower of the church, like so many in this part of Devon, is a landmark on account of its elevated position. From the church the most picturesque route is by the road overlooking the Harbour to **Rickham,** proceeding along the coast-watchers' path to **Prawle Point,** which may also be approached by road. Four miles along the coast is **Start Point,** 146 feet above sea level. The permanent aerials are of the BBC transmitting station. The **Lighthouse** *(Weekday afternoons)* guards the Skerries, a dangerous bank off the coast.

KINGSBRIDGE TO DARTMOUTH

The route from Kingsbridge to Dartmouth, a distance of 15 miles, skirts the **Dodbrooke** side of the inlet, and the villages of **Charleton** (before which a creek of the Salcombe estuary is crossed), **Frogmore, Chillington,** and **Stokenham** are passed, the coast being reached at Torcross.

Torcross is on the margin of Start Bay, four miles north of Start Point. It has become popular on account of its bathing and its salt and freshwater fishing. North and south of the village are leys (or lakes), **Slapton Ley** and **Widecombe Ley,** well stocked with pike, perch, and roach.

Slapton village is about half a mile inland and has a Decorated and Perpendicular **Church,** with low tower and spire, a screen, a sanctuary ring, and notably remains of a chantry (beside the *Tower Inn*), founded by Sir Guy de Brian, who bore the standard of Edward III at the siege of Calais.

Slapton Sands comprise the northern portion of the sandy beach which extends for about seven miles to Start Point. The beach consists mainly of coarse sand mixed with shingle. Half way along the Sands at a point almost opposite the Slapton road is the granite pillar set up by the United States Army authorities and "presented to the people of the South Hams who generously left their homes and their lands to provide a battle practice area for the successful assault in Normandy in June, 1944".

Northward of the *Ley* the road ascends to the hamlet of **Strete,** and then dips down a steep hill to **Blackpool.** The road again rises to **Stoke Fleming,** with an imposing 13th-century church tower erected as a landmark for ships making for Dartmouth, which is reached in a farther two-and-a-half miles.

Dartmouth (Pop.: 7,000. Hotels: *Royal Castle, Queen's, Manor House, Dart,* etc.) is one of the most picturesque old towns in the country. Snugly situated on the hillside, just within the mouth of the *Dart,* it is beautiful at all seasons; the deep sheltered harbour provides magnificent anchorage. The **Butterwalk,** Duke Street, west of the Quay, is a row of houses built 1635–1640. Restored, they stand as a splendid example of the style of architecture evolved in the reign of Elizabeth I and her Stuart successors. The first floor of Number 6 Duke Street is now used as a **Museum**—Historic and Maritime *(weekdays, fee).* St. *Saviour's Church* is partly of Decorated architecture, with a plain embattled tower. *St. Clements Church,* the parish church, a mile north-west of the town, stands as a prominent landmark on Boone Hill.

Dartmouth Castle *(fee),* overlooks the estuary. Its remains include a round tower and a square keep with embrasures for cannon. Adjoining is the Church of St. Petrox. The nearby coves, Castle Cove, Sugary Cove and Compass Cove are all suitable for bathing. **Kingswear** *(ferries from Dartmouth),* across the river is of great antiquity. Its church stands well up overlooking the estuary. The castle dated from 1480 but has been rebuilt as a private residence.

Totnes (Pop.: 6,500. Hotels: *Royal Seven Stars, Fairseat, Chateau Bellevue),* is an old town in the *Dart* with a regular summer service of boats to and from Dartmouth. From the bridge, Fore Street rises steeply to the quaint old East Gate spanning the roadway. In Fore Street is the *Brutus Stone,* traditionally that on which Brutus of Troy first set foot in Britain. Nearby is the *museum.* The Parish *Church of St. Mary* is a grand and impressive red sandstone edifice of the 15th century, in the Perpendicular style, with a massive square tower surmounted by crocketed pinnacles. The **Guildhall** stands to the north of the church, and is mainly 16th–17th-century date. In the main hall will be seen the old stocks, a man-trap and the old bull ring; at one side is the doorway of the old lock-up. A few steps from the church, and near the **North Gate** of the town, are the well-preserved ruins of **Totnes Castle,** of red sandstone *(daily, fee).* The circular keep with 15-foot walls, occupies a lofty mound, from the top of which are extensive views.

To Dartington Hall. A walk of under two miles. The Dartington Hall estate lies in a large bend of the River Dart. The 14th-century manor-house is an interesting example of careful restoration. The estate is now a Trust with agricultural and commercial enterprises formed into several companies. Endowed departments are Dartington College of Arts, a co-educational boarding school and the Adult Education Centre. In the garden the fine trees and flowering shrubs, and the terraces overlooking the old tilt-yard are of particular interest.

To Buckfastleigh and Buckfast Abbey. Totnes is a convenient centre for Buckfastleigh, a small town with a 13th-century church, standing high up away from the town. **Buckfast Abbey** is a Saxon foundation of 1018. In 1147 the Abbey was affiliated to the Cistercian Order, to which it remained attached until the Dissolution under Henry VIII in 1539. From that time onwards the buildings were gradually dismantled. In 1882 a group of French Benedictine monks bought the place with a view to its complete restoration. The Abbey church was rebuilt by the monks themselves, was completed in 1938. In 1967 a small preparatory school was inaugurated.

Brixham (Pop.: 11,200. Hotels: *Northcliffe, Berry Head, Parkway House, Smuggler's Haunt, Quayside,* etc.), is a place of considerable historical and archaeological interest. It is divided into two parts, **Higher** and **Lower Brixham,** as they are generally shown on a map, but **Brixham Churchtown** and **Brixham Quay,** as they are called locally. The town is situated, facing north-east, about a mile-and-a-half west of Berry Head, the southern horn of Torbay. It is easily accessible by rail and road, but the best approach is by sea from Torquay. The hills rise so steeply on either side of the harbour that steps are mostly used instead of lanes to connect each terrace with that above or below.

Brixham has retained its essential character of a working harbour of fishing people. In spite of its popularity as a holiday and artistic centre, it has not commercialized its beautiful setting.

On the quay is the fish market, where auctioneers do a thriving business with piles of newly-caught fish.

The Harbour. The Brixham roadstead is well known owing to its accessibility in every state of weather, wind and tide, and for its deep water and the excellence of its anchorage. The Breakwater is 3,000 feet in length.

All Saints' Church is the parish church of Lower Brixham. Its first incumbent was the Rev. Henry Lyte, who wrote the beautiful hymns, "Praise my soul, the King of Heaven" and "Abide with me". **St. Mary's Church,** the parish church of High Brixham, is a large 14th-century building, built over and outside an earlier structure, and surmounted by an embattled tower, 103 feet high.

The **Brixham Cavern** *(fee),* in Mount Pleasant Road, leading up from Fore Street, is one of the most perfect caves in the country. Many fine stalactites and stalagmites are to be seen.

Berry Head forms the southern extremity of Torbay with magnificent views in all directions. On a clear day these extend northwards right round Torbay across Torquay to Teignmouth and north-eastwards as far as Portland Bill. To the north-west and west the heights of Dartmoor may be distinguished, while to the south Scabbacombe Head and the estuary of the Dart seem very close at hand. The **Lighthouse** on the Head has a very short stature, the lantern being quite near the ground. **St. Mary's Bay** lies below the Head. Bathing is pleasant from a shingle and sand beach.

Paignton

Bathing.—At Paignton, Preston, Goodrington, and Broadsands.

Boating.—Motor- and rowing-boats from Paignton Harbour and Beaches. Motor-boats at Goodrington Park.

Early Closing Day.—Wednesday.

Entertainments.—Theatre and Festival Hall, Cinemas, Zoo.

Ferry.—From Promenade (Goodrington Cliff Gardens) to Brixham and Torquay (summer only).

Fishing.—In Torbay, for whiting, pollock, mackerel, etc. Freshwater fishing in the rivers *Dart, Teign,* etc. Sea Anglers' Club at harbour.

Hotels.—*Redcliffe, Palace, Harwin, Grosvenor, Coverdale, Hunters Lodge, Oldway Links, Queen's, Hydro, Marine, Ocean, Middlepark, Alta Vista, Ebor Towers,* and many others.

Population.—30,289.

Post Office.—Palace Avenue.

Sports.—Bowls, tennis, cricket, boating and sailing.

Paignton is a flourishing seaside resort with a resident population of over 30,000. During July and August this population is almost doubled, and there is also an increasing number of winter visitors. Possessing fine stretches of golden sands, it is an ideal resort for family holidays.

The broad promenade is closed to all vehicles during the summer, making it an excellent strolling place. Separated from the sea only by the promenade is Paignton Green, a fine stretch of grass—ideal as a children's playground. In the Festival Hall, on the Green, seasonal shows are performed.

Huts and cabins are available for hire at Goodrington, Preston, Paignton and Broadsands. The Pier, projecting 800 feet out to sea, is the starting point of the motor boat trips. Fishing boats go out in the bay for dabs, whiting and mackerel.

The Parish Church is mainly early 15th century. Among the many features of interest are the magnificent Norman west door, the 11th-century font, the skeleton monument in the south aisle, and the exquisite Kirkham chantry.

In nearby Kirkham Street is **Kirkham House** *(daily, except Sunday mornings),* an interesting example of west country medieval domestic town architecture.

Southward from the harbour and separated from Paignton sands by Roundham Head, is **Goodrington** a most attractive bathing spot. There is a large park, terraced walks, lawns, garden, and a childrens' Peter Pan playground.

Berry Pomeroy Castle *(daily, fee)*, is a picturesque ruin at the head of a lovely glen down which the Gatcombe brook flows to join the *Dart*. The older portion of the ruin seen now—the Gatehouse with guard-room, and Lady Margaret Tower dates from the end of the 13th century. The more beautiful portion which was never completed was the work of the Seymours, to whom the property passed in the reign of Edward VI.

Torquay

Distances.—Berry Head, 10; Bovey Tracey, 12; Brixham, 9; Dartmouth, 11; Dawlish, 12; Exeter, 23; Kingsbridge, 22; Newton Abbot, 7; Plymouth, 32; Totnes, 9.

Early Closing.—Wednesday, higher part of town; Saturday, lower part of town.

Hotels.—*Palace, Grand, Cavendish, Devonshire, Rosetor, Victoria, Queen's, Abbey Lawn, Livermead House, Lincombe Hall, San Remo,* *Imperial, Palace Court, Osborne, Toorak, Templestowe, Kistor, Torbay, Belgrave, Vernon Court, Bute Court.* Many others and a great many guest houses of all grades.

Information Bureau.—At 9 Vaughan Parade.

Population.—52,000.

Post Office.—Fleet Street.

Sports.—All sports facilities available in parks and clubs. Fishing, boating, sailing, golf.

Torquay is at the northern end of Torbay. From Berry Head to Hope's Nose is a distance across the bay of rather more than four miles. The town of Torquay, facing due south, is sheltered from the east by the hills on which a greater part of it is built. The Seafront sweeps northwards from Corbyn Head, a charming view-point. Below the Head is one of the fine bathing beaches. South of Corbyn Head is the most southerly of the beaches, Livermead Sands.

Inland are the King's Gardens, with a bowling green and a large shallow pond.

Torre Abbey *(daily)*, was founded in 1196 (temp. Richard I) by Lord Brewere, who owned the barony of Tor. He richly endowed the Abbey, and bestowed it on monks of the Praemonstratensian order, founded by St. Norbert in 1120. The remains show that it was a magnificent edifice. The Abbey now contains the *Municipal Art Gallery*. The grounds are superbly laid out and have facilities for tennis, bowls and miniature golf.

The Harbour, enclosed by the Haldon and Princess Piers, embraces Inner and Outer Harbours together, a water area of over 40 acres. At the head is the Strand with shops and the bus shelter. High on the hillside is **St. John's Church** a spacious and impressive building designed by G. E. Street. The west window is by Burne-Jones. In Babbacombe Road is the **Museum** of the Torquay Natural History Society.

To Kent's Cavern *(daily, fee)*, one of the oldest recognizable human dwellings in our country. The most direct road is by way of the Babbacombe Road and Ilsham Road, the Cavern being about a mile-and-a-quarter from the Strand. The Cavern consists of two parallel caves, connected in one place, and divided into chambers. The natural ventilation of the cave is remarkably good, and the temperature remains constant at 52 degrees F. Flood-lights enhance the beauty of the colouring, and has led to the development of small ferns, which contrive to exist on the limestone wall. Stalactites of all sizes hang from the roof.

To Cockington the western portion of Greater Torquay, long beloved by artists and photographers. The best approach is along Cockington Lane, which branches at right-angles from the main road to Paignton, about 300 yards beyond Corbyn Head. The Forge, a quaint old building, has been committed to canvas times without number. Nearby is the thatched and timber-fronted lodge from which a drive leads to *Cockington Court*, the gracious 16th-century manor house, now a restaurant.

To Anstey's Cove and Bishop's Walk. The walk over Warberry Hill (448 feet above sea-level and the apex of Torquay) involves a preliminary clamber, but gives grand views of

161

TORQUAY–BABBACOMBE–WATCOMBE

Torquay and its surroundings, and towards Dartmoor one sees Rippon Tor and the rocks of Haytor. **Anstey's Cove** is situated at the end of a deep ferny combe and sheltered by lofty cliffs. **Bishop's Walk** is so named because it was the favourite walk of Henry Phillpotts, who, although Bishop of Exeter, preferred to establish his palace near Torquay; the palace has now become the *Palace Hotel*.

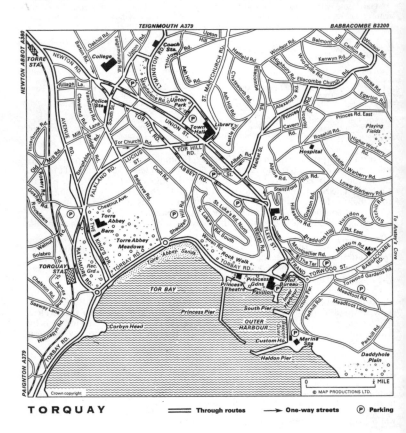

TORQUAY　　　━━━ **Through routes**　　━▶ **One-way streets**　　Ⓟ **Parking**

Babbacombe adjoins Torquay on the north. Few spots charm a visitor more than Babbacombe Downs, a breezy plateau perched so high that on a clear day Portland Bill— full 40 miles away—may be seen. The Downs are laid out with public gardens, promenade, shelters, and concert hall; the beach far below can be reached by the steep descent of Beach Road, at the foot of which is a stone jetty where boats from Torquay and Teignmouth call. From the other end of the Downs, a Cliff Railway *(daily 10 to 6 or later)*, or alternatively a road with hairpin bends, descends to **Oddicombe Beach.**

Watcombe may be reached by bus from the Strand or Castle Circus to Easterfield Lane with a half-mile walk to the cliff path. Or by bus to St. Marychurch, and thence by Petitor

162

Road and the Cliff Path. Watcombe Beach, pretty and secluded, is at the foot of the **Valley of Rocks,** with the famous **Giant Rock** towering at the head of the combe.

Maidencombe, a mile beyond Watcombe, is reached by road (bus service) to Maidencombe Cross, then a right turn down Sheep Hill to the secluded hamlet nestling at the foot of this fine unspoilt valley or combe. The hamlet contains a fine old specimen of the rare Judas tree. A steep footpath leads down to the sheltered beach.

To Marldon and Compton. From Cockington a road runs uphill from the Forge, leaving the church and manor-house on the right. In about one-and-a-half miles a road junction known as Five Lanes is reached, and from there the road on the right leads to the village of Marldon where the church has a massive embattled tower and monuments of the Gilbert family. **Compton Castle** (N.T., *Mons, Weds, Thurs, Apr.–Oct., fee),* one of the finest remaining examples of a fortified manor-house, was built about 1329 by Geoffrey Gilbert, Member for Totnes in the Parliament of 1326.

Newton Abbot (Pop.: 18,630. Hotels: *Globe, Queen's, Bradley, White Hart),* is a thriving market town with various light industries, pottery and clay-pit workings. The town stands in the beautiful vale of the river *Lemon,* which flows into the *Teign. Forde House,* a late Tudor manor-house of historic interest, lies to the east of the railway. **Wolborough Church** is prettily situated on a slope, from which may be seen some of the tors of Dartmoor. Opposite the lych gate is a good path which, passing the *Mackrell Almshouses,* leads to Wolborough Street and the centre of the town, conspicuous objects of which are the Market Place and **St. Leonard's Tower,** about 60 feet high, all that was spared in the demolition of the Church of St. Leonard in 1834. **Highweek Church,** on a commanding site, is a Perpendicular building dating from the early 15th century. The modern **Church of St. Mary,** at Abbotsbury, contains some fittings from the former chapel-of-ease of St. Mary in Highweek Street. The Technical Schools and Public Library form a fine block at the corner of Highweek and Market Streets. A short distance from Highweek is the *Seale-Hayne Agricultural College,* a beautifully situated and well-equipped centre of agricultural education and research.

Bradley Manor House (N.T., *Weds in summer, fee),* reached by a pleasant walk of half-a-mile along the bank of the *Lemon,* is one of the oldest inhabited houses in Devon. Mostly 15th century, and incorporating an earlier house, this home is a good specimen of a small manor-house of the West Country type.

TORQUAY TO EXETER

The coast road A379 runs through Watcombe, past Maidencombe and Labrador. Inland on the left is **Stoke-in-Teignhead,** a picturesque agricultural village with a 14th-century church. The coast road now falls to Shaldon with Ness Point on the Ness estate away on the right.

Shaldon, municipally part of Teignmouth, has a shelving beach of shingle and red sand and pleasantly situated houses. The bridge and a ferry connect with Teignmouth.

Teignmouth (Pop.: 12,500. Hotels: *Royal, Beach, London, Portland,* etc.), is situated on the broad sandy estuary of the *Teign.* The chief attractions are its sea front, the river, and the varied beauties of the surrounding country. Facing the sea is the **Den,** six acres of green turf laid out with flower beds. At the northern end is the Pavilion and bowling green, and towards the southern end putting and tennis courts. A well-stocked Aquarium is a further attraction.

Dawlish (Pop.: 7,800. Hotels: *Charlton House, Brooklands, Elizabeth,* etc.), is an attractive small resort three-and-a-half miles north of Teignmouth. North and south, towering red cliffs sentinel the town, and between them the parade, pleasant at any season. A feature of Dawlish is the neatly kept **Lawn,** with its trim gardens, between the Strand and the "Brook"—as the Dawlish Water is locally called.

Inland is the ancient church whose first recorded vicar was Capelanus in 1272. Bounded by a sea wall and the railway the beach of reddish sand extends from Boat Cove to Langstone Cliffs.

Beyond Langstone is the **Warren**, a low, sandy bar almost blocking the mouth of the *Exe,* and noted for its wild bird life and for certain rare flowers. A mile-and-a-half-long stretch of fine, sandy beach, washed by the tide, offers safe bathing, boating and relaxation. Near at hand is an amusement centre.

North of the Warren along the west bank of the *Exe* is **Starcross** from which a ferry crosses the *Exe* to Exmouth.

Kenton possesses a church built in the reign of Edward III, with pinnacled buttresses and tall red sandstone tower. The magnificent rood screen is believed to date from 1455. From Kenton it is a pleasant walk over the hill north-west of the church and up the valley to **Kenn,** where is an almost equally noteworthy church.

Powderham Castle *(daily except Sats, Apr.–early Sept., fee)* is the beautiful country seat of the Earls of Devon. The oldest parts date from the end of the 14th century. The park is of great extent, and is thickly planted with oaks; on its highest ground is a tower, called the Belvedere, erected in 1773. The Church is a 15th-century building.

From Powderham it is an easy drive of five miles to **Exminster,** a large village, the history of which goes back to Saxon times.

Exeter (Pop.: 93,000. Hotels: *Rougemont, Great Western, Royal Clarence, Queen's, Imperial, White Hart,* etc.), is an ancient and fascinating city. In the days of the Romans, and later under the Saxons, it was a frontier outpost against the western Celts. Later came the Norman Castle, the Cathedral, the Guildhall and other medieval buildings, and the steady growth of the city up to our times. In 1942 air raids inflicted widespread destruction. Much of great beauty and interest was lost, while the main shopping centre was almost wiped out. Much has been rebuilt in a style which is spacious and modern. An inner by-pass has done much to relieve traffic congestion.

Those spending only a short time in Exeter should make a point of visiting the Cathedral, St. Nicholas Priory, the Guildhall, the Castle, and Northernhay, with a glance at the old walls and some of the medieval parish churches.

The Cathedral. The best exterior view of the Cathedral is perhaps that which is obtained from the Cathedral yard, or Close. The Norman Towers are the most noticeable features. They are similar in general form, but differ in detail. The north tower contains an ancient astronomical Clock. The south tower contains 13 of the Cathedral Bells. They are the second heaviest peal in England, and very rich in tone. In the north tower hangs the Peter bell weighing over six tons.

The West Front consists of three storeys. The basement, or screen, containing the three portals, is entirely covered with niches filled with statues; above and behind this is the west wall of the nave, in which is a magnificent window, and above this, behind the parapet, is the gable of the nave, containing a window of much smaller dimensions. On the right of the centre entrance is the tiny chapel built by Bishop Grandisson as his mortuary chapel.

The Interior. The Cathedral consists of a long nave, with two aisles of the same length; north and south transepts under the towers; and, at its eastern end, the noble Choir and aisles. The Lady Chapel, and ten other Chapels, connect with the interior at various points.

The Nave. The great breadth and length, the rich windows, the uniformity of architecture, the beauty, excellence, and variety of every detail, and, above all, the form and plan of the vaulting, uninterrupted throughout the whole length of the Cathedral, are unrivalled in England. The roof is supported on each side upon an arcade of seven pillars and arches. Between every two arches is a rich corbel, composed of figures and foliage, of which no two are alike. They support slender reeded columns of stone, with highly decorated and studiously diversified capitals. This roof, there being no intervening central tower or lantern, is continued across the transept to the eastern extremity of the Choir in one unbroken line, and is the longest known stone vaulting in the Pointed style of architecture.

Projecting from the north wall of the nave is the **Minstrels' Gallery.**

From about here or perhaps a little higher up is the best view of the great **West Window,** with its magnificent 14th-century tracery. The glass was all destroyed in the raid of 1942 but has been replaced.

At the north-west angle of the nave, immediately to the left of the entrance door, is the **Chapel of St. Edmund the Martyr,** used as the chapel of the Devonshire Regiment.

In the south aisle is the **Font** of Sicilian marble. On the south wall, a little to the west of this, hangs the Sledge Flag carried by Captain Scott on his first expedition to the Antarctic, and a little farther east a five-light window commemorates men of Devon who died in South Africa, 1899 to 1902; 467 in all. Below the window are tablets to commanders who earned fame in the same campaign—General Buller, Major-General Kekewich, defender of Kimberley.

The **Trancepts** form the lowest stages of the old Norman towers, a feature shared by no other cathedral in England. **St. Paul's Chapel** (the *Children's Chapel*) is to the east of the north transept and **St. John the Baptist's** to the east of the south. Beneath the clock in the north transept is the **Chantry Chapel of William Sylke,** a precentor of the Cathedral. Nearby are the old works of the clock.

The **Choir Screen** erected by Bishop Stapledon, who died in 1326, is a magnificent example of the style which then prevailed, and is, as a screen, almost unrivalled in England.

The Choir. In the centre of the screen is the door to the Choir. From it the very fine **East Window** may be seen to advantage. It is a nine-light Perpendicular replacement (1391) of the original window.

Probably the most imposing feature of the Choir is the **Bishop's Throne,** of carved oak and with a pyramidal canopy of open carving rising nearly to the height of the vaulting, 52 feet. Round the base are modern paintings of the four Bishops who did most to make the Cathedral what it is. The oak Stalls and Pulpit are modern, and elaborately carved with Decorated work.

On the north of the High Altar is the tomb of *Bishop Stapledon* (*d.* 1326) who did so much to beautify the Choir. The Bishop was murdered in Cheapside on account of his partisanship of Edward II. The table tomb near, with the indent of a lost brass on it, commemorates Bishop Lacy (*d.* 1455).

Beyond the Choir and Reredos is the **Lady Chapel,** thought to cover the site of Leofric's Saxon monastic church; it affords a burial place for several of the Bishops of Exeter.

The **Cloisters** were originally built in a quadrangle south of the Cathedral. They were destroyed during the Commonwealth, and only a portion, at the south-east angle, was rebuilt in 1887. The Cloister Room gives access to the old library above, which houses the Capitular Archives and Precentor Cook's Collection *(admission on application to new Cathedral Library).*

The **Chapter House** *(shown only on application to the Vergers),* was built by Bishop Bruere (1224–1244) in Early English style of architecture, but the walls were heightened and the present Perpendicular windows and roof placed there nearly two centuries later.

The **Bishop's Palace,** to the south-east, stands in beautiful grounds which command the best view of the south side of the Cathedral. Here is the new Cathedral Library open to students Monday to Friday.

The quaint little **St. Martin's Church** was consecrated in 1065, but almost completely rebuilt in the 15th century. The oak barrel-vaulted roof, the west window, font, Jacobean altar rails and west gallery are all of note.

The **Priory of St. Nicholas** *(Apr.–Sept., weekdays),* in The Mint, is possibly the finest surviving English example of a monastic guest house.

The **Guildhall** was rebuilt in 1330 and restored about a century later. It is thought the oldest municipal building in England. The Elizabethan portico which projects across the footway was added in 1595.

Rougemont Castle adjoining Northernhay, close to the Central Station, and approached from High Street by way of Castle Street, was built by the Conqueror, and probably received its name from the red sandstone of which it was composed. The ancient gateway has been restored, and beyond it is the old castle yard. Round the castle yard run the ramparts, on the two outer sides forming part of the old City Wall.

High Street is the chief street of the city. New Bridge Street, Fore Street, High Stret, East Gate, Sidwell Street, and Tiverton Road, extend from the Exe Bridge to the north-eastern suburbs of Exeter and may have been the main Roman road.

The centre of Roman Exeter, where North Street and South Street join High Street, was formerly known as the Carfax (Lat. *quadrifurcus*) or cross-roads. The western extension of High Street originally bore left at the Guildhall and ran down Stepcote Hill to the river *Exe*. The old waterfront is worth a visit, with its *Custom House* dated 1681, and containing fine ceilings and a Charles II coat-of-arms.

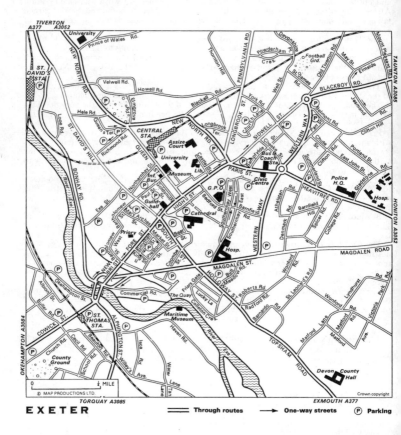

EXETER

Through routes → One-way streets ⓟ Parking

Across Exe Bridge, is the **Church of St. Thomas,** whose vicar in 1549 was hanged on the tower as a rebel.

In West Street is the parish church of **St. Mary's Steps,** founded in the 12th century. Outside the south face of the tower are clock jacks which strike the hour and quarters. Close by the church some 15th-century merchants' houses have been preserved and restored. Two stand at the foot of **Stepcote Hill,** which in medieval times was the main street into the city from the west. The third, thought to be one of the oldest timber-framed houses in Europe, was removed bodily in 1961 from its site in Edmund Street 300 feet up the slope to its present position on the corner of West Street. Adjacent to this house are the remains of the West Gate, and part of the west wall of the city.

The **Royal Albert Memorial Museum and Art Gallery** houses one of the largest collections in the region with fine paintings and water-colours, collections of costumes, silver and glass, and sections on ethnography, foreign archaeology and natural history.

The Underground Passages. A unique feature in Exeter is the complex of medieval underground water courses from which the City was supplied with wholesome water from the Well of St. Sidwella outside the City Walls. Open most afternoons in summer and on Saturdays in winter or by arrangement with the Director of Museums and Art Gallery.

The **City Library** is in Castle Street. It was burnt out in the war and a new building was opened in 1965. The search rooms of the City Record Office adjoin.

The University. Developing from the University College of the South West and obtaining full university status in 1955, the University now caters for some 3,300 students. Although the original College Building, in Gandy Street in the city centre, still houses some departments most of the University has moved to the 270-acre Streatham Estate, a wooded site about one mile to the north of the city centre.

EXETER TO LYME REGIS

About five miles down-river from Exeter is **Topsham,** formerly an important seaport and now incorporated in the city. From Topsham the eastern bank of the *Exe* can be followed via Exford, Exton and Lympstone to Exmouth.

Exmouth (Pop.: 22,000. Hotels: *Imperial, Devoncourt, Grand, Cavendish,* etc.), stands at the mouth of the *Exe* where the sea sweeps in round Straight Point, strewing the shore with yellowish sand that threatens at times to block the estuary. It is popular as a "family holiday" resort, with an equable climate, extensive sands, and fine sea front. On the broad, well-kept Esplanade is a large Concert Pavilion in front of which are the Beach Gardens. On the landward side of the Esplanade are the Madeira and Plantation Walks forming part of an almost continuous background of green slopes, wooded cliffs, gardens and sports fields. The **Maer,** a sandy, tussocky stretch with a path sloping up towards Orcombe, is one of Exmouth's greatest attractions. This path gives glorious views. It can be followed over fields close to the cliff and across the peninsula of Straight Point.

To Withycombe and St. John-in-the-Wilderness, rather less than three miles by way of Withycombe Raleigh. At Bystock, a mile-and-a-half to the north-east, is the Church of St. John-in-the-Wilderness.

To Littleham, some two miles east of Exmouth by the cliff path or by way of Douglas Avenue. The church is the ancient parish Church of Exmouth. Among the memorial tablets is one in the chantry chapel to the memory of Lady Nelson, wife of the hero of Trafalgar. She lived for many years at the Beacon, Exmouth.

To Lympstone. The route is by the Exeter Road. In one-and-a-half miles is Courtlands toll-house (bus stop), where Summer Lane on the right leads past **À-la-Ronde** a circular house built in 1798 by two maiden ladies. There are interesting prints, engravings, silhouettes and samplers. A little higher up the lane a path on the right leads across an adjoining field to the almshouses and chapel of **Point-in View,** commanding views of great beauty.

Lympstone is a picturesque village about two miles north of Exmouth, just off the main road to Exeter. One long straggling street leads down to the waterside. Lympstone's recreation ground, the Cliff Field, now belonging to the National Trust, commands a beautiful prospect to the west over the river.

North of Lympstone is Woodbury, a picturesque village of cob-walled and thatched cottages. The Church of St. Swithin dates back to the 13th century. About a mile east of the village is *Woodbury Castle,* the name given to a series of earthworks of British origin.

Budleigh Salterton (Pop.: 4,000. Hotels: *Rosemullion, Rolle, Otterbourne, Links-Pinewood*, etc.), lies near the mouth of the *Otter*, a sparkling trout stream. The beach of large pebbles about two miles in extent is open to the Channel. The town has developed from a long street sloping gently from Knowle Hill down to the sea. By the side of the street flows a small stream, which gives the town a quaint appearance, not lessened by the little bridges that span it to give access to the houses. The Marine Parade slopes up eastwards to a little red sandstone bluff overlooking the saltings and the marshy vale of the *Otter*. From the car park, just beyond the War Memorial, a footpath on the left leads up the valley and by bridge across the river to Otterton. Westward from the Parade a broad path climbs the cliff, passing at the end of the houses the open space known as Jubilee Park. Rounding Sherbrooke Chine, a break in the cliffs, the path eventually reaches **Westdown Beacon,** one of the most delightful points of vantage for sea views in this part of Devon.

To East Budleigh, a typical Devon village two miles north of Budleigh Salterton. The oldest part of the Church—the north aisle—is probably 13th century. **Hayes Barton** *(June–mid-Sept., weekdays, fee)*, a mile west, was the birthplace of Sir Walter Raleigh *c.* 1552.

To Otterton. Eastward from East Budleigh is Otterton, a picturesque village, with many "cob" cottages and a fine chestnut grove.

To Bicton, less than a mile north of East Budleigh. About half-way, at four cross-roads, is a curious brick obelisk, its sides inscribed with scriptural texts. Nearby is Bicton Park. **Bicton Gardens** *(daily in summer)*, were laid out in 1735 to designs of Le Notre who planned the gardens at Versailles. There is a Pinetum, an 18-inch narrow gauge railway and a Countryside Museum.

Sidmouth (Pop.: 12,200. Hotels: *Belmont, Victoria, Bedford, Royal York*, etc.), is an attractive and dignified town which has preserved much of its 19th-century architecture. The beach is shingle, with sand at low tide and beyond Chit Rocks. The Esplanade is about a third of a mile in length and overlooks the bathing beach. Westward from the Esplanade are the Connaught Gardens. Adjoining them is Jacob's Ladder bathing beach, a sandy expanse where children may safely bathe and play. The coastal footpath leads to Peak Hill which shelters the Royal Glen, the former home of Queen Victoria. Abutting on the Esplanade is the Cricket Ground, and also splendid croquet lawns and tennis courts. At the eastern end of the Esplanade is the ornamental Alma Bridge, beneath which the river *Sid* trickles down to the sea. Salcombe Hill (500 feet) is a fine viewpoint.

Branscombe is a scattered village of picturesque cottages and interesting houses. It lies in a narrow valley, the houses nestling in several wooded combes, and sheltered to the east and west by towering chalk cliffs. The upper village with many old thatched cottages, slopes along the side of the winding valley towards the old Church, just below which is a picturesque smithy. Opposite is the Old Bakery. A quarter-mile lower down, the lower village lies where the valley curves seaward. The Church is of great age, and beloved by antiquaries.

Beer is a straggling village street, a gurgling streamlet flowing down first one gutter, then the other, descending almost to the beach, terminating in a small open space. On one side of the enclosure is a way to the beach with its nets and fishing boats, and on the other a path curves round to the cliff and a minature promenade overlooking the bathing-tents.

Seaton (Pop. 4,000. Hotels: *Royal Clarence, Bay, Esplanade*, etc.), is a pleasant somewhat retiring small resort at the mouth of the *Axe*, with a shingle beach. The Esplanade extends from the Red Haven Cliff near the river mouth to the foot of the White Cliff near Beer.

The western end of the Esplanade runs below rising cliffs on which is *Seahill*, a popular sports ground, with tennis courts, bowling greens and miniature golf courses.

To Ladram Bay. From the west end of the Esplanade at Sidmouth via Peak Hill the cliffs can be followed most of the way to Ladram, where the action of the waves on the red sandstone has detached enormous blocks from the cliffs.

To Ottery St. Mary, six miles to the north east, via Bowd, a pleasant town with a population of about 4,500 and the birthplace of the poet Coleridge. The Church is the glory of the town and of the surrounding country. There are some pleasant Georgian houses east and north of the churchyard and several interesting houses in the neighbourhood. A mile north-west of Ottery is **Cadhay** *(mid-July–Sept., Weds., Thurs, Bank Hol. Suns, and Mons)*, a fine specimen of Elizabethan domestic architecture.

Sidford has a modern church, but its most notable building is Porch House, dated 1574, at which, it is said, the fugitive Charles II found refuge after the battle of Worcester. **Sidbury,** a mile farther northward, is a typical Devon village. The very interesting church has a Norman tower. West of the village are the remains of a British camp known as *Sidbury Castle.*

To Colyford and Colyton. Two miles to the north of Seaton, on a sparkling tributary of the *Axe* is the village of Colyford. It was created a borough *c.* 1231 and there was a bridge over the *Coly* here in 1254. A mile farther north is **Colyton,** an even older foundation, for it is recorded as a Saxon settlement before A.D. 700. It stands by the *Coly* near its junction with the *Axe.* The town clusters round the fine old church of St. Andrew.

Honiton consists mainly of one long street along which are a number of pleasant Georgian houses. A weekly market is held here and the local industries are lace and pottery.

Between Seaton and Lyme Regis lies four miles of tumbled, broken ground known as the Landslip. Most is now covered with trees, bushes and turf. A path runs through from end to end, but note that the only ways into and out of the Landslip are at the ends.

Lyme Regis (Pop.; 3,500. Hotels: *Royal Lion, Alexandra, Three Cups,* etc.) is a picturesque little town that occupies a valley running steeply down to the sea about six miles east of Seaton. There is a car park at the foot of the main street and adjacent to the Parade—the only level promenade in the town unless one includes the picturesque stone pier known as the **Cobb** enclosing the harbour. The **church** was built in 1500 but shows part of an earlier structure. Owing to the steepness of the hillside, the floor is on three levels. Of interest in the town are the **Museum** with relics of Monmouth's Rebellion and the quaint **Peek Memorial Chapel** once a stable.

LYME REGIS TO BRIDGWATER

The way is through **Uplyme** to the A35 and **Axminster,** a town long famous for carpets. It is also an important market centre for a large rural area. It has an interesting church with a Norman doorway and much 13th-century work. **Chad** is a small town across the Somerset border seven miles north of Axminster. It has a notable Town Hall and a fine old Grammar School dating from 1583. Within the church are several interesting monuments.

Taunton (Pop.: 37,370. Hotels: *Castle, County, Creech Castle, George,* etc.) is the county town and a busy market and business centre set in the rich vale of Taunton Deane with the little river *Tone* flowing through its centre. These are two fine parish churches and the ruins of a castle built about 1100. Eleven miles north-east on the A38 is Bridgwater.

The River Thames

from London to the Source

The navigation of the *Thames* is, generally speaking, free to everyone; so too are the towpaths, and also the fishing as far up-stream as Staines. Most of the riverside land and property, however, is private and, beyond the freedom of the towpath, these rights must be respected. The *Thames* still follows its old course from the source to the sea, running a total length of 210 miles. It rises at Thames Head in Trewsbury Mead in the parish of Coates in Gloucestershire, about three miles from Cirencester. There are 16 principal tributaries, these being the *Churn, Cole* and *Coln*, above Lechlade; the *Windrush* and *Evenlode*, between Lechlade and Oxford; the *Cherwell, Ock, Thame* and *Pang* between Oxford and Reading; the *Kennet, Loddon, Wye* and *Colne* between Reading and Staines; and the *Bourne, Wey* and *Mole*, between Staines and Teddington. In the river above Teddington there are 44 lock installations. At Sunbury there are two locks and at Teddington three locks. A fourth lock is on the *Kennet* at Reading. Maintenance of an adequate level of water is made possible by 138 weirs. From its source to Teddington jurisdiction of the river is the responsibility of the Thames Conservancy whose headquarters are at Nugent House, Vastern Road, Reading. Below Teddington the Port of London exercise control (Port of London Authority, Trinity Square, London E.C.3).

PUTNEY TO KINGSTON

The stretch of the river from Putney Bridge to Hammersmith Bridge is the heart of London's boat racing, and many rowing clubs, great and small, have their headquarters here. Also, the *Oxford and Cambridge Boat Race* is rowed annually from Putney to Mortlake. From the south side of Putney Bridge a towpath, running alternately on either bank, extends for over a hundred miles to Lechlade. On the northern side of the bridge is *Fulham Palace*, the official residence of the Bishop of London. Beyond is *Fulham Football Ground*.

From the boat houses at Putney, the towpath passes *Barn Elms Park*, now playing fields. Barn Elms mansion was the residence of Walsingham, State Secretary to Elizabeth I, who often visited him here. Later visitors were Evelyn, Pepys, Cowley, Cowper, Fielding and Handel. The site is now occupied by the *Ranelagh Club*. The towpath then skirts reservoirs to *Hammersmith Suspension Bridge*, opened in 1887. **Hammersmith,** a busy suburb of London, is the headquarters of several boating organisations. At **Chiswick** is **Hogarth House** *(daily, fee)* containing interesting mementoes of the artist. The grounds of Chiswick House are now a public park. Chiswick Mall has delightful old houses, and a picturesque mid-stream island. **Mortlake** and **Strand-on-the-Green** were once riverside villages, but now consist mainly of blocks of flats. Kew Bridge, officially styled *Edward VII Bridge,* was opened in 1903. The triple island is *Brentford Ait.* The Surrey towpath borders **Kew Gardens** for about a mile. As the Royal Botanic Gardens and Arboretum the gardens cover nearly 300 acres, and combine the attractions of a museum, park and formal gardens *(daily, fee).* **Brentford,** across the river, has a monument on the site of the old *ford,* commemorating historical events from 54 B.C. Facing Kew Gardens is **Syon House** *(certain times, fee)* a residence of the Duke of Northumberland and the interior of which is a fine example of the work of Robert Adam. Nearby is the Syon Park **Garden Centre** which includes a Great Conservatory, an aviary and aquarium and other attractions. Here too is a museum of old London buses, trams and other transport. In *Old Deer Park* adjoining Kew Gardens is *Kew Observatory.* Richmond Lock only operates at low tide.

Richmond-upon-Thames *(Richmond Gate, Richmond Hill, Ivy Hall)* is a popular resort. The towpath has been converted to a promenade and fine gardens created. The graceful bridge connects with **Twickenham.** Near the top of Richmond Hill a fine Terrace gives extensive views of the Thames Valley. At the highest point of the hill is the *Star and Garter Home* for severely disabled service men. Adjoining is **Richmond Park,** 2,400 acres in extent and ten miles in circumference. Large herds of deer roam the park, which was first enclosed by Charles I. *White Lodge* was the early home of Queen Mary, and the birthplace of the late Duke of Windsor. *Pembroke Lodge,* once the seat of Lord John Russell, and now a restaurant, has fine gardens open to the public. There are two golf courses and a polo field.

From Richmond to Kingston is a popular reach of the river extending for four-and-a-half miles. A ferry to the Middlesex bank is available at *Marble Hill.* The mansion at Marble Hill was built by George II for Mrs. Howard in 1723. At *York House* in **Twickenham** Queen Anne was born in 1664: the building now serves as the Town Hall. On the opposite bank is **Ham House** *(daily except Mons),* a fine Jacobean building now furnished and maintained by the Victoria and Albert Museum. In the 18th century Twickenham was a country resort for the aristocracy, painters and writers. Horace Walpole's mansion at *Strawberry Hill* was famous. At **Teddington** the *Thames* ceases to be tidal, and three locks are needed to cope with the heavy traffic. The *National Physical Laboratory,* adjoining *Bushy Park,* is one of the largest State laboratories in the world. The one-and-a-half miles reach from Teddington to Kingston is extremely attractive, with riverside villas, boat houses, gardens, and *Steven's Ait,* an island with good moorings for picnic parties.

KINGSTON TO WINDSOR

Kingston upon Thames is a thriving community with historic links dating from Saxon times. Near the modern *Guildhall* and the 12th-century *Clattern Bridge* is the famous *Coronation Stone*—traditionally that on which seven Saxon kings sat for their coronations in the 10th century. Other buildings of interest are the *Market House* (1706); the restored 14th-century *Church*; and *Cleave's Almshouses.* The *Lovekyn Chapel,* founded in 1309, is now used as a library by Kingston Grammar School. From the river, little is seen of the town, except the towpath, which is bordered by gardens and a promenade. Kingston Bridge, with five graceful arches, was opened in 1828. The original wooden bridge of 1219, replacing the ancient ford, was the first to be built above London. From Kingston there are daily river excursions during the summer between Kingston Pier and Oxford

(Folly Bridge). Passengers may board the steamers at any lock or regular stopping place. Boats may be hired, and there is an annual Regatta.

On the Middlesex side of the bridge is **Hampton Wick.** On the Surrey side, the large residential district of **Surbiton** adjoins Kingston, and above Surbiton is **Thames Ditton,** a popular mooring place. Opposite is the *Home Park* and the riverside walk of *Hampton Court Park*. **Hampton Court Palace** and its beautiful gardens are open daily. In the Palace are fine pictures and tapestries, and the *Great Gatehouse* and *Clock Court* of the original building. Henry VIII and many subsequent monarchs have resided in the Palace. Adjacent is Bushy Park—noted for its deer and fine Chestnut Avenue, and extending to Teddington and Hampton. Below Hampton Court Bridge the river *Mole* enters the *Thames. Molesey Lock* is the second largest on the river. Above *Tagg's Island* is **Hampton** with Garrick's Villa and Garrick's Ait. Between Hampton and **Sunbury,** reservoirs line the banks, with *Sunbury Lock* a prominent feature. In one-and-a-half miles, *Walton Bridge* crosses the river, which then winds its way past *Lower Halliford* to **Shepperton,** where is a fine riverside manor house, and a picturesque square with an ancient church. Into the back water of Shepperton Lock flows the river *Wey*. Two miles upstream is **Chertsey** with a bridge and a lock. An abbey founded in 666 once stood on the island where the abbey stream ran into the *Thames.* Here the body of Henry VI rested for two years on its way from St. Pauls to Windsor. Beyond **Laleham** is **Penton Hook** with a lock and marina.

At **Staines** the Romans had a crossing on their road from London to the west. It was probably a ford or simple bridge of logs. Now there are two modern bridges. On the old Middlesex–Buckinghamshire boundary is the famous *London Stone* erected in 1285 and marking the former limit of the jurisdiction of the City of London and the rights of the City Corporation in the *Thames.* Today it has a significance for anglers in that below the stone fishing is free, but private to landowners above. In the Staines area there are large and important reservoirs.

From Bell Weir Lock the river flows through the meadows of **Runnymede** (N.T.), the historic site of the signing of Magna Carta in 1215. In the meadows is the *Magna Carta Memorial* presented by the American Bar Association and, on the hill above, the *Memorial to Air Forces of the Commonwealth*. The well-known *Bells of Ouzeley* stands at the county boundary of Surrey and Berkshire, and a ferry connects the busy Windsor–Staines road with **Wraysbury** on the Buckinghamshire side. Half-a-mile upstream is old Windsor Lock and, beyond, the Albert Bridge marks the beginning of **Windsor Home Park.** At **Datchet** the Victoria Bridge connects the village with Windsor. The village of Old Windsor on the Staines road was a seat of the Saxon kings. Romney Lock is famous for water pageants and for the annual "Swan-upping" ceremony when the young cygnets on the river are counted or marked. From the towpath a promenade leads to Windsor Bridge.

Windsor (Pop.: 30,100. Hotels: *Castle, Old House, Harte and Garter, Royal Adelaide*) was made a Royal Borough in 1922 but is an ancient town having received its charter from Edward I in 1277. The Guildhall completed by Sir Christopher Wren and the Church with carvings by Grinling Gibbons are of interest. Most famous building however is—

Windsor Castle *(in absence of the Court, daily, fee)*. The castle, famous as the residence of the British Sovereign, was founded by William the Conqueror. Originally in wood, it was continued in stone by Henry II, and has been extended and altered by subsequent monarchs. It encloses 13 acres and is the largest castle in England. There are three main parts—the *Lower Ward,* in which are St. George's Chapel, the Albert Memorial Chapel, the Horseshoe Cloisters, and the residences of the Knights of Windsor; the *Upper Ward* with State Apartments, private apartments, and a south wing where guests are accommodated. Between these is the *Middle Ward* with the massive Round Tower, from the summit of which are magnificent views.

The main entrance is through Henry VIII's Gateway (1511) to the beautiful *St. George's Chapel*, begun by Edward IV and completed by Henry VIII. In the richly decorated choir are the stalls of the Knights of the Garter. A subterranean passage leads to the *Royal Tomb House*. The Albert Memorial Chapel, at one time presented to Cardinal Wolsey, was restored by Queen Victoria in memory of the Prince Consort. The *State Apartments*, in which

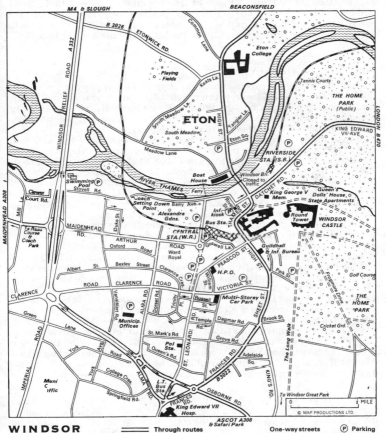

WINDSOR ═══ Through routes　　One-way streets　　Ⓟ Parking

foreign rulers visiting Her Majesty are accommodated, are beautifully furnished. Much of the carving was done by Grinling Gibbons, and there are pictures by Rubens, Rembrandt, Van Dyck and others. The *Waterloo Chamber*, used for banquets and theatrical performances, has portraits associated with Napoleon. Near the State Apartments is *Queen Mary's Dolls' House*, designed by Sir Edward Lutyens on the scale of one inch to the foot.

The **Home Park** of 500 acres adjoining the Castle contains *Frogmore House* and the *Royal Mausoleum* where rest the bodies of Queen Victoria and the

Prince Consort. To the south, **Windsor Great Park** of 2,000 acres, extends from the Castle to *Snow Hill,* on which is the Copper Horse, an equestrian statue of George III. Beyond the *Long Walk* is Royal Lodge, the private home of the Queen Mother. **Virginia Water** at the southern end of the Great Park, has an artificial lake more than one-and-a-half miles in length.

Eton, across Windsor Bridge, is famous for **Eton College** *(guided tours in summer)* founded by Henry VI in 1440. The beautiful *Chapel* has 15th-century wall-paintings; the *Cloisters* date from 1443; and the *Dining Hall* from 1450. The School has more than 1,100 pupils, and is noted for its "Wall Game" and for its aquatic festivals on Speech Day, held on the Saturday nearest to 4th June.

WINDSOR TO HENLEY

From the bridge, the two-mile reach to *Boveney Lock* is popular for rowing. On the Berkshire side is **Clewer,** with a restored Norman church. The mill stream cuts off an island on which is the *Windsor Race Course.* Beyond, the beautiful grounds of castellated Oakley Court border the river, which is next divided by a series of islands. Of these *Monkey Island* is a popular resort.

Beyond the modern road bridge is Bray lock. **Bray** *(ferry)* is a charming village, popular with boating parties. The celebrated Vicar of Bray adjusted his religion three times to retain the living of Bray Church, which dates from about 1293 and has fine brasses and monuments. The picturesque *Jesus Hospital,* founded 1627, houses 26 elderly residents. Beyond Brunel's railway bridge and Maidenhead bridge of 13 arches, built in 1772, we reach Maidenhead, with Taplow on the opposite bank. **Maidenhead** (Pop.: 47,220) is an excellent centre for excursions, and begins a popular and beautiful reach of the *Thames.* The town received its first charter in 1582, and the attractive almshouses near the bridge were founded in 1659. From Taplow a road via **Burnham** leads to the woods of *Burnham Beeches.*

The charming *Boulter's Lock* is one of the longest and deepest on the *Thames,* and the river front to *Cookham Lock* is surpassingly beautiful, with the lovely woods of the **Cliveden** estate (N.T.) and *Dropmore.* The river divides here into four channels, two of which encircle **Formosa Island,** the largest on the *Thames.* On leaving Cookham Lock the four streams re-unite and the river is spanned by *Cookham Bridge.* **Cookham** is a pretty village of some historical interest, with a village green surrounded by picturesque houses, and famous old hotels in the High Street. The ancient church has a superb tower and many other features of interest. The river can be crossed at **Bourne End,** by infrequent ferry or by the railway bridge. The Bourne End Sailing Week is held in June. Between Bourne End and Marlow there are several islands, frequented by numbers of wild fowl. Marlow Lock is about 300 yards below Marlow Bridge.

Marlow (Pop.: 11,700) is a pleasant old town with good shops and hotels and attractive houses. With its fine Suspension Bridge built 1836, and pinnacled church spire, the town shows up well from the river. As a market town it dates from Saxon times, but the buildings are now mostly modern. The house in West Street in which Shelley lived and wrote the "Revolt of Islam" still stands. About a quarter of a mile from Marlow, on the Berkshire bank, is the ancient Bisham Church. A short distance farther upstream is **Bisham Abbey,** a well-preserved Tudor residence with an interesting history: it is now a National Sports Centre.

About one-and-a-half miles above Marlow Bridge is *Temple Lock,* a reminder that the Knights Templar were once associated with this area. A farther half-mile or so brings one to *Hurley Lock.* On the Bucks side is *Harleyford Manor,* with lawn and woodlands backed by hills. At Hurley there are a number of islands, picturesque backwaters, and an extensive weir. The restored Norman church (partly pre-Conquest) is on the site of a Benedictine monastery.

Upstream on the Buckinghamshire bank is *Medmenham Abbey,* built 300 years ago on the site of a 13th-century Cistercian monastery. In the 18th century a fashionable club, burlesquing monastic life, occupied the mansion. Known as the *"Hell Fire Club",* it became notorious for blasphemous orgies. **Medmenham** village has picturesque cottages and an interesting church. *Magpie Island* is in a pretty backwater navigable by small craft.

Beyond Aston ferry is *Hambledon Lock,* close to the Berkshire bank. On the opposite bank is *Greenlands,* a 17th-century mansion now an Administrative Staff College. Farther inland is the pleasant village of **Hambledon.** Round the bend of the river is *Temple Island,* the starting point for the famous *Henley Regatta.* On the Berkshire side is **Remenham,** and just below Henley Bridge is the Leander Club boathouse.

Henley (Pop.: 11,400) is believed to be the oldest town in Oxfordshire. It stands at an attractive part of the *Thames,* in pleasant surroundings. The handsome arched bridge with sculptured masks dates from 1786. In 1829 the first Oxford and Cambridge Boat Race was rowed between Hambledon Lock and Henley Bridge. In 1839 *Henley Regatta* was established and immediately became popular. The pleasant town is well supplied with hotels and inns, many dating from coaching days. The church has a square turreted tower and contains features of interest. The *Chantry House* beside it, and the adjacent *Red Lion* inn date from the 14th century. Facing the wide market-place is the Town Hall, built to commemorate Queen Victoria's Diamond Jubilee.

HENLEY TO OXFORD

A mile upstream from Henley is Marsh Lock, with a picturesque weir and wooden bridge. A short distance above the lock is the delightful *Hennerton Backwater,* one-and-a-half miles long, which rejoins the river at **Wargrave,** a secluded pretty village frequented by artists. Just beyond the railway bridge is the lock at **Shiplake,** where the little river *Lodden* joins the Thames. In Shiplake church, Tennyson was married in 1850. *Shiplake Reach* extends for one-and-a-half miles; there are several islands and the rushing backwater of *St. Patrick's Stream,* a mile from which is the charming village of **Sonning.** In Saxon times this was the centre of the diocese of the Bishops of Salisbury, who had their palace here. The present church replaced the Saxon cathedral. Sonning Lock, with the picturesque mill and trees, claims to be the prettiest on the river. Two miles beyond Sonning, the river *Kennet* joins the *Thames.* At Caversham Lock the steamers land passengers for Reading. **Caversham** has many attractive houses on a picturesque stretch of the river. Above the lock are several boathouses and swimming baths. The concrete bridge (1966) has a span of 457 feet.

Reading (Pop.: 135,000. Hotels: *Great Western, Caversham Bridge, Ship, Post House*) is a prosperous industrial, residential and University town. It has a riverside promenade, parks, and many open spaces. Industries include food manufacture, electronics and centrifugal pumps. The University has more than 5,500 students. The Museum of English Rural Life *(Tues–Sats)* is a national centre for the collection of material relating to every aspect of the countryside. Adjoining Forbury Gardens are remnants of a 12th-century abbey where Henry I was buried in 1136 and John of Gaunt was married in 1359.

A mile upstream is **Mapledurham** where by the lock are a picturesque mill and weir. The surrounding wooded country is quite unspoiled and very beautiful. **Mapledurham House** *(fee)* was the manor house of the Blount family, whose tombs are in the church which is well worth a visit. Just over half-a-mile above the lock is Hardwicke House with Elizabethan associations. **Whitchurch** is a pretty village with a toll bridge across the river to **Pangbourne** attractive with thatched cottages. The *Pang* stream is famous for its trout. At **Basildon** three miles farther on is *Basildon House* a former home of Viscount Fane (1770).

Next come **Goring** and **Streatley,** attractive river resorts connected by a bridge. At Goring is a lock, and a church which has a Norman tower, an ancient porch, and fine brasses. The pretty village of Streatley is at the foot of *Landon Chase*

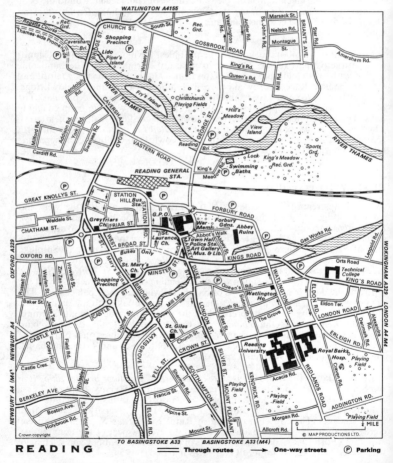

READING

═══ **Through routes** ⟶ **One-way streets** Ⓟ **Parking**

(N.T.) and *Streatley Hill* with its slopes of juniper. The distance from Goring Lock to *Cleeve Lock* is a little over half-a-mile, and the river is dotted with small willow-clad islands. About one-and-a-quarter miles above Cleeve Lock is **South Stoke** on the north bank, connected by ferry with the ancient village of **Moulsford,** picturesque with old cottages and a restored 14th-century church. The gabled manor house is now a training school for nurses. A mile beyond Moulsford railway bridge is **North Stoke,** a tree-embowered village in which Dame Clara Butt lived. In another two miles is Wallingford Bridge. The busy town of **Wallingford** (Pop.: 6,130) lies back from the river in a thriving agricultural area. It is a historic town with earthen ramparts, narrow streets, old houses, a medieval bridge and a 17th-century Town Hall. **Crowmarsh Gifford,** on the Oxford bank a quarter-of-a-mile inland, is notable for its Norman church.

From **Benson Lock** *(ferry)* to the next bridge at **Shillingford** there are good views of the twin hills of *Sinodun*. Two miles farther on, the *Thames* is joined by the river *Thame.* In another mile one reaches *Day's Lock,* with **Little Wittenham** (or Abbot's Whittenham), and beyond on the north shore **Dorchester.** This quiet little town of pleasant houses was formerly a Roman station, a Saxon town, and a Cathedral city. It was once the largest diocese in England. The magnificent *Abbey Church* near the bridge over the *Thame* is over 200 feet long, with a famous Jesse window, and a Norman font and shrine. From Day's Lock the river curves, passing on the right **Burcot,** and **Clifton Hampden** with its ancient church and inn. By Clifton Lock a straight *Cut* by-passes a bend in the river which skirts the attractive village of **Long Wittenham.** From **Appleford** railway bridge it is one mile to Culham Lock, connected by a bridge with the charming old village of **Sutton Courtenay** on the backwater. Half-a-mile beyond *Culham Cut* is Old Culham Bridge which dates from 1430.

Abingdon (Pop.: 18,800. Hotels: *Upper Reaches, Crown and Thistle*) is an ancient picturesque town which grew up around the powerful Abbey founded in the 7th century and refounded by the Benedictines in A.D. 955. Until 1870 it was the county town of Berkshire but is now in the new Oxfordshire. It has a beautiful bridge, medieval gabled houses, Tudor and Georgian buildings, and an arcaded *County Hall* dating from 1677—in which is a *Museum (daily)*. Facing the County Hall is the remarkable Norman door of *St. Nicholas Church.* The surviving parts of the abbey buildings include the *Abbey Gateway* rebuilt about 1460, and the *Checker Hall,* now used as a theatre. Adjoining this is the *Checker,* i.e. Exchequer or Treasury, with its 13th-century chimney and groined undercroft. Beyond is the 15th-century *Long Gallery.* *St. Helen's Church* has a 13th-century tower with a fine spire, five aisles, a Jacobean pulpit, and a unique 14th-century painted ceiling in the Lady Chapel. By the church are picturesque *Almshouses* built in 1446, and *Christ's Hospital* founded in 1553.

From Abingdon Lock, the river winds through attractive scenery. Beyond the railway bridge **Nuneham Woods** stretch for two miles along the river bank. On the south side is **Radley** where, concealed by high banks, is *Radley College.* The College boat-house is at nearby Sandford Lock, the deepest on the *Thames.* In half-a-mile is *Kennington Island,* then Iffley Lock. On the right is **Iffley** church, an excellent example of Norman architecture. On the one-and-a-half mile reach between Iffley and Folly Bridge the "Eights" and "Torpid" boat races take place. Beyond *Christchurch Meadow* is the steamer landing place at Folly Bridge, Oxford.

OXFORD

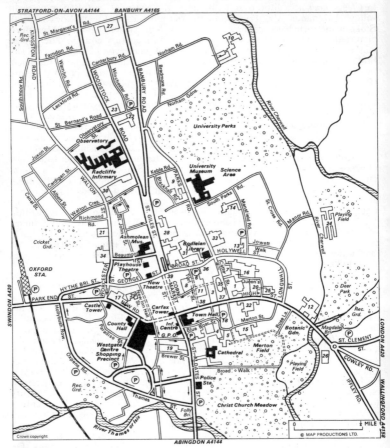

OXFORD ═══ **Through routes** ⟶ **One-way streets** Ⓟ **Parking**

1. All Souls, 1438
2. Balliol, 1263
3. Brasenose, 1509
4. Christ Church, 1525
5. Corpus Christi, 1517
6. Exeter, 1314
7. Hertford, 1874
8. Jesus, 1571
9. Keble, 1870
10. Lady Margaret Hall, 1878
11. Lincoln, 1427
12. Magdalen, 1458
13. Manchester, 1888
14. Mansfield, 1886
15. Merton, 1264
16. New College, 1379
17. Nuffield, 1937
18. Oriel, 1326
19. Pembroke, 1624
20. Queen's, 1340
21. Ruskin, 1899
22. St. Anne's, 1952
23. St. Antony's, 1948
24. St. Catherine's, 1963
25. St. Edmund Hall, 1238
26. St. Hilda's, 1893
27. St. Hugh's, 1886
28. St. John's, 1555
29. St. Peter's, 1929
30. Somerville, 1879
31. Trinity, 1554–5
32. University, 1249
33. Wadham, 1612
34. Worcester, 1714
35. Radcliffe Camera
36. Sheldonian
37. St. Mary the Virgin Ch.
38. St. Martin & All Saints
39. St. Michael 'Northgate

Oxford

Boating.—On the *Isis (Thames)* and *Cherwell.* Boats may be hired at Folly Bridge, Magdalen Bridge etc. Salter's steamer trips to Abingdon, Henley, Kingston etc. leave from Folly Bridge.

Car Parking.—There are numerous official off-street car parks. Within the central Disc Zone, parking at on-street car parks is free for two hours, but a parking disc must be displayed on windscreen.

Distances.—Banbury, 23; Bath, 62; Cheltenham, 42; Malmesbury, 43; London, 57; Reading, 27; Stratford-upon-Avon, 40; Warwick, 42; Windsor, 39.

Hotels.—*Eastgate, Excelsior, Randolph, Royal Oxford, Oxford, Melville, Linton Lodge* and others.

Information Centre.—St. Aldates—starting point for guided walks and coach tours *(daily).*

Library.—Westgate.

Population.—109,000.

Post Office.—St. Aldates.

Oxford lies for the most part between the *Isis (Thames)* and the *Cherwell.* It is a county town and an industrial centre but is best known as the seat of an ancient University and the home of beautiful architecture. A town existed here before the Norman Conquest; references to a university date from the 12th century, and the oldest of the existing colleges was founded 1249.

Eastward from the station the first quarter-mile is frankly dull, but when New Road is reached one sees *Nuffield College* on the left, and the *Castle Mound* and *County Hall* on the right. The road continues as Queen Street to the crossing at Carfax.

Carfax (of Lat. *quadrifurcus,* Fr. carrefour) implies a cross-roads. Approaching this one from *Queen Street,* the right hand fork is *St. Aldate's,* the left fork is *Cornmarket Street,* and the road straight ahead is *High Street.*

Following each of these in turn:

St. Aldate's runs southward, with the **Town Hall** on the left, and then on the same side **Christ Church,** with **Tom Tower** and the **Cathedral.** One may continue to *Folly Bridge,* with a view downstream of Salter's boat yard and the College "barges" and boat houses. Or one may turn left after passing Christ Church, and by way of **Broad Walk** and **Rose Lane** (by the Botanic Garden) emerge in High Street opposite **Magdalen College** (pronounced "maudlin").

Cornmarket Street. At the north-west corner of Carfax stands a 14th-century tower which is all that remains of the former City Church of **St. Martin.** At the north end of Cornmarket is **St. Michael's Church,** and beyond, in **Magdalen Street,** are **St. Mary Magdalen's Church,** the **Martyr's Memorial,** and on the left the **Taylor Institute** and **Ashmolean Museum.** Still farther north is the **City War Memorial** and **St. Giles' Church,** at the junction of Woodstock Road and Banbury Road. Returning past **St. John's College** and the west front of **Balliol,** turn left into **Broad Street.** On the left are **Balliol College, Trinity College** and the **New Bodleian Library;** on the right **Exeter College,** the **Old Ashmolean,** and the **Sheldonian Theatre.**

High Street—or to follow local usage "the High"—is a beautiful street gently curving to Magdalen Bridge. On the left are **All Saints' Church, Brasenose College, St. Mary's Church, All Souls College, Queen's College, St. Edmund Hall,** and **Magdalen College.** On the right are **Oriel College, University College,** the **Examination Schools,** and the **Botanic Garden.**

Turl Street, a turning north from the High by All Saints' Church, has **Lincoln** and **Exeter** colleges on the right, and **Jesus College** on the left. *Cattle Street,* also a turning northward, passes the **Radcliffe Camera** and **Old Schools** on the left. On the right are **All Souls College, Hertford College,** and beyond this—if one continues to **Parks Road**—are **Wadham College** and the *University Museum,* with **Keble College** opposite, on the left. **Oriel Street,** southward from the High opposite St. Mary's Church, leads to **Corpus Christi** and **Merton** colleges.

OXFORD COLLEGES

The Colleges of Oxford

Oxford now has 34 Colleges, in addition to lesser collegiate institutions. There are more than 11,000 students, the majority being of undergraduate status. Of the two dozen men's colleges, dates of foundation vary from University College (1249) and Balliol (1263) to St. Catherine's (1962). It should be noted that from 1974 several of the men's colleges have admitted a limited number of women undergraduates.

There are five women's colleges, the oldest being Somerville and Lady Margaret Hall, and also five graduate colleges of fairly recent foundation and open to both sexes. These are Nuffield (1937), St. Antony's (1950), Linacre (1962), St. Cross (1965) and Wolfson (1965).

In addition there are certain *Halls,* licensed under a Statute of 1918, whose students are subject to University regulations, and are mainly theological students. The Halls are **Campion, St. Benet's** and **Greyfriars** (Roman Catholic); **Mansfield** (Congregationalist); and **Regent's Park** (Baptist). These should not be confused with the medieval halls of residence, of which only one survives (**St. Edmund Hall,** a College since 1957).

Not incorporated with the University are **Ruskin College** (founded in 1899 as a "working men's college") and certain theological institutions such as **Ripon Hall, St. Stephen's Hall, Wycliffe Hall, Manchester College,** and **Pusey House.**

Most of the college precincts are open to visitors, at least in the afternoons. When in doubt, enquire at Porter's Lodge.

All Souls College. Founded by Archbishop Chichele in 1438 and dedicated in particular to those killed in the Hundred Years War. It is unique among the older colleges in that there are no undergraduates—only Fellows. The *Front Quadrangle* is the oldest and most attractive of three. In the *Great Quadrangle* are the twin towers by Hawksmoor, a pupil of Wren. The modern carvings over the gateway represent the co-founders Archbishop Chichele and Henry VI. The *Hall* and the *Codrington Library* are 18th century.

Balliol College. Founded in 1263 by John Balliol, of Barnard Castle, Balliol remained a minor college until the 19th century, when it developed under the influence of Jowett and others. The frontage facing Broad Street is by Alfred Waterhouse and was built 1867–68 in Scottish baronial style. The *Library* (formerly the Hall), the old library, and the oriel window of the Master's lodging are all 15th-century work.

Brasenose College (B.N.C.) was founded in 1509, and covers the site of nine medieval Halls. It has a fine *Gate Tower* and *Dining Hall.* A "brazen nose" over the gateway facing the Radcliffe Camera is 16th century; the original knocker from Brasenose Hall now adorns the High Table. The newest quadrangle, with an attractive High Street front, was completed in 1909.

Christ Church ("the House") founded 1525 by Wolsey, and, refounded by Henry VIII in 1546. From St. Aldate's one enters *Tom Quad,* the largest of Oxford's quadrangles. Over the gatehouse the famous bell *Great Tom* is housed in Wren's domed tower. Every night at five minutes past nine o'clock it strikes 101 notes. From the south-east corner of the quadrangle one approaches the magnificent *Hall*—the largest in Oxford—and the **Cathedral.** When Wolsey destroyed St. Frideswide's Priory to build the college, he left sufficient of the original monastic church to form what now functions both as the Chapel of Christ Church, and as the *Cathedral* of the City of Oxford. The interior shows much 12th-century work, and the 15th-century vaulting of the Choir is exquisite. The Cathedral is open daily from 7.15 a.m. to 6.45 p.m.

Corpus Christi College ("Corpus"). This is one of Oxford's smaller colleges. It was founded in 1517, and the first *quadrangle, Hall, Chapel* and *Library* are of that date. In the front quadrangle is a curious 16th-century *Sundial.*

Exeter College. Founded 1314. Of the early building, only the former gatehouse, *Palmer's Tower,* remains. It stands beyond the *Chapel,* an elaborate structure built 1856–59 by Sir Gilbert Scott and based on the Sainte Chapelle in Paris. The fine *Hall* (1618) has a collar-beam roof. The block at the corner of Turl Street and Broad Street was rebuilt in 1964.

Hertford College (1874). The college takes its name from Elias de Hertford who founded *Hart Hall,* one of several medieval Halls that occupied the present site. After a chequered career, the foundation was revived in 1874, with financial endowment by the banker S. C. Baring. Most of the buildings are modern.

Jesus College. Founded in 1571 by Queen Elizabeth I, at the cost of Dr. Hugh Price, Treasurer of St. David's. The college has always maintained a close Welsh connection, and the *Library* has a valuable collection of Welsh manuscripts.

Keble College (1868). Founded in memory of the Rev. John Keble, who died in 1866, to provide a college life on Christian principles for men of limited means. The College is of red and polychrome brick, and is dominated by the impressive *Chapel*.

Lady Margaret Hall (L.M.H.). Founded 1878. The first of the Women's Colleges in Oxford, Somerville being second in 1879. L.M.H. was restricted to members of the Church of England, and was named after the mother of Henry VII—Lady Margaret Beaufort.

Linacre College (1962). A post-graduate college, non-residential. It occupies the former buildings of St. Catherine's Society, between Christ Church and Folly Bridge.

Lincoln College. Founded in 1427 by Richard Fleming, Bishop of Lincoln. The Turl Street front is attractive. The *Gate Tower, Hall,* and first quadrangle are 15th century. John Wesley was made a Fellow in 1726.

Magdalen College. Founded 1458, and has beautiful buildings in a riverside setting. The graceful *Bell Tower* (1492–1501) is one of Oxford's best known features. The quads are all attractive, especially that surrounded by cloisters and overlooked by the *Founder's Tower.* To the north are the attractive 18th-century *New Buildings,* and beyond is the *Grove* with its noble elms and grazing deer.

Merton College (1264). Though University and Balliol Colleges have earlier foundation dates, Merton claims to be the first college with resident students. (The original establishment was at Malden, in Surrey.) The old buildings are attractive. *"Mob Quad"* (the oldest quadrangle in Oxford), *Chapel, Hall,* and *Library* all show 14th-century work. The *Garden* overlooks to the south a stretch of the old City wall.

New College (1379). Founded by William of Wykeham (who also founded Winchester College for boys). The 14th-century *Gatehouse* is in New College Lane. The original quadrangle has been disfigured by a 17th-century battlemented upper storey. A passage to the left leads to *Cloister, Chapel* and *Bell-tower.* In the ante-chapel is Epstein's sculpture "Lazarus". The *Garden Quadrangle* leads to the garden, which is bounded by the north-east curve of the old City wall.

Nuffield College. Founded in 1937 by Lord Nuffield. This is a graduate society for both sexes. The college is on the site of the old Oxford Canal Wharf, and is built in Cotswold style, with tower and spire.

Oriel College. Founded 1326, but nothing remains of the original building. The *front quadrangle, Hall* and *Chapel* are mid-17th century, with Jacobean gables. The third quadrangle was originally *St. Mary's Hall,* absorbed in 1902.

Pembroke College. Founded 1624, replacing the medieval *Broadgates Hall,* whose refectory forms part of the present *Library.* In 1962 a new and attractive quadrangle was completed by the incorporation of *Beef Lane* which formed the northern boundary of the college.

Queen's College (1340). The queen in question was Philippa, wife of Edward III, but the founder was her chaplain Robert Eglesfield. The buildings are late 17th and early 18th century. The splendid High Street front and cupola are after the designs of Hawksmoor. The college has always maintained strong connections with the North Country.

St. Anne's College (1952). The youngest of the women's colleges. It began in 1879 as a society for home students, and was incorporated as a College in 1952. A new dining hall was built in 1959, and the *Wolfson Building* added in 1964.

St. Antony's College. Founded in 1950 as the result of a benefaction from a French merchant, Antonin Besse. This is a post-graduate college specialising in Modern Studies. It occupies the site of a former Anglican convent in Woodstock Road.

St. Catherine's College (1962). A new college, developed from the former St. Catherine's Society for non-collegiate students. The architect Arne Jacobsen has designed a highly modern structure of glass, concrete and bronze on the east bank of the *Cherwell.* The ancient *Church of St. Cross* now serves as the college chapel.

St. Cross College (1965). Another recent post-graduate college, in course of erection immediately to the south of *St. Cross Church.*

St. Edmund Hall (1270). This is the last of the medieval *Halls* still remaining, but since 1957 it has ranked as a College. Its attractive small quadrangle is in part 16th century. Extensive modern additions were made in the early 1970's. The adjacent disused church of St. Peter-in-the-East has been adapted as a college library.

St. Hilda's College. Founded for women students in 1893 by Miss Beale, Principal of Cheltenham Ladies College, and incorporated by Royal Charter in 1926. It lies to the south of Magdalen Bridge, and was the first college east of the *Cherwell.* It has now over 300 undergraduates and about 80 graduates.

St. Hugh's College. Founded 1886, and a college since 1926. Its buildings, between the Banbury and Woodstock roads, are perhaps the best among the women's colleges. They were opened in 1916, and later additions include the *New Building* (1966), followed in 1968 by the *Wolfson Building*.

St. John's College. Founded in 1555 by Sir Thomas White, a wealthy Merchant Tailor, who took over the Cistercian monastery of St. Bernard. The west front and first quadrangle are 15th century. *Chapel* and *Hall* have been much restored. The cloistered sides of *Canterbury Quad* were built when Archbishop Laud was Chancellor of the University. A special feature of St. John's is the beautiful *Garden*.

St. Peter's College. Founded 1929 as *St. Peter's Hall*, in memory of Dr. F. J. Chavasse, at one time Rector of the parish church of St. Peter-le-Bailey, now the *Chapel*. The foundation, on the site of one of the oldest medieval Halls, has grown rapidly and was incorporated as an independent college in 1961.

Somerville College was established in 1879 as the undenominational counterpart of Lady Margaret Hall, and was incorporated by Royal Charter in 1926. It was named after Mary Somerville, the mathematician. There have been many additions, the most recent being the Vaughan and Wolfson buildings opened in 1966 and 1967.

Trinity College. Founded 1555 on the site of *Durham College*, set up about 1286 for Benedictine monks. From Broad Street one enters the *Front Quadrangle* and passes to the *Chapel Quadrangle*, whose east side embodies the remains of the earlier foundation, including the old Library (1417–21). The Chapel is late 17th century. The *Garden Quad* opens by an iron grille to the *Garden*. Access may also be obtained to Trinity from St. Giles, through the modern *Dolphin Gatehouse* between Balliol and St. John's.

University College (1249). The oldest of the colleges, but only on its present site since 1330. The buildings are 17th-century Gothic, with a fine curving façade on the High Street. The *Shelley Memorial* is in the near right hand corner of the first quadrangle.

Wadham College (1610). The buildings are attractive and substantially unchanged. The fine *Hall* has a hammer-beam roof, and over the entrance are statues of James I, and of the founders Nicholas and Dorothy Wadham. New buildings were added in 1952 and 1972. The *Garden* is notable for its fine views.

Wolfson College. Founded in 1966. A post-graduate college; so far non-residential but the new buildings between Banbury Road and the *Cherwell* were completed by 1973, and are destined to accommodate not only unmarried graduates of both sexes, but also married graduates and their families.

Worcester College. Founded in 1714, and built on a site occupied by Benedictines since 1283. On entering the main quadrangle, the 15th-century buildings of the old foundation may be seen on the left. They form a contrast to the classical 18th-century range on the north side. Worcester is noted for its park-like *Gardens* and picturesque *Lake*.

University Institutions etc.

The Sheldonian Theatre. This was built in the 17th century to house secular functions of the University. It will seat 1,500 people. The original plan was by Wren, but later additions have been made. The weathered stone heads (said to represent Roman emperors) that used to line the railings have now been replaced by new carvings. Adjoining is the *Clarendon Building*, long the site of the University Press, which was removed to Walton Street in 1830.

The Old Ashmolean (now *Museum of the History of Science*), was built to house the miscellaneous collection inherited by Elias Ashmole from the Tradescants, and also to provide a Natural History School and the first chemistry laboratory in this country. It was opened by the Duke of York, later James II, in 1683. Most of the contents were later transferred to the *New Ashmolean* (see below). Since 1935 it has built up a magnificent collection of early scientific instruments, notably astrolabes.

The Radcliffe Camera. Dr. John Radcliffe, physician to William III, left a bequest for the erection of a library, and eventually the noble circular "Camera" with dome and lantern was completed in 1748, the architect being James Gibbs. Since 1860 the building has been used as a reading room for the *Bodleian Library*. An underground tunnel connects with Old and New Bodleian libraries for the transfer of books.

The Bodleian Library was organised and endowed by Sir Thomas Bodley, who died in 1613. The Library gradually extended to occupy all the *Old Schools* (immediately south of the Clarendon Building), and finally the *New Bodleian* building, formally opened in 1946. This building, opposite the *Sheldonian*, has 11 floors of bookstacks, and also reading and exhibition rooms. The Bodleian, like the British Museum and several other libraries, receives a free copy of every book printed in the U.K. It now houses over 3,000,000 volumes.

The **Old Schools quadrangle** gives access not only to the Library, but also to the *Divinity School*, with its marvellous 15th-century stone vaulting, and to *Convocation House*.

Ashmolean Museum and **Taylor Institute.** The building at junction of St. Giles and Beaumont Street fulfils two functions. The "Taylorian" was the result of a bequest by Sir Robert Taylor, an architect, for the teaching of foreign languages. The University decided to build an institute for this purpose, but to combine it with new galleries to house overflowing treasures of the Old Ashmolean. The western wing, entered from Beaumont Street, forms the *Museum*, with its matchless collection of art and antiquities, musical instruments, coins etc. One of its greatest treasures is a beautiful gold and enamel jewel once owned by Alfred the Great. The Taylorian faces St. Giles, and contains lecture rooms and a library for language students.

The **University Museum,** in Park's Road, is a Ruskinesque pile built after the introduction in 1850 of an Honours School of Natural Science. Numerous scientific departments have proliferated from the original building, and the Science Area now covers the south-west portion of the Parks. Among the Departments are those of the various branches of Chemistry, Physics, and Medicine; and of Geology, Zoology, Botany and Forestry. More recently the Science Area has extended to the Keble Road Triangle. Here are the Departments of Engineering and Metallurgy, and the striking Nuclear Physics Laboratory (Ove Arup, 1970).

The **University Botanic Garden,** adjoining Magdalen Bridge, was originally a "physick garden" for medicinal plants, for which the land was given in 1621 by the Earl of Danby.

The **University Theatre** *(Playhouse).* Under University control since 1961. University and college dramatic societies share the theatre with a resident professional repertory company.

Municipal Buildings etc.

The **Castle.** Apart from the *Mound,* all that remains of Robert d'Oilly's castle of 1074 is the tower and crypt of the *Chapel.* The Castle once covered a large area. Here Matilda was besieged by her cousin Stephen in 1142, during their struggle for the monarchy.

County Hall. An imposing block of buildings near the Mound. Behind County Hall stands H.M. Prison.

Town Hall, St. Aldate's, in Neo Renaissance style, replaces the old Town Hall, demolished 1892. It has a fine *Council Chamber, Assembly Room,* and a fifteenth-century *Crypt.*

Martyrs' Memorial, in St. Giles' Street, was erected in 1841 by Sir George Gilbert Scott. The figures in the niches represent Cranmer, Ridley, and Latimer; the site of their martyrdom at the stake is marked in nearby Broad Street.

City War Memorial, to the dead of both Wars, is a handsome structure in front of St. Giles' Church. A light cross springs from a pedestal with carved shields, the whole on a broad base of six steps.

The **New Theatre,** in George Street, was rebuilt in 1933, and is a fine and well-equipped building. The other Oxford theatre, the *Playhouse,* is now under University control.

The Churches of Oxford

(for *Cathedral* see under Christ Church).

St. Mary the Virgin. This is the University Church. Its bells are pealed on certain University occasions, and the University sermon is preached here on most Sundays in term. Here Cranmer withdrew his recantation before being burnt for heresy. The tower dates from the 13th century, and the spire from the 14th. The baroque south porch, with its twisted pillars, was added in 1637.

All Saints'. Now redundant, and houses the library of Lincoln College. Until 1971 this was the City Church, a title now transferred to St. Michael's. It was built in 1707–10 on the site of an ancient church.

St. Aldate's is a very ancient foundation, much rebuilt. The south aisle and crypt are 14th century, and at the east end of the north aisle are five arches removed from the Norman chancel.

St. Michael-at-the-North-Gate. Since 1971 this has become the City Church, and civic services, attended by the Mayor and Corporation, are held several times each year. The Saxon tower of this church is the oldest building in Oxford. The tower adjoined the north gate of the city wall, and over the gate was a prison known as Bocards.

THE THAMES ABOVE OXFORD

St. Peter's-in-the-East contains much Norman work, and an impressive Crypt, now entered from outside the church.

St. Giles' situated just north of the City War Memorial, is one of Oxford's most distinctive monuments. The nave is 12th century, and most of the remainder 13th and 14th centuries.

St. Mary Magdalen's. A church has stood on this site since Saxon times. It was enlarged in 1194 by Hugh of Lincoln. The present building is mostly modern work.

St. Ebbe's, near Pembroke College, is an ancient foundation but rebuilt in the last century. The tower is 13th century, and a 12th -century doorway is preserved.

St. Thomas the Martyr. Near the Station. The chancel, with three Norman windows, dates from the 12th century. Nave and tower were rebuilt about 1500.

The Thames above Oxford

The young *Thames* upstream as far as **Cricklade** (42 miles from Folly Bridge) is well worth exploring. Between Oxford and **Lechlade** it is navigable by motor launches, but beyond this it is only suitable for boats of shallow draught.

A popular trip is downstream from Cricklade by canoe or rowing boat, and for this reason it will be better to consider the route in this direction.

Cricklade is an agricultural town with a history extending back to Saxon times. The river runs parallel with the derelict *Thames and Severn Canal,* past **Castle Eaton** (4 miles) and **Kempsford** with its 14th-century church and ruined castle, to **Inglesham** (10 miles) where canal and river join. Very soon after comes Lechlade (11 miles).

Lechlade, on the Gloucestershire bank, is an attractive small market town. About half a mile beyond the bridge, the river *Cole* enters from the right; then there is a lock (the first on the *Thames*) and a bridge—*St. John's.* A short distance on is *Buscot Lock,* then **Kelmscott** on the Oxfordshire bank, *Radcot Bridge* and *Radcot Lock* (18 miles). In another two and a half miles is the picturesque *Rushey Lock* and weir (whence a cut to Shifford). Thence to *Tadpole Bridge* (21 miles), *Shifford Lock* (25 miles), past *Harrowden Hall* rising steeply from the right bank, to picturesque *New Bridge,* over 700 years old and the scene of a battle during the Civil War.

Bablockhythe (31 miles) recalls Matthew Arnold's "Scholar Gipsy". Then past *Pinkhill Lock* and *King's Lock* to *Godstow Lock* (39 miles) with the famous *Trout Inn* and the remains of *Godstow Nunnery* where Fair Rosamund, mistress of Henry II, was educated and buried. Now follows a peaceful stretch of river, with the splendid expanse of *Port Meadow* on the left, and we arrive at *Osney Lock* (41 miles), a convenient place to land for Oxford.

The Chilterns

The Chilterns form a range of hills extending from their northern limit near Luton and running southwest to the *Thames* near Henley. The western face of this range, for most of its length, is a cliff-like escarpment clearly defined, with Ivinghoe Beacon (756 feet) dominating its northern edge, and overlooking the Vale of Aylesbury. Eastwards the land slopes gently down towards Rickmansworth and the Colne Valley towards the former Middlesex border.

The A40 London to Oxford road cuts across this area in the south.

High Wycombe (Pop.: 59,300. Hotels: *Falcon, White Lion*), is spread three miles along the valley of the river *Wye* and is the premier furniture-manufacturing town of England. The industry stems from the prolific beechwoods of the area. The oldest buildings of the town are picturesquely grouped near the tall-towered parish church at the town centre, and include the Guildhall (1757) and the Market Hall (1761).

Hughendon Manor (N.T., *Feb.–Dec., daily except Tues, fee*), is the former home of Benjamin Disraeli who is buried in the little church in the grounds. The house with its contemporary decoration is a typical example of a Victorian country seat and contains many relics of the statesman.

West Wycombe, two miles along the Oxford road, is a completely unspoiled village entirely owned by the National Trust. A distinguishing feature is the huge golden ball surmounting the church on the hill above, with the Mausoleum of the Dashwood family adjoining. Below the hill are **West Wycombe Caves** *(daily Apr.–Sept.)*, owned by the Dashwood family and with exhibits recalling the Hellfire Club founded by Sir Francis about 1750.

West Wycombe Park (N.T., *Mons–Fris, in June. Daily except Sats, July and Aug., fee*), is a large mansion built in 1750 and the home of the Dashwood family. The Palladian house has fine frescoes and painted ceilings. The grounds with lake and classical temples are notable.

Bradenham, a pretty village with a large green and little church, lies off the A4010 road (which leaves the A40 at this point) and the fine *Bradenham Manor (not open)*, was the boyhood home of Disraeli. This main road runs through the beautiful Saunderton Valley, with Bledlow Ridge to the south and the heights of Naphill and Lacey Green to the north. At Pink Hill is the *Pink and Lily Inn*, a favourite rendezvous of the poet Rupert Brooke and his friends, and on the edge of the Chilterns can be seen *Whiteleaf Cross* cut into the chalk of the hills in Saxon times to mark the presence below of the ancient Icknield Way that follows the line of the Chilterns.

Princes Risborough is a pleasant market town immediately below the cross with ancient half-timbered houses near the church and little market hall (1824) standing on pillars. The **Manor House** (N.T., *Tues and Weds, free)*, is a handsome building of 1670 with a spectacular double staircase.

From Princes Risborough the road divides past the Market Hall. **Little Kimble** lies three miles north and has a small church with an extraordinary collection of 12th-century wall paintings. It adjoins the extensive grounds of **Chequers** *(not open)*, the official home of the Prime Minister. The other main road (A4129) runs west across flat country into Oxfordshire.

Thame *(Black Horse, Spread Eagle)*, is a handsome market-town with a wide High Street, Cornmarket and Buttermarket setting off the variety of Tudor and Georgian buildings that abound. Notable is the 15th-century *Birdcage Inn* and the very large parish church on the western edge of the town. From the church the road (B4011) crosses the river *Thame* back into Buckinghamshire. Three miles south-west of Thame is the **Rycote Chapel** *(daily, fee)*, a small 15th-century building with notable benches and pews and barrel roof.

Long Crendon two miles north-west along the B4011 is another village of medieval charm with a wide range of interesting architecture and a large church. In the **Courthouse** (N.T., *free*), the manorial courts were held from the time of Henry V until recent times. From the village Angle Way turns right off the main road to the pretty hamlet of **Chearsley** and into country with a wealth of delightful villages.

Cuddington, with its village pump on the Green, has several notable stone buildings including the splendid *Tyringham Hall (not open)*, at the lower end of the village.

Nether Winchendon, reached by a footpath across the water-meadows of the *Thame*, consists mainly of a group of ochre-washed cottages surrounding a tiny green with the unspoiled parish church alongside. The church has a gallery and a good three-decker pulpit as well as medieval Flemish stained glass and a fine clock dating from 1740.

Nether Winchendon Manor *(certain Suns)*, is the home of the Spencer-Bernard family, one of whose ancestors was the first Governor of Massachusetts. There are fine portraits and furnishings and interesting documents including some signed by Oliver Cromwell.

The road high on the hill above the village eventually joins the main A41 from Aylesbury to Bicester. **Waddesdon** is a Rothschild village, having been acquired by Ferdinand Rothschild in 1872 and rebuilt. The family arms can be seen on many of the houses.

Waddesdon Manor (N.T., *Apr.–Oct., Weds–Suns and Bank Hols, fee*), at the western end of the village is a fantastic architectural amalgam of the French "chateau" style and houses the superb collection of paintings, furnishings, tapestries, carpets and objets d'art collected by the owner during his lifetime. The grounds are wooded and extensive and include an aviary.

Also on the southern heights which define the Vale of Aylesbury are the little villages **Brill, Ludgershall** and **Wotton.**

Wotton House *(June–Sept., Weds, fee)*, in Wotton Underwood, was built in 1704 on the plan of the original Buckingham House in London. The interior decorations were carried out by Soane after a fire in 1820.

North of the Vale of Aylesbury are the Claydon group of villages *(see Index)*. Eastward from the Claydons the Vale runs to **Quainton** with its picturesque almshouses and sloping village green and, a mile south, the headquarters of the **Quainton Railway Society** *(Bank Hol. week-ends)*, with a fine collection of steam locomotives and stock.

Aylesbury (Pop.: 41,288. Hotels: *King's Head, Bull*), is the county town of Buckinghamshire. Despite its rapid growth it still retains a picturesque central Market Square with the fine buildings of the County Hall (1740) at the southern end. The only other picturesque part of the town is round the parish church at the hilly and cobbled Parson's Fee, Temple Street, Castle Street and Rickford's Hill. **Hartwell House** *(Apr.–July, Weds)*, two miles west on the Thame road, was the residence between 1807 and 1814 of the French Bourbon king Louis XVIII during the Napoleonic Wars. It is now an international secretarial college for girls. It has an unusual staircase carrying carved heads of famous figures and some superbly decorated rooms.

Wing, eight miles north-east of Aylesbury on the road to Leighton Buzzard, has the only Saxon church in Britain retaining its original 7th-century crypt and polygonal apse above.

Ascott (N.T., *Apr.–Sept., Weds, Sats, Bank Hols, and Suns, in July–Aug., fee)*, is a fine Elizabethan mansion on the east side of the village. Here is the major portion of Anthony de Rothschild's collection of French and Chippendale furniture, paintings and porcelain. Extensive grounds.

Wendover, on the A413 to the east of Aylesbury, is situated at what is virtually the only gap in the Chilterns, with Aston Hill and Hauton on the north and, to the south, the continuing line of the Chilterns marked by the highest point at **Coombe Hill** (842 feet). This is National Trust property. The monument commemorates those who died in the Boer War. Several good nature trails organised by the Bucks, Berks and Oxon Naturalist Trust begin here.

Near Coombe Hill is **Chequers** *(not open)*, the official residence of the Prime Minister, and *Hampden House (not open)*, home of John Hampden, whose refusal to pay taxes levied by King Charles I led to the Civil War in 1642. He is buried in the church nearby.

Great Missenden lies along the valley of the *Misbourne*, the tiny river which starts its life just outside the village and gives its name to this wide and beautiful valley. **Little Missenden**, two miles east, is just off the main road and is a place of idyllic charm and quiet with a church containing some of the most important medieval wall-paintings in England.

Amersham has its old town, wide High Street and old Market Hall of 1682 in the valley, with the new town a mile away. Also in the Misbourne valley are **Chalfont St. Peter** and **Chalfont St. Giles,** the latter with its village green, pond and Norman church.

Milton's Cottage *(Feb.–Oct., daily except Tues)*, at Chalfont St. Giles was the retreat of the poet John Milton during the Great Plague in 1665. It is now a museum of Milton relics.

Six miles south of Amersham on the Oxford road is **Beaconsfield**. The older portion has a tree-lined main street and a large parish church with the grave of Edmund Waller. Near the station is **Bekonscot Model Village** *(daily)*.

Jordans and its Quaker Meeting House and *Mayflower* barn, is two miles east, and a mile north of the A40. This road leaves Buckinghamshire four miles on at the picture-postcard village of **Denham. Gerrards Cross** is also on this road, and immediately south are Hedgerley, Fulmer and Farnham Common, with **Burnham Beeches** and its ancient trees and delightful walks.

Just north of Slough is **Stoke Poges** and the "country churchyard" of Grey's Elegy in which the poet is buried.

From Denham the A412 runs north between **Rickmansworth** and **Chorley Wood,** in Hertfordshire.

Chenies is over the border in Buckinghamshire and is a "model village" built by the Dukes of Bedford. The *Bedford Chapel (on application to the Bedford Settled Estates, London WC1)*, adjoins the parish church and has tombs of the family dating from the 15th–20th century.

Three miles east are **Croxley Green** and the industrial complex of **Watford** on the A41, and north-west along this road are the New Town of **Hemel Hempstead** and the very old town of **Berkhamsted.** At Berkhamsted are a well-known boys' public school and the extensive ruins of a **castle** *(daily)*, once the home of the Black Prince.

Ashridge Park *(certain weekends, Apr.–June, July)*, now a Management Training Centre, is a fine mansion built in florid "Gothick" style by James Wyatt in 1806 for the Duke of Bridgewater. Most of the grounds and deer park are N.T. property.

Below the hill is **Aldbury** with its pond, stocks, village pump and green. From **Ivinghoe Beacon** there are superb views over **Ivinghoe** village, **Edlesborough,** and **Mentmore** (another Rothschild village), towards Leighton Buzzard.

Tring, to the south on the A41, was once famous for its silk mill and includes *Tring Park (not open)*, a former Rothschild mansion. The **Museum** *(daily)*, a branch of the British Museum, has a fine collection of stuffed birds and of insects.

Dunstable, on the A5 Holyhead road, has the ruins of a large monastery and the nave of a Norman abbey standing in the middle of industry and tower office-blocks. Dunstable Downs, to the south, is a famous centre for gliding.

Whipsnade *(daily, fee)*, three miles south-west, is the "Country Zoo" of the Zoological Society where the animals roam the hillsides in large paddocks and enclosures.

Woburn Abbey *(daily, fee)*, is the historic home of the Duke of Bedford, an 18th-century mansion remodelled by Flitcroft in 1747. The house contains magnificent collections of furniture and art treasures. In the grounds are many modern attractions including the Wild Animal Kingdom administered by the Chipperfield family of circus fame.

Luton, a vast sprawling industrial complex, is devoted chiefly to the manufacture of cars and road vehicles but once was famous for its straw-hat industry. Its busy airport lies to the south-west.

Luton Hoo *(Apr.–Sept., daily except Tues and Fris, fee)*, three miles south, houses the Wernher Collection of art treasures including the Fabergé jewels and a unique Russian collection. The gardens are very beautiful.

Hitchin, north-east of Luton on the Icknield Way, is an old town that still preserves its charm in the old houses that skirt the Market Place and the lovely parish church bordering the river *Hiz*.

The northern tip of the Chilterns ends in the Barton Hills, near the village of **Barton,** said to be the original of the "Delectable Mountains" of Bunyan's "Pilgrim's Progress".

North Bucks (Vale of Aylesbury)

The Vale of Aylesbury, which extends along the A41 from Aylesbury to the county boundary near Bicester, is bounded on both sides by gentle, green hills and includes some of the finest pasturage in the south of England. This is an area of fine houses, with little villages often on the edge of their grounds, dignified parish churches and quiet, unassuming inns. As the land rises to form the southern edge of the Vale, the windmill of Brill can be seen stark against the sky from many points on the A41. **Brill** is perched on the hilltop close to the 17th-century post-mill. From the grass-covered ridges of an old encampment between there are widespread views over Oxfordshire.

At the top of Tram Hill, in the wide High Street is an unusual memorial in the form of a barometer to Sir Edward Verney of Claydon for many years a County Councillor. A little way down the High Street the village green and square are happily overseen by the parish church which, though restored and virtually rebuilt by Oldrid Scott in 1888, still preserves some Norman work and has a 13th-century chancel arch and 14th-century window.

South of Brill is **Chilton,** another village with a hilltop church, this one much lighter and less altered than Brill and showing the care which has been expended on it by the local family of Aubrey-Fletcher. It has a huge memorial entirely blocking the west wall and extolling the attributes of another important resident, Chief Justice Carter, who had it placed in position before he died in 1755. High on the outside wall of the tower is a figure of a knight.

Down in open rolling country is **Dorton** where Dorton House *(Sat. p.m. May–July)*, a handsome 17th-century residence with a Long Gallery enormous fireplace and decorated ceilings, is now a school. A chalybeate spring rises in the woods nearby. Attempts to develop the place as a spa proved a failure.

On the other side of Brill, almost into Oxfordshire, is the lonely and isolated **Boarstall Tower** (N.T., *not open*), the moat-encircled gatehouse of a former 14th-century fortified manor. **Boarstall Duck Decoy** *(daily except Mons, Feb.–mid-Sept.)* is an old decoy restored by the Wildfowlers' Association in 1969.

Across-country four miles away towards the A41 is the breezy and isolated hamlet of **Ludgershall,** with its little church of which John Wycliffe had the living in 1368. Two miles east of Ludgershall is **Wotton House** *(Wed. afternoons, June–Sept.)* with its two flanking Pavilions *(not open)* dating from about 1704 and rebuilt by Sir John Soane in 1820. The village of **Wotton Underwood** is mainly a small group of farm cottages and a little church.

Across the A41 near Kingswood is **Grendon Underwood,** a long, straggling village with the fine Tudor *Shakespeare's Farm* at the eastern end. It is said that the poet often stayed here while travelling between Stratford and London and wrote much of a "Midsummer Night's Dream" in Grendon, the characters of Bottom and other rustics being based on villagers he knew.

Between the A41 Bicester and A413 Buckingham roads lie the **Claydon** group of villages. They comprise Botolph, East, Middle and Steeple Claydon.

Claydon House (N.T., *Mar.–Oct., daily except Mons, fee)*, home of the Verney family, was built 1752–68 on the site of an older house. The stone-faced west wing, all that remains of a more ambitious scheme, contains magnificent rococo state rooms with fine wood carvings. Florence Nightingale spent her last years here and her room, furnishings and letters are to be seen. In the little chapel are several monuments of the Verneys.

North of the Claydons stretches a remote and unfrequented part of Buckinghamshire, more pastoral and far less wooded than in the south. It includes **Winslow**, on the A413, a quiet little town with an attractive Market Square surrounded by Georgian buildings and on the corner, the handsome *George Inn* with a wrought-iron balcony. As the road bends south of the village the large red-brick Winslow Hall *(not open)* can be seen over its wall, built in 1700 for William Lowndes, Secretary to the Treasury to Queen Anne.

Tucked away behind the *Bell Hotel* is **Keach's Chapel** *(key from cottage opposite)* built in 1695 and containing pews and furniture from the early 1700s. Keach was a Baptist and in his early days at Winslow got himself into trouble by suggesting that the solemn and round-eyed little children who faced him each Sunday in chapel might be allowed some small degree of relaxation on the Sabbath. For this he was tried at Aylesbury for sedition and put in the stocks for two hours, whilst his "Child's Instructor and Primer" was publicly burned in the Market Square.

Six miles west of Winslow stands the beautiful and lonely church of **Hillesden.** It is almost entirely 15th century, having been rebuilt (except for the west tower) between 1493 and 1500 on instructions from the bishop of Lincoln. It was the sight of this church that so impressed the youthful Gilbert Scott when he lived at nearby Gawcott where his father was vicar. Scott determined to be an architect and re-create Gothic design, and a drawing made by the boy when he was 15 can be seen in the room over the church porch. Inside, the church is light and graceful, with the enormous private pew of the Denton family who were kinsmen of the Verneys. Their great house in the field near the church is entirely destroyed, and Hillesden continues alone, with only the parsonage and a handful of cottages around it.

Due south of Winslow lie **Granborough,** where the church has unusual wall-paintings by a Victorian vicar in an attempt to revive the medieval custom, and **North Marston,** once a centre of pilgrimage. In the church preached Master John Schorne, sent from Monks Risborough in 1314 as parish priest, who effected miracles at the famous "holy well". The church became very rich from the donations of the pilgrims and the relics were transferred to Windsor in 1478. The well is still there, though now covered-over, and North Marston sleeps quietly under its thatch and dreams of days long past.

Back on the A413 **Whitchurch** lies midway between Aylesbury and Winslow. It is a quiet village of stone and half-timbered housing with a church set on a hill at its northern end. Behind the church are the Creslow Pastures containing one of the largest single fields (300 acres) in England. In Elizabethan times Creslow Pastures was the main source of beef and mutton for the royal kitchens, and the church has a memorial to John Westcar, a leading agriculturist of the 19th century and the first man to send cattle to Smithfield by the newly-opened Grand Union Canal, in 1801. His monument shows him standing with a bull and sheep surrounding him.

Buckingham (Pop.: 5,100. Hotel: *White Hart*) the former county town is picturesquely placed on the banks of the *Ouse.* Ravaged by fire in 1725 it has few old buildings to show. Part of the rebuilding included the curious castle-like structure (now a restaurant) on Market Hill built as the town gaol in 1748. Hidden away up an alley off Market Hill is the **Chantry Chapel** (N.T., *key at 4 West Street)*, rebuilt in 1475 but still showing a fine Norman doorway. The church

(1770) stands away from the town centre on the site of the old Norman castle. Other interesting buildings include Trolly Hall in Castle Street and the *White Hart* on Market Hill.

Just west of Buckingham, on the A422 to Brackley, a by-road branches right and enters the two-mile tree-lined avenue that leads to **Stowe.** The avenue ends at the Corinthian Arch, and the road turns left and bears round to the entrance lodges of Stowe House, now one of the most famous public-schools in England. The house was inherited by Viscount Cobham in 1697, who laid out **Stowe Gardens** *(open during the Easter and summer-holidays),* for which he enlisted the services of William Kent, James Gibbs and many others. The result is an extraordinary mixture of lawns, lakes, temples, grottoes and follies including the Temple of British Worthies, and the first use of the "ha-ha"—a device for hiding a fence in a ditch so that the view from the house provides a vista of lawns unmarred by artificial boundaries.

East of Buckingham we are in rapidly-changing territory, for here, based on the tiny hamlet that gives it its name, is **Milton Keynes,** the new town destined to house a quarter of a million people by 1991. It will embrace several villages such as Woughton, Simpson and Loughton as well as Stony Stratford, on the A5 coaching road. **Stony Stratford,** with its *Cock Inn* and *Bull Inn* (from where the expression "a cock-and-bull story" originates), is a pleasant town, rich in history and, like Buckingham, a victim to two disastrous fires in the 18th century which destroyed one church and damaged the other.

Bletchley, seven miles south on the A5, had already "developed" before Milton Keynes was even thought of, and today is an ugly and featureless conglomeration of shops along a road from the busy railway station. In the middle of the urban sprawl is the handsome parish church on an island of green. Between Bletchley and the A5 is **Fenny Stratford** church, much restored in 1700 by the Bucks historian, Browne Willis, in memory of his parents. Both Willis's father and grandfather died on the 11th of November, in different years, and in his will Browne Willis left money for the firing of several small cannon in the churchyard on the anniversary of the event. These are the well-known "Fenny Poppers" which, to this day, are fired in the churchyard at intervals during the 11th November.

On the main line from Euston just north of Bletchley is **Wolverton,** a typical railway-town with long rows of Victorian houses and the home for many years of railway carriage works. It is still an important railway centre, and the vast sheds still house the Royal trains. The Grand Union Canal runs through the town, and just north of the railway crosses the *Ouse* by means of a tubular bridge known locally as the "tin trunk".

Newport Pagnell (Pop.: 6,350. Hotels: *The Swan Revived*), close to the M1 has a large graceful church well restored. Various light industries, vital but unobtrusive, include the only factory in Britain making genuine parchment. Across the iron Tickford Bridge are the remains of Tickford Abbey.

North of the town, on the A50, is *Tyringham House,* once the home of William Praed, banker, MP for St. Ives, Cornwall and a financier connected with the construction of the Grand Union Canal. The house, built by Sir John Soane in 1782 but much altered, is now a health centre. On the other side of the road, two miles on, is **Gayhurst** where the church represents a fine example of church architecture in the classical tradition of 1728 and the years following. Greyhurst House *(private)* is a fine Elizabethan mansion standing back from the main road and approached by the extraordinary-looking Victorian *Sir Walter Raleigh* inn, once a gatehouse at the beginning of the long drive. Gayhurst was the home of Sir Everard

Digby who, though not a Roman Catholic, allowed his house to be used by Guy Fawkes and Robert Catesby and paid the penalty when the "Gunpowder Plot" was discovered in 1604.

The A526 (A50) from Newport Pagnell goes to Northampton. Another road, A509, strikes north for Wellingborough, crossing the *Ouse* at **Olney.** Here, in the massive and tall-spired church the rector in the 18th century was the famous John Newton, and friend of the poet William Cowper, with whom he collaborated in writing the "Olney hymns". The little town, famous once as a centre of the lace-making industry, has a single straight High Street of prim frontages. Near the church, on the village green is the house where Cowper lived from 1768 to 1786 and now the **Cowper & Newton Museum** *(daily, except Mons, Easter–Oct. Nov.– Easter, afternoons only).*

At **West Underwood,** a mile west of Olney, are the **Flamingo Gardens and Zoological Park.** *(Weds, Thurs, Sats, Suns, Bank Hols, Easter–Sept. fee.)*

In Hertfordshire and Bedfordshire

ST. ALBANS AND DISTRICT

Hertfordshire. The complicated contours of the Hertfordshire border make it difficult to define the county accurately. In the south the old Middlesex boundary pushes a deep wedge into it at Enfield and Potters Bar, and, in the west, Herts itself penetrates deep into Buckinghamshire at Tring and Long Marston. Fortunately the county has four trunk roads which, beginning in London, fan across it like the widening spokes of a wheel and so give it cohesion. They are the A1, the A5, the A6, and the A10.

The A1, when it was still called the Great North Road, entered the county at the bottom of the long hill leading up to **Barnet.** Though the A1 of today is the by-pass, Barnet is still very much alive, busy with shops and shoppers, the traffic constantly grinding to a halt at the traffic-lights in the town centre. Here the road divides, the A411 going to Elstree to the west, while through the town the A1081 to St. Albans branches off the A1000 to Hatfield.

On the A1081 the historical significance of Barnet is perpetuated by the stone obelisk at **Hadley Green** marking the site of the Battle of Barnet during Easter 1471. This was one of the bloodiest battles in what came to be known later as the Wars of the Roses (a name first used by Sir Walter Scott) and the culmination of the long struggle between the houses of York and Lancaster. Ostensibly the struggle was between Henry VI of Lancaster and Edward IV of York, but the prime mover was the Earl of Warwick who was slain at Barnet, the price he paid for attempting to act as "Kingmaker" to both sides. Today **Hadley Green,** surrounded by charming Georgian houses, seems peaceful enough, and **Monken Hadley,** on the Hatfield Road, is reminded of those grim and gory days only by the presence of a fire-basket on the roof of its church, placed there as a beacon warning in 1494.

This atmosphere of rural calm is characteristic of this stretch of ground between North London and the adjacent counties where tracts of wooded landscape, like **Totteridge Park,** create a "green belt" far more real and durable than any administrative invention of the planners. A similar stretch is along the A411 between Barnet and **Elstree,** the latter famous for film-making in England which began there in 1913. Beyond the vast expanse of water represented by **Aldenham** reservoirs, and past Elstree Aerodrome, is *Aldenham School,* founded by Richard Platt, a brewer, in 1597. On the other side of **Letchmore Heath** and Aldenham village is another old scholastic foundation, *Haberdasher Aske's School,* moved here in 1950 from Hampstead and occupying Wall Hall, a house once owned by the American millionaire J. Pierpoint Morgan. Aldenham church shows Norman architecture, a 13th-century font and a 14th-century oak parish chest 10 feet long and hollowed out of a single tree-trunk.

Across-country east of Aldenham is **Radlett,** once a brickmaking village on the Roman Watling Street (A5). On the main road is a *Coal Duty Post,* one of the few remaining examples of the posts erected in 1861 by the City of London Corporation to mark the points at which tax had to be paid on coal coming into the capital by road.

Between the A5 and the A6 is **Shenley,** with its 18th-century circular lock-up beside the village green. In the church is the tomb of Nicholas Hawksmoor, the 18th-century architect and pupil of Wren.

Both main roads cross the river *Colne,* the A5 at **Colney Street** and the A6 at **London Colney,** before they meet briefly and separate again at St. Albans.

St. Albans

Distances.—London, 21; Aylesbury, 24; Dunstable, 13; Luton, 11.
Early Closing.—Thursday.
Entertainment.—Abbey Theatre. Concerts in City Hall.
Hotels.—*Great Red Lion*, High Street; *White Hart*,

Holywell Hill; *Sopwell House*, Cottonmill Lane.
Population.—52,000.
Post Office.—St. Peter's Street.
Sport.—Swimming (open and covered), golf (18-hole municipal course), bowls, tennis.

St. Albans is an old and picturesque town at the meeting of two great roads 21 miles north-west of London. It is a favourite residential area with several light industries, busy shops and markets.

In A.D. 304 Alban, a Roman, was executed for his conversion to the Christian faith. In the 8th century Offa II of Mercia built a church on the spot and called it St. Albans. It became an important centre of pilgrimage, the church was raised to the status of an abbey and a new town developed.

The present **Cathedral** raised to that dignity in 1877, incorporates much of the original building and the great Norman pillars and arches are some of the most massive in the country. With a length of 550 feet it is second only to Winchester in this respect. The massive Norman tower is 145 feet high. The earliest parts, which include Roman tiles from Verulamium, date from about 1080. The fine painted ceiling of the choir is medieval. Other features are the St. Alban Chapel with marble-based St. Alban's Shrine, the chantry tomb of Humphrey, Duke of Gloucester, son of Henry IV, and a fine chancel screen.

Verulamium, the former Roman city, lies a little to the west on the banks of the *Ver*. The Museum *(daily, fee)* houses an important collection of Roman remains including hypocaust, mosaic flooring, parts of a theatre, and of the city wall. Verulamium was the only "municipium", or privileged town with equal rights to Rome, established in this country by the Romans. It was sacked by Boadicea in A.D. 61 but rebuilt to become the third largest centre in Britain.

The steep Holywell Hill runs down from the crossroads at the Market Place in which is the 15th-century **Clock Tower** *(weekdays, Spring Bank Hol.–mid-Sept.)* which contains a bell cast in 1335 and a collection of medieval glass and pottery. Through the Market Place is the wide St. Peter's Street, where today's market is held at week-ends. A plaque on the wall of the National Westminster Bank, formerly the Castle Inn, records the death there in 1455 of Edmund Beaufort, Earl of Somerset. Nearby in French Row is the 13th-century *Fleur-de-Lys* inn. Many coaching inns survive in the town including the 15th-century half-timbered *White Hart* in Holywell Hill, and the *Peahen,* while down by the river is the *Fighting Cocks,* once a fishing lodge attached to the monastery and one of the oldest inns in England.

St. Albans was the scene of two important battles during the Wars of the Roses, in 1455 and again in 1461. The first took place at the spot now called Key Field and the other at Barnard's Heath a little to the north.

Many interesting mementoes of St. Albans in past history can be seen in the **City Museum,** Hatfield Road *(weekdays, except Mons and Tues in winter)*. The museum includes the Salaman Collection of tools and implements illustrating local crafts and industries.

Gorhambury House *(May–Sept., Thurs, fee),* three miles north near the A5, is the seat of the Earls of Verulam of whom the most famous representative was Francis Bacon, Elizabethan poet and statesman. The present house dates from *c.* 1780.

North-west of St. Albans the A5 leaves Hertfordshire just past **Markyate,** an unassuming village with a pleasant church at the end of an avenue of limes. The poet Cowper, born in Hertfordshire at Berkhamsted, came to Dr. Pitman's School here in 1740, an experience that gave him a hatred of schools and schoolmasters for the rest of his life.

The A6 leaves St. Albans by St. Peter's Street and runs north to **Harpenden** *(Harpenden Arms)*, with its wide and beautiful common of gorse and heather that narrows down to a picturesque if slightly self-conscious High Street. On the west side of the Common is the *Rothamsted Experimental Station,* a world centre for agricultural research established in 1843 by Sir John Lawes whose family owned the original mansion. (Technical visitors only by application to the secretary.)

Five miles east of Harpenden is the village of **Wheathampstead,** on the parallel B651 from St. Albans. *Mackery End Farm* was well-loved by Charles Lamb, who wrote a famous essay about it. The church contains the tomb of Hugh and Margaret Bostock, the chapel to the Garrard family, and a small sculpture of Apsley Garrard a member of Scott's Antarctic Expedition in 1913.

From Wheathampstead a minor road leads to **Ayot St. Lawrence** where George Bernard Shaw lived from 1906 until his death in 1950. His home, **Shaw's Corner** *(daily, except Tues. Closed mid-Dec.–mid-Jan.)* is now a museum and kept much as it was in his lifetime. His ashes were scattered in the garden. The twin village of **Ayot St. Peter** is on a hilltop and provides fine views as the lane drops down to the old village of **Welwyn.** This was once an important place on the old coach road, but today has been allowed to sleep quietly and dream of its past whilst the traffic roars along the A1 (M) that by-passes Knebworth and Stevenage. Slightly to the south, on the other side of the main road, is **Welwyn Garden City,** the second development of Ebenezer Howard who had created Letchworth Garden City in 1903. Welwyn was begun in 1920 and is a distinct improvement on Letchworth, with its wider roads, fine parks and more attempt at individuality than was present in Howard's first development. It was officially designated a New Town in 1948.

South of Welwyn Garden City on the old Great North Road (A1000) is **Hatfield** *(Comet, Stonehouse, Salisbury)* now transformed into another "New Town" alongside the main road and leaving the old High Street to stagnate or so it might seem.

Hatfield House *(Apr.–Sept., daily except Mons, fee)* the ancestral home of the Cecils, earls of Salisbury, is a great mansion built in 1611 beside the remains of a Tudor palace of the Bishops of Ely and acquired by Henry VIII chiefly as a residence for his children. The house contains a wealth of Tudor and Jacobean treasures.

Close to the Gatehouse of the Old Palace the parish church of Hatfield contains the tombs of Lord Melbourne, Prime Minister to Queen Victoria, and his eccentric wife Lady Caroline Lamb.

Knebworth House *(Easter–Sept., daily except Mons, fee)*, three miles north of Welwyn off the old coach road, was built in the early 1500's as the home of the Lytton family and enlarged by the 1st Lord Lytton. Its furniture and paintings form a panorama of five centuries of English history. The beautiful grounds and deer park have portions laid out for picnic and pleasure grounds.

Still on the great North Road (A1000) the old-world village of **Stevenage** sits side-by-side with the vast development known as Stevenage New Town.

Not surprisingly perhaps, the relationship is a happy one, for Stevenage had its first "new town" as far back as the 13th century when the abbot of Westminster uprooted the village from its original site near the parish church and transplanted it astride the main road. The Stevenage Development Corporation have been wise and in this development have carefully avoided the soul-destroying acres of identical streets and houses, with only one centre for shopping, that was a feature of earlier housing experiments. At Stevenage the various hamlets that have been engulfed have been allowed to retain not only their names, but also their identity, the result being that while Stevenage is justifiably proud of its fine pedestrian-only New Town Centre, each part of this great sprawl of housing also has its own shops, churches and pubs in a modern form. Names like Sheppall, Chells, Pin Green and Almonds Spring all preserve the identity of these lost villages and help to foster a wealth of local activities and associations that do not have to depend on the facilities offered by the Corporation. Sometimes the combination of old names and new associations can be slightly unfortunate, as in the Bedwell Happy Wives' Club, but this is probably an improvement on that other classic from Essex, the Ugley Women's Institute.

Hitchin, five miles to the north-west, is a very different place from Stevenage. Here the ancient town has grown up around the church and market place (*see* "Chilterns section") and it is farther north, on the county boundary at **Letchworth,** that we find the first experiments in artificial urban growth as conducted by Ebenezer Howard in 1903. A curiosity of this town was that until a few years ago it was entirely "dry" though a hostelry, tactfully called *The Skittles,* supplied no beer but only soft drinks from the very early days.

Baldock *(George and Dragon)* is an ancient town along the even more ancient Icknield Way (A505) at a point where it crosses the Great North Road. The staggered road junction at its centre is still a busy place, though the wide streets preserve the many handsome Georgian frontages from the vibrations of traffic as happens in some less fortunate towns. *Wynne's Almshouses* of 1621 have had a Victorian restoration that has scarcely improved them. The churchyard has a touching epitaph to a small boy killed at play in 1821.

The area round Hitchin and Baldock, with its wide horizons, straight roads rising and falling over the chalk of the downs, has many villages well worth exploring. **St. Ippollits,** for example, which takes its odd name from the dedication of its little church to the 3rd-century Roman martyr who miraculously cured horse ailments. **Clothall,** still with the cultivation-terraces of the Saxons growing wheat and the quaint group of raised pews at the back of the village church: **St. Paul's Walden,** birthplace of the Queen Mother and famous for the 600-year-old fragments of stained glass in the window of the tower.

Through **Cottered** and **Sandon** the land is high and drops down to **Royston** and the A10 to Cambridge. The A14 from Royston runs dead straight to Huntingdon, crossing into Cambridgeshire just north of the town.

BEDFORD AND DISTRICT

Bedfordshire. The wide range of scenery and activities that combine to make up this county does not strike the visitor immediately. His first impression is likely to be shaped by the direction from which he enters it. Along the Icknield Way, through Dunstable, he is immediately conscious of the thriving car industry of Luton, its busy Airport, the hotels grouped round the access roads to the M1 and the steep streets and roadways of this hilly town up which lorries grind incessantly.

Coming from the Hertfordshire boundary and the Great North Road via Hitchin the impression is completely different. Bedfordshire here appears to be a county of high, rounded hills, green and inviting, with Sharpenhoe Clappers and its woods rising out of the countryside around it as the most northerly outcrop of the Chiltern Hills which start by the *Thames* in the far south.

Yet a third aspect of the county is seen along the A418 from Leighton Buzzard to Bedford, where, on approaching the county town, the land seems flat and sullen, only the tall chimneys of the brickworks around Kempston and Elstow relieving the monotony of this featureless lunar landscape.

All of these are Bedfordshire, yet none of them are typical of the county any more than are the herds of Père David's deer in Woburn Park or the baboons who remove your windscreen wipers in the Wild Animal Kingdom. If anything is typical of Bedfordshire it is its untypicality—its refusal to conform to accepted ideas of what the English countryside should look like, its juxtaposition of industry and rurality and a blending of the old and the new in startling contrast.

The A1, the A5 and the A6, fanned out this distance from London to encompass the county from east to west, make it easy to explore.

Bedford

Distances.—Aylesbury, 30; Buckingham, 27; Dunstable, 20; Huntingdon, 21; London, 51; Luton, 19.
Early Closing.—Wednesday.

Hotels.—*De Parys, County, Swan, Embankment.*
Population.—73,000.
Post Office.—Dame Alice Street.

Bedford, the county town, is of pleasing architectural contrasts, well-known for its schools and association with John Bunyan who lived in the town from 1655 until his death in 1688. The main A6 road from London enters the town by the bridge over the wide *Ouse,* tranquil and serene, and immediately plunges into a vortex of one-way streets and traffic lights that gives one little opportunity to look at the variety of ancient and historic buildings that make up this town. Once across the bridge, for example, the traffic system gyrates around St. Paul's Square, with the church in the middle of it. St. Paul's Church is an old and large building though much of it is the result of too-enthusiastic Victorian restoration during the town's peak period of prosperity in the early 19th century. It still retains some old and important monuments, notably a brass to Sir William Harpur, one of Bedford's greatest sons, founder of the Grammar School and Lord Mayor of London in 1570.

Harpur's benevolence gave rise to the Harpur Trust who now control four schools and several almshouses in the town, including *Bedford School,* De Parys Avenue, the *Boys' Modern School,* Harpur Street, *Girls' High School,* Bromham Road, and *Dame Alice Harpur School,* Cardington Road.

Outside the church is a statue to John Howard, prison reformer.

For the visitor one of the most pleasant and rewarding new buildings in Bedford is the **Public Library** in Harpur Street, gleaming with light and efficiency, and with a coffee-bar and lounge provided. It houses the *Bunyan Memorial Library Collection* of Books on Bunyan and his times. In Mill Street is the **Bunyan Museum** *(Tues–Fris)* in a building known as the Bunyan Meeting built on the site of a former barn in which he preached. Among its treasures are copies of "Pilgrims' Progress" in some 150 different languages. The **Bedford Museum** *(daily except Sun mornings)* is on the Embankment by the *Ouse* and shows collections of local interest. Nearby is the **Cecil Higgins Art Gallery** *(daily except Sun mornings)* with a good art collection and a series of English water colours.

Just south of Bedford is the village of **Elstow,** near where Bunyan was born in 1628, and there is another collection of items associated with him in the 15th-century Moot Hall *(daily, except Mons).* Elstow also has an important parish church which was once part of a Benedictine nunnery founded in 1075.

Two miles due east of Elstow (though visible for many miles) is **Cardington,** with its great black hangars which once housed the R.101 airship before its tragic maiden flight to India in 1930 in which it crashed. It is one of the few places in England where the war-time barrage balloons can still be seen, for they are used at this RAF base in the training of parachutists. John Howard lived at Cardington, in lonely splendour after the early death of his wife and before he embarked on his life's work of prison reform. On the Green in the village is *Howard's House (not open).* Howard's friend, the brewer and philanthropist Samuel Whitbread, also lived in the village and, in fact, paid for the bridge over the river which he commissioned from the great engineer William Smeaton, builder of the Eddystone Lighthouse. The large village church has one of the only two black basalt fonts in England (the other is at Essendon, Herts).

Six miles south of Bedford on the A418 is **Ampthill,** a lovely village set amid hills and with criss-cross streets that have something of interest to reveal at every turn. From the churchyard of St. Andrew's are wonderful views of the surrounding countryside and inside the church is a curious effigy to Richard Nicholls (*d.* 1672) incorporating the cannonball that killed him! Once there was a castle here, to which Henry VIII sent his first wife, Catherine of Aragon, while arranging his divorce from her. During her stay she is said to have introduced the Spanish lace-making art into this part of the country. The grounds surrounding the castle are now **Ashburnham Park,** in which the public are free to wander, though the house now on the castle site is a Cheshire Home. *Houghton House,* a mile north of the village, is the shell of a large mansion said to have been built in 1615 for the Countess of Pembroke. In the 18th century it was bought by the Duke of Bedford whose family decided to dismantle it in 1794. It is thought to have been the inspiration for Bunyan's "House Beautiful".

At Silsoe, four miles south-east of Ampthill is **Wrest Park** *(Apr.–Oct., Sats, Suns, Bank Hols)* where the Department of the Environment maintains a formal canal garden of great charm.

Four miles to the east of Bedford is the village of **Willington.** The massive barn-like building just north of A603 is a **dove-cote** (N.T., *daily. Key from cottage opposite church*) and, with the adjoining range of stables, dates from the 16th century. It has accommodation for 1,500 pigeons each with its own nesting-box. Even stranger than this, for many, is the outline of the docks that can still be traced down by the *Ouse,* where the Danes cut a channel and installed a boat-repairing yard over a thousand years ago. On the same road, but across the river *Ivel* and the Great North Road, is **Sandy,** a name that indicates the kind of soil found in this part of Bedfordshire and accounts for its value for market-gardening, of which Sandy is a centre. North of Sandy, where the A428 joins the A1, is **Roxton** where the *Ouse* is crossed at Tempsford Bridge. There are some lovely buildings including the delightful Congregational Chapel with its verandah of tree-trunks and roofed with thatch. It was converted from a barn in 1808 by Charles Metcalfe who, as lord-of-the-manor, built a "model" estate nearby for his workers in a similar style.

Another model village of mid-Victorian vintage is found at **Old Warden,** two miles west of Biggleswade, built by Lord Ongley in the 1850s and whose influence can also be traced in the 12th-century parish church, one of the oldest in the county, but irretrievably spoiled by his lordship's virtual rebuilding of the interior. On the old airfield here is the **Shuttleworth Trust Collection** *(daily)* of historical aircraft and cars. Demonstration flights of some of the veteran aircraft are given on Sundays from April to September.

If any village can be called typical of the Bedfordshire countryside it is probably **Podington** north-west of Bedford and close to the border with Northamptonshire. With its warm stone buildings it is certainly typical of north Bedfordshire. Its church is Norman and has a good 14th-century "Doom" and other wall paintings.

Just over a mile south of Podington, almost on the county boundary, is **Hinwick House** *(Bank Hol. Mons only, otherwise by written application)* built in the reign of Queen Anne and housing a private collection of furniture and paintings including some by Kneller, Lely and Van Dyck.

At Stagsden, five miles west of Bedford on the A422, are the **Stagsden Bird Gardens** *(daily, fee)* a large bird zoo and breeding establishment with over 1,300 specimens, and a fine display of shrub roses.

East Anglia

LONDON TO SOUTHEND

The A13 road to Southend leaves London via **Barking,** a town which, despite its present appearance, has a long and important history. It is separated from the metropolis by the river *Roding* which enters the *Thames* at Barking Creek two miles downstream from the Royal Group of Docks. Barking was famous for its Benedictine Nunnery as far back as A.D. 670 and the Abbess of Barking exerted a powerful influence until the Reformation. None of the original abbey buildings now remain, but at the entrance of the parish church is the two-storey Firebell Gate built in the 12th century, and the church itself has many interesting brasses and monuments dating from the 15th century. In Tudor Road, south of Ripple Road (A123) is **Eastbury House** (N.T., *not open*) an attractive Elizabethan building built in 1572.

The A13 continues eastwards to **Dagenham,** a vast area of municipal housing which includes the *Becontree Estate,* begun in 1921 and, with a population of over 100,000, the largest undertaking of its kind. In its early days an attempt was made to move the indigenous Chinese population of Limehouse to Becontree, but at each attempt the Chinese returned to Limehouse, walking back with their belongings piled on handcarts, and the project was abandoned. Dagenham is also famous for the presence of the giant Ford Motor Company factory, established there in 1932 and employing nearly 20,000 people. It has its own docks and railway and at night the enormous illuminated sign bearing the company name can be seen for many miles.

The A13 skirts the uninspiring village of **Rainham** and continues to the Thames-side town of **Purfleet** dominated by the tall chimneys of the Tunnel Cement Company. Local industry also includes the Thames Board Mills, producing paper and cardboard, but despite the commercial activities Purfleet retains a certain 19th-century charm in its riverside inns such as the *Royal Hotel* and other examples of Georgian architecture. These include the handsome Government Powder Magazine transferred across the *Thames* from Greenwich about 1760. Between Purfleet and West Thurrock to the east is the northern entrance to the *Dartford Tunnel,* that long-awaited link between Essex and Kent.

West Thurrock has a surprisingly beautiful little 14th-century church, once isolated on the marshes. The church provides a minor mystery in that excavations have revealed that it stands on the site of an earlier circular church of which the origins and unusual shape have never been explained. **Grays** is a busy riverside town, modern north of the railway but Georgian or earlier between railway and river.

From Grays the A13 to Southend runs inland, but a lower road (A126) keeps roughly parallel with the river and enters **Tilbury** by way of the 100-acre dock system which, though 20 miles from it, are part of London Docks. **Tilbury Docks** have recently been modernised and continue their function as the departure-point for the P & O Line and other companies serving India and the Far East. Before the docks were built in the 1880s Tilbury had a population of less than 400, though, like Barking and West Thurrock, evidence of it being an ancient settlement is to be found. The parish church includes 13th-century material and the town was certainly in existence in the 7th century when it was converted to Christianity by St. Chad.

On the marshlands west of the town stands **Tilbury Fort** *(daily, fee)* built in 1682 to repel the expected invasion by the French and Dutch. It was largely rebuilt in Victorian times and continued to serve as a useful vantage point from which to survey the Thames Estuary both in the 1914–18 War and in World War II. Just north of the Fort is the site of *Tilbury Camp* where, in 1588, Queen Elizabeth I made her famous speech to her assembled troops at the time of the Armada.

The villages which stretch along this part of the Essex shore are not very picturesque, many with slightly off-putting names like **Coryton, Mucking** and **Fobbing.** This area also includes **Canvey Island,** separated from the mainland only by a narrow creek and once the haunt of smugglers.

The B1014 road from Canvey Island joins the A13 at South Benfleet and runs into Southend via Leigh-on-Sea and Westcliff.

Southend-on-Sea

Distances.—London, 42; Colchester, 37; Romford, 25; Chelmsford, 19.

Early Closing.—Wednesday.

Entertainments.—Pier Pavilion, Cliffs Pavilion, Kursaal, Dolphinarium, Peter Pan Childrens' Playground, Historic Aircraft Museum.

Hotels.—*Royal,* Royal Terrace; *Kia-Ora,* Palmeira Ave; *Mayflower,* Royal Terrace; *Boston Hall,* The Leas, Westcliff; *Ellesmere,* Penbury Road, Westcliff; *Wooburn Guest House,* Thorpe Bay.

Library.—Victoria Ave, Southend; Broadway West, Leigh-on-Sea; London Road, Westcliff.

Population.—165,000.

Post Office.—Weston Road.

Sports.—Riding, Golf (Municipal Golf Course, Belfairs Park), archery, bowls, athletics Stadium.

For more than a hundred years Southend has been the favoured week-end retreat of generations of Londoners. The result is a prosperous and bouncing town, full of life and vitality and, like its northern counterpart, Blackpool, brash, self-confident and raucous. Its most famous feature is its **Pier,** a mile and a third in length and the longest in the world. There is a floral clock 60 feet in diameter, and along the front every other shop seems to be selling fish-and-chips, cockles, whelks and that true Cockney favourite—jellied eels. Yet Southend began as a royal watering-place in 1809, when the Prince Regent decided that the seaside village of *Prittlewell* would be healthier for his bride, the Princess Caroline, than her embarrassing proximity in London. Caroline stayed at the south end of Prittlewell—and Southend it soon became in its own right. Its popularity grew, until today the borough has engulfed not only Prittlewell but the neighbouring towns of Westcliff, Leigh-on-Sea and Thorpe Bay.

West Cliff and **Thorpe Bay** represent the rather more "genteel" parts of Southend for those who do not wish to admit to staying in the town itself. Westcliff is older and retains a certain character of its own, but Thorpe Bay is modern and slightly prim compared with its more rumbustious neighbours. From Thorpe Bay Esplanade one can look across the Thames Estuary almost 10 miles to Sheerness on the Kent coast.

Leigh-on-Sea already existed before Southend became popular. It is an old fishing village, well-used to smugglers in its time, and even today carrying on a healthy business in boat-building, sail-making and the catching and cooking of cockles fished from the estuary in small boats known as "bawleys". Peculiar to this part of the Essex coast is the trade of bait-digging, the bait in this case being the ragworm or "Southend worm" much prized by anglers.

From Leigh-on-Sea to the Esplanade at Thorpe Bay is a total distance of seven miles, all of which is accessible to the public, a fact which explains in part the district's attraction for the Londoner. Past Thorpe Bay the road from London ends at **Shoeburyness,** an old town today dominated by the Army gunnery-range nearby. The coastal area north of Shoeburyness is **Foulness,** the projected site of London's third airport.

Immediately north of Southend, on the A127 alternative road to London, **Prittlewell** still reminds one of its antiquity by the presence of its handsome 15th-century parish church and the remains of *Prittlewell Priory,* a Benedictine monastery established in 1100. Past Southend Municipal Airport on the B1013 is **Rochford,** an attractive old market town of half-timbered and weather-boarded houses standing on the river *Roach.* Nearby are the ruins of *Rochford Hall,* built about 1545 and once owned by the parents of Anne Boleyn whom Henry VIII may well have visited here.

The B1013 runs past **Hockley** to the large and spreading village of **Rayleigh,** another attractive market town with a wide High Street, castle ruins and a curious stump of a windmill devoid of sails but decorated with battlements! *Rayleigh Mount* (N.T.) is the site of an 11th-century motte-and-bailey castle built to guard this vulnerable underbelly of Essex from marauders from the sea. South of Rayleigh the A129 joins the main road (A127) to Southend or London.

Two rivers cut deep into this part of Essex. The *Roach* comes in as far as Rochford, but north of it is the larger river *Crouch.* Between the two rivers exist a whole series of isolated villages which are probably the reason why many people think of Essex as being flat. Certainly this remote area is, but it has a character all of its own. **Canewdon,** for example, has an ancient and surprisingly large parish church for such a sparse population. At **Hullbridge** is the first ferry across the *Crouch* at a point nearly 15 miles inland from the sea.

LONDON TO COLCHESTER

At Whipps Cross, **Leytonstone,** the two routes from London to East Anglia separate, the A11 to Newmarket and Norwich bearing left while the A12 to Colchester continues on to **Wanstead.** At the crossroads here stands an old coaching inn, *The George,* on the corner of which is a curious plaque erected "In memory of cherry pye, eaten here the fifteenth of July 1753". Between Wanstead and Manor Park is **Wanstead Flats,** an extensive and welcome lung of this part of suburban London.

The A12 skirts **Ilford** and **Romford** to reach *Gallows Corner,* where the road to Colchester branches left and the A127 to Southend-on-Sea continues on what was one of the first "arterial roads" built in the London area.

Past Harold Wood open country is at last reached, and at **Brentwood** one feels that the real Essex has begun and London is far behind, though it is only 15 miles from Aldgate Pump, the traditional point from which distances to the Eastern Counties are measured. Brentwood still has the air of a pleasant country town. In Ingrave Road the old walls of the Grammar School built in 1568 can be seen, while in the High Street are the even older ruins of St. Thomas's Chapel dating from 1221. As an important stop on the old coach road to Colchester, Brentwood has several old inns and even a few Georgian shop-fronts can be found amidst the depressing similarity of the modern multiple businesses who, paradoxically, attempt to assert their individuality by this means.

South of Brentwood is beautiful Warley Common, and **Warley** Village has the famous Barracks that have been the HQ of the Essex Regiment since 1742.

From the centre of Brentwood a road (A128) runs north to **Kelvedon Hatch,** with its two fine Georgian mansions, and then to **Chipping Ongar.** This pretty village, with its old picturesque bow-fronted shops and steep High Street, still manages to preserve its attractive atmosphere of changeless age despite the fact that it is now the terminus of the Central London Line.

One mile west is **Greensted.** Here the church of St. Andrew is one of the smallest and most interesting churches in Britain. It was built in 1013 to house the body of the martyred St. Edmund on its journey from London to Bury St. Edmunds, in Suffolk, and its walls are built entirely of split oak tree-trunks, the rounded sides being placed outward. Many of the trees used in the construction of this unique church were already two centuries old when the church was built.

Immediately outside Brentwood, at **Shenfield,** a branch road (A129) runs south-east to **Billericay** and **Wickford,** both old market towns whose individualities have been almost obliterated by development as commuter areas.

The A12 continues past the handsome and well-preserved windmill at **Mountnessing** and enters **Ingatestone.** This long village has a most interesting 15th-century Parish Church, and nearby is **Ingatestone Hall** *(Apr.–Oct., Tues.–Sats, free),* a fine Elizabethan house of 1545 containing exhibits of armour, portraits and documents of Essex life.

Just east of the village, on the B1007, is **Stock,** considered by many to be one of the most attractive of Essex villages. Its main delight is the charming timber belfry and white wooden spire of the church, while round it are grouped the old almshouses, the village green and pump all combining to make a picture which lingers long in the memory.

Between the main road and the B1007 lies the upland area of *Galleywood Common* with its gorse, ferns and splendid views, giving the lie to the theory that Essex is flat. Here is the famous Galleywood Racecourse in use since 1759.

Chelmsford

Angling.—River *Can,* Central Park, Chelmsford *(free),* Lille Baddow Lock, River *Chelmer,* Hoe Mill Lock *(daily tickets).*
Distances.— London, 33; Colchester, 22; Southend, 19; Bishop's Stortford, 18; Dunmow, 12; Braintree, 11.
Early Closing.—Wednesday.
Entertainments.—Civic Theatre, Chancellor Hall,

Chelmsford & Essex Museum. Cinemas.
Hotels.—*County,* Rainsford Rd. *Beechcroft* (Pvte). New London Road. *Plough,* Duke Street.
Library.—Civic Centre.
Population.—60,000.
Post Office.—High Street.
Sports.—Cricket, fencing, boating, weight-lifting club, archery, netball, rifle-club.

Chelmsford is the county town of Essex and has been of importance since 1100, when the Bishop of London ordered the building of a new bridge across the river *Chelmer* leading to its growth and later status of an assize town. Though the town has spread enormously in latter years, the centre still indicates its antiquity and importance in the many handsome buildings such as the 18th-century Shire Hall and the attractive Corn Exchange nearby. The 15th-century church was elevated to the status of a **Cathedral** in 1926 and contains an ornate tomb to the Mildmay family who were important local landowners. Opposite the Shire Hall is a statue to another illustrious resident, Sir Nicholas Tindal, who became Lord Chief Justice of England in the early 1800s. The Essex County Museum *(weekdays)* is situated in Moulsham Street. In Springfield Road are the high brick walls of the County Gaol, first opened in 1822 but altered in 1848 to conform with the plan of the "New Model Prison" in London at Pentonville.

Two miles west of Chelmsford is **Writtle,** for ever associated with Marconi and his first experiments in wireless telegraphy. The Parish Church contains an impressive monument to a local worthy depicting the Parable of the Sower and including effigies of two girls wearing wide straw hats, asleep instead of working. The village has another of those attractive greens which are such a feature of this area, and several beautiful old houses including the 15th-century timber-framed Moor Hall, Aubyns, also timber-framed and built about 1500, and Mundays, a dignified 17th-century house. All are privately owned.

Great Baddow, two miles south-west of Chelmsford, is a place of elegant Georgian and early-Victorian houses and was obviously the place where the wealthy of Chelmsford elected to live in its palmiest days. The handsome Parish Church is beautifully sited on top of a hill.

Maldon

Angling.—Good facilities for both fresh and salt-water fishing.
Distances.—London, 43; Southend, 20; Colchester, 16; Chelmsford, 10.
Early Closing.—Wednesday.
Entertainments.—Embassy Cinema; Marine Lake; Boating Pool.

Hotels.—*Blue Boar*, Silver Street; *Swan*, High Street; *King's Head*, High Street.
Library.—St. Peter's Room, High Street.
Population.—14,000.
Post Office.—High Street.
Sports.—Yachting, bowls, tennis (8 municipal courts), golf (9 holes).

Reached from Chelmsford by A414, Maldon with the adjoining Heybridge Basin, a mecca for yachtsmen, is situated on the estuary of the river *Blackwater*. Though mentioned in the Domesday Book, the name of Maldon is of Saxon origin and was obviously of importance long before the Normans came. Quaint and narrow streets with old inns, like the *Blue Boar* in Silver Street, make this town attractive in its own right even for those who have no hankering for the nautical life. At one time Maldon had three churches, the present Parish Church being that of All Saints at the top of Market Hill. Lower down is the sole surviving tower of St. Peter's Church which fell into ruin and was abandoned in 1665. In 1700 a native of the town, the celebrated Dr. Thomas Plume, purchased the old church and built a school and a library on the site of the nave, incorporating the tower into the structure. This is now the Plume Library and contains over 6,000 of the doctor's books. **Heybridge Basin** is devoted to sailing, either for pleasure or for a living, the result being an astonishing variety of craft to be seen including examples of the fast-disappearing Essex sailing barge.

From Maldon the B1008 runs through Latchingdon to **Burnham-on-Crouch.** This is another favourite yachting centre, devoted more to pleasure-sailing than to commerce. The terraced houses along the Quay, centred on the dignified *White Hart Hotel,* provide much of the distinctive atmosphere of this little port. Here the estuary is the rather narrower one of the *Crouch*, and its popularity for yachtsmen is indicated by the modern white buildings of the Royal Corinthian Yacht Club, one of five sailing-clubs having their headquarters here. During the annual Yachting Week Burnham is thronged with yachtsmen and visitors and at times as many as 3,000 craft may be gathered in the estuary.

The area of land between the *Blackwater* and the *Crouch* is a flat and lonely region of wildfowl and salt-marshes. North of Burnham the only town of any size is **Southminster** whose church was once of importance in this area. After the death of Nelson at Trafalgar his chaplain became rector here, and in the vestry are preserved several relics of the admiral, who was born in Essex. East of the B1021 lie the desolate *Dengie* and *Tillingham* marshes, part-covered at high tide and visited by few.

Of great interest in this almost-forgotten and lonely area is **Bradwell,** on the southern bank of the *Blackwater* estuary. Here is the small and simple Saxon church of *St. Peter-on-the-Wall*, built in 654, and one of the oldest surviving buildings in the country. The walls of a Norman fort can be seen close at hand, and in this region of wide horizons and endless space even the presence of a nuclear power station scarcely seems to intrude. Between here and Chelmsford are several isolated villages, and between **Steeple Wick** and **St. Lawrence** is a chapel labelled "The Peculiar People", once an outpost of the short-lived religious sect of that name founded in London in 1838.

Past Chelmsford the A12 continues through **Boreham,** where an odd-looking church containing both Norman and Roman work gives it more than passing interest. The straight Roman road runs through **Wittham,** a fine large village with a wide High Street and several attractive coaching inns including the *Spread Eagle* and the *White Hart*. The Parish Church is almost entirely 14th century.

A sharp double bend in the A12 heralds the approach to **Kelvedon,** another small town well-known to travellers on this important road. Today it is by-passed and has reverted to its former quiet and elegance represented by such charming buildings as the Ormonde House, the half-timbered houses of the High Street, many of them with later Georgian shop-fronts, and the many-arched bridge that carries the main road over the *Blackwater*.

At **Marks Tey** the A12 is joined by another Roman road, Stane Street (A120) coming from Braintree, and finally enters the great Roman town of Colchester.

Colchester

Distances.—London, 56; Chelmsford, 22; Braintree, 15; Ipswich, 18.
Early Closing.—Thursday.
Entertainments.—Colchester & Essex Museum; Minories Art Gallery.
Hotels.—*George,* High Street; *Red Lion,* High Street; *Cloisters,* Maldon Road.
Library.—Stockwell Street.
Post Office.—Head Street.
Population.—74,000.
Sports.—Golf, swimming (indoor), cricket, hockey, tennis.

With its centre sited on top of a steep hill, Colchester is justifiably proud of being the oldest named town in Britain.

Its original name came from Camulos, the Saxon war-god and at the time of the Romans this part of Britain was ruled by Cunobelin, the "Cymbeline" of Shakespeare. As *Camulodunum* it was of the greatest importance to the Romans in repelling the attacks of the neighbouring Iceni, and in A.D. 61 the redoubtable Boadicea gained her greatest victory when she attacked and sacked the town. The Romans fortified and strengthened the bastions and today the walls they built, in some places 10 feet thick, can still be seen. At one point they are pierced by the massive Balkerne Gate, one of the largest town gates in Britain.

The Castle *(daily).* Colchester seems to have done many things on a grand scale, and the ruins of Colchester Castle, built by the Normans, has the largest keep in England and one of the largest in Europe. It houses the *Castle Museum* which contains the largest collection of Roman remains ever assembled.

More history can be seen at the **Seige House** near the East Bridge over the *Colne,* where cannon-balls are still embedded in the timbers as a result of the seige of the town in 1648 during the Civil War.

Colchester has a long military history and is still a garrison town. But it was also commercially of great importance and boasts several large inns of which perhaps the finest and most picturesque are the *Red Lion,* the *George* and the *Marquis of Granby.* Much of the town's wealth came from the trade in oysters centred on The Hythe, from where the white-sailed dredgers fished the estuary of the *Colne* for the famous Colchester "natives" which were highly-valued even before the coming of the Romans. The town has a total of 23 churches—something of a problem in these days of small congregations. The problem has been successfully solved in at least one instance where the former All Saints Church has now become a Natural History Museum *(weekdays).* A church still very much performing its intended function is St. Botolph's which, though built in 1837, adjoins the ruins of the Norman priory of the same name.

From Colchester several roads run radially inland and to the coast. The A12 continues north-east to reach the "Constable Country" at **Dedham** on the river *Stour* before entering Suffolk. Here Castle House was the former home of Sir Alfred Munnings RA and is now an art gallery *(May–Oct., Weds and Suns).*

Eastwards the B1027 leads towards the Essex coast, with a branch to **Brightlingsea,** a small resort at the mouth of the *Colne* with a long tradition of fishing and sailing. The tower of the 13th-century church is 94 feet high and one of the finest in the Eastern Counties. The road continues past the ancient ruins of **St. Osyth's Priory** *(May–Sept.)* and enters Clacton-on-Sea.

Clacton-on-Sea

Bathing.—From sandy beach.
Distances.—London, 71; Ipswich, 24; Harwich, 16; Colchester, 15.
Early Closing.—Wednesday.
Entertainments.—Gaiety Arcade, Pier Avenue. Funfair, Pavilion.
Hotels.—*Royal*, Marine Parade; *Ebor Lodge*, Marine Parade; *Duncan*, Beach Road; *Argyll*,

Colne Road; *Windsor*, West Avenue; *Clifton Lodge*, Marine Parade and many others.
Library.—Station Road.
Population.—35,000.
Post Office.—High Street.
Sports.—Cricket, cycling, football, hockey, judo club, shooting, tennis.

The visual atmosphere of Clacton is largely that of a Victorian-Edwardian suburb. It was a fairly late developer in the seaside stakes and only within recent years has it become a minor and less ostentatious version of Southend. Nevertheless it has charm, good cliffs and walks and a *pier*, complete with bandstand, of which it is inordinately proud. Clacton is distinguished for its sands and the very beautiful *Floral Gardens* which stretch along the road towards **Holland-on-Sea,** another but smaller resort much favoured by those in retirement. South of the town is **Jaywick Sands.**

On this exposed part of the Essex coast it is no surprise to find several Martello Towers, erected during the Napoleonic Wars to repulse the expected invasion by the French. A curiosity of the area is Moot Hall, a house which looks purely 15th century but in fact is comparatively modern, the old beams having been brought from Suffolk and re-erected to a new plan on the site.

From Holland-on-Sea the B1032 runs inland through Great Holland to Kirby Cross where it joins the B1033 to Frinton. Developed between 1890 and 1900 **Frinton-on-Sea** has attained a certain reputation for a rather self-conscious exclusiveness due to the determination of the authorities to bar public transport. The result is a town that is pleasant and quiet, trim and well-ordered, with tree-lined roads and greensward leading to the cliffs, and an air of respectability. There is good bathing and sailing and a tennis club with many grass courts *(tournaments)*.

Two miles along the coast is **Walton-on-the-Naze,** a resort both in size and character midway between the slightly raffish air of Clacton and the exclusiveness of Frinton. Walton was a comparatively early seaside resort and many of its buildings date from the beginning of the 19th century. The bathing here is safe and there is good sea-fishing. Just north of the town the **Naze** forms the most easterly point on the Essex coast. It is surmounted by the 80-foot *Naze Tower,* with battlements on top, built in 1720 by Trinity House as a beacon to mariners and a signal of the approach to the estuary of the river *Stour* and the port of Harwich. The area behind the Naze is broken-up by a series of creeks and islands, like **Hamford Water** and Horsey Island, which today provide interest for bird-watchers.

Harwich, with Parkeston Quay, is a somewhat faded town though it can provide visual interest in some of its Georgian buildings, notably the enormous former Great Eastern Hotel, now the Town Hall. Also of interest is the Guildhall, dating from 1769 and the High Lighthouse built in 1818. The Redoubt was built in 1808. It is a massive circular fort nearly 200 feet in diameter, with walls eight feet thick and surrounded by a moat. South of Harwich is the modern development of **Dovercourt,** unsophisticated enough to be pleasant and relaxing, while west of the town is **Parkeston Quay,** the jumping-off point for journeys which may end in Vienna, Moscow or Berlin by way of the Hook of Holland.

From Parkeston the B1352 runs alongside the estuary past **Wrabness** to **Mistley,** where two Lodges by the roadside built by Robert Adam in 1782 mark the entrance to Mistley Hall. This was the home of Richard Rigby whose grandiose scheme to turn the village into a fashionable health resort came to nothing.

At **Wivenhoe,** on the banks of the *Colne,* the craft of boat-building has been carried on for centuries. The famous actor, Sir John Martin-Harvey was born here in what he describes in his Autobiography as "an atmosphere of tar and Oregon pine". Between the village and Colchester, in Wivenhoe Park, stand the functional buildings of the University of Essex.

BISHOP'S STORTFORD TO COLCHESTER

The river *Stort,* which formerly marked the boundary between Essex and Hertfordshire for most of its length, also had the effect of dividing **Bishop's Stortford** in two. Now the boundary has been altered and the town is entirely in Hertfordshire.

Some archaeologists think that Stortford was the final burial-place of Harold, last of the Saxon kings, who fell at Hastings. Whether or not this is true, there is no doubt that it was the birthplace of Cecil Rhodes, founder of modern Africa. His birthplace is now the **Rhodes Memorial Museum** *(weekdays)* and presents a fascinating collection of items dealing with the life and adventures of that complex personality. The centre of the town is at the top of a steeply-sloping hill and marked by a pseudo-Greek Corn Exchange of 1828, but plenty of good and more genuine Georgian shop-fronts can still be seen. The tall tower of the church, on the summit of the hill, is a landmark for many miles, and amongst its monuments is one to the Rev. Francis Rhodes, vicar of the church and father of the explorer, who died in 1878 before his son's greatest schemes came to fruition.

From the Corn Exchange the old Roman Stane Street (A120) plunges downhill, crossing the *Stort* and then climbing upwards back into Essex through **Hockerill** to **Takeley.**

Four miles out of the town a side-road (B183) branches right towards Hatfield Heath and Hatfield Broad Oak, both situated in the thousand acres of the ancient royal hunting Forest of Hatfield, now owned by the National Trust.

Southwest again are the **Rodings,** a group of eight villages all taking their second name from the river *Roding* that meanders through this lovely part of Essex before it joins the *Thames* in the unglamorous ambience of Barking Creek. But here London seems very far away. It is Essex at its best round here, rolling timbered country, unspoiled and peaceful because it has to be sought-out. The village of **Matching,** as an example, with its church and rectory, village pond and dovecote, is a rural idyll that hides itself away in the manner typical of Essex villages in these parts. It is two miles south of Hatfield Heath, the same distance west of Abbess Roding, and is reached by a lane that leads nowhere else!

Through Takeley the A120 runs on through **Great Dunmow** which, with **Little Dunmow,** will always be associated with the Dunmow Flitch. This was the flitch, or side of bacon, presented annually to the couple who could prove to the satisfaction of a "judge" and "jury" of locals that they had never wished themselves unwed for a year and a day. The first recorded presentation was in 1444, and the custom continued almost unbroken to Victorian times, when it finally lapsed. It was revived at a Whit-Monday fête at Ilford during the 1920s and has since been adopted by other towns, possibly in the hope of stemming the rising tide of divorce.

Six miles north of Dunmow is **Thaxted,** on the A130, once one of the most prosperous towns in the south of England. Its wealth was founded on wool, cloth and cutlery, and the last is preserved in the name of **Cutlers Green,** a village nearby. Thaxted has a famous and beautiful Guildhall at the top of Town Street, twin-gabled and half-timbered, its upper storeys leaning precariously over the massive timbers supporting the building which formerly provided accommodation for the weekly market. Its beauty is enhanced by its island site, and the whole of Town Street, in fact, is a repository of the changing face of English architectural styles. Behind the Guildhall is the vast Parish Church, known often as "the cathedral of Essex" and another indication of the former grandeur and wealth of this little town.

Quiet as Thaxted may seem today it has been the scene of at least two *causes celèbres,* both of them centred on the church. In 1647 a pitched battle between rival factions took place in the church when the mayor and most of the townspeople attempted to eject the new minister, Edmund Croxon, a notorious drunk and lecher. In 1922 more trouble was caused when the then incumbent, the Rev. Conrad Noel, declared that he was a "Christian Communist" and made the Red Flag the chief form of decoration in the church.

Four miles north of the town is **Hempstead,** where the famous highwayman Dick Turpin was born in his father's butchers shop. East across the oddly named river *Pant* is **Finchingfield,** that jewel of the Essex countryside considered by many to be the prettiest village in England. Certainly the pond and green, with their white-painted posts and fence, the little cottages grouped around and the squat Norman church watching over it all, makes a breathtaking picture.

The winding B1053 follows the course of the *Pant,* crossing it at **Shalford,** and finally comes through **Bocking** into Baintree, of which it is now part.

From its position on Stane Street at a point where the important pilgrims' road from Walsingham crossed it, **Braintree** has been accustomed to providing accommodation for travellers for many centuries and has rather more inns, as a result, than other places of comparable size. But its real source of wealth was from the cloth trade, established there in the 17th century and given added impetus in 1816 when the Courtauld family began the making of silk at Bocking. Since then the industry, which pioneered the production of man-made fibres, has grown enormously. The company has shown its appreciation to Braintree and Bocking in real and practical terms, and over the years has provided a hospital, public gardens and a recreation-ground, an institute and a museum.

From the other Roman road north of Bocking the A131 branches to **Halstead** on the river *Colne,* a town with a splendid steep High Street rising up from the bridge at its foot. Though several half-timbered buildings survive most of Halstead is Georgian or later and even the 14th-century Parish Church has a tower added in 1850. The convolutions of the Victorian mind also account for the presence of the chapel in Fremlins Brewery, built in 1833, which all workers were made to attend daily.

On the Essex side of the boundary with Suffolk created by the river *Colne* are **Earls Colne** and **Wakes Colne,** the latter worth visiting if only for a view of the great railway viaduct with its 30 arches, over 100 feet long, which was built in 1847 to carry the line over the Stour Valley.

From Earls Colne the B1024 runs due south to join the A120 at **Coggeshall,** another former centre of the wool trade. At one time a flourishing Cistercian Abbey existed here, founded in 1139, but a victim of the Reformation. The most notable building in the town is **Paycockes' House** (N.T., *Weds, Thurs, and Suns, afternoons, Apr.–Sept.*). It dates from about 1500 and is notable for its magnificent panelling and woodcarving. The Paycockes were wealthy merchants in the town for several generations, and their brasses may be seen in the Parish Church.

From Coggleshall it is just four miles to Marks Tey, where the A120 joins the A12 to enter Colchester.

Ipswich and District

Ipswich

Distances.—Aideburgh, 25; Clacton, 26; Colchester, 18; Harwich, 22; London, 72; Lowestoft, 44; Felixstowe, 12.
Early Closing.—Wednesday. Also all day Monday.

Hotels.—*Great White Horse, Crown and Anchor, Post House.*
Population.—123,000.

Ipswich is the biggest port between the *Thames* and the *Humber* and stands at the estuary of the *Orwell* and *Gipping* (from which latter river the town derived its old name of Gippeswic).

The Normans built a castle here, and ravaged the town in reprisal for the fact that it was owned by the sister of King Harold, whose other brother, Gyrth, was reputed to have killed the Conqueror's horse under him.

The town featured largely in many naval campaigns in medieval times, but its peaceful activities were concerned chiefly with the export of manufactured cloth, and later of corn, together with the import of coal.

Ipswich is associated with many famous men, but its most illustrious son is Cardinal Wolsey, Chaplain to Henry VII and born in the town probably in 1485. In 1528 he began his great project for a Royal College which might have rivalled Eton or Winchester, but his sudden death in 1530 after his arrest for high treason brought the scheme to an end. Today only the massive red-brick gateway, with the royal coat of arms, reminds us of this great prelate who had already founded Christ Church College, Oxford.

Ipswich is largely Victorian in appearance today, but here and there picturesque old buildings stand out. Most notable is the **Ancient House** in the Butter Market, a magnificent specimen of a 16th-century timber-framed building decorated with an extraordinary amount of pargeting. This form of decoration, consisting of designs in bold relief on the plastered walls is typical of Essex and Suffolk and found, in a much less dramatic form, in many old towns.

In Tavern Street stands the *Great White Horse* hotel, immortalised by Dickens in Pickwick Papers where a bedroom at the inn was the scene of Mr. Pickwick's unfortunate adventure with "the lady in yellow curl-papers". The figure which denotes the sign was described by Dickens as "resembling an insane cart-horse", and a far from flattering description of the inn, after Dickens had stayed there covering the local elections, almost resulted in an action for libel by the proprietor. Today it is one of the most comfortable and best-appointed hotels in the Eastern Counties.

The **Quay** at Ipswich is picturesque and always busy. There is the handsome Custom House, built in 1842, and an odd-looking granary, complete with turrets, at Stoke Bridge.

In the centre of the town is the beautiful and extensive Christchurch Park, with the fine Tudor mansion set in it built in 1548. **Christchurch Mansion** *(daily)* stands on the site of the former priory and was added to during the 17th century by the provision of handsome Dutch-style gables. Part of the house contains the *Wolsey Art Gallery,* with paintings by Constable and Gainsborough, opened in 1931 to mark the 400th anniversary of Wolsey's death.

For those interested in medieval church architecture, Ipswich is a rich field of exploration, for it has 12 churches dating from the 15th century or before. Many, including the parish church of St. Mary-le-Tower, have suffered at the hands of

Victorian restorers including Sir George Gilbert Scott, who probably did more damage to English parish churches than did Henry VIII and Cromwell combined.

Between Ipswich and Colchester lies the Valley of the *Stour* which includes the "Constable Country" made famous by the painter John Constable (1776–1837). **East Bergholt,** where the painter was born, is still largely unspoilt, and his parents are buried in the church. The village is famous for its bell-cage in the churchyard—an alternative to the more normal tower and bells which, tradition insists, was never completed due to lack of funds on the death of Wolsey. **Flatford Mill,** probably the most famous subject that Constable painted, is preserved, together with the equally well-known **Willy Lott's Cottage,** providing a tourist attraction that is somewhat marred by the inevitable tourist "amenities" of cafés and gift-shops. On the Essex bank of the river, which may be crossed by a wooden bridge, the scene is much more as it was in Constable's day when his family owned the mill.

Hadleigh, 10 miles from Ipswich on the A1071, has a long and pleasing High Street exhibiting several fine examples of pargeting and a varied mixture of architecture. The most beautiful building, however, is the 15th-century Guildhall *(Weds, except during Aug.)* which was restored in the 18th century and includes a charming Assembly Room of the period and a musicians' gallery.

South-east of Ipswich on the A45 is Felixstowe.

Felixstowe

Angling.—Off piers, off shore in boat and off beaches.

Distances.—London, 86; Colchester, 30; Ipswich, 12.

Early Closing.—Wednesday.

Entertainments.—Amusement Park, Childrens' Playground, Miniature Steam Railway, Pier Pavilion, Organ Concerts, Spa Pavilion, Cruises.

Hotels.—*Hotel-de-Novo,* Orwell Road; *Burlington,* Beach Road West; *Cavendish,* Sea Front; *Dolphin,* Beach Station Road; *Rosebery,* Sea Front.

Library.—Crescent Road.

Population.—19,000.

Post Office.—Hamilton Road.

Sports.—Bowls, cricket, croquet, golf (18-hole), roller skating, riding, tennis, water ski-ing.

Built almost entirely during the present century, Felixstowe has become one of the most pleasant of East Anglian resorts due mainly to its sheltered position between the rivers *Deben* and *Orwell,* and its south-facing aspect. Its lush almost sub-tropical vegetation has given it the title of "The Garden Resort of the East Coast" and it is certainly remarkable for the number and high standard of its parks, floral gardens and rockeries. The very small tidal movement here makes Felixstowe exceptionally safe for bathing, and therefore an ideal resort for young children. An interesting International Folk Festival organised in association with the English Folk Dance and Song Society was inaugurated in 1971.

IPSWICH TO LOWESTOFT

From Ipswich the A12 runs almost due east for a few miles before it is joined by the A1093 from Felixstowe coming in at **Martlesham.** The village has a handsome inn—the *Red Lion*—with the sign made from a ship's figure-head said to have been salvaged from a wreck in 1672.

The main road by-passes **Woodbridge,** but it would be most unwise for the explorer to do so, for Woodbridge is probably the most unspoilt small town in Suffolk. As has happened so often in this kind of place, the predominantly 16th-century buildings round Market Hill have been given Georgian shop-fronts —a sign of prosperity and a demand for goods and services among the gentry of the early 19th century.

Edward Fitzgerald, the poet who translated Omar Khayam, lived here from 1860 to 1873, and at the *Bull Inn* his friend Alfred, Lord Tennyson, lodged while visiting him.

North of Woodbridge, before the A12 is once more reached, a road to the right runs to the Saltings across the *Deben* estuary to **Sutton Hoo,** where in 1939 was discovered the famous burial-grave of a Viking ship, one of the most important finds ever made relating to that era. Eleven burial mounds were discovered, and are slowly and carefully being excavated.

The main road runs inland for some miles, but between it and the coast are several attractive villages which, through the centuries, have seen invasion by Romans, Angles and Danes coming up from the shallow shores that offer so little protection. Constant erosion is the reason why the main highway runs so far inland, and has also produced the curious peninsula of **Havergate Island,** the only breeding-ground in Britain of the rare avocet, and a paradise for bird-watchers. Havergate Island is an extension of **Orford Ness,** and a little inland is the tiny village of **Orford** with its monumental castle built in 1160 of which only the 18-sided keep remains *(daily throughout the year).* The gradual silting-up of the estuary contributed to Orford's decline, which had a population of over a thousand in the 13th century, but the river *Butley* still provides oyster-beds, and salmon and trout are plentiful. Also to be seen nearby is the sole surviving relic of *Butley Priory,* the large gatehouse of 14th-century construction incorporating baronial emblems and heraldic devices.

On the B1069 to Snape stand **The Maltings,** a restored medieval range of buildings which has become the centre of an Arts Festival, of which the prime mover was Benjamin Britten, and which was destroyed by fire on the first night of the 1969 season. Rebuilt, it continues to increase in prestige as a centre of musical culture.

Aldeburgh is a small town on the coast with a charm and quiet that refuses to give way to pressure from developers. Early in the 19th century the vicar was George Crabbe, whose collection of poems, "The Borough", was the inspiration for much of Benjamin Britten's work including the opera "Peter Grimes". In common with many coastal towns in this area Aldeburgh has gradually been swallowed by the sea, and the area of the town as shown in 16th-century maps is twice what it is today. Aldeburgh was a port a century before the reign of Elizabeth I, and the restored Moot Hall is a reminder of those spacious times.

Back on the A12 are **Wickham Market** and **Saxmundham,** both quiet little market towns of ancient origin on this important Roman road. To the west lies **Framlingham** with its fine castle ruin *(daily, fee)* built in the time of Edward I, and an imposing church containing splendid monuments.

Just past **Yoxford,** a charming village of bow-windows and balconies, a lane branches off to **Westleton** to the right, where there is a post-mill and several grand houses, including the all-white brickwork of The Grange. Just south, on the B1122 is **Theberton,** where the church has a memorial to the crew of a German zeppelin brought down in the First World War.

Near the coast and along it, in this area, are several towns and villages of interest. **Leiston,** on the B1122, has the ruins of 14th-century *Leiston Abbey (daily)* and is the cradle of the agricultural engineering trade in Suffolk. Higher up the coast was once the flourishing port of **Dunwich,** granted a charter by King John and the right to the proceeds of all wrecks in return for an annual levy of 500 eels! Once it had nine churches, a population of over a thousand, and 80 "great ships". But a storm at sea in 1327 destroyed three churches and 400 houses, and the sea has never given up since. Now only a few cottages and the bare bones of the former chapel and leper colony mark this town which the sea has claimed for ever.

Blythburgh, where the B1125 rejoins the A12, has also lost much of its former grandeur due to the silting-up of the river *Blyth.*

The A1095 bears right for **Southwold,** a cheerful and invigorating little seaside town of Edwardian vintage, with a lighthouse apparently rising from its back gardens. But it is not entirely Edwardian, for on Gun Hill there is a fine Elizabethan cannon and the 15th-century church has a curious contemporary wood figure, known as "Southwold Jack" which strikes the hours on a bell.

Southwold Museum *(Tues, Weds, Fris, afternoons, Apr.–Sept.; Thurs in addition in Aug.)* has a good collection of items of local interest including relics of the long-defunct Southwold Light Railway. Across the *Blyth* can be seen the tall tower of the ruined church of **Walberswick,** still a mark for mariners.

Joining the A12 once more at **Wrentham,** the route continues past **Kessingland,** where the caravans and camping-grounds herald the approach of Pakesfield and Lowestoft, but where there is also a *Wild Life Park* which includes a special zoo for children.

Lowestoft

Angling.—Oulton Broad for perch, bream, rudd and pike. Sea-fishing off pier for whiting, cod and flat-fish.
Bathing.—From sand beach.
Distances.—London, 117; Aldeburgh, 27; Norwich, 27; Gt. Yarmouth, 10.
Early Closing.—Thursday.
Entertainments.—Sparrows Nest Theatre & Gardens, South Pier Pavilion, Claremont Pier, Kirkley Cliff Amusement Gdns., Somerleyton Hall (replica of Crown Jewels), East Anglia

Transport Museum, River buses on Oulton Broad.
Hotels.—*Ashurst,* Claremont Pier; *Annandale,* Kirkley Cliff; *Victoria,* Kirkley Cliff; *Strathleven,* Wellington Esplanade; *Windsor,* Kirkley Cliff.
Library.—Suffolk Road (near station).
Population.—53,000.
Sports.—Powerboat racing, tennis, cricket, sailing on Broads, bowls, golf, bellringing (Lowestoft, practice night Mondays 8 p.m.—Pakefield, practice night Fridays 8 p.m.).

Lowestoft is the most easterly tip of England, and proud of it. So proud, in fact, that it lists "The Dawn" as one of its chief amenities! It has been a fishing-port from the 16th century but its modern importance stems from the arrival of the railway in 1847 and the extension of the Harbour to its present 63 acres. The Old Town is separated from South Town by a swing-bridge, and at the northern end of the Old Town a lighthouse rises from the main road! The Fish Market is of great interest *(permits to view from Docks Manager)*. The cliffs here are indented by "scores" or gashes, near which some of the old herring curing-houses survive. Lowestoft looks inland as well as to the sea, and **Oulton Broad** is the first of the great series of inland waterways which are normally associated with Norfolk. Oulton is the only broad connecting directly with the sea. One of Lowestoft's most recent and imaginative amenities is the **East Anglia Transport Museum,** Carlton Colville *(Sat. afternoons and Suns in summer)*.

Six miles north of Lowestoft is the appropriately-named village of **Herringfleet** with a fine weather-boarded, octagonal smock-mill complete with fantail and sails. Farther along the lane that marks the boundary with Norfolk are the ruins of **St. Olave's Priory,** established in the 14th century by the Austin canons.

Fritton, on the A143 to Great Yarmouth, Norfolk, has a Norman church with a rare three-decker pulpit, an even rarer duck decoy and, in **Fritton Lake,** the largest lake in England outside the Lake District.

Due west of Lowestoft on the A146 is **Beccles,** a picturesque little town with its church perched high above the banks of the river *Waveney*. There is much to remind the visitor that Beccles was once a hive of industry, with its little quay concerned with the handling of corn, malt and coal as was common in this area for centuries. Today the town has found a new outlet in printing, particularly of colour work, and in the manufacture of machinery for the thriving fodder beet industry on which so much of the agricultural economy of East Anglia is founded. An oddity of the church is the detached campanile containing a ring of 10 bells.

Five miles westwards along the *Waveney* the county boundary forms a sudden loop to include **Bungay** where the powerful Hugh Bigood built his castle in the 12th century *(daily— keys available at Kings Head and Swan inns)*. There is a restored 13th-century gatehouse

211

and a drawbridge and several handsome buildings in the town including a theatre of 1828 which later became the Corn Exchange and is now a laundry. Whether or not H. G. Wells had the name of the town in mind when he wrote his novel "Tono-Bungay" dealing with the marketing of a patent medicine, Bungay has had a tradition of health since 1730 when a local apothecary, John King, established baths here and later published his famous "Essay on Hot and Cold Bathing".

Once past Bungay, the A116 from Beccles joins the A143 from Great Yarmouth and crosses to the Norfolk side of the *Waveney* for the remainder of its way.

IPSWICH TO NEWMARKET

The A45, curving in a quarter-circle from Felixstowe through the heart of Suffolk, provides more character and interest than any other road in the Eastern Counties.

Six miles north-west of Ipswich it enters **Needham Market,** though no market has been held here since the plague struck in 1685. It is a quiet town of Georgian frontages and comparative peace, not unlike Stowmarket another four miles on. **Stowmarket** is bigger and more bustling and obviously the shopping centre for the wealthy of this rich agricultural district. Many fine Georgian and Regency fronts have been carefully preserved, and the Abbots Hall Museum *(afternoons, Apr.–Oct.)* houses a collection of items reflecting the rural life of Suffolk through the centuries.

Stowmarket is virtually the geographical centre of the county, though the boundary between East and West Suffolk lies another three miles west.

South-west of the town, towards the Essex boundary, one can reach the delectable village of **Kersey,** its famous High Street, full of half-timbered and plastered houses, running down both sides of a valley to the river *Brett* below, an essential ingredient for the "Kersey" cloth made here in the Middle Ages. South again is **Hadleigh,** another beautiful pink-washed and timbered town with a spectacular Cloth Hall of about 1430 with double overhanging upper storeys, as at Thaxted.

The river *Stour,* dividing Suffolk from Essex, imposes its own special character in this area, not only in the more famous **locale** of Constable, but in the quieter villages along its banks, like **Stoke-by-Clare** and **Stoke-by-Nayland,** the latter at the highest point of this lovely valley. The church spire is a landmark for miles, and the church itself is rich in ornamentation and tombs to the wealthy landowners of the past who form part of the fabric of English history. Over the south porch is a remarkable 17th-century library, and the south door is still complete with tiny carved figures 500 years old.

Still by the river, **Bures,** once a royal capital in the far-off days of the Saxons, is the town in which the young King Edmund was crowned on Christmas Day in the year 855. St. Stephen's Chapel, dedicated by Stephen Langton in 1218, has magnificent tombs of three earls of Oxford including that of Richard, a commander at Agincourt under Henry V.

Little Cornard and **Great Cornard,** with its timber church spire more typical of the other side of the river in Essex, has given its name to a fine hymn-tune by Martin Shaw and can also show some good Elizabethan wall-paintings.

Like a bastion between the two counties, **Sudbury** stands at the junction of five roads and gives an impression of bustle and importance, as it has done for generations. There is much to see and admire in this busy place including the house in which the painter, Thomas Gainsborough, was born *(daily except Mons)*.

North of Sudbury, on the A134, is **Long Melford,** reputedly the longest village in England and even in medieval times considered one of the loveliest. Its enormously wide village street and green provides a perfect setting for the wealth of half-timbered cottages, handsome houses and inns, such as *The Bull,* and the long, graceful lines of the parish church. **Melford Hall** (N.T., *Apr.–Sept., Weds, Thurs and Suns. Also Bank Hol. Mons)*. On the parallel road, B1070, some three miles cross-country is **Lavenham,** with Kersey probably one of the most-photographed towns in England. Its great church stands at the top of the curved and descending High Street, the houses straight on the pavements. East of the High Street, behind the ancient *Swan Hotel,* the Market Square stands hidden, though on an eminence, dominated by the fairy-tale front of the Corpus Christi Guildhall built in 1520 *(daily—key from caretaker at 1 Lady Street).*

The B1070 from Lavenham and the A134 from Long Melford join at *Cross Green,* and five miles on meet the A45 just outside Bury St. Edmunds.

Bury St. Edmunds (Pop.: 26,000. Hotels: *Suffolk, Angel, Everards, Cupola House*) has many claims to importance, both locally and nationally, but none more unexpected than its claim to be the birthplace of Magna Carta.

Though Runnymede was the place of the actual signing of this document, the decision of the barons to force King John to ratify the Charter was made in 1214 on oath on the high altar of the great Abbey of St. Edmundsbury, at that time a place of holy pilgrimage. Today, though the provisions of the Magna Carta still exist, the abbey in which it was conceived is gone, only the great Gateway on Angel Hill remaining with the gardens behind where can be traced the outline of the former range of buildings.

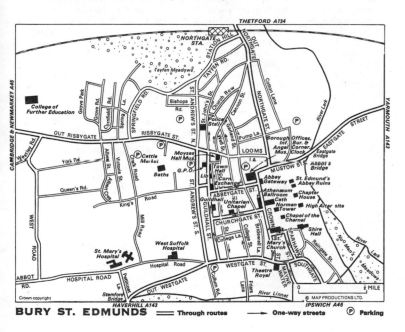

BURY ST. EDMUNDS ═══ Through routes ⟶ One-way streets Ⓟ Parking

But Bury St. Edmunds as a town continues to exist in the same plan of four-square streets centred on Butter Market and Cornhill, with the Traverse between, as it has done since first planned by the Normans. The town slopes down towards the Abbey Gate, and the gradual fall of Angel Hill between with its open space provides a picture that caused even the critical William Cobbett (1762–1835) to call it "The nicest town in the world". And not only is it nice to look at but nice to listen to: names like Looms Lane, Out Westgate, Garland Street and Hatter Street all evoke a sense of rural charm, the whole being contained by the rivers *Lark* and *Linnet.* The inns are prosperous and have regained their former prestige

213

of the great coaching days. Cupola House, in the Traverse, is perhaps the best 17th-century house in Bury (it is now an hotel) and once housed Daniel Defoe, as a plaque records. The oldest domestic building in the town, and probably in all East Anglia, is the 12th-century **Moyses Hall** *(weekdays)*. The Town Hall designed by Robert Adam in 1771 was built on the site of the medieval Market Cross. Of interest is the Gershom-Parkington Memorial Collection of Clocks (N.T., *weekdays*) on Angel Hill.

The A45 to Newmarket leaves Bury by Risbygate Street and the Cattle Market and heads into wooded and undulating countryside past **Risby** to **Kentford.** It is a lonely, wooded road, once terrorised by highwaymen. At the crossroads leading to **Moulton** and **Chippenham** a grassy mound marks the "Boy's Grave", still carefully tended and decorated with flowers by gypsies in memory of the poor shepherd lad who lost one of his sheep, and hanged himself rather than face his cruel master. Now the country has become flat and open, typical "paddock" country, in fact, for the thriving racing fraternity based on Newmarket and its famous Heath. **Newmarket** *(Rutland Arms, Bedford, White Hart)* forms almost an island in the surrounding county of Cambridgeshire, tenuously clinging to Suffolk by the thin ribbon of road marking the junction of the A45 and the A11 from Norwich. It is a wide and airy town, opulent houses, tall horses and little men abounding in that peculiar atmosphere of racing that is so difficult to describe. The first race here was in 1619 and (for those interested in ornithology) the last British bustard was seen on the Heath in 1840. Newmarket is the headquarters of the *Jockey Club* and, perversely, the racecourse itself is over the county boundary in Cambridgeshire.

South of Newmarket the mighty earthwork known as the **Devil's Ditch** crosses the main road before the road divides once more, continuing as the A45 to Cambridge on the right, and the A11 to London to the left. Back on the Norwich side of Newmarket, off the A11, is **Mildenhall,** with one of the noblest churches in Suffolk—and remembering Lavenham, Kersey and Long Melford this is something very noble indeed.

From Mildenhall the A1065 runs across the beginning of the brecklands to **Brandon,** a quiet town with an unusual variety of local materials used in its buildings including chalk, flint, brick and plaster, and with many roofs constructed of pantiles. A fine avenue of elms connects the church with the High Street.

London to Cambridge

The old coach-road to Cambridge left London by way of Tottenham, Edmonton and Enfield, crossing into Hertfordshire at Waltham Cross. The present A10 takes a slightly different course, cutting between the congested suburbs of Enfield and Chingford and regaining the old road near Wormley and its acres of water and glass-houses.

One advantage of the new A10 is that it runs nearer to Theobalds Park, Cheshunt where, 14 miles from Charing Cross, stands the entrance to the City of London! This apparent anomaly is accounted for by the presence in the park of old Temple Bar, the stone archway which for two centuries stood at the junction of Fleet Street and the Strand and marked the boundary of the City of London, where even today royalty must stop and request permission of the Lord Mayor before entering. Temple Bar was designed by Wren, but because of traffic congestion was dismantled and removed in mid-Victorian times and was subsequently purchased by Sir Henry Meux in 1888 and re-erected in the grounds of his home.

On the opposite side of the old main road (now the A1010) is **Waltham Cross,** separated from its famous Abbey two miles away in Essex by the river *Lea* that marks the boundary between Herts and Essex. Waltham Cross is an ancient town taking its name from one of the three remaining Eleanor crosses erected in the 13th century to mark the nightly resting place of the body of Queen Eleanor, wife of Henry III, from Lincoln to London, where Charing *(chère-reine)* Cross is the 12th and final cross. The High Street is narrow and congested, and is bridged by the sign of the *Four Swans* inn that spans the road.

Waltham Abbey, across the *Lea,* was founded by King Harold in 1030 as a collegiate church and was raised to an abbey in 1177. Much of the Saxon architecture remains, and even more 13th- and 14th-century work. The tower was built in 1556 after the Dissolution to indicate the change back from a monastery to a parish church. The fine Abbey Gateway still survives leading to the 14th-century Harolds Bridge, and in the undercroft of this large church is a museum *(daily)*. The little town grouped round the Abbey still preserves an identity of its own, with handsome half-timbered buildings like the *Welsh Harp Inn* and the little range of yellow-brick houses called Paradise Row.

The area on both sides of the *Lea* is given over to market gardening, with large tracts of water predominating and many greenhouses glittering in the sun. It is not a very beautiful part of England but still a prosperous one as it approaches **Hoddesdon,** once an attractive town on the coach road but now given over almost entirely to the developers, shopping precincts and multiple stores. But no place can ever lose all its character if it is on a river, and Hoddesdon still benifits from the *Lea* and provides good boating and fishing. One or two old buildings have survived, including the 16th-century *Golden Lion,* and in the High Street is a house which was once St. Monica's Priory and dates from 1622. A mile north of the town the gatehouse and a few crumbling red-brick walls are all that is left of *Rye House,* the centre of the famous Rye House Plot of 1683 to assassinate King Charles II and his brother James.

On the eastern side of the A10 the A602 to Hertford branches off, passing on its way *Haileybury College,* a famous public school founded in 1862 out of a college established for Civil Servants of the East India Company. In the First World War it provided no less than four VCs and also sustained a loss of 577 ex-scholars, a record of which it must surely be proud.

Hertford (Pop.: 20,400. Hotel: *White Horse Inn)* is the county town of Hertfordshire, and still has an old-world character despite the complex system of one-way ring roads and what must surely be one of the most hideous multi-storey carparks in the country. Narrow streets and old frontages make it easy to believe that this is an ancient place, once the seat of the Saxon kings, though little is left of the castle in the town centre built about 913 and recorded in the Anglo-Saxon Chronicle. In this education-conscious area one of Hertford's most famous schools is the *Christ's Hospital School for Girls,* the female section of the famous "Bluecoat School" the other half of which is at Horsham in Sussex. Hertford is fortunate in having four little rivers at its disposal—the *Lea,* the *Rib,* the *Beane* and the oddly-named *Mimram.* Along the *Beane,* on a fir-clad hillside called the Warren, is the second oldest building in the town after the Castle—St. Leonard's Church. At **Hertingfordbury** the composer Haydn stayed with the Brassey family in 1792.

East of Hertford the A119 runs for two miles to Ware, where it joins the A10 to Cambridge which has come up via **Great Amwell.** Through the park and the valley here flow the waters of the *New River,* the creation of Hugh Myddleton, friend of Sir Walter Raleigh, who determined to end London's chronic shortage of water by constructing this extraordinary 40-mile long channel which empties itself into a reservoir at Islington, at that time a country village just north of the capital.

Coming into **Ware** the predominating features are the tall granaries along the river *Lea* and its canal housing the barley which has long been an important factor in the economy of the town. The most handsome of these is the Canons Maltings built about 1600. The Parish Church is large but has suffered from Victorian restoration.

The A10 leaves Ware and continues north along the line of the Roman Ermine Street through **Puckeridge, Buntingford** and **Royston** passing the unfortunately-named village of **Nasty.** Buntingford is full of quaint and picturesque houses with overhanging storeys and a delightful set of almshouses founded in 1684 by Seth Ward, born nearby, who later became Bishop of Salisbury and was a friend of Sir Christopher Wren.

Eight miles north **Royston** stands at the junction of the Roman *Ermine Street* and the Saxon *Icknield Way,* and a two-ton boulder of stone, called Royse's Cross, stands in the Market Place. The square socket on its top face once held the cross which stood at the junction of these two important highways. The chief curiosity of this busy and pleasant town, however, is the 28-foot deep cavern under Melbourn Street, 17 feet in diameter and decorated with an incredible collection of wall carvings, cut in the chalk, depicting saints, kings, crusaders and various scenes from the bible. It was discovered in 1742 and the reason for its existence is unknown.

The road divides at Royston, straight ahead to Huntingdon as the A14, while the A10 to Cambridge bears right through Melbourn after crossing into Cambridgeshire. In this area three counties meet—Hertfordshire. Cambridgeshire and Essex through which runs the other main road to Cambridge, the A11, which is in fact the Norwich Road and passes south-west of the university town as a fast but undulating road through Six Mile Bottom to Newmarket.

The countryside between the A10 and the A11 is full of quiet, forgotten villages with little churches and crowded churchyards. Places like **Standon, Puckeridge** and **Much Hadham,** in which little has changed over the years. On the A11 north of Bishop's Stortford is **Stansted,** a village largely off the main highway and with a steeply sloping High Street which climbs quickly up again to reach the busy *airport* which creates much of the work for locals, though which does not make itself felt quite so aggressively as does Luton or Gatwick.

Apart from the thundering traffic along the A11 the atmosphere of these Essex villages is tranquil enough, and even the village of **Ugley** remains unconcerned about the endless jokes caused by its name. **Newport** is delightful with its wide High Street and sleeping houses, and the fine town of **Saffron Walden** can boast some of the best examples of pargetting on its houses to be seen for miles. The town grew up around the saffron-growing industry of medieval times, a type of crocus used medicinally and as a dye. The church is the largest in Essex and there are some fine half-timbered inns including the *Sun*. The town also has a good **Museum** *(daily except Suns in winter)*.

Just south of Saffron Walden is the magnificent **Audley End House** *(daily, except Mons, Apr.–mid-Oct.)* set in its park and making a beautiful sight from the main road. The original house was built by the Earl of Suffolk in 1603. It contains many fine treasures including paintings by Canaletto, furniture by Chippendale and Hepplewhite and plaster-work designed by Robert Adam.

At **Great Chesterford,** north of Saffron Walden, the A11 swings away towards the right to Newmarket, running for a while parallel with the A10 which continues into Cambridge.

Cambridge

Angling.—Controlled by the Great Ouse River Authority, Clarendon Road, who issue licences to fish the *Cam* and the *Great Ouse*.

Distances.—London, 54; Bedford, 29; Chelmsford, 41; Colchester, 48; Ely, 16; Newmarket, 13; Norwich, 61; Oxford, 81.

Early Closing.—Thursday.

Entertainments.—Cinemas (5), ADC Theatre, Arts Theatre, Dancing (Guildhall and Old Corn Exchange).

Hotels.—*University Arms,* Regent Street; *Garden House,* Granta Place; *Royal Cambridge,* Trumpington Street; *Milton Arms,* Milton Road; *Station Hotel,* Station Road.

Library.—Central Library, Wheeler Street; County Library, Shire Hall.

Population.—99,000.

Post Office.—St. Andrews Street.

Sports.—Cricket, fishing, football, golf, horse-racing, gliding, boating and punting, bowls, hockey.

Though Cambridge is world-famous for its University and Colleges, it was already in existence in A.D. 70 when the Romans established a township on the river they called the *Granta*. Through the years the name became modified to *Grantebrigg, Caunterbrigge, Caumbridge* and finally Cambridge. By 1610 the river had become the *Cam,* by a curious process of back-change, though part of it still keeps its name of *Granta,* just as part of the *Thames* at Oxford is called the *Isis.*

The river has played an integral part in the commercial development of Cambridge from the earliest times, as a vital artery for Fenland traffic, and in Roman times Cambridge stood on the *Via Devana,* the important highway between Colchester and Godmanchester. In 1086 William the Conqueror built a mighty castle here when he used Cambridge as a base against the East Anglians led by Hereward.

The first college of learning was founded at Cambridge when dissident students from Oxford transferred their allegiance to the busy town on the *Granta,* and in 1284 established Peterhouse as a place of residence, for previously students had lived in lodgings scattered about the town. Peterhouse was followed by seven other colleges during the 14th century, and in Tudor times further colleges were added as Cambridge increased in prestige as a seat of learning. The number has continued to grow, until today there are 29 colleges, 21 for men, five for women only and three for both sexes.

The womens' colleges are comparatively new, and the first was Girton, established in 1871, and at first rigorously excluded from the life of the university and built two miles from the town centre. The result is a rather lower percentage of women students at Cambridge than at Oxford.

Cambridge, because of its comparatively isolated position in East Anglia has never succumbed to the pressures of industrialisation as has Oxford. In Cambridge one is constantly conscious of the college buildings, white and clean, lining the banks of the *Cam* and creating the beautiful and famous "Backs" where undergraduates and the general public can relax. But, of course, the domestic life of Cambridge as a town continues throughout the year, whereas the academic year during which the colleges are in use by undergraduates consists of less than half of the 52 weeks of the calendar year. The influx of some 8,000 undergraduates during term makes a fundamental change to Cambridge life, but the buildings that are associated with learning remain a permanent feature and underline the impression that Cambridge is predominantly a centre of learning, with commerce and industry taking second place.

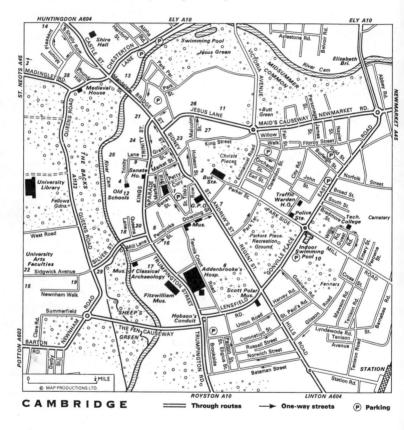

CAMBRIDGE ══ Through routes ➔ One-way streets ℗ Parking

1. *Guildhall & Inf. Bureau*
2. *Churchill, 1959*
3. *Christ's 1505*
4. *Clare, 1326*
5. *Corpus Christi, 1352*
6. *Downing, 1749*

7. *Emmanuel, 1584*
8. *Fitzwilliam.*
9. *Gonville & Caius, 1349*
10. *Hughes Hall, 1885*
11. *Jesus, 1497*
12. *King's, 1441-43*

13. *Magdalene, 1542*
14. *Newhall, 1954*
15. *Newnham1875*
16. *Pembroke, 1347*
17. *Peterhouse, 1280*
18. *Queen's, 1446*

19. *Ridley Hall,1879*
20. *St. Catharine's, 1473*
21. *St. John's, 1511*
22. *Selwyn, 1882*
23. *Sidney Sussex, 1588*
24. *Trinity, 1546*

25. *Trinity Hall, 1350*
26. *Wesley Ho., 1925*
27. *Westcott Ho.*
28. *Westminster, 1899 and Cheshunt, 1905 (on Westminster site),*
29. *Darwin College, 1964*

Notes are given on some of the most interesting buildings beginning with the older colleges:

Peterhouse (1284). The oldest of the colleges, established by students from Merton College, Oxford. The poet Thomas Gray was in residence here in 1742.

Clare (1338). Originally founded in 1326, the college suffered two disastrous fires and the present buildings date from 1638. Famous for the beauty of its gardens.

Trinity Hall (1350). Founded by the Bishop of Norwich and traditionally a lawyers' college.

King's (1441). The founder was Henry VI who intended it for students from Eton which he had founded the same year. King's College Chapel is undoubtedly the most striking building in Cambridge externally and internally and has a long tradition of choral music. Treasures include "The Adoration of the Magi" by Rubens.

Queen's (1448). Named after its original founder, Margaret of Anjou (wife of Henry VI) and Elizabeth Woodville, wife of Henry IV, who refounded and endowed it in 1465. Noted for the Mathematical Bridge across the *Cam*, built in 1729 of wood without a single nail on mathematical principles.

St. John's (1511). Founded by the Countess of Richmond and enlarged in 1598 by the Countess of Shrewsbury. Has four courts of which one, New Court, is across the river and reached by the Bridge of Sighs, an 1831 replica of the 16th-century Venetian bridge.

Magdalene (1542). Owes its existence to monies acquired from the Dissolution of the monasteries by Henry VIII. Samuel Pepys was a student here and bequeathed to the College his magnificent Library and the six volumes of his coded diary. N.B. The name of this college is pronounced as written. It is Oxford's Magdalen College which is pronounced "Maudlin").

Trinity College (1546). An amalgamation of four ancient colleges organised by Henry VIII shortly before his death. As a result it is the largest college with buildings grouped round the two-acre Great Court by Thomas Nevile in 1610.

Emmanuel (1584). Founded by Sir Walter Mildmay, a Chancellor of the Exchequer to Queen Elizabeth I. It has strong American associations, for here studied John Harvard who later founded his own university in Massachusetts.

From 1596, when **Sidney Sussex** was founded, no new colleges were built in Cambridge for over two centuries, when **Downing College** came into being in 1800.

The first women's college was **Girton,** established first in Hitchin (Herts) in 1869 but allowed to transfer to Cambridge in 1871, but even then carefully sited two miles from the town centre for reasons of propriety. In that same year a second women's college was created as **Newnham,** and the third women-only college came with the building of **New Hall** in 1954. The full list of Cambridge Colleges with dates of foundation is as follows:

Peterhouse 1284; Clare 1338; Pembroke 1347; Gonville 1348; Trinity Hall 1350; King's 1441; Queen's 1448; St. Catherine's 1473; Jesus 1496; Christ's 1505; St. John's 1511; Magdalene 1542; Trinity College 1546; Caius (pronounced "Keys") 1557; Emmanuel 1584; Sidney Sussex 1596; Downing 1800; Girton 1871; Newnham 1871; Ridley Hall 1879; Westcott House 1881; Selwyn 1882; Fitzwilliam House 1887; St. Edmund's House 1896; Westminster 1899; Cheshunt 1905; Wesley 1921; New Hall 1954; Churchill 1959.

With the increased number of students at Cambridge many colleges have had to expand, and the juxtaposition of new architecture and old and mellow buildings is one that has exercised the minds of many architects since World War II. A fine example of fusion of styles is found in the Cripps Building at **St. John's,** while **New Hall,** the women's college built in 1954, is in white concrete set amongst trees and a typical example of 20th-century architecture.

The visitor to Cambridge is fortunate that, in most cases, he can wander through the courts and gardens of the colleges at will and explore the Backs. As at Oxford the college buildings have no corridors, but the undergraduates' rooms are reached by worn spiral stairways with the names of the occupants listed at the entrance. These rooms may NOT be visited by the general public, but this is hardly a severe imposition when there is so much else to see.

As might be expected Cambridge has many fine churches apart from those associated with specific colleges. The most ancient by far is **St. Benet's,** the tower of which is the oldest building in Cambridge. It is also a mecca for bellringers, for it was as a member of the ringers of this church that Fabian Stedman evolved his system of methods and change-ringing that exists in no other country in the world. The **Round Church** (St. Sepulchre's) is the oldest (12th-century) of the four remaining round churches in England. Ruthlessly restored in 1841. **Great St. Mary's,** rebuilt in 1478, is the University Church and provides a dignified background for the open market held in the square in front three times a week. Visitors may climb the tower to view the spectacular scenery of the surrounding countryside.

In the narrow streets of the university town may be found many bookshops hidden in quaint corners, such as that in Argyle Passage, and art galleries are also plentiful.

Museums, too, are numerous in Cambridge and include:

Fitzwilliam Museum, Trumpington Street.
Archaeology and Ethnology, Downing Street.
Classical Archaeology, Little St. Mary's Lane.
County Folk Museum, Castle Street.
Scott Polar Research Institute, Lensfield Road.
Sedgwick Museum of Geology, Downing Street.
Whipple Museum of the History of Science, Free School Lane.

Modern Cambridge, with its multiple stores, snack-bars, discotheques and other trappings of civilised existence is found chiefly in St. Andrew's Street and Regent Street, and in the residential areas west of the *Cam* between the Madingley and Barton roads.

Excursions from Cambridge

Probably the best-loved village in the immediate vicinity of Cambridge is **Grantchester** three miles to the south. At the rectory lived Rupert Brooke, whose poem about this village was written in Berlin just before the First World War. The church has a beautiful 14th-century chancel. The nave and tower are Perpendicular. A woodland path leads to *Byron's Pool.* At **Trumpington** farther south the early 14th-century church is noted for its graceful interior.

Three miles south-east of Cambridge are the *Gog and Magog Hills,* rising up to 300 feet and giving splendid views.

Four miles west of Cambridge is the *American Military Cemetery* at **Madingley** *(daily).* The beautifully-landscaped hillside site contains the graves of 3,811 U.S. servicemen based in Britain and a Roll of Honour on the wall of the Memorial lists a further 5,125 names of those whose graves are unknown. The chapel contains a fine mural depicting the European theatre of operations and there is also a small war museum.

Two miles north of the A45 between Cambridge and Newmarket at Lode is **Anglesey Abbey** (N.T., *May–mid-Oct. on Weds, Thurs, Sats, and Sun. afternoons and also Bank Hol. Mon.*). This handsome house was built in 1600 but has a crypt of a much earlier date (probably about 1270) representing the remains of an Augustinian monastery on which the house was built.

Soham, on the A142 Newmarket–Ely road, has a massive church with a ring of 10 bells and every year mounts an imaginative and colourful Arts Festival. South of the village at **Wicken Fen** there is a fine example of the type of windmill once used to drain the Fens. There is also an interesting Nature Trail designed to demonstrate the flora and fauna of the Fens in the years before drainage. Visitors wishing to follow the Nature Trail must first report to the Warden at Lode Lane, Wicken.

North of Cambridge

North of Cambridge the **Fens** begin, that vast, flat and hedgeless area of black earth bright with flowers in the spring but dark-green with beet and other crops during summer and autumn. Once the land between Cambridge and the Wash had been almost entirely flooded, raised patches of land forming the islands that still survive as place-names in the area such as the Isle of Ely, Thorney Island and others. The Romans were the first to build raised causeways across these dangerous marshes, but nothing further was done until well after the Norman Conquest.

From the 13th to the 17th centuries determined efforts were made to drain the land by the provision of canals or "cuts", notably by Charles I and also by the Earls of Bedford, who owned land round Whittlesey and Thorney. In 1651 the fourth Earl of Bedford engaged the services of the famous Dutch engineer Vermuyden, an expert on land-reclamation and drainage, and with the later use of windmills to pump water out of the ditches the Fens were gradually transformed into the fertile soil we see today.

In the early 1800s steam power was used to pump the water and at **Stretham,** on the A10 is preserved one of the first hammerbeam steam engines used *(daily, all year)*. Though a diesel unit was installed in 1925 the original steam engine is still used in emergencies.

Ely (Pop.: 10,000. Hotel: *Lamb*) lies four miles north of Stretham and 16 miles from Cambridge. From the road there is a view of the red roofs of the little town clustering at the foot of the cathedral.

Ely Cathedral was built in 1083 on the site of a Saxon Benedictine abbey. In 1322 the tower collapsed and was replaced by the beautiful "lantern" which adds so much to the building and can be seen from many miles around. The splendid Galilee Porch is a fine example of Early English architecture. The great West Tower is of six stages crowned by an octagon, the lowest stage being Transitional Norman, the others Early English. The octagon is of the Decorated period. Ely is one of the longest churches in England. The long narrow nave measures 248 feet and is a fine example of late Norman work. The west window is Perpendicular.

The original three-storey abbey gateway still survives, and is incorporated into the fabric of King's School which claims descent from the original monastic school attended by Edward the Confessor. The **Isle of Ely** derives its name from the eels which once proliferated on this island, and were the staple diet of the Saxons.

North-west of Ely, at the end of the "sixteen-foot drain" is **Chatteris,** and, almost on the county boundary is **Ramsey Abbey Gatehouse** (N.T., *not open*) the sole remnant of the large Benedictine Abbey that once stood there. Further north is **March** on the *Nene* and a long straggling town, with a 15th-century church noted for its superb hammerbeam roof decorated with carvings of some 200 figures of angels, each with wings outstretched in flight.

In the north-west of the county is **Wisbech,** the centre of a flourishing area where fruit and flowers are the main industry. Visually Wisbech is the most attractive town in these parts after Cambridge itself, and, as in most well-to-do country towns, the houses and shops are kept in perfect condition and the introduction of new buildings carefully controlled. Along the banks of the *Nene* are several dignified houses of which the most important is **Peckover House** (N.T., *Apr.–Oct., Weds, Thurs, Sats, Suns and Bank Hol. Mons from 2 to 6 p.m.)*. It was built in 1722 by Jonathan Peckover, with a richly ornamented interior of plasterwork in rococo style. Peckover was the owner of a local private bank now incorporated into Barclay's.

At **Tydd St. Giles,** five miles from Wisbech, the curate was once Nicholas Breakspeare who later, as Adrian IV, was the only Englishman to become Pope (1154–1159).

Norfolk

Norwich

Distances.—Cromer, 25; Dereham, 16; Holt, 22; Ipswich, 43; King's Lynn, 44; London, 111; Southwold, 30; Yarmouth, 20.
Ealy Closing.—Thursday.
Entertainment.—Cinemas, Maddermarket Theatre.
Golf.—At Hellesdon, 2 miles.

Hotels.—*Castle, Lansdowne, Maid's Head, Nelson, Royal, Bell, Eiger, Town House, Windsor, Cumberland,* and others.
Population.—120,000.
Post Office.—Bank Plain.

The ancient and famous city of Norwich is situated in a loop of the *Wensum,* near the junction of the river with the *Yare.* A Saxon settlement, it acquired a Castle and a Cathedral under the Normans, and by the 14th century, its city walls enclosed an area almost as great as did those of London. Always an agricultural centre, its industries were stimulated by a constant influx of Flemings, Huguenots and others bringing their skills of weaving, dyeing, shoe-making and other trades. The narrow winding streets and old houses are gradually giving way to wider thoroughfares and high buildings, but Norwich as a city has the best of both worlds.

From the east, Norwich is entered by the 13th-century Bishop Bridge over the *Wensum,* whence Bishopsgate leads past the Great Hospital (an almshouse founded in 1249) to the Cathedral precincts.

Norwich Cathedral. No other English cathedral, save Durham, is so completely a Norman structure. The See of East Anglia, founded in the 7th century, was later removed to Norwich, mainly through the agency of Bishop Herbert de Losinga. This prelate began the building of Norwich Cathedral in 1096, together with a Benedictine priory for 60 monks. Choir, transepts, and lower stages of the tower were built in his lifetime, and the nave was completed in 1150. Notable features of the exterior are the apsidal east end with its flying buttresses, the Norman tower with a spire exceeded in height only by Salisbury, and the great window of the west front.

Entering from the west end, one is struck by the massive Norman pillars supporting the arches of the *nave,* and by the long range of the roof. The 328 bosses in the nave vault are carved with scriptural scenes. The aisles of the nave are Norman, as are the clerestory windows. The nave altar, hallowed in 1947, replaced the medieval altar. The organ case erected in 1950 is one of the finest in England.

The *South Transept* shows further architectural glories. The walls, especially the west side, show a profusion of arches, arcades, and ornament. Passing eastward from the south transept, one sees on the right the *Bauchun Chapel* dating from the early 15th century; the roof is somewhat later. Next is Losinga's beautiful *Chapel of St. Luke.* The retable behind the altar dates from 1381. At the east end is *St. Saviour's Chapel,* built (on the site of a Norman chapel) in 1931 as a war memorial to Norfolk men. It is now the regimental chapel of the Royal Norfolk Regiment. Then comes the *Jesus Chapel,* restored in 1966. Note the low arch with painted ceiling over the processional path; from it the church relics were displayed to pilgrims. West of this arch, in the choir, is the tomb of Sir Thomas Erpingham, the "good old knight" of Shakespeare's Henry V, and the donor of the Erpingham Gate.

The *Presbytery,* carried eastward into a semi-circular apse, retains its original Norman ground plan. It is the ancient episcopal *Throne,* erected in the Saxon period and restored to its original form in 1959. A blue slab in front of the altar rails covers the traditional burial place of the founder of the Cathedral. His elaborate tomb was destroyed during the Commonwealth. From the Presbytery there is a fine view westward, of the roof in particular.

Descending the steps, note on the left the modern *Bishop's Throne,* and enter the *Choir.* The 62 stalls are the ancient monastic seats; the misericords and carved canopies are worth examining. From the choir one can regain the south aisle and pass by the Prior's Door into the *Cloisters.* These replace the original cloisters damaged by tumultuous citizens in 1272, and their re-building occupied the next 130 years. They were again renovated in 1938, and the coloured bosses repay close examination. Outside the quadrangle stood the Chapter House, refectory, infirmary and other parts of the monastery.

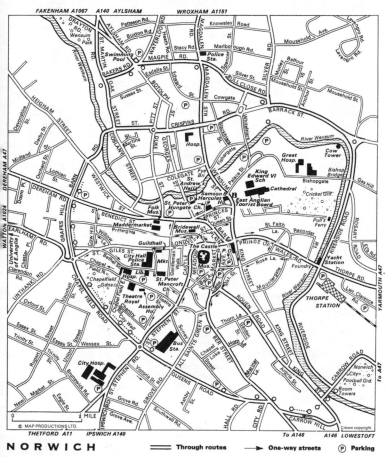

N O R W I C H ═══ Through routes ➤ One-way streets Ⓟ Parking

Those who on leaving the Cathedral walk round the Close towards the eastern end should continue down Lower Close to **Pull's Ferry,** the picturesque and ancient water-gate of the city. Near the north-west corner of the Cathedral is **King Edward VI School,** founded in 1325 and refounded by Edward VI. Opposite the West Front of the Cathedral is the beautiful **Erpingham Gate,** built in

1420, leading to the busy thoroughfare known as Tombland (from "toom" meaning empty). Facing the Gate is the gabled Samson and Hercules House and to the right is the *Maid's Head Hotel,* a 15th-century hostelry. Crossing Tombland into Wensum Street, turn left into Elm Hill, a medieval street with its memories of the Pastons and its charming old houses, including the 16th-century Stranger's Club—the "strangers" being earlier immigrants. At the top of Elm Hill is **St. Peter Hungate Church Museum,** since 1933 a museum of church art. On the right Princes Street leads to **St. Andrew's Hall.** Originally the nave of a 15th-century Dominican Church, this has served many purposes and is now a civic hall. Separated from it by the organ loft is Blackfriars Hall, the chancel of the old church. Opposite, in St. Andrew Street, is *Suckling House.* This was the house of a 15th-century merchant, and has a fine open roof with king-post. Behind St. Andrew's Church is the **Bridewell Museum,** once a prison and now a museum of Norfolk's crafts and industries. Farther along St. Andrew Street, on the left, is the street called St. John Maddermarket, which recalls the dyeing industry. Near by is the **Maddermarket Theatre,** built in Elizabethan style and the home of the Norwich Players. In Charing Cross, continuing the line of St. Andrew Street, is **Stranger's Hall,** a 14th-century house now a museum of domestic life from Tudor to late Victorian times. The narrow lane beside **St. Gregory's Church,** just beyond the Hall, leads to Pottergate. South of this is St. Giles Street and the Market Place. The old market square has been expanded into a spacious City Centre, the fine City Hall, opened in 1938, occupying the western side. Below the steps a Garden of Remembrance forms a setting for the City War Memorial. At the northern end of the market place is the 15th-century flint-built **Guildhall,** and at the opposite end is the stately **Church of St. Peter Mancroft.** Across the adjoining car-park is the Central Library and Record Office, and beyond this is the **Assembly House,** a fine example of 18th-century architecture. From the church cross Hay Hill and take the pedestrian way behind a large modern store to Orford Hall and the Castle.

Norwich Castle *(daily, free)*. This great Norman fortress, superbly sited on a lofty mound, dominates the city. Since 1894 it has been the principal civic *Museum and Art Gallery.* Many of the displays illustrate the social and cultural history of Norfolk and its natural setting. There is a famous collection of pictures by Artists of the Norwich School; also collections of Lowestoft porcelain and Norwich silver. The Dioramas are especially popular with children, as are the Mammal Gallery (with sound effects) and the Aquarium. From the central Rotunda there is access to all exhibition galleries and also to the interior of the Norman Keep, 90 feet square.

Norwich has many picturesque narrow streets, which often open out into squares, or "plains". Ancient churches are numerous. North-west from the Cathedral and across the Wensum is **Colegate,** with three fine medieval churches. In this area, too, are Nonconformist and Quaker places of worship, associated with the Gurneys, the Martineaus, and other literary figures of the last century. Magdalen Street has recently been restored to its former beauty. **Wensum Lodge,** the former Music House, in King Street, dates from the 12th century and is the oldest dwelling house in Norwich.

The heights of **Mousehold Heath,** familiar from the pictures of old Crome and the writings of George Borrow, lie to the north-east of the city and can be reached by bus. **Earlham Hall,** one-and-a-half miles west of Norwich, was once the home of Elizabeth Fry. It is now the administrative building for the University of East Anglia, which was opened in 1963 and has now 3,000 students.

At **Caister St. Edmund,** three miles south of the city, are remains of the Roman town of *Venta Icenorum*—the administrative centre of the Iceni. The brick and flint town wall is now grass grown but the face of the wall can be seen in places. Within the walls is the parish church, with a fine font and wall paintings.

224

THE BROADS

Broadland covers roughly the area between Norwich and the east coast. Here are about 100 miles of navigable rivers, linked with the meres and lakes locally known as "Broads". Holidays on the Broads are increasingly popular, whether by motor-cruiser or yacht, or at a riverside inn or bungalow. The three main rivers are the *Bure* (with its tributaries *Ant* and *Thurne*), the *Yare,* and the *Waveney.* All three rivers unite at **Breydon Water,** near Yarmouth, and continue as the *Yare* to the sea via Yarmouth Harbour. The Broads differ considerably, but all have their charm. The river system forms a connected waterway, so that all parts could be visited in a single cruise. There are a number of cruising centres among which are Norwich, Wroxham, Potter Heigham and Oulton Broad, near Lowestoft. The most popular river is the *Bure.*

The Bure and its Tributaries

The navigable part of the river *Bure* begins at **Coltishall** village. From here the river follows a winding course for five miles to **Wroxham,** a village with a 14th-century church, a large store, hotels, and boat-hire establishments. About one mile below the bridge one may enter **Wroxham Broad** and from its south-east corner rejoin the river. This Broad has an area of 120 acres, surrounded by woodland and meadows. A Regatta is held here in late July. Farther down river one comes to **Salhouse Broad** and **Hoveton Broad,** and beyond these is **Horning,** an attractive village in picturesque surroundings. Beyond Horning, Ranworth Dyke gives access to the tree-lined **Ranworth Broad,** a popular mooring spot. The inner Broad is a nature reserve. **Ranworth** Church dates from 1370. It has an exquisite rood screen and other treasures; and from its tall tower there is a fine view. Next the tributary *Ant* comes in from the left and then the ruins of **St. Benet's Abbey,** a once-celebrated monastery founded *c.* 955. Almost opposite the Abbey, Fleet Dyke leads into **South Walsham Broad.** Two miles below the Abbey, the *Bure* is joined by the tributary *Thurne,* which connects with a northerly group of Broads. A few miles beyond *Thurnemouth* the *Bure* is crossed by **Acle Bridge,** one mile from the village of **Acle.**

Acle Bridge is about 12 miles by river from Wroxham; the remaining 11 miles to Yarmouth is rather dull, across level marshlands until the *Bure* reaches the tidal **Breydon Water** at Great Yarmouth.

To the north-east of Acle are several beautiful Broads—**Ormesby, Rollesby** and **Filby**—not easily reached by water, but well worth visiting by road.

The Rivers Ant and Thurne

Entering the *Ant* from the *Bure,* we reach **Ludham Bridge** one mile upstream. Beyond this the ancient and reed-thatched church of **Irstead** can be seen among trees to the left, and three miles from Ludham Bridge one enters **Barton Broad,** a beautiful stretch of water about one mile long. At the north end Stalham Dyke leads to **Stalham,** a small but busy market town with an interesting old Church.

Up the Thurne to Hickling

The *Thurne* is a wider river than the *Ant,* and flows through a wild and secluded area of the Broads. About three miles up the *Thurne,* after passing the village of **Thurne,** and the picturesque **Womack Water,** one comes to the medieval Heigham Bridge. The large village of **Potter Heigham** lies about one mile inland. It has an old church and some fine houses, and a yachting centre has grown up near the Bridge. A farther one-and-a-half miles upstream is *Heigham Sound* leading to **Hickling Broad**—largest of the Broads—and **Horsey Mere.** Returning to the

Thurne and continuing up river for one-and-a-half miles, **Martham Broad** is reached.

The River Yare, Yarmouth to Norwich

The *Yare* rises near East Dereham, joins the *Wensum* at Norwich, and flows east for 20 miles to join with the *Waveney* and form the broad estuary of Breydon Water.

Starting from Yarmouth, at *Haven Bridge*, the view along Breydon Water is at first uninteresting except for the sea-birds and waterfowl. Herons can usually be seen at the margins of the flats. About half-mile east from the junction of *Waveney* and *Yare* are the remains of **Burgh Castle**, a well-preserved Roman fort that formed part of the defences of the "Saxon Shore". Continuing for about five miles up the *Yare*, one comes to the New Cut linking with the *Waveney*. Just beyond is **Reedham**, with a fine church and an old inn. A farther one-and-a-half miles upstream the tributary *Chet* comes in from the left. (Shallow craft may make a pleasant diversion up this stream to Loddon). Two miles farther along the *Yare* brings one to **Cantley**, a popular angling resort with a busy beet-sugar factory. On the opposite side and a little farther on Langley Dyke leads to **Langley** and the remains of an Abbey founded in 1198. The *Yare* continues to **Buckenham Ferry**, a spot much favoured by anglers. Next comes **Rockland Broad**. This is shallow, and cruisers should keep to the marked channel. About two miles on is the village of **Brundall** and **Surlingham Broad** which is rather silted up. At **Bramerton** the left bank rises in a wooded escarpment. The *Yare* continues past **Postwick** and **Whitlingham**, and then comes **Thorpe St. Andrew** the delightful riverside village that adjoins Norwich, at the foot of a wooded hill. The banks are fringed with vessels, ocean-going and otherwise. On bearing right to the river *Wensum* one sees the towers and spires of Norwich begin to appear.

The River Waveney and Oulton Broad

The *Waveney* rises a few miles west of Diss. For most of its length it forms the boundary between Norfolk and Suffolk. Two miles from the coast it turns northward away from Lowestoft, and joins with the *Yare* at Breydon Water, near Yarmouth.

From a point where the *Waveney* is nearest to the coast, Oulton Dyke leads into **Oulton Broad**, connected by Lake Lothing with Lowestoft Harbour and the sea. Oulton Broad is a popular boating centre, and though just in Suffolk it is a good starting point for the Norfolk Broads.

Great Yarmouth

Distances.—Aldeburgh, 36; Beccles, 15; Bungay, 20; Cromer, 35; London, 124; Lowestoft, 10, Norwich, 20, Sandringham, 60.
Early Closing.—Thursday.
Entertainment.—Amusements, cinemas, dancing, Theatres, Pier Pavilion. Tyrolean Biergarten.

Circus.
Hotels.—*Royal, New Beach, Carlton, Bath, Norfolk, Cavendish, Sandringham, Star, Central, Marine View*, and many others.
Population.—52,000.
Post Office.—Regent Street.

A broad stretch of clean sands extending for miles to north and south, a sea-view affording an almost constant panorama of outward and homeward-bound vessels; a sea air not to be excelled even along this healthy East Coast for its pure and bracing quality; this is Yarmouth to which tens of thousands of visitors return summer after summer, thinking of it during the intervals between their visits as a familiar and loved friend. The Marine Parade is a broad and attractive thoroughfare extending for three-quarters of a mile between the piers. On one side are hotels and guesthouses, numerous arcades, a maritime museum and places of entertainment, including the Tower centre with attractions including a ballroom; on the other side the sands, the Marina, gardens, swimming pool, the shelters, piers, and beyond them all the sea. The *Nelson Monument*, on the South Denes, is surmounted by a figure of Britannia. Nelson was born at Burnham Thorpe, Norfolk in 1758. *St. Nicholas Church* in area is one of the largest parish churches in England. Burnt out in 1942 it was except for the outer walls rebuilt in 1960. Along South Quay are some Elizabethan houses including one housing a *Museum of Domestic Life*. The **Tolhouse** is an old and curious building of 13th-century date. The *Rows* are a distinct feature of the old town. There were originally 145 Rows with a total length of seven miles, all of them built at right angles to the sea.

Gorleston is Yarmouth's southern neighbour and a highly popular resort. There is an excellent sandy beach, shelving rather more than that at Yarmouth. A modern steel and concrete pier forms the southern protection to the entrance to Yarmouth harbour. The church is a large 13th-century structure.

Caister-on-Sea, three miles north of Yarmouth, is an ancient Roman port and fishing village proving popular as a seaside resort. **Caister Castle** *(May–Sept., daily, fee)*, a picturesque ruin, was built about the middle of the 15th century. Near the southern corner of the moat is *Caister Hall*, its walls contemporary with the castle. Roman remains have been discovered near the main road to Acle.

Mundesley-on-Sea *(Royal, Manor, Continental)*, is a popular holiday village set on a low cliff below which spreads a firm expanse of sand. A long sea wall forms a pleasant promenade. The church was restored and re-roofed in 1904. There is good bathing, angling, bowls and tennis, and a golf course.

Pleasant villages in the Mundesley neighbourhood include **Gimingham,** three miles north-west. The church is ancient but unremarkable except for the porch which is an excellent example of 15th-century flintwork. **Trunch,** just over a mile south from Gimingham, has a church with an almost unique font cover of richly carved oak resting on pillars. **Knapton** is situated on comparatively high ground two miles from Mundesley. The simple but lofty interior of the church is dominated by a magnificent roof, unrivalled by any other parish church in England. Constructed of Irish oak in 1503, it has double hammer-beams and bears richly carved figures of prophets and angels. **Paston,** a little over a mile from Knapton, was long associated with the Paston family, though the original Paston Hall no longer exists. The present hall has no connection with that family. The most noteworthy features of the church, reed-thatched, are the 15th-century rood screen and some medieval wall paintings. **Bacton,** a long mile east of Paston, is a rapidly growing caravan centre and bungalow town. The seafront is small but there are wide and beautiful sands and some inns and cafés. Near at hand are the ruins of *Bromholm Priory* now almost obliterated. The church like that of Paston is partially thatched. **Happisburgh,** seven miles from Mundesley, is an old village with fine sands and excellent bathing. The red-banded *Happisburgh Lighthouse*, the lantern of which is 136 feet above high water, gives three white flashes every half minute. The church has a fine tower and a font of great beauty.

North Walsham *(King's Arms, Black Swan, Cross Keys)*, is an old country town with a threefold attraction in its Church, Grammar School and Market Cross. The church is a noble building for the most part early Perpendicular rising imposingly above the town. The windows at the east end of the aisles are beautiful specimens of the Decorated style. The Market Cross, rebuilt in 1600, is a kind of covered pavilion with a cobbled floor. The Paston School was founded in 1606. Horatio Nelson was a one-time pupil.

In the low-lying country between North Walsham and the coast are small scattered villages connected by narrow winding roads. **Ridlington** has a lovely brick and thatch barn with Dutch gable ends. The church has an octagonal font and an old door with immense keys. **Crostwight** church has a 15th-century low tower. The *Ant* rises in Antingham Ponds near Bradfield about four miles north of North Walsham.

Worstead, three miles south-east of North Walsham, is an agricultural village with a wide square flanked by fine houses, while the church owes its origin to the worsted weavers. The lofty embattled tower is in four stages and reaches a height of 109 feet.

Cromer

Distances.—Dereham, 28; Norwich, 25; London, 133; Yarmouth, 35.
Early Closing.—Wednesday.
Entertainment.—Pier Pavilion (concert party), cinema, dancing. Zoo.
Hotels.—*Cliftonville, Colne House, Hotel de Paris,*

Ship Inn, Overstrand Court, Cliff House, and others.
Population.—5,500.
Post Office.—Church Street.
Sports.—Angling, bathing, bowls, tennis, golf, riding.

Cromer, on the coast due north of Norwich, was a small fishing town (still famous for crabs and lobsters) which has developed into an attractive resort. It is appreciated by those preferring an outdoor holiday—walking in the well-wooded country, riding, swimming, fishing, golf and tennis. The massive sea-wall is the basis for wide Promenades. At the head of the Pier is the *Lifeboat Station* one of the most importance on the coast. On either side of the Pier stretches a shore of sand and low cliffs. *Lighthouse Cliff,* at the eastern end of Cromer, affords a fine all-round view. The Lighthouse gives five white flashes every 15 seconds. Nearby are the 18-hole Golf Links. The Parish **Church** is a large Perpendicular structure dedicated to the SS. Peter and Paul, and dates from the early 15th century. The south doorway is probably of this date. The church is faced with square flints and the 160-foot tower once served as a lighthouse. The most interesting feature of the interior is the hammer-beam roof.

There are excellent cliff walks and inland walks near Cromer. **Northrepps, Southrepps** and **Felbrigg** all have interesting churches. **Felbrigg Hall** (N.T., *Apr.–mid-Oct., Tues, Weds, Thurs, Suns, Bank Hols, fee*), is a well-preserved Jacobean house, in 1,000 acres of park and woodland. **East** and **West Runton** lie on the coast between Cromer and Sheringham, and inland from them is the heath known as *Roman Camp.*

Nearly 11 miles south of Cromer is **Aylsham,** a pleasant market town on the *Bure.* A short distance north-west of Aylsham is **Blickling Hall** (N.T., *Apr.–mid-Oct., Tues, Weds, Thurs, Sats, Suns, Bank Hols, fee*), a fine quadrangular Jacobean mansion, designed by the same architect as Hatfield House, and formerly the seat of the late Marquess of Lothian.

Eastward along the coast from Cromer one passes **Overstrand, Sidestrand** and **Trimingham.**

Sheringham

Distances.—Cromer, 4; Norwich, 28; London, 130; King's Lynn, 40; Wells, 17; Yarmouth, 40.
Early Closing.—Wednesday.
Entertainment.—Little Theatre (repertory), band concerts.
Hotels.—*Burlington,   Uplands,   Southlands,*

Beaumaris, Two Lifeboats, and others.
Population.—4,680.
Post Office.—Station Road.
Sports.—Angling, bathing, bowls, tennis, golf, putting.

Sheringham lies four miles west of Cromer, and like the latter was a fishing village until the coming of the railway. It is now a popular holiday and residential centre, with good sands and a sea-wall Promenade at the foot of low cliffs. Sheringham is set in pleasant surroundings; *Beeston Hill,* on its eastern outskirts, affords a good view of the area. About half-mile from the sea-front and reached by Holt Road, is *Franklin Hill* another pleasant view-point. **Upper Sheringham,** one mile inland, is a delightful village with a fine 14th-century Parish Church, with a wonderful collection of bench-end carvings. Close by is *Sheringham Hall* in its fine Park.

Leaving Sheringham by Holway Road it is three-quarter-mile to Sheringham Woods, 77 acres owned by the town. Just beyond the woods *Pretty Corner,* at the cross-roads, justifies its name. A short distance east of Sheringham, and best reached from the Cromer road, are the ruins of **Beeston Priory,** founded in the reign of King John. Between the railway and the sea is the lovely little Beeston Regis Church.

Westward from Sheringham the road runs past a string of interesting coastal villages. **Weybourne,** picturesquely situated in a dip; **Salthouse,** which has suffered many inundations by the sea—the last being in 1953; and **Cley-next-the Sea,** once a flourishing port, though now one mile inland owing to the silting up of the estuary. Cley has curious old houses and alleys, and the size of its ancient church is an indication of its former greatness. Another of the church towers dominating the low-lying marshland is one-and-a-half miles west of Cley, at **Blakeney,** the only remaining port on the *Glaven* estuary, and now a popular sailing centre. The fine church of St. Nicholas has fine woodwork and hammer-beam roof. The chancel was built in 1220, and on the north-east corner is a slender turret that used to contain a beacon light for shipping. Fragments of a Carmelite friary (1296) can be seen near the Church.

Blakeney Point (N.T.) which includes the salt marshes and sands to the north and north-west, is interesting for its bird and plant-life. At its extremity is a bird-sanctuary. Motor-boat trips to the Point are organised from Blakeney and also from Morston, one mile farther west.

Inland from Blakeney are some delightful villages, notably **Wiveton, Glandford, Letheringsett** and **Langham. Stiffkey** (Stukey) on the coast, is only four miles from Wells but a diversion can be made by turning inland at Stiffkey to see the ruins of *Binham Priory,* founded in the 11th century. The nave was spared at the Dissolution of the Monasteries for use as a parish church.

Some nine miles to the west of Cromer is the small market-town of **Holt,** with a spacious market-place. The town was rebuilt after the fire of 1708. The original Gresham's School founded in 1555 is now housed in extensive modern buildings. **Fakenham,** 12 miles farther along the A148, has a high church tower and two coaching inns. Between here and Swaffham (16 miles) a short diversion to the right at Newton brings one to the village of **Castle Acre,** situated on a steep slope above the river *Nar.* Little remains of the Norman castle, built on pre-existing earth-works. Beyond the ancient parish church are the remains of a Cluniac Priory founded in 1090 by William de Warenne, son-in-law of the Conqueror.

Swaffham *(George)* is a pleasant market town, with a domed Market Cross, an old Church, and 18th-century red-brick buildings. Twelve miles east of Swaffham, on the road to Norwich, is the busy market town of **East Dereham,** whose history begins with the founding of a Nunnery in 654 by St. Withburga. The Church is the second largest in Norfolk. The poet Cowper lies buried here and George Borrow was born at Dumpling Green, within the parish.

Eight miles south-east of Norwich, by the A11, is **Wymondham** (pronounced Windham), a market town with some old houses and a market cross. The dominant feature is the Abbey Church founded in 1107. The western front still stands and is the parish church; it has a square western tower and an octagonal east one. The interior displays all the splendours of Norman architecture.

Beyond Wymondham the A11 continues to **Thetford** *(Bell, Anchor),* near the county border. Thetford is a Breckland town in an area of heath and pinewoods. It has attractive old houses, and the ruins of an old Castle and a Cluniac Priory. In medieval times Thetford was a town of great importance. Its thirty parish churches are now reduced to three.

Wells-next-the-Sea *(Crown, Tinkers'),* is a north Norfolk fishing port that retains a coastal trade, and has attained some popularity as a quiet resort and a camping site. At the centre of the town is a long Green known as the Buttlands, flanked by some fine 18th-century houses. Narrow streets lead down to the busy Quay, with its quaint old houses and inns. Wells affords good sailing, fishing, and wildfowling. About a mile from the quay is the Beach of fine yellow sand backed by grassy sand dunes.

To the west of Wells lies Holkham Park, once a barren waste, converted to pastures and woodland by that famous patron of agriculture "Coke of Norfolk", Earl of Leicester (1752–1842). **Holkham Hall** *(Thurs, June–Sept., and also Mons, July–Aug., fee)*, built in 1734, is in severe Palladian style. Continuing westward one comes to the Burnhams, a group of villages of which the largest is **Burnham Market. Burnham Thorpe** was the birthplace of Horatio Nelson, whose father was rector of the Parish Church. No memorial of Nelson existed until 1890, but since that time the church has become almost a Nelson museum. A few miles south are the ruins of *Creake Abbey*, founded in 1206. **Burnham Overy** has an ancient flint Church with tower and a bell cupola. From the little quay, *Overy Staithe*, expeditions can be made to the bird sanctuary at Scolt Head. **Burnham Market** (or Burnham Westgate) has a wide main street with some good houses. **Burnham Norton** has a church whose flint tower has overlooked the marshes since Norman times. The interior of the church is of great interest. **Burnham Deepdale** is the most westerly of the Burnhams; in its church is a font with 11th-century carvings of the Seasons.

South of Wells, half-way to Fakenham, is **Little Walsingham,** a beautiful village whose streets are bordered with medieval and Georgian houses. An ancient archway gives access to the ruins of an Augustine Priory founded in the 12th century. For centuries there was a constant stream of pilgrims to this spot to the Shrine of "Our Lady of Walsingham", built at the place where the Virgin Mary is said to have appeared to the lady of the Manor, in 1061. Many miraculous cures were reported. At the Dissolution of the Monasteries all was destroyed or stolen, and pilgrimages were not resumed until our own times. There are now two restorations of the Shrine, or "Holy House"—the Anglican Shrine (1931–37), a Church with red brick tower, which claims to be on the original site; and the Roman Catholic Shrine, about a mile to the south, in the restored Slipper Chapel, where earlier pilgrims removed their shoes to walk the last mile barefoot.

Hunstanton (Pop.: 4,140. Hotels: *Golden Lion, Neptune, Le Strange Arms,* etc.), unlike other East Anglican resorts, faces west, overlooking the Wash. It takes its name from the fishing village now called Old Hunstanton a mile north of the new town. There is a central Green, with hotels and Victorian houses of brown carrstone. The sands are extensive and backed by stratified cliffs; and there is a pier, a promenade, and the usual seaside amenities. North of the Pier is the Old Lighthouse, beyond which the cliffs slope to the marram dunes of the old village. **Old Hunstanton** has mellow houses, winding lanes, and an 18-hole golf course. A short way farther north is **Holme-next-the Sea,** where Peddar's Way, the pre-Roman track that comes from Suffolk via Castle Acre, reaches the sea.

Southward from Hunstanton, the Lynn road passes through the attractive village of **Heacham.** In the church is a memorial to Pocahontas, the Red Indian princess who married John Rolfe, of Heacham Hall. A farther two miles brings one to **Snettisham,** and beyond this **Dersingham,** both with interesting churches. Near Dersingham is **Sandringham House,** a country residence of the Royal Family. It was purchased in 1861 by Queen Victoria for the Prince of Wales. Both George V and George VI died here. The grounds are usually open to the public. The main road next passes through **Castle Rising,** an almost medieval village with castle, market cross, church and almshouse. Dominating the village is the Norman **Castle** *(daily, fee)*, built in 1150 on huge earthworks. Here Queen Isabella was confined for 30 years for her part in the murder of Edward II. The Keep is still well preserved. Opposite the restored 12th-century church is the interesting *Trinity Hospital* founded in 1614 to be an almshouse for 10 women. The old ladies still attend church on Sundays in red cloaks and pointed black hats.

King's Lynn (Pop.: 30,650. Hotels: *Duke's Head, Globe, Cozens*), is an ancient town on the *Ouse,* three miles from its outflow into the Wash. Once a gateway of the medieval wool trade and the home of merchant princes, it still, retains streets of fine old houses, and buildings of historic interest. And it is still a busy port, with coasting and continental trade. King's Lynn was already a market town and port when Bishop Losinga founded St. Margaret's Church in 1101. Some years later St.

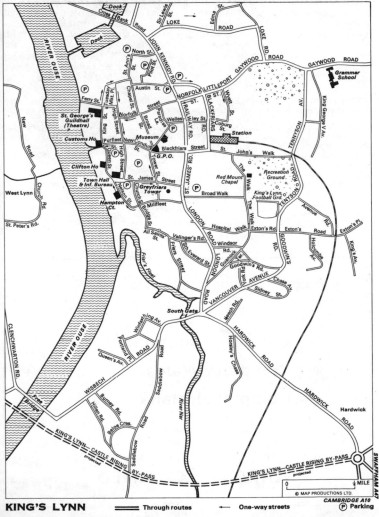

KING'S LYNN ═══ Through routes ← One-way streets

CAMBRIDGE A10 Ⓟ Parking

Nicholas's Church was built as a chapel of ease to St. Margaret's. Around these two centres the town steadily expanded. **St. Margaret's Church** contains some notable brasses, and a remarkable leaning arch of the original Norman church. Adjoining the Church is the Saturday Market Place, and opposite is the Guildhall built in 1421. A short way east of the Church is the lofty Greyfriars Tower, and beyond this are the Walks, fine avenues of limes and chestnuts. Here also are the octagonal Red Mount Chapel (*c.* 1485) and fragments of the Town Wall. About half-mile down the London Road are the remains of the Southgate (*c.* 1440), and midway is the Roman Catholic Church, containing a replica of the famous Walsingham Shrine. From the Saturday Market, Queen Street, joining with King Street, leads to the large Tuesday Market Place. Near the junction, on the quayside, is the beautiful 17th-century Custom House. North-east of the market place is the *Church of St. Nicholas,* with a fine south porch, an angel roof, and some good carving.

Eleven miles south of King's Lynn is **Downham Market,** a small town on high ground bordering the Fens. Its carrstone Church has a lofty tower.

Between King's Lynn and Downham Market, away from main roads and on either side of the *Ouse,* are four small villages, **Wiggenhall St. German, Wiggenhall St. Peter, Wiggenhall St. Mary Magdalen,** and **Wiggenhall St. Mary the Virgin.** Even in this county of famous churches, these villages are worth visiting for the sake of their ancient and curious churches.

Northampton and Peterborough

The A5, Thomas Telford's great coach road from London to Holyhead, crosses the Ouse just outside **Stony Stratford** to enter Northamptonshire. Almost immediately the A508 branches right towards Northampton passing near the Grand Union Canal at **Cosgrove.** Here, on the high ground surrounding the church, splendid views can be obtained in a wide circle around. The road keeps west of the Canal for four miles until it crosses it by a hump-back bridge at **Stoke Bruerne.**

Over the bridge a narrow lane leads left into the **Waterways Museum** *(daily all year)*. Here there are locks, a canalside inn, and in a handsome three-storey warehouse a fascinating collection of pictures, photographs and models of everything to do with the life of the "narrow-boat people" of the canals. A prominent exhibit is a full-size reconstruction, in authentic colours, of a narrow-boat cabin complete with decorations in the mysterious "roses and castle" design whose origin is unknown. In the shop adjoining a range of canal souvenirs may be bought.

Also at Stoke Bruerne is **Stoke Park** *(Sats and Suns, July and Aug.)* containing the 17th-century twin Pavilions *(exterior view only)*, all that remains of the fine house attributed to Inigo Jones which was destroyed by fire in 1884.

A short distance along the canal from Stoke Bruerne is the entrance to **Blisworth Tunnel,** one and three-quarter miles long, the longest canal tunnel still in use. The construction of Blisworth Tunnel held up the completion of the Grand Union Canal for five years, from 1800 to 1805, and even after its opening it was not provided with a towpath. The narrow-boats were propelled through by men known as "leggers" who lay flat on the boat deck and forced the boat through by pushing on the canal wall with their legs.

The A508 crosses the M1 at Junction 15 and enters Northampton by the South Bridge over the river *Nene.*

Northampton

Distances.—Aylesbury, 36; Huntingdon, 37; Leicester, 32; Luton, 35; London, 66; Oxford, 41; Peterborough, 40; Rugby, 20; St. Albans, 45.
Early Closing.—Mondays and Thursdays.
Entertainment.—*Repertory Theatre,* Guildhall Road; *New Theatre,* Abington Street;

cinemas; *aquadrome.*
Hotels.—*Westone, Grand, Angel, Plough, Ram, Bull and Butcher.*
Market Day.—Wednesday and Saturdays.
Population.—126,600.
Post Office.—St. Giles's Street.

Northampton is the county town and has for centuries been a centre for the manufacture of shoes. During the Civil War it supplied the boots for Cromwell's New Model Army, the result being that at the Restoration Charles II demolished its town walls and castle. The old tanneries which once supplied the tannin from oak bark can still be seen along the river. Northampton was severely damaged by fire in 1675 and most of its buildings are therefore 18th-century or later. It has a fine cobbled **Market Square** and several interesting churches the most important of which is the round church of **St. Sepulchre's.** It was built in 1115 by Simon de Senlis, a returning Crusader, and is one of only four round churches in England dating from that period and modelled on the Church of the Holy Sepulchre in

Jerusalem. The Victorian **St. Matthew's Church,** in the Kettering Road, has close ties with the art world and shows Graham Sutherland's "Crucifixion" and the stone "Madonna and Child" of Henry Moore. In the town centre is the striking-looking pillared façade of **All Saints' Church,** with its stone parapet, in the middle of which is an odd-looking statue of Charles II wearing Roman armour and a full-bottomed wig. Nearby, in Gold Street a survival of the fire is *Hazelrigg House,* a handsome building with curved gables built about 1665. In Guildhall Road is the **Central Museum and Art Gallery** *(weekdays).* As well as exhibiting many items of archaeological interest and pictures it has one of the world's finest collections illustrating the history of the boot and shoe trade including Queen Victoria's wedding shoes and shoes worn by Nijinsky and other famous dancers. Along the Wellington Road is **Abington Museum** *(weekdays throughout year, and Sun. afternoons from Apr. to Sept.)* a 15th-century house which has rooms in various period furnishings and also a section devoted to the history of the Northamptonshire Regiment.

South-west from Northampton

Just across the river on the A50 is **Delapré Abbey** *(Thurs and Sats; grounds daily)* where are kept the county records and muniments. The A43 strikes off opposite to cross the M1 *(no access)* and in nine miles reaches Towcester. **Towcester** *(Brave Old Oak),* was the *Lactodorum* of the Romans on Watling Street and is still an important stop on the A5 London–Holyhead road. Its coaching-inns are therefore numerous and picturesque and include the *Saracen's Head* and the *Talbot.* The parish church has an ornate organ of 1760 from Fonthill Abbey and a rare "Treacle" Bible ("treacle" being used instead of "balm" in the passage concerning Gilead). Towcester has a popular racecourse.

Five miles south-west is **Silverstone** with a well-known motor-racing track on a former airfield. The A43 passes through **Syresham,** a small village with a wide and pleasant main street, and then drops down to **Brackley.** This picturesque town, with its long tree-lined High Street and stone houses, has played a large part in English history. It is closely associated with Simon de Montfort and also with Magdalen College, Oxford, who in 1447 bought the 12th-century Hospital established by the Earl of Leicester. At the Dissolution it became *Magdalen College School* and has continued so ever since. The large Town Hall with a cupola in the High Street was built by the Duke of Bridgwater, of canal fame, in the 18th century. From the road to Buckingham can be seen the many arches of the viaduct carrying the old Great Central Railway from the Midlands south to London.

Two miles south of Brackley the A43 meets the B4031 on the county boundary, and three miles west of the junction is **Aynho** a lovely village of stone-built houses with apricots growing on the walls. The apricots are a reminder of the days when rents to the lord of the manor were paid in this fruit.

Aynhoe House *(May–Sept., Weds, Thurs, fee)* is a 17th-century mansion much altered by Sir John Soane. Part is now flats but the remainder is a most gracious series of rooms exhibiting pictures and a fine collection of ceramics.

A mile away, in a wood, is Pestwood House (not open) where the villagers were isolated during the Plague, food for them being left outside in the grounds.

North from Aynho leafy, winding lanes lead through **Charlton** and **Farthinghoe** to **Middleton Cheney,** on the Banbury–Brackley road (A422). The village seems in danger of being engulfed by Banbury, though the older part of stone walls and cottages still preserves its identity. The parish church is well known for the surprising number of stained-glass windows designed by pre-Raphaelites including Rossetti, Burne-Jones, Ford Madox Brown, William Morris and Philip Webb. Burne-Jones, it seems, was a friend of the rector.

Off the A422 the B4525 runs five miles into **Sulgrave,** a village of great interest to American visitors in being the home of George Washington's ancestors, and from where his great-grandfather emigrated in 1656.

Sulgrove Manor *(daily except Weds, fee)* was built in 1560 by Lawrence Washington and is a beautiful example of a small manor house of Tudor times. There are numerous relics and mementoes of the Washington family, but perhaps of greatest interest to Americans is the family coat-of-arms carved above the main doorway. This consists of three stars and two stripes and is said to be the origin of the American flag.

In the 14th-century church is a brass to Lawrence Washington, his wife and their four sons and seven daughters.

Due north of Sulgrave is **Woodford Halse,** known to every railway enthusiast as the former important junction of the Great Central Railway and still keeping its rows of brick railway cottages as at Crewe, Swindon and Wolverton. The road runs through **Hinton** and joins the A361 at **Byfield,** where the stub of the ancient market-cross stands on the village green. From here it is six miles through **Charwelton** (where the river *Cherwell* rises and also acquires its pronunciation) past the 13th-century packhorse bridge to Daventry.

Just south of the main road before the town is reached is *Fawsley Park,* where Charles I hunted before the Battle of Naseby when staying at the now-ruined Dower House set in the Great Park with its spectacular chain of lakes. The isolated medieval church in the Park has a fine tomb of 1539 and carved 14th-century bench-ends.

Around Daventry

Daventry, 12 miles west of Northampton is a small and peaceful town for ever associated with the early days of broadcasting and still ringed around with tall radio masts. But its true age is seen from the site of these same radio masts—on high ground, with a splendid view all around and on earthworks which mark the site of a Bronze-Age fort. At the ancient *Wheatsheaf Inn* in the town Charles I is said to have stayed before the Battle of Naseby. The squat, stubby ironstone parish church is in Classical style, and, like much else in Daventry, is good, solid and unimaginative.

Braunston, about three miles north-west of Daventry on the A45, is an important place on the Grand Union Canal where the original Grand Junction Canal from London joined the Oxford Canal. From this point six other waterways can be reached including the Coventry Canal and the *Trent* and *Mersey* to Manchester, the Trent Navigation to the *Humber,* or south on the Oxford Canal to the *Thames* and London. Also on the Grand Union, three miles north-east of Braunston, is **Long Buckby Wharf,** once a busy commercial canal centre and the home of the gaily-painted cans that featured so largely on the narrow-boats. **Ashby St. Legers,** on the B4038 north of Daventry, was the ancestral home of the Catesby family, implicated in the Gunpowder Plot (1605). The church is one of the few in Northamptonshire to have escaped the attention of Victorian restorers and has some 14th-century wall-paintings. On the eastern side of the M1, midway between Daventry and Northampton, is the village of **Great Brington.** Just outside is **Althorp Hall** *(Suns during May, and on Tues, Weds and Suns from June to Sept.).* This 15th-century mansion was the home of the Spencer family, whose many portraits can be seen in the house, and was greatly altered by Henry Holland and others in the 16th, 17th and 18th centuries. The main picture gallery is 115 feet long and there is a fine collection of furniture.
Northampton to Naseby. Naseby is reached from Northampton either by the A50 or by the northbound A508 and turning to the left a mile short of Kelmarsh. Six miles up the A508 is

Brixworth where are the kennels of the Pytchley hunt, and an ancient Saxon church, one of only three in England based on the Roman basilica and where the circular apse still survives. Near the village are the extensive *Pitsfood reservoirs* reaching to **Holcot** where in the church are faint medieval wall-paintings.

Across-country, between the A50 and the A508 near Great Creaton, is **Cottesbrooke** with a church noted for the completeness of its 18th-century fittings including box-pews, a three-decker pulpit, family pew and reading desk. *Cottesbrooke Hall (see notices)* is an 18th-century mansion standing in extensive grounds and plantations of cedars, and is the possible original of Jane Austen's "Mansfield Hall".

Four miles north a lane leads to **Naseby** and a mile outside the village is the site of the famous battle of 1645. A small modern memorial marks the actual site of the encounter, which changed the course of English history. The larger obelisk put up in 1823 is incorrectly placed. In the church is preserved a table at which a party of Royalists were surprised by Roundheads the night before the battle.

To Castle Ashby. The A428 Bedford road runs south-eastward in seven miles to Yardley Hastings from which a left turn leads to **Castle Ashby** *(Suns, Bank Hols, Apr.–Sept. Additionally Thurs, Sats, June–Aug.)*, seat of the Marquess of Northampton. Fine paintings, furniture, Greek vases.

To Wellingborough. Just off the A45, six miles out is **Earls Barton** with a great square castellated Saxon tower to its church dominating the village. The church is Norman, the battlement on the tower having been added in the 15th century. **Wellingborough** has seen a great deal of growth during the latter half of the 19th century and its main industries are shoemaking and the manufacture of clothing. It stands at the junction of the *Nene* and *Ise* and was once a busy centre for the extraction of iron ore found locally. Despite Victorian expansion it still has some old and colourful buildings such as the Old Grammar School, the 17th-century *Golden Hind* and the old parish church of St. Luke with carved misericords.

East of Wellingborough, **Higham Ferrers** and **Rushden** both owe their expansion to the shoe trade. Higham Ferrers, however, has not become totally drowned in the sea of Victorian red brick and the church and the odd-looking Bede House of 1428 preserve its character. Equally, **Raunds**, on the A605, though still an industrial town, is saved by its church with its 15th-century wall-paintings and curious medieval 24-hour clock-face supported by angels.

Kettering and Corby

Burton Latimer, on the A6 to Kettering, is an oasis of stone amid Victorian brick and has not only an interesting church but a Jacobean schoolhouse and Hall. The A6 is joined by the A604 from Cambridge just a mile outside Kettering.

Kettering *(George)* is a busy industrial town with footwear and clothing factories and a population of some 42,600. The Industrial Revolution brought prosperity and with it a surge of rebuilding and restoration and little of the old place remains. The restored 14th-century church has a tall and beautiful spire.

Rushton Hall *(see notices)*, property of the Royal National Institute for the Blind, is a fine Tudor mansion. It dates from about 1500 with considerable additions.

At **Geddington** five miles north along the A43 is one of the three surviving Eleanor Crosses marking the resting places of that Queen's coffin on its journey from Harby in Lincolnshire to London in 1290.

Corby (Pop.: 47,700. Hotel: *Strathclyde*) has developed rapidly from a small village to an important steel-making town due to exploitation of the nearby ironstone quarries.

Rockingham Castle *(Easter–Sept., Thurs, Suns, Bank Hols)*, to the north of Corby almost on the county boundary, was a Royal castle until 1530 when it passed to the Watson family who still own it.

The great Forest of Rockingham once stretched almost to Oundle in the east and was richer in venison than even the New Forest in the days of Charles I. There are still considerable remains of this 6,000-acre forest providing opportunities for picnics and walks. At **Gretton** is the eerie façade of **Kirby Hall** *(daily, fee)*, a fine house built in 1570 but allowed to fall into disrepair until now. Though it still looks habitable it is like the back-drop to a theatrical production, with no depth or substance.

Just west of Corby is **Deene Park** *(see notices)* home of the Brudenelle family since 1514. It was the home of the 7th Earl of Cardigan who led the Charge of the Light Brigade at Balaclava in 1854.

Between Corby and Stamford the river *Welland* marks the boundary between Northamptonshire and what was formerly Rutland—the smallest county in England. Now the planners, with their ruthless determination to destroy individuality in the name of progress, have obliterated Rutland, which has become administratively part of Leicestershire. It is an area of good hunting, of rolling, peaceful countryside, and in many ways a microcosm of all that is best in rural England.

Oundle (Pop.: 3,750. Hotel: *Talbot*) reached from Kettering or Northampton via Thrapston, is a pleasant market town surrounded on three sides by the river *Nene* which adds to its already considerable charm. There are a number of old houses and inns and round the 14th-century church are grouped the mellow buildings of the famous public school. Nearby are the attractive 17th-century *Latham Almshouses*.

Four miles south-west of Oundle is **Lyveden New Bield** (N.T. *Mar.–Oct., Weds, Thurs, Sats, Bank Hols, fee)*, the uncompleted shell of a two-storey house in the shape of a Greek cross, begun in 1600 by Sir Thomas Tresham. Sir Thomas became involved in the Gunpowder Plot and the work was never completed.

Cotterstock Hall *(garden open. House on written application)* a mile and a half north of Oundle is a 17th-century stone house having associations with Dryden the poet. There are pleasant gardens. Further north is the hamlet of **Fotheringhay.** Only a mound in a field marks the site of the castle where Mary, Queen of Scots was tried and executed in 1567. The church has a noble lantern tower and monuments of Yorkist princes.

Huntingdon (Pop.: 16,500. Hotels: *Old Bridge, George*) linked administratively and, by a bridge over the *Ouse*, with Godmanchester, is a quaint and fascinating place, a market town since Saxon times. It is famous as the birthplace of Oliver Cromwell (1599–1658). The *Cromwell Museum* in Market Hill is in the old grammar school in which both he and Pepys were educated. His birthplace, Cromwell House incorporated with a later building, stands in High Street. Around Market Hill are several pleasant Georgian buildings. The *Ouse* gives good fishing and boating.

At **Buckden** three miles south are the remains of *Buckden Palace (Suns, July–Sept.)*, once the palace of the Bishops of Lincoln. It retains a Tudor gatehouse and tower of about 1490. West of the A1 is the extensive **Grafham Water** *(fishing)* with many walks and picnic spots in the vicinity.

St. Neots (Pop.: 15,150. Hotel: *Bridge*) on the *Ouse* nine miles south of Huntingdon, is an interesting market town with a number of flourishing light industries including milling, brewing, paper-making and timber processing.

St. Ives (Pop.: 7,150. Hotels: *Slepe Hall, Pike and Eel*) on the *Ouse* six miles east of Huntingdon, was once called Slepe but changed its name in 1050 when a priory dedicated to St. Ivo was established. A chapel, rebuilt 1689, stands on the little bridge crossing the *Ouse*. In the market place is a statue of Cromwell who lived for a time in the town. North of St. Ives across the A141 at Warboys is the 15th-century gatehouse of **Ramsey Abbey** *(daily, fee)*. To the north is an area of flat fenland where roads are few and horizons distant. Instead, dykes and "drains" abound with names like Forty Feet Bridge indicating the width of the canal at that point. Ten miles away to the north-west amid pylons and the tall chimneys of factories processing the local sugar-beet can be seen the outline of Peterborough and its cathedral.

Peterborough (Pop.: 70,000. Hotels: *Great Northern, Bull*) is an ancient city, and the see of a bishop since 1541, on the river *Nene*. Much of its prosperity has been due to the establishment of railway and steel works and extensive brickworks, particularly at Fletton. It is thunderously busy with traffic at most times, and many old buildings which have been shaken to their foundations have been replaced by modern office-blocks and impersonally efficient shopping centres. Good buildings solid enough to resist the march of progress are the 17th-century Guildhall in the Market Place and the Customs House by the river bridge. A number of old stone houses can be seen in Priestgate, off Bridge Street. Among them is the Museum *(weekdays)* interesting for its Roman remains and items of local interest.

The **Cathedral** is a vast and high building considered one of the most impressive Norman churches in Britain. The elaborate West Façade with recessed arches, gables and sculptures was a later addition. It is the third church on the site the first having been founded by Penda, King of Mercia in 656 as the church of the Benedictine monastery of *Medeshamstede*. The oldest part now standing is the Choir dated about 1140. The fine central tower was built in 1886 replacing a 14th-century tower which became unsafe. Two queens of England were buried here—Catherine of Aragon in the north choir aisle, and Mary, Queen of Scots after her execution at Fotheringhay. The unhappy Mary was later re-interred in Westminster Abbey by her son, James I. The monuments of both were destroyed by the Puritans but tablets, subscribed for by "Catherines" and "Marys" are placed nearby.

Close against the county boundary and a mile south-east of Stamford is **Burghley House** *(Apr.–Oct., Tues, Weds, Thurs, Suns, Bank Hols, fee)* seat of the Marquess of Exeter and by far the largest Elizabethan house in England. The interior is richly decorated and there are many paintings and treasures. The well-known Burghley Horse Trials take place in the spacious grounds in early September.

Into Leicestershire

The large expanse of country stretching from Peterborough almost to Leicester is the hunting country of the Shires. It is the home of one of the oldest hunts in England—the Cottesmore—established about 1780, though organised hunting had begun some 50 years before.

It is hunting that has given much of the area its characteristic appearance. In the early years of the 19th century, at the time of Surtees' famous character, Jorrocks, the rich land-owners planted copses or coverts between their fields as places where the fox could breed and so provide constant good sport. These copses have now grown extensively, and it is difficult to realise that this beautiful countryside, with coverts and open fields alternating to the horizon, is largely man-made. Many of the roads, too, owe their characteristic appearance to the march of progress. In this case the progress was that of the stage-coaches which, in this notoriously muddy part of the Midlands, were frequently literally "bogged-down" in the mire of the roads they had to use. As a result during the winter the tracks became wider and wider, as coaches tended to go round the muddier areas, until in some cases what had begun in the spring as a track 10 feet wide had become, by the end of winter, an enormous morass often 60 or 80 feet in width. When the metalling of roads came about the permanent hard surface could revert to its former narrow width, but many of the roads in the Shires have retained, as a legacy from those uncomfortable days, their attractive strip of greensward down each side.

Over the county boundary from Northamptonshire at **Caldecott,** the A6003 runs north four miles to Uppingham.

Uppingham *(Falcon, Central)* famous for its school, is a town of quiet warm stone which seems still to be part of the 19th century with its atmosphere of bow-fronted shops and Georgian architecture. Yet the same frontages often hide a far older Tudor exterior, as can be seen at the *Falcon* and *Unicorn* inns. The School, founded by Robert Johnson in 1584, is grouped near the church with many quadrangles and passages. Five miles north on the main road is—

Oakham (Pop.: 6,400. Hotel: *George),* a rather livelier place than Uppingham with much of its charm though fewer stone buildings. Of its castle there remains a fine late-Norman banqueting hall with a collection of horseshoes on the walls extracted as a toll from visiting notabilities since medieval times. Adjoining is the Museum devoted mainly to local history. Close to the church are the School (founded 1587) and the old Butter Cross and stocks.

Pleasant villages near Oakham include **Brooke,** two miles south-west, where the church has a fine interior, **Whissendine** on the *Eye* four miles north-west, **Exton,** eight miles east in a rich ironstone area, and **Egleton** two miles south-east where the church shows good Norman work.

The road from Oakham north-east towards the Great North Road seven miles away climbs up through **Burley** and provides some of the best views obtainable of the surrounding Vale of Catmose. The mansion of *Burley-on-the-Hill* (not open) stands in fine parkland. Further along is **Cottesmore** the village from which the famous hunt takes its name, though the kennels are now at Ashwell two miles west. The church has a chapel dedicated to R.A.F. and American Air Force men stationed nearby in the 1939–45 War.

At **Market Overton** to the north, excavations have unearthed many Roman coins and traced the outlines of typical earthworks indicating a Roman settlement of some size. Finds are now housed in Oakham School Museum. Two miles away at **Thistleton** the church incorporates an arch from a previous 10th-century building and the wide green gives the place a feeling of great age and mellowness.

Melton Mowbray (Pop.: 19,900. Hotels: *Bell, George, Harboro*), is an ancient and prosperous hunting centre. It has been famous for its pork pies. The church is a fine Early English building. A 15th-century house once owned by Anne of Cleves is now a restaurant. There are some lovely almshouses and pleasant walks along the river.

Stapleford Park *(Easter and May–Sept., Weds, Thurs, Suns, Bank Hols, fee)*, five miles east, is a fine mansion restored in 1633 with pictures, tapestry and fine furniture. In the grounds is a miniature railway.

Belvoir Castle *(Apr.–Sept., Weds, Thurs, Sats, Suns, Bank Hols, fee)*, the seat of the Duke of Rutland, stands at the northern tip of the county seven miles west of Grantham. There are some notable pictures and art treasures.

At **Bottesford** the church contains a large number of monuments to various owners of Belvoir.

Leicester

Angling.—Coarse fishing in *Soar*.

Distances.—Ashby-de-la-Zouche, 17; Birmingham, 39; Derby, 28; Grantham, 30; London, 98; Market Harborough, 15; Northampton, 32; Peterborough, 41.

Early Closing.—Thursday.

Entertainment.—*Phoenix* and *Little* Theatres; *De Montfort Hall* (concerts); *Granby Halls* (exhibitions); *cinemas*.

Hotels.—*Grand, Abbey, Belmont, Royal, Post House, Hermitage*.

Library.—Bishop Street.

Population.—283,600.

Post Office.—Bishop Street.

Sport.—Bowls, tennis, swimming pool, roller-skating. Horse racing at Oadby. Flying at Stoughton.

Leicester, the county town, stands on the *Soar*. It is a busy industrial city, centre of the hosiery trade, and active in numerous light industries, particularly footwear production. In the modern centre at the intersection of five main streets is a *Clock Tower* (1866) with effigies of Simon de Montfort and other benefactors of the city. To the west through High Street and facing on to the modern St. Nicholas Circle, is *St. Nicholas Church* with a Norman tower and thin Roman bricks in the clerestory. To west of the churchyard is the *Jewry Wall*, chief Roman relic in Leicester and probably part of a temple. Nearby is a Museum *(daily)* with many Roman exhibits. South of the Circle is *St. Mary de Castro* which exhibits architectural styles from Norman to late-Perpendicular. Adjoining is the site of the former *Castle* nothing of which remains except the restored Hall. Beyond the ruined *Turret Gateway* is the *Newarke* an addition to the castle with *Trinity Hospital* almshouses founded in 1331. The *Newarke Houses Museum* displays fine collections of shoes and clocks. In the *Magazine Gateway* (reached by subway) is the museum of the Royal Leicester Regiment. On the east side of the Circle is the *Guildhall* with fine interior woodwork particularly in the Mayor's Parlour. Here also is the Town Library. In Peacock Lane is **St. Martin's Cathedral,** its status raised from a civic church in 1926. Eastward is the newly-covered *Market Place* to the south of which are the *Town Hall* and *Central Reference Library*. Across Belvoir Street is King Street left of which diverges New Walk leading to the *Museum and Art Gallery (daily)* with notable collections. New Walk continues to University Road and the *University* (1957). Here the School of Engineering is a striking example of the modern use of aluminium, for which the designers won an award in 1963.

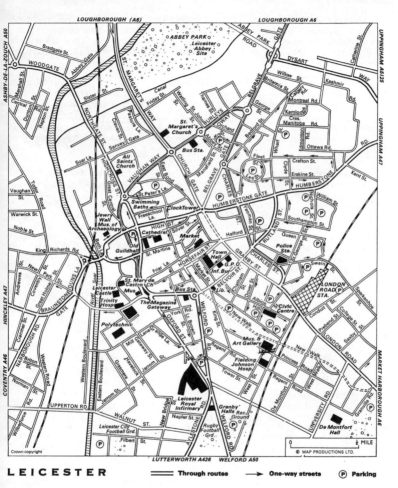

LEICESTER ═══ Through routes ➝ One-way streets Ⓟ Parking

In the north of the city is the pleasant *Abbey Park* with a lake and the scant remains of **Leicester Abbey** where Cardinal Wolsey died in 1530. Two museums of note lie to the north—The *Museum of Technology* in Corporation Road and *Belgrave Hall* with period furniture off Belgrave Road.

Beaumont Hall, Stoughton Drive, in the south-eastern suburbs, is a fine 10-acre botanical garden with rock and water gardens and fine floral displays.

Due east of Leicester, eight miles along the A47 road to Uppingham, is **Billesdon** a pleasant village with remains of Iron Age earthworks and in the oldest part of the village a school dating from 1650.

Market Harborough (Pop.: 14,500. Hotels: *Angel, Grove Motel*) lies on the A6 close to the county border 15 miles south-east of Leicester. In the wide main square is the quaint Grammar School (1614) standing on pillars. A market town since 1203 it has several old inns including the *Three Swans* with an ornate 18th-century wrought iron sign.

Foxton, a little north of Market Harborough, stands on the Grand Union Canal and is a favourite centre for lovers of canals and locks. Here the canal is raised a total of 75 feet by two successive tiers of locks each of five double-locks.

Stanford Hall *(Easter–Sept., Thurs, Sats, Suns, Bank Hols.)* eight miles south-west on A427 where the *Avon* serves as the county boundary, is a fine William and Mary house dating from 1690. It houses fine furniture and paintings and a museum of vintage motor cycles and cars.

Lutterworth, still on the A427 just west of the M1, was an important staging post on the old A5 coach road and retains several half-timbered houses and inns and a 15th-century church with wall paintings.

The south-west border of Leicestershire is formed by the A5, the Roman Watling Street, as it runs past **Hinckley,** a large town devoted to shoe-making, and from here the A447 runs due north to **Market Bosworth,** a picturesque stone-built town approached by a pleasant avenue of trees. Nearby is the site of the battle of Bosworth Field where Henry Tudor defeated Richard III in 1485. A stone cairn stands over Dick's Well, where Richard is reputed to have paused for a much-needed drink during that decisive battle.

Charnwood Forest. North-west of Leicester is the area of the old Charnwood Forest, some 30 square miles of heathland and with some of the oldest crags and rock-formations in Britain. There are fine views over ridges, hills and woods from the higher points such as Bardon Hill, 912 feet near Coalville, and Beacon Hill, 818 feet near Woodhouse Eaves. At Bradgate Park are the ruins of the hall where Lady Jane Grey was born in 1537.

Ashby-de-la-Zouche (Pop.: 8,300. Hotels: *Royal, Holywell House*), is an old town in pleasant surroundings on the western edge of Charnwood Forest. The old castle built in the time of Edward IV (1461–83) and now a ruin *(daily)*, was visited by Mary, Queen of Scots but is best known for its role in "Ivanhoe". In the church is a rare pilgrim's effigy. The town has several good half-timbered Tudor houses.

At **Measham** on A453 south of Ashby is the *Midland Motor Museum.* At Appleby Parva a little south is Sir John Moore's School (1693).

Four miles north-east of Ashby is **Staunton Harold,** with a church that has the rare distinction of having been built in 1653 during the Commonwealth. It preserves the quaint custom from those days of segregating men and women on opposite sides of the church during services. Nearby is one of the most beautiful houses in Britain, *Staunton Hall* (not open) with its classical Palladian façade and surrounded by parkland. Since 1955 it has been a Cheshire Home.

On the A453, six miles north of Ashby, **Breedon-on-the-Hill** provides not only extensive views over the Trent Valley but also, in the church, has a rare statue from the former Saxon monastery on the site destroyed by the Danes in 885. In the village there is also an entertaining conical stone lock-up built in the 17th century.

Between the M1 and the A6 in the northern corner of the county is **Long Whatton** where the main interest is the 25-acre park of **Whatton House** *(Suns and Bank Hols, Easter to Aug.)*. The gardens contain a profusion of bulbs, a 100-

yard long herbaceous border and a unique Chinese Garden. From here it is less than four miles south to Loughborough.

Loughborough (Pop.: 45,900. Hotels: *King's Head*), is a sprawling, largely Victorian town, highly industrialised but given character by the open spaces of the University (1964) which spread between the town and the M1. At least one of its industries is almost unique—that of bellfounding. On the eastern side of the town is the famous foundry of Taylor & Co., one of only two bell foundries in Britain (the other is the Whitechapel Bell Foundry in London). The foundry has produced some of Britain's heaviest and most important bells and carillons, and supplied the carillon to America's Washington Cathedral and more recently the 53-bell carillon at Canberra, Australia. The town's War Memorial in Queens Park has a carillon of 47 bells cast by Taylor's.

South-west of Loughborough on the A6 is **Quorn,** or Quorndon, which gives its name to the famous hunt. Further along the road is **Mountsorrel** with good views over the *Soar* which here forms part of the Grand Union Canal. There are extensive quarries in the neighbourhood.

Nottingham and District

Nottinghamshire presents three faces to the visitor. The southern part of the county is dominated by Nottingham with its thriving business life, shops and historical background. In the northwest, towards Derbyshire, is the coal-belt area with its tips and slags—the land of D. H. Lawrence and the grim kind of background which produced his kind of writing. The third part, of the most interest to the visitor, is the area north of Nottingham. This includes Sherwood Forest and some beautiful countryside around, although beautiful countryside does not exist in a watertight compartment in the county—it infiltrates the coal tips and, indeed, one of the advantages of Nottingham itself is the ease with which one can reach open country from the town.

From Loughborough the A60 runs north and enters Nottingham as it joins the A52 and crosses the river *Trent*.

Nottingham

Distances.—Ashby-de-la-Zouch, 22; Birmingham, 50; Derby, 16; Grantham, 24; Lincoln, 36; London, 123; Mansfield, 14; Newark, 20; Stamford, 40; Worksop, 28.

Early Closing.—Mondays and Thursdays.

Entertainment.—*Playhouse, Theatre Royal, Arts Theatre, Albert Hall* (concerts). *Film Theatre*, cinemas. Ice Stadium.

Hotels.—*Albany, Bridgford, Strathdon, George, Victoria, Edwalton Hall, Portland, Flying Horse* and others.

Libraries.— *City Library,* Sherwood Street. *County Library,* West Bridgford.

Population.—299,750.

Post Office.—Queen Street.

Sport.—Bowls, tennis, boating. County Cricket ground, Trent Bridge. Golf at Wollaton Park.

Nottingham, the county town, and noted centre of the tobacco, pharmaceutical and lace and hosiery industries is situated on the north bank of the *Trent*. The ground rises gently from about 90 feet above sea level on the river plain to about 420 feet on the highest ground in the northern suburbs. It is situated in the middle of England, at the edge of a vast coalfield and is a hub in a great system of inland waterways.

The centre of Nottingham is the Old Market Square a great open space of nearly six acres overlooked on the east by the Council House (1928). Behind is a modern shopping arcade. The market is now housed under cover at King Edward Street near which is the gigantic Victoria Centre.

The **Castle,** reached by Friar Lane, occupies a commanding position on the west side of the town 150 feet above the *Leen*. Outside are bronze statues of Robin Hood and his men. In its present form it is a palatial building in the Renaissance style occupied by the **City Museum and Art Gallery** *(daily)*. The caves and passages that honeycomb the hill on which the castle stands may be viewed by prior appointment. Beneath the walls is the ancient *Trip to Jerusalem* inn which actually runs into the hill.

To the south-west near the University is Wollaton Park laid out with various sports facilities and a golf course. The fine mansion houses the **Natural History**

NOTTINGHAM ══════ **Through routes** ➔ **One-way streets** Ⓟ **Parking**

Museum. In the University Park is the **University Art Gallery** *(daily)* in which changing exhibitions are mounted.

At Trent Bridge is the County Cricket Ground (venue of Test matches). Notts County is the oldest Football League club in Britain while Nottingham Forest is a strong rival club. Both sport and the arts are strongly provided for. The *Nottingham Playhouse* opened in 1963, is a modern and progressive theatre.

St. Mary's Church south-east of the Centre is a cathedral-like building of the 15th century. It has a striking embattled tower and is remarkable for the number and size of its windows. The Roman Catholic Cathedral west of the Centre is a fine building by Pugin.

At Colwick Park on the south side of the Trent is a race course.

To Hucknall. Hucknall Torkard six miles north of Nottingham is a colliery town of little interest except for the church where Lord Byron is buried in the family tomb. The grave is marked by a marble slab given by the King of Greece in recognition of Byron's services to that country. Close to Hucknall is the **Sherwood Zoological Park** *(daily)*.

To Newstead Abbey, nine miles north of Nottingham on the A60 Mansfield road. In this great house *(Easter–Sept., daily, fee)*, purchased by Sir John Byron in 1540 are many Byron relics, pictures and furniture. The gardens are extensive and attractive.

To Eastwood. Across the M1 on the A608 one can see around Eastwood the juxtaposition of colliery, tip and countryside that did so much to colour the writing of D. H. Lawrence who was born in the town in 1885.

Southwell and Newark

North-east from Nottingham the A612 road runs in 13 miles via Burton Joyce and Lowdham to—

Southwell (Pop.: 4,300. Hotel: *Saracen's Head*) a pleasant small town with a very large and noble Minster which became a cathedral in 1884. One of the oldest buildings here is the *Saracen's Head*, already an inn in 1396 and where Charles I stayed before his surrender in Newark. Southwell is also the home of the Bramley apple for it was in the garden of Bramley Cottage here that the first tree was raised. South of the Cathedral are the remains of the former *Palace* of the Archbishop of York originally dated 1360. There is trout fishing available in the *Greet* stream.

Southwell Cathedral is cruciform in plan and one of the few early churches in England which have three towers. The central tower is both a lantern and a campanile. The appearance of the West front is marred by the large Perpendicular window which was inserted in the 15th century, but the two western towers are typically Norman as also is the fine great doorway. The nave is very impressive with massive circular pillars and lofty triforium. The transepts are similar in design to the nave without the aisles. In the north transept is the fine elaborate tomb of Archbishop Sandys of York (*d.* 1588). Over the door here is a fragment of Saxon sculpture. The Choir is a beautiful Early English structure. The brass lectern is old and once belonged to Newstead Abbey. The lower part of the great East Window is partly of glass about 500 years old and came from the chapel of the Knights Templars in Paris. The Chapter House is an octagonal structure with no central pillar. The leaf sculpture here is marvellous.

Newark-on-Trent (Pop.: 24,600. Hotels: *Ram, Robin Hood*) is a well-built, picturesque town of considerable antiquity with many historical associations. The **Castle** was almost entirely reconstructed in 1125 and has a fine Norman gatehouse. King John often lived here and died at the castle in 1216. **St. Mary's Church** is notable for its fine tower and the octagonal spire, 252 feet high. The lower portion of the tower is Early English and the upper part and spire 14th-century Decorated work. The nave, transepts, north aisle and chancel were built at the end of the 15th century. The oldest portions, the central piers and the unfinished crypt, were begun about 1167. In the Market Place are everal interesting buildings including the Town Hall. The **Museum** occupies the old Grammar School building in Appleton Gate, the school having moved to Earp Avenue. At the junction of Carter Gate with several other streets is the *Beaumont Cross* of late Gothic design. At the southern end of the town is the *Queen's Sconce,* military earthworks remnants of the town's defences during sieges in the Civil War.

Three miles north of Newark on the eastern side of the Trent is the village of **Holme** with a church rebuilt in 1485 still with its contemporary fittings. A mile further is **Cromwell**, from which says Carlyle, "without any ghost to teach us, we can understand that the Cromwell kindred all got their name." Two miles south of Newark is **Hawton** church which contains magnificent carving, but is specially famed for its Easter Sepulchre, one of the most beautiful examples in England.

On the western outskirts of Newark on the A6056 the high ground above **Kelham** gives fine views along the river valley. Kelham Hall *(not open)* is a spiky Victorian Gothic construction with a resemblance to St. Pancras Station, London. It is used by a theological college. At **Averham** is the *Robin Hood Theatre* at one time a "folly" built by a former rector.

The A46 south-west from Newark runs to the east of Nottingham. After crossing the A52 it runs through pleasant rolling countryside with sudden, unexpected hills to give added interest.

MANSFIELD AND DISTRICT

Mansfield (Pop.: 57,600), in the centre of the rich north Nottinghamshire coalfield, is a busy industrial town. Among its major industries are stone-quarrying, cotton and wool processing, footwear manufacture, tin-box making, toy making and the manufacture of electrical, radio and radar equipment. **Mansfield Woodhouse** is chiefly involved with coalmining and stone quarrying, some of its stone have been used in Southwell Cathedral. The church has several memorials and effigies. To the north-west is the rugged Pleasley Vale. South-east is Fountain Dale traditionally the home of Friar Tuck. A mile further is **Blidworth,** a colliery town on raised ground set in Sherwood Forest with strong associations with Robin Hood. Will Scarlet is said to have been buried in the churchyard.

Hardwick Hall (N.T., *Apr.–Oct., Weds, Thurs, Sats, Suns, Bank Hols.*), six-and-a-half miles south-west of Mansfield, was built in 1597 for the Countess of Shrewsbury, mother of the first Duke of Devonshire. It is a beautiful example of Elizabethan domestic architecture. There is notable furniture, needlework and tapestries and attractive gardens.

Bolsover Castle *(daily, fee),* eight miles north on the Chesterfield road, was built by Sir Charles Cavendish, father of the first Duke of Newcastle, in the early part of the 17th century. The Keep shows ornate marble chimneypieces. Some of the roofs of the buildings are very handsomely groined.

Edwinstowe, seven miles north-east of Mansfield, and close to the Forest, derives its name from the time of Edwin King of Northumbria, who had been killed in battle at Hatfield, Yorkshire, and was buried here.

The church has a good 13th-century tower and lofty spire. The *Maun* and *Moden* streams run through the village. In the forest tract of Birklands is the famous old *Major Oak.*

Two miles east is **Ollerton** in a well-wooded valley on the high road. It has greatly developed in recent years and is a popular centre for excursions in the Forest area. There is a fine avenue of beech trees known as Ollerton Beeches. Three miles south is Rufford Abbey *(no admission)* formerly the seat of Lord Savile.

Thoresby Hall *(Easter–Sept., Weds, Thurs, Sats, Suns, Bank Hols, fee),* four miles north of Ollerton just west of the Bawtry road and the home of Countess Manvers, is a fine mansion built by Salvin in 1864 and is the only remaining great house in the Dukeries still occupied as home of the original family. The State apartments and Great Hall are lavishly decorated in Victorian style. Around the terraces are beautiful formal gardens. Of interest is the Frank Bradley Exhibition of Toy and Model Theatres.

North-west of Thoresby and reached by A6005 to Carburton, a by-road leads to **Clumber Park** (N.T.) a huge landscape design created by the Dukes of Newcastle out of heathland bordering on Sherwood Forest. The house is now demolished but the stable block survives with pleasure grounds along the large lake. The neo-Gothic church was built by Bodley. The famous lime-tree avenue between Apley Head and Carburton Lodge is a public highway.

Welbeck Abbey *(not open)* north of Cuckney is now a military establishment. The estate previously belonged to the Duke of Portland.

Worksop (Pop.: 36,000. Hotel: *Lion*), is a busy industrial town on the verge of the coalfield. Many light industries have developed and the town is less dependent than formerly on the collieries. The town has long been a centre for excursions through what is known as the Dukeries. The *Priory Church* was founded in 1103 but only the nave and aisles of the old church are now standing. It has however been added to and now serves as parish church. To the south is the 14th-century *Gatehouse*. Worksop Manor *(not open)* to the south-west belonged to the Duke of Newcastle but much has been pulled down. Worksop has a swimming pool, greyhound track and golf club. Two miles west is **Steetly Church** a beautiful specimen of Norman work.

Sherwood Forest. Once an extensive royal forest stretching from Nottingham to Worksop. The name is known wherever the English tongue is spoken through many an old ballad and tale of Robin Hood, the prince of outlaws. Much diminished by the coalfield there are still many beautiful tracts of health and woodland. The district known as the Dukeries, between Worksop and Ollerton, is one of the best preserved parts. Its title was derived from the fact that within its borders were the princely homes and estates of five Dukes—Duke of Portland (Welbeck), Duke of Newcastle (Clumber), Duke of Norfolk (Worksop), Duke of Leeds, and the once Duke of Kingston (Thoresby).

East Retford developed as a busy market town and an important rail junction. On one side of the market square is the Town Hall in front of which is the *Broad Stone,* the base of an old cross where during the Plague the townspeople left money to be exchanged for food.

Lincolnshire
Fens and Wolds

Lincolnshire, the second largest of the English geographic counties after Yorkshire is one of the least explored. Every county has characteristics that mark it from its neighbour, but in Lincolnshire these differences are more apparent than are usually found. Its coastline is indented by two sides of the Wash forming an area of dunes and marram-grass called the Marsh. South of the Wash the Fens have been reclaimed from the sea providing a type of soil found almost nowhere else in Britain and supporting a flourishing flower and bulb-growing industry. North of the Fens, up to the river *Humber* that divides the county from Yorkshire, a rolling countryside dotted with little villages and few trees forms the Wolds of Lincolnshire, and near the western boundary the Ridge, a "spine" of high ground runs due north and south and carries the old Roman Ermine Street from Barton-upon-Humber to Lincoln and beyond.

For most visitors it is the Fens that are Lincolnshire, and it is to the area round Spalding that they come each year in April and May to see the glorious display of colour made by the millions of flowers and bulbs, an industry which provides employment for thousands.

Spalding (Pop.: 16,950. Hotels: *Red Lion, White Hart*) is the most Dutch-like of all Fenland towns. Its architecture reflects this influence and the river *Welland* flows through a deep channel in the town centre. Along the banks stand prim houses of mellow red brick reminiscent of the canalsides of Amsterdam. **Aysconghfee Hall** *(daily)* contains a Bird Museum and in the public grounds open-air aviaries. *Springfield Gardens (early Apr.–mid-May)* is a show garden of the local bulb growers. In Broad Street is the museum of the Spalding Gentlemen's Society, the oldest provincial scientific and literary society in England.

Holbeach, 12 miles east of Spalding on the A152, is a much smaller town with a single street and a church with a 180-foot high tower that is a landmark for miles. It has been a market-town since the 13th century and is also a centre for bulb-growing. To the north is the desolate Holbeach Marsh.

The eastern edge of the bulbfields is marked by the little town of **Long Sutton**. It has an impressive church with Norman nave but is known chiefly for its unusual lead spire, of great height, which surmounts a detached campanile containing eight bells.

Crowland (sometimes written *Croyland*) south of Spalding on A1073 close to the county boundary is famous for its ruined *Abbey* built in the 8th century by King Ethelbald. The north aisle of the original Norman church serves as the parish church. There is a fine Perpendicular west tower with a good peal of bells. In the centre of the town is the quaint triple-arched *Triangular Bridge* now high and dry. The effigy came from the abbey.

West of Crowland on the Bedford Level are the Deepings, little hamlets of **Market Deeping, Deeping St. James** and **Deeping Gate.**

249

BOURNE–STAMFORD–GRANTHAM

Bourne (Pop.: 6,460. Hotel: *Angel*) on the western side of the Fens, is a busy little market town at the junction of the A151 from Spalding and the A15 to Peterborough. The Town Hall has an exterior staircase while the Priory church has notable Norman arcades.

The associations of this town provide the sort of contrasts which are such a feature of the county. Once the headquarters of Hereward the Wake in his doomed but valiant attempt to resist the invading Normans, Bourne today is more noted for being the home of BRM racing cars. The *Burghley Arms* was formerly an Elizabethan house in which was born Sir William Cecil, powerful Lord High Treasurer to Elizabeth I, while 300 years later, in 1825, another child was born in the town who was destined to be famous in a very different way. He was Frederick Worth, later to become a dress-designer and friend of the Empress Eugénie, and founder of the fashion and perfume house that still bears his name.

Stamford (Pop.: 14,485. Hotel: *George*) in the south-west corner of the county with a by-pass on the A1, is a famous old market centre. Built mainly of the local stone the town presents an appearance that has changed little since its period of greatest prosperity in Georgian times. From this era date the Town Hall, the Assembly Rooms, and many fine houses and inns which give the town its air of solid well-being.

By the side of the *Welland* tall warehouses stand that were once filled with wool, and many of the houses in the town have much older cellars beneath them once used for the same purpose. Everywhere narrow lanes run into handsome squares, some, like St. Mary's Place, still cobbled.

In the 15th century Stamford was trading with the Wool Staple of Calais through its numerous wealthy merchants. One such was William Browne who, in 1485, founded **Browne's Hospital** *(weekdays)* for ten poor men and women. He supplied a chapel for them, and in addition built two churches in the town—*St. John's* and *St. Margaret's*. Later the Cecil family, earls of Salisbury, were presented with the manor of Stamford by Elizabeth I and their sumptuous tombs may be seen in *St. Martin's Church*.

Woolsthorpe Manor (N.T., *Mons, Weds, Sats, fee*) at Colsterworth 11 miles north of Stamford, is a small 17th-century house, the birthplace of Sir Isaac Newton.

Grantham (Pop.: 27,900. Hotels: *Angel and Royal, White Hart*) is an ancient town on the *Witham* well-known for its fine old coaching inn the *Angel and Royal*. Of the town's many inn-signs the oddest must be that of the *Beehive*, in Castlegate, which has for its sign a real beehive in a tree outside. Westgate, with its Dickensian shops and old houses is probably Grantham's best-preserved street, though what is left of Vine Street also has much charm. *St. Wulfram's Church* has a fine Decorated tower surmounted by a beautiful 281-foot high crocheted spire. In the church is a notable chained library. **Grantham House** (N.T., *Apr.–Sept., Weds, Thurs, fee*) is a late 14th-century building later refurbished. Its extensive garden provides a fine open space in the centre of the town. Other features are the Market Cross and Town Conduit. Before the Guildhall is a statue of Sir Isaac Newton.

The name of Vine Street is a reminder that in the days of the Romans this area and that of the Isle of Ely were famous for their vineyards. In fact, one still exists just on the county boundary south of the A17 near Newark at **Stagglethorpe** *(Vinery open Sat. afternoons in Aug.)*. It is the most northerly vineyard in Europe and produces some 2,000 bottles annually.

Fourteen miles north-east of Grantham on the A15 is **Sleaford,** an old town on the river *Slea* but largely Victorian in aspect. Not that this detracts, for its public buildings are very handsome and include the Sessions House (1831), the Union (1838) and the Corn Exchange (1857). In Carre Street is an interesting building labelled "Navigation Office—1792", a relic of Sleaford's ill-fated attempt to canalise the *Slea* for navigation. Sleaford is situated at an important road junction between Ridge and Fenland. Due east of the town the A17 runs towards Boston which may be reached by branching left onto the A52 at **Swineshead**. It was here, in 1216, that King John spent several days at the Abbey after losing most of his possessions in the treacherous marshes and waters of the Wash.

Boston (Pop.: 26,000. Hotels: *White Hart, New England*) an ancient town and port on the *Witham,* is dominated by its famous "Stump"—the tower of the church of St. Botolph, reminiscent of the belfry of Bruges, which visually holds together this Fenland area and can be seen from the Norfolk side of the Wash.

Boston had strong links with the Hanseatic ports, such as Hamburg, in the 13th century, until the discovery of the New World and subsequent opening of trade shifted the emphasis to Bristol and other West of England ports. Several Boston men were among those on the *Mayflower* on its historic voyage in 1620. Ten years later another expedition of seven ships to America contained so many Boston men that they gave its name to the new township that became the capital of Massachusetts.

Boston is still a busy port, dealing mainly with bananas and timber, and its picturesque quays still hum with activity. The Market Place is a focal point from which many of its best buildings can be seen. Much is 18th- or 19th-century but several older buildings include the restored half-timbered *Shodfriars Hall,* now an arts centre. In narrow Spain Lane are ruins of the refectory of a 13th-century Dominican Friary and nearby is the cobbled Spain Court. In South Street stands the fine 15th-century **Guildhall** *(weekdays)* now a museum and art gallery, but containing the original tiny room in which Brewster and the Pilgrim Fathers were tried in 1607. Next-door is the elegant 18th-century *Fydell House (daily during term)* used as the headquarters of Pilgrim House, an adult education offshoot of Nottingham University, and owned by the Boston Preservation Society. Along the river towards the Wash is **Skirbeck,** still part of Boston, with a 13th-century parish church.

Towards the Wash winding lanes lead towards the saltings of *The Haven,* where notices on the sea-wall warn of the dangers of exploring the marshes alone. The hard paths through the saltings are few, and known only to the locals, and even so the swiftly incoming tide can bring disaster to the unwary. **Frieston Shore,** looking out across the Wash and Boston Deeps, is a mecca for bird-watchers, particularly in the winter, when many birds visit the area after the Arctic summer.

Ten miles north-west of Boston, on the canalised river *Blain* is **Tattershall.** The Castle (N.T., *daily, fee*) was built about 1440 by Ralph Cromwell, Treasurer of England. The 100-foot-high tower is a good example of a fortified brick dwelling of the period. The stone Gothic fireplaces were sold in 1911 but were recovered by the Marquess Curzon. The *church* was completed by William Waynflete, Bishop of Winchester and founder of Magdalen College, Oxford. Near the 15th-century market cross are the buildings of Lord Cromwell's choir-school.

From Coningsby a mile east of Tattershall the B1192 runs north to **Woodhall Spa** *(Petwood Moat House).* Suddenly the scenery changes and the light and sandy soil, supporting rhododendrons, pine and heather, give it an appearance more of Surrey than of Lincolnshire. Woodhall came into prominence at the end of the Victorian era when, in 1891, a project to mine for coal failed, but uncovered springs of water said to contain "free iodine". The mining project was therefore transformed into plans for a spa, and a number of hotels were immediately built. The health-giving properties of the water were presumably valid, for the spa still exists, people still visit the pump-room and the County Health Service recommends and uses the baths. The hotels are still there, of which the most sumptuous and richly Edwardian is the *Petworth,* though Woodhall's attractions today are centred mainly on its famous golf-course with its own luxury *Golf Hotel.*

From Woodhall Spa B1191 leads to **Horncastle** a small market town on the site of the walled Roman *Banovallum* at the confluence of the rivers *Bain* and

LINCOLN

Waring. The church, heavily restored, has several good brasses and a collec.ion of weapons from the Civil War.

Two roads lead north from Horncastle, the A153 to Louth and the A158 to **Wragby,** busy with the timber industry, and on to Lincoln.

Lincoln

Angling.—On the *Witham* to Grantham and on the Fossdyke Navigation Canal.

Distances.—Boston, 35; Grantham, 25; Grimsby, 36; Horncastle, 21; Louth, 26; London, 132; Newark, 16; Scunthorpe, 29.

Early Closing.—Wednesday.

Hotels.—*White Hart, Annesley, Eastgate, Grand,*

Moor Lodge, The Queen.

Population.—74,200.

Post Office.—Guildhall Street.

Sports.—Boating, swimming, bowls, tennis. Point to Point racing.

Theatre.—*Theatre Royal.*

There is never any doubt that you are approaching Lincoln. From every direction the great triple-towered cathedral, set on its hill at the centre of the town, stands up from the rooftops around bidding you come nearer. A Roman settlement *Lindum Colonia,* established on the hilltop in A.D. 71, was walled and fragments remain including the Newport Arch at the northern end of Bailgate.

The Cathedral *(limited parking in Minster Yard),* shows examples of every style of architecture from early Romanesque to Victorian Gothic, but the greater part of the building dates from the period between 1192 (St. Hugh's Choir) and 1280 (Angel Choir).

Approaching from the west by the Exchequergate arch, one is confronted by the Norman façade which was largely rebuilt after a fire of 1141, but incorporates parts of the first cathedral, completed in 1092. An earthquake of 1185 brought ruin to the Norman church and its successor was begun, under St. Hugh, in 1192.

The most important external features are the 12th-century frieze of sculpture on the west end, the elaborate Judgement Porch on the south side of the Angel Choir, the great east window (the earliest and largest eight-light window in Britain) and the decagonal Chapter House with its massive flying buttresses.

The interior is full of interesting features, including the Tournai marble Norman font (comparable with that at Winchester), the fine 14th-century chancel screen, the carved oak work of the Choir which is the finest and most complete collection of 14th-century wood-carving in England, executed by the same craftsmen who made the stalls in Chester Cathedral, the wealth of 13th-century stained glass in the great transept and choir aisles, the interesting 18th-century "Gothick" stonework round the high altar and the plinth on which once stood the shrine of St. Hugh's head.

In the north choir aisle is the *Treasury,* containing a changing exhibition of plate from churches in the diocese and the best of the four surviving originals of Magna Carta. Passing through the north-east transept, one reaches the *cloister,* with an interesting wooden vault and fine roof bosses, dating from *c.* 1300, but the north range of the cloister, with Dean Honywood's valuable Library above, is the work of Sir Christopher Wren and was built in 1674–75. The *Chapter House* is entered from the east walk of the cloister. This is the earliest and largest multangular chapter house in Britain, the vault of which springs from a graceful central pillar, giving the impression of a great palm tree.

There is a wealth of minor sculpture at Lincoln. Outside, the figures of Edward I and Queen Eleanor, to the east of the *Judgement Porch,* and the "Lincoln Pilgrim" over one of the pairs of lancet windows of the Consistory Court (facing the Galilee Porch) are particularly notable. Inside, there is the unrivalled collection of elaborate roof bosses, much superb stiff-leaf foliage moulding and many individual stone carvings, chief of which are the angels in the spandrels of the triforium arches of the *Angel Choir.* Beneath one of these and above the easternmost free-standing pillar on the north side is the small grotesque figure popularly called the "Lincoln Imp".

Lincoln, like York, is a foundation of secular canons and the Chapter owns almost all the property in the Minster Yard, including a number of extremely interesting 18th-century houses and several containing extensive medieval features.

Almost facing the west approach to the Cathedral precincts is the gateway of the **Castle** *(daily, fee)*. All that now remains of the fortress founded by William the Conqueror are the outer walls and some towers.

There are several examples of Norman domestic buildings still standing, and in The Strait is the *Jew's House* (now an antique shop) built in 1170 and one of the

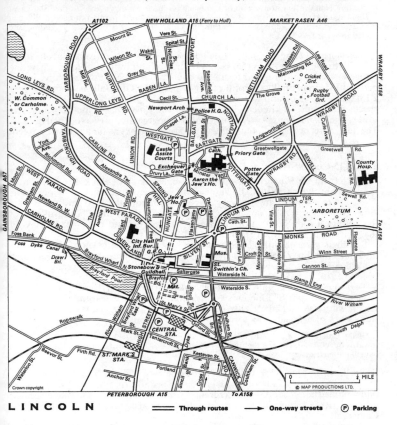

L I N C O L N   ══ **Through routes**   → **One-way streets**   Ⓟ **Parking**

oldest secular buildings still in use. In an age when the Normans were seeking the assistance of the Jews to finance their building projects there were several large houses with Jewish owners, another being the *House of Aaron,* also 12th-century, at the beginning of the cobbled Steep Hill from the Cathedral to the lower town, or "Below Hill". In Broadgate a former monastery dating from the 13th century is now the *Greyfriars City and County Museum (daily)* of natural history as well as antiquities associated with the city. A museum devoted to rural life in the county is the *Museum of Lincolnshire Life* in Burton Road *(afternoons except Mons, all year)* which gives a comprehensive picture of country life and manners from

Elizabethan times to the present. The *Stonebow*, once the chief gate of the city, dates from the 15th century. Above the arch is the Guildhall with the corporation insignia. The *High Bridge* dates from Norman times. Off High Street south of the bridge is the *Church of St. Mary le Wigford.*

Aubourn Hall *(Jun.–Aug., Weds, fee)*, seven miles south-west of Lincoln near the A46 is an interesting 16th-century house with fine panelled rooms and a magnificent carved staircase.

Doddington Hall *(May–Sept., Weds, fee)*, five miles west of Lincoln, is a fine Elizabethan manor house with collections of furniture and china. There is a beautiful gatehouse and walled rose gardens.

Gainsborough (Pop.: 17,400. Hotel: *White Hart*) reached from Lincoln in 18 miles by the A57 and the A156, is an old market and industrial town where the bridge of 1787 over the *Trent* forms the boundary with Nottinghamshire. In the midst of Victorian brickwork of the town centre is the **Old Hall** *(daily from 2, fee)* a 15th-century black and white manor house with a fine hall, mellow rooms and spectacular medieval kitchens. The *Church of All Saints* has a late-Perpendicular tower. The *John Robinson Memorial Church* (Congregational) was opened in 1897. The tidal-bore, or "eagre", that runs up the *Trent*, reaches as far as Gainsborough.

THE LINCOLNSHIRE WOLDS

South from the *Humber* is a widening, 40-mile stretch of chalk downs, high for Lincolnshire, which flattens down again to the Fens just south of Horncastle. These are the Wolds—an area very different from both the Fens and the coastal strip around the Wash—and thought by many to be the most beautiful part of this county. From the edge of the Fens the higher ground begins at Spilsby on the A116 midway between Horncastle and Skegness.

Spilsby is a small and pleasant town and was the birthplace of the explorer Sir John Franklin, whose statue stands in the Market Place. In the parish church is his flag and the seven massive tombs of the Willoughby family ranging from 1349 to 1610.

Two miles west of Spilsby is **Bolingbroke,** birthplace of Henry IV, with the remains of the Earl of Lincoln's *Castle (daily, free)* later captured by John of Gaunt who also built the richly decorated parish church. Today it stands in a framework of neat early-Victorian and Georgian houses.

Gunby Hall (N.T., *Apr.–Oct., Weds, Thurs, Fris, Bank Hols, fee*) on the south side of A158 towards Burgh-le-Marsh, is a dignified red-brick house of 1700 with a beautiful staircase and panelling, portraits by Reynolds and a delightful formal garden.

North-west of the A158 towards Horncastle is the village of **Somersby,** where the poet Tennyson was born in the parsonage in 1809 *(not open)*. Nearby is the oddly-named hamlet of **Ashby Puerorum** ("Ashby-of-the-boys") so called because ground rents from the village were once used to finance the choirboys of Lincoln Cathedral.

Across the Wolds at **Tealby,** near Market Rasen, are more associations with the Tennyson family. The village is attractive with a large church on one side, and on the other the remains of Bayons Castle, once the home of the Tennyson family.

Market Rasen is a quiet Victorian town known chiefly for the steeple-chase meetings now held on the racecourse.

West across the wide sweep of the Wolds along the A631 is **Louth,** the splendid 300-foot spire of the church being visible for miles before the town is reached. The spire was completed in 1509 and is in the honey-coloured Ancaster stone that lends itself so well to the changing light of this area. The town is a mixture of many styles, from Elizabethan in the centre to modern factory developments on its edge. Much of it is Georgian, notably Westgate with its beautiful bow-fronted house with curving double stone steps leading up to the central front door. Unfortunately the church has suffered internally from the ravages of a citizen of the town, the Victorian architect and "restorer" James Fowler, the effect of whose work can be seen in so many Lincolnshire churches. Down by Riverhead are several old warehouses at the end of the Louth Navigation Canal connecting the town with the sea near Grimsby.

The rolling countryside of the Wolds north of Louth makes fine grazing for sheep which figure prominently both in the scenery and in the economy of the area. North-west towards Caistor the main cultivation is wheat and peas, the latter grown intensively and harvested with mechanical expertise for the frozen-food factories round Grimsby.

Caistor is another town that was well-known to the Romans and parts of the old town wall still survive. From here the A1084 drops down to the flat countryside round **Brigg** (made famous by Delius' "Brigg Fair") and on to the busy steel town of **Scunthorpe** which obtained its prosperity from the discovery of iron-ore in the 19th century and now supplies 11% of all the steel made in Britain.

North of Brigg is **Elsham Hall** *(Park and Design Centre, daily)* featuring garden design and various aspects of rural craftsmanship.

Epworth, 16 miles south-west of Scunthorpe on the A161, is the village famous as the childhood home of John and Charles Wesley at the rambling *Old Rectory (daily, fee)*.

THE COASTAL STRIP AND THE HUMBER

The long coastline of Lincolnshire stretches from the Wash at Gibraltar Point to the *Humber* past Grimsby. It is a coast of dunes and wide, gently-sloping sands where bathing can be dangerous owing to the sudden fogs that descend causing the stranger to lose all sense of direction as the tide comes swiftly in. The low coast and absence of cliffs makes the area liable to flooding and at Sutton-on-Sea can be seen the massive concrete sea-wall built in 1953 after the disastrous floods that took such a toll of life and property.

At Gibraltar Point there is a Nature Reserve, and three miles north is **Skegness** (Pop.: 13,550. Hotels: *Crown, Links, North Shore*) with its fine stretch of sands and pier. It is the most southerly of the three Lincolnshire seaside resorts so popular with people from the Midlands and has a short but memorable season. Holiday camps and caravans abound in this area.

A little inland from Skegness is **Burgh-le-Marsh** on the A158 which has a fine working windmill and Windmill Museum *(daily, all year)*.

Seven miles north of here on the B1196 is **Alford,** where is Britain's last commercially-operated windmill *(3rd Sat. in June, July & Aug.)*.

Mablethorpe, reached from Alford eight miles along the A1104, is on the coast and has fine sands and a good golf-course. Inland the surprisingly large church of **Theddlethorpe All Saints** has been called the "Cathedral of the Marsh" while nearer the coast at **Theddlethorpe St. Helen** is an important Nature Reserve and Conservation Area.

Saltfleetby (pronounced "Sollerby") **St. Peter** is one of three villages with the same patronymic and has a curious leaning tower which, on inspection, proves to be a Folly. From here the flat coast and wide foreshore continue past **Saltfleet**

Haven while the A1031 runs back a mile or so to join the A18 and enters the fine holiday resort of **Cleethorpes** (Pop.: 35,780. Hotels: *Kingsway, Darley's, Dolphin*). Here we are almost into Grimsby, and Cleethorpes is a splendid vantage point to view the shipping entering the *Humber*.

Grimsby (Pop.: 95,700. Hotel: *Humber Royal*) is one of the world's busiest fishing-ports and also does a healthy business in coal, grain and timber. The enormous fish-quays, working non-stop each of the 24 hours, is a fascinating and exciting spectacle. In the Town Hall of Grimsby is the *Doughty Museum (Tues–Sats throughout year)* showing a wonderful collection of models of 18th- and 19th-century ships together with pictures and china.

Six miles along the coast is **Immingham** an important oil port and a terminal of the car ferry services to Gothenburg. As the *Humber* narrows towards Hull on the northern bank a link with Yorkshire is provided by the *car-ferry* that crosses from Hull to **New Holland,** and where the motorist has the unusual experience of driving along the station platform to reach the road.

South of New Holland and four miles south-east of **Barton-upon-Humber** is **Thornton Abbey** *(daily, fee).* The ruins of the abbey itself are dwarfed by the stupendous remains of the Abbey Gateway. A fortified bridge 120 feet long spans a dry moat and leads to the massive façade of the Gateway, built in the 14th century, while behind are over 100 acres of monastic ruins spread over the flat fields.

The Cotswolds

The Cotswold Hills form a watershed between the lower *Severn* and the *Thames* and extend across Gloucestershire from near Bath to the border of Warwickshire. The steep western scarp overlooks the fertile valleys of Gloucester and Evesham. On the other side there is a gradual slope, furrowed by river valleys, to the south-east. The sub-soil is composed of oölitic limestone; woodlands are predominantly of beech and the lesser flora is also that characteristic of limestone country.

To define the area popularly known as The Cotswolds is more difficult. In general, the term is understood to apply to the area bounded on the west by the Stroud-Winchcombe escarpment, and extending to, and slightly beyond, Chipping Sodbury in the south-west; Chipping Campden in the north; and Witney to Chipping Norton in the east.

The name Cotswold is derived from the Anglo-Saxon *cote*—a sheepfold, and *wold*—open uncultivated land. On the grassy slopes sheep were bred, and by the 14th century a flourishing wool industry had developed. The prosperous merchants built gracious manor-houses using the local yellow-grey stone, with fine tithe barns and magnificent churches. Many of these beautiful buildings still stand, their attractiveness enhanced by the loveliness of the surrounding countryside.

One gateway to the Cotswolds is **Witney**, a market town busy with blanket making and light engineering. The 17th-century pillared Buttercross incorporates part of an old market cross, and the Blanket Hall (1721) has a curious clock. At **Cogges,** a mile to the south-east, the church (1100), vicarage, and manor house (*c.* 1250) are of interest.

WITNEY TO BURFORD

From Witney the main road westward leads to **Burford** (11 miles). A more interesting and leisurely route is by the minor roads and lanes that traverse the Windrush Valley, gained by turning right two miles from Witney to **Minster Lovell** and then passing through a series of delightful hamlets and villages. From Minster Lovell with its interesting church and fine manor house, follow the road to **Asthall Leigh** and there turn left. A mile further on a road to the left runs down the valley to a bridge over the *Windrush,* commanding a lovely view of **Asthall** village. Beyond its Elizabethan manor house the road rises and displays a long reach of the Windrush Valley. Across the meads on the right is **Swinbrook,** a scattered village whose church has effigies arranged on shelves, and medieval carvings on the chancel stalls.

From Swinbrook to Burford there is a choice of routes—along the south bank of the *Windrush,* or over the hill to **Fullbrook,** less than a mile from Burford.

Burford (*Bull, Inn for All Seasons, The Winters Tale, Lamb*) in the Windrush Valley, is a picturesque town with a main street sloping steeply down to a fine old bridge across the river. The stone houses present endless varieties of local style, some with mullioned windows and spandrelled doorways; yet the result achieved is one of complete harmony. The Church, dating from Norman times, is a fascinating building to explore. Adjoining the churchyard are the Almshouses, founded in 1457 by Richard, Earl of Warwick—the Kingmaker. Facing them is the Grammar School, founded in 1571 for boys. Burford Priory, a 13th-century religious house, was rebuilt in Elizabethan days. It became untenanted and neglected for many years, until restored during this present century; it is now occupied by an Anglican community for women.

Burford, well served by bus and coach services, is a good centre for exploring the surrounding countryside. The **Forest of Wychwood,** famous for its deer and magnificent trees, once extended from Burford to Bourton-on-the-Water and to Charlbury. Most of the area is now privately owned; the remaining land has become a National Nature Reserve.

Four miles along the road to Chipping Norton is **Shipton-under-Wychwood** an extensive and quietly pleasant place with good houses and an old inn, the *Shaven Crown.* The church, among trees below the village, has a palimpsest brass on the wall of the south aisle, and 15th-century stone pulpit and font. **Ascott-under-Wychwood** has a small church with a tower topped by a diminutive bell-cote. **Charlbury** is an attractive little town on the *Evenlode* river. Lee Place, a residence of the Marquis of Blandford, is 17th century, and a Friends' Meeting House has the date 1779.

BURFORD TO NORTHLEACH

The main Oxford–Northleach road touches the southern extremity of Burford. A pleasanter route from Burford to Northleach is to follow the Windrush Valley by either of the following roads:
(1) that following the south bank of the river (for this turn along Sheep Street, Burford, and follow the river to Little Barrington. Or
(2) cross Burford Bridge and turn left to Taynton and Great Barrington, then re-cross the river to Little Barrington.
Continue west to Windrush and Sherborne, thence to Farmington and Northleach. Alongside the route are attractive villages: **Taynton** set among trees, with a church, manor house and cottages built of the famous Taynton stone; **Great Barrington,** a small village with an 18th-century mansion situated in a fine deer park; **Windrush** with a notable church; **Sherborne,** a beautiful village of Cotswold cottages with stone roofs and dormer windows; and **Farmington,** a peaceful hamlet with a Georgian mansion and rectory, and a church dating from 1150.

In less than two miles is **Northleach** *(Wheatsheaf),* a market town and former wool trade centre. The magnificent Church has a high tower and pinnacled roof, and a notable South Porch. The interior has many features of interest, including fine brasses, mainly to woolstaplers—hence the representation of sheep and woolpacks. In the main street are 17th-century almshouses.

From Northleach cross-roads, a minor road runs north-west to the delightful villages of **Hampnett,** where a lovely small Norman church nestles amid barns and houses; **Turkdean,** on wooded slopes; and secluded **Notgrove.** A mile from this last village is *Notgrove Barrow,* "a tomb in the grand style of the cult of the dead".

Eastward is **Aston Blank** (Cold Aston) with attractive houses. In less than two miles is **Bourton-on-the-Water,** where the road joins the Roman *Fosse Way*—the direct route from Northleach to Stow-in-the Wold.

Bourton-on-the-Water *(Old New Inn, Old Manse, Brookside)* is a pleasantly situated small town. Through its centre flow the clear waters of the *Windrush,* with lawns and footpaths on each side, and crossed by a series of low built footbridges. The Church has a Georgian tower with a curious dome, and retains its 14th-century chancel. Other attractions include trout fishing, a "model village", a botanical garden and aviary, and a museum of witchcraft.

Clapton is reached by field path or by a turning off the Sherborne road. It consists of a handful of houses including a gabled manor and farms set on the hillside. The simple Church is one of the smallest in Gloucestershire. About half-a-mile south of Clapton a left-hand turn from the Sherborne road leads to the road linking Bourton with **Great Rissington,** which has an attractive church, rectory, and farmhouse. The Church is mainly Early English, but among evidences of Norman work are the four tower arches. The main street, with widely spaced houses, runs up to the village green. Beyond is an R.A.F. airfield.

A mile or so to the north lies **Little Rissington** on the hillside above the *Dikler*. Its church stands on a spur a little apart from the village. **Wyck Rissington,** still further north, divides naturally into two sections—the houses and farms near the church, and a series of cottages bordering an extensive green. The Church is considered to have the best 13th-century east end of any church in the county. The tower is Norman, on a possibly Saxon base. The Norman font dates from 1080.

Above Wyck Rissington, to the north-east, **Icomb Hill** rises 800 feet above sea level and forms a grand viewpoint. Below is **Icomb** village, in a sunny valley. The interesting church dates from 1220, and possibly earlier, for it was Offa, King of Mercia, who gave Icomb to the monks of Worcester. Icomb Place is a fine medieval manor house, probably built for the Sir John Blaket (*d.* 1431) whose tomb is in the church.

Three miles eastward across the fields, or reached by road from Stow, is **Bledington,** an attractive village clustered round a large green. The Church has many interesting features and should not be missed.

Stow-on-the-Wold *(Talbot, Unicorn, Fosse Manor)* "where the winds blow cold" is a hill town of typical stone-built houses. The lofty Church, with its 14th-century tower was originally dedicated to Edward the Martyr (the King murdered at Corfe Castle) but was later re-dedicated to Edward the Confessor. Medieval wool merchants raised the tall tower, and extended the interior.

The large open central area of the town includes the Market Place, with a market cross, and the old stocks in the shade of an elm. For centuries, Stow was famous for its immense fairs—20,000 sheep were sold on one occasion.

Seven roads radiate from Stow, through lovely scenery and attractive villages. To the south-west are **Upper Slaughter,** with a notable Elizabethan manor house; and the neighbouring **Lower Slaughter** with picturesque old bridges over a stream flowing through the village. **Upper Swell** and **Lower Swell,** a short way west of Stow, are a mile apart. From the bridge at Upper Swell a beautiful view is obtained of Cotswold houses, great barns, trees and a now silent mill-wheel. The gabled manor house dates from 1600. The church has retained some Norman features. Lower Swell has picturesque cottages, and the interesting little church is on the site of a Roman crematorium.

Nine miles east of Stow is **Chipping Norton,** in Oxfordshire. This picturesque town, with a population of 4,500 *(White Hart, Crown and Cushion, Fox)*, is on the southern slopes of the valley carved out by a tributary of the *Evenlode* river. The Church is noted for its chancel, tombs, and brasses. Of interest are the 17th-century Almshouses, a fine old inn *The White Hart,* and attractive 18th-century buildings lining its wide streets. Four miles north are the **Rollright Stones** —a famous prehistoric stone circle. Five miles to the north-west is **Chastleton** village, where stands the Jacobean Chastleton House dated 1603 and open daily to the public. The village of **Churchill,** the birthplace of Warren Hastings in 1732, is three miles south-west of Chipping Norton. It has a fine church tower and village fountain.

From Stow-on-the-Wold, the Fosse Way runs direct to **Moreton-in-Marsh** (4½ miles), and forms its exceptionally wide main street. Moreton-in-Marsh lies at the edge of the Northern Cotswolds, and has pleasant old houses and inns in its tree-lined streets. Charles I slept at the *White Hart* in July 1644. In the Curfew Tower opposite the Market Hall, is the original curfew bell. Remains of a secret passage leading from the old manor house to the church 300 yards away may still be seen.

Chipping Campden *(Noel Arms, Cotswold House, King's Arms, Seymour House)* north-west of Moreton, has been described as "the most beautiful village street in England". The wide curving thoroughfare is an outstanding example of harmony in architecture. There are 14th-century houses and inns, a 15th-century Grammar School, 17th-century Almshouses and Market Hall, and an 18th-century Town Hall. For nearly 200 years Campden was a busy centre of the Cotswold wool trade. The Market Hall still dominates the centre of the main street. The word *chipping* is derived from the old word *ceapen*, meaning market.

The impressive 15th-century Church reflects the opulence of former days. In this spacious building are fine brasses and sculptured memorials, and in large glass cases there are magnificent examples of medieval embroidery. In the High Street, almost opposite the end of Church Street, is *Grevel's House*, which was built in 1380 by a rich wool merchant who did much for Campden. It is a beautiful small domestic building with a Gothic doorway and lovely bay windows and gables. One mile to the north-west is **Dover's Hill,** where the famous Cotswold Games were formerly held. *Scuttlebrook Fair* is still celebrated in Campden on the Saturday after Whitsun. Two miles east is **Ebrington,** a lovely village of thatched cottages. Further north is **Hidcote Bartrim,** where the seventeenth-century **Hidcote Manor** (N.T.) has beautiful gardens open to the public on certain days.

Broadway *(Lygon Arms, Broadway, Swan, Dormy House)* five miles west of Campden, is the principal Worcestershire village of the North Cotswolds, and a famous show place. Picturesque old houses line the wide grass-bordered street. The *Lygon Arms* hotel dates from the 17th century, and there is a notable Tudor House. The Parish Church is modern, but St. Endburgha's Church on the Snowshill road dates from Norman times. To the south-east is **Broadway Beacon** (1,024 feet) crowned by a Tower that is a landmark for many miles around.

South of Broadway

From Broadway a road leads to **Snowshill,** three miles south. This is an attractive secluded Cotswold village. **Snowshill Manor,** a lovely Tudor mansion with terraced gardens (N.T.) is open to the public on certain days.

From the western end of Broadway the A46 runs south-west, skirting the western heights of the Cotswolds, to Winchcombe and Cheltenham. Before following this route, it would be as well to give some description of the central area lying between Broadway and Bourton-on-the-Water. The most direct road between these points follows the line of the ancient trackway known as *Buckle Street.* Keeping to the high ground, and starting by Broadway Tower, Buckle Street then passes to the east of Snowshill, and reaches its highest point at *Cutsdean Hill,* more than 1,000 feet above sea-level. It continues high above the upper Windrush Valley, crosses the Stow-Andoversford road, and reaches Bourton at the bridge.

An alternative route is to take the road from Broadway to Snowshill, continuing to **Cutsdean,** a village still just within the borders of Worcestershire. Less than a mile further on is the hamlet of **Ford.** From here the road runs parallel with the infant *Windrush* river to **Temple Guiting,** a charming village set among trees and once the property of the military order of Templars.

The road continues to follow the valley southward, through the hamlets of **Kineton** and **Barton,** and passes on the right a turning to **Guiting Power**—a pretty village at the junction of two streams—finally reaching the straggling village of **Naunton.** From here the river is followed for a further mile or so, when the road strikes left for Bourton-on-the-Water.

BROADWAY TO CHELTENHAM

From Broadway to Cheltenham by the A46 is just over 15 miles. The road runs along the Vale in a south-westerly direction, with occasional turnings on the left leading to hill villages. Such a turning one and a half miles from Broadway, leads to **Buckland,** an attractive small village whose church contains fine panelling and benches, 15th-century glass, a mazer—the "Buckland Bowl", and medieval tiles. Buckland can also be reached from Broadway by a walk of two and a half miles through Burhill Woods and fields.

A mile beyond the turning to Buckland, another diversion from the main road brings one to **Stanton,** a well-preserved village at the foot of Shenbarrow Hill. There are many old houses. Warren House, once the manor house, was built in 1577. Stanton Court, a beautiful Elizabethan mansion, has been carefully restored.

Stanway, one and a half miles to the south, is a charming village of gabled houses; medieval church and tithe barn; and **Stanway House,** a beautiful Tudor mansion with an impressive Jacobean gatehouse and beautiful gardens *(open)*.

The main road may be rejoined via **Didbrook,** worth visiting for its fine old church, and another turning almost immediately leaving the A46 crosses the railway and leads to **Hailes** (or Hayles).

Alternatively a field-path runs from Didbrook to Hailes Church, built in 1130. In the church are 14th-century wall paintings and medieval stained glass. Near the church are the ruins of the Cistercian **Hayles Abbey,** founded in 1246, and in the Middle Ages the goal of pilgrims, who came to see its precious relic, a phial of the Holy Blood—vouched for by the Pope and by the Patriarch of Jerusalem.

> "By goddes precious herte, and by his nayles,
> And by the blode of Crist, that it is in Hayles".
> Chaucer: *The Pardoner's Tale.*

In 1936 the site was presented to the National Trust. Excavations have been carried out, and many finds are exhibited in the small museum.

At just over eight miles from Broadway, the A46 arrives at **Winchcombe** (Pop.: 4,000) a small market town of great antiquity. Its 15th-century Parish Church has a battlemented tower, many grotesque gargoyles, and an altar cloth embroidered by Katherine of Aragon. The *George Inn* was used by pilgrims to Hayles Abbey, and still retains part of its medieval gallery.

To the south-east of Winchcombe is **Sudeley Castle,** built in the reign of Stephen, rebuilt in the 15th century, and given to Henry VIII's widow Katherine Parr and her husband Seymour in 1547. The Castle was dismantled during the Civil War, rebuilt in 1837, and is still occupied. The Gardens and part of the Castle are open daily except Mondays, but open Bank Holidays.

High in the hills between Winchcombe and Cheltenham is the important Stone Age burial mound called **Belas Knap.** When this long barrow was opened in 1863–4, 38 skeletons were found. The burial chambers have been carefully restored.

From Winchcombe the road runs west and south via **Postlip** with its beautiful Elizabethan manor house, to **Cleeve Hill,** the highest point in the Cotswolds (1,031 feet) and a magnificent view-point. Near that point of Cleeve Common known as *Cleeve Cloud* is a British Camp now scheduled as an Ancient Monument. The main road descends to **Southam,** noted for its manor house and for a splendid tithe barn (at *Pigeon House Farm),* and **Prestbury** (with its racecourse), to Cheltenham.

THE SOUTHERN COTSWOLDS

The Coln Valley

From Northleach the Fosse Way runs south-west for 10 miles to Cirencester. About two and a half miles along this road is Fosse Bridge, where the road crosses the river Coln. A turning to the left, just before the bridge, follows the beautiful Coln Valley and passes through a number of attractive riverside villages— **Coln St. Dennis** with its ancient church; **Coln Rogers**; **Winson**; **Ablington**; and **Bibury.** At Bibury the stone cottages of *Arlington Row* (N.T.) are a famous feature of the village; they date from the early 17th century and were once used as a wool factory. The Church shows Saxon and Norman work, and there is a Jacobean manor house, Bibury Court.

From Bibury a road runs south-west to Cirencester, but alternatively the Coln Valley road may be continued to **Coln St. Aldwyn,** on the hillside, and to **Quenington,** with its stone-built cottages and attractive houses. The main road is reached at **Fairford,** an ancient market town famous for its trout fishing and for the wonderful 16th-century windows in its church. Twenty-eight windows illustrate biblical scenes from the Creation to the Last Judgement. There are some interesting houses and a fine old mill. John Keble, one of the leaders of the "Oxford Movement" was born at Fairford in 1792.

From Fairford a road runs 9 miles due west to Cirencester, passing the three Ampneys—**Ampney St. Peter, Ampney St. Mary,** and **Ampney Crucis.** These are named after the *Ampney* stream which flows into the *Thames* near Cricklade.

CHEDWORTH and the ROMAN VILLA

Leaving Northleach as before, turn right immediately after passing Fosse Bridge. In less than a mile a turning on the left leads to Chedworth, but for the Roman Villa keep straight on.

Chedworth is a picturesque village spreading over two hillsides, with a rippling brook which is a tributary of the *Coln.* The **Roman Villa** (N.T., *daily*) is about a mile away, in Chedworth Woods, and is one of the most complete and charmingly situated of our relics of the Roman occupation. The stone-built villa had forty to fifty rooms on the ground floor, and in parts there was a second floor. Some rooms had mosaic flooring and central heating. Some of the original walls still rise several feet above ground. There is a Museum, and some rooms have been roofed over and their original purpose indicated.

Cirencester

Distances.—Bath, 34; Bristol, 37; Cheltenham, 16; Gloucester, 17; Malmesbury, 12; Oxford, 36; Stow-on-the-Wold, 19.
Early Closing.—Thursday.
Golf.—18-hole Cirencester Golf Club on Cheltenham road (2 miles).

Hotels.—*King's Head, Fleece, Crown, Stratton House.*
Market Day.—Friday. Cattle market on Tuesday.
Polo.—Cirencester Park, Sunday afternoons in summer.
Population.—13,000.
Post Office.—Castle Street.

The district where Cirencester now stands was once occupied by the British tribes known as the *Dobunni*. Recent archaeological work indicates that the tribal centre was at Bagendon, three miles to the north. During the 400 years of Roman occupation it developed as a military post, becoming a focal point at the intersection of the great Roman highways Ermin Street, Fosse Way, and Akeman Street. As the city of *Corinium* it built defensive walls and gateways, within which were fine temples, houses with exquisite sculpture and mosaic floors, a colonnaded Forum, and a Basilica. Little of Corinium remains above ground today, but remains of Roman buildings are still being uncovered; since 1960 there has been a considerable amount of fresh excavation work. Outside the line of the walls is the site of a large amphitheatre.

Corinium was plundered and burnt by the Saxons in 577, but was never entirely deserted. Under Norman rule Cirencister (as it was now called) became increasingly important. A castle was built, and an abbey was founded by Henry I in 1117. No trace remains of the castle, and of the great abbey only a gateway still stands; the abbey was deliberately destroyed during the Dissolution of 1534. Today Cirencester is a busy market town with a famous parish church facing a spacious market place, delightful old inns and houses, and a fascinating museum of Roman antiquities.

The **Parish Church** (dedicated to St. John the Baptist) is a magnificent structure of graceful proportions. It was built in Norman times to replace a Saxon church that was demolished to make room for the Abbey. The considerable additions made in the 14th and 15th centuries bear witness to the prosperity of the local wool trade. The fine tower, which shows up so well at a distance, dates from 1400. The three-storey south porch—a rebuilding of that erected in 1500—has beautiful fan-vaulting. There is a notable window at the east end of the nave, above the chancel arch; and the early 16th-century pulpit is of the wine-glass shape found in many Gloucestershire churches. Both St. Katherine's Chapel and Trinity Chapel have magnificent vaulting.

The **Corinium Museum** is in Park Street, and is open daily, June–August inclusive. The present building was erected in 1938 and has an unrivalled display of Roman antiquities, mostly from the locality of Corinium. Exhibits include sculptures, tessellated pavements, and the various minor articles of everyday life in Roman England.

Adjoining Cirencester is the magnificent **Park** of 3,000 acres which has been in the possession of the Bathurst family since 1690. The Park, which includes a considerable area of farmland, is open daily to the public, and there are occasional Hunt meets and polo matches.

A little outside the town, between the Fosse Way and the road to Stroud, stands the Royal Agricultural College founded in 1846.

Malmesbury *(Old Bell, George, Stainsbridge)*, in Wiltshire, lies 12 miles south-west of Cirencester. The small town is a place of great antiquity and was long celebrated for its magnificent **Abbey**, which became a place of pilgrimage. St. Aldhem, at one time its Abbot, was buried here in 705. Most of the noble Abbey dated from the 12th century, but at the Reformation all but a fraction was pulled down, leaving only the nave and aisles of the Abbey Church, which were retained to form the present **Parish Church of St. Mary.**

The imposing fragment of the **Abbey Church** that remains, now the Parish Church, is notable for its richly carved south porch, one of the finest remaining examples of Norman work in this country. Projecting from the south triforium wall of the nave is what was probably a "watching loft" used by the Sacristan when guarding the Abbey treasures and relics. In the north aisle is a monument to King Athelstan *(d.* 940) who according to tradition was buried in the Abbey.

The 12th-century historian William of Malmesbury was a monk of the Abbey; and Thomas Hobbes the philosopher (1588–1679) was a native of the town.

Near the church is a **Market Cross** dating from the time of Henry VII and restored in 1954. It forms a shelter rising to a pinnacle 40 feet in height. South of the market cross the High Street, flanked by pleasant houses and picturesque inns, leads to **St. John's Bridge.** Near by in Lower High Street stands the remains of what in the 13th century was the Hospital of St. John of Jerusalem. The *Old Bell Hotel* is built on the site of the 12th-century castle which was demolished in the following century.

Tetbury *(Snooty Fox, Close)* five miles to the north-west of Malmesbury and back in Gloucestershire, is a picturesque small market town on a hill, with wide streets and a Town Hall (formerly Market Hall) standing on pillars. Tetta, an abbess of Wimborne founded a monastery at Tetbury, and for centuries it was a flourishing centre of the wool trade; some of the fine houses built by the merchants still stand. The Church, originally Norman was entirely rebuilt in 1787; tower and spire were reconstructed in 1890. The interior of the church is interesting for its tall wooden pillars and its box pews entered from narrow corridors.

Chipping Sodbury *(Cross Hands)*, the most southerly of the three Cotswold Chippings, lies half-way between Tetbury and Bristol. It has an exceptionally wide, stone-built main street which seems to confirm the aptness of the name, for "chipping" here as elsewhere meant "market". Although much of the surrounding district is still rural, there has been marked industrialisation during the last twenty years. A Mop Fair is held twice yearly. The Church dates mainly from the 15th century.

Old Sodbury, less than two miles to the east, also has an ancient church. Above the village is an extensive British encampment within which a Roman camp was built later. On a clear day the outlook from here is magnificent.

Eastward again, a road (A4040) runs to **Acton Turville** a short distance north of which is **Great Badminton.**

Badminton House *(June–early Sept, Weds, fee)*, for three centuries the home of the Beauforts, stands in a magnificent park celebrated for its trees. It is a fine Palladian mansion and contains valuable collections of paintings and furniture. For many years Badminton has been famous for the Three Days Event Horse Trials.

The road north from Badminton leads through Little Badminton to Hawkesbury Upton near which is **Hawkesbury** where the hill is crowned by a lofty tower in memory of Lord E. H. Somerset *(d.* 1842). The church dates from Saxon times and shows good Norman work. To the south lies **Horton** where is *Horton Court* (N.T., *Apr.–Oct., Weds and Sats)* a typical Cotswold manor house with a 12th-century hall and detached ambulatory.

From Chipping Sodbury a road runs four miles due north to **Wickwar,** where are a 15th-century church, a pack-horse bridge, and a 17th-century grammar school. Still further north, via **Charfield,** one comes to **Wotton-under-Edge,** a small town (Pop.: 3,500) in a hilly setting. Once this was a busy centre of cloth-weaving; indeed, the name is held to be derived from "Wool-town". From its main street one has a view of woods and green slopes on the far side of the valley. The predominant feature of this High Street is the ancient *Tolsey,* its tiled pyramidal roof crowned by cupola and weather-vane. From here Market Street leads to the market-place still known as The Chipping. St. Mary's Church has a lofty pinnacled tower, and contains interesting old brasses. The Grammar School is one of the earliest scholastic foundations in England, dating from 1384. Among former residents of the town were Edward Jenner, who introduced vaccination, and Isaac Pitman, of shorthand fame.

Within walking distance to the east of Wotton are **Newark Park** (N.T.) and **Ozleworth,** whose Norman church has a tall hexagonal tower. Neighbouring **Boxwell** derives its name from a great wood of box trees covering 40 acres.

From Wotton the road northward to Stroud first passes through **Nailsworth** (Pop.: 3,700) a small town at the foot of a steep valley. Here, as at Stroud, some cloth is still manufactured, but the town is mainly residential. The hill known as "Nailsworth Ladder" with a gradient at times of 1 in 2, is a scene of motor-cycle trials. Four miles to the north of Nailsworth is Stroud.

Stroud *(Imperial, Stratford, Bear of Rodborough).* The town is not unattractive, with its steep narrow streets, and is a shopping and business centre (Pop.: 19,100). The Town Hall, in Church Street, still preserves some of its 16th-century features.

In medieval times the famous Cotswold wool was mainly exported, via the "Staple" at Calais, for manufacture abroad. In the reigns of Edward II and Edward III the importation of cloth was prohibited, and its manufacture encouraged, so that by Tudor times most of the wool exported was in the form of broadcloth. Stroud and its neighbourhood became increasingly devoted to the manufacture of broadcloth, the river *Frome* and its tributaries providing the water supply for fulling and dyeing processes. Fine West of England cloth is still manufactured at Stroud, but a variety of other industries, notably in plastics, have now established themselves.

Stroud is well provided with open spaces—Stratford Park, Bank Gardens, Park Gardens, and Victory Park. From many parts of the town one can look southward across the valley of the *Frome* to Rodborough Fort, a castellated mansion at the northern end of **Rodborough Common.** Both this Common and the more extensive **Minchinhampton Common** that adjoins it, are now National Trust property.

Minchinhampton is a pleasant small town that was once a centre for the wool and cloth trade. It has a picturesque Market Hall dating from 1698, with an interesting list of toll charges displayed. Holy Trinity Church has a curious truncated steeple crowned with pinnacles.

Two miles to the south-west of Stroud, at **Woodchester,** is the site of the largest **Roman villa** in the Cotswolds. It consisted of two courts, bounded by colonnades and buildings, and covers 26 acres. The site was first excavated in 1793–96, and foundations of 65 rooms were exposed. Nothing is now to be seen, except when the great tessellated pavement—49 feet square and normally covered with sand and soil to preserve it—is uncovered for a few weeks and open to public view.

BETWEEN STROUD AND CIRENCESTER

The Frome Valley. From Stroud to **Sapperton,** halfway to Cirencester, lies the "Golden Valley" of the *Frome*. Though peaceful today, this valley was once busy with industry and an incessant stream of barges passed along the *Thames and Severn Canal,* laden with coal or bales of cloth. From Sapperton a line dips steeply to the foot of the valley, crossing the now derelict canal near the entrance of the tunnel, two-and-a-half miles long, that carried its waters under the Cotswolds. Up to the right we climb through beechwoods, presently coming to a road leading to **Edgeworth,** with its church sheltered by. tall trees. A mile further on is **Miserden** (named after a family called Musard who held it in the 12th–13th centuries). The church shows Saxon and Norman features. East of Miserden, across the valley, is **Winstone,** an ancient and straggling village only a mile from the Roman *Ermin Street* between Cirencester and Gloucester.

The Dun Valley. To the south of Winstone, the little river *Dun* on its way to Cirencester gives its name to three interesting little villages—**Duntisbourne Leer, Duntisbourne Abbots,** and **Duntisbourne Rous.** A little farther downstream is **Daglingworth,** whose church is outstanding for its Saxon stone carvings and its Norman altar.

The Churn Valley. Although the Ordnance map marks the source of the river *Thames* as **Thames Head Bridge** on the Fosse Way, three miles south-west of Cirencester, the fact that this source is frequently dry lends support to the contention that the *Thames* really starts life as the *Churn*.

From Cirencester a road closely follows the *Churn* stream to its source near Coberley, some 10 miles to the north. Starting from Cirencester we pass through the villages of **Baunton, Bagendon, North Cerney** (with a notable church), **Colesbourne, Cowley** (with a fine manor house) and **Coberley.** At Coberley the church contains interesting monuments, including one to Lady Joan de Berkeley, the mother of Dick Whittington, thrice Lord Mayor of London.

A little to the north of Coberley is **Seven Springs,** with its inscribed plate:

HIC TUUS
O TAMESINE PATER
SEPTEMGEMINUS FONS.

Here is the highest source of the *Thames;* tree-shaded and by-passed by a new road, it provides a quiet resting place for travellers.

STROUD TO CHELTENHAM

The direct route from Stroud to Cheltenham is 14 miles. The route described below is a mile or so longer.

From Stroud follow the A46 road northward for some four miles to **Painswick.** Away to the left·of the road, before reaching Painswick, rises **Haresfield Beacon** (800 feet) one of the finest viewpoints along the western edge of the Cotswolds.

Painswick has been called "Queen of the Cotswolds". It is a charming unspoilt town with typical stone-built houses. The Church is a beautiful building, mainly 15th-century—the heyday of the wool trade. The churchyard is also notable for its clipped yews (said to number 99), its interesting modern lych-gate, and the iron "spectacle" stocks at the south-east corner of the churchyard.

Two beautiful houses are the old Court House, and the Palladian mansion Painswick House half-a-mile to the north.

Two miles north of Painswick, in a hollow on the left, is **Prinknash Abbey,** formerly the residence of Abbots of Gloucester, now occupied since 1928 by monks from Caldey Island and greatly enlarged. Also on the left is **Painswick Beacon** (922 feet) and the remains of a hill fort known as *Kimsbury Camp.*

Opposite Prinknash, leave the Cheltenham road and bear right through the lovely Buckholt Woods to **Birdlip.** On the Gloucester road to the left is the steep descent of Birdlip Hill; but from Birdlip follow the A417, crossing the A436 at the *Air Balloon Inn,* and entering Cheltenham via Leckhampton.

Cheltenham

Airport.—Air charter services at Staverton Airport, four miles.

Angling.—Apply to Secretary, Cheltenham Angling Club.

Bowls.—*Cheltenham Bowling Club* has greens in Suffolk Square; *Cheltenham Spa Bowling Club* in St. George's Square; and *Whaddon Bowling Club* in Whaddon Road.

Cricket.—Cricket Festival in August, on College ground.

Early Closing.—Wednesday for most shops.

Entertainments.—*Everyman Theatre,* Regent Street,

The Playhouse, Bath Road. Annual Musical Festival in July.

Golf.—*Cotswold Hill Golf Club,* Cleeve Hill; *Lilley Brook Golf Club,* Charlton Kings.

Hunting.—Nine packs meet within easy reach of Cheltenham.

Information Bureau.—At Municipal Offices, The Promenade.

Population.—70,000.

Races.—Course adjoins the Evesham road.

Swimming.—Open-air pool at Sandford Park. Large covered swimming baths at Alstone Baths.

Cheltenham is a town of trees and open spaces, of elegant Regency buildings and imposing modern ones. At one time an inland spa, its medicinal waters have now become of very minor importance, and Cheltenham is noted principally as a delectable residential and educational town, a festival centre for the Arts, and a holiday resort from which to explore the Cotswolds. Like many other towns, it has acquired a traffic congestion problem.

The oldest part of Cheltenham is the long High Street running north-west to south-east, with the Parish Church on its south-side and the Grammar School (rebuilt) on the other. The High Street is now busy with traffic and lined with modern shops; *The Plough,* an old coaching inn, is now a hotel.

Running southward from the High Street is the spacious **Promenade,** with its double avenue of horse-chestnuts. On one side are luxurious shops, and on the other an attractive Regency terrace which now houses the Municipal Offices. The terraced houses, with their delicate ironwork balconies, are typical of the older private dwellings in all parts of the town.

A hundred yards east of the Promenade is the **Town Hall,** a handsome Renaissance building which is the centre of the town's social and cultural activities. Also in the Town Hall is the Central Spa and Lounge, where if so inclined one may still sip the Cheltenham waters. Adjoining the Town Hall are the terraced **Imperial Gardens,** and a little further south, beyond the *Queen's Hotel,* are the **Montpellier Gardens,** typical of the many pleasant little parks that characterise Cheltenham. Across the road is the **Rotunda,** with its domed roof; built originally as a Pump Room, it is now occupied by a bank.

Returning almost to the High Street, on the left one comes to Clarence Street, where is housed the **Library, Art Gallery and Museum.** Near by and somewhat concealed by shops and houses—although its spire is prominent in distant views— is the **Parish Church,** lying in the angle formed by Clarence Street and High Street. The Church is a spacious and dignified building, and has a number of

CHELTENHAM ═══ Through routes ➤ One-way streets ▒ Disc Parking Zone Ⓟ Parking

notable glass windows. To many visitors not the least interesting feature of Cheltenham Church and churchyard is the number of quaint memorial inscriptions that may be found.

To the north of the High Street is Pittville Street, leading in half-a-mile to Evesham Road running between **Pittville Park** and **Pittville Gardens.** The former, 18 acres in extent, lies to the west of the Evesham Road, and can be entered from the road or by means of a subway from the Gardens across the way. Pittville Gardens, east of the road, are laid out in a more formal manner, and at the far end is the beautiful **Pittville Pump Room,** with its Ionic colonnade. The ground floor assembly hall and adjoining rooms are in constant use for presentation of social attractions, conferences and banquets. The "healing waters" are now only available at the Town Hall.

As an educational centre, Cheltenham is of high standing. In addition to Cheltenham College, the Ladies' College, the Grammar School, and various other schools, there is a fine Technical College and two Training Colleges for teachers.

The Cheltenham Waters. The exploitation of Cheltenham's natural waters is said to have started with the observation in 1716 that pigeons liked the grains of salt which formed on the ground near a spring. Hence the prominence of pigeons on the town's coat of arms and crest.

In 1738 the first spa was built by that versatile seaman Captain Skillicorne, so fulsomely commemorated in St. Mary's Church. The event which set the seal upon the success of the Spa was the prolonged visit in 1788 of George III, whose physician had advised a course of the waters. Much has been written about fashionable Cheltenham of the period. In 1816 an **Assembly Room** was opened by the Duke of Wellington. The roll of talented writers, musicians and artists who have stayed or resided at Cheltenham is a long one, and the atmosphere of the town takes on an added dignity with the memory of the many gay, witty and wise men and women who have lingered in the Promenade or looked down on the town from the neighbouring hills.

From Cheltenham the A40 runs eastward to **Northleach,** via the residential district of **Charlton Kings** to **Andoversford** (6 miles).

Before Andoversford is reached, the road passes between Dowdeswell Wood and **Dowdeswell,** reached by a turning on the right. Dowdeswell has a beautiful little church (note the dove-cotes let into the four panels of its tiny spire); beside it stands one of the most delightful of Cotswold houses.

A short distance towards Andoversford, a road to the left leads to **Whittington,** whose church stands on the lawn of Whittington Court, an Elizabethan house restored in 1866. The church has interesting Norman and medieval features, and in the churchyard is a 14th-century cross. Between Whittington and **Syreford,** a mile or so to the east, there was once a Roman settlement; among remains excavated was a fine statuette of Mars.

Shakespeare Country

Stratford-upon-Avon

Car Parks.—Bridgefoot, Waterside, Arden Street, Rother Street, Windsor Street, Bridgefoot Garage.

Distances.—Banbury, 20; Birmingham, 24; Cheltenham, 31; Evesham, 14; London, 92; Oxford, 40; Shrewsbury, 64; Worcester, 25.

Early Closing.—Thursday.

Entertainment.—Cinema, Festival Club, Royal Shakespeare Theatre.

Hotels.—*Shakespeare, Welcombe, Alveston Manor,* *Arden, Falcon, Swan's Nest, White Swan, Barwyn,* and others.

Information Centre.—High Street.

Library.—Public Library, Henley Street.

Market Day.—Cattle, Tues; General, Fris; Farm produce, Mons, Weds, Fris.

Population.—19,280.

Post Office.—Bridge Street.

Sport.—Boating, bowls, cricket, fishing in Avon, golf (Tiddington Road), putting, riding, tennis. Racecourse (National Hunt). Regatta.

The town of Stratford-on-Avon was established in 1196 by King John as a market centre for Warwickshire. The *Mop Fair* held annually in October is a survival from these early times. Stratford is world famous, for here William Shakespeare was born, lived and died (1564–1616). The town preserves many links with its interesting past and attracts visitors and literary pilgrims from many countries. The central streets of this orderly compact town bear the same names as when Shakespeare knew them. Picturesque half-timbered houses associated with Elizabethan and Jacobean times provide an appropriate setting for his life and work.

Interest in the poet began shortly after his death and steadily increased through the years. In 1769, the actor David Garrick, organised the first Shakespeare Festival in an octagonal wooden building in front of the present theatre. The Festival Season now spreads over seven months each year, attracting large audiences. Many buildings and relics connected with Shakespeare are now in the care of a Shakespeare Trust. An inclusive ticket for admission to Shakespeare's Birthplace, New Place, Anne Hathaway's Cottage, Hall's Croft, and Mary Arden's House can be obtained from any of these properties. *Each of these buildings are open daily. Suns in winter from 2 p.m.*

Shakespeare's Birthplace. The Birthplace in Henley Street where William was born on April 23, 1564, was the family home of the Shakespeares. The house has altered little over the centuries and contains much of the original timber. On the death of his father, John Shakespeare, William inherited the property which passed successively to his daughter and grand-daughter. In 1847, the house was purchased by public subscription for preservation as a memorial to the poet. It contains fascinating architectural features and many objects of interest. The garden at the rear is devoted mainly to trees, flowers and herbs mentioned in Shakespeare's works. The building at the side of the garden houses the library and record collections of the Birthplace Trust. Publications, books and view cards are on sale. The Trust also arranges exhibitions, sponsors lectures, and promotes a poetry festival.

New Place (adjacent to the Guild Chapel). The site and part of the foundations are all that remain of New Place, the house to which Shakespeare retired in 1610 and in which he died in 1616 at the age of 52. The building adjoining was the home of Thomas Nash who married Shakespeare's grand-daughter. Nash's House is now **New Place Museum** with an interesting collection of historical, archaeological and local exhibits.

The **Knott Garden** beyond is an enchanting colourful replica of an Elizabethan garden, from the far end of which a gate leads into the Great Garden of New Place *(daily, free)*. Shakespeare owned and cultivated this large beautiful garden, which is now maintained as a memorial to him. The old mulberry tree on the lawn is claimed to have grown from a cutting planted there by Shakespeare.

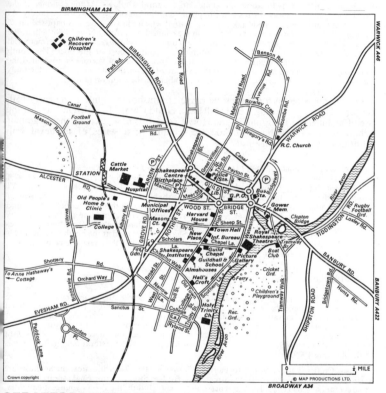

STRATFORD-UPON-AVON ═══ **Through routes** ⟶ **One-way streets** Ⓟ **Parking**

Hall's Croft, near the Parish Church, was the home of Shakespeare's daughter, Susanna and her husband, Dr. John Hall. This fine half-timbered residence with a walled garden is an excellent example of a Tudor town house with some later additions. It possesses many features of unusual interests and contains rare furniture and period exhibits. Part of the building is equipped as a Festival Club. It is also the local centre of the British Council, which welcomes overseas visitors and organises lectures, hospitality etc.

The Royal Shakespeare Theatre along Waterside was opened in 1932. It replaced the theatre built in 1879, which burnt down in 1926. There is comfortable seating for an audience of over 1,300, good acoustics, spacious foyers and a licensed restaurant and bars overlooking the river. Adjacent are the *Memorial Library,* devoted to Shakesperian literature *(weekdays, apply to Librarian)* and the *Picture Gallery and Museum.* Portraits, paintings, sculpture, relics and a collection of costume designs are on view.

271

STRATFORD-UPON-AVON

A short walk along Waterside leads to—

Holy Trinity Church. Apart from its associations and beautiful situation, this Parish Church of Stratford has intrinsic interest as a spacious, handsome building, parts of which date from the 12th century. On the north entrance door is a remarkable 13th-century *sanctuary knocker*. Within are rich carvings in wood and stone and beautiful windows. At the entrance is the Parish Register, containing entries of the baptisms and burials of the Shakespeare family. At the west end, on a modern pedestal, is the *old font* at which Shakespeare was baptised on 26 April, 1564. The curiously carved oak *Stalls* in the chancel date from about 1480. Behind the rail on the floor of the sanctuary are the five *Tombs of the Shakespeares* with memorial inscriptions. On the north wall is a sculptured and painted bust of the poet. The South Window contains glass bought with contributions from American visitors and is called the *American Window*. The *Clopton Chapel* at the east end of the north aisle was formerly the Lady Chapel. It contains memorials to the various members of the Clopton family.

On Church Street is a picturesque range of almshouses, built in the early 15th century. The neighbouring **Guild Hall** has a Guild Chapel founded in 1269 for the use of members of the Guild of the Holy Cross. It is now used by the Grammar School as a school chapel. Inside are remains of a series of medieval wall paintings. *(open free when not in use.)*

The Grammar School and Guild Hall *(Weekdays during Easter and Summer holidays only— 2–4.30).* The Grammar School was originally established in 1269 for teaching the sons of members of the Holy Cross. Following the suppression of the Guild, King Edward VI refounded the School in 1553, and it is very probable that Shakespeare, as the son of Stratford's leading burgess, received his early education here. In the 16th century the ground floor of the Guild Hall served as a local government centre, and for performances by travelling companies of actors. The impressive Upper Hall has been used for school purposes since 1553. The desk, said to have been used by Shakespeare stood at the northern end, and is now preserved in the Birthplace. The Pedagogue's House, built in the courtyard below in 1427, is still in use as a classroom.

Stratford has a wealth of historic buildings.

The *Falcon Hotel* and the *Shakespeare Hotel* in Chapel Street, are ancient hostelries where many famous people have stayed. In High Street are timbered fronts dating from Elizabethan days. **Harvard House,** elaborately carved and with projecting windows is of particular interest to Americans as the maiden home of the mother of John Harvard, founder of Harvard University, U.S.A. Built in 1596, it fell into decay in succeeding centuries until Marie Corelli, the novelist, who lived in Stratford, supervised the restoration and furnishings of the house in 1909.

Mason Croft, in Church Street, formerly the home of Marie Corelli, is now the Shakespeare Institute. At the corner of High Street and Bridge Street is the **Shakespeare—Quiney House**—for 36 years (1616–1652) the married home of Judith, the Poet's youngest daughter. It is now a tea-room. In Sheep Street are picturesque 16th- and 17th-century buildings including the **Shrieve's House** (No. 40) the home of William Rogers, who was probably the original of Shakespeare's Sergeant in the *Comedy of Errors.* At the corner is the Town Hall built 1769 on the site of an old market house.

Clopton Bridge with fine arches spanning the *Avon,* and built by Sir Hugh Clopton in the reign of Henry VII, replaced an earlier wooden structure. In the gardens near by, is the *Shakespeare Monument*; the poet and four of his principal characters are gracefully represented in bronze.

Shakespeare Villages

A mile west from the town centre is the picturesque hamlet of **Shottery,** now part of Stratford. Here is **Anne Hathaway's Cottage,** the home of Shakespeare's wife before their marriage. It is a spacious timber-framed house, with irregular walls, thatched roof and tiny latticed windows. The earliest parts date from the 15th century with walls of wattle and daub. The furniture, utensils and relics were used by successive generations of Hathaways until 1892 when the Trustees purchased the property for preservation. Three miles north-west of Stratford is **Wilmcote** village, in which is the homestead of Mary Arden, the mother of Shakespeare. This 16th-century farmhouse is open daily. The picturesque house has many interesting features and relics. Behind are old out-buildings, a farming museum, and a square stone dovecote.

Within easy reach of Stratford are **Temple Grafton,** four and a half miles west, where is Hillborough Manor, a 16th-century house. A mile north-west of Temple Grafton is **Exhall**—with stone and timber-framed cottages and an interesting church. **Wixford,** one mile south-west of Exhall, is a pleasant angling village, dating from 974. The ancient church contains splendid monuments. A short distance west is **Ragley Hall** *(daily except Mons and Fris from Apr. to Sept. 2–6)*. This fine manor of the Seymours dating from 1680 contains collections of paintings, china, furniture and books. The extensive park has gardens and a lake.

Alcester, two miles north of Wixford is a picturesque market town with timber houses and a Town Hall dated 1641. Roman and Anglo-Saxon relics have been found here. Two miles north of Alcester is **Coughton Court,** the family seat of the Throckmortons since 1409. The Court, now the property of the National Trust, contains Jacobite relics. *(Weds, Thurs, Sats, Suns, and Bank Hols. Apr.–Sept. 2–6. Oct., Sats and Suns only. Fee.)*

Bidford, four miles south of Alcester with traditional Shakespeare associations, is notable for its lovely 15th-century bridge and unusual church with beautiful stained glass.

Hillborough, two miles east from Bidford, is a tiny hamlet with a Tudor Manor House, a Grange and a quaint mill on the banks of the *Avon.* A mile further east is **Welford-on-Avon**—a pretty village with thatched cottages, a maypole on the Green, an ancient mill, and a church with Norman features and ancient lychgate.

Clopton House *(daily, fee),* one and a half miles north of Stratford, dates from Tudor times and has associations with Shakespeare and the Gunpowder Plot. It contains period furniture and paintings. *St. Peter's Chapel* was built in 1453.

Snitterfield, four miles north of Stratford, is a charming village having historical associations with Shakespeare and Charles II. The church is notable for its 14th-century font and carved scroll work.

The village of **Hampton Lucy,** four miles north-east of Stratford, is one of the prettiest in Warwickshire. The church was rebuilt 1822–26 and is an architectural gem.

Charlecote (N.T., *daily except Mons, Apr.–Sept, fee*) has been the home of the Lucy family for over 800 years. The house is famous for its alleged association with Shakespeare, who was accused of stealing deer from *Charlecote Park*. Except for the Gatehouse, the family mansion was rebuilt in 1551–58 with later additions. It contains a wealth of paintings, tapestry, pictures, furniture and relics of the Lucy family.

Charlecote Church rebuilt on the site of an ancient edifice in 1853 is one of the most ornate and interesting in the county.

Warwick

Distances.—Stratford-upon-Avon, 8; London, 91; Coventry, 11; Birmingham, 21; Oxford, 42; Worcester, 33.
Early Closing.—Thursday.
Fishing.—In Avon.

Hotels.—*Lord Leycester, Warwick Arms, Woolpack, Crown.*
Population.—18,300.
Post Office.—Old Square.
Tennis and bowls in St. Nicholas Park.

The county town of Warwick is beautiful and impressive with archaeological and historical associations. The streets are attractive with many old timbered fronts and gables. There are gardens and parks with sports facilities, riverside walks and boat excursions on the *Avon*. The principal show places are Warwick Castle, St. Mary's Church with the Beauchamp Chapel, and the Lord Leycester Hospital.

The Castle *(weekdays, Suns in summer, fee)* perched high above the *Avon*, is the home of the Earl of Warwick and one of the few medieval fortresses still inhabited. The existing building dates from the 14th and 15th centuries. The oldest parts are the curtain walls and the massive towers. *Guy's Tower* is 128 feet high with walls 10 feet thick and *Caesar's Tower,* polygonal in shape, rises to a height of 147 feet. The moat is now dry, but the 14th-century gateway still has the ancient portcullis. The rooms are splendidly furnished and contain priceless treasures. In the State Dining-Room are paintings by Van Dyck and Rubens and some fine sculptures. The 16th-century Great Hall contains a collection of armour and *Guy's Punch Bowl*— an enormous cauldron believed to have been made originally about 1350 and used as a garrison cooking-pot. The Cedar Room with panelled and carved walls and a unique Adam chimney-piece, displays Van Dyck portraits of Cavaliers, including the well-known one of

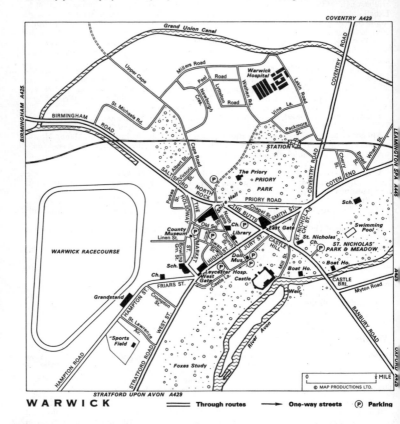

Charles I. The State Bedroom has walls hung with Brussels tapestry made in 1604. The furniture and the bed of Queen Anne were presented to the Warwicks by George III. A fine collection of ancient and medieval armour lines the Armoury passage. The chapel occupies the site of a 6th-century building. The grounds cover about a square mile, with several acres laid out as lawns and gardens.

In the greenhouse is the celebrated *Warwick Vase*. This beautiful white marble vase is over five feet high and holds 163 gallons. It was probably made by Lysippus a Greek artist, in the 4th century B.C. It was discovered among the ruins of Hadrian's Villa at Tivoli in Italy. The ambassador to George III brought the vase to England and sold it to the second Earl of Warwick. The vase is in excellent preservation.

Castle Bridge leads via Castle Hill to the **East Gate** one of the four main gates of the ancient town and of which only two survive. It is surmounted by St. Peter's Chapel dating from Henry VI's reign. North-east is Smith Street with half-timbered buildings and *Landor House*, now a school. It was the birthplace of Walter Savage Landor, the poet, in 1775. Facing the East Gate is Jury Street the main thoroughfare through the town centre. The **Court House** on the corner with Castle Street, erected in 1725, is used for civic and social functions. High Street leads to the **West Gate**. It is strongly vaulted and formed part of the 12th-century fortifications. Above the gate is the tiny *Chapel of St. James*, built in 1123; it has a beautiful east window. The embattled tower dates from 1450. The chapel is now used by the inmates of the adjoining building—Lord Leycester Hospital.

Lord Leycester Hospital *(daily, fee)* is a picturesque building dating from the reign of Henry IV. In 1571, the Earl of Leycester donated it for use as a hospital to accommodate 12 old soldiers hurt in the wars. It is still in use as a home for retired or disabled ex-service-men and their wives. These "brethren" wear badges which are duplicates of those originally provided by Lord Leycester, and bear the names of the first holders and the date 1571. Inside the building are separate apartments for each brother and his wife, the *Great hall* and *Guildhall* (now a museum).

Bowling Green Street leads to the Market Place. In the Market Hall, con-structed in 1670, is the *Warwick Museum*, with collections on the history, natural history and archaeology of Warwick and the surrounding area.

Eastward is **St. Mary's Church,** with a commanding tower 174 feet high. This interesting building of Norman origin has a 12th-century crypt beneath the choir. A disastrous fire in 1694 destroyed much of the building. The Beauchamp Chapel, built 1443–64 is an architectural gem with beautiful carving and fan vaulting. It contains the rich tomb of Richard Beauchamp and interesting monuments including those to the family of Robert Dudley—the favourite of Queen Elizabeth I.

In Church Street is the Public Library; near by in Castle Street is the timber-framed *Oken's House,* an Elizabethan house now containing the Warwick Doll Museum, an interesting collection of dolls and clothing.

North-west of Warwick is a chain of interesting villages: **Hatton** has a church with a fine lychgate, a 15th-century tower and a west window of Flemish glass. Old Hatton House (1578) with Tudor chimneys, has been converted for cottagers on the estate. **Haseley** has a Norman church with medieval glass, unusual brasses on the tomb of the Throckmortons, ancient bells and a 15th-century font. At **Wroxall** is a splendid park, in which are the ruins of a 12th-century abbey. The large house which replaced an Elizabethan Manor is now a boarding school. **Baddesley Clinton** has an interesting church; the town, built about 1500, has a turret stairway and eight gargoyles. Baddesley Clinton Hall is a pre-Elizabethan family mansion in a lovely setting with an ancient gateway, a moat and a bridge. A mile north is **Temple Balsall** a manor given to the Knights Templars in the 12th century who built the splendid church. In 1863 after restoration by Sir Gilbert Scott it became a parish church. **Knowle,** two miles north-west of Temple Balsall is an attractive small town with interesting houses and a church with notable carvings. The ancient Guild House (1412) was well restored in 1912.

Leamington (Pop.: 45,000. Hotels: *Manor House, Regent, Clarendon, Apollo, Angel, Amersham, Park),* is a pleasant modern town and health spa on the river *Leam,* with wide, tree-lined avenues, riverside walks and pleasure grounds. Following the discovery of the medicinal value of its spring water, many Regency houses were built in the late 18th century. In 1813 the Pump Room was installed and Baths built to provide hydropathy and physiotherapy services, and swimming facilities. The Pump Room Gardens and Jephson Gardens, at either side of Victoria Bridge, are splendid riverside retreats with floral displays. Concerts are held at the Pump Room and the Town Hall (festival in June). In Avenue Road is the Library, Museum and Art Gallery *(daily, free)*. There is a cinema and facilities for various sports. All Saints' Church built 1843–96 has a tower, a beautiful east window and stone tracery.

Interesting villages in the neighbourhood include **Lillington** where an oak tree believed to be over 900 years old grows in a spot claimed to be the exact centre of England. **Cubbington,** two miles north-east of Lillington has an ancient church. **Offchurch,** three miles east of Leamington is traditionally linked with King Offa who founded the church. Three miles south is **Chesterton,** a Roman Camp on the Fosse Way. There is a remarkable stone windmill, erected in 1632 and an interesting church. Six miles east of Leamington is **Long Itchington,** noted for a picturesque village green and gabled half-timbered architecture. **Southam,** two miles south of Long Itchington has a 14th-century old Mint House—now an inn—and a half-timbered house where King Charles I slept on his way to Edge Hill. Five miles east of Southam are the **Shuckburghs.** The manor house at **Upper Shuckburgh** has been owned continuously by the Shuckburgh family since the 12th century. A pleasant excursion is to **Guy's Cliffe** and the *Saxon Mill,* set in beautiful scenery between Leamington and Warwick. According to legend, Guy of Warwick, an Earl of Saxon England, became a hermit, and built a cave in which he lived and died. The grounds, chapel and caves may be viewed on application at the lodge. Northward is the wooded height of *Blacklow Hill.* On the summit is a stone monument, surmounted by a cross to King Edward II's unpopular favourite Piers Gaveston, who was beheaded here in 1312.

Each of the roads radiating from Stratford, Leamington and Warwick pass through exceptional scenery or places of historical significance.

Compton Verney, mentioned in Sir Walter Scott's novel "Kenilworth", was acquired by the Verney family in the reign of Henry V. The present house, built in 1720, stands in a beautiful park, commanding fine views. Two miles away along the Banbury road is **Kineton**—originally the King's Town of Saxon times. In the town are ancient stone houses and a church with a beautiful doorway. Four miles south-east on the Banbury Road is **Edge Hill**—a ridge five miles long where the battle of Edge Hill was fought in 1642. The Round Tower (1750) on the summit of the hill is now the *Castle Inn* (teas) from which are splendid views.

Compton Wynyates, about 15 miles from Stratford, is a fine Tudor manor house *(Weds, Sats and Bank Hols: Suns, June to Aug., fee)*. The house—built between 1481 and 1515 has twisted chimneys, gables, turrets and battlemented walls. Inside are fine ceilings, a minstrel gallery, panelled rooms with pictures and family portraits. The chapel attached to the house was rebuilt about 1665.

On a hill above is *Compton Pike,* a stone spire erected about 1640, in which a light was placed to guide people to Compton. **Long Compton** village, a short distance south, has an ancient church and lychgate. A mile away on the Oxfordshire border, are the Rollright Stones—about 70 in number. They are probably of Druidical origin.

Banbury, famous for its "Nursery Rhyme" cross and cakes, is an ancient wool town. The cakes are still sold in a 17th-century cakeshop. The cross is modern, replacing the original destroyed by the Puritans.

Seven and a half miles north-east **Sulgrave Manor** *(daily except Fris, fee)*, the ancestral home of George Washington, attracts many American visitors. The House was built by Lawrence Washington in 1560, but was partly altered and rebuilt in 1920–30. It contains portraits and possessions of George Washington. In the 14th-century church are memorials and the arms of the Washington family.

Kenilworth—four and a half miles from Warwick or Leamington, is a straggling attractive village commanding roads in all directions.

It is famous for its **Castle** *(daily),* built in the reign of Henry I by his chamberlain, Geoffrey de Clinton (*c.* 1122). Within the following decades the Keep and the walls of the inner court were added. John of Gaunt, son of Edward III received the castle as part of his wife's dowry in the 14th century. He added the fine banqueting hall, state apartments and domestic quarters. In 1563, Queen Elizabeth conferred the Castle upon her favourite, Robert Dudley, Earl of Leicester, who enlarged the property. He built the great Northern Gate-House, and the Leicester Block with mullioned windows which can still be seen. Queen Elizabeth I paid several visits to Kenilworth, where she was entertained by Leicester on a scale of sumptuous magnificence. The Keep was partly destroyed in the Civil War by Cromwell's officers, who dismantled the towers, drained the lake and destroyed the park.

After the Restoration the Castle was never reoccupied. In 1937, it was presented to the nation by Sir John Siddely, later created Lord Kenilworth, and is preserved as a national monument.

Across the Abbey Fields is **St. Nicholas' Church,** dating from the 13th century. The Norman west-doorway displays exquisite carving. The windows, tower and spire are 14th century and the font is dated 1664.

The village of **Stoneleigh** two miles north-east has some attractive old houses and a 12th-century church. Stoneleigh Abbey is a seat of Lord Leigh.

West Midlands

RUGBY TO COVENTRY AND BIRMINGHAM

Rugby (Pop.: 59,370. Hotels: *Three Horse Shoes, Crescent, Grand*), is a busy engineering and railway centre twelve miles south-east of Coventry and best known for its famous public school.

The **School** was immortalized by one of its old boys, Thomas Hughes (1822–1896) in "Tom Brown's Schooldays". The school was founded in 1567 with a bequest of £100 left by Lawrence Sheriff, a local lad who won fame and fortune in the grocery trade in London. Famous past pupils include the poets Matthew Arnold (1822–1888), Arthur Hugh Clough (1819–1861) one of whose poems is "Say Not that the Struggle Naught Availeth", Rupert Brooke (1887–1915) and C. L. Dodgson (Lewis Carroll) (1832–1898). The present buildings have no great architectural distinction and date mostly from the early 1800s. Dr Thomas Arnold (1795–1842), father of Matthew, revolutionized English public school education while he was headmaster from 1818 to 1841 and produced many a great leader for the British empire. In the elm-lined area known as the Close there is a plaque on the Doctor's Wall commemorating one William Webb Ellis who in 1823 "with a fine disregard for the rules of football as played in his time" picked up the ball and ran with it thus inventing rugger. Dr Arnold's classroom is above the main gate. Across the quadrangle an iron-studded door leads to the dining room and the fireplace where the bully Flashman in Hughes's novel had young Brown "roasted".

The 19th-century chapel is a red-brick structure with a 16th-century stained glass window from Louvain depicting the Adoration of the Magi. There is also stained glass from Rouen in the transept. Dr Arnold is buried beneath the chancel steps, his grave marked by a simple slab bearing his name and a cross. In the south transept there is a "poets' corner" dedicated to Arnold, Clough, Brooke and Carroll. Brooke died during the First World War on the Greek island of Skiros where he lies buried in an olive grove. The house where he was born is in Rugby at 5, Hillmorton Road. The Carroll memorial features the Mad Hatter, the March Hare and other members of that company in "Alice in Wonderland".

Newbold on Avon, north-west of Rugby and reached along the B4112 has an unusual collection of statues of the Boughton family in its parish church which date from the 16th and 17th centuries. Note Thomas Newbould, doughty warrior armed with two swords and his dog at his feet.

The road (A428) from Rugby to Coventry passes through **Church Lawford** where the church has 300-year-old woodcarvings such as the sea-serpents on the pulpit. At **Binley**, just before Coventry, is a church designed by the Adam brothers dubbed by some for its lightness as in "the ballroom style". From Binley it is only a mile to the north for **Coombe Abbey** which stands on an old Cistercian site. Its gables and tall chimneys can be seen from the road. The building was erected mainly in the Elizabethan age.

Coventry (Pop.: 334,840. Hotels: *Leofric, Allesley, Smithfield, Bradford, Beechwood*), is one of England's most ancient cities. It prospered in the Middle Ages with its cloth industry and is now a major centre for the manufacture of motor vehicles. The city's centre was almost completely destroyed in a fierce air raid on the night of 14 November 1940. The area has now been largely rebuilt within an elevated ring road. The history of Coventry begins with the Benedictine priory founded in 1043 by Leofric, Earl of Mercia. His wife, Godgyfu, or Godiva, has come down in legend as having ridden naked through Coventry to induce her husband to relent on the severe taxation he had imposed on its citizens. There is a statue of Godiva on her horse in the gardens of Broadgate,

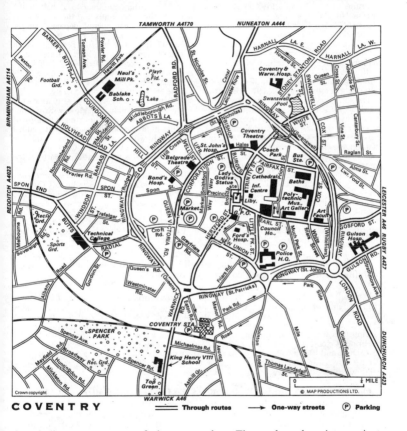

COVENTRY ═══ Through routes → One-way streets Ⓟ Parking

the rebuilt centre, an area of pleasant gardens. The modern shopping precinct lies on the west side of Broadgate. To the east there is a view of two of Coventry's famous spires. The nearest belongs to Holy Trinity and is 237 feet high. The taller rises to 303 feet and belongs to what was the parish Church of St. Michael which was destroyed in the great raid. This spire is the third-tallest in England after Salisbury and Norwich. and dates from the 14th century. The third spire away to the south rises to 204 feet and was part of Christ Church which was also destroyed in the raid.

COVENTRY CATHEDRAL

Holy Trinity is in the Perpendicular style. The roof and tower lantern date from 1667 and there is a 15th-century stone pulpit inside. *Christ in Majesty*, a window by Hugh Easton, was designed in 1955. William Siddons married Sarah Kemble in this church in 1773.

The Cathedral. The magnificent new Cathedral in the heart of Coventry has risen beside the ruins of the old one. Five bombs reduced the 14th-century building to a shell in the terrible November air raid of 1940 and since then only the outer walls and the magnificent tower still stand. The modern-day Cathedral, designed by Sir Basil Spence, departs from the old tradition and is built of pink Hallington sandstone. Entrance is by a door in the magnificent West Screen of glass engraved by John Hutton. The interior is brilliant with colour. On the far wall is the enormous tapestry designed by Graham Sutherland, a masterpiece in vibrant green, brilliant yellow and fiery red which entailed over 30,000 hours in the making. To the right is John Piper's glorious Baptistry window with its colours radiating from a central point of white and gold. Beneath the window is the font hewn from a Bethlehem hillside. To the left is the entrance to the star-shaped *Chapel of Unity*.

The full glory of the nave windows is best seen from the choir stalls. Five pairs of tall windows on each side representing the development of Christian life glow with colour. The 80-foot high ceiling is very fine, with slender concrete columns supporting a canopy of concrete lattice ribs and slatted spruce panels. On the high altar is the magnificent guilded cross designed by Geoffrey Clarke. Made in silver overlaid with gold and weighing a quarter of a ton, the cross is shaped like a bird on the wing. In the centre is a small "Cross of Nails", the symbol of Coventry Cathedral's Ministry of International Reconciliation. Nearby is the impressive lectern made from satin-finish bronze and Afrormosia wood. The fine cast-bronze eagle surmounting it is by Elizabeth Frink. Beneath the tapestry is the *Lady Chapel* and, adjoining, the beautiful little *Chapel of Christ in Gethsemane*. A symbolic Crown of Thorns dominates this quiet corner. The *Chapel of Christ the Servant*—now known as the Chapel of Industry is circular and has tall glass windows with a centrepiece comprising an aluminium cross surrounded by a Crown of Thorns.

Outside is the massive bronze sculpture of St. Michael, patron saint of the Cathedral, defeating the devil. This sculpture, by Sir Jacob Epstein, is near St. Michael's porch which links the 14th-century and 20th-century buildings.

South of the cathedral is **St. Mary's Hall,** the city's old Guildhall, a mellowed building in soft red sandstone dating from the 1300's.

The vaulted porch, reached through an entrance arch, covers a carving of the Coronation of the Virgin and another of the Annunciation. There are other carvings but they have been blurred by time and erosion. The 14th-century kitchen is still partly used for its original purpose. Note the statue on the window sill: Henry VI. Nearby is a whipping post with a carving of a weird, grinning human figure. Above the kitchen is the Great Hall with the celebrated Coventry Tapestry, an example of early 16th-century Flemish work. The tapestry is 36 feet long and 10 feet wide. The six panels portray various saints including John the Baptist, Peter, George and Mary Magdalene, all in Tudor dress. The hall also has a 15th-century window with nine lights, each showing a king.

Outside the Hall, Jordan Well leads to the **Herbert Art Gallery and Museum.** In the entrance is a 1920 Alvis motor car and other locally produced goods such as a gold watch of 1690 and a 13th-century face pitcher. On the upper floor the exhibits include a bust by Jacob Epstein and a painting by the landscapist David Cox.

To the west of St. Mary's Hall, High Street leads to Greyfriars Lane and *Ford's Hospital,* founded as an old peoples' home in 1509. The two-storey timbered building has a 40-foot frontage and stands on a stone base.

Southwards from Jordan Well are the cloisters, chapter house and dormitory of *Whitefriars,* a Carmelite friary founded in 1342. The foundations of the church were found in 1962 and indicated that the building was 300 feet long, the largest of its order in England.

North of Jordan Well rises the residential tower block of **Lanchester College of Technology,** a branch of Warwick University. Going north along Priory Lane and left into Fairfax Street one comes to Hales Street where a section of the old city wall and two gates can be seen.

Meriden, six miles west of Coventry was regarded as the traditional centre of England and an oak tree planted in the village green marks the spot. The tree commemorates the opening of the by-pass (A45) "whereby Meriden became a village again". From the church on the hill there are views of the hills of Staffordshire, Worcestershire and Shropshire. The church is mainly 14th and 15th century but the chancel is Norman. A piece of early vandalism can be seen on the effigy of a knight: the initials M. H. and the date 1676.

At Stone Bridge a right turn leads to **Coleshill,** beyond the M6. This small town has kept several medieval characteristics such as the five-arched bridge and the grim pillory, whipping post and stocks. The church on the hill dates from the 14th century but the font is Norman. There various effigies of the Digby family and a crucifixion scene on the seven lights of the east window.

About a mile to the east of Coleshill is **Maxstoke Castle,** built in 1346 by the De Clinton family. It has one of the largest barns in England. Richard III spent the night here before his death on the battlefield at Bosworth. Among the interesting objects on display are a pair of stockings that belonged to Queen Elizabeth I. They are salmon pink and have minuscule feet.

From Coleshill join the M6 at Junction 5 and leave it at Junction 6 for **Erdington** in the Birmingham suburbs. Here is situated Warwickshire's oldest inn *The Green Man,* opened in 1306 and considered the 9th oldest in England.

Birmingham

Distances.—Coventry, 18; Derby, 40; Evesham, 30; Gloucester, 53; Hereford, 52; Leicester, 39; Lichfield, 16; London, 110; Nuneaton, 22; Shrewsbury, 43; Stafford, 27; Stratford-upon-Avon, 24; Warwick, 21; Worcester, 27.

Early Closing.—Wednesday/Saturday.

Entertainment.—*Alexandra Theatre,* Suffolk Street; *Repertory Theatre,* Station Street; *Birmingham Theatre,* Hurst Street; *Crescent Theatre,* Cumberland Street. Many cinemas. Night clubs and dancing. Town Hall (concerts: Birmingham Symphony Orchestra; organ recitals). City Art Gallery (concerts).

Hotels.—*Albany, Midland, Royal Angus, Arden,* *Apollo, Cobden, Norfolk, Imperial Centre, Wheatsheaf Motel, Excelsior Airport,* and others.

Population.—1,103,366.

Post Office.—Victoria Square.

Sports.—Almost every sporting pastime is catered for with many clubs available. Many swimming baths and lido at Stechford. Tennis in parks. and clubs. Warwickshire Cricket Ground, Edgbaston. Ice rink, roller skating, bowling. Greyhound racing. Association football: *Birmingham City* (St. Andrews), *Aston Villa* (Villa Park), *West Bromwich Albion* (Hawthorns). Municipal and private golf courses.

Birmingham, Britain's second city and famed as "the workshop of the world" lies at the heart of a nexus of highways which include the motorway interchange point at Gravelly Hill aptly nicknamed "Spaghetti Junction" from its writhing appearance seen from the air. Birmingham is Britain's foremost metal-working city and its industrial fame is worldwide. It has more than 1,200 industries which produce, among other things, pen-nibs, marine engines, turbines, motor cars and bicycles. It is difficult to believe that this huge city was overshadowed by Coventry until the late 1700s when Birmingham suddenly became one of the hotbeds of the Industrial Revolution. For this reason the city has few really old parts. One of these is the roadway in the south-eastern central district that begins as Deritend and becomes Digbeth which leads to the Bull Ring. In Digbeth is the *Old Crown House,* a crooked inn dating from the Middle Ages. The **Bull Ring,** once a lively livestock market place, is a mighty centre of trade with its complex of multi-level, air-conditioned supermarkets, car parks and pedestrian precincts all dominated by the *Rotunda,* a lofty cylindrical office block. Dwarfed by it all is the Church of St. Martin.

St. Martin's Church was rebuilt in 1875 to the original plan of the 1300s. The two statues in niches in the 200-foot tower are of Richard the Lionheart and St. Martin giving half of his cloak to a beggar. The hammer-beam roof in the nave is a copy of the ancient one in Westminster Hall, London. Inside the church the funerary statues include a fine representation of Sir William Bermyngham who is believed to have built the original church. In the south transept there is a beautiful window designed by Sir Edward Burne-Jones (1833–1898), the pre-Raphaelite painter born in Birmingham. The window was made by William Morris (1834–1896).

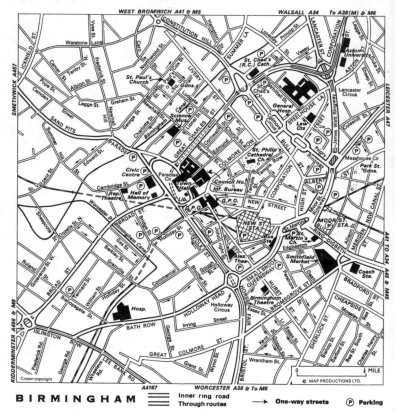

BIRMINGHAM — Inner ring road / Through routes · → One-way streets · Ⓟ Parking

Corporation Street and New Street are the traditional shopping streets with many fine shops and stores. In New Street is the fine Hudson's Bookshop. At the far end of New Street is **Victoria Square,** the geographical centre of the city.

The **Town Hall,** a massive neo-classical pile, a copy of the Temple of Jupiter Stator in Rome, dominates Victoria Square. Designed by E. Welch and Joseph Hansom (of Hansom cab fame) construction began in 1832. The 40 Corinthian columns are each 36 feet tall. In the Great Hall is one of England's finest organs. It was in this hall that the composer Felix Mendelssohn conducted the first performance of his oratorio *Elijah* in 1846. Outside the hall stands Brock's statue of Queen Victoria (1899) and a statue of James Watt (1736–1819) by Alexander Munro. Watt developed his steam engine in Birmingham.

On the south side of Victoria Square in the **General Post Office,** is a statue of Sir Rowland Hill (1795–1879), originator of the penny post and the son of a Birmingham man.

The **Council House** on the north side of the square is an English Victorian interpretation of Italian High Renaissance. The fore section with the dome was built in 1874. The clock tower is 160 feet tall and known locally as "Big Brum". The rear section of the building was added in 1919. On the upper floors is the **Corporation Art Gallery and Museum** one of the finest collections in England. Two local artists, Burne-Jones and David Cox, are honoured with fine collections. There are also paintings by Botticelli, Guardi, Hogarth, Pissarro, Sisley and Sutherland. There are sculptures by Donatello and Rodin.

From Victoria Square Colmore Row leads to central Birmingham's only sizeable piece of greenery, the yard of **St. Philip's Cathedral.** The church was built in 1715 as parish church by Thomas Archer. The four beautiful windows, designed by Burne-Jones, who was born nearby and christened in the church, and made by Morris, depict the Nativity, the Crucifixion, the Ascension and the Last Judgment.

On the west side of the Town Hall is the new **Central Library** which has more than a million volumes and many relics of Watt, including the old leather bag in which he carried his lunch.

Further technical exhibits can be seen at the **Science and Industry Museum** in Newhall Street to the north of Victoria Square. The exhibits include ancient steam engines and the motor car in which John Cobb reached 400 miles an hour in 1947.

In Edgbaston, in the south-western outskirts of the city, stands the Roman Catholic **Oratory of St. Philip Neri.** It was established in 1847 by Cardinal Newman (1801–1890) and is a memorial to him. The mosaics were laid by Italian craftsmen and depict the Coronation of Mary and St. John the Baptist and St. John the Evangelist. The marble pillars supporting the nave are each 18 feet tall and made from single blocks of Italian marble.

Birmingham University lies south of Edgbaston and three miles south of the city centre. The University was incorporated in 1900 and houses the Barber Institute of Fine Arts. Here can be seen a magnificent collection of sculptures by Della Robbia, Rodin and Degas as well as paintings by Bellini, Rembrandt, Constable, Turner, Gauguin and Toulouse-Lautrec.

Also in Edgbaston are the **Botanical Gardens** which are more than 100 years old and considered second only to Kew Gardens for their specimens of trees and plants. On view are a magnificent alpine garden, aviaries and a zoo.

Birmingham's second university is at **Aston** in the northern part of the city. Nearby is **Aston Hall** *(daily, Suns in summer only),* a red-brick Jacobean mansion built between 1618 and 1635. It has fine plaster-work ceilings, sumptuous carved fireplaces and a majestic grand staircase.

Blakesley Hall, four miles east of Birmingham, is a half-timbered house built in 1575 and housing a museum of local history.

Bournville, four miles south of Birmingham, is an example of capitalist benevolence toward the workers. This is a chocolate factory set in garden surroundings. It was built by the Cadbury family in 1879 and has served as a model for municipal housing and welfare. The Day school has a carillon of 42 bells ranging from sopranos weighing 15 pounds to basses of two tons. Selly Manor and Minworth Greaves are 14th-century houses brought to Bournville and re-erected to embellish the already pleasant surroundings. The latter has an enormous oak table 22 feet long.

COVENTRY TO NUNEATON

A mile north-west of Coventry is **Wicken** where, amid the factories built over an old coalfield, is a church with a 14th-century tower and a Norman west door. The unusual feature of the church is the huge mural painting of the late 1400s that was discovered in 1956 behind a layer of plaster which had concealed it since 1547. The painting is on the north wall and shows St. Christopher carrying the infant Christ on his shoulder across a stream against a stiff breeze. Note also the late 16th-century Flemish carved chair with its two winged men carrying knapsacks and riding dragons.

Bedworth, three miles north of Coventry, marks the beginning of the north Warwickshire coalfield. Only the tower remains of the 15th-century church, the rest having been rebuilt in the late 1800s and the almshouses about a century before.

Chilvers Coton is in the heart of the country associated with George Eliot, the pseudonym of Marian Evans (1819–1880) author of such great novels as *Adam Bede, Silas Marner* and *The Mill on the Floss*. She was born at South Farm, Arbury, two miles south-west. The place is marked with a blue obelisk. Chilvers Coton Church where the authoress was christened was almost entirely destroyed in an air raid in May 1941. German prisoners-of-war volunteered to rebuilt it and finished the task in 1946. The new font was made from the shattered pillars of the old church. Eliot's parents are buried in the church just south of the figure of *Resurrected Christ*.

Arbury Hall *(Easter–Oct., Suns and Bank Hols, Mons and Tues, fee)*, which appears as Cheveral Manor in Eliot's writings, is the grey stone mansion of the Newdegate family who owned the estate on which the authoress was brought up. The exterior is Gothic of the late 1700s. Inside the outer structure and its battlements is an Elizabethan house. Sir Christopher Wren designed the stables with the sundial over them bearing the legend "Life's but a walking shadow" as well as the great porch. The saloon has a magnificent ceiling of fan-vaulting based on that of the chapel of Henry VII at Westminster Abbey in London. There is also a painting of the young St. John the Baptist by Sir Joshua Reynolds and a Newdegate family portrait by George Romney. See also the fine oak carvings in the chapel by Grinling Gibbons.

Nuneaton is a manufacturing town producing bricks, textiles and hats. *St. Mary's Church* in Manor Court Road has the remains of a 12th-century Benedictine nunnery from which Nuneaton obtains the prefix to its name. The church was built in 1878 but has four massive granite Norman piers supporting the old tower. The piers are carved with grotesques and foliage at their base. Much of the old nunnery was depredated during the Middle Ages for building stone. Relics include a huge stone coffin with a carved cross. Henry VIII granted the nunnery to Sir Marmaduke Constable whose effigy rests at the parish church.

St Nicholas Church originated in the 1200s but much of the outer structure was built a century later. It is in Early English style and stands amid clipped yew trees. The nave roof is very handsome with panels and carvings, some going back 500 years. Corbels of heads and foliage decorate the high arch to the chancel. The reredos has canopied saints and angels. St. Nicholas is one of the niched figures at the altar and appears again on the carved pulpit. The figure of Sir Marmaduke Constable is in a recess in the chancel. He is dressed in the armour of the 1560s. At his feet there are a lion and a helmet with a sailing ship as its crest. In the church grounds there is a memorial garden to George Eliot.

NUNEATON TO ATHERSTONE

The road (A444) passes **Weddington,** a northern suburb of Nuneaton. The church was first built in the 13th century but was extensively altered in 1733 and 1881. The north transept, which is part of the original building, has a modern oak screen carved with birds and foliage. Two ancient features are the painting of the Crucifixion and the 12th-century font.

Caldecote, about a mile north, lies close to the Leicestershire border and is a pleasant village of charming cottages, a small church and the remains of a great house. *Caldecote Hall* is now an apartment block but it was formerly the home of the Purefroy family. The only relic of the old mansion is the oak door, now in the church nearby. The door with massive hinges believed to have been made in the 1200s is pitted with bullet marks.

At **Mancetter,** on the southern fringe of Atherstone, is a wealth of slate tombstones in the churchyard offering a broad anthology of verse epitaphs. The church is mainly 13th century and has a brilliant east window 600 years old. There are memorials to two martyrs, a man and a woman, who died at the stake in the reign of Mary Tudor in 1555 and 1557. The description of the sublime manner in which these two tragic persons underwent their final torment is most moving.

Atherstone is an old market town strategically situated in relation to certain major centres of England. A sign outside the *Red Lion Inn* gives the distance to London as 100 miles—the same as to Liverpool and Lincoln. Hat-making was the chief industry and the town still produces headgear, though no longer for the slave trade as it once did. The parish church is mostly modern but the chancel is 14th century. It was in the chancel that Harry Richmond, later Henry VII, took communion before his victory at Bosworth Field which brought him the crown of England. The 15th-century east window depicts the Crucifixion, the Annunciation and other New Testament scenes.

From Atherstone the B4116 passes through Leicestershire before re-entering Warwickshire at **Grendon,** a peaceful village with a 14th-century church ornate with intricately carved oak. There is a 17th-century canopied pew with a figure of Mercury holding a staff in one hand and a falcon in the other.

Polesworth, about two miles along the road, is a mining town and the birthplace of Michael Drayton, a poet who was a contemporary of Shakespeare but never achieved wide fame. The church has a Norman arcade and eight Norman windows. The female effigy in the tomb of Sir Richard Harthill is thought to be Sara de Manchester, head of the Abbey here in the 1200s. The effigy is regarded as the oldest stone sculpture in England.

North of Polesworth follow the sign to **Austrey** where the delicate broach spire of the 14th-century church can be seen through the trees before the village itself becomes visible.

Newton Regis, the most northerly parish in Warwickshire, is named after Henry II. Charles I prayed at the altar before fighting the Cromwellians at nearby Seckington. The gold and blue altar frontal was first laid on the altar at Westminster Abbey in London. The occasion was the planned coronation of Edward VII which was stopped through the king's illness.

Sutton Coldfield, 13 miles to the south-west, is reached along the A453 which passes through part of Staffordshire. Sutton Park is 2,400 acres of heather, gorse and woods. Henry VIII gave the land to John Vesey who was born in Sutton in 1452 and became Bishop of Exeter, served Henry at the Field of the Cloth of Gold and was tutor to Mary Tudor. Vesey died at the age of 102 and his effigy is in Sutton Coldfield Parish Church. The track that runs alongside the western side of Sutton Park is the Icknield Way built by the Romans. The Parish Church is Early English and is rich in elaborate decoration such as the 24 carved angels in the nave roof. There is a Norman font and many oak carvings such as the 17th-century Italian choir seats and the 18th-century pulpit.

Old Moor Hall once was the residence of the Bishops of Lichfield. *New Hall,* one-and-a-half miles south-east, dates from the 1200s despite its name.

SOLIHULL TO KENILWORTH

Solihull is a pleasant town now generally regarded as a residential suburb of Birmingham. The school was founded by Edward VI in 1560. Dr Samuel Johnson applied for the post of master here. He was refused because of his grotesque manner and uncouth appearance. Instead the Doctor went off to London where he found much greater fame. The Manor House in the high street is Tudor and serves as a meeting place for various Solihull organizations. Solihull church is dedicated to St. Alphege, an early Archbishop of Canterbury martyred by the Danes. The spire is 168 feet tall and has a peal of 10 bells. The chancel was built in the 13th century. St. Alphege himself is buried in one of the five chapels and his martyrdom is portrayed in a window. Beneath the St. Alphege Chapel in the vaulted crypt is a pre-Reformation altar stone. The pulpit is Jacobean and there is a 15th-century stained-glass window in the transept.

From Solihull the B4102 leads to **Hampton-in-Arden,** a pleasantly situated village with a 15th-century packhorse bridge of five arches spanning the river *Blithe.* On an eastern pier there are the remains of a cross marking the parish boundary with the initials H.B. The church, situated on a hill, was built in Norman times. The nave arches are 700 years old, the base of the tower 14th-century and the windows a century later. Note the wasp-waisted font and the stone seat at the south wall probably dating from the late 1200s. The spire of the steeple was destroyed by lightning in 1643. The clock is 17th century but no longer functioning. The east window commemorates Elizabeth Peel, daughter-in-law of the Prime Minister Sir Robert Peel, and a niece of the poet Shelley. The window portrays the poets Langland, Chaucer, Shakespeare, Milton, Dryden, Cowper and Shelley.

Berkswell, two miles south-east, derives its name from the stone tank at the church gate. This was probably used for christenings. The village stocks are curious in that they have an odd number of ankle holes. Local legend has it that one notorious village wrongdoer was one-legged. The church has a Norman nave arcade. The carvings include one of Hugh Latimer, the bishop burned at the stake in the reign of Mary Tudor. The *Bear Inn* has a Russian gun captured in the Crimean War, brought to the village and fired before a ceremonial dinner that cost the participants 3s. 6d. each.

Bickenhill, about a mile to the north of Hampton-in-Arden, has a church with some rare 13th-century glass, a sculptured stone screen and a timbered roof previously concealed behind a layer of plaster.

Staffordshire

Staffordshire is renowned mainly for its industries such as the Potteries in the north where the fine products of Stoke, Burslem and other centres are exported throughout the world and locks and keys of Wolverhampton in the south. The county also has coal mines and engineering industries and the southern portion forms part of that powerhouse of industry known as the Black Country.

However the county is not entirely without stretches of open country. The Dovedale region on the border with Derbyshire is an area of great beauty. Cannock Chase is a fine tract of woodlands and heath. There are many attractive small market towns, pretty villages and the old cathedral city of Lichfield.

LEEK TO UTTOXETER AND RUGELEY

Leek (Pop.: 19,370. Hotel: *Three Horse Shoes*), on a hillside amid fine scenery is regarded as the moorland capital. The town manufactures silk, an industry brought here by the Huguenots in the 1600s. To the north the stony outcrop known as *The Roches* rises to 1,500 feet. St. Edward's Church has a 14th-century tower. The cross beams in the nave roof are each made from a single oak trunk. A Saxon cross stands in the churchyard. The Market Place has several interesting 18th-century houses.

The remains of the *Dieulacresse Abbey* lie about one-and-a-half miles to the north. This former Cistercian monastery is believed to have been founded in 1214 by Ranulph, Earl of Chester, a renowned crusader who served with Richard the Lionheart and is mentioned in *Piers Plowman*.

Some three miles north-west of Leek is **Rudyard Lake,** a reservoir after whom the celebrated writer Rudyard Kipling was named. His parents went for long walks in the vicinity during their courtship.

Flash, about seven miles north of Leek along the A53, has a unique characteristic and a curious history. It is the highest village in England being 1,525 feet above sea level and often cut off by snowdrifts in winter. It derives its name from a 19th-century word meaning fake coins. Its position near the border with Cheshire and Derbyshire made it a favourite haunt of counterfeiters fleeing the attentions of legal officials who did not have the authority to cross the county boundaries and arrest the criminals.

South of Leek is **Cheadle** which has some attractive timbered and gabled Tudor houses at the Market Cross and a fine Roman Catholic church designed by A. W. Pugin and completed in 1846. The red-stone church is in the Decorated style and has a 200-foot spire. The triptych in the north aisle depicting the last days of Christ is by a Flemish craftsman of the 15th century.

To the east of Cheadle, overlooking the Churnet Valley, is a nature reserve on Hawksmoor. This comprises 250 acres overgrown with wild flowers and plants and frequented by many species of wildlife.

On the A50 is **Checkley,** a village with a church first built in the 1200s and with a 15th-century tower. In the churchyard are three shafts of Saxon crosses each five feet high. The chancel windows include scenes of seasonal tasks such as netting, pruning, hay-making and feeding the pigs.

Uttoxeter (Pop.: 9,034. Hotel: *White Hart*), is an old market town with farm machinery manufacturers and a racecourse. Dr Johnson in his later life did penance in the market square for an earlier disobedience to his father. The town is also the birthplace of Mary Howitt (*b.* 1804), authoress of many children's stories and who collaborated with her husband William Howitt in writing *The Literature and Romance of Northern Europe* published in 1852. The parish church dates from 1350 with a re-modelling in neo-Gothic style in 1828.

The B5013 south passes **Abbots Bromley** known for its Horn Dance which takes place every year in early September to celebrate some old hunting rights. The road crosses Blithfield Reservoir an attractive lake created in 1953 by damming the river *Blithe*.

Blithfield Hall *(Easter–Sept., daily, fee)*, is a fine Elizabethan house with Georgian and Gothic additions, the home of the Bagot family. There is a fine carved 17th-century staircase. On display is a satin cap embroidered in gold and silver thread which Charles I once wore. The Paradise Room contains a collection of toys used by successive generations of Bagot children. The church nearby dates from the 1200s and 20 generations of Bagots lie buried there.

B5013 continues to **Rugeley,** a pleasant town in the Trent Valley backed by the hills of Cannock Chase. Rugeley has an interesting old church, much reduced since it was first built in the 1300s but still used as a place of worship.

In the yard of the Parish Church, built in 1822, is a headstone to John Parsons Cook whose "life was taken away" in 1855. Cook was one of the victims of the notorious poisoner William Palmer (1824–1856). Palmer attended Rugeley Grammar School and worked as an apprentice to a druggist in Liverpool. He returned to Rugeley and practised medicine at a house opposite the *Talbot Arms*.

DUDLEY TO LICHFIELD AND BURTON-UPON-TRENT

Dudley (Pop.: 185,535. Hotels: *Station, Ward Arms*), is dominated by the ruins of its castle on the hill. The gatehouse is Norman and there is a Norman arch in one of the walls. The courtyard, approached through three gatehouses and a barbican, is surrounded by a 14th-century wall which is eight feet thick in places. The stable area is 17th century, the chapel 14th and the great hall with its mullioned windows is Tudor. From the keep there is a view of seven English counties. There is a well stocked zoo in the castle grounds. Dudley's oldest church is St. Edmund's, built in 1724. The ruins of a Cluniac priory dating from the 1200s are located west of the castle.

West Bromwich, three miles east of Dudley, is a metal-working town but there is a fine Tudor building known as Oak House which has survived the tide of modern industry. The house is south-west of the town centre and dates from the early 1500s. It has an unusual lantern turret and a fine cluster of Tudor chimneys. The house is open to visitors and contains period furniture and fine panelling.

Taking the A461 from Dudley we come to **Wednesbury** which is believed to be the site of a battle between the Saxons and the British in 592. Farther on is **Walsall,** an old town with many handsome parks some of them reclaimed from waste ground left by disused collieries. The town hall was built in 1902 in the Renaissance style. In Bradford Street a tablet marks the house where the writer

Jerome K. Jerome, author of the humorous classic *Three Men in a Boat* (1859–1927) was born. Dorothy Pattison (1832–1878) who won the town's love and respect for her nursing work under the name of Sister Dora is remembered by the bronze statue on a granite pillar at the bridge. There is also a statue and a stained glass window to her in St. Matthew's Church. The church is situated on a hill from which there are views of Cannock Chase and the Wrekin. The church tower is 15th-century but the nave was rebuilt in 1821. The spire dates from 1951. The nave arcades are in cast iron.

There is an art gallery in Lichfield Street and nearby, in the Central Library, a museum of leathercraft.

Lichfield lies ten miles along the A461 past **Rushall** where the ruins of the old hall still show signs from the cannon balls fired at it during a Civil War attack in 1643 led by Prince Rupert. **Wall,** reached by turning right on to the A5 at Muckley Corner, was the Roman *Letocetum* and has the remains of Roman baths.

Lichfield (Pop.: 22,670. Hotel: *Angel Croft*), has two claims to fame—its cathedral and Dr Samuel Johnson (1709–1784), who was born here. His statue stands in the market place together with that of his illustrious biographer James Boswell (1740–1795). The Johnson Museum on the corner of Market Street marks the doctor's birthplace. The museum has many important relics and a major library of Johnsoniana. Nearby is the birthplace of another distinguished son of this cathedral city, Elias Ashmole (1617–1692), marked with a tablet. Ashmole bequeathed his collection of scientific rarities to Oxford where they are now housed in the Ashmolean Museum.

Lichfield market place saw the burning of the last man in England for heresy. He was Edward Wightman and he perished at the stake in 1612. George Fox, founder of the Society of Friends—the Quakers—(1624–1691) stood in the market place and condemned Lichfield for its "sinfulness" when he was released from prison in 1651.

From the market square, Dam Street leads to the cathedral. An antiques shop marks the Dame's school where Dr Johnson learned to read and write. In Bore Street are the Guildhall and the David Garrick Theatre. Bore Street leads into St. John Street with its Grammar School attended by Ashmole, Garrick, Johnson and Addison. Opposite is St. John's Hospital built in 1495 by Bishop William Smyth who also founded Brasenose College, Oxford.

The **Cathedral** is probably the finest example of a small medieval cathedral in England. Dedicated to St. Mary and St. Chad it is distinguished by its three spires known as the Ladies of the Vale. The central spire is believed to be the work of Sir Christopher Wren. The cathedral is built of red sandstone quarried from Borrowcop Hill half a mile to the south-east. Much of the church's interior was badly damaged during the ravages of the Civil War from 1643 to 1646. The west front was begun in 1275 but only five statues of the original 113 remain. They are in the top row of the north-west tower. The remainder date from the 1800s.

Inside the cathedral there is an uninterrupted view for 370 feet beneath the lofty nave arches as far as the 14th-century **Lady Chapel,** resplendent in Decorated style. The chapel's seven east windows contain 16th-century glass from the Cistercian Abbey of Herkenrode in Belgium. The two west windows are of Flemish glass brought to Britain after the French Revolution and kept in storage until bought for the cathedral in 1895. There is also some Herkenrode glass in the choir aisles. Much of the other glass in the cathedral is modern as in St. Stephen's Chapel.

Approaching the Lady Chapel one sees on the right the lovely sculpture by Sir Francis Chantrey (1817) known as "The Sleeping Children". This memorial to the children of a Cathedral cleric who perished in a fire in 1812 is the finest of Chantrey's early works. The statue of Bishop Ryder, who died in 1836, situated opposite in the north aisle, is also by Chantrey and one of his last sculptures.

The ten-sided **Chapter House** on the north side was built in 1249 and has a finely vaulted roof. The **Library** contains rare bibles, manuscripts and the 7th-century St. Chad's Gospels. There is also a copy of South's sermons which has been marked by Dr. Johnson who used it while compiling his famous dictionary. The **Sacristy** on the south side is reached through a minstrel gallery. On the upper floor is the simply decorated **Chapel of St. Chad** dating from 1225. From here relics of the saint were displayed to the faithful gathered below. **St. Stephen's Chapel** in the north transept, was built in about 1230. It was once used as an organ loft. **St. Michael's Chapel** in the south transept serves as a war memorial with busts of Johnson and Garrick.

The Bishop's Palace in the Cathedral Close was built in 1687 and is now a choir school.

From Lichfield the A38 to Burton-upon-Trent passes near **Barton-under-Needwood,** birthplace of John Taylor. Taylor, one of triplets born to a poor family, became private secretary to Henry VIII and later Master of the Rolls. He presented the church built in 1517. Inside the Taylor coat-of-arms displays three infant boys' heads representing the triplets.

Burton-upon-Trent (Pop.: 50,175. Hotel. *Midland*), is renowned for its beer and more than three million barrels of the beverage are produced every year. Brewing has been carried on here on a major scale since the 1700s. The celebrated "clear water" used is drawn from deep wells in nearby gravel pits. The bronze statue opposite the Town Hall is of Michael Bass, the brewer whom Prime Minister Gladstone created Lord Burton. In Guild Street there is a museum with British and Roman exhibits. Very little is left of the abbey founded before the Norman Conquest. It stood near the Church of St. Modwen which was rebuilt in 1726. The font dates from 1662 and comes from the previous church as does a large 16th-century chest.

WOLVERHAMPTON TO THE POTTERIES

Wolverhampton (Pop.:' 268,850. Hotels: *Connaught, Mount, Fox, Park Hall, Castlecroft* and others), is the chief town of the Black Country, an extensive area of coal and iron production. Producing all manner of hardware it has long been famous for its locks. The town is named after Wulfruna, sister of Edgar II. She founded a church here in 994.

Near Queen Square on a wooded hill is the **Church of St. Peter.** The tower is 15th century and rests on 13th-century arches. The church has a notable octagonal font and pulpit, both carved and both 15th century. The west gallery was built in 1610. There is a tomb to John Lane (*d.* 1667) who helped Charles II escape after the battle of Worcester. In the south transept is a good bronze statue of Admiral Sir Richard Leveson by Le Sueur. In the churchyard is the *Dane's Cross* a 12 foot-high carved stone shaft believed to date from the 9th century.

In nearby Lichfield Street the **Art Gallery and Museum** has enamels and pottery as well as paintings by Romney, Gainsborough, Turner, Cox and Morland. West of St. Peter's is the **Town Hall** built in 1870 and the **Civic Hall** built in 1938.

Moseley Old Hall (N.T., *Mar.–Nov., Weds, Thurs, Sats, Suns and Bank Hol. Mons and Tues, fee*), four miles north, is a fine Elizabethan house where Charles II went into hiding after the battle of Worcester.

Penkridge, nine miles north of Wolverhampton, is worth a visit for its 13th-century church with its memorials of the Littleton family complete with wives and multitudes of children.

Eastward from the road lies **Cannock Chase,** the largest stretch of unspoilt countryside in the county. The Chase comprises 50 square miles of moors which rise to 500 feet above sea level. The Staffordshire coalfield lies under the northern tip of the Chase and Cannock is a mining town. The Chase was the hunting ground of the Mercian kings and was also the haunt of wolves and the hiding place of outlaws.

Stafford (Pop.: 54,890. Hotels: *Swan, Vine*), the county town is an ancient place dating from the days of the Mercian kingdom in the 700s. It has associations with Henry VII who stayed here on his way to wage battle with Richard III at Bosworth Field and win the crown of England. Another monarch to visit the town was Queen Elizabeth I who accepted the gift of a silver cup from the citizens. Stafford is the birthplace of Izaak Walton (1593–1683), the genial author of *The Compleat Angler*. The Irish-born dramatist R. B. Sheridan, author of *The Rivals* and *The School for Scandal* was member of parliament for Stafford from 1780 to 1806. Footwear is the main industry of the town, a trade of which Sheridan made the celebrated epigram "May the trade of Stafford be trod underfoot by all the world".

Greengate Street has several buildings of architectural and historical interest. *High House,* a four-storey, gabled, half-timbered house, was built in 1555. Charles I lived here in 1642 while he was raising troops under his banner. Nearby is the *Swan Hotel* which Dickens described as a "Dodo" because he found it quiet and dead but which George Borrow described as being constantly busy in his novel *The Romany Rye.* Borrow worked here as an ostler. Chetwynd House now used by the General Post Office, was a base of the Duke of Cumberland in 1745 when he pursued the broken ranks of Bonnie Prince Charlie's Highlanders northwards to their defeat at Culloden Moor. The house was also the home of Sheridan when he stayed in his parliamentary constituency. Nearby is the small **Church of St. Chad** which has several interesting Norman features and unusual carvings. The parish **Church of St. Mary's** has an unusual octagonal tower the foundations of which date from the 1200s. The doorway to the north transept dates from the 14th century. Walton was christened in the Norman font and his bust is in the north aisle. The foundations of the *Chapel of St. Bertelin* (1000), the Mercian prince who established a hermitage here, are near the church. The **William Salt Library** is in a fine 18th-century house in Eastgate Street. It has a good collection of books and manuscripts relating to Staffordshire.

From Stafford the A34 (no exit on Motorway), leads north to **Stone,** the birthplace of the painter Peter de Wint (1784–1849) and Richard Barnfield, the poet who was a contemporary of Shakespeare. John Jervis, Earl of St. Vincent, the great naval commander one of whose junior officers was Nelson, was born in Stone and died in his 89th year in 1823. He is buried in the churchyard.

Stoke-on-Trent is the result of the 1910 amalgamation of the "Five Towns" immortalized by Arnold Bennett (1867–1931). There are actually six towns beginning with Longton in the south, then Fenton, Stoke, Hanley, Burslem and Tunstall. The chief industry is pottery and the area is renowned the world over for the quality of its products with such names as Wedgwood, Minton and Spode.

The **Church of St. Peter** was rebuilt in 1839 but the remains of the cross in the churchyard date from the 900s. The great potters of the district are remembered in the church. Josiah Wedgwood, who died in 1795 and was buried here, has a medallion by Flaxman in the chancel. The **Spode-Copeland Museum** in Church Street has many interesting early specimens of Staffordshire pottery. Etruria, the factory founded in 1769 by Josiah Wedgwood, is between Hanley and Newcastle-under-Lyme. Etruria Hall, built in 1770 as Josiah Wedgwood's home, is now the offices of an iron company. The Wedgwood factory is at Barlaston, four miles south of Stoke. There is also a Wedgwood museum and both establishments can be visited by arrangement.

Hanley is the birthplace of Arnold Bennett. He spent his early childhood at 205 Waterloo Road, Cobridge, now a museum. A plaque marks his birthplace at the corner of Hope Street and Hanover Street. The *Museum and Art Gallery* in Broad Street contains the largest collection of Staffordshire figures in existence.

Newcastle-under-Lyme, about three miles west of Stoke, is an old industrial town which had Simon de Montfort and John of Gaunt as lords. The Guildhall in the High Street was built in 1714 and modified in 1854. *St. Giles Church* was built in 1876 but the lower part of the buttressed and pinnacled tower dates back to the 13th century. The *Museum and Art Gallery* at Brampton Park, by the Wolstanton Road, exhibits textiles, pottery and objects of local historical interest.

Keele, some five miles west, is the site of the *University College of North Staffordshire*. It was founded in 1962 and the new buildings include the Library (1962), the Students' Union (1963) and the Chapel (1965).

Chester and District

Chester

Angling.—Salmon, trout and coarse fishing in *Dee* and *Clwyd*.

Distances.—Birkenhead, 16; Crewe, 24; Liverpool, 18; London, 182; Manchester, 38; Preston, 48; Stafford, 48.

Early Closing.—Wednesday.

Entertainment.—Gateway Theatre, cinemas.

Zoological Gardens. River trips.

Hotels.—*Grosvenor, The Queen, Blossoms, Mollington Banastra, Oaklands, Pied Bull, Dane.*

Population.—62,700.

Post Office.—St. John Street.

Sports.—Bowls, football, golf, dog-racing. Rugby Union.

One of the most ancient and picturesque cities in Britain, Chester is famous for the large number of black-and-white timbered medieval buildings that abound, its two-mile circumference of Roman walling round the original city, most of it still intact, and its Rows—galleried shopping arcades above the ground-floor shops in certain streets. The walls of the city, built by the Romans and strengthened and enlarged in later centuries, form a striking example of a fortified medieval town. The circuit along the top of the ramparts provides wonderful panoramas in all directions, and at various points are the great gateways and watch-towers that once guarded the entrances to the city. Two of these towers are now museums, **King Charles' Tower** *(daily Apr.–Sept.)*, containing plans and diagrams relating to Chester in the Civil War and the **Water Tower:** *(daily Apr.–Sept.)* with models and dioramas of Chester in Roman and medieval times.

The large number of striking black-and-white timbered buildings ('magpie' houses) that exist are one of Chester's most attractive features, and such houses are found all over Cheshire. Like the towers on the city walls, some houses have been converted into museums. These include **Bishop Lloyd's House** *(Mons to Fris, but not Bank Hols)*, dating from 1615 and with strong connections with the United States of America. Bishop Lloyd's eldest daughter married twice, first to Thomas Yale, whose family later founded the famous American university, and then to Theophilus Eaton, founder and first governor of New Haven. **Stanley Palace** *(Mons to Fris, but not Bank Hols)*. Built in 1591 and enlarged in 1700 it is now the headquarters of the English-Speaking Union in Chester. Other highly picturesque buildings which are still in use as shops, inns or private residences are the *Falcon* (1626), the *Bear & Billet Inn* (1664), the **Old Leche House** (1570), the *Old King's Head* (1640), and the *Tudor Inn* (a reconstruction of 1503).

The **Grosvenor Museum** *(daily throughout year)* is housed in a Victorian building and contains one of the finest exhibits of Roman remains in Britain and is particularly rich in relics and data concerning the Roman Army. An annexe displays furniture and costumes through the ages.

In Watergate Street is *God's Providence House* dating from 1652 but since rebuilt with the same materials.

CHESTER

Chester's famous **Rows,** which form galleried walks along the tops of the ground-floor shops, with additional shops of their own, have never been adequately explained. They add a unique and additional dimension to the interest of this fascinating town. They are first mentioned in the 14th century and are thought possibly to have been built to screen the extensive Roman remains that had been neglected for centuries since the departure of the Romans.

In the centre of the city the **Cross** takes its name from the former medieval High Cross which was demolished during the Civil War. Parts were later discovered and the cross has now been reconstructed and stands in a garden by the Newgate.

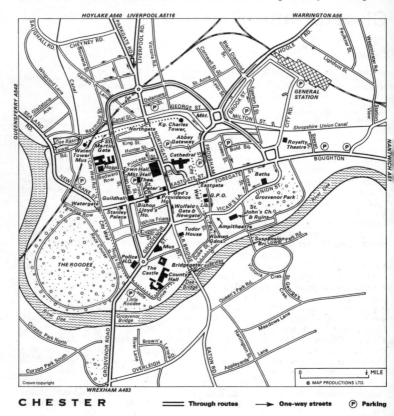

C H E S T E R ════ **Through routes** → **One-way streets** ℗ **Parking**

The former castle, close to the city walls in the south-west corner of the old town, has been replaced by an early-Victorian group of buildings which houses the County Offices. One surviving medieval portion is the Agricola Tower *(daily)*, which contains the fine vaulted **Chapel of St. Mary de Castro** and on a lower floor the **Museum of the Cheshire Regiment** with relics of Sir Charles Napier and many campaign honours.

Apart from the massive block of the New County Hall at this spot, Chester's two most prominent buildings are the vast Victorian **Town Hall** (open at irregular times when not in use) completed in 1869, and opposite, across Northgate Street, the cathedral.

The Cathedral was rebuilt by Hugh, Earl of Chester, a nephew of William the Conqueror, in A.D. 1093, for a community of monks of the Benedictine Order, on the site of an earlier Church of secular canons, founded by Ethelfleda, daughter of Alfred the Great, and containing the shrine of Saint Werburgh, the daughter of Wulfere, King of Mercia, in the 7th century.

The building was restored by Sir Gilbert G. Scott; its unusually warm tone is due to the use of the red sandstone of the district. The principal portions were erected during the 13th, 14th, 15th and 16th centuries, although considerable remains of the Norman structure still exist. The western entrance is formed of a Tudor arch under a square head, and above it is a fine Perpendicular window. The roof of the **Nave** is composed of panelled oak, its bosses being ornamented with coats-of-arms, mainly of persons connected with the city and its history. The wall of the north aisle of the nave is lined with mosaics.

The **North Transept** contains the organ and the tomb of the learned Bishop Pearson, who died in 1686. The adjacent bay contains a War Memorial to the Cheshire Yeomanry. At the entrance to the north choir aisle are interesting relics of the Norman church: the base of a pillar and a Norman capital which was inverted and used as a foundation by later builders.

Chester Cathedral is smaller than many, but the observant visitor will notice many beautiful details: a favourite view is that across the **Choir** from the north choir aisle. Over the stalls in the choir are some of the finest oak canopies in England. Some of the misericords are very quaint. The bishop's throne in the choir is also worthy of attention.

The easternmost portion of the cathedral, the **Lady Chapel**, is entered from the north choir aisle. On one of its bosses is depicted the murder of Thomas à Becket. In the Lady Chapel, immediately behind the High Altar, stands all that is left of the shrine of St. Werburgh.

The **South Transept**, which is as large as the choir, was formerly the parish church of St. Oswald. In one of the chapels are the colours of the Cheshire Regiment and the flags flown by H.M.S. *Chester* at the Battle of Jutland, 1916.

The **Cloisters,** entered by a door in the north aisle, should on no account be missed. In recent years they have been lovingly restored. In the east walk of the Cloister is the entrance to the vestibule of the **Chapter House,** both the vestibule and the chapter room being fine specimens of Early English at its best. Many of the literary treasures of the Cathedral are here displayed; and there is a beautiful oak cupboard with doors decorated with 13th-century ironwork. In the north walk is the chief entrance to the old **Refectory,** which still contains a fine reader's pulpit approached by a staircase in the wall. The Refectory has been restored at a cost of £10,000, and is used for conferences and gatherings of all kinds and for meals in connection therewith.

Parallel with the West Cloister runs the Great Cellar—a massive Norman work. In the south-west corner are the steps leading to the beautiful little **Chapel of St. Anselm.**

Other interesting churches in the city are **St. Peter's Church,** at the Cross, and the **Church of St. Mary on the Hill** with its fine timber roof. Just outside the Newgate is the Church of **St. John the Baptist,** next to the cathedral the most interesting ecclesiastical edifice in the city. It was begun about 1075, and was intended for the cathedral of the diocese that included Lichfield and Chester, but Coventry was chosen to be the seat of the bishop.

The **Roodee,** Chester's famous racecourse, stands close to the river on the south-west of the city. **Chester Zoo** *(daily, fee),* is at Upton, two miles, on the A41. The gardens are notable.

North-west of Chester stretches the Wirral Peninsula, a tongue of land reaching to the Irish Sea and bounded on one side by the *Dee* and on the other by the *Mersey.*

Port Sunlight, 10 miles from Chester on the A41 alongside the *Mersey,* is a model village and factory complex created by Lord Leverhulme in the early years of the present century. The **Lady Lever Art Gallery** *(weekdays and Sun. afternoons)*, has collections of china, English furniture and pictures by many English masters.

Ellesmere Port, six miles due north of Chester on the Mersey estuary and Manchester Ship Canal, is one of Britain's largest oil ports and an important industrial town. East of Ellesmere Port, a little inland from the estuary, **Helsby Hill** (462 feet) has part of an Iron Age promontory fort with wide views across the *Mersey* north and to the Welsh mountains to the west.

Runcorn, where the estuary narrows to the beginning of the *Mersey* proper, is being developed as one of Britain's "new towns" and though highly industrialised for a century will benefit from enlightened planning and the provision of good housing estates, open spaces and golf courses. South-east is **Halton Hill,** another prominence with extensive views over the *Mersey,* while Halton Village, on its slopes, has a romantic 11th-century ruined castle and several fine houses including a Georgian vicarage and the 18th-century *Castle Inn*.

Daresbury, three miles due east, was the birthplace in 1832 of Lewis Carroll (Rev. C. L. Dodgson), author of "Alice in Wonderland". The parish church, set amid fields, has a colourful stained-glass window in which Alice and many of her friends such as the Mad Hatter and the Cheshire Cat are depicted.

Northwich, south-east of Runcorn on the A533, is one of two towns in this district where rock-salt is mined and several parts of the town show signs of subsidence due to the extensive workings below. Just north is that remarkable example of Victorian industrial enterprise, the *Anderton Boat Lift* built in 1874. This lift, the only one now working in Britain, raises boats 50 feet from the river *Weaver* to the *Trent and Mersey Canal* in huge water-filled caissons. Originally worked hydraulically by an ingenious system of counter-balances it is now operated electrically.

Knutsford (Pop.: 13,760. Hotels: *Royal George, Heatherfield, Rose and Crown*), north-east of Anderton is a very different place. Standing on rising ground it is a quiet, charming little town of "magpie" houses and narrow, winding streets and is the original "Cranford" of Mrs. Gaskell. The writer is buried behind the 17th-century Unitarian chapel.

Tatton Park (N.T., *Apr.–Oct., daily except Mons, fee*), three-and-a-half miles north of Knutsford, is a fine 19th-century house formerly owned by the Egerton family with collections of pictures, furniture and silver. In 1935 the last Lord Egerton built an annexe to display his immense collection of sporting trophies and curiosities collected during a lifetime of world travel. The house stands in two-thousand acres of parkland including lakes and large formal gardens.

This north-east corner of Cheshire is close to the densely populated Lancashire border. **Stockport,** already virtually connected with Manchester, is a hilly and highly industrialised town where the *Goyt* and *Tame* merge to become the *Mersey*. But even in this area open country is not far away, and two miles south is the fine timber **Bramall Hall** *(daily, except Thurs)*, with a chapel dating back to 1400.

Alderley Edge lies southward and is another fine viewpoint. Just over a mile to the south on the east side of A34 is **Alderley Old Mill** (N.T., *Apr.–Oct., Weds and Suns, fee*), a restored 15th-century corn-mill that was operating up to 1949.

Lyme Park (N.T., *see notices*), dates from Elizabethan times but the fine Palladian exterior is due to the Italian architect Giacomo Leoni. The Hall is furnished with period furniture and there is an extensive deer park.

Jodrell Bank radio telescope *(afternoons daily, Easter–Oct., Sat. and Sun. afternoons only during rest of year)* is situated off the A535 south of Alderley Edge. It was built for Manchester University in 1957. In the Concourse Buildings adjoining can be seen many items connected with radio-astronomy. There is also a fascinating planetarium.

Macclesfield (Pop.: 44,240. Hotels: *George, Bull's Head, Queens*), is a thriving industrial town on rising ground above the river *Bollin*. At one time a centre of silk manufacture it retains its association with the clothing trade in its modern factories devoted to the production of man-made fibres. The parish church is on high ground above the river and is connected to the river bank by terraces and flights of steps of which Church Side, with its 108 well-worn steps, is the most picturesque. One of the oldest buildings is the Unitarian Chapel in King Street, built in 1689 immediately after the accession of William of Orange, and bearing a plate certifying it as a "Publick Place of Religious Worship for Protestant Subjects Dissenting from the Church of England". Eastwards from Macclesfield are high moorlands rising to the Peak District, and on the county boundary the *Cat and Fiddle*, isolated and, in its setting 1,690 feet above sea-level, claims to be the highest inn in England.

Gawsworth Hall *(daily afternoons Mar.–Oct.)*, is three miles south of Macclesfield and is a fine Tudor mansion in which lived Mary Fitton, possibly the "Dark Lady" of Shakespeare's sonnets.

Adlington Hall *(Easter–Sept., Suns, Bank Hols. Also Sats, July–Aug., fee)*, five miles north of Macclesfield on the Stockport road (A523), dates originally from 1450, though its black-and-white half-timbered portion was added in 1581.

Congleton, eight miles south-west of Macclesfield, has a fine parish church of 1742 unspoilt by restorers and still retaining its galleries and box-pews. But the greatest architectural glory in this part of Cheshire is four miles to the south-west. This is the incredible Little **Moreton Hall** (N.T., *daily except Tues, Mar.–Oct.)*. Completed about 1589 it is one of the most astonishing and perfect examples of black-and-white domestic architecture of the period. It has huge, overhanging half-timbered gables, a wainscoted gallery within and a private chapel, and the whole range of buildings is surrounded by a moat.

Sandbach, between Congleton and Crewe, is a quaint old market town famous for its two remarkable 7th-century Saxon crosses side-by-side in the market place. They are covered with carvings and are said to represent a royal wedding in Saxon times. Everywhere in Cheshire is the contrast between rurality and industry—between the ancient and the modern.

Crewe *(Crewe Arms, Royal)*, is an example of a town that owes its existence entirely to the coming of the railways in 1837. It became the main locomotive works of the LNWR in the great days of steam, and produced many locomotives famous in the annals of railway development. It is still a railway centre, quite apart from the fame of its junction, and today produces many diesel locomotives. A good deal of Crewe's industry is devoted to transport, both by rail and road and also to pharmaceuticals and veterinary products. In this background of Victorian industrial progress it is hardly surprising that Crewe has little antiquity with which to impress the visitor. The "magpie" houses of the rest of Cheshire are noticeably absent, but for those interested in architecture it has much to offer, from the cheerful early-Victorian Municipal Offices, through the delightful Crewe Theatre saved from demolition by an enlightened borough council, to the striking modern buildings of the present Civic Centre or the industrial blocks like the fine Satec Factory at Weston Road. Oddly enough one of the most modern industries, the manufacture of vaccines and other pharmaceuticals, continues in the only old mansion in the town—Crewe Hall with towers, pinnacles and rampant lions at the gates.

Nantwich, south of Crewe on the river *Weaver,* is the second salt-mining town in Cheshire. It is old and has several attractive houses of which the most interesting is *Churche's Mansion (daily)*. This is a particularly fine example of a Tudor merchant's house with superb oak panelling. The 14th-century parish church has a remarkable stone-vaulted roof and there are good almshouses of 1638.

The flattish area of Cheshire running north of Nantwich saw the development of the canal system in the late 18th and early 19th centuries which, in time, became as complex and involved as the railways were to do half a century later. At Hurlestone Junction four canals converge to become the *Chester Canal* giving access to the *Mersey* and the sea. There is little doubt that Cheshire is a happy hunting-ground for the student of industrial archaeology, though there are many areas where commerce seems never to have penetrated.

Malpas, for example, in the south-west corner of the county on the Shopshire border seems always to have been outside the range of industry and mechanization, preferring to earn its living from agriculture. It is a quiet, hilly town on the river *Dee,* offering fine panoramic views into Shropshire towards the Wrekin and westwards to the mountains of Wales. The church has some interesting medieval stone carving and a parish chest in constant use since the 13th century.

From the Shropshire border the A49 runs north, passing east of the 13th-century ruins of **Beeston Castle,** *(daily),* perched on the summit of the Peckforton Hills. A curiosity is the sham modern "medieval" castle built on the hillside a little below the original.

Tarporley, three miles north, is an ancient town in what was once the fox-hunting centre of the county. From its churchyard there are wide views ranging over the Peckforton Hills to the south, while to the north are the 4,000 acres of **Delamere Forest** with its meres, thickets and glades—a constant reminder of what much of Cheshire must have been like before the advent of industry. In the quiet rectory garden of Delamere village Charles Darwin once planted a tree. In the same garden is a mulberry tree planted long before Darwin's time, in 1620 to be precise, which is still bearing fruit. Not far from the village are various forest nature trails and a Forestry Museum *(daily)*.

Gloucester and District

Gloucester

Distances.—Bath, 38; Bristol, 35; Cardiff, 56; Cheltenham, 9; Evesham, 24; Malvern, 25; Hereford, 28; London, 105.
Early Closing.—Thursday.

Hotels.—*New County, Fleece, Longford Inn, Double Gloucester.*
Population.—90,150.
Post Office.—King's Square.

Gloucester, the county town, stands at the junction of the navigable *Severn* with the wide and deep water of the Sharpness Ship Canal and is a considerable port busy in handling coal and iron, timber and grain. The first definite appearance of the town in history is in connection with the Romans of whom it bears marks to this date in its four chief streets—Northgate, Southgate, Eastgate and Westgate.

The **Cathedral** is in essence Romanesque dating from 1089 to 1160 but the exterior has been transformed with 14th–15th-century Perpendicular work. The most striking change was the replacement of the apse by "the world's largest window, 72 feet by 38 feet". An attractive feature of the exterior is the Tower built 1450–60 and standing on the pillars of its successor. It is 225 feet high to the top of the pinnacles the light and graceful tracery of which gives a special character to the exterior.

The nave's vast plain pillars, over 30 feet high, are most impressive; their arches and triforium are also Romanesque; the vault was added 1242–45. Two western bays rebuilt 1421–37. Here is the monument of Jenner, inventor of vaccination. The south aisle vault and windows, being in danger, were rebuilt in elegant Decorated style, 1318–29, ornamented with "ball flowers". At the east end of this aisle is the chantry of Abbot Seabroke with alabaster effigy; opposite is a tomb of a knight and his lady.

The south transept is of unique interest as the reputed birthplace in 1331 of Perpendicular Gothic which soon spread all over England (though not abroad); the whole, though still Romanesque, is covered throughout with a veil of vertical mullions continuous from floor to vault, with horizontal transomes, whilst the vault is rare in having no bosses. The builders went on, 1337–50, to veil the whole of the space under the tower and the presbytery east of it with a richer version of the same design, and to crown it with a vault 86 feet high, richly adorned with bosses, those in the eastern bay forming an orchestra of angels with musical instruments. The vault's western bays continue under the tower and are supported each side by unique slender arches. Enter the presbytery by its south aisle. On the pulpitum or choir screen, largely rebuilt in 1820, stands the organ. Its main case was built, 1663, whilst the smaller Choir Organ on the east side may be 16th century. The choir stalls are 15th century, with a 13th-century fragment. In the centre of the presbytery is the fine wooden 13th-century effigy of Robert of Normandy, William I's eldest son, *d.* 1134. The glass of the east window, 1350, commemorates local heroes who fell at Crecy, 1346, and Calais, 1347; it shows our Lord crowning our Lady, with saints, kings, and abbots around. Re-enter the south aisle. The apsidal east end, repeated in the crypt and triforium, recalls the original typical Romanesque form which the east window replaced. The Lady Chapel, 1457–83, is a superb creation of late Perpendicular, with fine glass and elegant two-storey chapels.

299

Continue along the north aisle. On the left are; the 16th-century tomb of Osric, a Mercian prince who founded Gloucester Abbey, 681; next, the tomb of Edward II, 1327, with superb canopy work and figure, once a great pilgrimage centre; third, the tomb prepared for Abbot Parker, 16th century. The north transept was remodelled, 1368–74. Monuments in the north aisle include John Stafford Smith, son of a Gloucester Cathedral organist, and who wrote the tune taken for the American National Anthem "The Star-Spangled Banner".

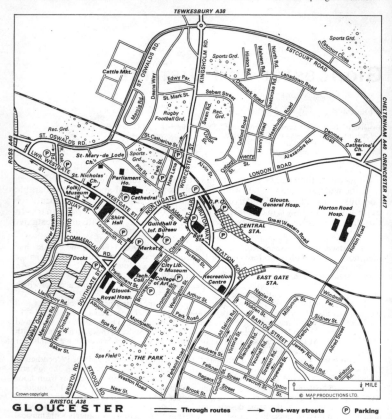

GLOUCESTER ===== Through routes → One-way streets Ⓟ Parking

The cloisters show superb work of 1370–1412, with early fan-tracery vaulting; the Romanesque chapter house and slype are to the east, the monastic washing place and entry to the infirmary cloister are in the north walk, and carrells or places for copying books in days before printing are in the south walk.

Gloucester contains several interesting ancient churches and various historical houses.

Near the west gate of the Cathedral Close is **Bishop Hooper's Statue,** standing on the spot where, in 1555, he was burnt to death by three successive fires of green wood.

The statue stands in the grounds of the mother-church, **St. Mary de Lode.** From the relics discovered during excavations, the site of the church is believed to have held a Roman temple.

St. Nicholas's Church, in Westgate, is traditionally said to have been built by King John. Much of the structure may be the work of his reign, but there are fragments of greater age. Opposite in Hooper's House is a *Folk Museum* with relics of Bishop Hooper who was burnt at the stake in 1555. Adjoining is the Gloucestershire *Regimental Museum.*

The Church of **St. Mary de Crypt,** in Southgate, owes its curious name to the existence of two large crypts, and is notable as the scene of Whitfield's first sermons and the burial-place of *Robert Raikes,* the founder of Sunday Schools. A cottage still standing in St. Catherine Street was one of the first houses used for this purpose, but **Raikes's House** is in Southgate, opposite the old "Crypt" Grammar School which adjoins the church.

In Northgate, near "the Cross," is the **New Inn,** built about 1450 and remarkable for its courtyard and galleries, characteristic of 15th-century hostelries.

Slimbridge Wild Fowl Trust *(daily, fee),* 11 miles south-west off A38 beyond Frampton-on-Severn is an interesting breeding ground of many species of wildfowl.

Farther south-west is **Berkeley,** a small Severnside town. **Berkeley Castle** *(Apr.–Sept., daily except Mons, and Suns, only in Oct., fee),* south of the town, the home of the Berkeleys for over 800 years, was the scene of the murder of Edward II in 1327. The Early English church contains several Berkeley effigies.

The **Forest of Dean** occupies a triangular plateau between Gloucester, Ross and Chepstow. Formerly part of Crown lands it is now Forestry Commission property. The present area subject to forest law is 22,000 acres including 18,000 acres of woodland which now forms part of one of England's National Forest Parks. **Cinderford** on the east, once a centre of the coal-mining industries of the Forest, is a market town of 8,000 people whilst **Coleford** is an industrial town on the western side of the Forest. Centre of the Forest is *Speech House,* now a hotel, but part of the building dates from 1680; and former head-quarters of the Court of Verderers who administered Forest laws.

St. Briavels is a village close to the *Wye* on the Tintern road with a church and castle of interest. The remains of the *castle* (youth hostel) date from about 1250.

Tewkesbury (Pop.: 8,740. Hotels: *Royal Hop Pole, Tudor House, Swan*), is a fine old town on the Warwickshire *Avon* close to its meeting with the *Severn.* Famous in history because the last battle of the Wars of the Roses was fought here in 1471, the town has a magnificent Norman abbey and many half-timbered houses of the 15th and later centuries.

The Abbey by tradition originated in the cell of a British recluse called Theoc his hermitage being named Theresburia in time converted to Tewkesbury. The present structure however was begun in 1092 by Robert FitzHamon. The work was continued by Robert, the great Earl of Gloucester, a natural son of Henry I, and in succeeding years by the de Clares, Despencers, Beauchamps and Nevilles.

Most prominent is the tower rivalled only by the twin towers of Exeter. It rises 148 feet to the top of the pinnacles which were added in 1660. The West Front is splendid Norman work with a late Perpendicular window and a remarkable sevenfold arch, 34 feet wide, rising to 65 feet and flanked by turrets. The arcades of the nave are Norman but the roofs of both nave and aisles have Decorated groining. The roof bosses are beautifully carved. The major part of the choir is Decorated work. The 14th-century windows display in stained glass a series unique in England of scriptural subjects and figures of past benefactors. Off the choir are a number of beautiful chapels containing tombs and monuments of great interest.

Tewkesbury is the "Nortonbury" of Mrs. Cruik's "John Halifax, Gentleman" and many of its older houses are referred to in that novel. Opposite the Abbey Gates is the *Bell Hotel,* once Abel Fletcher's house, with its bowling green. The old Abbey Mill, now a café, has been restored. In Church Street is the *Hop Pole Hotel* immortalized by Dickens in "Pickwick Papers" and opposite, *Warwick House.* Farther north, in High Street, are *Tudor House,* interesting to Americans as the site of a Presbyterian Academy, founded in 1712 by the Rev. Samuel Jones of Philadelphia, *Clarence House* and the *Wheatsheaf Inn,* now a café.

Deerhurst, four miles south of Tewkesbury, is famed for its Priory, once an abbey, and of interest for the Saxon work it contains. The plan of the present church comprises a western tower, a nave and north and south aisles. The door in the tower and the greater part of the chancel belong to the Saxon period, the masonry consisting of alternate layers of large and small stones. The font may date from the 8th century or earlier. There are some early and well-preserved brasses including a very fine one to Sir John Cassey (*d.* 1400) and his wife. Towards the river is **Odda's Chapel,** relic of a Saxon chapel consisting of a nave only 25 feet long by 16 feet wide. Adjoining a fine Tudor style farmhouse the chapel was discovered in 1885. It was built by Odda and belonged to the Saxon manor.

Herefordshire

ROSS-ON-WYE AND DISTRICT

Herefordshire with its peaceful villages, orchards and rich farmlands where the famous white-faced cattle browse, still remains one of the least spoilt English counties. The county forms the southern portion of the Welsh border region, being bounded on the north by Shropshire, the west by the Welsh mountains, on the east by Worcestershire and Gloucestershire, and on the south by Monmouthshire. The river *Wye*, a famous salmon-fishing river, flows through the county via Hereford and Ross to reach its supreme loveliest at Symonds Yat. With the exception of Hereford, the county town, there are few large towns, but each and every village or hamlet with its distinctive black-and-white houses and old inns is a delight to the eye. There are numerous prehistoric remains and much evidence of Roman occupation, and many abbeys, castles and manor houses reflect bygone days.

Ross-on-Wye

Distances.—London, 131; Abergavenny, 23; Monmouth, 11; Gloucester, 16; Worcester, 28; Cardiff, 47; Hereford, 14; Birmingham via M50 and M5, 59, via Hereford, 76.
Early Closing.—Wednesday.
Entertainments.—cinema; concerts.
Hotels.—*Royal, Cedars, Walford, Chase, Swan, Rosswyn.*
Information Bureau.—Gloucester Road.
Population.—6,570.
Post Office.—Gloucester Road.
Sports.—Boating, cricket, golf, hunting, tennis, angling.

A few miles from the Gloucestershire and Monmouthshire border, Ross is a good centre for touring the Wye Valley and surrounding areas. The town stands on high ground on the left bank of the *Wye* and from the Prospect, a public garden, there are fine views of the horseshoe bend of the river. The red sandstone arcaded *Market Hall* was built during the reign of Charles II and the weekly market is founded on a charter granted by King Stephen. The town's **Parish Church of St. Mary** dates from the 13th century, but has undergone various alterations. At the entrance to the churchyard is the *Plague Cross*, an old churchyard cross with an inscription recording the burial of 315 victims of the Plague or Black Death which swept through the town in 1637. The church has good Early English windows but the chancel, being of a later date, has Perpendicular windows; much of the glass in the east window dates from the 15th century. Inside there are several monuments to the Rudhall family and also the tomb of John Kyrle, the Man of Ross, who died in 1724.

John Kyrle, born in 1637, spent most of his life in Ross and was celebrated for his philanthropy and public spirit; Alexander Pope praised his good works in his essay, *Of the Use of Riches*. Kyrle's house became an inn after his death and later was turned into two shops, now occupied by a chemist and the *Ross Gazette*. Over the chemist shop is a medallion of the Man of Ross. and in the garden behind is **John Kyrle's Summer House** *(view by permission)*. The public works of Kyrle include the Prospect and John Kyrle's Walk, a footpath with views of the river and Wilton Castle.

Another celebrity associated with Ross is Charles Dickens. In the *Royal Hotel* the author first met his friend and biographer, John Forster, and the town was also the home of Mr. Dolby, the secretary and manager of Dickens' reading tours.

To Wilton and Bridstow. Wilton is about half-a-mile from Ross on the Monmouth and Hereford road. The six-arched bridge spanning the *Wye* dates from 1599 and nearby there are the remains of *Wilton Castle*. The ruins of the castle date from the 13th century, but both Leland and Giraldas Cambrensis state there was a castle in the time of King Stephen. Less than a mile north-west of Wilton Bridge is **Bridstow** Church, founded by King Harold, "the last of the Saxons", The structure, save for the west tower, was completely rebuilt in 1862.

To St. Weonards, Garway and Kentchurch. West of Ross, on the A466 between Monmouth and Hereford, is the old village of **St. Weonards.** The church here has fine stained-glass windows in its Myners Chapel which date back to the early 16th century. **Garway,** not far from St. Weonards, near the Monmouthshire border, has a church founded by the Knights Templars. There is also a massive 14th-century dovecote, its circular walls four feet thick and with nesting holes for 666 birds. To the north is the village of **Kentchurch** on the banks of the *Monnow* and across the river in Monmouthshire are the ruins of Grosmont Castle. Kentchurch Court *(by appointment, preferably to parties of four or more, fee)* for centuries the home of the Scudamore family was largely rebuilt by John Nash and has some notable woodwork attributed to Grinling Gibbons.

To Weston-under-Penyard. "The garden village of south Herefordshire", Weston-under-Penyard, lies due east of Ross. You can walk there through Penyard Woods passing Alton Court, a 17th-century half-timbered manor house, and also the ruins of the old Penyard Castle. The old church at Weston-under-Penyard has a fine 14th-century tower and a Norman arcade. Also in the village is *Lower Weston,* a beautiful Elizabethan manor house of soft red sandstone and mellow tiles, with armorial bearings over the porch.

Goodrich *(Ye Hostelrie)* is a pleasant village on the west bank of the *Wye,* a short distance below Ross, well-known for its castle.

The **Castle** *(daily and Sun. afternoons, fee),* stands on a wooded hill above the river. The oldest part of the castle, the square keep, is thought to have been built about the middle of the 12th century, and the rest of the ruins date from about a century-and-a-half later. During the Civil War the castle was a Royalist stronghold and in 1646 fell to Cromwell's troops after a seige of four-and-a-half months. Parliament, later, ordered the "slighting" of the defences and the castle remained a ruin from that time. It was in this castle that Wordsworth is said to have met a little girl of whom he wrote in his well-known poem "We are Seven".

The **Church** has good stained-glass windows and some fine oak panelling taken from the former Goodrich Court. During the 17th century Dean Swift's grandfather was vicar of the parish.

Below the village is *Kerne Bridge* and a barn, notable as the only remnant of Flanesford Priory, founded in 1346. Down river at **Welsh Bicknor** is *Courtfield,* traditionally the childhood home of Henry V and now a residence for retired Roman Catholic priests. The 19th-century church contains some excellent carving and also the 14th-century tomb of Margaret Montacute.

Symond's Yat is about seven-and-a-half miles south of Ross and one of the most famous beauty spots on the river *Wye.* The river flows in a great horseshoe bend for some five miles around Huntsham Hill, looping back to within about 400 yards of its original course. From the "Top Rock", over 500 feet high, there are magnificent views of the valley and surrounding countryside. Symond's Yat is a good centre for rambling and boating trips.

ROSS TO HEREFORD

This route is for those who are not in a hurry and want to see some of the interesting places along the river *Wye*. Motorists with less time to spare should take the main road.

The road from Ross passes the attractive village of Brampton Abbots and meets the river at the point where a small suspension bridge crosses it to Foy. The village church here has some fine oak timber work, especially the roof and screen; there's also an east window filled with 17th-century glass. From the suspension bridge the road runs past the *Hole in the Wall* and follows the river to **How Caple** with its impressive 14th-century church. Over the chancel screen is a fine oak carving of the arms of William III. Bearing left at How Caple the road passes the lane for the lonely Fawley Chapel (John Kyrle once lived in the Elizabethan-style Fawley Court), and by way of **King's Caple** rejoins the river at **Hoarwithy.** This village's richly decorated Victorian church is well worth visiting.

Farther up the river, through pleasant scenery, the road passes the high grounds of Carey Wood and *Ballingham Hill,* and reaches Holme Lacy House, founded in the reign of Henry III and for centuries the seat of the Scudamore family. The present house dates mostly from the 17th century and is now a hospital. The village church (St. Cuthbert) is of Norman origin and is notable for its medieval choir stalls, and there are also monuments of the Norfolk and Scudamore families. South-west of the village is **Aconbury** with its prehistoric, hilltop camp and an interesting church which is part of a 13th-century nunnery. Overlooking the river, west of Holme Lacy, is **Fownhope,** an attractive village with black-and-white houses and an ancient inn. The church has a Norman tower and near the churchyard there are the old village stocks and a whipping post.

The road from Holme Lacy runs east to the bridge at Even Pits, leading to **Mordiford,** where the *Lugg* joins the *Wye*. Between Mordiford and Hereford the *Wye* is overlooked on the south by Dinedor Hill and the road passes through the village of **Hampton Bishop.**

Hereford

Distances.—London, 133; Birmingham, 57; Bristol, 67½; Cardiff, 53¾; Cheltenham, 37; Ledbury, 14; Leominster, 12½; Manchester, 131; Monmouth, 18; York, 216¾.
Early Closing.—Thursday.
Entertainments.—cinemas; dancing.
Hotels.—*Green Dragon, Graftonbury, Somerville,* *Hope Pole, Queen's Arms, Tabard, City Arms, Castle Pool.*
Information Bureau.—Town Hall.
Post Offices.—Broad Street, St. Peter's Street.
Sports.—Swimming, bowls, putting, tennis, horse-racing, angling, golf (5½ miles).

The city of Hereford, one of the most interesting places in the west of England, is set in a fertile district noted for its wooded vales, green pastures, hop gardens and rich orchards. In Saxon times the city was the capital of Mercia. There was a powerful fortress here, probably built before the Conquest, but very little remains today; its site is now a garden known as Castle Green. The city walls ran from the castle along the lines of the present Mill Street, Bath Street, Blue School Street and Victoria Street, and sections may still be seen.

Hereford's shopping centre is the open space known as High Town. Here can be found the stone-fronted Market Hall with its clock tower. The market, locally known as the Butter Market, to distinguish it from the cattle and other markets elsewhere, is held on Wednesdays and Fridays. Opposite the Market Hall is a fine old black-and-white, half-timbered building, the **Old House** *(daily in summer, fee),* dating from 1612, and the only building on Butchers Row. It has a fine collection of Elizabethan and Jacobean furniture. Nearby, at the end of the High Street, is **All Saints' Church** with its slightly bent tower (212 feet high) crowned by England's largest weathercock. Inside the church there is some elaborate 13th-century stonework, richly carved 14th-century canopied stalls with carved misericords, and a chained library with around 300 volumes. The church register contains the entry of the baptism of David Garrick, who was born in nearby Widemarsh Street.

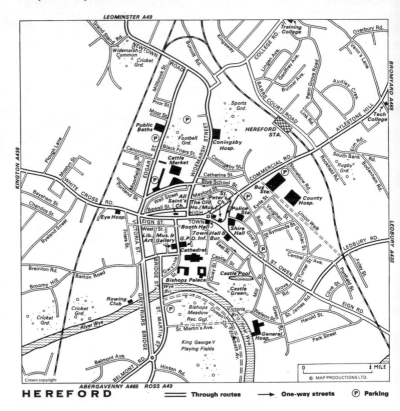

HEREFORD ═══ Through routes → One-way streets Ⓟ Parking

The Cathedral. The See of Hereford, one of the oldest in the country, most probably dates from the 7th century, but the present church was begun much later in the 11th century by the first Norman bishop, Robert de Lorraine. An earlier church built round the tomb of St. Ethelbert, the martyred King of East Anglia (794), was destroyed during a Welsh invasion about 1050. Work was continued on the cathedral by Bishop Reynelm and others during the 12th century and the Lady Chapel was added around 1225. The North Transept was rebuilt in the middle of the 13th century and the great central tower (165 feet high) was erected about 1325. In the 15th century there were alterations to the South Transept and chantries by Bishop Stanbury and Bishop Audley. The beautiful outer porch at the north door was the last ancient addition erected in about 1530 by Bishop Booth. In 1786 the western tower fell and destroyed the west end of the nave; rebuilding was carried out by James Wyatt and in

1842 a thorough restoration of the cathedral was begun. Wyatt's West Front was replaced at the beginning of this century by a new front designed by J. Oldrid Scott.

On entering the cathedral attention is at once attracted by the massive Norman pillars and arches of the **Nave** and aisles, with the curious carving round their capitals. In the **Choir** with its carved stalls of the Decorated period is the 14th-century Bishop's Throne and also King Stephen's Choir said to have been used by the king himself. Both aisles of the choir have bishops' tombs and in the north choir aisle is one of the cathedral's greatest treasures, the *Mappa Mundi* (Map of the World). This map (*c.* 1300) is drawn on a sheet of vellum (65 in. by 53 in.) and shows Jerusalem as the centre of the world. Opening off the aisle is the beautiful Chantry of Bishop Stanbury whose tomb is opposite.

Among the many monuments in the east aisle of the North Transept is the shrine of St. Thomas Cantilupe, a 13th-century Bishop of Hereford, whose tomb became a famous place of pilgrimage. There are more interesting tombs and brasses in the north-east and south-east transepts between which is the Lady Chapel with its fine Early English windows. In this chapel is the entrance to the **Crypt** and the two-storeyed Audley Chantry.

Some of the best Norman work can be seen in the South Transept including an ancient fire-place, a rarity in a church. Of note in the South Aisle is the Jacobean oak pulpit, the fine alabaster tomb of Sir Richard Pembridge and the Norman font. Off the south aisle of the nave is the Bishop's Cloister and the ruined Chapter House, and from the south wing of the south-east transept the Vicar's Corridor leads to a porch and cloistered quadrangle of the 15th-century Vicars' College.

The **Cathedral Library** is now housed in two sections. The Chained Library over the aisle of the North Transept *(small charge)* is the world's largest collection of chained books. Among the 1,444 volumes are fine manuscripts, works by Caxton and the Nuremberg Chronicle (1493). The rest of the library is housed in the West and South Cloisters.

Adjoining the Cathedral Close, is the old Deanery and **Canon's Residence;** the **Bishop's Palace,** which still has some of the original Norman timber pillars is near the Cathedral's west front.

A short way to the east of the cathedral is the ancient *Cathedral School* and also **Castle Green,** a public garden, the site of the ancient castle demolished by order of Parliament in 1652. In the centre of the gardens is the **Nelson Column** (the great naval hero was a Freeman of Hereford). Next to the steps leading to the Victoria Bridge is a stone cider mill given to the city by Lord Chesterfield and near the Green is Castle Cliff House which dates from the 13th century and was once used as a Bridewell.

On the other side of the cathedral, in Broad Street, is the **City Library, Museum and Art Gallery** which has Roman antiquities excavated from Magna Castra (Kenchester) as well as a large number of old farming implements and a good collection of English watercolours. In nearby Church Street is the house where actress Sarah Siddons lived and in a narrow lane close to the old stone **Wye Bridge** a brass tablet marks the reputed birthplace of Nell Gwynne. North of the Cathedral is the oldest parochial place of worship in Hereford—**St. Peter's Church.** Founded by Walter de Lacy under the patronage of William the Conqueror, the church was used by fugitives as a place of sanctuary up to 1514. It is remarkable for its 15th-century choir stalls and its fine, large, Early English chancel with a rood-loft staircase.

In Widemarsh Street not far from the *Livestock Market,* one of the largest in England, and the *Fruit and Produce Market,* are the Coningsby Almshouses (restored), founded in 1614. The chapel and dining hall of the almshouses are part of the old Order of St. John of Jerusalem building, dating from the 13th century. In the garden behind are the ruins of the 14th-century *Blackfriars Monastery* and also a stone *Preaching Cross* dating from 1350.

To Dinedor Hill. Dinedor Hill, almost 600 feet high, is just two-and-a-half miles south-east of the city and is reached via Lower Bullingham. From the summit, the site of an Iron Age camp, there are extensive views. The camp is said to have been used by the Roman general Ostorius Scapula when fighting Caractacus.

To Belmont Abbey and Clehonger. About two miles from Hereford on the Abergavenny road, a secondary road, marked by the signpost to Ruckhall, leads to **Belmont Abbey.** The abbey consists of a modern monastery, a school and a church with beautiful carving. Less than a mile along the same road is **Clehonger.** Its attractive church has a beautiful Norman doorway, a fine nave roof, an ancient altar stone and some interesting monuments and brasses.

To Kilpeck. Nine miles south-west of Hereford is the village of **Kilpeck** with its remarkable Norman church, one of the finest examples of Romanesque architecture in England. Except for the addition of some Early English windows and a door, the church has changed little since the 12th century. The south doorway is richly ornamented with symbolic carving and zigzag moulding, and the shaft and heads of the west window have an intricate, interlaced decoration. Other interesting features include a sculptured chancel arch, grotesquely carved corbels, a large Norman font and a Saxon stoup. West of the church are the remains of the Norman castle, consisting of earthworks, a moat and parts of the keep.

To Holmer. Holmer is on the A49, less than two miles north of Hereford. The church dates from the 12th century and is notable for its 13th-century detached tower which has a black-and-white, half-timbered upper storey.

HEREFORD TO HAY-ON-WYE

The direct route to Hay-on-Wye is the A438 via Willersley giving good views over the *Wye.* An alternative, longer, route is the B4352 via Bredwardine.

A mile to the west of Hereford, just off the A438, is **Kenchester,** the site of the Roman city of *Magna Castra.* The walls enclosed about 20 acres. A large amount of pottery, coins and jewellery have been found here, and in Hereford museum are tessellated pavements. The main road passes near the villages of **Byford** and **Monnington-on-Wye,** and continues to **Willersley** where the A4112 Leominster road comes in on the right.

.A pleasant diversion from Willersley is to **Eardisley** on B4111, a pretty village with many black-and-white houses. Its 13th–14th-century church has a finely sculptured Norman font with carvings around the bowl portraying figures in contemporary costume engaged in symbolical scenes of combat. In the surrounding district there are traces of British and Roman camps, and also the remains of a castle.

About three miles west of Willersley is **Whitney** where the road crosses a toll bridge *(small fee)* across the *Wye.* To the left of the road, less than two miles from the toll bridge, are the ruins of **Clifford Castle,** the birthplace of "Fair Rosamund", the mistress of Henry II. Her real name was Jane de Clifford, but because of her beauty she became known as Rosa Mundi, the "Rose of the World". The remains of the cliff-top castle include massive fragments of the north wall and a round tower, and although there are no traces left of Fair Rosamund's home, parts of the ruins date back to the reign of Edward I. About half-a-mile from the village is the ancient parish church which has a fine, 14th-century oak effigy of a priest.

The *alternative* route to Hay-on-Wye is a few miles longer than the more direct A438, and runs south of the river. Leaving Hereford on the Abergavenny road (A465) you can turn right on a secondary road, by the signpost marked Ruckhall, and visit Belmont Abbey and Clehonger. Farther along this secondary road is the pleasant village of **Eaton Bishop.** Its interesting church has a 13th-century nave, and a notable east window filled with 14th-century stained glass. Less than a mile from Eaton Bishop the road joins the B4352 and then continues on to **Madley.** This village's well-preserved large church dates mostly from the

13th and 14th centuries and in addition to some finely carved woodwork and elaborate tombs, has an impressive east window with 14th-century glass. Every year, usually in June, the church is the setting for a music festival organised by the parishioners.

Tyberton, about two miles to the west, has a brick church, rebuilt in 1720 but retaining its Norman doorway. Inside the church there are some interesting monuments and an elaborately carved reredos, and in the churchyard stands a 14th-century stone cross. Just off the B4352, about three miles away, is *Moccas Court,* a house designed by Robert Adam, set in lovely woodland, water and mountain scenery. In the grounds of the house there's a fascinating Norman church, built of "tufa", supposed to have been obtained from a nearby dripping well and petrifying springs. The church has some interesting stonework and 14th-century stained glass.

A few miles to the north-west the road passes through the lovely village of **Bredwardine** with its old six-arched bridge spanning the river *Wye.* Near the bridge is the ancient St. Andrew's Church which has curious Norman carvings and an elaborate effigy of that Vaughan of Bredwardine and Tretower who was killed at Agincourt and is said to be the original of Shakespeare's Flellen. Francis Kilvert, the diarist, was vicar at Bredwardine until his death in 1879. Adjoining the churchyard are the foundations of a castle and on Merbach Hill, about a mile away, is the cromlech, *King Arthur's Stone.*

After Bredwardine the road runs between the *Wye* and Merbach Hill and about five miles from the village joins the B4348 some two miles from Hay-on-Wye.

Ledbury

Distances.—Cheltenham, 22; Gloucester, 17; Hereford, 15; Ross-on-Wye, 12; London, 119; Worcester, 17.

Early Closing.—Thursday.
Hotels.—*Feathers, Old Talbot, Royal Oak.*
Population.—3,700.

Despite its small population Ledbury is one of the four chief towns of Herefordshire. There are a number of picturesque half-timbered houses in the town especially in cobbled Church Lane which opens onto the Market Place. The most notable black-and-white building is the **Old Market House** which stands in the square of the main street. Built by John Abel in 1633, the house is still supported on its stout wooden pillars. The Almshouses, or **St. Katherine's Hospital,** in High Street, were founded in the 13th century, but were rebuilt in 1822. They are on the site where the palace of the Bishops of Hereford once stood.

The **Church,** dedicated to St. Michael and All Angels, has an impressive detached tower with a lofty spire. Parts of the building date from the 11th century but numerous alterations and additions have been made through the centuries. The west door and part of the chancel are Norman, and the bell tower dates from about 1230; north of the choir is the early Decorated chapel, now used as a baptistry. The church has many interesting memorials, brasses and fragments of old glass in the windows. In the churchyard is the grave of Jacob Tonson, the celebrated publisher of Addison, Steele, Dryden and Pope, who died in 1736.

The Poet Laureate, John Masefield was born in Ledbury, and another literary figure associated with the town is Elizabeth Barrett Browning. She once lived at nearby "Hope End" in Colwall, and her father and mother are buried in the church.

To Stoke Edith. This attractive village is midway between Ledbury and Hereford. It is said to derive its name from St. Edith the natural daughter of King Edgar. The church, rebuilt in 1740, is notable for its three-decker pulpit and marble font.

To Eastnor. The **Castle** *(Bank Hols and Suns, June–Sept., or by appointment, fee)*, about two miles east of Ledbury, is set in an attractive park and contains fine collections of paintings, armour, tapestry and furniture. It was built in 1812 by the first Earl Somers on the site of an older house. Eastnor **Church** was rebuilt in 1851 but retains its medieval tower and some 12th-century stonework. Inside the church is a fine alabaster monument to the 3rd Earl Somers, and also a "Crucifixion" by Van Dyck.

To Bosbury, Colwall, Mathon and Cradley. The picturesque village of **Bosbury** with its half-timbered houses is about four miles north of Ledbury. Its ancient church has a massive detached 12th-century tower about 80 feet from the main building. The nave dates from the same period as the tower, but near the chancel is a beautiful Late Perpendicular chapel. Objects of interest include a Saxon font in the baptistry and slabs in the south aisle dedicated to Knights Templars. The tomb of Edna Lyall, the novelist, is in the churchyard and also the shaft of the cross mentioned in her story "In Spite of All".

At Colwall, east of Bosbury, Elizabeth Barrett Browning spent her childhood at Hope End. Her house no longer remains but the beautiful Malvern countryside with the "Beautiful, beautiful hills..." can have changed little since she was a girl. A footpath runs from the village to the **Herefordshire Beacon** (1,114 feet high) which has the remains of a large Iron Age camp. **Mathon,** farther north, is sheltered by the Malvern hills and set in an area of orchards and hop fields. The church dates from Norman times and has some fine 14th-century woodwork in the roof of the nave. A mile away is **Cradley** with its attractive black-and-white cottages and 15th-century parish hall.

To Much Marcle and Sollers Hope. Much Marcle, southwest of Ledbury on the A449, has three historic houses, one of which is open to the public. *Homme House,* an Elizabethan mansion with a round tower and embattled parapet; *Hall Court,* built by Sir John Coke in 1608 with fine timber framing; and **Hellen's** *(Suns, June–Sept, and Bank Hols, fee)*, a manorial house dating back to the 14th century. The Great Hall can still be seen and the house also has a collection of carriages and a 17th-century pigeon house with a quaint roof. The village church is also worth a visit to see its fine monuments.

To the west is **Sollers Hope** which claims to be the birthplace of Dick Whittington, an honour to which Pauntley in Gloucestershire also aspires.

HEREFORD TO LEOMINSTER

The most direct road to Leominster is the A49, however there's a pleasant alternative route via Stretton Sugwas and Weobley.

The first places of interest on the route are **Stretton Sugwas** with its 17th-century timbered church tower and **Credenhill** where the 17th-century Border poet, Thomas Traherne, was once rector. The village church merits a visit, and on the crest of the hill there's an ancient hill-camp. Just off the main road (A480) about a mile north-west of Credenhill is Brinsop Court, a 15th-century moated manor house where the poet Wordsworth stayed on a number of occasions. The nearby village church has a 14th-century oak screen and memorial windows to Wordsworth.

At **Norton Canon,** about a mile and a half past the small village of **Yazor,** there's a road on the right leading direct to Weobley, but if you continue on the A480 you can visit Sarnesfield and a few of the interesting villages nearby. **Sarnesfield** has an attractive 13th-century church with the tomb of John Abel whom Charles I dubbed "the King's Carpenter".

About two miles south-west of Sarnesfield on the A4112 is **Kinnersley.** The church dates from Norman times, but has been much altered during succeeding centuries. Its interior is rich in woodwork and there's a fine monument to the Smalman family, who once owned Kinnersley Castle, the manor house near the churchyard. A mile north of the village at **Almeley,** is the mound and earthworks of a castle built during the reign of King John. The church has a tower dating from 1200 and the roof of the nave is painted with Tudor roses. There are some interesting houses in and around the village including a 17th-century, black-and-white Meeting House.

Weobley, just off the A4112 about two miles from Sarnesfield, is a most attractive village of black-and-white, half-timbered houses—some dating from the 15th century. There's also a 14th-century church and earthworks of an ancient castle. At the west end of the village, reached by the lane on the left, is *The Ley,* a 16th-century manor house, now a farm. An interesting feature of this house is a priest's hole.

Leominster is reached by the A4112 via Dilwyn.

THE GOLDEN VALLEY

The little river *Dore* flows down the peaceful Golden Valley, on the eastern edge of the Black Mountains, to meet the river *Monnow* near Pontrilas. The Welsh name of this river is *Dwr* (dore), meaning water, and it is thought to have been mistaken by the Normans for their D'or—of gold—and so the valley came to be called Golden.

The village of **Dorstone,** at the northern end of the valley, is about 15 miles west of Hereford, just off the B4348. The church (St. Faith) was founded by Walter de Brut, a Norman soldier to whom William gave land in recompense for help. Built in 1890, the present building replaced an earlier structure; during the rebuilding a tomb of a tall man, thought to be the founder, was discovered. The coffin was reburied, but a pewter chalice found with it, was placed in a recess in the wall. The name of the parish is said to be a corruption of Thorstein or Thor's Stone, a prehistoric burial chamber known as Arthur's Stone. The tomb is on Merbach Hill about a mile from the village; from this hill there are extensive views of the lovely Wye Valley.

Peterchurch, nine miles south, has a fine Norman church with a double chancel and lofty Norman arches. To the west of the village are the ruins of the ancient castle of Snodhill.

Farther down the valley are the attractive villages of **Turnastone** and **Vowchurch** standing near each other, on either side of the river. According to legend the village churches were built by two sisters, one of whom is supposed to have said, "I vow I will build my church before you will turn a stone of yours." Both churches date from Norman times and Turnastone's church is well worth visiting to see its fine woodwork.

At nearby **St. Margaret's** there's an interesting church with a wonderful lace-work wooden screen, and farther south **Bacton's** church contains a monument to Blanche Parry, Maid-of-Honour to Queen Elizabeth I. Blanche Parry was born in Bacton and like the queen she served, she never married.

Abbeydore, towards the southern end of the Golden Valley, owes its name to a Cistercian abbey founded in the middle of the 12th century. After the dissolution of the monasteries the abbey fell into neglect but part of the original structure survived, and the choir and transepts are still used as parish church.

At the southernmost end of the valley is **Ewyas Harold** with traces of a Norman castle, and at nearby **Rowlstone** there's an interesting medieval church with some notable stone carvings and fine 15th-century iron candelabra.

LEOMINSTER AND DISTRICT

Leominster

Distances.—London, 138; Brecon, 38; Hereford, 13; Ledbury, 22; Worcester, 26; Ludlow, 11.
Early Closing.—Thursday.

Hotels.—*Royal Oak, Talbot.*
Information Bureau.—Grange Court.
Population.—6,930.

The busy market town of Leominster lies in a beautiful valley, surrounded by rich meadowlands, orchards and hopfields. The *Lugg* flows through the town and there are other small rivers nearby. According to Leland, the town derives its name from a minster or monastery founded about 660 by the King of West Mercia. Other authorities, however, suggest the name comes from "the minster of Leof or Leofric, Earl of Mercia"; in the Domesday Book it is known as Leofminstre. At one time Leominster was a thriving centre of the wool trade renowned for its high quality wool "Lemster Ore". Nowadays the town is famed for its **Priory Church** of St. Peter and St. Paul. The church dates from Norman times and is remarkable for the possession of three naves. In the early 13th century a new nave for the use of the townspeople was built beside the original Norman nave, and in the following century a third nave of the same size as the others was added. The *Original Nave,* consecrated in 1130, is considered one of England's finest examples of Early Norman work. The western door, with its fine Norman carvings, is particularly beautiful; the doors themselves are modern and were made locally in 1953 to commemorate the coronation of Queen Elizabeth II. The *Central Nave* is remarkable for its great west window (45 feet by 23 feet), and in the 14th-century nave, now known as the *South Aisle,* there are more splendid windows renowned for their lavish ball-flower decoration. The church possesses one of the few perfect Ducking stools left in England. It was in use as late as 1809. Another church treasure is a beautiful silver-gilt chalice and paten said to be well over 400 years old.

Parts of the Priory can be seen in the old Priory Hospital on the north side of the church, while in The Grange, a park adjoining the churchyard, there's the *Old Town Hall,* or Grange Court. This fine timbered house was once known as the Market Hall or Buttercross and was built by John Abel in 1633. The building got in the way of the 19th-century traffic and was moved from its original site and re-erected in the park in 1853. There are other fine old houses in High Street, Broad Street, Bargates, Bridge Street and Corn Square. In Bargates are picturesque 18th-century almshouses which were rebuilt in 1874. In an alcove on their front is the quaint figure of a man holding a hatchet and beneath him a tablet inscribed with a verse.

To Eardisland, Pembridge and Kington. About five miles west of Leominster is the lovely little village of **Eardisland** with its black-and-white houses clustering near the bridge over the river *Arrow.* One of the finest buildings is the half-timbered *Staick House* which dates from the 14th century. Beside the river there's a quaint old dovecote and adjoining the bridge is a black-and-white timbered house—formerly the Grammar School—with an old Whipping Post fixed to one side. The ancient stone **Church** (St. Mary's) is built in the Early English and Decorated styles and has a 12th-century nave. The tower and roof are modern but many other original features have been preserved. Not far from the village is **Burton Court** *(Weds, Thurs, Sats, Suns and Bank Hols, Whitsun–Aug.)* The present house was rebuilt in the early 19th century but parts of the old manor house, notably the 14th-century hall, can still be seen today.

Pembridge, two-and-a-half miles west of Eardisland, is another picturesque village with black-and-white houses. The 14th-century church has one of the country's finest detached bell towers. Also in the village is an ancient Market Hall with eight massive oak pillars supporting its stone tiled roof. Opposite is the *New Inn*, an incongruous name for such a fine timbered building which dates back to the 16th century.

Fourteen miles along the A44 from Leominster, is the small border town of **Kington,** set in attractive hilly country beside the river *Arrow*. The church, dominating the town, has a Norman tower and some good Early English and Decorated work. Inside is the effigied tomb of Thomas "Black" Vaughan who was killed at the Battle of Banbury (1469), and his wife Ellen the Terrible. She is said to have been given the name after avenging her brother's death by shooting an arrow through her murderer's heart during an archery tournament which she had entered disguised as a man. Two interesting sights in the neighbourhood of Kington are a section of Offa's Dyke, and the gardens and park of **Hergest Croft** *(daily, May 20 to June 18, fee)*, which have a notable collection of trees and flowering shrubs.

To Bromyard. The small market town of Bromyard is 12 miles east of Leominster in the valley of the river *Frome*. Its church dates from Norman times, and in the winding streets are many fine old half-timbered buildings, notably the *Falcon Inn*. Just two-and-a-half miles from the town is **Lower Brockhampton** (N.T., *Mons, Weds, Fris, Sats, Suns and Bank Hols, fee*), a small half-timbered manor house, dating from the 14th century, notable for its well-preserved 15th-century gatehouse over the moat.

To Dinmore. About six miles south of Leominster is the 16th-century house, **Dinmore Manor** *(daily, Apr.–Sept., fee)*. In 1190 Richard I gave Dinmore to the Knights Hospitallers of St. John of Jerusalem and the detached chapel dates from this period, though it was rebuilt in the 14th century. Reconstructed cloisters, music room and gardens. From nearby Dinmore Hill, overlooking the Lugg valley, there are extensive views of the countryside.

To Stretford and Dilwyn. Stretford, five miles south-west of Leominster, is notable for its church which is almost as broad as it is long, and is unique in having two naves covered by a single gable roof. Inside is a Jacobean pulpit and two pairs of 14th-century effigies. Farther west, on the A4112, is **Dilwyn** with its quaint black-and-white houses and large church, an amalgam of Norman and medieval architecture. There are some fine old houses near the village, including the 17th-century *Luntley Court* with its gabled dovecote and two-storeyed porch.

To Eyton, Kingsland and Shobdon. Eyton, two miles north-west of Leominster, has an interesting Early English church with a beautiful 15th-century screen. A farther two miles away at **Kingsland** there's another noteworthy church, dating from the 14th century. There's some good early 14th-century stained glass, and an almost unique feature is the Volka Chapel adjoining the north porch with its variety of windows and a tomb recess containing an open stone coffin. North of Kingsland is *Mortimer's Cross*, where a pedestal with a long inscription commemorates the battle between Yorkists and Lancastrians fought here in 1461. **Shobdon,** a few miles away, along the B4362 towards the Radnorshire border, has a church dating from the 12th century but largely rebuilt in the "Gothic" style.

To Yarpole and Croft. Yarpole, five miles north of Leominster, is notable for its church which has a detached medieval bell tower, the lower storey of which is built of stone and the top of wood. A short distance from the village is **Croft Castle** (N.T., *Easter–Sept., Weds, Thurs, Sats, Suns and Bank Hols, fee*), set in a large park with splendid avenues of oak, beech and Spanish chestnuts. The castle has been the home of the Croft family since the Conquest, although it did pass from their hands in 1750 for a period of about 170 years. Close to the castle is the small church with memorials to the Croft family, including the elaborate tomb of Sir Richard Croft who died in 1509. On a high-point in the park is the Iron Age fort of *Croft Ambrey*, named after the British king Aurelius Ambrosius (481–508) who is said to have once occupied it.

To Berrington Hall and Eye Manor. Berrington Hall (N.T., *Easter–Sept., Weds, Sats, and Bank Hols, fee*), about three miles north of Leominster, was built in 1778–83 by Henry Holland. The house has a marvellous interior with especially noteworthy painted ceilings. The park surrounding the house was laid out by "Capability" Brown in 1780. A mile to the west is **Eye Manor** *(Apr.–June, Weds, Thurs, Sats, Suns, July–Sept., daily, fee)*, built in 1680 and with fine plasterwork and interesting collections of costumes, straw work and other crafts.

LEOMINSTER TO LUDLOW

Motorists have a choice of roads to the historic town of Ludlow. The most direct routes are the picturesque road (B4361) through Richard's Castle and the more busy A49 which runs through Brimfield. However, those who have plenty of time can take a roundabout route, over 20 miles, by the A4110 and A4113, and visit some of the interesting places in northern Herefordshire.

If you travel on the A49 it's well worth making a diversion to Middleton-on-the-Hill. This village has an unpretentious little church dating from Norman times and also a 16th–17th-century moated house, Moor Abbey, which once belonged to the monks of Leominster.

Just off the B4361, some four miles north of Leominster, are Berrington Hall and Eye Manor, and farther north are the black-and-white houses of **Orleton** village. Two famous, though widely differing, personalities are connected with this village. Adam of Orleton, the 13th-century bishop who forced Edward II to abdicate, was born here, and the village is also the birthplace of Sir Arthur Keysall Yapp, the secretary of the YMCA who introduced the Association's Red Triangle. The village's medieval church has a timber spire and porch, and contains a fine carved Norman font. On the Shropshire border the B4361 passes through **Richard's Castle** where a mound, earthworks and fragments of wall are the only remnants of a castle founded about the time of the Norman Conquest, one of the first to be built in England. Nearby, on the same hill, is the old church with its 14th-century detached tower. From Richard's Castle the road runs past Moor Park into Overton, where it joins the A49 about a mile from Ludlow. The woods before Overton are part of the "wilde wood" of Milton's "Comus".

If you choose to travel by the longest route you pass through **Kingsland,** and about a mile from Mortimer's Cross come to the village of **Aymestrey.** The church has a particularly fine 16th-century screen with beautiful carvings. About two miles north is the attractive village of **Wigmore** with the remains of a castle, once the seat of the powerful Mortimer family. Near the village are the fragments of *Wigmore Abbey* founded in the 12th century; part of the abbey buildings have been incorporated in the old farmhouse of Wigmore Grange.

Not far from Wigmore the A4110 meets the A4113.

About a mile west of the junction is **Brampton Bryan** where there is a 14th-century gatehouse, all that remains of the castle destroyed by Royalists, despite its brave defence by the redoubtable Lady Brilliana Harley. The church, destroyed at the same time, was rebuilt in 1656 by Lady Brilliana's widower.

Along the A4113 is **Leintwardine.** The village is said to stand on the site of the Roman city of *Bravinium*. The church with its impressive tower contains some fine woodwork and there's also a monument to Sir Banastre Tarleton, who was present at the surrender of Yorktown during the American War of Independence. About five miles from Leintwardine the road joins the A49 and from there it is only a few miles farther south to Ludlow.

Worcestershire

Worcester

Distances.— Birmingham, 27; Evesham, 16; Gloucester, 27; Great Malvern, 8; Hereford, 26; Kidderminster, 15; London, 113; Oxford, 57; Stratford-upon-Avon, 25; Tewkesbury, 16.
Early Closing.—Thursday.

Hotels.—*Gifford, Crown, Star, Ye Olde Talbot, Diglis.*
Population.—73,450.
Post Office.—Foregate Street.
Racecourse.—The Pitchcroft.

The cathedral city of Worcester is situated mainly on the eastern bank of the river *Severn*. Apart from the cathedral, Worcester is famed for its fine porcelain. There is also some heavy engineering industry and the city's amenities include the county cricket ground and the racecourse. Formerly *Hwiccwaraceaster,* the camp of a west Midland tribe, it was known to the Romans as *Vigornia*. It had a turbulent history until the 17th century having been laid waste successively by Romans, Danes, Saxons and Roundheads. Many of the old Tudor and Georgian buildings have been cleared away in the modernization of the city's centre to make way for modern structures like the precinct with its hotel, shops and roof garden facing the cathedral.

The Cathedral. Its origins lie far back in the year 680 when a band of missionaries came from the monastery at Whitby. A small wooden church, long ago vanished away, was built by them near the site of the present great Cathedral. Later, this Christian centre became the Cathedral of Bishops of Worcester. Notable among the earlier ones was Oswald, who became Bishop in 961. and subsequently went on also to become Archbishop of York. He determined that the clergy serving the Cathedral church should live as monks under the strict rule of St. Benedict. Thus Worcester Cathedral became the church of a monastery and so continued for nearly 600 years down to the Dissolution of the Monasteries in 1540.

It was the great Wulstan, however, who in 1084 began the creation of the present building. Parts of the original church built by St. Wulstan are still visible. The most notable is the crypt, one of the finest of its date in Europe.

In the 14th century Worcester Cathedral and monastery were very largely rebuilt, much being added to the previous building works of Bishops Silvester, William de Blois, and Cantelupe. It is to Bishop de Blois that we owe the Lady Chapel. Thus by the middle of the 13th century the Choir and Lady Chapel were built in a beautiful Early English style, with carved foliage and Purbeck marble pillars. The rest of the church, the Transept and Nave, remained Norman and was probably in need of repair. To this was added a beautiful Choir. A problem was to make the Nave harmonise with the Choir, and it was therefore necessary to reconstruct the Nave.

Work began under the direction of Bishop Cobham between 1317 and 1327. It was in this period that the first two eastern bays on the north side of the Nave were taken down and rebuilt in a Decorated style.

The North aisle was vaulted in stone. After his death, the work begun by Cobham was continued and the whole of the Norman work on the north side of the Nave, except the two western bays, was pulled down and replaced by the beautiful pointed arches and decorated columns as they exist to this day.

One other notable Bishop who made a great contribution to Worcester Cathedral as it now is should be mentioned. This was Bishop Wakefield, in whose time, from 1375–1380, the tower, the great Transept and the whole Nave were vaulted with stone, the refectory was rebuilt (it is now used as the assembly hall of the Kings School) and the central tower erected in 1357. In 1386 the North Porch was built. This completed the structure of the Cathedral as we see it today; a great work of restoration was also completed in the 60's and 70's of the last century.

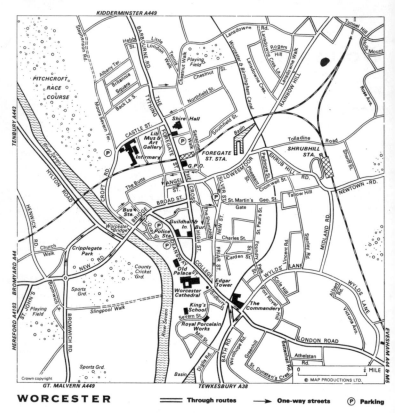

WORCESTER   ═══ **Through routes**   ➔ **One-way streets**   Ⓟ **Parking**

What has emerged from all these works across centuries is an amalgam of different styles of architecture, including Norman, Early English, Decorated and Perpendicular.

The interior of the Cathedral should be viewed firstly from the West End looking east, since the removal of the organ from the entrance to the Choir in the 19th century has made it possible to see the whole of the long building in one uninterrupted vista. Items of particular interest are the memorial to the composer Edward Elgar, in the north-west corner of the North Nave aisle, the tomb of King John in the Choir facing the High Altar, and the Chantry Chapel of Prince Arthur on the south side of the High Altar.

There is a notable series of carvings of the Last Judgment on the southern wall of the Deans' Chapel, and the magnificent Chapter House, leading off the cloisters, should on no account be missed.

From the cathedral High Street leads northward to the **Guildhall** situated on the left. This is a Queen Anne building dating from 1721 by Thomas White, a pupil of Sir Christopher Wren. The magnificent façade has a statue of Charles I on the left of the entrance and of Charles II on the right. Above is a statue of Queen Anne. Worcester was known for its loyalty to the Stuarts and earned itself the title of Faithful City. Hence the motto "Floreat semper fidelis civitas" (May the faithful city always prosper). On the southern side of the Guildhall is Copenhagen Street running down to the *Severn* and passing the tower and extraordinarily slender spire of the demolished *Church of St. Andrew*. The spire is 245 feet high and the third-tallest in England. Built in 1751, the spire has a base diameter of 20 feet and the top of the spire is about 7 inches across.

High Street continues into The Cross where a turn to the right at The Trinity leads to **Trinity House.** This half-timbered building belonged to the Guild of the Holy Trinity until the Reformation. Queen Elizabeth I spoke to the citizens from its balcony. The staircase leading to the balcony is the only form of access to the upper floor. When the old Trinity buildings were demolished in 1891 this house was moved 30 feet to its present site with the aid of powerful jacks and greased railway lines. The Trinity leads to Queen Street and the Cornmarket where stands **King Charles's House** with its inscription "Love God and Honor Ye Kinge 1577". Charles II is said to have hidden here for a time after his defeat at the battle of Worcester in 1651.

New Street leads into Friar Street, an area of timbered houses. *Greyfriars,* the largest, dates from 1480. It became a private residence after the Reformation and is now on public view. Friar Street leads to Sidbury and to the mainly Tudor building known as **The Commandery** *(Mons–Fris, fee).* This began in 1085 as the Hospital of St. Wulstan, an Augustinian community to help travellers. The building's fine features include the Great Hall, a beautiful minstrels' gallery and an oriel window containing 14th-century glass.

On the west side of the Foregate, a continuation northward of High Street, stands the *Berkeley Hospital* completed in 1703. It was built as a refuge for 12 men and three women with provision made for a distribution of money, coal and clothing. The statue of the founder, Robert Berkeley is over the doorway of the chapel. The **Royal Porcelain Works** were founded in 1751 and moved to their present site in Severn Street, 300 yards south-west of The Commandery, in 1840. There are extensive showrooms to which admission is free. Conducted tours of the works are available for a small charge.

Upper Broadheath, a hamlet two miles west of Worcester, is the birthplace of the composer Sir Edward Elgar (1857–1934). The cottage where he was born is a museum containing scores and portraits.

Spetchley, with its park, is three miles east of Worcester. *Spetchley Hall,* seat of the Berkeleys, was built in the neo-Classical style in 1811. The previous house was destroyed during the Civil war and only the stables remained from which the family made a new home. The house overlooks a spacious deer park with lakes *(Apr.–Oct., daily except Sats, fee).* The *Berkeley Chapel* in Spetchley church has the magnificent monument to Rowland Berkeley and his wife Katharine (1611). The couple lie under an arched canopy with an obelisk at each corner and decorations of red and gold roses. Their son, Robert Berkeley, is shown in judge's robes (1656).

MALVERN AND DISTRICT

Malvern

Distances.—Cheltenham, 23; Evesham, 22; Gloucester, 25; Hereford, 21; London, 119; Worcester, 8.
Early Closing.—Wednesday.

Hotels.—*Abbey, Foley Arms, Gold Hill, Broomhill, Cottage-in-the-Wood,* and others.
Population.—29,000.
Post Office.—Abbey Road.

Six places bear the name Malvern. Great Malvern, or Malvern proper, is the largest. An extension north forms North Malvern. Immediately below North Malvern is Malvern Link and West Malvern lies on the western side of North Malvern. Malvern Wells is south of the main town. It is the site of the Holy Well that brought fame to the area. Little Malvern lies beyond the Wells.

Great Malvern on the slopes of the Worcestershire Beacon developed as a fashionable spa from 1842. Most of the houses are early or mid-Victorian but there are also some attractive Regency residences.

Malvern Priory is well situated among cedars and yews in the older part of the town. The Priory church is Norman and Perpendicular. Its 124-foot square tower contains a peal of eight bells and is reminiscent of Gloucester Cathedral. The church once formed part of a Benedictine monastery founded in 1085. It was largely rebuilt in the first half of the 15th century but later became almost derelict until it was restored by Sir Gilbert Scott in 1860. It was sold to the local people at the time of the Dissolution for £20.

The **nave** roof is supported by six semi-circular Norman arches resting on massive round pillars. The great **West Window** is said to be the gift of Richard III and bears his arms. The nine lights are filled with glass that was once in other parts of the church. The church's 40 windows once all had stained glass but much of what is seen now is a collection of beautiful fragments saved down the centuries. Nevertheless the glass here is regarded as one of the finest collections of the 15th century in England.

The **Choir** is a good example of Perpendicular work. An interesting feature are the old encaustic tiles bearing some 200 different designs. These designs include coats-of-arms and images such as the pelican in its piety feeding its young from its own blood, representing the Eucharist. The tiles, dating from 1457, are among the oldest in England. The misericords on the stalls bear elaborately carved scenes of life throughout the year such as grass-cutting and a doctor visiting a patient in bed. There is also an amusing picture of three rats trying to hang a cat. The reredos, representing the Nativity, is in glass, mosaic and marble and presented in 1884. Behind it is a fine old stone screen partly covered in tiles with two fine oak doors. The altar was given to the church in 1907.

The very high Clerestory windows of the choir on the north side are the finest and most complete in the church. The glass depicts scenes from the life of St. Wulstan and the early history of the Priory. The great **East Window** once showed Christ's entry into Jerusalem and the Ascension but is now filled with fragments. There is some fine painted glass in the **Jesus Chapel** in the north transept. The North Window, representing the Joys of Mary, was damaged by a storm in the 18th century. The windows in the beautiful small chapel of St. Anne in the south chancel portray early Old Testament scenes.

The **Priory Gateway** in Abbey Road near the church is a fine example of Perpendicular architecture on its north side but is merely brick on the south.

The **Festival Theatre** next to the undistinguished Winter Gardens was where the premiere of George Bernard Shaw's *The Apple Cart* was performed in 1929. That was the first year of the Malvern Festival which takes place every year for four weeks from the last week in July.

Malvern College, founded in 1863, is one of the leading public schools in the country. It was designed by Joseph Hansom (1803–1882) of Hansom cab fame in the style known as Collegiate Tudor.

Jenny Lind (1820–1887) the "Swedish nightingale" who became the most celebrated soprano of the 19th century and who performed before the Victorians taking the waters locally, is buried in the cemetery near the station.

At **Little Malvern,** three miles south, is *St. Wulstan's Roman Catholic Church* where the composer Sir Edward Elgar (1857–1934) is buried.

Looking from north to south from Great Malvern the main summits of the Malvern Hills are: North Hill, Sugar Loaf, Worcestershire Beacon, Herefordshire Beacon or Camp Hill, Swinyard, Midsummer Camp, Raggedstone and Chase End Hill or Gloucestershire Beacon. The *Earl's Ditch,* or Red Earl's Dyke, which runs near the crest of the hills from end to end of the chain was probably first built by the ancient Britons.

The summit of **Worcestershire Beacon** can be reached in 30 minutes on foot from Great Malvern. At 1,395 feet it is the highest of the hills and the view extends over 15 counties in conditions of perfect visibility. The towers of Worcester cathedral can be seen eight miles away. Gloucester lies 26 miles away in the opposite direction. Hereford cathedral can also be seen. *St. Ann's Well,* one of the chief springs of the district, rises at 750 feet up on the slopes of the Beacon.

Herefordshire Beacon, four miles south of Malvern is 1,114 feet high and the site of a British Camp. The camp has a circumference of 2,970 yards and occupies an area of 44 acres which accommodated 20,000 men. The citadel with its thick walls is 50 yards across.

From Little Malvern a short excursion can be made along the A4104 to **Upton-on-Severn.** In Church Street there is a row of early 18th-century houses with characteristic pedimented porches. The *White Lion* in the High Street was the setting of one of Tom Jones's adventures. Only the 14th-century tower of the church remains. The tower has an octagonal cupola and dome topped by a lantern dating from 1755.

At **Ripple,** five miles south-east on the A38, there is a late 12th-century church with 14 stalls dating from the 15th century with perhaps the finest carved misericords of any village church in England. The carvings portray the various tasks month by month throughout the year. The nearby almshouses were built in 1701. The Hall has a late 18th-century façade.

WORCESTER TO EVESHAM

The road (A44) passes **Whittington** where is *Crookbarrow Hill* a fine example of ancient British earthworks. The Romans probably used it as a signal station to overlook Worcester and their camp at Kempsey four miles south of the city where pottery, coins and other relics have been found. On the other side of Kempsey Common is **Pirton Court** one of the finest examples of the half-timbered houses of south Worcestershire. Follow the road to **Croome d'Abitot** for **Croome Court,** seat of the Earl of Coventry. The grounds were made into their present beautiful form by Lancelot "Capability" Brown, the 18th-century landscape architect. An inscription on an urn records how Brown "formed this garden scene out of A MORASS". The church has monuments of the Coventry family and its interior is the work of Robert Adam.

Pershore (Pop.: 5,180. Hotels: *Angel Inn, Manor House*), nine miles from Worcester, is a Georgian town in the heart of fruit-growing country. Though named after its celebrated pears, Pershore now concentrates more on plums as a crop. Much of the Georgian character of the town remains. The High Street has buildings with attractive balconies or bow windows in brick and stone. These include the *Three Tuns* with its cast-iron verandah and *Perrott House,* the town's most elegant building. A 14th-century bridge, recently reinforced, crosses the river *Avon* in the south of the town.

Pershore Abbey in the west of the town is situated in a meadow. It was formerly much larger than its present cruciform Norman structure. The Abbey was originally founded in 689 and came into the Benedictine order in about 984. The present structure occupies only the choir and part of the transepts of the original building. The two flying buttresses on the west side were added in 1913. The remains of Norman arcading can be seen around the south transept. In that section there are also a late 13th-century tomb commemorating some unknown knight and an altar tomb bearing the effigy of an abbot dating from the late 1400s. The complete Haselwood tomb in the south transept is late 16th century. Another Haselwood memorial in the west transept is dated 1610. The original Norman font of the Abbey is also in the north transept.

The **Church of St. Andrew** is eastward of the Abbey and dates from the reign of Edward the Confessor. The main feature is the tower but much of the building has been restored.

Elmley Castle, now in ruins, four miles south-east of Pershore, was the earliest of the Beauchamp family's seats. The church which is in the Perpendicular style has

EVESHAM

Through routes   One-way streets   (P) Parking

some good monuments of the Savage family who were Lords of the Manor from 1512 to 1822.

Nearby is **Bredon Hill,** an outlier of the Cotswolds. Near the summit at 960 feet is *Kemerton Camp,* one of a chain of 27 forts that extended from Clifton to Bredon Hill. The camp was probably British and later adapted by the Romans. The *Bambury Stone* in the camp is believed to have been an altar used in sacrificial rites.

Cropthorne, just off to the left from the A44, is considered to be one of England's prettiest villages. It is worth a visit for its black-and-white cottages and Norman church.

Evesham (Pop.: 13,850. Hotels: *Mansion House, Northwick Arms, Park View*), pleasantly situated on the river *Avon,* began as an abbey named after one Eoves, a swineherd who had a vision of the Blessed Virgin. In 1265 it was the scene of the battle in which Simon de Montfort, the first man to call a parliament that also represented commoners, died after being defeated by Prince Edward, son of Henry III. The **Bell Tower** (1539) is one of the few remains of the abbey. The tower is believed to be the last architectural work of any importance by English monk-builders.

The two churches near the Bell Tower are **St. Laurence,** built in the 15th century for the pilgrims visiting the shrine of Simon de Montfort and **All Saints** which was used by the people of Evesham. St. Laurence has a splendid east end exterior. Its best feature is the Lichfield Chantry or chapel famed for the beauty of the fan-vaulting of its roof. All Saints has traces of its original Norman structure but dates mainly from the 14th and 15th centuries. It also has a chantry for the Abbot of Lichfield with a fine Tudor roof of fan-tracing and superbly carved.

Lay buildings of interest in the town include the *Star Inn* in the High Street and *Dresden House,* built in brick with a richly-carved cornice. The wrought-iron brackets of the porch date from 1692. The Market Place is situated near the junction of High Street with Bridge Street. At the entrance is an ancient structure of wood and plaster called Booth Hall dating from the 15th century. It was replaced as a meeting place by the Guildhall on the other side of the Market Place. The **Almonry** in Vine Street, a broad tree-lined road, once formed part of the Abbey and was later used as a jail. It now houses a museum one of the exhibits being the Abbot's Chair.

WORCESTER TO KIDDERMINSTER

The road (A449) leads to **Ombersley,** a picturesque village of half-timbered houses. The *King's Arms Inn* dates from 1450. King Charles II is said to have slept in the bedroom on the night before the battle of Worcester. *Ombersley Court* is Regency stucco (1812) on the exterior but early 18th century within.

Areley Kings is a scattered village with an attractive grouping of church, rectory and half-timbered church house. Layamon, the "earliest writer in the English language" as distinct from Anglo-Saxon and Norman French, was priest here from about 1189 to 1200.

Stourport *(Swan),* was dubbed the Venice of the Midlands because of its importance as a junction in the busy days of the Staffordshire and Worcestershire Canal, opened in 1771. The canal was the work of James Brindley, the near-illiterate son of a Derbyshire farmer. The canal basin is flanked by the plain brick façade of the *Tontine Inn* and a fine Georgian warehouse with a wooden clocktower. The iron bridge over the *Severn* was built in 1870. Bridge Street, New Street and York Street have several Georgian brick houses. The parish **church** was designed ambitiously by Sir Gilbert Scott in 1875. Funds ran out and the ends of the uncompleted nave had to be blocked up. It was not until 1965, 80 years later, that the work was completed though not to Scott's original plans.

The B4195 leads to **Bewdley,** one of the most beautiful small towns in England as its old Norman name "Beaulieu" (beautiful place) inferred. The town is situated on a slope above the western bank of the *Severn*. The river is spanned by Telford's three-arched bridge completed in 1801. Stanley Baldwin was born in 1867 in Lower Park House in Lower Park Street. This street continues into High Street which probably has one of the best ensemble of buildings of architectural merit in the country. These include the Cooke Almshouses (1693), the Queen Anne Manor House and two black-and-white buildings at Nos. 68 and 69 dating from 1610. Much of the timberwork in Bewdley's old buildings is from oak from the Wyre Forest. There are four very old inns in Load Street which runs west to east down to the river. One of these is the half-timbered *George Hotel,* an old posting house. The 18th-century **Church of St. Anne** has a pretty exterior but the interior is spoilt by unsightly stained glass. *Tickenhill Palace,* west of the town, was where Henry VIII's brother Prince Arthur married Katherine of Aragon by proxy in 1499. The building is now faced in Georgian brick.

Kidderminster (Pop.: 47,250. Hotel: *Park Attwood*), is the world's largest carpet-manufacturing centre. The factories, in mock-Renaissance style, are about the only unusual architectural feature of this industrial town. In the Bull Ring in the town centre there are statues to Richard Baxter, the 17th-century divine who suffered imprisonment for his religious beliefs, and Sir Rowland Hill, founder of the penny post who was born in Kidderminster and is buried in Westminster Abbey in London. The **Church of St. Mary and All Saints** is situated on a hill. It has a 15th-century tower and nave and a 14th-century chancel. There is a fine monument under a Perpendicular canopy of Sir Hugh Cokesey (*d.* 1445) and his wife. **St. George's Church** in Coventry Street is in 1824 Perpendicular and impressive for the soaring quality of its pillars and buttresses.

DROITWICH AND BROMSGROVE

Droitwich (Pop.: 12,760. Hotels: *Worcestershire, Raven, St. Andrews House, Chateau Impney*), seven miles north of Worcester along the A38, boasts the strongest natural salt water known. The springs have been known and used for more than a 1,000 years. Droitwich became a busy spa in 1836. That was four years after an outbreak of cholera. During the epidemic fresh water ran out. It was found when patients were washed in the Droitwich brine they showed signs of improvement. The salt solution is about 12 times stronger than in the ocean and about 40% than in the Dead Sea. The water is so dense that bathers find it impossible to sink in it which leads to much amusement when taking the waters.

St. Andrew's Church, opposite the Town Hall, dates from the 13th century. There is Early English arcading in the nave and a Tudor roof over the chancel. *Priory House* in No. 1 Friary Street is Elizabethan with Queen Anne chimneys. **St. Peter's Church** in the south-eastern outskirts of the town has a Norman chancel and Decorated nave and north transept. Note the curiously apt inscription above the south doorway: "Remember Lot's wife". The south transept is Early English.

Chateau Impney, a mile north of Droitwich, is an opulent Victorian version of the style of Louis XIII with its scarlet bricks, mansarded roof and elaborate gables. It was designed by a French architect for John Corbett, the "Salt King" of Droitwich and is now a hotel.

Hanbury Hall (N.T., *Apr.–Sept., Weds, Sats, fee*), three miles east of Droitwich, is a red brick house built in 1701 by Thomas Vernon. The staircase is painted by Sir James Thornhill and shows episodes from the life of Achilles. In the garden is a Queen Anne orangery.

Bromsgrove is a pleasant market town which also produces clothing, buttons and fishing tackle. The **Church of St. John the Baptist** situated on a hill and surrounded by pollarded lime trees dominates the town. The beautiful tower and spire were built in the 1300s. There are good monuments to Sir Humphrey Stafford and his wife (1450) and Sir John Talbot and his two wives (1550). Buried side by side in the graveyard are two young victims of an accident in the early days of the railways. The tombstones bear a picture of an ancient steam locomotive.

Redditch, six miles east of Bromsgrove, is a major supplier of needles and fish-hooks. The Roman Catholic church was built in 1834 by Thomas Rickman. This was the architect who coined the terms Norman, Early English, Decorated and Perpendicular. His church is a modern version of the Perpendicular.

Salop

Shropshire is an attractive border county flanked on the west by the Welsh regions of Clwyd and Powys and by Cheshire, Staffordshire, Hereford and Worcester on its English side. The river *Severn* divides the county into two geographical regions with hills in the west and south and rolling plains in the north-east. The hilly region contains some of the oldest rocks known to man, such as the pre-Cambrian formations of the Long Mynd and the Wrekin. The varied landscapes, the celebrated, centuries-old black-and-white houses and the pleasant towns such as Shrewsbury, Ludlow and Church Stretton make Shropshire an interesting area for touring. The economy is based mainly on farming but there are ironfounding and engineering industries which recall the days of the late 18th century when Shropshire was the major iron producer in England. The ancient history of the county is revealed in its place names such as Llanyblodwell (Celtic), Wroxeter (Roman) and Donington (Saxon). But even before these places arose the region was peopled in prehistoric times as witnessed by such remains as barrows and stone rings.

Shrewsbury

Distances.—Bridgnorth, 21; Chester, 40; Hereford, 52; London, 153; Ludlow, 28; Newtown, 32; Oswestry, 18; Welshpool, 19.
Early Closing.—Thursday.
Golf.—At Meole Brace.
Hotels.—*Lion, Prince Rupert, Britannia, Load Hill,*

Beauchamp, Abbey Gardens, Pengwern and others.
Library and Museum.—In Old School, near station.
Population.—56,150.
Post Office.—Pride Hill.

Shrewsbury, the county town, is at the very heart of Shropshire. It has a fine setting on rising ground on the peninsula formed by a sweeping meander of the *Severn.* At its narrowest point is the bright red sandstone **Shrewsbury Castle** which with the watery ring of the *Severn,* seems to complete the defensive ring round the city. The Castle was founded by the Norman lord Roger de Montgomery in 1070 and rebuilt during the reign of Edward I. Telford, the great 18th-century technocrat and ironmaster, modernised it and it now serves as a council chamber.

Opposite the castle are the **Library and Museum** *(weekdays)* well-established in buildings previously occupied by Shrewsbury School. One interesting and prized relic is the cloak which King Charles I wore at his execution in 1649. In front of the building is the statue of Charles Darwin (1809–82), the eminent scientist who fathered the theory of evolution and who was born in Frankwell across the river.

Castle Street leads to the centre of old Shrewsbury with its attractive black-and-white houses some going back 500 years. This district has long been busy with shoppers and tradespeople as witnessed by road names such as Milk Street, Butcher's Row and Fish Street. It helps to make Shrewsbury one of England's finest Tudor towns but there is nothing of the museum atmosphere and the buildings are still in use. The cluster of spires belong to St. Alkmund's, St. Julian's and St. Mary's which are set amid a maze of narrow lanes, the result of natural growth rather than planning. The Perpendicular-style spire of **St. Alkmund's Church** soars almost 200 feet towards the sky. The spire is 15th century but the rest of the church was largely rebuilt toward the end of the 18th century when its brasses were stripped and sold as scrap. The steeple of **St. Julian's Church** is older, dating from the 13th century but its nave is 18th-century although there are some 500-year-old timbers. **St. Mary's Church,** just off Castle Street, is the finest of the three and consists of a medley of styles from the 12th century to the 17th. The spire is 220 feet high atop a Norman tower. The nave belongs to the transitional period between Norman and Early English. The transept is Early English. A 16th-century window in the north of the chancel has scenes from the life of St. Bernard. The great Jesse window contains English glass, dating from the mid-14th century, that was originally in the Friary of the Grey Friars.

St. Mary's Street leads to the quaintly named medieval road of Dogpole. The Guildhall on the left was built in 1696. Mary Tudor once lived in the Olde House nearby. Charles Dickens stayed at the *Lion Hotel* and the great violin virtuoso Paganini gave a performance there. Next door is another half-timbered structure, Tudor House. This is where Harry Richmond, later King Henry VII, is reputed to have stayed while on his way to vanquish King Richard III at Bosworth.

In High Street are two very fine half-timbered houses—*Ireland's Mansion* and *Owen's Mansion* the latter erected in 1592 by a wealthy member of the Drapers' Company.

Along the High Street and to the left is the **Square** with the picturesque **Market Hall** erected in 1596. It is one of the finest buildings of its kind and is supported on columns: the upper portion was used as a market for the flannel from Wales which used to be brought on the backs of ponies. A statue here commemorates Lord Clive who represented Shrewsbury in Parliament and was the town's mayor in 1762. Returning by High Street we come to **Wyle Cop** another thoroughfare of old houses which leads to the **English Bridge** linking the Shrewsbury peninsula with the English side of the town. The bridge was built in 1769 and widened in 1927. Across the bridge is the Technical College on the left, while Abbey Foregate leads straight ahead to the **Abbey Church.** The building is made of the characteristic dark-red local stone and was first founded in Norman times but much of it was rebuilt in the 19th century. A fine Early English arch divides the nave from the tower. Outside is the *Reader's Pulpit* dating from the 14th century. It is kept in an enclosure near the road and is one of the last relics of the monastery.

Back on English Bridge, Beeches Lane and Town Walls give on to Belmont, a road of elegant 18th-century houses. There is Old St. Chad's, a church of Norman times which collapsed in 1788. It still has among other things its 17th-century beams, an 18th-century pulpit and two kneeling figures in Stuart dress complete with lace ruffs.

New St. Chad's was built after the catastrophe about a quarter of a mile to the west in 1792. It is a round church with a cupola tower 154 feet high. It has an imposing portico of Doric columns while Ionic columns support its gallery. The church overlooks **The Quarry,** a 25-acre park named after its former function. It was here that local red stone was obtained. The park is now a fine recreation ground with an ornamental lake frequented by many varieties of birds. In August there is a two-day musical and floral festival held here. Across the river is **Shrewsbury School** approached by the Kingsland (Toll) Bridge. The school was founded in 1552 by Edward VI but the present buildings were erected here in 1822. The institution is one of England's leading public schools. Its former pupils include Jeffreys, the "Hanging Judge", Darwin and Samuel Butler, author of *Erewhon* and headmaster of the school from 1798 to 1836. On the northern side of the peninsula is the **Welsh Bridge** which was built in 1795. Across the bridge the road rises to **Darwin House** where the great pioneer was born. The Welsh Bridge, of course, is the beginning of the gateway to Wales. In former times, Shrewsbury was a rampart to withstand any attack from the Principality.

SHREWSBURY TO LUDLOW

The road (A49) passes through **Baystonhill,** mainly a dormitory suburb of Shrewsbury. Nearby, hidden among trees, is Bomere Poll, one of Shropshire's many meres or small lakes.

Dorrington is the birthplace of John Boydell (*b.* 1719) engraver and publisher who won fame by employing such eminent artists of the day as Reynolds and Fuseli and was elected Lord Mayor of London.

About a mile to the north-east is **Condover Hall** *(daily in Aug.)* now a school and home for blind children. North-west of Dorrington is **Stapleton** with a red sandstone church unusual for its two different storeys knocked into one. The lower level was probably a storage place when the church was first built in about 1200 and was incorporated into the rest of the building in 1786. A little to the south of Stapleton is *The Moat House,* a half-timbered farmhouse surrounded by a moat. At Pitchford, three miles east, is **Pitchford Hall,** built in 1473 and the finest half-timbered house in the county.

Longnor the next village on A49 has a late 17th-century hall *(not open).* **Leebotwood** is in Shropshire's hill country and the great mass of the Long Mynd can be seen to the south. Leebotwood has several pretty black-and-white houses and a thatched inn dating from 1650 complete with beams and Jacobean panelling.

Church Stretton (Pop.: 2,900. Hotels: *Longmynd, Denehurst*) is situated at 650 feet above sea level at the heart of Shropshire's hill region. It lies in the valley between the Long Mynd in the west and the Caradoc Hills in the east 13 miles south of Shrewsbury. The town was formerly much favoured as a spa offering invigorating air and relaxing surroundings. Its importance as a health resort has diminished but it still offers magnificent scenery to the visitor. The church has a version of the *Sheila-na-gig* over a blocked Norman doorway. This stone carving is usually an impudent female fertility symbol. In this case the figure is male but no less provocative. Just outside **All Stretton** there is a drinking fountain with an inscription recalling the days when the district was a spa. The Strettons— Church Stretton, Little Stretton and All Stretton—owe their common name to the Roman road or street and the line of Watling Street from Leintwardine to Wroxeter is not far to the east.

The **Long Mynch** rises away to the west. Its summit, almost 1700 feet above sea level, is covered in moorland with great stretches of heather and whinberries. From the top are extensive views over the dark rocky ridge of the Stiperstones to the Welsh counties beyond. The **Cardingmill Valley** extends to the north-west of the town. **Caer Caradoc** (1,500 feet), two miles north-east, has an old British encampment and a cave where Caratacus, the bitter foe of the Roman occupiers of Britain, is reported to have taken shelter.

Wistanstow is a quiet village at the southern end of Wenlock Edge. It is named after St. Wystan, who renounced the crown of Mercia for a life of religion but was later murdered by envious relatives. The village has a church dating from the 12th century.

Craven Arms *(Craven Arms, Stokesay Castle)* is an important junction and a centre for the sheep farming conducted on the surrounding hills. Just south before Ludlow is **Stokesay Castle** *(daily except Tues)* a fine example of a fortified manor house. Built about 1280 it has fine panelling and fireplaces of the period.

Onibury has a church that is beautifully simple with its plain stone exterior and whitewashed walls inside contrasting with the rich woodwork of the gallery and the unusual criss-cross pattern of the screen. **Bromfield** has the remains of a 12th-century priory and Ludlow racecourse is nearby. Henry Hill Hickman (1800–30), a pioneer of inhaled anaesthetics, is commemorated in a plaque in the church which dates from the Elizabethan era.

Ludlow

Distances.—Birmingham, 40; Gloucester, 48; Hereford, 24; Leominster, 11; London, 143; Worcester, 30.
Early Closing.—Thursday.
Hotels.—*Feathers, Angel, Bull.*
Market Day.—Monday.

Museum.—Butter Cross.
Population.—7,080.
Post Office.—Corve Street.
Sports.—Rowing, tennis, bowls, putting, swimming pool, golf at Bromfield (2 miles).

Ludlow is one of the most picturesque towns in England and is beautifully situated on a hill overlooking the *Teme*. The old town is dominated by its ancient castle and cathedral-like church.

The **Castle** *(fee)* was once the seat of the Lords Presidents of the Marches who ruled the border country and Wales and was part of a line of defences that ran from Chester to Chepstow. It was begun in 1086 by the Norman lord Roger de Lacy. Built of pink sandstone it offers a magnificent view from its 110-foot-high Norman keep. There are also a beautiful round Norman chapel and the Great Hall, now roofless, where John Milton's masque *Comus* was first performed in 1634. Shakespearian plays are staged in the castle in summer.

The town has several beautiful old buildings. Spanning Broad Street is the only remaining gate of the seven which originally pierced the strong walls of the town. Beyond the Town Hall is the old Butter Cross with its portico and bell-turret.

St. Laurence Church has much detail of interest—the stalls in the choir, with restored canopies, the reredos displays excellent wood carving. St. John's Chapel with fine panelling, and the 14th- and 15th-century glass in the east window of the south transept. The font is probably Saxon, though the cover is modern. The tower is 135 feet high and gives a splendid view. The porch is hexagonal and unique except for St. Mary Redcliffe at Bristol.

Eastward is the venerable timbered **Reader's House** *(daily, fee)*—the reader was an official of the ancient Palmers' Guild who read the prayers.

In Corve Street is the *Feathers* a half-timbered inn. Other old inns are the *Angel* and the *Bull*. Among old buildings are *St. Giles's Hospital, Lane's Hospital*, the *Tolsey* and *Ludford House*.

SHREWSBURY TO BRIDGNORTH

The A5 road eastward from Shrewsbury goes through **Atcham** *(Mytton and Mermaid)* with its sandstone bridge across the *Severn* and red 13th-century church. Just north of the road is **Attingham Park** (N.T., *Easter–Sept., Weds, Thurs, Bank Hols, fee)* with extensive parkland. The house, famous for its interior decoration, was designed by George Steuart in 1785 for the first Lord Berwick. In a mile the B4380 runs off right for **Wroxeter** where are the remains of the Roman town of *Viroconium* including part of a basilica, baths and a colonnade *(daily, fee)*. Roman stone was used for part of the construction of Wroxeter church which has a Saxon nave.

Eight miles farther on is **Ironbridge,** the centre of a fascinating region that was once a power house of industry. Ironbridge itself rises on the northern slope of the *Severn* and is dominated by its pink-stone church. Spanning the river is the celebrated bridge—the "stupendous iron arch"—the first construction of its kind in the world. The bridge was designed in 1774 by T. F. Pritchard and cast in the specially enlarged furnaces of Abraham Darby (1677–1717) at nearby **Coalbrookdale** which was then the cradle of England's iron industry.

Coalport, famous for its china and porcelain, is two miles south-east of Ironbridge. Not far from Coalport is **Broseley,** strangely pretty despite its former industrial functions. Near Broseley is **Benthall Hall** (N.T., *Easter–Sept., Tues, Weds, Sats, Bank Hols)* a 16th-century stone house with fine stairway and ceilings. Caughley has the distinction of giving birth to the famous "willow pattern" which has graced countless thousands of tea-sets. **Madeley,** north of Coalport was also a pottery town from 1828 to 1840. Much of this area is being preserved as an open-air museum of the early days of the Industrial Revolution in England. The brick kilns and the old furnaces as at Coalbrookdale still present an impressive sight though their fires no longer light up the night sky.

From Ironbridge the B4373 to the north leads to **Dawley** where Captain Webb, the first man to swim the English Channel in 1875, was born. Dawley is now part of **Telford,** a new town named after Thomas Telford (1757–1834) designer of the Menai Bridge and builder of many canals, waterways, ports and harbours.

Little Wenlock lies about two miles to the west of Dawley and has The Old Hall, being the remains of an Elizabethan mansion. In the churchyard, as in many others in this region, there are many iron tombstones. Little Wenlock is rather an isolated village cowering under the bulk of the **Wrekin,** the 1,334-foot cone marking the grave of an extinct volcano. Though modest in height compared to Alpine peaks, the Wrekin stands out in contrast to the relative flatness of the surrounding landscape. From the summit there are fantastic views.

Much Wenlock, situated at the north-eastern tip of Wenlock Edge, the limestone ridge that flanks Clun forest, is five miles south-west of Ironbridge. The Guildhall still has wrist fetters outside where wrongdoers were once shackled and whipped. Inside the building are the old stocks. The nearby ruins of **Wenlock Priory** *(daily, fee)* were once a nunnery founded in the 7th century.

From Much Wenlock the A458 leads to **Morville,** a beautiful village nestling amid cornfields and trees. The gilded domes belong to Morville Hall, an Elizabethan house rebuilt in the 18th century. Aldenham Park is the home of the Acton family.

Bridgnorth presents a striking appearance. It is really two separate units: the High Town perched 200 feet up on the right bank of the *Severn* and the Low Town on the opposite side of the gorge which is a continuation of the one at Ironbridge upstream. At the south end of the High Town there is a remarkable leaning tower, the last relic of a 12th-century castle. Telford took time off from his bridges and canals to design the church of St. Mary Magdalene which dates from 1797. Other interesting buildings are the *Governor's House* (1633) and the *Town Hall* (1652) which stands on arches.

There are many interesting strolls to be had through the narrow lanes of the town and up and down the steps to and from the river connecting the High and Low Towns. There is also a cliff railway that climbs a giddy gradient of $1:1\frac{1}{2}$.

Clun and the Stiperstones

Clun is a quiet little village in the south-east of Salop. The village has the rather grim ruins of a Norman castle and a museum displaying a selection of flints and arrowheads found in nearby Clun Forest. The Hospital of the Holy Trinity was founded in the early 1600s by the Earl of Northampton. It is a single-storey stone structure built round a grass courtyard. Clun's church is Norman with some remains of earlier Saxon features. There are unusual carvings on the pillars and a host of angels with outspread wings.

Clungunford, away to the east half-a-mile from the Roman Watling Street, has a prehistoric barrow near its church. The Church dates from the 14th century but the tower, which is almost detached from the main building, was erected in the 19th century. Note the massive oak bolt in the Priest's Door. It is four inches square and 600 years old.

To the west of Clun, Clun Forest is as much desolate open land as it is trees. The forest is mainly the work in recent times of the Forestry Commission. Through the forest region runs a portion of Offa's Dyke, a remarkable man-made earthen rampart that once extended for 140 miles from the *Wye* to the *Dee*.

North on the A488 is **Bishop's Castle,** a small market town of irregular streets. No trace of the castle is left but the *Castle Hotel* stands on the old site. The *Three Tuns* is the oldest hostelry in the town and dates from 1642. Another interesting building is the *House on Crotches* which is supported by wooden posts. Follow the A488 north to where *Corndon Hill* rises to 1,684 feet in the west. Some six miles from Bishop's Castle and off to the right is **Shelve,** one of the remote villages that lie under the *Stiperstones*. This rocky mass was once the site of thriving lead mines worked by the Romans. Pigs of lead bearing Hadrian's seal have been found here. Another Stiperstone village is **Pennerley** which is near the grimly-named *Devil's Chair* on the ridge of the Stiperstones, some 1,731 feet above sea level. **Snailbeach** is another relic of the old lead mines with its backcloth of spectacular slag heaps glittering with barytes. **Pontesbury** is also in the shadow of the Stiperstones on the A488 to Shrewsbury. Nearby is the site of a battle between the Kings of Mercia and Wessex. Mary Webb, the Shropshire writer who wrote *Gone to Earth* and *Precious Bane* and died in 1927 lived in Pontesbury for two years.

If the B4387 is followed from **Ploxgreen** one comes to **Westbury** which has the ruins of a castle destroyed in the Civil War. Follow the B4387 to the A458 and turn left for **Wollaston.** Near this village which nestles under the Breiddin Hills was where Old Parr was born in 1483. A brass plate in Wollaston Church records that in his reputed 152 years on earth the old boy lived through the reigns of ten English kings and queens from Edward IV to Charles I. With a diet of rancid cheese and hard bread this ancient rustic first married at the age of 80 and had two children from the match. He was also reputed to have married again at 120 and his untimely death came from dissipation after he went to London by Royal Command.

OSWESTRY TO MARKET DRAYTON AND NEWPORT

Oswestry (Pop.: 12,100. Hotels: *Wynnstay, Queen's*) is an ancient border market town with an embattled history of tumult, raids and local wars. St. Oswald, after whom the town is named, was murdered by King Penda of Mercia in 642. But long before that people lived just to the north on the summit of a hill that now bears the remains of an Iron Age camp known as Old Oswestry. Oswestry has some good examples of half-timbered houses. The best of these are the Llwyd Mansion and the Headmaster's House which dates from the 18th century though the school itself was founded in 1407. Sir Henry Walford Davies (1869–1941), composer and Wilfred Owen (1893–1918), the young poet, were born in the town. **Whittington,** three miles north-east along the A495, has a picturesque ruined castle with swans gliding in the moat.

Ellesmere *(Black Lion)* lies in the heart of the Shropshire "lake district". There are seven stretches of water known as "meres". Each is the haunt of wildfowl and a paradise for anglers and those fond of sailing. The town is a jumble of narrow streets and there are several picturesque half-timbered buildings.

On the northern border of the county stands **Whitchurch** a pretty little market town that has not been too much spoiled. The church is well set at the top of a hill with old almshouses nearby. In the church is the monument to that John Talbot, first Earl of Shrewsbury, dubbed by Shakespeare in "Henry VI" as "the scourge of France". Sir Edward German (1862–1936) was born in Whitchurch. In the High Street is a three-storey shop building made entirely in cast iron.

From Whitchurch follow the A41 to Tern Hill and then take the A53 to **Market Drayton.** This is another old town with a goodly share of 17th-century half-timbered houses and Georgian buildings. Lord Clive (1725–74) the East India Company clerk who went on to conquer India for the British Empire, was born at Syche, two miles north-west of Market Drayton. As a boy he lowered himself down the steeple of Market Drayton church and perched on one of the gargoyles. The famous **Hodnet Hall Gardens** *(Apr.–Sept., daily, fee)* lie five-and-a-half miles south-west. These beautiful grounds cover 60 acres.

South-eastward on the A41 is **Newport** a busy market town in a thriving agricultural area. The town stands on the Shropshire Union Canal. Newport is interesting for its old inns and the fine *Royal Victoria Hotel* dating from about 1830. The Guildhall, built in 1615, survived the fire of 1665 when much of the town was burned.

South of Newport are **Oakengates** and its near neighbour **Wellington** a considerable market and manufacturing town. Wellington has a well-known public school, Wrekin College. Together with **Shifnal** both towns are now incorporated in the new town project of **Telford.**

East of Shifnal with entrance across the border at West-under-Lizard is the magnificent **West Park** *(daily except Mons and Fris, fee)* seat of the Earl of Bradford, with fine gardens and parkland.

Liverpool and District

Merseyside. The administrative metropolitan county of Merseyside is mainly of an industrial nature and includes the two major shipping centres of Liverpool and Birkenhead beside other large towns, notably Bootle and St. Helens. These busy centres contribute greatly to the prosperity of a region that is one of the most densely populated areas in Britain. The coastal strip north of Formby to Southport and Banks on the Lancashire border, and the sector contained within the Wirral peninsula, excepting Birkenhead, constitute the non-industrial, and therefore the most popular parts of this county so far as visiting tourists are concerned.

Liverpool

Distances. — London, 197; Southport, 20; Manchester, 35; Birkenhead, 2 (Tunnel); Preston, 30; Chester, 18; Bolton, 29.
Early Closing. — Wednesday (suburbs).
Entertainments. — Theatres: *Royal Court, Everyman* and *Playhouse* (repertory), *Empire. Philharmonic Hall* (concerts of Royal Philharmonic Society). Numerous cinemas. Liverpool Show (mid-July) at Wavertree east of city. "Merseyside Sound" originated at Cavern Club (Matthew Street).
Hotels. — *Adelphi, Exchange, St. George's, Lord*

Nelson, Stork, Shaftesbury, Bradford, Hunts and others.
Population. — 606,800.
Post Office. — Victoria Street.
Sports. — Golf: courses at Allerton, Bowring, Woolton, Childwall, Blundellsands and West Derby. Liverpool Racecourse at Aintree (5 miles). Bowls, tennis etc. in city parks. Liverpool Football Club play at Anfield, Everton F.C. at Goodison Park. Swimming baths, ice rink and dog track.

Dominating Liverpool's seven-mile-long water front and dock area are three massive buildings, the Royal Liver Building, the Custom House, and the Dock Board offices. The most impressive of these, the offices of the Royal Liver Friendly Society (1910), reaches a height of 295 feet with a frontage of 301 feet though architecturally the Dock Board building can justifiably claim to be the forerunner of the three. The Custom House, perhaps the best known though still often referred to by its old name of Cunard Building, was completed in 1916. Fronting these buildings is the Pierhead with a series of hinged bridges connecting to the Landing Stage, a vast floating quay stretching along the waterfront for close on half-a-mile. Ocean-going liners use the downstream portion, Prince's Landing Stage, whilst the upstream section, George's Landing Stage, is used by a constant stream of ferry vessels. Ferry services to Birkenhead and Seacombe across the *Mersey* run approximately every 15 minutes. In the vicinity of the Pierhead in Chapel Street is the *Church of Our Lady and St. Nicholas* the original parish church of Liverpool dating from 1360 but rebuilt in 1952 after enemy bombing in the Second World War. It is best noted for its very fine woodwork. Behind this famous church and running parallel to Chapel Street is Water Street which in turn, leads us into Dale Street for the *Town Hall* (1754) and, close by, the Liverpool *Stock Exchange*. Still closer to the city centre in Dale Street are the *Municipal Offices* and, beyond them, the entrance to the two-and-five-eighths mile long

Mersey Tunnel linking Liverpool with Birkenhead. Well worth seeing slightly east is the imposing *St. George's Hall* (1854) near the city's principal rail station, Lime Street. This building with 60-foot high Corinthian columns houses both a concert hall with a magnificent organ, and law courts. To the north the *Walker Art Gallery* generally acknowledged as having the best collection outside London, not least of paintings, is especially noted for its early Italian and Flemish works and the fine

LIVERPOOL

━━━ Through routes   → One-way streets   Ⓟ Parking

░░░ Parking Meter Zone

Roscoe Collection. Immediately adjacent is the *Museum and Central Library* comprising three buildings containing valuable material and treasures (see part of the Sassoon collection of ivories), first editions, prints and fine-art books. The *Sudley Art Gallery* in Mossley Hill Road is also well worth a visit on account of its collection of British paintings.

The **Roman Catholic Cathedral** (Metropolitan Cathedral of Christ the King) in Mount Pleasant was originally planned to be the largest place of worship in Europe though this in fact never materialised. The present structure was built between 1962 and 1967 when it was officially consecrated. Probably of greatest interest is the shape of the building itself which, tent-like in appearance, rises to a height of 270 feet with an overall diameter of 200 feet. Such is the area within the perimeter that up to 3,000 of a congregation can be accommodated with a further section to the north of the Cathedral being used for open-air gatherings. The main Entrance Porch, the lantern filled with coloured glass and the several chapels—notably St. George, St. Patrick, St. Thomas Aquinas, St. Columba and the Lady—constitute the most rewarding aspects of the Cathedral so far as the sightseer is concerned.

The **Anglican Cathedral** conspicuously sited in St. James's Mount is destined when complete to be the largest Anglican cathedral in Britain. In addition to its great size it is also one of the most interesting of all British cathedrals with possibly the most notable feature being the tunnel-shaped aisles. Although the foundation stone was laid in 1904 it was not until six years later that the beautiful Lady Chapel was completed and consecrated. Sir Giles Gilbert Scott, the architect who was responsible for the original largely Gothic design, gave much of his life (1880–1960) to the work which he was still supervising up to his death. Possibly the most noteworthy features of the Cathedral are to be found in the Central Space which houses the transepts, the Vestry Tower rising to a height of 331 feet, the War Memorial Chapel, the Choir containing what is said to be the largest organ in the world and the magnificent stained glass in all windows, not least that in the Bishops' Window in the nave.

Liverpool University (founded 1903) is situated a little way east of the R.C. Cathedral while the *Philharmonic Hall* (Royal Philharmonic Society) whose accoustics are among the best in the country, stands in Hope Street roughly equidistant between the two cathedrals. Other points of interest within the city are *The Old Bluecoat School* dating back to 1717 and now known as Bluecoat Chambers in Church Alley. The former School has for some time been an arts centre which is open to the public; *St. John's Beacon,* a 450 feet tower with a restaurant and observation gallery, near St. George's Hall, and the vast area (2,046 acres) which comprise the Docks. Here, from the 38 miles of quays is handled close on 30 million tons per year. It is further claimed that the Liverpool of today is Europe's greatest Atlantic seaport. Of the many parks and open spaces which lie on the city's periphery, **Sefton Park** (269 acres) in the south-east is both the finest and the most attractive. *Otterspool Park* and *Stanley Park* both offer fine views, the first-mentioned being near the start of Liverpool's most impressive roadway, namely the seven miles-long Queen's Drive which terminates near Everton Football Club's ground.

Speke Hall (N.T., *daily, fee*), eight miles south-east of the city centre and close to *Liverpool (Speke) Airport* is a fine 16th-century half-timbered house primarily famed for its carved wainscoting, elaborate plasterwork, Great Hall and tapestries.

Hale three miles west of Speke is a quaint place described by Carlyle's wife as "the beautifullest village in all England". It has attractive old low-roofed cottages and a 17th-century church.

ACROSS THE MERSEY

Birkenhead (Pop.: 137,700. Hotels: *Central, Woodside, Riverhill*), is a busy seaport directly opposite Liverpool of which it is in fact an integral part. Its 10 miles of docks and quays are combined with those of Liverpool under the control of the Mersey Docks and Harbour Board, the shipyards have provided the port with many of its ships whilst the suburbs are a popular dormitory for many whose work is on the other side of the Mersey. Access is by the ferry services and by the Mersey rail and road tunnels. The *Williamson Art Gallery and Museum* (1928) has a particularly fine collection of English watercolours. Ceramics, notably the Knowles Boney Collection, are a feature of the Gallery. The *Town Hall* (1887) is impressive as too is the *Central Library* in Borough Road. *Birkenhead Park* (180 acres) and the still larger *Arrowe Park* (425 acres—bird sanctuary) are both owned by the Corporation while north-west of the town Bidston Hill has, in addition to a very old windmill, a direction indicator to assist the enjoyment of the extensive views of the surrounding countryside.

Some four miles north of Birkenhead is **New Brighton,** a coastal resort popular with residents of the industrial belt of Merseyside and beyond. The town, amalgamated with Wallasey, has a fine promenade stretching along the banks of the Mersey estuary as far as **Seacombe** and well-organised amenities such as can be expected from most other seaside resorts. There is a good stretch of firm sand and what has been described as "one of the largest sea-water swimming pools in the world". As one might expect the seafront affords excellent views of the shipping which passes in and out of the Mersey. **Wallasey,** terminal point of the M53 motorway, is also important in that from here the new Mersey Tunnel (opened 1971) runs for over five miles to eventually emerge just north of Liverpool's Exchange Station. Excellent bathing can be had at Wallasey Beach backed by sand dunes and facing out to the Irish Sea.

Hoylake (Pop.: 32,200. Hotel: *Stanley*), situated at the western tip of the Wirral peninsula, is noted for its bracing air and the championship course of the Royal Liverpool Golf Club over which many major tournaments have been played. A seaside resort with good beaches and extensive promenade and rather quieter than New Brighton it is a popular residential town for commuters to Liverpool. **West Kirby** *(Dee),* eight miles from Birkenhead is, like Hoylake, another residential and seaside resort offering good facilities, not least the bathing. Facing west across the *Dee* estuary it is more sheltered and consequently milder than Hoylake. There are good walks in the neighbourhood, notably to the Grange and Caldy Hills. The *Hilbre Islands* lie a mile offshore from Hilbre Point and are frequented by many species of birds, particularly waders.

Thurstaston is a quaint old village on A540 running south-east from West Kirby to Chester. Thurstaston common together with Harrock Wood and Inby Heath comprise an extensive area of heathland now in National Trust hands. Farther south-east **Heswall,** near the southernmost boundary of the new Merseyside county where it meets Cheshire, is an attractively set little place facing out across the estuary of the *Dee* and the North Wales coastline in Clwyd county.

Aintree, six miles north of Liverpool's city centre and reached by the A59, has a famous racecourse, venue of the Grand National Steeplechase held each March–April while a little way to the east and reached by the A57 road passing Prescot (6½ miles) is *Knowsley Hall* seat of the Earls of Derby (Stanley family) since the 14th century. East of the 2,000 acres Park (the largest in Merseyside county) which contains the Hall (15th century) is the manufacturing town of **St. Helens** famed the world over on account of its glass industry. A Glass Museum depicting the history and manufacture of glass in all its forms is in Prescot Road within the offices of Pilkington Bros. while also worthy of note in this industrial town of over 100,000 inhabitants is the Church of St. Helens, Windleshaw Abbey ruins, the Friends' Meeting House and Seddon's Cottage.

From Liverpool the A565 Southport road skirts the eastern shore of the *Mersey* for three miles to **Bootle** (pop. 74,310) a large industrial town at the mouth of the estuary. The extensive docks here are the largest and most modern of the Mersey Dock Boards complex. Northward are **Seaforth** and **Waterloo,** dormitories for Liverpool. The latter has a well-planned front and a fine expanse of sand uninterrupted for several miles northward. The road continues through **Blundellsands** and **Crosby** where are the Merchant Taylors' schools. **Formby,** nine miles from Liverpool, has a good golf course and is a pleasant residential development popular with Liverpool business people. Of interest are St. Luke's Church, the Beech Walk and several attractive Tudor-style cottages. Seaward are extensive sand dunes forming the *Ainsdale Nature Reserve* (N.T.). **Ainsdale,** four miles south of Southport on the A565 is, in fact, amalgamated with the municipality of that town. Here, on the periphery of the new county of Merseyside where it meets Lancashire, is an 18-hole golf course of some merit and a church, St. John's, with an unusual east window depicting "Sunrise at Jerusalem on the first Easter Morning".

Southport

Distances.—Liverpool, 20; London, 210; Manchester, 39; Preston, 17; St. Helens, 19; Wigan, 20.

Early Closing.—Tuesday and Saturday.

Entertainment.—Cinemas, theatres, dancing etc.

Hotels.—*Prince of Wales, Clifton, Brunswick, Royal, Scarisbrick, Metropole,* and many others.

Population.—84,350.

Post Office.—Lord Street.

Sport.—Bowls (crown and flat greens), boating and bathing, cricket at Birkdale, golf (six courses including the famous Birkdale course), tennis.

Southport, the seaside "Garden City", is situated on the sandy coast of Lancashire, near the estuary of the *Ribble,* 20 miles by road north of Liverpool and the same distance south-west of Preston. It has, in Lord Street, a well-planned tree-lined boulevard with good shops and a pleasant promenade. There is also an extremely long pier with entertainment pavilion. The beach, a six-mile stretch of firm sand, is often busy with day visitors during the height of the season. Particularly attractive aspects of the town are the avenue of grafted elms in the *Botanic Garden,* and the beautiful *Hesketh Park* with its unique garden for the blind. The famous Southport Flower Show takes place each August in Hesketh Park attracting growers from far and wide. Other points of interest in the town are the *Art Gallery, Museum, Model Village, Zoo* and the fine *Marine Lake.* Bordering the flat coast are extensive sand dunes ideal terrain for the many golf courses in the vicinity and best known of which is the famous *Birkdale Golf Club.* The parish church, St. Cuthbert's 1730, a mile-and-a-half north-east of the town centre, contains some remarkable wood carving brought here from St. Peter's, Liverpool. Southport has, in addition to its first-class sports and entertainments facilities, good provision in hotels and accommodation of all grades and has developed in recent years as a popular conference centre.

Manchester and District

Greater Manchester like Merseyside a metropolitan county is similar in the respect that both are densely populated more especially in their southern parts. This county, largely industrial with the exception of the north-eastern area around Littleborough and along part of the Yorkshire border, is the mecca of cotton spinning and all things allied to it.

Manchester

Distances. — Barnsley, 36; Leeds, 40; London, 184; Liverpool, 35; Rochdale, 11; St. Helens, 23; Warrington, 18; Wigan, 19.
Early Closing. — Wednesday or Saturday.
Entertainment. — Opera House, Palace Theatre, Library Theatre, Forum Theatre, University Theatre. Free Trade Hall (Hallé Orchestra) Peter Street. Belle Vue Gardens, cinemas, dancing. Many night spots and restaurants.
Hotels. — *Piccadilly, Midland, Grand, Mitre, Simpsons, Willow Bank, Queens, New Millgate,* *Lansdowne,* and others.
Population. — 541,470.
Post Office. — Spring Gardens.
Sports. — Good facilities for bowls, putting, tennis, swimming and a complete range of indoor sporting activities. County cricket ground at Old Trafford. Association football at Stretford (Manchester United) and at Maine Road (Manchester City). White City Stadium, Old Trafford. Belle Vue, Hyde Road.

Manchester, sometimes described as one of the world's most important industrial areas, is also, if nowadays to a somewhat lesser extent than formerly, the focal point of the English cotton industry. The city stands at the confluence of the rivers *Irwell, Irk* and *Medlock,* the first-named separating it from Salford, a large cotton-spinning town of 131,330 inhabitants. The famous *Manchester Ship Canal,* opened 1894, which runs from the south-west of the city to the *Mersey* at Eastham, a distance of some $35\frac{1}{2}$ miles, has been solely responsible for making Manchester the third largest seaport in England.

Around the city centre, Piccadilly, there are several buildings of note. Westward from Piccadilly Gardens (Bus station) along Market Street is the *Royal Exchange,* scene often of great activity among the buyers and sellers of cotton, and, slightly north of it in Victoria Street, the Cathedral.

Manchester Cathedral, the former old parish church, is a 15th-century sandstone structure in Perpendicular style with a square tower rising to a height of 130 feet. For its short length of 220 feet it is unusually wide at 112 feet the nave having double aisles. Within its confines the most interesting features are the Choir (see ornate cornices, roof and Stalls), the three Chapels (St. John's, Manchester Regimental and Lady), the Nave wherein is the exquisite pulpitum and, not least, some very fine brass and ironwork. The Cathedral, in spite of bomb damage during the early 1940s, has undergone considerable restoration and is today in a good state of repair throughout.

Slightly north of the Cathedral is **Chetham's Hospital** which, after a checkered existence since its foundation in 1653, now houses a public library with upwards of 80,000 books in part of the building. It is claimed that this was, in fact, the first free public library in England and possibly Europe. The imposing *John Rylands*

Library (1899) reached from the Cathedral by following the main thoroughfare of Deansgate for approximately three-quarters of a mile has, in addition to its close on three-quarter of a million books, an outstanding collection of extremely old manuscripts not least important of which is that part of St. John's Gospel written prior to A.D. 150. Outstanding too are some very fine jewelled bindings dating back to medieval times.

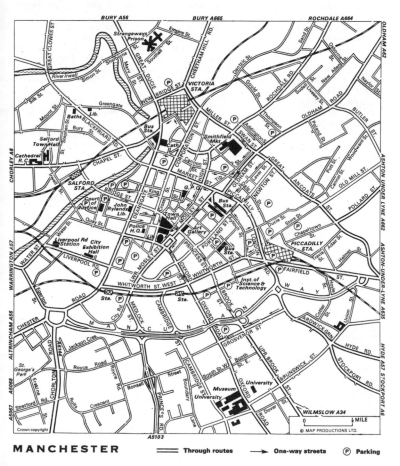

MANCHESTER ═══ Through routes → One-way streets Ⓟ Parking

East from the Rylands Library along Brazennose Street is the triangular-shaped *Town Hall* (1876) conspicuous on account of the 281-feet high clock tower (see the great hall with its twelve frescoes by Ford Madox Brown depicting Manchester's past and the fireplace in the reception room). Close by, in Mount

Street, is the *Central Library* and, in Peter Street, the *Free Trade Hall,* home of the world-renowned Hallé Orchestra. The *City Art Gallery,* built 1825–29, midway along Moseley Street is one of Manchester's finest buildings. Owned by the Corporation it contains several thousand items among which the most notable are paintings by Dughet, Courbet, Fantin-Latour, Forain, Gauguin, Pissarro, Vlaminck, Max Ernst and Leger (French School) and exceptionally fine works from the Italian, Flemish and British Schools. Sculptures of note include Henry Moore's "Mother and Child".

South of the famous Mancunian Way, that great dual carriageway which traverses the city from east to west, are the sprawling buildings which constitute the **University,** Oxford Road, famous for the discovery of the neutron and Sir John Cockcroft's first machine used for splitting the atom. Close to the University's main entrance, and also in Oxford Road, is the **Manchester Museum,** well worth visiting on account of its famed Lloyd Japanese collection. **Whitworth Art Gallery,** south of the Museum, is best noted for its exceptionally fine collection of English watercolours. The *Athenaeum Annexe* in Princess Street, close to the Art Gallery, has fine collections of pottery, porcelain and material depicting local history.

In the north of the city near the A56 Burnley road is Manchester Prison (Strangeways) which, along with Liverpool's Walton Prison, witnessed the last two judicial hangings (13th August, 1964) in Britain before the abolition of capital punishment.

Belle Vue, south-east of the city is, in addition to being a vast entertainments complex (84 acres in all), home of one of the country's most famous Zoos whilst similarly situated with regard to Manchester's Piccadilly, though to its south-west, is the *Old Trafford Cricket* Ground, well known as one of the venues for Test Matches.

Manchester's **Ringway Airport,** distinctive with its hall of chandeliers, and the largest municipally-owned airport in the United Kingdom is situated 10 miles south of the city centre, close to the southernmost extremity of the new Greater Manchester county boundary with Cheshire.

Wythenshaw Hall *(daily, free)* seven miles south of the Altrincham–Stockport road, is a fine half-timbered house set in parkland and noted for its collection of 17th-century furniture and pictures.

Platt Hall *(daily, free),* in Platt Fields, Rusholme, two miles on the Wilmslow road, has a notable collection of English costume from the 17th century to the present day.

Heaton Hall *(daily, free),* at Prestwich, six miles north, was once the home of the Earls of Wilton, designed by James Wyatt in 1772. It displays 18th-century furniture and pictures and contains a notable organ by Samuel Green.

Several great cotton-manufacturing towns and centres of industry lie within a 20-mile radius of Manchester and although at first sight they would appear to hold little of interest to the would-be sightseer, many have features of considerable note. **Oldham,** seven miles north-east important for its textile machinery, has an art gallery containing valuable British watercolours and paintings; **Stockport,** six-and-a-half miles south-east, formerly in Cheshire, houses a museum noted for its "Blue John" window which consists of 250 pieces of amethystine spar from the Castleton mine in Derbyshire; **Wigan,** oldest town in Lancashire, lying between the M6 and M61 motorways and **Bolton,** 10 miles north-east of it have in *Haigh Hall,* Museum and Art Gallery, and the *Hall i' th' Wood,* a folk museum, two much-visited buildings. *Smithills Hall,* two-and-a-half miles north-west of Bolton is acknowledged as being one of the oldest manor houses in the North of England. *Turton Tower* in this same area is noted for its interesting collection of arms, furniture and a great many items of local significance. **Bury,** eight-and-a-half miles from Manchester by the A56, has the Wrigley Collection of paintings, watercolours and engravings in the town's Art Gallery and Museum.

Rochdale, just north of the M62 Pennine motorway which crosses to Leeds, is famous for its blankets, calicoes and flannels. Notable in the town are St. Chad's Church, the Town Hall, Art Gallery and Museum and the original Co-operative Shop (1844) in Toad Lane. Gracie Fields, the "Lassie from Lancashire" was born in Rochdale. At Blackstone Edge to the east on the Halifax road is one of the best surviving sections of Roman road in England.

Ashton-under-Lyne on the eastern periphery of Manchester lies close to the lovely Medlock Vale (N.T.) and has a church notable for its stained glass.

Eccles, four miles west of the city and originator of the famous cakes has a 15th-century church and the Monk's Hall museum and art gallery. Of interest is the nearby Barton Swing Bridge and aqueduct over the Manchester Ship Canal.

Salford, sometimes erroneously thought to be a part of Manchester proper is, in fact, separated from that great city by the river *Irwell*. Although set in the heart of a highly industrialised region Salford attracts its own sightseers principally on account of its fine Roman Catholic Cathedral of St. John (1848), its Art Gallery, Science Museum and Georgian houses. Salford Docks, which are important in their own right, lie on the Manchester Ship Canal.

Lancashire

Lancashire west of the M6 motorway is vastly different from its corresponding section to the east. In the west are the important holiday resorts of Lytham and St. Anne's, Blackpool, Fleetwood, to a lesser extent, and Morecambe. Lancaster, the county town, in the north and Preston some 22 miles to the south also contrast one with the other in the sense that Lancaster is steeped in history while Preston, albeit the site of the Battle of Preston in 1648 at which Cromwell defeated the Royalists, is nowadays probably best known as an engineering town and important rail centre. Ormskirk in the south of the county 18 miles from Preston is basically an agricultural market town forming the centre of a potato-growing district.

East of the constantly busy M6 motorway which carries the bulk of traffic from Scotland to the Midlands and London is *east* Lancashire with its many industrial towns in the southern half—Blackburn, Accrington, Burnley, etc.— and its vast Forest of Bowland and the lovely valleys of the rivers *Ribble* and *Lune* in the north.

WEST LANCASHIRE

Preston (Pop.: 97,365. Hotel: *Bull and Royal*), is an engineering and cotton industry town on the *Ribble* with extensive riverside docks. There are several substantially built houses of the late Georgian period while a modern feature is the new shopping area with its pedestrian precinct. The *Harris Museum and Art Gallery* has a notable collection of 19th- and 20th-century paintings. Richard Arkwright the inventor was born at Preston in 1732. Six miles south-east is Hoghton Tower, a 16th-century fortified manor house. **Samlesbury Old Hall** *(Suns, Easter–Sept.)*, four miles north-east, dates from the 14th century and contains a collection of watercolours and some antique cabinets.

Leyland, south of the *Ribble* estuary and just off the M6 motorway, is an industrial centre noted for its production of lorries and other large commercial vehicles—a place which, indeed, has given its name to the vast organisation known as British Leyland.

Ormskirk (Pop.: 27,600), 18 miles south-west of Preston, is a market town with an unusual church, mainly Perpendicular, with a tower and spire alongside each other. Here are buried the Stanleys, Earls of Derby. There are some 12th-century monuments. Two miles south-west is **Aughton** where is *Cranford (Apr.–Oct.)* an unusual shrub and rose garden.

Scarisbrick Hall, four miles north-west, is a notable example of Gothic architecture. Two miles south is **Halsall** one of the prettiest villages in the whole area with a well-preserved 14th-century church with unusual porch and several effigies.

Rufford Old Hall (N.T., *daily except Mons; and Weds, Thurs, in winter, fee*), to the east of the A59 five miles north of Ormskirk, is a beautiful late medieval house of half-timber and plaster panels with a remarkable hammer-beam roof and a massive movable screen. Village museum, many pieces of arms and armour.

Lytham St. Anne's

Beach.—Firm sands stretching six miles.
Early Closing.—Wednesday.
Entertainment.—Summer shows, cinemas, Two piers.
Golf.—Royal Lytham and St. Anne's Golf Club; St. Anne's Old Links Golf Club; Lytham Golf Club, Fairhaven Golf Club. Miniature course on South Promenade.

Hotels.—*Crown, Chough's Nest, Lynton Cottage, Hoe, Ye Olde Cottage Inn, Sandrock, Combe Park,* and many others.
Population.—40,000.
Post Office.—Clifton Drive South, St. Anne's; Clifton Square, Lytham.
Sport.—Bathing, boating on Fairhaven Lake, bowls, tennis, golf.

The twin towns of Lytham and St. Anne's two miles to the west are amalgamated to form an essentially quiet coast resort catering for a quite different type of holidaymaker than is the case with the much gayer Blackpool or Morecambe to the north of it. There are several fine hotels, a splendid beach with wide sands and excellent golf course at hand, including the famous championship course of the Royal Lytham and St. Anne's Golf Club. In and around the combined towns the main points of interest are the *Carnegie Library,* the *Parish Church, Lifeboat Memorial, Lowther and Ashton Gardens, Fairhaven Lake, Old Windmill* and the wooded avenue on Green Drive.

North of the town is Squires Gate (Blackpool) Airport and a huge holiday camp. Immediately north lies Blackpool.

Blackpool

Distances.—London, 228; Preston, 17; Lancaster, 26; Liverpool, 46; Manchester, 47; Leeds, 73; Carlisle, 93.
Early Closing.—Wednesday.
Entertainments.—Numerous theatres, three piers, dance halls, Waxworks, circuses, icedrome, several bathing pools, Zoo, Illuminations, Pleasure Beach, etc.
Hotels.—*Imperial, Clifton, Cliffs, Savoy, Queen's*

Hydro, Carlton, Headlands, Gables, St. George, Beulah, and many others.
Population.—151,300.
Post Office.—Abingdon Street.
Sports.—Golf: four courses. Association Football: Blackpool F.C. Limitless facilities available for boating, bowling, putting, tennis, swimming and complete range of indoor sporting activities.

Blackpool, probably the most highly organised seaside resort in Britain, is a town of many contrasts for, apart from the candy-floss atmosphere which permeates the ever-bustling Pleasure Beach, the three famous piers and the vast complex of entertainments housed within the Tower buildings (Zoo, Aquarium, Ballroom) there is the totally different aspect of peaceful parks and gardens, notably the vast 288-acre *Stanley Park* with its exquisite gardens, conservatories, golf course and well-kept bowling greens. The town does, of course, owe its success to the ever increasing number of facilities in the sense of "mass media entertainment" which it offers to close on eight-and-a-half million visitors who pass through every year. The *Tower,* erected 1889, rising to a height of 519 feet dominates the scene and is Blackpool's most famous landmark. The Corporation's tramway service, the last to remain in the country and also the first to be inaugurated is a feature of the town. The dazzling spectacle that constitutes the Illuminations, an annual event in October, results from many months of work and planning by a special section of the Corporation engaged in the mammoth job of preparing the various tableaux. There are some extremely good shops, countless hotels, boarding houses and licensed premises and, for indoor swimming the fine Derby Baths. Also worthy of note in the town is the *Grundy Art Gallery,* Queen Street, for its good collection of 19th- and 20th-century British paintings

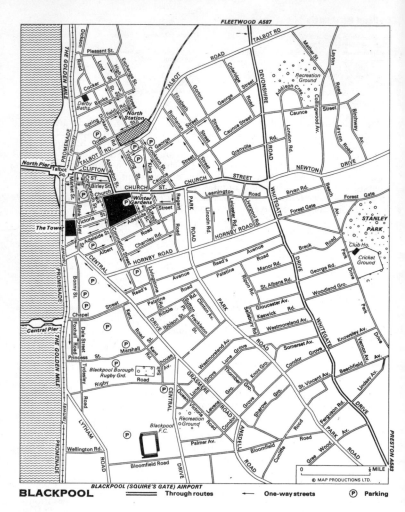

BLACKPOOL   ═══   Through routes   ◀—   One-way streets   Ⓟ Parking

and drawings. The *Winter Gardens,* Coronation Street, is much in demand as a venue for large conferences.

Thornton Cleveleys (Pop.: 26,900. Hotels: *Royal, River House*), five miles north of Blackpool, is a popular resort comprising **Cleveleys** with fine promenade, sandy beach and entertainments and **Thornton** a mile-and-a-half inland, a little county town on the *Wyre.*

Fleetwood (Pop.: 28,600. Hotels: *North Euston, Mount*), four miles north, is both a thriving fishing port and a holiday resort. The fish dock *(permits from Dock manager)* covers over 11 acres. From the quay near the station starts the boat service to the Isle of Man. There are facilities for bowls, tennis, putting and golf, pier, and a fine model-yacht pond. A ferry runs from Fleetwood across the *Wyre* to Knott End. Three miles south of Fleetwood is *Rossall School* a famous boys' public school at which the late Sir Thomas Beecham was a pupil.

Lancaster (Pop.: 49,500. Hotel: *Royal King's Arms*) the county town stands on the *Lune,* just west of the M6 motorway. The *Castle* high above the river has a fine Norman Keep (restored *c.* 1585), a Well Tower and Hadrian's Tower with a small museum. John of Gaunt made considerable additions to the structure and one turret is named "John of Gaunt's Chair". Other buildings include the *Priory Church of St. Mary* (1431), the *Old Town Hall* built in 1873 with a fine museum, *St. John's Church* (1754), and the old *Custom House* (1764) on the quay. Also of note are the Roman Catholic Cathedral in East Road, the modern Town Hall and the *Storey Institute and Art Gallery.* Williamson Park, where is the Ashton Memorial, offers extensive views of the surrounding countryside. Skerton Bridge which spans the *Lune* to the north of the town centre dates back to 1788. Fishing on the *Lune* attracts many anglers to the town.

The A589 runs west for four miles to reach:

Morecambe (Pop.: 41,850. Hotels: *Midland, Elms, Clarendon, Park*) a popular resort and probably the best organised holiday centre in north-west England with a multitude of amenities and entertainment for visitors. Like Blackpool there are notable Illuminations in the autumn. There is a fine seven-mile-long promenade, several first-class hotels, a great deal of other accommodation, a good beach and bathing pool. *Marineland* has performing dolphins and sea lions and an extremely good aquarium. Bathing-beauty contests of some importance have long been associated with the town. Linked with Morecambe is **Heysham** with a vast Entertainments Centre. Heysham is a terminal of the Belfast mail steamer service and of a service to the Isle of Man. Above the town the ruin of St. Patrick's Chapel, a 9th-century oratory, contrasts with the ultra modern nuclear power station which, when finished, will occupy a site to the south of the harbour.

Near the extreme north-west corner of the county is **Carnforth** but a mile from the M6 motorway. **Leighton Hall** *(May–Sept., Weds, Suns, Bank Hols)* two-and-a-half miles north at Yealand Conyers is a fine mansion set in extensive grounds. It contains notable furniture and pictures.

EAST LANCASHIRE

Lancashire, east of the M6 motorway and north of the Greater Manchester county boundary, is vastly different from its neighbouring section west of that great highway. It is, too, quite dissimilar in the physical make-up of its southern half, largely industrial—in a line roughly from Preston to Colne and the Yorkshire boundary—from its northern area where the great Forest of Bowland with its moors and the delightful valleys of *Ribble, Hodder* and *Lune,* make for a scene of spacious tranquillity.

Chorley (Pop.: 31,600), nine miles south of Preston and just west of the M61 motorway continuing into Manchester is a cotton-weaving and engineering town having several interesting associations with the past. Here was born Henry Tate (1819) the sugar refiner. **Astley Hall** *(daily except Suns in winter)* near the centre is an Elizabethan house with fine furniture, tapestry and pictures. South-east across the motorway are the Anglezarke and Rivington reservoirs of Liverpool's water supply. From nearby Rivington Pike (1,192 feet) are extensive views.

Blackburn (Pop.: 101,130) a world centre of cotton-weaving, has the fine *Lewis Textile Museum* depicting the development of spinning and weaving. The parish church was raised to cathedral status in 1926 since when the transepts have been rebuilt.

Ribchester Museum (N.T., *Weekdays except Fris, Dec.–Jan., Sats only*), seven miles north-west of Blackburn, occupies the site of the Roman fort of *Bremetennacum* constructed by Agricola about A.D. 80. Notable is the replica of the Ribchester Helmet (original in British Museum) and the tombstone of a Roman soldier. There is also an excavated granary in the grounds and a Roman well in the nearby gardens.

Whalley lies on the *Calder* seven miles north-west of Blackburn. The remains of the *Whalley Abbey* date from 1296 with the two gatehouses, one transept and the cloister still remarkably well preserved. There are also remains of the abbots' lodge part of which has been restored for use as a diocesan conference centre. In the parish churchyard are pre-Norman crosses. Three miles north-west is *Stonyhurst* a well-known Roman Catholic school for boys founded by Jesuits of St. Omer in 1593. The stately manor house, library, observatory and museum may be visited by prior appointment. North of Stronghurst is *Browsholme Hall* noted for its fine collection of art treasures.

Accrington, five miles east of Blackburn, is another cotton-weaving town. The *Haworth Art Gallery* has a notable collection of Tiffony glass and some fine English watercolours.

Burnley (Pop.: 76,480. Hotels: *Keirby, Sparrow Hawk*) is an industrial town busy with cotton spinning, collieries and other industries. The 14th-century *Towneley Hall* is now an Art Gallery and Museum housing a fine collection of paintings, antique furniture and ceramics, and shows good plasterwork. St. Peter's Church—see remains of the old stocks and crosses in vicinity—is notable. **Gawthorpe Hall** (N.T., *Easter–Sept., Mons, Weds, Sats, free*) at Padiham three miles west, and a college of further education, houses the Kay-Shuttleworth Collection of textiles. The Jacobean house has been the home of the Shuttleworth family since the early 14th century.

Colne with close on 20,000 population is a market town seven miles north-east of Burnley close to the Yorkshire border. The church in Perpendicular style dates originally from 1122. Of interest are the wheeled stocks in the churchyard, the

Hartley Memorial and the market cross. The now derelict Wycoller Hall two miles south-east has associations with Charlotte Brontë's "Jane Eyre".

Rawtenstall, seven miles south-west of Burnley, has a good art gallery and a museum of local crafts.

The **Forest of Bowland** an extensive area of fells and moors and officially an area of outstanding beauty may be reached by B6478 from **Clitheroe** to Waddington, Newton and the attractively situated **Slaidburn,** a village which has in its church a well-preserved Jacobean screen. The *Trough of Bowland* is a pass separating the Bleasdale moors from the forest area. To the south and reached by a subsidiary road leading off the B6243 running west from Clitheroe is **Bleasdale** where have been discovered many archaeological relics, notably a wood circle. **Chipping** is a charming village to the south-east.

Hornby is a small village nine miles north-east of Lancaster and a good angling spot. The castle has a good 13th-century tower with additions by Sir Edward Stanley who was also responsible for the tower of the church.

From Hornby the A683 from Lancaster continues northward through **Melling** and **Tunstall** on the site of a Roman fort and on to Kirkby Lonsdale on the county border.

Into Cumbria

THE KENDAL DISTRICT

Kendal

Hotels.—*County, Kendal, Rainbow, Woolpack, Roebuck, Black Swan, Golden Lion.*

Population.—21,500.
Post Office.—Stricklandgate.

Kendal is often ignored in the holiday rush for the Lakes, which is a pity, because it is an interesting old town. Once a thriving centre of the woollen industry, (home of the famous Kendal green), its main occupation now is the manufacture of boots and shoes. There are several fascinating old buildings, like the 14th-century *Castle Dairy,* and *Abbot Hall,* a fine example of Georgian architecture, now an art gallery and Museum of Lakeland Life and Industry. Romney, the famous portrait painter, who served his apprenticeship in Kendal, lived at *Romney House* on Milnthorpe Road, and there are several portraits of him in the Town Hall. Katherine Parr, Henry VIII's last and luckiest wife, is believed to have been born in Kendal Castle, the ruins of which are a conspicuous landmark in the valley. The most interesting building is the 13th-century parish church, which has been very well restored. The 80-foot tower has one of the finest peals of bells in the north. From the Kendal Fell Lands, near the beautiful Serpentine woods, is practically unrestricted access to Cunswick Scar and along the cliffs to Scout Scar. Kendal has golf, cricket, tennis, bowls, putting and excellent fishing, but above all it is a marvellous centre for exploring the Lakes, with good local bus services, and within easy reach of many of the most popular places in the area. Windermere is only eight miles away.

About two miles west of the Town Hall is **Scout Scar** a very fine viewpoint over the glorious panorama of the Lakeland giants.

Sizergh Castle (N.T., *Apr.–Sept., Weds. Gardens only Tues and Thurs, fee*) three miles south of Kendal is the ancient home of the Strickland family. The oldest part is the 14th-century pele tower. It has fine panelling and ceilings.

Levens Hall *(May–mid-Sept., Tues, Weds, Thurs, Suns, fee)* five miles south of Kendal on the Milnthorpe road, is a fine Elizabethan house rich in oak carvings and pictures. There is a fine topiary garden.

Kirkby Lonsdale *(Royal, Green Dragon, Sun, Fleece,* etc.) just in the county border and 15 miles from Kendal, is an attractive market town with splendid scenery and idyllic stretches of the river *Lune* both below and above town. The old bridge with its modern companion beside it dates from the 13th century. The church dates from the reign of Stephen and is notable for its three Norman diamond-patterned pillars.

Sedbergh *(White Hart, Bull, Golden Lion)* is a quaint old town 10 miles north of Kirkby Lonsdale well-known for its public school which grew out of the ancient grammar school founded by Henry VII. There is golf, some fishing and plenty of easy hill-walking.

Orton *(George)*, six miles south-east of Shap, is built in the form of a rough square looking on to an island of pasture land. Its streams and bridges are a pretty feature. The old Hall is much as it was in 1604, the date over the door.

SHAP AND DISTRICT

Shap *(Greyhound, King's Arms)* is a typical moorland village, bare, bleak and grey, but the air is like a tonic. Shap was once an important coaching station, and there are one or two old houses bearing 17th-century dates, though the only building which could possibly be called picturesque is the *Moot Hall* near the Market Place. Bonnie Prince Charlie spent a night at West Farm during the '45 rebellion, and had an inflated bill to prove it. It is a stern, uncompromising place where Bibles and prayer books are still annually distributed under the terms of Lord Wharton's will. He fought against Charles I at Edge Hill, and his are the initials, P.L.W., carved in an oak frame in the old parish church.

Shap Abbey *(daily, free)* is about a mile from the village on a lane off the Bampton road, and dates back to the 12th century. The first sight of those imposing ruins is unforgettable—the massive tower in the peaceful Lowther Valley, against a background of the Mardale Hills.

To Wasdale Crag. The beautiful felspathic granite comes from the quarries at Wasdale Crag, about four miles south of Shap. You pass the granite works en route, and a Druid's Circle is half-way between Shap and the Toll Bar near the railway.

To Bampton. It is a pleasant walk through the fields, via Rosgill and Hegdale, to this quiet village by the river *Lowther*. Good fishing. Interesting church.

To Swindale and Mardale. Known locally as the "corpse road", the three-and-a-half mile walk over the fell via Shap Abbey is far pleasanter than it sounds. The name comes from the days before Mardale church was demolished (to prepare for the flooding of the site when Haweswater became a reservoir for Manchester) and the dead were carried to Shap for burial.

To Gunnerkeld. You take the Penrith road over Skew Bridge and follow the Sleagill sign post. A footpath leads through the fields to Gunnerkeld Bottoms and the Druid's Circle. The inner circle is clearly marked, the outer less well defined.

ON MORECAMBE BAY

Fourteen miles by road south-west of Kendal is:

Grange-over-Sands *(Grand, Grange, Crown, Netherwood, Commodore)* rivalling Morecambe as a seaside resort, and beautifully situated on the lower slopes of *Yewbarrow*, with magnificent views across Morecambe Bay. Sheltered on the north and west by hills, Grange has a higher temperature in spring than any other place in the north of England. About a mile south of Grange is *Kent's Bank* where the ruined Abbot's Hall is supposed to have been built to accommodate the Abbot of Furness when he crossed the treacherous Morecambe Sands.

Cartmel, two miles west of Grange, was originally Caermoel an ancient British "camp among the hills". Cartmel is a cathedral city in miniature, with a fine old priory church, one of the few which escaped destruction during the Dissolution of the Monasteries. The *Priory Church* was founded in the 12th century and has a fine oak screen and choir stalls and a valuable library. The gatehouse (N.T., *daily, fee*) is a picturesque building over the street.

Holker Hall *(Easter–Oct., daily except Sats, fee)* a little north of Cark-in-Cartmel, dates from the 16th century with later additions. It has fine gardens and an extensive deer park.

Ulverston *(Sun, King's Arms, Bay Horse, Railway, Queen's)*, on the northern shore of Morecambe Bay, is the market town for the Furness District and an admirable centre for exploring the Lakes. It is near the sea, surrounded by beautiful countryside. Above the town is *Hoad Hill* (435 feet) with a monument, a replica of Eddystone lighthouse, to Sir John Barrow (*b.* 1764). *Conishead Priory* is two miles south of Ulverston. *Swarthmoor Hall,* which dates back to the 16th century, was the home of the famous Quaker, George Fox. There is an interesting parish church at *Aldingham,* five miles from Ulverston, with the ruins of *Gleaston Castle* nearby.

To Furness Abbey. The direct route from Ulverston is via **Dalton-in-Furness** where George Romney, the portrait painter was born in 1734. *Dalton Tower* (N.T., *key at 18 Market Place*) is a 14th-century pele tower in the main street.

Furness Abbey *(daily, fee)* was founded in the 12th century by Stephen, Count of Boulogne and Martain, afterwards King of England, and became immensely powerful and rich. From the ruins it is possible to get an accurate idea of the size and scale of the buildings, and the splendour of the style.

Barrow-in-Furness (Pop.: 64,000. Hotels: *Duke of Edinburgh, Victoria Park, White House*) is a busy industrial town with armament works and shipbuilding yards and docks. A bridge connects with Vickerstown on the **Isle of Walney,** a 10-mile-long spit of land running parallel with the coast.

Broughton-in-Furness *(Old King's Head)* is a small market town at the head of the *Duddon* estuary. It has a 19th-century church on the site of the original Norman building of which only the south door remains. *Broughton Tower* was largely rebuilt in the 18th century, but the tower of the ancient castle and part of the dungeons remain.

Broughton is a good centre for excursions, and a favourite starting point for the **Duddon Valley.** The river *Duddon* was the subject of at least 34 of Wordsworth's sonnets, and runs through wild and beautiful country. At **Ulpha** a road strikes off steeply to the west and goes over Birker Moor to Eskdale. Across the river two miles farther on is **Seathwaite** an attractive hamlet where "Wonderful Walker", the curate made famous by Wordsworth, is buried in the churchyard, near a 200-year-old yew tree. **Black Combe** rears up about five miles west of Broughton. Going via Broadgate and Swinside you pass a fine prehistoric circle, and follow a steep path to the summit (1,969 feet). A descent can be made by the southern slope to return to Broughton via **Silecroft** with its fine sands.

The Lake District

The Lake District is in the north-west of England, within the administrative county of Cumbria. It is a spectacularly beautiful mountainous region, with rugged peaks soaring to well over 3,000 feet, magnificent lakes, forests, tranquil valleys and wild lonely moors, and little glassy mountain tarns. The whole area is roughly 30 miles from north to south, by 25 miles from east to west, much of it a National Park—all of it one of the greatest natural playgrounds in the country.

To begin with it is a walker's Paradise, but unless you are going to settle for a gentle stroll by the lake, remember that mountain walking needs mountain equipment—proper boots, protective clothing, map, compass, iron rations. Remember too, that mountains should be treated at all times with respect. Lakeland weather is changeable, and when it rains, it *rains,* and mist can shroud a mountain suddenly, out of a clear sky. Rock climbing in the Lake District is for the experts, and if you are not sure of yourself, don't try. Great fishing in the rivers, especially in the western region, and the lakes (salmon and sea trout in the *Leven, Derwent, Cocker, Duddon, Esk, Irt, Calder,* and brown trout nearly everywhere in lakes, rivers and becks). The best pike fishing is in Esthwaite Water, and Bassenthwaite is famous for its perch.

Windermere, home of the Royal Windermere Yacht Club is the headquarters for sailing, though there is boating on many other lakes, notably Coniston Water and Derwent Water. Bathing can be an icy dip in a mountain pool, or swimming at an organised lido like Millerground or Waterhead on Windermere, or the Isthmus on Derwent Water. Apart from bowls and tennis at most of the larger resorts, there are fine golfing facilities, with 18-hole courses at Grange-over-Sands, Kendal, Ulverston, Windermere, and best of all at Seascale and Penrith. There are also some fierce local games, like Fell Races to the top of Butter Crags and Back, and Cumberland and Westmorland wrestling (at the famous Grasmere Games). Sheepdog Trials, and Hound Trials, especially on Applethwaite Common, near Windermere, and Rydal, Keswick, Patterdale.

Accommodation in the Lake District ranges from the luxury hotels of the principal centres like Windermere and Ambleside to off-the-track farm houses and cottages, and little village inns, but it is a wise precaution to book in advance, especially for July, August and early September. This is good camping and caravanning country, with many well-appointed sites.

WINDERMERE AND DISTRICT

Windermere and Bowness

Bathing.—Near Millerground landing.
Early Closing.—Thursday.
Hotels.—At Windermere: *Windermere, Elleray, Langdale Chase, Applegarth.* At Bowness: *Burnside, Windermere Hydro, Old England, Royal, Stag's Head,* and many others.
Population.—8,530.
Post Office.—Crescent Road, Windermere.
Sports.—Bathing, boating, bowls and tennis. Golf and putting.

Windermere and Bowness are two villages which together form a small town on the eastern side of the lake, about four miles from its head. Bowness is the real "port" of the lake, centre for fishing and boating, and headquarters of the Royal Windermere Yacht Club. It is a maze of little streets, and very much the holiday resort. Windermere is about a mile-and-three-quarters from Bowness, and rather more residential. The parish of Windermere includes the bottom of the lake and all the islands. St. Martin's Church near the lake, has some of the finest stained glass in Britain, including one pane showing the Stars and Stripes—the arms of a 15th-century ancestor of George Washington. Lake Side Station is about six miles away, near the foot of the lake.

The best way to get some idea of the size of Windermere (largest lake in England, approximately 10 miles long and a mile at its widest part), is to take the boat trip from Lake Side to Waterhead. The scenery is beautiful and infinitely varied.

Lake Side to Waterhead. Sailing up the lake you pass *Blake Holme,* and *Silver Holme,* which guard the little bay formed by the rocky promontory of Long Tongue. Helvellyn comes into sight on the northern horizon almost as soon as you leave the pier, with a grand array of mountains from Fairfield to Ill Bell. Past *Grass Holme* and *Rawlinson Nab* with *Cunsey Wood* behind it; *Ling Holme* at the mouth of the Cunsey Beck, and glimpses of the Langdale Pikes, Coniston Fells, Bowfell and Scafell Pike on the western skyline. Just beyond Ramp Holme is *Ferry House,* with the largest island straight ahead—*Curwen Island,* or Belle Isle. The scenery becomes grander when you leave Bowness pier, sailing past *St. Mary's Island* (or Lady Holme), *Rayrigg* and *Elleray* woods, *Queen Adelaide's Hill,* and *Millerground* (where there is boating and bathing). *High Wray* is passed on the western shore, with the ruins of *Wray Castle* farther north, then on to the head of the lake, past *Dove Nest* and *Wansfell Holme,* with the brooding mass of mountains in the background.

Many delightful footpaths in the woods between Windermere village and the lake, and enjoyable short walks with rewarding views to: Biskey Howe, and Post Knott, descending to the Kendal Road at Burnside; to School Knott by Lickbarrow or Droomer; to Adelaide Hill and Miller Brow past Rayrigg Hall; to the Elleray woods to the Troutbeck road; to the Ferry by the public park and Cockshot Point, and across by the ferry to Ferry House.

To Orrest Head. This is a spot just north of Windermere village, and a walk which should not be missed. The view is unforgettable—the full length of the beautiful lake, with its green and wooded shores, against the background of the rugged wall of mountains.

To Newby Bridge. This quaint old bridge across the *Leven,* about a mile from the foot of the Lake, is a favourite spot with anglers. A mile farther on, where the river splashes and tumbles over three picturesque waterfalls, is the village of **Backbarrow,** home of two ancient cottage industries—swilling, and oak-spale basket making. *Cartmel Fell Church* is well worth a visit on this walk. The easy way back is by boat from Lake Side to Bowness.

To Troutbeck Valley. This beautiful valley stretches for about eight miles south from the foot of High Street to Calgarth Park and Windermere. You take the Troutbeck road at Cook's House crossroads, about half-a-mile from Windermere. The village of Troutbeck is about three miles farther on, clustering on the western slope of the valley. There is some good stained glass (by Burne-Jones) in the parish church. Only the inn sign on the modern hotel reminds you that this was once the famous *Mortal Man Inn.* From Troutbeck there are many easy, delightful tracks to the head of the valley, and perhaps the best is the one to the right of Troutbeck Tongue.

To Kentmere. The lower part of the valley was actually a lake, until the mere was drained over a hundred years ago. The best route is past the Windermere reservoir to the Garburn Pass. Wonderful views from the summit, of Troutbeck Valley and Kentmere. There is a rough path along the upper part of the valley, but the reward is a splendid view of Rainsborrow Crag falling almost sheer from Yoke.

To Kirkstone Pass. The pass lies between Red Screes and Caudale Moor and is allegedly named after the Kirk Stone, a huge rock near the summit of the pass. Contrary to its claims, the *Kirkstone Pass Inn* is *not* the highest pub in England (*Tan Hill* in Yorkshire, and Derbyshire's *Cat and Fiddle* are both higher) but at 1,468 feet the *Kirkstone* deserves an honourable mention. From the pass, it is a steep three-mile descent to Ambleside.

Ambleside *(Salutation, White Lion, Vale View, Wansfell Tower)* is on the lower edge of Wansfell, about five miles from Windermere. There are good local and long-distance bus services, and a boat station at Waterhead, three-quarters-of-a-mile south of the village. The 19th-century parish Church of St. Mary has some interesting stained glass and a modern mural celebrating the famous Rush-Bearing Ceremony. The quaint building at the other end of the village, over Stock Beck, is the 200-year-old *Bridge House* (N.T.). **Waterhead** is the headquarters of sailing and boating at the head of the lake, and northern terminus of the boat service. Between Waterhead and Rothay Bridge is the site of a Roman camp, excavated, but now re-covered.

To Stock Ghyll Force. The fall is about half-a-mile from the town, and one of the finest of its kind in the district. The path leads uphill, past the *Salutation Hotel,* and then through the park entrance on the left. The force is magnificent—rushing water tumbling down the rocky glen, making three spectacular leaps from a height of 70 feet. Stock Ghyll can be included on a longer walk to Wansfell, or the Kirkstone Pass, by Grove Farm.

To Jenkin Crag. From Jenkin Crag (signposted off the main Windermere road) a track leads through the woods to High Skelghyll and Troutbeck, a short, and very pleasant walk.

To Scandale. By the Kirkstone road from the market cross, and by High Sweden Bridge to Scandale are fine views over Rydal Vale, and the scenery round Scandale Beck is delightful. The round walk, returning by Low Sweden Bridge, is about four miles.

To Skelwith Force and Elterwater. This is not one of the largest falls in the Lake District, but very attractive. The road runs through Clappersgate and up the beautiful Brathay Valley and beyond the falls, you can take the riverside path through the fields to Elterwater. Views of Wetherlam and the Langdale Pikes on this route are unsurpassed. A mile south of Elterwater village is *Colwith Force,* one of the finest falls in the district. (Alternative approach, and more direct, is from the Skelwith Bridge—Coniston road.)

Rydal Water is one of the smallest, and loveliest, of all the lakes, but to appreciate it, you need to leave the main road. There is no better guide to the beauty of the lakes than Wordsworth, and *his* favourite stroll began at Rydal Church, went behind his home, Rydal Mount, and followed the secluded path along the foot of Nab Scar. *Wordsworth's Seat* is the low rock just outside the village on the Keswick side.

To Loughrigg Fell. An idyllic walk round this rocky, fern-clad plateau begins at Market Place. Just beyond St. Mary's Church take the footpath across Rothay Park to Miller Bridge, then north to Pelter Bridge, and back to Loughrigg Tarn and Clappersgate. The most beautiful, though not the shortest, route to Grasmere is via Pelter Bridge and Loughrigg Terrace.

Grasmere *(Prince of Wales, Swan, Dale Lodge, Hollins, Red Lion)*. Entrancingly pretty—a beautiful jewel in a beautiful setting—Grasmere is widely held to be the most beautiful of all the lakes. This is the heart of Wordsworthland where the poet did some of his finest work. *Dove Cottage,* just off the main Ambleside–Keswick highway, is still as it was when he lived there, and the Wordsworth Museum *(weekdays)* contains several original manuscripts of his poems, as well as many portraits of Wordsworth, and his family and friends. His memorial is in Grasmere Church, and he is buried in the south-east corner of the churchyard.

To Easedale Tarn. The tarn is 915 feet above sea level, by a picturesque route by Sour Milk Ghyll.

To Grisedale Tarn by Tongue Ghyll. The Tongue Ghyll turning is about a mile-and-a-half from the village, off the Keswick road. Fairly rough uphill going beyond the tarn. About a hundred yards from the tarn, at the head of Grisedale, is *The Brothers' Parting*. This is where Wordsworth said goodbye to his brother John, who was drowned shortly afterwards in the wreck of his ship. Two of the verses from a poem which Wordsworth wrote in his brother's memory are carved on the rock face.

Round Grasmere and Rydal Water. A pleasant six-mile walk following the Ambleside road as far as the footbridge at the foot of Rydal Water, crossing the *Rothay,* returning by Loughrigg Terrace and joining the Langdale–Grasmere road at Red Bank.

Round Thirlmere. Following the Keswick road you begin the steep ascent of *Dunmail Raise,* which looks down on Grasmere from a height of 783 feet. *Helm Crag,* on the way up the pass, is famous for the weird rock formations of its rugged summit. The round of the lake is described in the Keswick section.

Elterwater. This very underrated lake is reached from a path about a mile from the village on the western side of the lake, via Hunting Stile.

To Dungeon Ghyll. Easiest route to this fine ravine is by Allan Bank and Score Crag, crossing the ridge at Yew Crag. A more ambitious path is by Easedale Tarn and Codale Tarn, then over the ridge to Stickle Tarn. Return by Hunting Stile.

The Langdale Pikes. The finest mountain panorama in the whole of the Lake District. The ascent from Grasmere should be made by Blea Rigg.

Coniston *(Sun, Crown, Black Bull, Ship Inn)* is an attractive village on the north-western shores of Coniston Water. The lake is five-and-a-quarter miles long and half-a-mile wide and its banks are beautifully wooded. There are two small islets, *Peel Island* and *Fir Island.* It was on Coniston Water that the late Donald Campbell made his ill-fated water speed record in 1967. A memorial to him stands in the village. The 19th-century parish church where John Ruskin is buried, is plain and unpretentious, and about a hundred yards from the church is the *Ruskin Museum.*

To Tarn Hows. Just off the Hawkshead road is a wooded lane, which leads to bracken-covered slopes, and suddenly, surprisingly, the enchanting little lake.

To Tilberthwaite. The Tilberthwaite road runs off the Yewdale road about a mile-and-a-half from Coniston. Despite the rough and stony track, this steep-sided ravine is well worth the effort.

To Grisedale. A longer excursion (about 15 miles). Best to start from Lake Bank. This fine wooded valley is Forestry Commission land. There is an interesting *Deer Museum,* marked nature trail, picnic site and camp site.

Hawkshead *(Queen's Head, Red Lion, Sun, Ivy House),* the ancient county town, is now only a village, but with some fascinating old buildings. The most interesting is the 16th-century Grammar School where Wordsworth was educated. He is accused of carving his name on a bench. There was a church in Hawkshead in Norman times, but the present church of St. Michael probably dates from the 15th century. The ancient building just north of the village, near Hawkshead Hall, was originally a Court House of the monks of Furness Abbey.

To Esthwaite Water. A pretty little lake about two miles long and half-a-mile at its widest. The round pond at the head of the lake is known as the *Priest's Pot,* allegedly because it would hold just enough good liquor for a thirsty priest to drink. Esthwaite flows into Windermere by the Cunsey Beck.

To Sawrey. *Hill Top Farm,* immortalised by Beatrix Potter, is at Near Sawrey, a place of pilgrimage for fans of Peter Rabbit and Mrs. Tiggywinkle.

KESWICK AND DISTRICT

Keswick

Bathing.—Bathing at north end of Derwent Water.
Early Closing.—Wednesday.
Hotels.—*Keswick, Derwentwater, Royal Oak, Queen's, Lake* and others.

Launch trips on lake. Boats available.
Population.—5,169.
Post Office.—Main Street.

Keswick is a fairly large and prosperous town on the banks of the river *Greta,* close to the northern shore of Derwent Water, perhaps the most picturesque sheet of water in England. The town has excellent bus services, and is a popular centre for exploring the Lakes. Once a woollen manufacturing centre, Keswick's main industry today is the manufacture of lead pencils and other wood articles. There is a fine *School of Industrial Art,* and a *Museum and Art Gallery* which contains many original manuscripts, including the world-famous "D'Ye Ken John Peel". In the main street is the 19th-century *Moot Hall,* with its romantic bell. The novelist Sir Hugh Walpole is buried in St. John's churchyard, and there is a monument to Southey, with words by Wordsworth, in the parish *Church of St. Kentigern.* Both Coleridge and Southey spent several years at Greta Hall (now part of Keswick School), and when Shelley left Oxford in disgrace he came to Keswick with his first wife Harriet, and lived for a while at Chestnut Hill.

To the Falls of Lodore. The celebrated Falls are about three miles from Keswick, reached by a path just beyond the *Lodore Hotel.* Enchantingly beautiful ravine, the stream cascades down a chasm between towering walls of rock, where trees, incredibly, manage to grow.

To Castlehead (or Castlet). Of great geological interest, Castlehead is all that is left of the original volcano whose eruptions primarily created the Lake District. From the summit (529 feet), marvellous views of the lake, dotted with richly wooded islets, and if you're lucky, a glimpse of the mysterious *Floating Island.*

To Watendlath. A peaceful, secluded valley running parallel with Borrowdale on the east. On the edge of the woods beyond the picturesque Ashness Bridge, a path leads right down to the *Upper Lodore Falls,* which are well worth visiting for themselves, and for the fine views over Derwent Water.

To Grange Fell, the great buttress which overlooks the entrance to Borrowdale from the east. Superb views of some of the highest and most rugged mountains in England. The summit is called *King's How,* in memory of King Edward VII.

To the Bowder Stone and the Borrowdale Birches. This enormous rock, probably carried down from Scotland by glaciers, is a mighty "ship" of alien stone, amazingly balanced on the lower slopes of Grange Fell. You pass the famous Borrowdale Birches on the banks of the *Derwent* on this enchantingly beautiful walk to Rosthwaite.

To Castlerigg Stone Circle. Like a Druid circle, but believed to be a Bronze Age meeting place even older than Stonehenge. It is situated a little more than a mile away off the old Penrith road.

To Latrigg. From the summit (just a few minutes' walk by enclosed path), you have an almost "aerial" view of Keswick, apparently just at your feet.

To Skiddaw Terrace. You could combine this walk with Latrigg. According to Southey, the terrace road past **Applethwaite** to Millbeck provides the best general view of Derwent Water.

To the Vale of St. John, Threlkeld, and Brundholme Woods. Not the easiest walk, but rewarding, with fine views down the Vale of Keswick and Bassenthwaite. If you look back when you stop for a breather, you will see the summit of Skiddaw, invisible from Keswick. After Threlkeld, take care—it is easy for strangers to get lost here. Once in Brundholme Woods, the way is clear and simple.

To Portinscale, with Newlands or Braithwaite. It is about a mile to **Portinscale** from Keswick, by a pleasant path through the fields. **Braithwaite** is just over a mile farther on, but the better walk is to **Newlands.** A path leads through pretty woods to the base of Catbells. If you make it a round trip via the old mines and Little Town, the distance is about 11 miles.

Round Derwentwater. The round-the-lake walk is perhaps the most picturesque 12 miles in England, beginning with the magnificent view of nearly the whole of the lake from the Ruskin Monument on Friar's Crag. You pass **Broomhill Point** and **Walla Crag,** where the Countess of Derwentwater is supposed to have clambered up the deep cleft in the face of the 1,234-foot rock to escape Cromwell's men during the Civil War. Some women might have found the Roundheads less frightening than the awesome *Lady's Rake.* The road continues past Falcon Crag and the little path leading to the Falls of Lodore, south to the village of **Grange** with its double bridge over the *Derwent,* then north to the hamlet of **Manesty** and the windy heights of **Catbells** (1,482 feet). Glorious views of the lake, with Skiddaw and Saddleback in the background and below the stark contrast of the disused Brandlehow Mines and the charming *Brandlehow Park.* A footpath near an iron kissing gate leads to Portinscale and back to Keswick.

The Honister Round. Beyond Rosthwaite the valley divides on either side of Eagle Crag into the valleys of **Langstrath** and **Greenup.** A stiff climb from the hamlet of **Seatoller** over Honister Hause, and a fine view from the summit of the forbidding flanks of **Honister Crag.** This is where the famous Honister green slate comes from, and much of the face is honeycombed with quarries.

Buttermere. This gem of the lakes south-west of Keswick has a noble setting of mountains—Brandreth, Green Gable, Haystack, High Crag, High Stile and Red Pike, Buttermere Moss and Robinson, Fleetwith, Honister Crag and Dalehead. It is well worth spending a day at Buttermere for the joy of walking the fells. If time is limited, settle for Red Pike. Hotels in the village include *Bridge, Fish* and *Hashness.* There is a Youth Hostel.

The best short excursion from Buttermere village is to **Scale Force,** where the stream leaps nearly 100 feet in one clear fall between perpendicular walls of syenite. **Crummock Water** is passed on the way to Scale Force from Buttermere village, and if you have time, walk along the edge of the lake to **Ling Crag**—the view is superb. The short way back to Keswick is by **Buttermere Hause** (8 miles). There is a hair-raisingly steep descent into the tranquil valley of **Keskadale.** The distant mountain in front is Saddleback, and you see Newlands Valley and Little Dale and the imposing precipice of Eel Crags. The route winds through gentle wooded country by Swinside, and Portinscale to Crosthwaite and Keswick.

Round Thirlmere. The road runs along the side of the lake at the foot of Helvellyn, past Thirlspot, and the Straining Well of the Waterworks, designed to look like a castle. **Thirlmere** is the chief source of Manchester's water supply. You pass Wythburn, whose main claim to fame is that Wordsworth wrote about its "modest house of prayer". The western road back passes below the forbidding **Fisher Crag** and **Raven Crag.**

Round Bassenthwaite Lake. The delightful **Vale of Keswick** stretches from the head of Derwentwater to the foot of Bassenthwaite Lake. The route from Keswick lies through Portinscale and past **Braithwaite** at the foot of the Whinlatter Pass. Passing **Thornthwaite,** the road skirts the base of **Lord's Seat** and **Barf** with its *Bishop Rock* (whitewashed now and then to keep his lordship's surplice white). At the **Peel Wyke** end of the lake you have a fine view of Skiddaw's twin summit.

To Whinlatter Pass and the Vale of Lorton. The easiest route from Keswick to Crummock and Buttermere is via Whinlatter Pass (1,043 feet) and the hamlet of **High Lorton** through the beautiful Vale of Lorton.

To Caldbeck and Threlkeld. Not one of the most inspiring journeys through the Lake District, but what it lacks in scenery it makes up in history. Caldbeck is where John Peel lived and died and you can see the grave of the world's most famous huntsman in the village church yard.

On the Fells

A brief guide to the fells in the Keswick area with the best starting points and some indication of the terrain:

Skiddaw (from Keswick). With Carrock, Bowscale and Lonscale Fells, Carlside, Great Calva and Ullock Pike. Travelling throughout generally easy. Steep scree on the descent and some rock.

Saddleback (from Threlkeld). Travelling generally easy via Scales village, magnificent views, many crags and precipices at both ends of saddle.

Grasmoor (from Braithwaite). With Grisedale Pike, Eel Crag, Causey Pike. By the Force Crag (Coledale Pass) route, Grasmoor is the easiest mountain to ascend from Keswick and one of the finest view points in the Lakes.

Eel Crag, Dalehead, Hindscarth, Robinson (from Keswick). Walk through the woods south of Portinscale, or better still, row to Hause End or take the motor launch to Brandlehow for Catbells, and start your trip from there. Fine views of the Helvellyn Range and Newlands on this splendid 13-mile round walk.

Helvellyn (from Wythburn). Travelling is moderately easy, but take care when getting off the main mountain on to either Swirrel or Striding Edge.

High Raise (from Rosthwaite). The path goes up the near side of Lining Crag and but for the bad walking up the valley, over loose stones and moraine heaps, this would be an easier expedition than Grasmoor.

Lord's Seat and Barf (from Thornthwaite). The ascent is made from opposite the Swan Hotel. Skiddaw seen at its best from this point. The giant thimble of the Pike of Stickle is seen to the south.

Glaramara (from Rosthwaite). A massive mountain, very grand, with fine views, and one of the most confusing summits in the whole of the Lake District. To be avoided in bad weather, but the walking is exasperating at any time, through wild rough country with rocks, heather and swamp nearly all the way.

Buttermere Fells (from Buttermere). Travelling on the three principal fells is rather rough. Upper ridge precipitous towards Buttermere.

THE PENRITH DISTRICT

Penrith

Early Closing.—Wednesday.
Golf.—Beacon Hill (18 holes).
Hotels.—*George, Castle, Hussar, Station, Strick-* *land, Carleton,* etc.
Sports.—Golf, tennis, cricket, football, rugby, bowls, swimming, shooting, fishing, riding.

The ancient town of Penrith is the gateway to the Lake District from the north, and owes much of its turbulent history to the fact that the visiting Scots were not always as friendly as they are now. The town was sacked many times during the Border wars, and Penrith Castle has seen a lot of action. Richard III raised his standard there, and it was the scene of bitter fighting during the Civil War when it passed into the hands of the Parliamentarians. Now its gardens are a public park, and only the gaunt ruins of the building overlook the town. The Parish Church has some interesting stained glass and a tradition of giants, both real and imaginary. Warwick the Kingmaker, that mighty man, built the tower in the old part of the church, and the legendary giant Owen Caesarius is supposed to be buried in the church yard. The Giant's Grave is certainly enormous, and there's another stone nearby, called the Giant's Thumb, with massive indentations where he left his fingerprints. There are fascinating places to visit within easy reach, and Penrith is an excellent centre for exploring the northern lakes, with good local bus services to Ullswater, Haweswater, Pooley Bridge and Patterdale.

Brougham Castle *(daily, fee)*. The ruins of the 17th-century castle are about one-and-a-half miles south-east of Penrith. James I was a guest there, and many romantic stories are told about the De Clifford family. The outer walls with the massive Keep and Gatehouse, are well-preserved.

Lowther Castle. Once one of the stateliest homes of England, now only the ruins remain, but a mile from the castle (about five miles south of Penrith) is **Lowther Wild Life Park** *(daily in summer)*.

Askham. It is a pleasant walk through the park, past the fine old Lowther Church and Askham Hall, to this pretty little village. A public way leads off the Kendal road about four miles south of Penrith.

Long Meg and her Daughters. Meg, an 18-foot column of red freestone, watches over her 66 daughters in this important Druidical circle near little Salkeld, some six miles north-east of Penrith.

The Beacon. Fine views from the Beacon (966 feet) which is north of the station, about a mile from the town.

Penrith to Ullswater. The most picturesque road to Ullswater from Penrith is along the west bank of the *Eamont*, passing *Dalemain* and its handsome park. A bridge over the river at Eamont marks the old dividing line between Westmorland and Cumberland. This whole area is rich in archaeological remains. Near Eamont Bridge is an ancient earthwork, possibly a Bronze Age burial place, known as *King Arthur's Round Table*. Across the road and higher up the river is **Mayburgh** where a massive block of unhewn stone is believed to have been a place of Druidical judicature.

The road continues through the attractive village of **Tirril,** past Barton church (the ancient parish church and well worth a visit) and on to **Pooley Bridge,** and the boat station where you can take the boat to Howtown and Patterdale. The voyage up the lake takes about an hour.

Ullswater. A lovely lake, shaped roughly like a scythe, with the "handle" towards Pooley bridge, and the "blade" curving gently round to Patterdale. Ullswater is

356

about seven miles long and a mile wide at its broadest part, framed in majestic mountains. If you sail from Pooley Bridge you get some idea of the sheer splendour of the lake and the surrounding countryside. The wooded, conical hill close to the pier at Pooley Bridge is *Dun Mallet*, site of an ancient British hill fort. To the east, behind Barton Fell is *Moor Divock* (1,061 feet) and between Barton Fell and the lake is *Trestermont*, legendary home of Sir Tristram, one of the Knights of the Round Table. Beyond Howtown, to the west are the wooded slopes of *Hallin Fell*, with a monument to Lord Brougham at the summit (1,271 feet). The fierce crag which juts into the lake is *Kail Pot*. The middle reaches of the lake are possibly the most beautiful of all—*Hallsteads*, on Skelly Nab (from where the skelly fishermen used to stretch their nets to Geordie Crag, on the opposite shore); *Place Fell*, and the tranquil woods and dales watched over by the frowning mass of Helvellyn. *Silver Point* divides the second and third reaches of the lake and you'll see *Stybarrow Crag* against the massive background of *Stybarrow Dodd* (2,756 feet). Away to the left is *St. Sunday Crag, the* Ullswater mountain.

Patterdale (Pop.: 700. Hotels: *Brothers' Water, Bridge House, Ullswater, Glenridding*, etc.), is the main centre for Ullswater delightfully situated at the head of the lake, nestling on the wooded spurs of Helvellyn and St. Sunday Crag. St. Patrick is supposed to have visited the area (hence the name), and baptised his converts in a well near the village. The parish church is dedicated to him. A favourite starting point for the ascent of Helvellyn and the sail down the lake, Patterdale, with Glenridding, is also a very good centre for excursions farther afield—to Windermere by the Kirkstone Pass and the Vale of Troutbeck; to Grasmere by Troutbeck; to Haweswater by Pooley Bridge and Lowther Castle; to Keswick by Matterdale, Threlkeld and Castlerigg Stone Circle.

To Aira Force. The route passes *Stybarrow Crag*, where one of the Mounseys of Patterdale Hall fought off marauding Scots and earned himself the title of King of Patterdale. From the village to the spectacular waterfall and back is about six miles of easy walking, with many footpaths to choose from. In full volume the force is really impressive, leaping some 60 feet between sheer walls of rock. Near the lake is *Lyulph's Tower*, an 18th-century shooting box.

To Grisedale Tarn. There are many glorious Ullswater valleys—Deepdale, Dovedale, Bannerdale, Haweswater Ghyll and many more, but Grisedale is perhaps the finest of them all. It is an eight mile round trip from Patterdale to Grisedale Tarn (1,768 feet) and back. Given the weather—and the stamina—the return could be made over St. Sunday Crag to Elmhow, remembering always that this is a mountain to be treated with respect.

Helvellyn. Anyone who can walk in the Lake District seems to feel compelled to climb Helvellyn. Fortunately it is the most accommodating of mountains, and even if you choose to ascend by Striding Edge (which is not nearly as bad as its reputation) there should be no danger to anyone who can walk steadily. Other ascents are via Glenridding or over Dolly-waggon Pike from Grisedale Tarn. Helvellyn, the Hill of Baal, or El-Velin, is supposed to have been the sacred hill of ancient times. It also has a more recent claim to fame. A cairn just beneath the summit on the southern side commemorates the first aeroplane to land on a mountain in Great Britain. What's more, it took off again. There is another monument—to a faithful dog which guarded its master's body for three months. Very useful in bad weather, the memorial is about 50 yards above the "walk off" for Striding Edge.

To Place Fell. Helvellyn is seen at its best from here. Place Fell is easily reached from Boardale Hause. It is a delightful afternoon walk, returning to Howtown via Boardale, or following the ridge line towards Hallin Fell to Patterdale.

St. Sunday Crag. *The* mountain of Ullswater, with marvellous views of the lake. The ascent should be made by Grisedale Tarn. In fine weather, the walk could be carefully extended over Cofa Pike to Fairfield, then down to Grisedale Tarn and back to Patterdale.

To Brothers' Water. You can follow the Goldrill Beck to Brothers' Water, traditionally the scene of a double tragedy in the 19th century, when two brothers were drowned.

To Haweswater. You can go by Boardale Hause, Angle Tarn and Kidsty Pike, or by Hartsop and Hayes Water over High Street. The whole appearance of the lake was drastically changed when it was converted into a vast reservoir to help boost Manchester's water supply (Thirlmere having proved unable to quench the city's thirst). The dam is the only hollow structure of its kind in the country, 1,550 feet long and 120 feet high. *Gatescarthfoot,* near the head of the lake, is where the road ends and the mountain tracks begin.

High Street. The easiest ascent of the High Street range is by Kidsty Pike from Gatescarthfoot. A more sporting route is by Rough Crag, with Blea Water below on the left, gloomy and impressive. Tantalising views from the summit—glimpses of Windermere and Buttermere Fells as well as a fine mountain panorama. Even better views if you follow the summit line southwards to Thornthwaite Crag, returning to Mardale by the Nan Bield Pass.

To Harter Fell. Harter Fell dominates the head of Haweswater. Follow the Gatescarth Pass to the summit, returning by Nan Bield and then by Smallwater to Gatescarthfoot.

THE WESTERN DALES AND THE COAST

This wildly beautiful region includes some of the loneliest valleys in the Lake District, accessible only to walkers, and challenging mountains where climbers need to use hands and feet. It also includes important industrial towns like Workington, and the busy port of Whitehaven, with a regular steamer service to Belfast and the Isle of Man. Britain's first nuclear power station and the largest nuclear fuel re-processing plant in Europe is at Calder Hall, about 12 miles south of Whitehaven. The main centre for road and rail services is Cockermouth, at the junction of the rivers *Cocker* and *Derwent* on the north-western boundary of the Lake District National Park.

South of Whitehaven is **St. Bees** *(Queen's, Abbot's Court, Albert)* a good centre for exploring Wasdale and Ennerdale. There is bathing from the beach, golf, and sea fishing from the rocks below the Head. The abbey church, restored in the 17th century, is now the parish church. Archbishop Grindal founded the public school in 1583. **St. Bees Head** is the rocky promontory at the southern tip of the Bay of Whitehaven. It is a sheer wall of rock which soars to a height of well over 300 feet. The name comes from St. Bega, an Irish recluse, who built a monastery there in the 7th century.

Seascale *(Scawfell, Wansfell)* is one of the most popular holiday resorts on this coast, with good sands, backed by sand dunes, and quite the best sea bathing and golfing near the lakes. The 18-hole course extends more than three miles along the shore. Seascale is a good centre for Eskdale, Ennerdale and Wastwater.

To Gosforth. A fair sized village about two miles from Seascale. It has a notable ancient cross, believed to be around 1,000 years old, curiously inscribed.

To Calderbridge. From this village, about two-and-a-half miles north-west of Gosforth on the main road to Whitehaven, the new road leads to the Atomic power station at Calder Hall, and the old road leads to the ruins of Calder Abbey. **Calder Abbey** *(Summer, Sats, Suns).* The ruins of this 12th-century monastery are about a mile upstream from Calderbridge, set in woods. Founded by a colony of monks from Furness Abbey, the original building was destroyed by marauding Scots. After many trials and tribulations, the abbey was rebuilt in the 13th century by a second colony from Furness Abbey.

Ravenglass *(Pennington Arms)*, is a small village on the estuary of the river *Esk*, about five miles south of Seascale. It is a good centre for exploring Eskdale. The narrow-gauge **Ravenglass and Eskdale Railway** runs between Ravenglass and Dalegarth, near Boot. There is good fishing in the rivers Esk, Mite, and Irt. **Walls** is an interesting Roman ruin, including the baths, about eight minutes' walk from the village. Across the estuary is Ravenglass Galleries, a nature reserve, and round the coast at **Drigg** is a fine bathing beach.

Muncaster Caster *(Weds, Thurs, Suns, Bank Hols, fee; grounds daily)*, on the southern slope of Muncaster Fell, has been the home of the Pennington family for more than 500 years. Its greatest treasure is an enamelled glass bowl, known as the Luck of the Muncasters, a gift from King Henry VI who was given shelter in the castle after his defeat at the Battle of Towton in 1461. A stone monument just beyond the bridge marks the spot where a shepherd rescued the King and took him to the castle.

Waberthwaite Church the ancient chapel for Muncaster Castle is reached at low tide by a ford. Interesting pre-Norman cross shaft in the church yard.

Eskdale. The *Esk* rises on Great End and runs into the sea at Ravenglass where it widens into an estuary with the rivers *Irt* and *Mite*. The end of the Ravenglass–Eskdale miniature railway line is at Dalegarth Station, near **Boot**, an attractive little village in the dale with a quaint old corn mill by the waterfall. There is good fishing with the chance of salmon and sea trout.

Birker Force is an impressive waterfall in a tranquil setting. The stream rises in a small tarn on the western slope of Birker Fell and tumbles into the *Esk* about a mile south-east of Boot.

To Stanley Ghyll and Dalegarth Force. A magnificent ravine, deep and thickly wooded, about half-an-hour's walk from Boot. Just beyond Dalegarth Hall is the signpost to Stanley Ghyll. Rather rough walking up the ghyll, but worth it—Dalegarth Force leaps from a cleft in the sheer wall of rock, and falls 60 feet to the pool below.

Devoke Water. This tarn, more than half-a-mile long and famous for its fine red trout, is on the western edge of Birker Moor, across the main Boot–Ulpha road. The lake feeds *Lin Beck,* a small tributary of the *Esk.*

Upper Eskdale. You take the road for Hardknott Pass, past the *Woolpack Inn* and Butterilket Farm (the oldest holding in the valley, farmed by the monks of St. Bees Priory over 700 years ago). A well-marked track leads to Esk Falls, where you cross the bridge over *Lingcove Beck* and follow the main stream to the upper valley 500 feet above. Wild and desolate, with spectacular views of the awesome **Scafell Pike** (3,210 feet). There is a very fine waterfall, *Cam Spout.* The descent should be made from here to *Cowcove Beck,* then left to Taw House Farm (N.T.).

Wastwater by Irton Fell. Stupendous view of Wastwater. You take the track from Eskdale Green to Miterdale and follow a good fell path across the foothills of the Screes, and as you cross the ridge line the lake is dazzlingly below. Easy ascent to the top of Whin Rigg from here, followed by an interesting walk along the summit of Wasdale Screes to the highest point, Ill Gill Head. Descend to **Wasdale Head** via Burnmoor Tarn or Strands.

Crinkle Crags and Bowfell. The best route is to go via Butterilket Farm, and bear right at the bridge over *Lingcove Beck,* following the course upstream.

To Harter Fell. A challenging mountain, near Boot, between Duddon Valley and Eskdale, and not to be confused with Harter Fell at Haweswater.

Wasdale. The entrance to Wasdale is at Strands, and this western approach shows Wastwater in all its glory against a majestic mountain background. The Screes sweep down to the southern shores of the lake and the scenery becomes increasingly wild and grand. Prominent are Great Gable, Kirkfell, and the pike profile of Yewbarrow, on the approach to Wasdale Head (which boasts the highest mountain, the deepest lake and the smallest church in England).

Scafell. Most easily ascended from Wasdale, or from Eskdale via Eel Tarn, or from Boot via Burnmoor (very hard going). It is not advisable to try and pass from Scafell Pike to Scafell—the mountain has claimed enough victims already. **Scafell Pike** is the roof of England (3,210 feet), with the summit dedicated to the nation by Lord Leconfield as a memorial to the men from the dales who gave their lives in the First World War. From Wasdale, the easiest ascent is by Brown Tongue. The descent could be made over Broad Crag and Ill Crag to Esk Hause and back to Wasdale by the *Sty*. Any time, in any way, this mountain should be treated with respect.

Great Gable. Glorious Great Gable, one of the most perfect mountain forms in England, with superb views from the summit, where the peaks can be identified on the relief map engraved on the War Memorial. This bronze tablet near the summit cairn was presented by the Fell and Rock Climbing Club. The most direct ascent (also the steepest, but best because of the views) is from Sty Head. The descent is best made by Windy Gap.

Ennerdale. Ennerdale is a long, lonely valley, more inaccessible than Wasdale, bounded by Great Gable and the fine screes of the Buttermere Fells, Kirk Fell, Pillar Mountain and the wild crags of Steeple. It stretches for 10 miles from the foot of Ennerdale Water, and walking at the extreme head of the valley is rough. There is a path round the lake by Angling Crag, and a road of sorts as far as Gillerthwaite Farm. Beyond Gillerthwaite much of the land has been fenced off by the Forestry Commission.

Pillar Mountain. Usually ascended from Wasdale or Buttermere, but the ascent from Gillerthwaite in Ennerdale is well worth while if only for the fine views of the Steeple, a spur of Scoatfell. **Pillar Rock** on the north face of the fell, was thought inaccessible until 1826, but since then it has been repeatedly climbed—*by cragsmen only*. Anyone who wants to visit the rock will find a fairly reasonable approach by the climbers' path from Looking Stead direct to the base of the rock. If just looking is enough, the best view points are from Scarth Gap, the Gables, or Ennerdale itself.

Carlisle and District

Carlisle (Pop.: 71,500. Hotels: *County, Crown and Mitre, Central, Vallum House*) is an ancient border city on the *Eden*. It is the administrative head-quarters of Cumbria, seat of a bishop and an important railway centre. At Court Square is the *Citadel Station,* a busy junction and motorail terminal with extensive marshalling yards and, adjacent the *County Buildings* and *Court House.* These buildings conspicuous with their two huge drum towers incorporate part

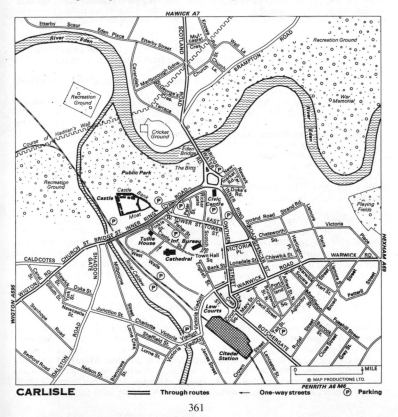

CARLISLE   ═══ **Through routes**   ← **One-way streets**   ℗ **Parking**

of the original Citadel founded by Henry VIII. At the end of English Street is the *Market Place* with a well-preserved 17th-century Cross and facing, the *Town Hall* (1717) much in contrast to the modern Civic Centre (1964) and nearby office blocks.

Carlisle Cathedral is a small red sandstone building completed in 1123. Originally the Church of the Blessed Virgin Mary it was raised to cathedral status in 1133 when the Carlisle diocese was founded by Henry I. The Choir, built in the Decorated style as opposed to certain other parts of the cathedral in the Norman, Early English and Perpendicular styles, was completed in 1362 after the original had been burned down some 70 years earlier. In the Choir are the Stalls (about 1400), some bearing 15th-century legendary painted scenes depicting the lives of the Saints Anthony, Cuthbert and Augustine and the magnificent East Window (1380) with its tracery lights and old glass part of which describes "The Last Judgement". This window, 58 feet high and 32 feet wide, is considered by many to be even finer in design than that of the famous West Window in York Minster. The Renaissance or Salkeld Screen dating from 1542 and the screenwork in St. Catherine's Chapel, are also very fine. The pulpit (1599) is somewhat unique in that it originally came from a church in Antwerp—until 1964 it had been in the church of Cockayne Hatley, near Potton, Bedfordshire. The arcade piers, in the Early English style, with their carved capitals depict the work of each month of the year and are a further feature of this much-visited cathedral wherein was married Sir Walter Scott in 1797. Access to the tower and clerestory is available to sightseers.

To the south-west of the cathedral are the *Deanery* and *Chapter Library* and the *Church of St. Cuthbert* (1778) where an old tithe barn (1490) has been restored for use as the parish hall.

Tullie House Museum (1689), in Castle Street, has many interesting paintings, antiquities and a natural history collection.

The **Castle** *(daily, fee)* was begun by William Rufus and consists of two wards, the outer ward with the Alma Block containing the county archives and the inner to the right comprising a well-preserved Norman keep completed by Henry II. The keep houses the *Border Regiment Museum* with relics associated with Mary, Queen of Scots' imprisonment.

From Carlisle A595 bears south-west towards Cockermouth passing the little village of **Thursby** and six miles farther the curiously named Red Dial crossroads. Nearby is the Roman fort of *Olenacum*. South-east of **Mealsgate** is **Boltongate** where the church has an unusual stone-vaulted nave of 15th-century date. At **Bothel** the A591 branches off south-east for Keswick.

Cockermouth (Pop.: 6,365. Hotels: *Trout, Globe, Appletree*) is famous as the birthplace of William Wordsworth. **Wordsworth House** (N.T., *Apr.–Sept., daily except Fris and Suns. In Oct. Mons and Weds only, fee*), in Main Street was built in 1745 and retains its original staircase, fireplaces and panelling. The Castle at the junction of the rivers *Cocker* and *Derwent* dates back to Norman times and is still occupied. The older part contains an example of the awful oubliette dungeon. Cockermouth has a good 18-hole golf course and there are salmon and trout in both rivers. At **Bridekirk** *(bus service)* two miles north, the church has two Norman doorways and a notable 12th-century sculptured font.

Workington (Pop.: 28,400. Hotels: *Green Dragon, Briery House*), is an industrial town and seaport at the mouth of the *Derwent*. The Helena Thompson Museum is of local interest. Mary, Queen of Scots stayed at Workington Hall in 1598.

The coast road north from Workington reaches in six miles **Maryport** a former centre for shipping coal and iron but now chiefly involved in plastics, chemicals and clothing. There is a beach with good sands. **Allonby,** farther north-east, a small resort with a pleasant beach, is within the coastal strip of land (extending along the Solway Firth through the seaside resort of **Silloth,** thence Abbey Town, Kirkbride and Burgh-by-Sands) now designated an "area of outstanding natural beauty".

Abbey Town reached by the B5302 from Silloth (4½ miles) is much visited on account of the *Holme Cultram Abbey* (remains), a Cistercian church founded in 1135. The parish church was built within the Abbey's original nave part of which still survives. Farther north at **Newton Arlosh** is a church with associations dating back to 1304. **Bowness-on-Solway** and **Drumburgh** mark the western extremity of the line of Hadrian's Wall.

Wigton, 11 miles south-west of Carlisle on the A596 Maryport road, has a fine 18th-century church, and an interesting fountain. Six miles north-west of Carlisle is **Burgh-by-Sands** with a fortified church of Roman origin and, north of the village, the monument marking the spot where Edward I died in 1307.

B6264 from Carlisle runs north-west to **Crosby** (the town's airport) and thence to Brampton. Just south of this and roughly parallel is the much busier A69 Carlisle–Newcastle road which reaches Brampton in nine miles and the Northumberland border five-and-a-half miles farther north-east. **Warwick,** four miles east of Carlisle via the second-mentioned road, has, in St. Leonard's Church, a well-preserved Norman apse and chancel-arch. **Brampton,** an attractive little market town, has several points worthy of attention, these being St. Martin's Church (Burne-Jones windows), Moot Hall, the stocks, Prince Charlie's House and the Church with Norman features one-and-a-half miles to the north-west.

The 14th-century **Naworth Castle,** three miles east of Brampton, part of which may be seen by prior arrangement, contains the Great Hall, the Library and some fine tapestry. **Lanercost Priory** *(daily, fee),* two miles north-east, was a house of Augustinian Canons founded about 1144. There are some fine arches and a 13th-century nave which is now in use as parish church.

Near **Gilsland,** a village on the border of Cumbria and Northumberland though just within the former and one mile north of A69, are some well-preserved sections of Hadrian's Wall and, additionally, two Roman inscribed altars. **Over Denton,** see church, possibly Anglo-Saxon, and **Birdoswald,** remains of a Roman fort, are also in this area.

A6071 north-west from Brampton reaches Longtown on the *Esk* in 11 miles and the Scottish border, formed by the river *Sark*, via that same road, some three-and-a-half miles farther on. Solway Moss, roughly equidistant between Longtown and Gretna Green, was the site of the battle at which the Scots were defeated by the English in 1542.

The flat uninteresting land between Carlisle and Longtown contrasts strongly with the region of Cumbria north-east of the Longtown–Brampton road. *Sighty Crag* near the Northumberland border reaches 1,702 feet. **Bewcastle,** reached by the B6318 from Gilsland to Kirkcambeck and thence by a minor road over remote moorland, is well worth visiting on account of its medieval castle remains, Roman fort and, more especially, its remarkable 14½-foot high inscribed Anglican Cross dating back to the 7th century.

Isle of Man

Routes to the Island

By Sea.—Through trains from principal centres to Liverpool connect with steamer departures, and time of crossing is 3½–4 hours. Also sailings to Douglas from Ardrossan, Belfast and Dublin; boats from Belfast and Ardrossan usually call also at Ramsey. Details from agents, British Rail, or the I. of M. Steam Packet Co., Douglas.

Car Ferries.—Car Ferry services from Liverpool and Ardrossan. Reservations must be made with I. of M. Steam Packet Co., Ltd.

By Air.—Airport at Ronaldsway, near Castletown. Services by Cambrian Airways and other lines.

Accommodation.—The Island is well supplied with hotels; an official list is issued by I. of M. Tourist Board, 13 Victoria Street, Douglas.

The Isle of Man caters for all tastes. The main centres have ample accommodation, fine beaches, and well-organised entertainments. Inland are hills and glens, woodland and moors, making a walker's paradise. Roads are uncrowded and excellent for motoring; some roads are "out of bounds" during the Tourist Trophy Motor Cycle Races held in June.

The Island measures roughly 33 miles × 12 miles, and has an area of 227 square miles of which more than half is under cultivation. The Calf of Man, at the extreme south-west, has an area of about 600 acres.

The Isle of Man is situated in the Irish Sea, rather less than 30 miles from England and from Northern Ireland, and only 16 miles south of Scotland. Most of the Island is hilly, the principal height being Snaefell, 2,034 feet. The mountainous regions are of the same geological structure as those in North Wales. Strata are much inclined—in places nearly vertical—but glacial action has rounded the mountain outlines.

Natural History. Sea-birds and river-birds abound, and the grey seal is found around the coasts. The fauna shows some surprising gaps, e.g. there are no foxes, squirrels, or moles. The Manx domestic cat is tail-less, and is becoming rather rare.

Native woodlands are sparse, but afforestation has long been the official policy, and there are now 3,500 acres of coniferous woodland.

History. In the 5th or 6th centuries missionaries from Ireland brought Christianity to the Isle of Man (*Ellan Vannier* in Manx), but in the 8th century Viking raids began the long period of Norse rule. As late as 1079–1095 Godred Crovan—"King Orry the Dane"—ruled not only the Island, but also the Western Isles of Scotland. In 1265 the Isle of Man became subject by purchase to Scotland but from 1333 Edward I assumed overlordship. About 1405 Henry IV granted it to Sir John Stanley, whose descendants as Earls of Derby were Lords of Man for many generations. In 1765 the Island was bought by the Crown.

Government. The Sovereign is represented by a Lieutenant-Governor, and the local legislature consists of two Chambers—the nominated Legislative Council, and the elected House of Keys with 24 members. No Act is valid until it has received the Royal Assent and has been formally proclaimed from Tynwald Hill. The Island has its own High Court of Justice, serious criminal cases being presided over by one of the two "Deemsters".

The Diocese of Sodor and Man is for administrative convenience counted as a diocese of the province of York.

Population and Industries. Population is approximately 50,000, of whom over 19,000 are resident in Douglas. Agriculture and the tourist trade are the main industries. Fishing has diminished in importance, and minor industries include textiles and light engineering.

Manx Arms and Manx Language. Paradoxically the arms of Man are legs—three of them, so disposed that one foot is always on the ground. The device is of uncertain origin, and at some time replaced the earlier ship device of the Norse Kings. The Manx language is closely related to Irish and Scottish Gaelic, with a Scandinavian influence noticeable in place-names.

Douglas

Angling.—Good sea angling from the pier.

Bathing.—Good bathing from firm sands. Public baths in Victoria Street include two salt-water swimming baths.

Distances.—Castletown, 10; Ramsey, 15; Peel, 11; Port Erin, 14; Port St. Mary, 14.

Early Closing.—Thursday.

Entertainments.—Dancing at *Palace Ballroom, Villa Marina,* and *Majestic Ballroom.* Cinemas: *Gaiety Theatre. Casino.*

Population.—19,250.

Post Office.—Regent Street.

Douglas is predominantly a holiday town, and its resident population of 19,000 is increased in the season by a further 50,000 or more visitors. It is the sea-port through which pass the bulk of visitors to the Island. The town is set on a rising hillside and faces east to a curving bay, with impressive headlands at either end. Little sign now remains of the fishing village from which the modern town has arisen. Visitors disembark at **Victoria Pier.** This and **Battery Pier** form the arms of the harbour, within which is the **King Edward VIII Pier** (completed in 1936). A restaurant, the *Crow's Nest,* at Sea Terminal Buildings, gives a fine panoramic view of the town.

The Sea Front. At the Jubilee Clock nearby is the junction of Victoria Street and the Loch Promenade. The latter forms the southern portion of the long promenade, still served by a horse-drawn tramway as well as by more modern motor-buses. Regent Street (containing the GPO) connects the sea-front with Strand Street, which with its continuation Castle Street forms the busiest part of Douglas. This continues as the Harris Promenade, and on the left is the *Gaiety Theatre* and the *Villa Marina*—eight acres of gardens with a Royal Hall used for dances, concerts and conferences. At this point Broadway runs inland, with buses for Laxey, Ramsey, etc. The sea-front continues as Central Promenade, with the vast *Palace Ballroom* and adjoining *Casino,* and is in turn succeeded by Queen's Promenade. This runs past the Holiday Camp and the Switzerland Sports Ground, to Summer Hill, just before the Tram Terminus and the station of the Manx Electric Railway. **Summer Hill Glen,** gaily illuminated by night, forms a pleasant walk. Beyond the station, the road ascends to **Onchan Head,** a fine viewpoint and the northern limit of Douglas Bay.

The Town. Near the top of Victoria Street is the Town Hall, and adjoining it the Public Library. To the right is Prospect Hill, leading to the **Legislative Buildings;** over the public entrance are the old arms of the Norse Kings—the ship with furled sails. Within, the Chamber of the House of Keys is on the ground floor and the Tynwald Court above. At the further end of Finch Road is the **Museum,** a comprehensive collection devoted entirely to Manx matters. Opposite the Legislative Buildings is the **Catholic Church of St. Mary of the Isle,** and at the further end of Hill Street is **St. George's Church,** the State Church of the Island, with some interesting memorials. A short distance south is the terminus of the Isle of Man Railway, which in summer serves many points of the Island. Nearby, the Stone Bridge crosses the *Douglas* and connects North Quay with South Quay. At the seaward end of North Quay are the Markets, buildings that replace the former open-air stalls; also the *Bus Station,* and the Swing Bridge crossing the harbour to Fort Anne Road.

From the shore end of Battery Pier a path with steps leads up to **Douglas Head,** whence there is a fine view of the town with its background of mountains dominated by Snaefell.

Excursions from Douglas

(1) **Kirk Braddan** (1¾ miles) by the Peel road, or by the Castletown road and the footpath passing between the grounds of the Nunnery and the river. The *Old Church of Braddan* is remarkable for its collection of Runic crosses. In summer, open air services are held on Sunday mornings in the natural amphitheatre at the back of the New Church that stands nearby.

(2) **Port Soderick** (3½ miles) by the Marine Drive, past rocky coast scenery of great grandeur.

(3) **Onchan, Clypse and Glencrutchery.** Onchan village may be reached by bus, and a pleasant walk from here is to take the road by the school, at the far end of the village. This descends to the upper **Groudle Glen** and follows the stream to a bridge, with the *Clypse Reservoir* on the right. Cross the bridge and ascend to Hillberry, returning by the Mountain Road to *Governor's Bridge,* on the outskirts of Onchan.

(4) **Groudle Glen** is reached by following the road beside the Electric Railway for two miles. The *Groudle* flows through a pleasant valley, and enters the sea through a rocky gorge.

(5) **Injebreck** (approx. 6 miles). Lovely Injebreck is a deep mountain recess at the centre of the Island. Walking distance can be cut by taking a bus to **Strang,** or if possible on to **Baldwin.** From Strang take road to *Mount Rule,* keeping right at fork. On the left as one descends to Baldwin are *Greeba* (1,383 feet) and *Slican Ruy* (1,570 feet). At the head of the West Baldwin Valley is the reservoir that supplies Douglas. As one proceeds up the valley *Colden* (1,599 feet) is seen on the left and *Carraghan* (1,640 feet) on the right. Extensive larch and pine plantations add to the charm of Injebreck.

(6) **Laxey and Snaefell.** Laxey can be reached in 30 minutes by the Electric Railway. By road it is eight miles via Onchan, now contiguous with Douglas, though independent.

Onchan (Pop.: 3,300) has developed from the nucleus of the old village, and now has modern hotels and a 20-acre Park complete with all sports facilities. From Onchan the road crosses the *Groudle* stream, and continues by the railway past *Garwick Glen* before turning sharply inland to Laxey. (The old road forks right and descends steeply to the old bridge, rising to rejoin the main road at the *King Orry.*)

Laxey (Pop.: 1,130). The old part lies by the harbour; the modern part is higher up the Glen and includes the pleasant *Laxey Glen Gardens.* The **Waterwheel,** about half-a-mile above the station has long been one of the marvels of Manxland. It was constructed in 1854 for pumping water out of the lead mines below, and is maintained purely as a show piece. The great wheel is 72½ feet in diameter. Beside it is a 75-foot platform reached by spiral steps, and from here there is a good view of Snaefell.

Snaefell by Electric Railway. For the first three miles from Laxey there is a clear view on the right of the Laxey Valley and the big wheel. At the *Bungalow* (1,400 feet) the railway crosses the Mountain Road, and mountain, moor, Ramsey and ocean become visible. When not obscured by mist, the view from the summit (2,034 feet) extends to England, Scotland, Wales and Ireland, and the Isle of Man is spread like a map at one's feet. The peak to the north is *North Barrule* (1,860 feet).

Douglas to Castletown, Port St. Mary, and Port Erin

The main road from the south end of Douglas Bridge passes the *Nunnery* grounds and in one mile gives a choice of routes. The A6, to the right, after a long climb passes Mount Murray, now the *Alex Inn,* and continues to Stanton Station and the village of Ballasalla. The road to the left (A25) is hillier, and passes through **Crogga** and **Santon,** to join the A6 before **Ballasalla,** once important by virtue of Rushen Abbey, the principal monastic establishment of the Island until the Dissolution of 1541. Little remains of the Abbey, but a short distance up the *Silverburn,* the 14th-century *Monks' Bridge* is still in good condition. The lower part of the *Silverburn Glen* is Manx National Trust property. The road south from Ballasalla soon passes the up-to-date Civil Airport at **Ronaldsway,** and *King William's College,* a famous boys' school. A mile further on is **Castletown** (Pop.: 2,378), an ancient small town at the mouth of the *Silverburn.* Until 1862 this was the capital of the Island, and seat of the Lord of Man or his representative. The impressive **Castle Rushen** is in an excellent state of preservation. The present building dates from 1350, an earlier structure having been largely destroyed in 1313 by Robert Bruce.

In 1651 the 7th Earl of Derby, fleeing from the battle of Worcester, was captured by the Parliamentary forces and executed. In his absence the Countess defended the Castle, but William Christian, Captain of the Manx militia, thought it expedient to come to terms with the Roundheads. The Countess vowed vengeance, and after the Restoration managed to get Christian tried and shot. A good account of this period of Manx history is given in Scott's stirring romance "Peveril of the Peak".

Castletown has also an interesting *Nautical Museum,* a museum of witchcraft *(Witches Mill),* and an ancient building once used as a Grammar School.

To **Port St. Mary** is about four miles. This quiet village was at one time the headquarters of the Manx fisheries. Above the village rises *Mull Hill* (556 feet). Interesting excursions can be made to the *Chasms,* to *Spanish Head* and to the **Calf of Man,** noted for its bird life.

Port Erin, on the western side of the peninsula, is only one-and-a-half miles from Port St. Mary. This unsophisticated resort is regarded by some as the most charming spot on the Island. It offers choice coast and hill scenery, boating and fishing, and unrivalled bathing from gently sloping sands. At the south side of Port Erin Bay is a *Marine Biological Station* under the control of Liverpool University. To the north of the bay is *Bradda Head* (400 feet) with the turreted *Milner Tower* on its summit.

Port Erin to Peel

The only railway communication between Port Erin or Castletown and Peel is via Douglas. Road distance via **Colby** is 14 miles. From Colby the road north ascends for five miles to *Round Table* (an ancient mound) with *South Barrule* (1,585 feet) on the right. (Round Table may also be reached from Port Erin by the picturesque mountain road, A36.) From here the road goes north-west to **Dalby,** and a short diversion may be made to *Niarbyl Point,* a fine viewpoint for coast scenery. Continuing north, the road passes through the picturesque village of **Glen Maye,** and so past **Kirk Patrick** to Peel.

Peel (Pop.: 2,750). The Ancient town of Peel combines the attractions of a holiday resort with the interest of a fishing port and the romance of a ruined castle. Its streets are narrow and winding, and a Marine Parade and sea-wall extend along the eastern end of the foreshore. The Harbour is busy with fishing boats: the local fleet is now small, but Scottish and Irish boats also bring their herring catches here, to be converted into the famous Manx kippers. The coastal scenery near Peel is best seen from the sea, and boating excursions are readily available.

At the mouth of the harbour is **St. Patrick's Isle,** covering seven-and-a-half acres, and now connected with the mainland by an extension of the West Quay. On the rocky island stand the remains of **Peel Castle,** of which a part forms the Cathedral of St. Germain.

The Castle. Some of the earliest Kings of Man occupied a fortress on this site, and by the 14th century a substantial stone castle had arisen. *St. Germain's Cathedral* within the walls, is the smallest cathedral of the Church of England, with a total interior length of 114 feet. A flight of steps in the south wall of the chancel leads to the crypt-prison. The square tower is 83 feet in height. Other features of the ruins are the *Palace of the Bishops; Fenella's Tower* (described in Scott's "Peveril of the Peak"); the roofless *Church of St. Patrick;* and the *Round Tower,* a defence tower whose top was originally conical.

Excursions from Peel

(1) **Corrin's Tower and Contrary Head:** From the West Quay several paths lead up the steep hill. From the top it is a pleasant walk of a mile to *Corrin's Tower,* a square building 50 feet high, built in the early 19th century and forming a useful landmark and viewpoint.

(2) **Glen Maye** is best reached by road via Kirk Patrick. The entrance to the Glen is through the grounds of the *Waterfall Hotel.*

(3) **St. John's** is a village two-and-a-half miles along the Douglas road, which here intersects the north–south road from Kirk Michael to Castletown. Its chief interest is the **Tynwald Hill,** an artificial mound in front of the church. Here on July 5th (old Midsummer Day) is held the ancient ceremony of proclaiming the laws.

Peel to Ramsey

The coast road from Peel passes *St. Germain's* and rises steeply as it reaches *Kirk Michael.* It then turns inland in flatter country via Ballaugh, Sulby and Lezayre to Ramsey. The railway route branches from St. John's, and then roughly follows the coast road.

An alternative route as far as Kirk Michael is by the road north from the *Ballacraire Hotel,* St. John's, via **Glen Helen** (which can be explored on foot to the picturesque *Rhenas Waterfall*), up *Creg Willey's Hill* and a long descent to **Kirk Michael,** a quiet village near the coast. Its church contains an interesting collection of Runic crosses and monuments. Here the main coast road (*see* above) is joined, continuing to *Bishops Court,* the seat of the Bishop of Sodor and Man, and *Ballaugh,* which marks the beginning of the Curragh area. A mile further is the entrance to the **Curragh Wildlife Park and Nature Reserve,** 26 acres acquired by the Manx Government in 1964.

Sulby stands at the northern end of the beautiful *Sulby Glen,* which has the most rugged scenery of all the Island glens. **Lezayre** has a pretty church, with Scriptural passages in the Manx language adorning its walls.

Ramsey

Access.—By bus or Electric Railway from Douglas (16½ miles).
Early Closing.—Thursdays.
Market Day.—Mondays.
Population.—3,880.

River Fishing.—The *Sulby* is an excellent trout and salmon stream.
Sea Fishing.—Whiting, mackerel and other fish are plentiful.

Ramsey is the second largest town on the Island. Much quieter than Douglas, it is popular both as a resort and as a residential area. It is situated at the mouth of the *Sulby* river, and faces a magnificent Bay with a sweep of 10 miles from *Maughold Head* to *Point of Ayre.*

The town is divided into two parts by the river and harbour, the southern portion being the older and busier. Parliament Street, the main business thoroughfare, runs from the *Town Hall* to the *Court House* (near the Electric Railway Station) and the *Market Place.* From here the East Quay leads to the harbour mouth and outlet of the *Sulby* river, bounded by North and South Piers of equal length. The *Queen's Promenade* extends from the harbour to *Queen's Pier,* nearly half-a-mile in length. South of the pier is the popular bathing beach.

The northern and more modern part of Ramsey is reached either by the *Swing Bridge* over the harbour, or by the *Stone Bridge*—built 1730—in Bowring Road. Northward from the Swing Bridge is the wide *Mooragh Promenade,* with extensive sands on one side, and on the other the wide expanse of *Mooragh Park,* one of the most attractive features of the town. A well-tended park of 40 acres has been furnished with sporting facilities, and contains a sea-water lake of 12 acres with an island at its centre.

The Golf Links at Brookfield Avenue are well known, and numerous competitions are held.

Excursions from Ramsey

(1) **The Albert Tower.** The 500-foot hill at the south end of Ramsey is surmounted by a granite tower, to mark the fact that the Prince Consort ascended it during a fleeting visit ashore in 1847 from the Royal yacht.

(2) **Sky Hill** (800 feet) is a picturesque eminence about one mile west of the town. In this direction also is *Glen Auldyn* a beautiful valley extending to the lower slopes of Snaefell.

(3) **Bride, Andreas and Jurby.** A longer trip, by car or bus, can be taken round the flat agricultural region north of Ramsey. At **Jurby** is a small civil airport. The **Point of Ayre,** north of Bride, is the northern extremity of the Island.

(4) **Maughold Head.** Maughold village is three miles from Ramsey. The Head rises behind the church, and its seaward face is the haunt of sea-birds. From the summit, 385 feet, there is a fine view. Celtic and Scandinavian stone crosses are preserved in the church yard, and near the east gate is buried Hall Caine, the novelist.

Ramsey to Laxey and Douglas

The Douglas road ascends from *Ballure Glen,* leaving first *Slican Lewaigne* and then *North Barrule* (1,860 feet) to the right, to *Cardle Farm* (opposite which a track leads to *Ballaglass Glen*). The road continues past *Corony,* leaving *Glen Mona* and *Dhoon Glen* on its seaward side, to the King Orry cross-roads just outside Laxey. Nearby is a Neolithic tomb known as **King Orry's Grave.**

The alternative route from Ramsey to Douglas is by the Mountain Road which skirts the western slope of *North Barrule* and the eastern face of Snaefell (Bungalow Halt), then descending by *Creg-ny-Baa* and *Hillberry* to Douglas (15 miles).

The Derbyshire Peak District

Buxton

Angling.—In reservoirs: apply Fly Fishers' Club or Borough Treasurer.
Distances.—London, 161; Derby, 33; Birmingham, 79; Sheffield, 29; Leeds, 63; Manchester, 25; Ashbourne, 21.
Early Closing.—Wednesday.
Entertainment.—Bingo, cinema, dancing, Playhouse Theatre.

Hotels.—*Palace, Leewood, Buckingham, St. Ann's, Hartington.*
Information.—St. Ann's Well, The Crescent.
Population.—20,300.
Post Office.—The Quadrant.
Sports.—Boating, bowls, cricket, fishing, golf, putting, swimming pools, tennis.

Buxton is an attractive holiday and health resort 1,000 feet above sea-level, yet protected by the beautiful surrounding hills. The town is compact and dignified, with gracious buildings, good shops, modern hotels, spacious conference halls, and many acres of parks and public gardens. Its rapid rise to popularity during the last hundred years was largely due to the radio-active thermal springs said to have brought relief to sufferers from rheumatism and allied complaints.

One of these springs is **St. Ann's Well,** in the centre of the town—at the foot of the terraced walks called the *Slopes*. This same well was used by the Romans 2,000 years ago. In the Middle Ages, when Buxton was still a mere hamlet, a chapel was built near the well; it was probably about this time that the well was dedicated to St. Ann. For many years sufferers made pilgrimages to St. Ann-of-Buxton, the cured leaving their sticks and crutches near the well, even after the destruction of the chapel in Henry VIII's reign.

Faith in the curative powers of "natural waters" has sadly dwindled in recent years, but the water may still be taken at St. Ann's Well, opposite the Crescent. The water is warm and has a pleasant taste. The building covering the well also houses the Information Office.

From the summit of the Slopes, near the well, is an excellent view of the town and its surroundings. Facing the well is the **Crescent:** this colonnaded promenade was built in 1780 on the site of a Roman bath. At the western end of the Crescent are the **Natural Baths,** shallow swimming pools supplied by the blue mineral water at a constant temperature of 82°F. from the town's thermal springs.

The Buxton waters issue from the limestone rocks at an elevation of 1,000 feet above sea-level at a constant temperature of 82°F. regardless of season. There is a steady flow of 200,000 gallons a day. The water is tasteless and odourless, bright and clear and of a pale blue tint, and remarkably soft to the skin. Since the time of the Romans it has been used as a curative agent in cases of rheumatism, gout, sciatica and neuralgia affections.

At the back of the *Old Hall Hotel* is the Square, to the left of which are entrances to the Pavilion Gardens and the Opera House (cinema). Up the hill is the Devonshire Royal Hospital, and another road leads to the chief Post Office. The Parish Church of St. John the Baptist was built in 1811. The Pavilion Gardens cover 23 acres through which runs the river *Wye*. There are facilities for various sports.

Poole's Cavern is a large cave in the hill **Grin Low** three-quarters of a mile from the Crescent with stalactites and stalagmites. Outside is a small museum.

BUXTON ═══ **Through routes** → **One-way streets** Ⓟ **Parking**

Walks Around Buxton

Gadley Lane. A short walk of two miles, via the Manchester Road behind the Devonshire Hospital to the Cavendish Golf Course. Descend the lane passing the Club House, cross a footbridge, then the stile on the left. The path leads to the Serpentine Walks and, by turning left, the town centre is reached.

To Grin Low Tower (Solomon's Temple). This conspicuous round tower crowns the summit of **Grin Low.** The name of the hill was originally borne by a barrow which served as the foundation of the temple. Standing 1,440 feet above sea-level, it commands a very extensive view, including Black Edge (beyond Buxton) with Kinder Scout to the right of it, Rushup Edge and the distinctive Mam Tor, the Peak Forest moorlands, the winding Wye Valley (to the east), the much-quarried Harpur Hill and Hind Low, and the long ridges of Axe Edge and Burbage Edge to the west.

371

The tower is reached by a footpath which leaves Green Lane exactly opposite College Road, a thoroughfare running south from Broad Walk; another path begins near the entrance to Poole's Cavern and ascends through Grin Low Woods; the two combined make a pleasant circular walk of about two-and-a-half miles.

To Cowdale and King Sterndale. Cowdale, two-and-a-half miles, is reached by a bridle path leading to the left of the Duke's Drive to **Staden,** and then across fields. A lane descends from here for a quarter of a mile to the Bakewell road (along which the buses run), opposite Pic Tor, about two miles from Buxton. By continuing eastward along the dale for another mile a steep, rough road is reached leading to the hamlet of **King Sterndale.** There is a picturesque green and the remains of an ancient cross.

To Axe Edge. The summit is more than 1,800 feet above sea-level and the high road along its eastern flank reaches an altitude of over 1,600 feet; but, as the lowest part of Buxton is about 1,000 feet high, the eminence does not seem so lofty as it really is.

The road (A53) to Axe Edge, along which the Leek buses pass, lies through Burbage. Opposite *Dove Head Farm* a flagged path leads to the source of the river *Dove.* The source of the *Manifold* is a little further on, behind the *Traveller's Rest Inn,* four miles from Buxton. The walk may be continued by descending from the Inn to **Three Shires Head,** where Derbyshire, Cheshire, and Staffordshire meet. From here follow the river *Dane* northwards to a path joining the Congleton road, where turn right. At the top of the hill, a track leads to the *Cat and Fiddle Inn* (see below).

To the "Cat and Fiddle". Leave Buxton by the Burbage road. At the War Memorial the main Macclesfield road keeps straight on, turning to the right by A537 about half a mile farther. Walkers, however, are recommended to bear to the right at the War Memorial and follow the old coach road. The two roads approach each other just above a reservoir, then they separate and finally meet again short of the Inn, which is four miles from Buxton by the Old Road, nearly five miles by the main road.

The *Cat and Fiddle Inn,* at the highest point on the Macclesfield road, is 1,690 feet above sea-level. The view westward from the Inn over the Cheshire Plain is remarkably fine; the Mersey and the giant telescope at Jodrell Bank are clearly visible.

To Wildboarclough. As the crow flies, Wildboarclough lies about six miles south-west of Buxton, but the walk is considerably longer.

Proceed by the Congleton road (A54) nearly to the sixth milestone, then turn to the right, downhill between trees and forking to the left in just over a quarter of a mile into **Wildboarclough,** the soft beauty of which is enhanced by comparison with the bleak scenes around. The place now consists only of the church, the post office, and a few residences.

The road to the right from the church ascends a valley, overlooked by Shutlings Low, to the *Stanley Arms Inn,* about nine miles out from Buxton. From here a path leads to the right for about one-and-a-half miles to the *Cat and Fiddle.*

To the Goyt Valley and Jenkin Chapel. From the top of Long Hill on the Manchester Road a rugged mountain road on the left leads downhill to **Goyt's Bridge.** From the bridge there are several routes:

(1) By going along the road to the left one follows the *Goyt* towards its source, finally meeting the old coach road near Burbage.

(2) A pleasant walk northward skirts the western side of the newly formed lake to Taxal and Whaley Bridge (4 miles), whence Buxton can be regained by bus.

(3) The narrow road climbing north-westwards from the Bridge is an old Roman road, and leads uphill and then down to the curious **Jenkin Chapel,** a Gritstone small building with box pews and a three-decker pulpit.

To Combs Lake and Chapel-en-le-Frith. A delightful walk of about six miles, returning by bus from Chapel-en-le-Frith. The route lies along the Long Hill road for about a mile, then along a lane on the right which passes over the moor. Near White Hall a path across a field to the right leads into a steep lane that goes down into the pretty hamlet of **Combs,** a short distance beyond which, reached by the road to the right of the *Bee Hive Inn,* is the lake, picturesquely situated among the hills. The lane leads into the Stockport road less than a mile to the west of **Chapel-en-le-Frith** *(King's Arms)* an old market town once "the chapel in the forest." The Church was first built in 1225 by the keeper of the royal forest, who dedicated it to St. Thomas Becket. Some traces of the original chapel remain in the chancel walls. The nave is probably late 14th century and the font is 15th century. Chapel-en-le-Frith has old inns, stocks and a market cross.

To Chee Dale and Miller's Dale. Follow the Bakewell road for just over three miles, or travel by bus as far as **Topley Pike,** then opposite the entrance to **Deep Dale** (to the right) take a bridle path to the left and cross the river by a footbridge. Turn to the right, then keep on beside the river. The path leads through the lovely **Chee Dale,** one of the best bits of limestone scenery. On the south side is **Chee Tor** a vertical crag rising 300 feet. The going is rather rough through the narrowest part of the dale.

Beyond the Tor the path issues into the Tideswell road, a good six miles from Buxton by this route.

Miller's Dale forms the next part of the valley of the *Wye* and extends eastward from the hamlet of the same name. At **Litton Mill** the water of the *Wye* is pent up by a weir. It is a very delightful walk on to **Cressbrook,** and thence by the river path and through **Monsal Dale** to the Bakewell road (buses) about nine miles from Buxton.

To Deepdale. The entrance to Deepdale is on the right of the Bakewell road just over three miles from Buxton. Deepdale is a typical dry limestone valley, a mile-and-a-half long. Rain and frost have splintered off pieces of rock, and these slipping down the steep sides, have formed immense screes, backed by limestone cliffs.

Deepdale Cavern, in the upper portion of the valley, is about 100 yards long. It has yielded relics of the Romano-British period. Some of which may be seen in the Buxton Museum.

Deepdale and its rightward continuation, **Back Dale,** communicate with the Ashbourne road near *Brierlow Bar Farm,* about three miles south-east of Buxton (buses).

If the walk is to be extended to **Chelmorton,** Deepdale should be left by a footpath shortly before the Cavern is reached. This is the highest village in the county, the Church being 1,209 feet above sea-level. A path leads north-east to **Taddington,** on the Bakewell–Buxton road (buses).

To the High Peak. For walks in the upland plateaux areas of Kinder Scout and Bleaklow, the best starting point is Edale or Hayfield, both readily reached from Buxton.

Other Excursions from Buxton

To Leek and Rudyard Lake. The Leek road runs south along the flank of **Axe Edge.** About four-and-a-half miles from Buxton is the *Traveller's Rest* (1,535 feet). Just past the Inn a diversion may be made to the right to visit **Flash,** an interesting hamlet that was once famous as a place for forbidden sporting events such as prize-fighting and cock fights—being close to three county boundaries.

Returning to the main road continue southward to **Leek,** 12½ miles from Buxton (bus route). Leek is an old and important Staffordshire town with a population exceeding 19,000. Through Protestant refugees settling here Leek became a centre of silk manufacture. Its Wednesday Market is well worth a visit. The Parish Church was rebuilt in 1301 but retains its fine 11th-century tower.

About three miles to the north-west of Leek is **Rudyard Lake,** which is over two miles long and was constructed in 1793 to serve as a reservoir for the Trent and Mersey Canal. It takes its name from the neighbouring picturesque village. The parents of Rudyard Kipling were familiar with this district.

To Macclesfield. Macclesfield is a very ancient town, 12 miles west of Buxton and formerly surrounded by defensive walls. The present population is 44,000. It is famous as the seat of the silk industry, introduced about 1790. The most prominent building is St. Michael and All Angels' Church, founded in 1278 by Queen Eleanor. Narrow streets flank the church—one of them mounting by 108 steps. The West Park, situated on the outskirts of the town in Prestbury Road, has at its entrance a Museum containing many objects of general interest.

One of the most picturesque and romantic villages in the neighbourhood is **Gawsworth,** situated four miles south-west of Macclesfield by the Congleton road. Gawsworth is famous for its medieval church, a beautiful building in an incomparable setting. The chancel possesses splendid memorials to the Fitton family including the kneeling effigy of Mary Fitton, the supposed "Dark Lady" of Shakespeare's Sonnets.

To Beresford Dale and Dovedale via Alstonfield. Leave by the London Road which follows the straight line of an old Roman road for three miles to Brierlow. On the right are the steep heights of Parkhouse Hill (the nearer) and Chrome Hill.

The main road crosses the *Dove,* leaving Derbyshire, and climbs to **Longnor,** a small Staffordshire market town.

Beyond Longnor, continuing southward, we cross the *Manifold* and in three-and-three-quarter miles turn left and re-cross the stream at Hulme End, about 10 miles from Buxton, where the road divides. The branch to the left goes to Hartington, for Beresford Dale; that to the right goes on for three miles to **Alstonfield** an attractive parish with prehistoric barrows, a fine church with a pinnacled tower and an Elizabethan Manor House, now used as a farm house. There is good angling near Alstonfield and the district has associations with Charles Cotton and his friend Izaak Walton. The church of St. Peter was a Saxon foundation and, although the present structure is late Tudor in style, traces remain of earlier periods.

From Alstonfield the road bears to the left to drop into the valley of the Dove at **Lode Mill,** half a mile above Mill Dale and about midway between Dovedale and Beresford Dale. The village of Alsop-en-le-Dale lies a mile beyond the river.

A more direct route from Buxton to Dovedale is by the Ashbourne road as far as its nearest point to Alsop-en-le-Dale (about 15 miles). A footpath from here leads south-west past Hanson Grange to Dovedale.

To Tideswell and Eyam. Leave Buxton by the Bakewell road, which is followed for nearly five miles; then turn off to the left, passing Blackwell, and descend into Miller's Dale. Turn to the right, down the valley, and fork left at the *Angler's Rest Inn* and climb the hill to Tideswell. **Tideswell** is said to derive its name from an ebbing and flowing well. Market rights have existed here since the year 1250.

The grey little town is chiefly visited on account of its ancient Parish Church, a fine cruciform building known from its size and beauty as the "Cathedral of the Peak". (Well dressing Saturday before nearest Sunday to 24th June.)

The church was erected late in the 14th century, and there have been no additions to the main fabric since 1400. The font and the chancel screen and gates are all of that epoch.

In the south aisle, near the Lytton Chapel, is a perfect brass of Robert de Lytton and his wife (1488). In the de Bower Chapel are the recumbent effigies of Sir Thurston de Bower and his wife (about 1395), and also two windows worthy of notice. In the centre of the spacious chancel is the restored slab tomb of Sir Sampson Mevirill (1462) who fought against Joan of Arc. Just within the sacrarium is the tomb of Sir John Foljambe, who died in 1358. It is marked by a modern brass, the original having been lost nearly two centuries ago. At the eastern end of the chancel is the original stone reredos.

The principal road through Tideswell meets the main Manchester–Chesterfield road at the *Anchor Inn.* For Eyam turn to the right and one-and-a-half miles farther, at the *Three Stags' Heads,* fork left.

The road soon descends the beautiful little **Middleton Dale** with limestone rocks rising into towers and spires on its northern side. In two-and-a-half miles from the fork a road to the left ascends the wood-filled ravine of Eyam Dale to Eyam.

Eyam (pronounced to rhyme with "steam"), is a picturesque village which achieved fame by the heroism of its inhabitants during the Great Plague of 1665. The infection is said to have been transmitted in a box of clothing from London.

The pestilence soon spread, but the rector—William Mompesson—persuaded his flock to isolate themselves rather than to flee elsewhere and risk spreading the disease. Before the plague ceased five out of every six villagers had perished.

Eyam Church stands on a Saxon foundation and retains a Saxon font (in the vestry) in addition to the Norman font—other Norman traces are the two pillars on the north side. Note the original tie beams and the bosses of the roof and the squint behind the pulpit. The Churchyard contains a Saxon cross about eight feet high, and the tomb of Catherine Mompesson, the devoted and ill-fated wife of the heroic rector.

Eyam has a pleasant village green on which are well-preserved stocks. A well-dressing festival is held on the last Saturday of August, and a sheep-roast and carnival on the first Saturday of September.

Eyam lies on the southern slopes of the hills confining the western side of the Derwent Valley as it flows down from Hathersage. North of the Village the hill-tops comprise a fine heathery moorland, with splendid views across to the Pennine Edges.

THE HIGH PEAK DISTRICT

The High Peak District lies to the north-east of Buxton. It is readily accessible from Manchester and Sheffield by bus, but buses from Buxton do not approach nearer than Chapel-en-le-Frith, except by making a long detour.

Buxton to Castleton by Road. Buxton is left by way of Fairfield, two-and-a-half miles beyond which is the quarrying village of **Dove Holes** so called on account of the large number of small water-swallows in the neighbourhood. (A water-swallow is a hole in which a stream disappears into an underground channel and emerging to the surface at a distance). A little farther on, leave the Chapel-en-le-Frith road and branch right, past the *Ebbing and Flowing Well,* and uphill to the hamlet of **Sparrowpit.**

From Sparrowpit the road to Castleton lies straight ahead, leaving *Eldon Hill* (1,543 feet) on the right. At **Winnats Head** an old road descends the Winnats Pass to Castleton, but the main road continues between Mam Tor and the Blue John Mine round a hairpin bend and past *Treak Cliff Cavern*. Before reaching Castleton, a lane leads sharply back to the *Speedwell Cavern*.

Edale and Hope Valley

In the much tunnelled railway known as the Dore and Chinley Line, four miles of the 20 which lie between the two places are run below ground. The *Cowburn* tunnel begins some two-and-a-half miles from Chinley Junction. It is 3,700 yards in length, and lies 900 feet below the surface. A mile or so from the eastern end of the tunnel is the old-world village of **Edale** giving its name to the charming Vale of Edale. Radiating from here are delightful walks, through scenery unsurpassed in the Peak District.

Walkers should consult the *National Park Information Centre* at Edale, and should ensure that they are provided with both map and compass.

Walks in the Kinder Scout area

(1) **Edale to the "Snake Inn":** The route of roughly 12 miles leaves Edale by the road westward to Edale Head, and branches left by *Jacob's Ladder* and the Reservoir. (This point is more quickly reached if the start is made from **Hayfield,** seven miles west of Edale.) The Snake Path skirts the western side of the Reservoir and follows the stream in William Clough. From Mill Hill the footpath turns due east and in about three miles meets the Glossop road near the *Snake Inn.*

(2) **Rushup Edge and Mam Tor:** The best ridge walk begins about three miles from Chapel-en-le-Frith on the Castleton road. Here a path on the left leads to **Rushup Edge.** When the Edge ends at Mam Nick, cross the road, climb Mam Tor and continue along the ridge to Lose Hill where descend to Hope.

At the lower end of Edale is **Hope** *(Old Hall)* a very ancient village, near the junction of the *Noe* with the *Styx.* The Parish Church, built about the 15th century, has a squat tower surmounted by a broad spire. The shaft of a Saxon cross stands near the south porch. In the church are a Norman font and a well-preserved carved oak pulpit.

Overlooked as it is by **Mam Tor** (1,700 feet), and the curiously-named **Lose Hill** (1,563 feet) and **Win Hill** (1,523 feet), there is no vale in the Peak District more beautiful than that of Hope.

One of the most popular walks from Hope is north-eastward over Win Hill to Derwent Valley. Take the Edale road, beside the *Old Hall Hotel.* In a quarter of a mile, at a bend in the road, branch right, cross river and railway, and via Twitchill Farm ascend Win Hill. From the summit a track leads to the *Ladybower Reservoir,* and bears right to the great Dam and to Yorkshire Bridge spanning the Derwent. Ascend to main road and turn right for Bamford. From Hope village to Bamford station is about five miles.

Castleton *(Nag's Head, George, Peak)* two miles west from Hope is a convenient centre for the most mountainous part of the Peak District, whilst its remarkable caverns attract many visitors.

Among the old customs which still linger here is the holding of a carnival on May 29, called Garland Day to commemorate the Restoration of Charles II. There is a procession, with a mounted king and queen, morris dancers, and a Maypole on the market-place.

The Parish Church is dedicated to St. Edmund, and dates from soon after the Norman Conquest. The Church exhibits all the styles of architecture which have prevailed since that period. It has a 15th-century pinnacled tower at the west end, contains an ancient stone font, and there is a fine Norman archway between nave and chancel.

Castleton obtained its name from its close connection with the now ruined—

Peveril Castle *(daily, fee)* a fortress which towers above the small grey houses and is a conspicuous feature in any characteristic view of the village. The ruin is reached by a zig-zag path starting by a cottage near the south-west corner of the Square. The stronghold is inaccessible on every side save one, and even there the approach is artificial, to obviate the severity of the ascent.

Erected by William Peveril, whom the Conqueror appointed guardian of the Peak in 1068, it was one of the first Norman castles to be built of stone. The existing Keep was added by Henry II in 1176.

On the south side of the precipice on which the Castle stands is **Cave Dale** a beautiful and secluded valley reached by the road which starts from the south-east corner of the village Square and a narrow gap on the right through the limestone wall. The narrow floor is formed mostly of short soft turf. In the course of an ascent of the Dale delightful views varying with each upward step are obtained of the Castle and Hope Valley.

The Caverns *(daily, fee)*. The caverns shown are four:

The Peak Cavern. This is situated near the Castle. Below sheer limestone cliffs is a huge arch leading to a Hall 334 feet in depth. For 400 years this was used as a rope-walk. Beyond it is a stream called the Styx, and a series of other caves great and small.

The Speedwell Cavern. This mine is near the head of the Winnats, three-quarters of a mile from Castleton. Steps lead down to a subterranean canal, navigated by boat, and leading to an enormous "bottomless abyss". The noise of cascading water and the effect of reflected lights in this cave are most impressive.

Treak Cliff Cavern. This cavern, about one mile to the west of Castleton, rivals those of Cheddar in its profuse display of variously coloured stalactites and stalagmites. The hill in which it is situated is the only place in the world where the "Blue John" variety of fluorspar is found.

Blue John Cavern. This is reached by following the main road to a point just beyond the hairpin bend. A quicker route from Castleton is by the Winnats Pass. Visitors should note that there are 180 steps to descend and ascend. The mine takes its name from the bluish-purple variety of fluorspar that is found there. So rare is this mineral that tazzas and other objects made from Blue John grace palaces and famous houses all over the world.

The Winnats. A green track leading up to the right from the entrance to Blue John Mine goes to *Winnats Head Farm*, just above the head of this rugged gorge, a narrow rift in the limestone hills through which climbs the old road to Buxton from Castleton. "Winnats" is a corruption of Wind Gates, a name obtained from the gusts of wind which constantly sweep through. The view through the great rocky portals presents a scene of magnificent extent and beauty.

Mam Tor. Westward of Castleton and above the head of the Winnats rises Mam Tor, a hill of very singular aspect, much of the surface presenting the appearance of having been scooped out. The hollows are due to the disintegration of the siliceous shale and sandstone of which the hill is composed. The debris trickles down into the valley below, and on account of this movement the hill is often called the *Shivering Mountain*.

Bradwell is a picturesque village two miles south-east of Castleton by the Tideswell road and a path continuing at the foot of the hills, or three miles by the road south from Hope. The village nestles in rugged scenery and was for some years an important lead-mining centre. In 1807, the miners accidentally discovered the fine set of caves now known as the **Bagshaw's Cavern** *(weekends)*, a few minutes' walk from the centre of the village. This is entered from the hillside by a long flight of steps, cut in the rock; and it comprises a number of fantastic chambers, hung with stalactites and sparkling crystals.

Northward from the village, a path on the left of Bradwell leads in a mile to **Brough,** the site of the Roman station of *Anavio*. The Roman Road from Brough to Buxton runs through Bradwell and the *Grey Ditch;* a defensive earthwork can be traced from Bradwell Edge to Micklow Hill near the Bath Hotel, where are the remains of a Roman bath and a thermal spring. At **Camphill,** Great Hucklow, south of Bradwell, are the headquarters of the Derbyshire and Lancashire Gliding Club. South-east of Bradwell one fine walk is that over Bradwell Edge and via Robin Hood's Cross to **Abney.** South from Bradwell the road ascends Bradwell Dale, at the head of which are the remains of the fine Elizabethan manor house, Hazelbadge Hall, built by the Vernons in 1549 and now a farmhouse.

Hathersage *(George, Little John)* five miles east of Castleton, is a quaint old-world village on the slope of a range of hills which protect it from east winds. Hathersage claims to be the place in which Robin Hood's famous henchman, Little John, was born; a house, said to have been his, stood near the church. There is little doubt that a man of his stature was buried here. His grave, on the south side of the church, is marked by two small stones, with a yew at head and foot and enclosed by a low iron fence. On being opened in 1782 it disclosed bones of enormous size.

The fine old Parish Church, mainly 14th century, stands on a height above the village. It has a handsome clerestory, and a beautiful tower of three stages, surmounted by an octagonal spire. The interior contains the altar-tomb of Robert Eyre, of Highlow, who fought at Agincourt.

Near the church is a castle mound, known as *Camp Green.*

BUXTON TO BAKEWELL

The road runs first through Ashwood Dale and then climbs out of the valley of the *Wye*. Six miles from Buxton is the long village of **Taddington,** about 1,100 feet above sea-level. The restored 14th-century *Church* contains brasses and tombs of the Blackwall family and a stone lectern. In the churchyard is a tall ancient cross shaft. A mile-and-a-half from the village is *The Five Wells Tumulus,* an ancient burying place.

From Taddington the road descends between lovely woods of **Taddington Dale** (National Trust) to the southern end of—

Monsal Dale of a more open type than the typical Derbyshire Dale. The Dale is about two miles in length, curving round the hill known as **Fin Cop** (1,072 feet) to the village of Monsal Dale.

Ashford-in-the-Water, 10 miles from Buxton, stands on the *Wye*. It is popular with visitors, and in spite of a by-pass, has a considerable amount of through traffic. Well dressing and well blessing ceremonies are held on Trinity Sunday and during the week following. There are three beautiful bridges and several fine old mansions in the neighbourhood. The Church has a 14th-century tower.

Bakewell (Pop.: 4,200. Hotels: *Red Lion, Rutland Arms, Castle, Milford House)* is an attractive market town of some agricultural importance, sheltered by hills on the north, east and west; and overlooking rich meadowland to the south. It is the chief town within the Peak National Park, and is an excellent centre for exploring the surrounding countryside, and for visiting the beautiful grounds and mansions of Chatsworth and Haddon Hall.

The name is of Anglo-Saxon origin, and refers to the warm springs of the town. Traces of Roman occupation have been found.

There are some attractive buildings in the town. In the **Market House** are the heraldic shields of the Manners family.

Ivy House, in Church Street, bears the date 1743, and the **Almshouses** on the other side of the road date from 1709. The beautiful **Bakewell Bridge,** with its five Gothic arches and triangular quoins, is one of the oldest bridges in England.

The **Church** is a large cruciform structure standing on a commanding site, and dating from the beginning of the 12th century. It is an interesting mixture of various styles of architecture, for while specimens of the original Norman work may be seen in the two western arches of the nave and in the fine west doorway, the rest of the nave and aisles are in the Early English style, introduced in the 13th century. Architecturally the exterior is more satisfying than the interior. In the Vernon Chapel is a monument to Sir Thomas Wendesley killed in 1403 at the Battle of Shrewsbury. At the end of the south aisle is that of Sir Godfrey Foljambe and his wife. The font is early 14th century.

About one and a half miles south of Bakewell on the main A6 Buxton–Matlock road is—

Haddon Hall *(Hall and gardens, daily except Suns and Mons, but open Bk Hol. weekends from Good Friday or 1 Apr. to Sept. fee)* among the most attractive of the ancient manorial dwellings in England, exquisitely beautiful in its surroundings, picturesque in its architecture, and with a halo of romance. The house stands on a natural elevation above the banks of the *Wye*.

Haddon Hall shows traces of Norman origin, but dates mainly from the 14th to early 16th century, and has been considerably restored in the present century. It was long the seat of the Vernon family, including Sir George Vernon, who was known as "King of the Peak." Following the marriage in Tudor times of Dorothy Vernon with John Manners, son of the Earl of Rutland, the estates passed into the possession of the Manners family. Many romantic stories have been based on the dubious tradition that Dorothy eloped with her lover.

The north-west Entrance Tower stands at the top of a steep limestone slope and dates back mainly to the early 16th century, though parts of it and also the massive oak doors are of an even earlier date (1400). On climbing a few steps the visitors come to the stone-paved Lower Courtyard. On the east side is the 14th-century *Banqueting Hall* and *Porch*.

The Chapel is entered from the south-west angle of the courtyard. The south aisle is the oldest part of the building; dating from the 12th century, while the tower, west windows and north aisle were added about 1310. Between 1380 and 1470 the building was again enlarged and the chancel added. Entrance to the eastern range of buildings is gained from the Lower Courtyard by the 14th-century *Porch* of rather later date from the *Great Hall* and *Kitchens* to which it gives admittance. It has a stone bench on either side, the left one supporting a Roman altar found in the meadows between Haddon and Bakewell. The 14th-century **Banqueting Hall** still retains much of its ancient character. The **Dining Room** is of the Tudor period. The **Great Chamber**, reached by a stone staircase, has an oriel window looking out over the Upper Gardens.

The **Long Gallery** (17th century) measures 110 feet by 17 feet, and is panelled throughout. The plain work is oak and the carved work walnut, while the dark stripes in the columns are bog oak.

The fine gardens lead down to the bank of the *Wye* over which is *Dorothy's Bridge*.

Rowsley is a charming little village of grey stone cottages beloved of anglers and artists. It stands on a tongue of land at the confluence of the *Derwent* and the *Wye*. The *Peacock Hotel* here was originally a manor house built 1652.

Rowsley to Chatsworth. The road lies due north from Little Rowsley (beyond old railway station), alongside the Derwent (a footpath starting direct from Rowsley follows the river more closely). A mile and a half onward is **Beeley,** an ancient and somewhat smaller village than Rowsley. It is noted for the grindstones made from the local hard grit. The Church contains a Norman round-headed doorway, believed to have been removed from an earlier church. The embattled tower is 16th-century work.

About half a mile beyond the village Chatsworth Park is entered at Beeley Lodge. The House is a mile from the lodge, or three miles from Rowsley.

Chatsworth *(Apr.–Oct., daily except Mons and Tues but open Bank Hols. Gardens, daily, fee)* has been the principal seat of the Cavendish family since the 16th century. The present building with the exception of the later north wing was begun in 1687 by William Cavendish, Duke of Devonshire, and was completed in 1706. This great mansion has many rooms and innumerable treasures. Worthy of special note are: The **Painted Hall,** 60 feet long and two storeys in height, with a staircase ascending to the **State Rooms.** The **Chapel,** completed in 1692, with fine paintings and wood carving. The **Dining room,** with fine portraits by Van Dyck. The fine gardens feature a great glasshouse and notable fountains.

Edensor at the western limit of the Park, is a "model" village inhabited by Chatsworth estate employees. The Church, designed by Sir Gilbert Scott, replaced an older building, but the Norman south porch, four aisle arches and some window tracery have been preserved. Chief interest, however, centres in the monuments and memorials to the Cavendish family and others.

Half a mile beyond Edensor the road forks. The left branch leads to Bakewell and Ashford. The right branch drops down to the Derwent Valley again to reach, about a mile on, **Baslow,** a pretty village, charmingly situated on the eastern bank of the Derwent. The Church, on the bank of the river, has a low 14th-century tower, surmounted by a broach spire. The peculiar eastern clock-face commemorates Queen Victoria's Diamond Jubilee. Three-quarters of a mile east of

Baslow, where the Chesterfield and Sheffield roads divide, is the northern entrance to Chatsworth Park at Park Lodge. The house is one-and-a-half miles from the entrance gate. Buses run from Baslow to Matlock, Buxton and Chesterfield, Sheffield and Bakewell.

Bakewell to the Lathkill Valley. Leave Bakewell by the road ascending by the church. In one mile turn left on a road that climbs to **Over Haddon.** Before entering the village turn to the left for a short way for the sake of the splendid view over the Lathkill. The beautiful **Lathkill Dale** is only accessible to walkers, who may follow it for three miles westward from Over Haddon until it joins the main road half-mile from Monyash (5 miles from Bakewell). **Monyash,** though less attractive than Over Haddon has an interesting 12th-century church and an ancient market cross. *One Ash Grange,* near the top of Lathkill Dale, has associations with John Bright.

Matlock

Distances.—Ashbourne, 14; Bakewell, 8; Buxton, 20; Chesterfield, 10; Derby, 18; London, 143; Manchester, 46.
Early Closing.—Thursday.
Entertainment.—Children's Corner, cinema, dancing. Venetian fête in September.

Golf.—Matlock Golf Club (18 holes) on Matlock Moor.
Hotels.—*New Bath, High Tor, Crown, King's Head* and others.
Population.—19,700.
Post Office.—Bank Road.
Sports.—Boating, bowls, putting, tennis, swimming.

The Matlocks. Set in the vale of the river Derwent is a group of places known collectively as The Matlocks. By Matlock Bridge is the original settlement **Matlock Town,** on a hill above the eastern bank of the river. To the north is **Matlock Bank,** with parallel streets set on the terraces of a steep hill. A mile to the south of Matlock Bridge, on the west bank of the river and in a narrow gorge, straggles **Matlock Bath,** the most picturesque and popular of the Matlocks.

Matlock Bath consists mainly of a single long street which with the railway and the river almost fill the bottom of the steep-sided Matlock Dale. East of the river the cliffs are clothed with trees affording delightful views. A popular centre is the *Grand Pavilion* where dances, music festivals, and other entertainments take place. The adjoining café was formerly known as the *Pump Room,* a reminder that it was the local thermal springs which first brought prosperity to the district and made Matlock a spa.

Near the Pavilion is the landing stage where motor and rowing boats may be hired, a pleasure ground, a thermal water fountain, a well-stocked fish pond, and the *Petrifying Wells.* When the lime-laden water emerges into the open some of the carbon dioxide escapes. Unable to hold in solution the whole of the lime, the water throws off the excess upon anything it touches, coating the object with a thick layer. Thus are formed the Petrified "souvenirs," nests, eggs, toys, and other queerly selected objects.

South of the Pavilion are the *Derwent Pleasure Gardens,* which provide access across an attractive bridge to the Lovers Walks. At the *New Bath Hotel* is an open-air thermal swimming bath, available to non-residents. Facing South Parade is **Holy Trinity Church,** a fine cruciform structure with a crocheted spire, and a reredos of Derbyshire marble. Still farther south and visible from the main road near Cromford is **Willersley Castle,** built in 1788 by Sir Richard Arkwright, the pioneer of cotton spinning machinery.

To the north-west of the Pavilion are the **Heights of Abraham** with thickly wooded slopes and at the top (800 feet) the *Victoria Prospect Tower* (views).

Below the Tower is the entrance to the **Rutland Cavern** *(fee)* first found when sinking a shaft from the summit of the hill during early lead-mining operations. Originally known as the "Nestor" or "Nestes" mine, it was worked by the Romans for lead between 81 and 138 A.D.

At the summit too is the Masson Cavern *(fee)* a portion of another Roman lead mine. The sides and roof are covered with fossil shells.

Masson Hill (1,100 feet), one of the grandest features of the Matlock scenery, combines with **High Tor** (400 feet) on the other side of the Derwent to present a picture of great charm. Near the top of the Tor is *Fern Cave,* a deep winding fissure in the rock. The main road through the dale continues to Matlock Bridge. Over the bridge is—

Matlock Town. Causeway Lane, to the right from the bridge, leads to Hall Leys Park beside the river. From the park a path leads to *St. Giles' Church,* set high on the hill. Most of the building is modern, but the church was originally built in 1130.

Matlock Bank. The Town Hall and General Post Office are in the lower end of Bank Road. The large building at the top of Bank Road was for many years a well-known hydro, built by John Smedley—a hosiery manufacturer— 1852. This with the other later establishments made Matlock famous as a hydropathic centre. It is now used for County Council Offices.

Riber is a small hamlet on the summit of Riber Hill (853 feet) south-east of Matlock tower. In the castle grounds is a *Wildlife Park.*

Walks around Matlock

To Bonsall. Bonsall is one and a half miles to the west of Matlock Bath, or can be reached from Matlock Bridge via Masson Hill. It is an interesting old village situated at the head of limestone valley. The ceremony of well-dressing is observed at the beginning of August. The Church, built on a rock overlooking the village, has a 14th-century spire surrounded by remarkable "crowns". Also of interest is the Market Cross, a shaft rising for 13 steps, and dated 1671.

To the Via Gellia. The Via Gellia starts at the *Pig of Lead Inn,* halfway between Cromford and Bonsall, and runs westward through a steep and well wooded valley. The Latinized name commemorates the local family who originally constructed this part of the highway. After two miles there is a road junction, and the road turning back sharply to the left climbs steeply to **Middleton** and affords good views. Those who wish to avoid walking uphill may prefer to take the bus from Matlock to Middleton and to walk down to the Via Gellia and so to Cromford (about 3½ miles).

To Cromford via Starkholmes. A pleasant, though hilly, walk of two-and-a-half miles from Matlock Town by way of Starkholmes road which runs southward from near St. Giles' Church. Once the summit is reached there are interesting views of the Dale on the right, and later the valley towards **Whatstandwell** opens up on the left. At the foot of the hill is the fine old *Cromford Bridge,* with the church beyond. **Cromford** is the site of Arkwright's first cotton mill, and was once busily occupied with the traffic of the Cromford Canal and the High Peak Railway. To the south of the village is the curiously shaped outcrop known as the *Black Rocks,* which afford a fine view from the summit.

To Wingfield Manor. From Cromfield cross Cromfield Bridge and follow the road to the right, through Lea Bridge to Holloway. On the right beyond the village is *Lea Hurst,* for long the residence of Florence Nightingale (*d.* 1910). A little beyond Holloway is the hamlet of **Wakebridge,** then on the left is **Crich Stand** (942 feet) with a tower which is the War Memorial of the Sherwood Foresters. **Crich** itself was once a flourishing market town. It is of interest for its ancient church, and for its unique *Tramway Museum,* housed in a quarry. Near Crich is *Wingfield Manor,* a fortified manor which was one of the prisons of Mary Queen of Scots. There is a bus service from South Wingfield to Matlock.

To Tansley or Dethick. Just before reaching Riber, Carr Lane to the right leads to Alders Lane (left) for **Tansley**—one-and-a-half miles east of Matlock. Alternatively continue along Carr Lane and take the next turning on the right to **Dethick,** whose church dates in part from the 13th century. The tower was added in 1539 by Anthony Babington, who was executed for his part in a plot to put Mary Queen of Scots on the English throne. The farm next to the church retains portions of the Babington family home, Dethick Hall.

To Darley Dale. From Matlock the main A6 road runs north-west to that portion of the Derwent Valley known as **Darley Dale.** The old church of Darley lies to the left of the main road, but may be seen by a short detour to the left, about two miles from Matlock Bridge. The church has a Burne-Jones window, but is more widely known for its famous yew tree over 32 feet in girth. The church was founded in Saxon times.

To Winster, Rowtor Rocks and Stanton Moor. From Darley Dale take the road on the left to Winster, crossing the *Derwent* at Darley Bridge. **Winster,** a former lead-mining town and considerable market, has a fine 17th-century Market House (N.T.). On Shrove Tuesday a traditional pancake race is held in the main street. One mile to the north of Winster is the village of **Birchover,** with old stocks, a bull ring, and an interesting small museum. By the *Druid Inn* are the **Rowtor Rocks,** an irregular pile of large blocks with a "rocking stone" at the summit. To the west, across the valley, are the twin pinnacles known as *Robin Hood's Stride* and the sharply defined *Cratcliff Tor*.

To the north-east of Birchover lies **Stanton Moor** (N.T.), notable for its Bronze Age "urn burial" mounds and cairns. Some of the discoveries are displayed in the museum at Birchover. Among the many rock structures are two incomplete stone circles—*Nine Ladies* and *Doll Tor*. At the northern end of the ridge is the picturesque village of **Stanton-in-Peak.** From here a descent may be made to the Winster–Alport road, where one turns right to reach the main Bakewell–Matlock road.

To Youlgreave and Arbor Low. The road to Youlgreave branches from the Matlock–Bakewell road about one mile beyond Rowsley. **Youlgreave,** on the hillside above the *Bradford* is an extensive village with a fine Church, whose 15th-century tower is conspicuous from afar. There is an annual Well Dressing ceremony on the Saturday nearest to 24th June.

Some three miles due west from Youlgreave, and reached by the road known as *Long Rake,* is the finest stone circle in Derbyshire, **Arbor Low,** situated 1,200 feet above sea level. A circle of rough unhewn stones six to eight feet long is surrounded by a ditch and mound of 250 feet diameter measured from crest to crest. The circle probably dates from about 1700 B.C. The Long Rake continues, past a turning right to Monyash to join the Buxton–Ashbourne road.

Chesterfield (Pop.: 70,150. Hotel: *Station*), 10 miles north-east of Matlock is a busy and progressive town. The Church is noted for its 14th-century twisted spire, which is 228 feet high and leans 10 feet from the perpendicular. There are many monuments to the Foljambe (Earl of Liverpool's) family. Prominent men associated with Chesterfield include Charles Darwin the naturalist, and George Stephenson the father of railways. At Old Wittington, two miles north, is **Revolution House** *(Apr.–Sept., daily)* a little stone building furnished in the 17th-century style.

Wirksworth is an old market town two miles south of Cromford and one-time centre of the lead-mining industry. The church is an Early English structure restored by Sir Gilbert Scott. Remains of Norman and Saxon work have been pieced into the restoration. The well-dressings in Whitweek attract many visitors.

DOVEDALE

The river *Dove* rises near Buxton, and for most of its length forms the county boundary between Staffordshire and Derbyshire. By convention, the name **Dovedale** is usually restricted to the wooded limestone gorge extending about three miles northward from the village of **Thorpe.** The next five miles northward goes under the names of **Mill Dale, Wolfscote Dale,** and **Beresford Dale.**

The beautiful Dovedale can be traversed from the south end, or from the north end near Alstonfield or Alsop-en-le-Dale. The preferred approach is from Thorpe village, crossing the bridge to Thorpe Mill and then branching right to car-park and footbridge. From this point there is a footpath on each side of the *Dove*. Dovedale is a narrow valley whose wooded slopes run almost sheer to the crystal stream. It is the most beautiful of the limestone valleys. Here and there the walls of foliage are broken by limestone rocks that mimic every variety of architectural shape. The stream is broken by a succession of little weirs—partly artificial and holding back the water in a fashion only to be appreciated by the angler. In many places the stream may be crossed by *Stepping Stones*. The first of such crossings occurs soon after leaving Thorpe. Soon after one passes the crags known as the *Twelve Apostles*, and then the bare rock face of *Sharplow Point*. The dale then becomes narrower and more hemmed in by cliffs. After *Reynard's Cave*, on the right, the better path is on the Derbyshire side. Finally the dale passes between *Ilam Rock* and *Pickering Tor* to reach three huge-mouthed caverns known as the *Dove Holes*.

The Dove valley continues as **Mill Dale**, somewhat less wooded than Dovedale, and this in turn gives way to the grassy slopes of **Wolfscote Dale.** At the end of this a footbridge gives access to a path on the Staffordshire bank that marks the beginning of **Beresford Dale,** a mile-long stretch of great beauty. This dale forms the theme of Part II of Izaak Walton's "Compleat Angler" which was added by his friend Charles Cotton. At the northern end is the famous *Fishing House* built by Cotton in 1674—a one-roomed stone structure—which can just be seen from the public path. The path on leaving the Dale crosses a walled lane and bears right to reach **Hartington,** a picturesque village with a large square. The Church has a fine 14th-century square western tower. *Hartington Hall*, rebuilt in 1611, is now a Youth Hostel.

THE MANIFOLD VALLEY

The *Manifold*, whose source is near that of the *Dove*, has a valley of "many folds". At **Hulme End,** one-and-a-half miles to the west of Hartington, the *Manifold* cuts a spectacular gorge through the limestone, and continues to Ilam where it joins the *Dove*. Much of the valley is not readily accessible, and the best known part is that immediately west of **Wetton** (2½ miles south of Hulme End). Here is Thor's Cave, a cavern once inhabited by man.

The most remarkable feature of the valley is the existence near Wetton of "swallows", through which in dry weather the river disappears completely, to emerge four miles farther on in the grounds of Ilam Hall. **Ilam** is a trim model village. Ilam Hall is now a Youth Hostel. In the churchyard are two fine Saxon crosses. Ilam is less that one mile from Thorpe, at the foot of Dovedale, and two miles north-east of Thorpe is **Tissington,** an idyllic little village with a manor hall, a church with Norman doorway and a village green surrounded by trees and bright grey cottages. Tissington Hall, a fine Jacobean mansion of the Fitz Herberts, was built in 1609. The custom of well-dressing, though its origin is wrapt in mystery, is said to have begun at Tissington, which has no less than five clear springs from the limestone. Well-dressing is observed on Ascension Day, and all the wells are visited in turn.

Ashbourne (Pop.: 5,500. *Green Man*) a little over three miles to the south-east of Thorpe is a very ancient market town. The Church contains many interesting monuments and has a 14th-century spire 215 feet high. In the centre of the town is the quaint *Green Man and Black's Head Inn*, with the two-faced head set on a beam across the street (originally the Black's Head stood opposite the Green Man). Between here and the church are two Almshouses, the building of the old

Grammar School, and some fine old houses, including one in which Dr. Samuel Johnson used to stay when visiting his friend Dr. Taylor. On Shrove Tuesday and the following day, an annual fixture is a primitive kind of football match, with hundreds of players taking part, the goals set three miles apart, and practically no rules.

Derby (Pop.: 219,350. Hotels: *Pennine, Midland, York, Clarendon, Gables*) 18 miles south of Matlock, is a very ancient town on the *Derwent*, though its old-world aspect has given way to industrialisation. The *Cathedral Church of All Saints* was originally the parish church, rebuilt by James Gibb (the architect of St. Martin's-in-the-Fields) in the 18th century, and raised to cathedral status in 1927. Monuments include the tomb of the famous Bess of Hardwick (Countess of Shrewsbury). Of interest also are the old Bridge Chapel of St. Mary, the Central Library and Museum, and the Corporation Art Gallery. At Derby are the Rolls-Royce factory, the British Rail Research Centre, and the Royal Crown Derby China Factory.

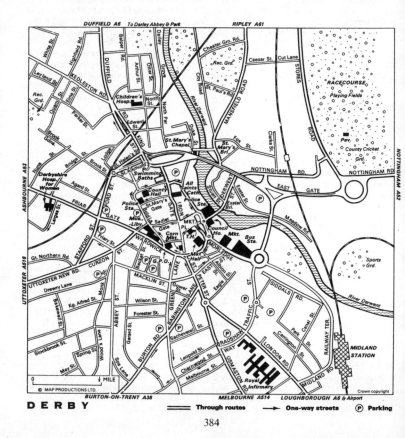

D E R B Y

═══ **Through routes**   ⟶ **One-way streets**   Ⓟ **Parking**

Yorkshire

York

Distances.—Bridlington, 41; Doncaster, 34; Driffield, 29; Filey, 41; Harrogate, 22; Hull, 38; Leeds, 24; London, 196; Ripon, 24.
Early Closing.—Monday or Wednesday.
Hotels.—*Abbey Park, Beechwood Close, Chase, Dean Court, Post House, Royal Station, Viking.*
Information Bureau.—Museum Street.
Market.—St. Sampson's Square.
Population.—107,150.
Post Office.—22 Lendal.

York, the *Caer Ebrauc* of the early Britons, and *Eboracum* to the Romans, and famous for its mighty minster and medieval city walls, stands on the River *Ouse*. A busy railway and commercial centre it still retains its air of medieval times with many quaint streets and corners.

York Minster *(daily conducted tours)*. The pride and glory of York is unquestionably the Cathedral, popularly called the Minster in common with a good number of large churches of Anglo-Saxon foundation that were never monastic. This stately edifice, the architectural magnificence of which at once strikes the eye, occupies a site in which a cathedral has stood since the year 627. It is indeed the fifth church that has held this site.

Historical Note.—On Easter Day (April 12th), 627, Edwin, the first Christian king of Northumbria, was publicly baptised on the spot where the Roman praetorium had stood. Almost immediately he began to build a stone church here, which St. Wilfred largely rebuilt in about 670. The building suffered from one of a long series of fires in 1069 when York was besieged by William the Conqueror. The cathedral rose again in Norman style but was again badly damaged in 1137 by a fire which destroyed much of York. Archbishop Roger restored it in the 12th century.

Walter de Gray, Archbishop in the reign of King John, began the construction of the present structure, a process which lasted for 250 years until 1472. Fire struck yet again in 1829, when the deranged Jonathan Martin started a blaze which completely gutted the choir. The building was restored in little more than three years and reopened in 1832. Just eight years later another blaze almost destroyed the south-west bell tower and the roof of the nave. Subsequent restoration included the installation of the peal of twelve *Bells* in the south-west tower, under a bequest from Dr. Stephen Beckwith. Later a huge bell bought by public subscription was placed in the north-west tower.

Among the Minster's greatest glories are the wonderfully preserved medieval windows, many of which were removed during the 1939–45 war and replaced in post-war years. Among the most splendid is the *Great West Window,* dating from 1338, in the Nave. Also outstanding are the twin *St. Cuthbert* and *St. William Windows* in the South and North Choir Aisles.

Cruciform in plan, the Minster is 524 feet in length; its width across the transepts is 249 feet. The central tower soars over 100 feet above the intersection of the Choir, Nave and Transepts and is 65 feet in breadth. The height of the twin western towers is 184 feet. The **Nave** is one of the longest in England. From the west door there is a most impressive view towards the beautiful stone screen, of Perpendicular design, which separates the Nave from the Choir.

In the **South Transept,** with its Rose Window, is the tomb of Archbishop Walter de Gray (who began the building of the Gothic cathedral), the tomb of Dean Duncombe and the regimental chapel of the West Yorkshire Regiment. From this transept access may be gained to the 234-foot Lantern Tower. In the **North Transept** is the *Five Sisters Window,* named from its five lancet compartments. There is a legend that the designs were first worked in tapestry by five young women who lived near the cathedral. Dating from 1260, this is the largest area of ancient grisaille glass in existence. Here also is the regimental chapel of the King's Own Yorkshire Light Infantry. In this transept is the *Astronomical Clock,* a memorial to 18,000 airmen stationed in the north-east who were killed in the 1939–45 war.

The octagonal **Chapter House,** reached from the North Transept via the Vestibule, contains various antiquities, but is chiefly interesting architecturally, as it employs external buttresses, rather than a central pillar, to support the downward thrust of the domed, leaded roof.

The **Choir** is seen against the background of the great East Window, 78 feet high by 32 feet wide. The largest area of early 15th-century stained glass in the world, it is in three divisions—(1) God reigning in Heaven; (2) Old Testament history to the death of Absalom; (3) the Apocalypse. In the Choir are the stalls of the members of the Chapter and others, with the throne of the Archbishop facing the pulpit. The pavement of the Sanctuary forms a memorial to the first Lord Halifax.

In the **South Choir Aisle** is the chapel of the Duke of Wellington's Regiment and the St. Cuthbert Window. Adjoining the South Choir Aisle is the Zouche Chapel, used for private prayer and meditation. The **North Choir Aisle** contains the tomb of Prince William of Hatfield, son of Edward III, and other monuments, together with the St. William Window.

Beneath the **Crypt** is the base of a Roman pillar. Here, traditionally on the site of the first York Minster, stands the font with its magnificent modern cover by Sir Ninian Comper. Here also are various altars and carvings, including the Norman *Doomstone,* which depicts the "cauldron" of hell.

The almost innumerable tombs and monuments in the Minster repay careful study.

To the east of the Minster is **St. William's College** *(weekdays, fee),* home of the Minster Chantry priests from the 15th century until the Dissolution; beyond the College is the only surviving gatehouse of those which gave access from Goodramgate into the Liberty of St. Peter, the Minster precincts, over which in former days the Minster police had jurisdiction. (The Minster police force today is thought to be the only ecclesiastical police force outside the Vatican.)

Just inside **Dean's Park** is the *Minster Library (free),* now part of the University. On the right of the cobbled roadway is the garden of the **Treasurer's House** *(Apr.– Oct., daily, fee)* containing period furniture, and, adjoining, Gray's Court. These were at one time a single building, house of the Minster Treasurer.

Along Aldwark is **Merchant Taylors Hall** *(free),* a medieval building restored in recent years, and showing some 17th-century glass and a minstrels' gallery. At the end of Aldwark is **St. Anthony's Hall** *(free),* formerly the hall of the Guild of St. Anthony, now the Borthwick Institute and part of the University.

Across the road is the ancient *Black Swan,* an inn for over 160 years. Henrietta Thompson, who lived here in childhood, became the mother of General James Wolfe, hero of Quebec. Back along Goodramgate is **Holy Trinity Church,** dating from the 13th century.

At the city end of Goodramgate is **King's Square,** south from which runs the **Shambles,** formerly the butchers' street. No. 35, once the home of the Roman Catholic martyr Margaret Clitherow (*d.* 1586), canonized in 1969 as St. Margaret of York, is a chapel to her memory. Nearby in Newgate is an open-air market.

The Shambles lead on to **Pavement** and **Herbert House** (Elizabethan). Notice at the side the narrow passage to *Lady Peckitts Yard,* named after the wife of John Peckitt, Lord Mayor in 1702. The Yard leads into Fossgate, at the northern end of which is the curiously named **Whip-Ma-Whop-Ma Gate.** On the west side of Fossgate is the **Merchant Adventurers' Hall** *(weekdays, fee),* a 15th-century guildhall. Fossgate crosses the *Foss* by the Foss Bridge to **Walmgate,** on the right of which is **St. Denys's Church** (12th-century glass). Further along on the left is **St. Margaret's Church** (Norman entrance porch). At the end of Walmgate is **Walmgate Bar,** through which turn right and follow the line of the walls past the Cattle Market in Paragon Street and into **Fishergate** and then fork left to re-cross the *Foss* by Castle Mills Bridge. Keeping to the right, bear into Tower Street.

Clifford's Tower *(daily, fee)* is unique in England in its design, being quatrefoil in shape.

Castle Museum *(daily, fee)* contains an entire street, "Kirkgate", of reconstructed old shops. An extension is housed in the former *Debtor's Prison* nearby. Here the old felons' cells have been converted to craft workshops.

Facing the Castle Museum are the Assize Courts, now the Crown Courts, built in the late 1770s.

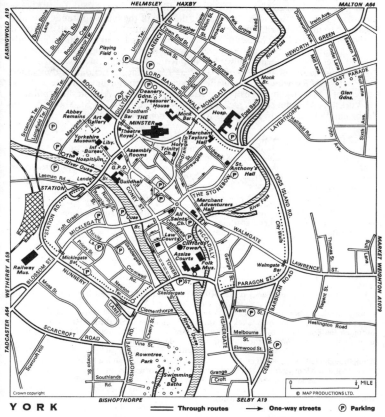

Y O R K ══════ **Through routes** ⟶ **One-way streets** Ⓟ **Parking**

Following the curve from Tower Street we arrive in Castlegate, where is **St. Mary's Church** one of the oldest churches in the city. Its graceful spire is 154 feet high, the tallest in York.

From the northern end of Castlegate, Low Ousegate gives on to Ouse Bridge and Bridge Street for **Micklegate,** one of the oldest streets in York with a number of Georgian houses and **Holy Trinity, Micklegate,** part of an alien Benedictine priory attached to the abbey of Marmoutiers in France. Parallel with Micklegate on the north is Toft Green, north of which is the **Railway Museum.** Leading off the right is Blossom Street which leads to Knavesmire, once the city's place of execution, and the racecourse. From the Railway War Memorial, Station Road leads to the graceful **Lendal Bridge** over the *Ouse* and so to Museum Street—note the 18th-century **Assembly Rooms** (entrance in Blake Street)—and **Lendal.** A few yards down on the left is the *Judges' Lodging,* a large Georgian building standing back from the road. At the end of Lendal is St. Helen's Square, named after **St. Helen's Church.**

The **Mansion House** (18th-century) is the official residence of the Lord Mayor during his term of office. The archway at the side of the building stands over the approach to the **Guildhall,** a restoration of a 15th-century Commonhall destroyed in 1942 in an air raid. Off Museum Street are the **Public Library,** from the grounds of which may be seen the well-preserved interior of the **Multangular Tower** which formed the western corner tower of the Roman fortress of *Eboracum.* The dominating feature of the **Museum Gardens** *(fee),* facing Lendal, is the ruined *Abbey of St. Mary,* which serves as the backcloth for the medieval Mystery Plays, nucleus of York's triennial Festival of Music and the Arts. Also in the grounds is the **Yorkshire Museum** *(daily, fee).* (The house of the Abbot of St. Mary's was in the original building now known as *King's Manor,* off Exhibition Square.)

York's ancient **city walls,** which afford interesting views of the city, are almost as great an attraction as the Minster. In their present form they date from the 14th century. A walk of $2\frac{1}{2}$ to 3 miles, along the walls, starting from Lendal Bridge, takes in:

Micklegate Bar, once the city's southern entrance, traditionally used by sovereigns on their visits to the northern capital; *Baile Hill,* formerly the site of a castle built by William the Conqueror as a companion of Clifford's Tower; *Fishergate Postern* (across Skeldergate Bridge), originally a look-out post; *Fishergate Bar; Walmgate Bar,* (the only one to retain its barbican); the *Red Tower* with walls in places nearly 4 feet thick; *Monk Bar,* tallest of the bars (reached via Foss Islands Road and Layerthorpe Bridge) and *Bootham Bar* (carved figures) at the city's northern entrance. Prominent during the wars against the Scots, Bootham Bar occupies the site of a Roman gateway.

YORK TO TEESSIDE

Thirteen miles north of York on the A19 to Yarn and Teesside is **Easingwold,** a charming small market town of irregular shape. Between here and York lies the "Forest of Galtres", no longer forested but formerly a royal hunting preserve. A pleasant drive round this area from the south end of the town takes one through **Stillington** to **Sheriff Hutton** with its castle. **Sutton on the Forest** is another picturesque village south of Stillington on the York road, further south along which is the turn-off west to **Skelton,** which has a beautiful mid-13th-century church. North up the A19, just before Shipton, is the turning off west to **Beningbrough Hall** (N.T., *Weds and Sats in summer*). Beningbrough is a hamlet some distance away. **Marston Moor,** scene of the battle, lies a few miles across the river. North of Linton one can cross the antiquated toll bridge at Aldwark and proceed to Boroughbridge.

Due east of Easingwold is **Crayke.** The Castle, now a private house, was formerly a palace of the bishops of Durham, and the whole parish was once an island of the county palatine of Durham in Yorkshire, for this land was a gift to St. Cuthbert of Durham in the 7th century. To the north-east is **Brandsby** on the slopes of the Howardian Hills.

To the north the York-Helmsley road takes one into Ryedale. **Gilling,** the next village, was for centuries the home of the Fairfaxes, a prominent Roman Catholic family. The castle is now a preparatory school to the boys' school, *Ampleforth College* and the home of the Abbot of Ampleforth *(grounds open on certain days during summer).* Across the valley lies the Benedictine Abbey and the College itself, reached by turning left off the main road a little north of Gilling, through Oswaldkirk. Further along the road are Ampleforth village, Wass and *Byland Abbey, Coxwold* and *Newburgh Priory (occasionally open in summer).*

Ten miles north of Easingwold on the A19 is **Thirsk** *(Golden Fleece, Royal Oak),* a busy market town with a recently recobbled market square. Its racecourse attracts great crowds.

Thirsk Hall, residence of the Bell family, lords of the manor, was refronted by Carr of York. Next to the Hall is *St. Mary's Church*, the most splendid Perpendicular building in the North Riding. To the south of the town there is a pleasant walk through meadow land between the beck and the adjoining village of Sowerby.

Nine miles north of Thirsk on the A168 lies **Northallerton** *(Golden Lion, Buck)*, county town of the North Riding. The principal feature is the long wide High Street which retains a late 18th- early 19th-century appearance. To the south the village of **Romanby** is now practically part of the town.

The Hambleton Hills

Thirsk and Northallerton lie in the Vale of Mowbray, a local name for the northern part of the Vale of York. Either of them is an ideal centre from which to explore the **Hambleton Hills,** the steep western slope of the North York Moors.

Due east of Thirsk on the main road to Scarborough is **Sutton under Whitestonecliffe,** the cliff from which it takes its name rising precipitously little more than a mile along the road; the one-in-four gradient of *Sutton Bank* brings the motorist to a most magnificent view across the vale to the Pennine Dales. Just below the cliff is the lake *Gormire*. A gliding club makes use of the thermals of the cliffs here.

Northwards from the top of Whitestonecliffe is the old drove road mostly a wide grassy track which passes above the Forestry Commission's plantations of Boltby and Silton Forests. The views are magnificent. In the north is "Black Hambleton" hill (over 1,300 feet). Below this hill the track joins a road from **Osmotherley,** largest of the Hambleton villages and close to which are the remains of **Mount Grace Priory** (reached from the A19). The best preserved ruin in England of a house of Carthusian monks, it is now in the care of the Department of the Environment; the house adjoining, which was the guest house of the monastery, then a private dwelling, is a National Trust Property.

Cod Beck Reservoir, near here is a popular picnic spot.

On the hill to the north-east of **Swainby** are the *Whorlton Castle* ruins. Two miles along the main road is the *Cleveland Tontine Inn* (1804). **Leake** Church, with its Norman tower, set in the fields beside the main road is about five miles south of Mount Grace.

On the return to Northallerton on the A684 it is worth turning aside a mile or two before the town to **Brompton,** where the church has a collection of Anglo-Danish hogback tombstones.

About six miles along the B6271 (which leads out of the north end of Northallerton, off the Darlington road across the railway crossing) lies **Kiplin Hall,** built for Lord Baltimore, founder of Maryland *(Suns. during summer)*.

The churchyard in the next village, **Bolton-on-Swale,** contains the grave of Henry Jenkins who died in 1670, supposedly aged 169. The Old Hall nearby has the remains of a pele tower. This B road, after passing near Scorton, joins the old Great North Road near Catterick Bridge, where there is a fine old hotel. Across the road is Catterick racecourse. Catterick Church is of particular interest because the contract for building it in 1412 has survived. Return to Northallerton by travelling five miles down the A1 to Leeming Bar. The small town of **Bedale** lies a mile or so to the west of this point with the imposing tower of the Church of St. Gregory. The A684 leads back to Northallerton across the bridge at Morton-on-Swale, favoured by anglers.

The South-West

The south-west region of Yorkshire has no need to assert its importance in the fields of industry and commerce. Sheffield is the steel capital of the world. The Yorkshire coalfield is the greatest in the country. Leeds and Bradford are internationally renowned for their clothing and woollen industries, while Hull is the third port in the kingdom. Too often the tourist passes them by, yet these areas have much more to offer than the muck and mills which have become cliché and caricature. Even the most industrial of Yorkshire's broad acres have often a striking and unique claim to beauty, whether of the natural countryside, of ancient houses or churches, or that strange, unconventional beauty that sometimes springs to surprise us from industry itself. Certain it is that the tourist who visits this part of Yorkshire with an open mind and a discerning eye will find the experience deeply enriching.

Sheffield

Car Parking.—Meters in central area, also off-street metered and other car parks. Multi-storey in Bank Street, Burgess Street, Eyre Street, Norfolk Street and Pond Street.

Distances.—Barnsley, 14; Doncaster, 18; Huddersfield, 26; London, 160.

Hotels.—*Grosvenor House, Hallam Tower, Harley, Kenwood, Montgomery, Roslyn Court, Royal Victoria, Rutland,* and many others.

Population.—519,700.

Post Office.—Fitzalan Square.

Sheffield is the phoenix of Yorkshire. Heavily bombed in the Second World War it has transformed itself from a "dark picture in a golden frame" into the showplace among Yorkshire cities, of which it is the largest, as well as being the fifth city in England.

The Cathedral. The cruciform Church of St. Peter and St. Paul in Church Street, Sheffield's cathedral since 1913, when the bishopric was founded, originated in the 12th century and was rebuilt in the 15th. As a result of bomb damage part of the church had to be rebuilt again. There is a wonderful coloured lantern passing through the roof to a height of sixty-two

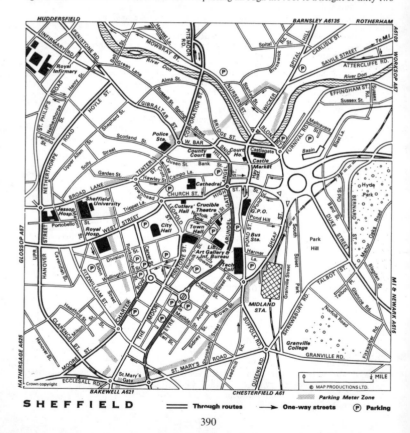

SHEFFIELD ═══ **Through routes** ⟶ **One-way streets** Ⓟ **Parking**

390

feet. Throughout the Cathedral the painted glass, illustrating scenes from the early history of the city, is a fascinating feature.

Cutlers Hall (1832), also in Church Street, was built as an administrative centre for the Cutler's Company in Hallamshire. Among its many fine rooms, the marbled main hall and the Regency-style banqueting hall are outstanding. The **Graves Art Gallery** at the Central Library, in Surrey Street, contains important oriental pictures as well as an extensive collection of European art. Among its most treasured possessions are the Grice Ivories. Also in Surrey Street is the **Town Hall,** whose tower, 193 feet high, is surmounted by a seven-foot bronze of Vulcan, symbolising the trades by which Sheffield lives. At Barker's Pool nearby is the **City Hall** containing the fine Oval Hall which can seat 2,800. Regular concerts are given here. **The Crucible Theatre,** near the junction of Arundel Gate and Norfolk Street is unique in Britain for its splendid audience facilities, the main auditorium seating 1,000 in steeply rising seats around three sides of a stage which projects 28 feet forward into the audience. There is also a small octagonal experimental theatre. The **University** of Sheffield was incorporated in 1905. The main buildings are in Western Bank less than a mile from the Town Hall.

Sheffield's many parks offer an immediate attraction. They range from the small but colourful gardens at Beauchief Abbey to Ecclesall Woods, only three miles from the city centre, offering 305 acres of natural woodland with bridle paths for horse riding.

The Huddersfield Road. The A616 runs north-west from Sheffield through moorland country dotted with reservoirs supplying water to the city. To the left is the Ewden Valley through which runs the *Ewden Beck.* Just beyond **Wharncliffe Side** are the impressive **Wharncliffe Crags** from the top of which are fine views. Wharncliffe Park *(Mons, Thurs, Sats)* provides good woodland walks. **Stocksbridge** is 9 miles from Sheffield in a rural area of small farms and rolling country which at its southern end runs into the Peak District National Park. Nearby **Deepcar** and **Bolsterstone** were at one time busy with glass manufacture. From **Langsett** *(sailing, fishing)* a right turn leads to **Penistone** once noted for its sheep market but now involved with steel. Along the A629 to Huddersfield the television masts of Emley Moor are prominent.

Rotherham (Pop.: 86,360. Hotels: *Brentwood, Brecon, Cross Kings, Station*), 6 miles from Sheffield, is a busy industrial town relying on steel, coal and iron-founding. The mainly 15th-century church of All Saints in the town centre is claimed to be one of the finest examples of the Perpendicular in the county. On the town bridge is the *Chantry Chapel of Our Lady* (1483) one of only three such chapels in England.

A mile and a half south-west of Rotherham is **Templeborough,** once the site of a Roman fort, finds from which can be seen in the museum, an 18th-century mansion at **Clifton Park.**

Four miles north of Rotherham is **Wentworth Woodhouse,** built by Flitcroft in the 18th century. Used as a teachers' training college it has the longest frontage (600 feet) of any English country house. The public may use the paths through the wooded grounds.

Along the A630 Doncaster road are **Thrybergh** with a good 14th–15th-century church and **Hooton Roberts** on a hillside above the *Don* and which has associations with Vaughan Williams. **Conisbrough** is a town of steep streets and intriguing corners dominated by a Norman castle *(daily)* made famous by Sir Walter Scott in *Ivanhoe* as the home of Athelstane. The cylindrical keep supported by six buttresses tapering to the top is unique in England.

Seven miles along the A631 is **Maltby** a colliery town and 1½ miles south-east of which is **Roche Abbey** *(daily, fee).* The ruins of this Cistercian abbey, founded 1147, are situated in a wooded valley and surrounded by lawns. The eastern part of the church still stands and a good deal of the vaulted gatehouse with its narrow arch for pedestrians and a broad archway for waggons is well preserved.

Barnsley (Pop.: 75,315. Hotels: *Queen's, Royal, Waverley, White Hart*) 14 miles north of Sheffield, depends largely on coal mining and glass blowing. Barnsley market, which dates from 1249, attracts visitors from a vast area. It was reconstructed in 1971–72. Joseph Locke, a Barnsley man who collaborated with George and Robert Stephenson in developing railways, is commemorated in one or two street names and by the 46-acre **Locke Park** at the southern end of the town. The Town Hall in Church Street is impressively massive occupying nearly 34,000 square feet and containing 140 rooms. Faced with Portland stone its four storeys are surmounted by a fine clock tower, 154 feet high. Contrasting with this comparatively modern building is the parish **Church of St. Mary,** whose embattled and pinnacled tower dates from the 15th century. The **Cooper Art Gallery** in the old grammar school in Church Street contains a good selection of English paintings and drawings.

North-east of Barnsley, at **Monk Bretton** are the remains of a Cluniac priory of 1153 *(daily, fee).*

Cawthorne is a charming village 5 miles west of Barnsley famous for its Cannon Hall Park, a favourite picnic spot. **Cannon Hall** *(daily, fee)* in the park is an excellent museum of the decorative arts containing fine collections of furniture, paintings, china, silver, glass and Victoriana. Since 1969 it has also been the home of the Regimental Museum of the 13th/18th Royal Hussars (Queen Mary's Own). Designed by John Carr, Cannon Hall was the home of the Squire of Cawthorne, Sir Walter Spencer-Stanhope. Among the family relics in the hall is the bow said to have belonged to Robin Hood's second-in-command, Little John.

Pontefract (Pop.: 31,165. Hotels: *Red Lion, Elephant, Malt Shovel*) is an ancient town well-known for its castle and for Pontefract cakes, though the liquorice from which the latter are made is no longer locally grown. Now only a ruin, the **castle** is steeped in memories of the many dark deeds once perpetrated within its massive walls. Here Richard II, deposed by Parliament, was imprisoned and died, probably murdered on the orders of Henry IV. Here Archbishop Scrope of York was executed for treason. James I, too, of Scotland was imprisoned here and many executions took place here during the Wars of the Roses. During the Civil War, Pontefract Castle was besieged three times and was the last Royalist stronghold to hold out against the Parliamentarians. On orders from Cromwell, the Town Council petitioned Parliament for its demolition, which was begun in March 1649. There is a small **museum** in the porter's lodge.

The oldest church in Pontefract, **All Saints,** still stands in South Baileygate in the shadow of the castle. Between All Saints and Ferrybridge Road on rising ground close to a playing field is the site of the *Priory of St. John,* founded in about 1090, and destroyed by Henry VIII.

North of the town is Pontefract Park, which contains the racecourse.

Ackworth, 2¼ miles south, is the home of the famous Quaker public school founded by Dr. John Fothergill in 1779 as a foundling hospital.

Wakefield (Pop.: 59,450. Hotels: *Cesars Wakefield, Cornhill Commercial, Grove House, Lupset, White Horse*) has many Georgian buildings, an impressive cathedral and one of the few chantry chapels in England. Cloth weaving, still an important industry, though secondary now to engineering, was practised at least as early as the 13th century. Wakefield was created a city in 1888, the year the See of Wakefield was formed, and its parish church became the cathedral. Its 247 foot spire is said to be the tallest in Yorkshire.

The medieval **Chantry Chapel of St. Mary** on Wakefield Old Bridge retains its beautiful original detail in spite of considerable restoration. It has had two new west fronts, one of them by Sir Gilbert Scott, who restored the chapel in 1847, and another in more recent years.

In Wood Street is the *Town Hall* with its impressive clock tower nearly 200 feet tall. Close by is *County Hall,* the impressive administrative headquarters of the West Riding County Council, which has a dome rising to 130 feet above street level. Well worth seeing is Wakefield's 19th-century *Court House,* with its splendid columns and statue of Justice.

At **Sandal Magna** within the city's southern boundary, only a few fragments remain of what in the 13th century was a great fortress, much favoured as a home by Richard III. It was destroyed in the Civil War. More recent excavations have revealed the great drum bases of the tremendously strong towers. At the foot of the hill is the impressively arched *St. Helen's Church,* mostly 14th century.

At **Kettlethorpe** off the Barnsley Road, is **Kettlethorpe Hall,** now a home for the elderly. The original frontage of the chantry chapel on Wakefield Calder Bridge was removed to Kettlethorpe Hall last century and used as a boat house.

Newmillerdam, a village about four miles south of Wakefield on the Barnsley road, has a lake and small museum *(weekends and Bank Hols, May to Sept.).*

Nostell Priory *(Easter–Oct., Weds, weekends, Bank Hols and daily in Aug. and part Sept., fee)* stands in a splendid park running across the Doncaster road, $6\frac{1}{2}$ miles south-east of Wakefield. It is especially famous for its fine collection of Chippendale furniture. Adjoining the park is **Wragby Church** notable for its medieval Swiss glass and fine woodwork.

Walton Hall, set in a pleasant village three miles south-east of Wakefield, is the former home of Charles Waterton the eccentric naturalist and traveller who created what is said to be the first wild life sanctuary in this country. **Heath Hall,** two miles east of the city on the Normanton Road (A655) was built in 1707 and extended by John Carr, the locally-born Georgian architect who became Lord Mayor of York *(open on certain days in summer, fee).* **Woolley,** seven miles south of Wakefield, is a pleasant village with a 15th-century church and *Woolley Hall,* now a teachers' college. **Bretton Park,** at West Bretton, a few miles west of Woolley, is a college for teachers of drama, music and the arts.

Leeds

Distances.—Bradford, 9; Doncaster, 21; Halifax, 15; Huddersfield, 15; London, 190; Manchester, 40; Rotherham, 29; York, 24.
Early Closing.—Wednesday.
Greyhound Stadium.—Elland Road.
Hotels.—*Faversham, Golden Lion, Great Northern, Griffin, Manston, Merrion, Metropole, Post House,* etc.
Population.—501,080.
Post Office.—City Square.
Theatres.—*City Varieties,* The Headrow; *Civic Theatre,* Cookridge Street; *Grand,* New Briggate; *Playhouse,* Calverley Street.

Leeds, England's sixth largest city produces clothing and wool textiles, furniture and leather goods and is a centre for printing, engineering and concrete manufacture.

Leeds is said to contain the oldest railway line in the world, instituted in 1758 to take coal to the river *Aire* from mines at *Middleton.* Its locomotives were designed by Matthew Murray, a brilliant engineer and inventor, commemorated by an obelisk in *St. Matthew's Church,* Holbeck and by the Middleton Railway Trust, formed in 1959, who have a collection of old locomotives which the public are allowed to inspect. On certain days they may also take a ride on the original 1758 route.

City Square contains Brock's mounted bronze of the Black Prince, whose companions are James Watt, Joseph Priestley, John Harrison and Dean Hook, as well as the eight so-called "nymphs", the bronze "flambeaux" figures of Morn and Even. *Mill Hill Chapel* (rebuilt 1847) where Dr. Joseph Priestley was minister for eleven years, is in City Square.

From City Square **Park Row** leads to **The Headrow,** on which stands the large and immediately impressive **Town Hall,** designed by Cuthbert Broderick. To the rear is the **Civic Hall,** with twin towers on which perch the owls (8 feet tall) which figure in the city coat of arms. Also on the Headrow is the *City Varieties,* said to be the oldest music hall in England. Leeds is a city of arcades, two of which, *Thornton's* and the *Grand Arcade* contain remarkable clocks with moving figures.

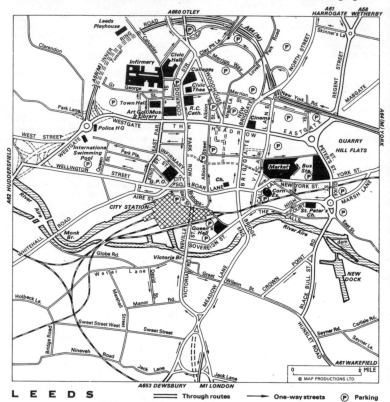

L E E D S   ════ Through routes   ──→ One-way streets   Ⓟ Parking

Leading north from the Headrow, **Cookridge Street** contains the *Civic Theatre,* designed by Broderick, the creator of the design for the Town Hall. Another of Broderick's buildings is the *Corn Exchange* now used as a market. Dating from 1863, it has an elliptical dome 75 feet high. North-west of the Civil Theatre, just off the Inner Ring Road is the *Playhouse.* The other Leeds theatre is the *Grand* in New Briggate with its fine large auditorium. From New Briggate, **Merrion Street** leads to the Merrion Centre, a shopping complex which includes an hotel, a dance hall and a bowling alley. Woodhouse Lane leads to the **University,** which contains the *Brotherton Library* with its priceless collection of rare and valuable books and letters. At **Headingley** is the famous cricket ground.

Roundhay Park (616 acres) with two lakes with fish and boats and an open-air pool is only one of many fine parks.

Temple Newsam House *(daily, fee)*. One of Yorkshire's and indeed England's treasures, Temple Newsam was owned by the Knights Templars from 1155 to 1308. The present house, set around three sides of a great court amid beautiful grounds, is in its oldest portions partly Elizabethan. Said to have been the birthplace of Darnley, husband of Mary Queen of Scots, it was acquired by Leeds in 1922 from Lord Halifax, whose family had owned it since Jacobean times. Temple Newsam is now used as an "extension" of the city's art gallery. Treasures from many ages are here: wonderful ceilings, furniture by Chippendale, gorgeous tapestry, fine pottery and paintings by the great artists.

Kirkstall Abbey. Via Abbey Road (65) buses from Corn Exchange. Industry seems to have grown up all round the remains of the early Cistercian buildings amid green lawns. The Abbey was founded in 1152 by Henry de Lacy, Lord of Pontefract, and built by Abbot Alexander. The church is roofless and the tower has collapsed but the chapter house and abbot's lodgings remain almost as they were built. A particularly fine ruin is that of the Abbot's house.

Abbey House Museum *(fee)*. The original Abbey Gatehouse contains, among much else of interest, three full-scale streets of 19th-century shops, houses and work places re-erected here from in and around Leeds.

Kirkstall Church contains the tomb of Richard Oastler, who helped to abolish child slavery in the factories and mines.

Some three miles due north-east of Kirkstall Abbey is **Adel**, where the lovely little church is one of this country's most perfect examples of Norman architecture. From Adel it is a pleasant walk to **Arthington**, a delightful Wharfedale village with some fine old houses.

Birstall. 7 miles from Leeds on A62 is Birstall, a little west of which is **Oakwell Hall** *(daily except Fris, free)* a charming Tudor house now owned by Batley Corporation, and where Charlotte Brontë stayed, afterwards including a description of the house in *Shirley* where she called it "Fieldhead". Birstall itself she renamed "Briarfield". Joseph Priestley, the discoverer of oxygen, was born at Birstall in 1733. A plaque marks the site at Fieldhead on one of the hills surrounding the town. Priestley's statue performs a perpetual experiment with candle and jar, in Birstall market place.

At Kirklees Hall near **Mirfield** (about 6 miles from Huddersfield) is the traditional site of Robin Hood's grave. The *Three Nuns Inn* at Mirfield is reputedly built on the site of an inn which was once the guest house for visitors to the Priory where Robin died. Mirfield is probably best known for the *Community of the Resurrection*, an order of Anglican brothers founded here in 1898 by the late Bishop Gore of Oxford, with the object of training priests.

Bramham Park *(Easter–Sept., Suns and Bank Hols, fee)* 11 miles north-west is a fine Queen Anne mansion with a collection of pictures by Reynolds and others. The gardens were designed after the style of Versailles.

Tadcaster (14 miles from Leeds) is generally known for its breweries and a plenitude of pubs to match! The *Ark Museum* in a 15th-century house near the church contains old brewing instruments and articles of local interest. From the seven-arched bridge over the *Wharfe* a fine view is had of the 15th-century riverside church built of white magnesium limestone which has been quarried here for centuries.

Towton, $2\frac{1}{2}$ miles south of Tadcaster on the A162 is remembered for one of the bloodiest battles of the Wars of the Roses, in which 30,000 men are said to have died on Palm Sunday 1461. At **Saxton cum Scarthingwell,** just south of Towton, the site of the battle is marked by a cross. A circular run out of Tadcaster can be extended beyond Towton to **Saxton,** at which church lie bodies of nobles slain in the battle, thence on to **Sherburn in Elmet,** the site of a palace of Aethelstan and capital of the British Kingdom of Elmet. Return can be made via **Cawood,** once a seat of the Archbishop of York. Only the gatehouse of the palace remains.

Huddersfield (Pop.: 130,050. Hotels: *George, Clare Manor, Saxon Inn*) is a hilly town on the edge of the Pennines and is probably equally famous for its fine worsteds and its choral singing. The Italianate Town Hall is frequently the scene of concerts, and the annual "Messiah" by the Huddersfield Choral Society is an imperishable tradition. Immediately impressive is the **Railway Station,** built in the Greek style, which looks out on the spacious George Square, containing a statue of Sir Robert Peel. In Kirkgate is the striking **St. Peter's Church** built in the style of the 15th century though dating only from the 19th. Among the newer buildings are the *Civic Centre,* the *Law Courts* and the *Market Hall* (opened in 1970).

To the east of the town at Mold Green, is **Ravensknowle Park** with the **Tolson Memorial Museum** which contains old textile machinery.

Castle Hill, Almondbury (900 feet) was the site of an Iron Age camp. The *Victoria Tower* on the hill gives good views.

Five miles from Huddersfield, **Kirkburton** (just off the A629) is notable for its beautiful old church. **Denby Dale,** a few miles away at the southern end of the A636 just before the junction with the A635 has a curious tradition of baking giant pies. One, baked in 1964 to raise money to build a village hall, weighed over six tons.

Holmfirth, six miles from Huddersfield, reached via the A616 and a branch road (right) from **Honley,** has a number of memorials to disastrous floods of past years. A few miles south-west of Holmfirth, the *Holm Moss Television Mast* stands on the moors, to the right of the A6024, about 1½ miles past the village of **Holme.**

A recently completed dam at **Scammondew** on the moors above Huddersfield is a popular sailing and picnic area. The dam wall carries the M62 motorway.

Halifax (Pop.: 91,040. Hotels: *Alan Fold, Blue Ball, Bull's Head, Feathers, Golden Lion, Star*) is a busy town in the Hebden Valley. In addition to carpets produced in one of the world's largest mills, Halifax manufactures all kinds of textiles, iron and steel tools and wire and the "Cat's Eyes" road studs invented by a local man, Percy Shaw. Also produced in Halifax are sweets, beer, stone, bricks and sanitary ware.

Centuries ago, Halifax was feared for its gibbet, an instrument of decapitation anticipating the French guillotine, which gave rise to the Thieves Litany—"From Hull, Hell and Halifax, good Lord deliver us." Its story goes back to the mid-14th century when Halifax cloth makers were granted the right to behead anyone caught stealing cloth worth more than 13½ pence. The Gibbet Law was retained until the middle of the 17th century and hundreds fell victim to its blade. All that remains of the gibbet is its base and steps, off Gibbet Street near the town centre.

Opened in 1779 as a cloth market, the **Piece Hall,** which contained 315 rooms set around a quadrangle and occupied a total of about 10,000 square yards, is now in use as a wholesale provisions market. It is scheduled as an ancient monument. **Wainhouse's Tower,** 270 feet high, is an ornate structure intended as a mill chimney but never used for that purpose. Wonderful views may be had from the platform at the top of the 400 steps inside the chimney. The tower is open for two days at the Spring and late Summer Bank Holidays *(fee).*

The Parish **Church of St. John the Baptist** is largely 15th century. A carved wooden figure known as *Old Tristram* stands near the west door beside the old pillar alms box. He is said to be modelled on a real beggar well-known in 17th-century Halifax. The *Old Cock Hotel* in Southgate contains an impressive Oak Room on the mantelpiece of which appears the date 1581.

Shibden Hall, once the home of the Lister family is now a folk museum in a delightful park. The **Bankfield Museum** in Akroyd Park concentrates on costumes and textiles. The **People's Park** near the town centre was designed by Sir Joseph Paxton and given to the town by Sir Francis Crossley, a local industrialist and benefactor, whose statue, along with others, adorns the park. The **Town Hall** has a sculptured clock tower and a spire rising 180 feet from ground level. It was designed by the architect of the Houses of Parliament, Sir Charles Barry.

There are many pleasant walks and drives around Halifax, particularly in the **Hebden, Shibden** and **Luddenden valleys** and in the more distant moorland areas.

One of the most popular local beauty spots is **Hardcastle Crags,** now owned by the National Trust.

Dean Head, Crag Vale and **Peckett Well** (a mile north of *Hebden Bridge*) are all well worth visiting; as are the moorlands at **Norland, Blackstone Edge** and **Wadsworth**, the **Ryburn** and **Blackburn** valleys and old villages like **Heptonstall, Midgley, Sowerby** and **Luddenden**.

Todmorden, about a dozen miles along the A646, has *Todmorden Hall* as its post office, a beautiful house over 300 years old. Two miles east of the town is *Stoodley Pike*, an obelisk raised in 1856 to replace a tower built in 1815 as a thank offering for peace after the Napoleonic wars.

At **Brighouse,** six miles east of Halifax, the *Art Gallery* in Rydings Park contains a room devoted to the work of an outstanding wood-carver, the late H. P. Jackson.

Bradford (Pop.: 294,740. Hotels: *Balmoral, Baron, Greycourt, Beechfield, Regency* and others) is the woollen market of the world. The **City Hall** has a 200-foot tower modelled on the campanile of the Palazze Vechio at Florence, and is equipped with a carillon. The **Wool Exchange** is nearby in Market Street. The heart of modern Bradford is **Forster Square,** named after William Edward Forster, the Bradford M.P. who founded free national education. The **Cathedral,** dating largely from the 15th century, was the parish church of St. Peter until Bradford became a cathedral city in 1920.

St. George's Hall in Hall Ings, is the setting for live musical concerts both by the Hallé Orchestra and Bradford's own choral societies. In Great Horton Road are the **University** buildings and the *College of Art*. Across the city at the eastern end of Hall Ings, just off Leeds Road, is the Bradford *Playhouse* (formerly the "Civic"), one of the best known amateur theatres in the North. There is also the Library Theatre.

In **Lister Park,** north of the city off Manningham Lane, is the *Cartwright Hall,* named in honour of Edmund Cartwright, inventor of the power loom, a splendid baroque creation built in 1904. It is now the city's **Art Gallery and Museum.**

To the south of the city on Bolling Hall Road is **Bowling Park,** with the beautiful **Bolling Hall,** one of the city's most historic buildings, now an excellent museum *(daily)* illustrating domestic life in Bradford from the 15th to the late 18th centuries.

At **Thornton** (B6145) on the city's western outskirts is the house, number 74 Market Street, where Patrick and Maria Brontë lived, when Patrick, the father of Emily, Charlotte, Anne and Bramwell, was the vicar of Thornton. The four Brontë children were all born in this small terrace house on the main street of the village.

Haworth is a place of pilgrimage for all Brontë lovers for here, from 1820 to 1861, the Rev. Patrick Brontë was the incumbent of the church, and at the adjacent **Parsonage** *(museum, daily)* his daughters lived and wrote. Also at Haworth is the museum of the *Keighley and Worth Valley Railway Preservation Society,* who run a train service between Keighley and Oxenhope.

The delightful village of **Tong,** four miles from the city centre, is reached by following a signpost left from Westgate Hill (A650). *Tong Hall* was built in 1702.

It is an easy walk from Tong to **Fulneck,** the Moravian settlement on a hillside, which is part of Pudsey. The Moravians settled here about the middle of the 18th century to establish a base for evangelism, naming the place after Fulneck in Moravia. The community buildings *(Museum: Weds and Sats)* form a long line overlooking a green valley.

Pudsey itself is a busy manufacturing town known for producing cricketers of the stature of Herbert Sutcliffe and Sir Leonard Hutton.

Shipley lies a little north of Bradford. There are some interesting old houses that contrast strongly with the new town centre with its strikingly modern clock tower. In Shipley Glen is a cable railway which climbs the wooded hillside. Shipley links Bradford with **Saltaire,** the model village created by Sir Titus Salt in 1855 in order to give his mill-workers the benefit of clean air and decent living conditions.

Doncaster (Pop.: 81,800. Hotels: *Danum, Acorn, Elephant*), the *Danum* of the Romans, is the centre of a great coal-mining area and is also concerned with the building of railway engines and rolling stock, as well as confectionery. Doncaster butterscotch is renowned. The Mansion House in High Street was designed by James Paine and completed in 1748. St. George's Church in St. Georgegate was built in 1818. Christ Church, in Thorne Road, is noted for its Belgian glass and for its steeple with octagonal lantern. Doncaster's famous **Racecourse** is situated on Doncaster Common to the east of the A638. Bloodstock sales take place at Belle Vue Stables.

Seven miles from Doncaster on the A18 is **Hatfield** with its lovely church, parts of which date from the 12th century. The village stands in *Hatfield Chase*, which was wild fenland teeming with game and ruffians until Cornelius Vermuyden, a Dutch engineer, drained it during the reign of Charles I. About three miles from Hatfield, **Thorne** seems more suited to Holland than Yorkshire. The waterway called *Dutch River* (cut by Vermuyden), which unites *Don* and *Ouse*, crosses the flat country to reach Goole, while the road takes a more roundabout route via **Rawcliffe**, once the home and now the burial place of Jimmy Hurst, a famous eccentric, who in the time of George III attempted among other exploits to fly with home-made wings.

Goole, a seaport 50 miles from the sea, announces its presence from a distance by the dockside cranes which tower over the flat country. There is a maritime feeling, too, in St. John's Church, built by the Aire and Calder Navigation Company in 1843. It contains memorials to ships and sailors. The oldest standing building is said to be the Georgian *Lowther Hotel* in Aire Street, but there is nevertheless a feeling of the past, for instance in the name of the *Vermuyden Hotel*.

Selby is 13 miles from Goole via A614 and A63. **Selby Abbey** is one of the finest monastic churches in England. Now Selby's parish church, its chief glories include two fine Norman doorways, east window with superb tracery and a fine tower, skilfully restored in 1909 after fire.

There is a toll bridge across the river on the York road (A63). In 1970 this modern bridge replaced a timbered bridge, erected around 1791.

Hull (Pop.: 285,472. Hotels: *Broadway, Dorchester House, Newland Park, Hull Centre, Royal Station*) or Kingston-upon-Hull, to give it its full title, ranks as the third English port in terms of cargo tonnage. It is also a terminal of the car-ferry service to Rotterdam and Zeebrugge. Although a great industrial centre, much of the city, rebuilt after war damage, is modern and attractive. **Wilberforce House** *(museum)* in High Street was the birthplace (1759) of William Wilberforce the slave emancipator. Also in High Street is the **Transport Museum.** In Pickering Park is a **Maritime Museum.** Running parallel with High Street is the old Harbour area where the wealthy merchants of bygone Hull lived and had their places of business. The first dock was completed in 1778. Filled in now, it provides a delightful open space in the city centre as Queen's Gardens. Hull is unique in this country in having its own municipal telephone service which has been most efficiently and economically run since 1904.

Almost halfway between Hull and Withernsea is **Hedon,** an ancient market town with a square-towered church called "The King of Holderness". The "Queen" is at **Patrington,** 4 miles south-west of Withernsea. **Withernsea** is a cheerful seaside town with good clean sands and offering a wide variety of entertainment.

The Yorkshire Coast

Bridlington to Redcar

No other stretch of the English coast can rival that of Yorkshire for beauty, variety and interest. Only a few miles inland are the Wolds and Moors, rich in prehistoric remains. The North York Moors National Park is an area of 553 square miles containing seven National Forests as well as secluded dales and valleys, rivers and becks, great houses and quiet villages. Ancient stone crosses are familiar sights on the moors. In addition to Lilla Cross, the most famous, there are John Cross and York Cross and the two Ralph Crosses to which reference is made on other pages.

Bridlington

Beach.—Extensive sandy beaches. Swimming pool.
Distances.—Filey, 11 ; Hornsea, 15 ; York, 41 ; Hull, 29 ; Scarborough, 18.
Early Closing.—Thursday.
Entertainments.—Dancing at Spa Royal Hotel and Burton's Buildings. Spa Theatre. Floral Pavilion (concerts).
Fishing.—First-class facilities from South Pier, beaches and boats. From North Pier in winter only. Annual Festival in September.
Hotels.—*Expanse, Brockton, Spa, Southcliffe, Shirley, Alexandra, Heatherlands, Regent, Monarch* and many others.
Population.—26,370.
Post Office.—Quay Road.
Sports.—Boating, bowls, putting, golf *(Belvedere Golf Club)*, tennis.

Bridlington is the principal resort on that flatter part of the coast which extends southwards from Flamborough Head. Its sands, like all those on this part of the coast, are clean, firm and extensive. Delightful sea-trips can be had along the coast. South of the harbour is **The Spa** where one can enjoy good music and entertainment. Opposite are the **Pembroke Gardens** and the *Yorkshire Yacht Club House,* as distinct from the Royal Yorkshire Yacht Club which is slightly nearer the harbour, and adjoining is the **Lifeboat House,** generally open for inspection.

A short bus ride, a pleasant walk northwards along the cliff-top or a saunter along the beach brings one to **Sewerby Hall** *(daily, fee),* a fine Georgian mansion containing restaurant and art gallery and a collection of trophies and awards of the pioneer airwoman Amy Johnson.

Bridlington Priory was founded in 1113. The only parts now in existence are the Church and **The Bayle,** the original gate-house of the monastery. In the Bayle is a **Museum of Antiquities** *(Mons to Fris in summer, fee).*

To Boynton and Carnaby. From the Old Town to Boynton is a straight road of less than three miles. About a mile from Old Bridlington is the hamlet of **Easton** (connection with Charlotte Brontë). Just beyond Easton, a public footpath leads near the park surrounding **Boynton Hall** *(by appointment, fee).* The Strickland family, to whom the seat belonged, are said to have introduced the turkey to Britain from America. Turning off opposite the Classical church and the vicarage is a bridle-path to Carnaby. In a garden at the Bridlington end of the village is a monument to the famous racehorse "Melbourne", bred at Carnaby House. The main road from Carnaby to Bridlington passes on the right the hamlet of **Bessingby.** Bessingby Hall is a finely situated mansion.

To Rudston and Burton Agnes (round trip of about 18 miles). Rudston is noted for the prehistoric Monolith in its churchyard. Here, also, is the grave of Winifred Holtby, the novelist. To the west, on the Kilham road, is the site of a *Roman Villa* discovered in 1933. In this area the Celts have left their traces in place-names such as **Cat Babbleton.** Near **Thwing** are over two hundred hillocks, 3 or 4 feet high, believed to be the graves of Danes slain in battle. Four miles north-west of Rudston, again near Thwing, is **Octon,** birthplace of Thomas Lamplugh, Archbishop of York (1688).

Burton Agnes, 5½ miles south-west of Bridlington, is reputed the prettiest village in the district. **Burton Agnes Hall** *(May to Oct., daily, Sats excepted, fee),* seat of the Boynton family, is a fine example of late Elizabethan architecture.

Harpham, half a mile south-west of Burton Agnes, is the birthplace of St. John of Beverley, after whom a spring in the parish is named. The church contains interesting glass.

To Barmston and Hornsea. From south of Bridlington, Kingsgate leads towards Carnaby Moor, Fraisthorpe, Barmston, and on by the coast towards Hornsea. **Barmston** has fine sands, water ski-ing and sailing and an interesting church. After Barmston comes **Skipsea,** once the seat of the Lords of Holderness, the remains of whose castle can be traced on a mound (Albemarle Hill) at Skipsea Brough. Six miles beyond Skipsea and 15 miles south of Bridlington is **Hornsea,** with all the requirements for a family holiday. Its *Mere* (yachting and fishing), the largest fresh-water lake in Yorkshire, is nearly two miles long.

There are pleasant walks from Hornsea to **Goxhill, Atwick, Skipsea, Aldborough, Sigglethorpe, Rise, Burton Constable** and **Ulrome.**

Great Driffield (Pop.: 7,000) is a busy centre on the edge of the wolds. Its church has a high Perpendicular tower.

Beverley (Pop.: 17, 320. Hotels: *Beverley Arms, King's Head, Lairgate, Angel*) is an attractive market town with a wealth of fine Georgian buildings. Although mainly concerned as an agricultural centre, there are several light industries now well established. In the Market Place, or Saturday Market, stands a fine Market Cross, an open octagonal structure.

Beverley Minster is considered to be one of the most beautiful examples of Gothic architecture in Europe. The great west window, of nine lights, is unusually fine. At the right of the altar is a curious relic of the old days of Sanctuary, the *Fridstol,* Freed Stool, or "Chair of Peace". The *Percy Tomb,* to the left of the altar is an exquisite specimen of Decorated work. Between the clergy desks in the nave is the grave of St. John of Beverley.

St. Mary's Church, almost a rival to the Minster in dimensions and beauty of architecture, is situated in the north part of the town, about half a mile from the Minster.

Five miles north of Bridlington is **Flamborough Head,** a bare, bleak promontory with high cliffs, precipitous and forbidding. But man has contrived to make two "landings"—North and South, of which the former is by far the most important and the site of the famous lifeboat station and of a station of H.M. Coastguard. The promontory is cut off from the mainland by *Danes' Dyke* an immense grass-grown entrenchment, extending for about two-and-a-half miles from the south to the north shore. **Flamborough Village** is chiefly inhabited by a small agricultural and fishing community. Much of the church is 13th-century. From the churchyard is to be seen the ancient keep or tower known as the *Danish Tower.* Close to the post office is a Fishermen's Memorial.

To Bempton and Speeton. Instead of turning towards the lighthouse from the North Landing take the cliff path in the other direction, northward. After descending a small ravine, ascending on the opposite side, and then, crossing a headland, we are faced with one of the grandest views on this coast. Two hundred feet or more below is **Thornwick Bay.** Then comes Little Thornwick Bay, with its massive overhanging rocks, backed by the straight walls of Bempton and Speeton Cliffs. Good walkers may continue by the path along the edge of the cliffs, lined in spring by thousands of sea birds. **Bempton,** about a mile inland, north of Flamborough village, has a Norman and Decorated Church, rebuilt in 1829. Nearby on the Speeton-Flamborough road is *Buckton Hall,* which has associations with many eminent men.

Filey (Pop.: 5,140. Hotels: *Beach, Belle Vue, Downcliffe, Hylands* and many others) is an ideal place for children and those who prefer a quiet bracing resort. There are good facilities for bathing, fishing, archery, riding, tennis, golf and bowls. The greater part of the town stands high above the sea on a somewhat precipitous cliff with a superb outlook over the expansive bay, with the great reef **Filey Brigg** as northern boundary and the chalk cliffs of Speeton, Bempton and Flamborough Head tapering away south-eastward. The wooded **Church Ravine,** runs steeply up from the sea at the northern end of the town. Above is the Parish Church, dedicated to St. Oswald, the patron saint of Northumbrian (or North of the Humber) fishermen.

Gristhorpe and Cayton Bay. About two-and-a-half miles along the Scarborough road or by cliff path. **Gristhorpe Bay** is a favourite ground for fossil-hunters. The prominent headland to the north is **Red Nab** (280 feet), which may be rounded at low tide to Cayton Bay.

Primrose Valley *(Southcliffe)* or Mile Haven, one mile south of Filey, is a favourite camping and picnic spot.

Butlin's Holiday Camp lies to the east of the main Bridlington road. Non-residents are admitted 10–6 daily except Sats.

Hummanby *(White Swan),* a pleasant walk or drive of four miles, is situated at the foot of the Wolds and has become an agricultural and shopping centre of some importance.

Reighton, five miles south of Filey, has a church dating from the 12th century. There is good bathing at **Reighton Gap** *(car park, caravan site, refreshments).* Along the Flamborough road is **Speeton** where the church stands isolated in a field.

Folkton Brow. A good drive or walk westward of seven miles via **Muston.** There is a long barrow on Folkton Wold.

Sledmere House *(not Mons and Fris)* situated on one of the highest parts of the Wolds, is the seat of Sir Richard Sykes, Bart. The Georgian house was built in 1751.

Kirkham Priory *(daily)* was a house of Augustinian canons. The remains include a fine Decorated gateway, part of the cloister and fragments of the church.

Castle Howard *(Easter–Oct., except Mons and Fris).* Magnificent mansion by Sir John Vanbrugh with tapestries, pictures and furniture. Lake in park (bathing and fishing).

Malton is a market town on the west bank of the *Derwent.* At **Old Malton,** the church incorporates part of a former Gilbertine priory.

Scarborough

Bathing.—Good firm sandy beach. Three bathing pools.

Distances.—Bridlington, 18; Castle Howard, 27; Filey, 7; Pickering, 18; Rievaulx Abbey, 34; Robin Hood's Bay, 14; Whitby, 21; London, 230.

Early Closing.—Wednesday.

Entertainments.—*Library Theatre* (plays); *Open-Air Theatre* (shows); *Floral Hall, Futurist* and *Spa Theatre* (variety); Peasholm Park (bands); *Spa Ocean Room* (dancing).

Hotels.—*Royal, Grand, Crown, Park Manor, Prince of Wales, Castle, Villa Esplanade, Bedford,* *Granville* and many others.

Museums.—*Scarborough Museum of Regional Archæology;* Museum Terrace. *Natural History Museum;* The Crescent. *St. Thomas's Museum;* East Sandgate.

Population.—43,061.

Post Office.—Aberdeen Walk.

Sports.—Angling and water ski-ing at the Mere, boating, bowls, putting, tennis. *South Cliff Golf Club,* Oliver's Mount. *North Cliff Golf Club,* North Bay. Regatta (Aug.).

Scarborough, one of the most popular resorts in the north of England, has a fine situation on slopes rising gently from the sea enclosed north and south by high cliffs. The South Cliff area is a highly favoured residential quarter with many hotels and boarding houses. Westborough, the street in which the Central Station stands is, with its continuations and the streets leading from it, the principal business quarter of the town. Half a mile down Westborough, Newborough and Eastborough is the harbour above which nestles the picturesque Old Town, the Scarborough of history and the home of the fishers and boatmen. Above stands the ancient castle ruins on a promontory beyond which is North Cliff with its gardens, hotels and holiday amenities. The town owes its popularity in great part to its saline and mineral springs discovered in 1620. Though the waters are no longer dispensed the **Spa** buildings include a Grand Hall, theatre, ballroom and other facilities for pleasure. The sands are clear and firm and provide good bathing and opportunities for beach games.

St. Mary's Church stands on a tongue of land separating South Bay from the north side. Most of the present structure is a rebuilding of 1669. The church is unique in England for the row of chantry chapels on the south side. **St. Peter's Roman Catholic Church** has some fine stained glass. **Northstead Manor Gardens** are beautifully laid out and there is an *Open-Air Theatre, Marineland* and *Zoo*.

The Castle *(daily, fee)* stands on a promontory nearly 300 feet above the sea. The fosse or moat which cuts off the height from the mainland is very deep and has beyond it, as an extra protection, the castle dike, a ridge formed of material thrown up when the moat was dug. The remains of the once noble pile are few, the tall battered Norman keep being the only remnant of consequence.

Oliver's Mount is the prominent hill overlooking the southern part of the town, and is distinguished by the impressive stone obelisk which represents Scarborough's tribute to those who fell in the World Wars. On the slopes is a motor-cycle circuit (road racing competitions in June and Sept.).

The **Mere,** south of the town, is a popular place for picnics, boating and fishing.

At the end of North Bay Promenade is **Scalby Mills** with a narrow glen with rugged boulders and steep banks between which a beck tumbles to the rocky shore.

Cloughton is a pleasant village six miles north. **Cloughton Wyke** is a pretty shingly inlet reached by a path from the high cliff surrounding the Wyke. At **Hulleys** about a mile NNW of Cloughton, is a "stone circle" believed remains of an early British smithy. **Hayburn Wyke** is popular for picnics. A steep sticky path leads down to a stony beach backed by cliffs.

Scarborough to Pickering and Helmsley. The road is via Falsgrave and Stepney Hill and in five miles to **Ayton,** where the *Derwent* is crossed at the south end of *Forge Valley* with a glimpse of the ruins of Ayton Castle on the right. Beyond **Hutton Bushel** and **Wykeham** is **Brompton** the native place of Mary Hutchinson, wife of William Wordsworth. Next comes *Snainton* in fruit-growing country. Snainton Church is Victorian, but still has its Norman lychgate from the original building. From Snainton a road by the inn leads into **Troutsdale** passing *Cockmoor Dikes* a series of earthworks with date so far undetermined. About a mile along the Pickering road is **Ebberston** where the church dates from Norman times. **Ebberston Hall** *(Easter–Sept., Sats and Suns)* is an elegant small villa built in 1718 in Palladian style to the designs of Colin Campbell. Beyond Ebberston is the old village of **Allerston,** then **Wilton** beyond which there is a descent into charming **Thornton Dale.** The village is an increasingly popular centre for walking and cycling. The Market Cross on the green is probably over 600 years old. The road to the right at the cross roads leads via Saltersgate to Whitby passing the *Fylingdales Early Warning Station* high on the moors. The church at **Ellerburn** contains both Saxon and Norman work.

Pickering (Pop.: 4,500. Hotel: *Forest and Vale*) stands at the head of the Vale of Pickering, a remarkably flat tract stretching 30 miles from east to west.

Pickering Church is of interest to American visitors for in the sanctuary is a memorial to Walter Hines Page, unveiled in 1924 by William Kellogg (author of the "Kellogg Pact"): this and another brass together commemorate the wartime association of Great Britain and America in 1917. The panelling in the chancel was given by Mrs. Page and members of another famous family associated with the American Embassy—that of Choate. The piece of old panelling is a memorial to Henry Ware Clarke, an American of Yorkshire origin who was killed at Cantigny in 1918. The church also contains an old memorial tablet in commemoration of two surveyors named King, both of Pickering, who helped to plan the City of Washington.

The Castle *(daily, fee)*, north of the town, is an attractive relic of great historical interest. The older parts date from the 12th century. The circle of walls is complete with three towers. Within the wards is the Keep (on a fine motte), chapel and traces of the hall.

Westward from Pickering are the villages of **Middleton, Aislaby, Wrelton** and **Sinnington.**
From the latter a branch road leads off right to **Cropton,** birthplace of William Scoresby the Arctic explorer, and **Lastingham** *(Blacksmith's Arms)* principally visited for the church where the crypt is unique in England with chancel, nave and side aisles. **Hutton-le-Hole,** a mile west, was a centre of the early Quakers. From here the moors to the north are easily gained and there are some splendid panoramas to be seen from Blakey Ridge. This road rises to 1,350 feet where it meets the road from Rosedale. Near the junction stand the two ancient stone *Ralph Crosses.* An old custom required a few coins to be left in the hollow at the top of one cross for travellers. South of Lastingham is **Appleton-le-Moors.** Its church is a good example of ornate Victorian Gothic.
From **Sinnington** the main road continues into **Kirby Moorside,** which once had two castles of which no trace remains.
Helmsley is a pretty little town on the *Rye* with a few old houses, ruins of a fine castle and an ancient church. Three miles north-west is Rievaulx Abbey (q.v.).
Southward of Helmsley is picturesque wooded country. **Hovingham Spa** is one of the prettiest villages in Ryedale. The church has a fine Saxon tower, Norman work and some early carvings. **Hovingham Hall** *(occasionally open)* built in 1760 is the seat of Sir William Worsley, Bt. Beyond **Slingsby** of a single street and the shell of an uncompleted castle, the main York road back to Scarborough is joined at **Malton.**

Ravenscar *(Raven Hall)* stands on a plateau 600 feet above sea level and commands a vast panorama of moorland, cliff and sea. Golf, tennis, bowls, fishing, riding, putting, dancing, and an excellent swimming pool are available. Several good walks include that to **Tan Beck,** a miniature glen.
Robin Hood's Bay (Pop.: 1,200. Hotels: *Victoria, Grosvenor*) 14 miles from Scarborough and seven from Whitby, nestles in a stream-cut ravine at a point where the cliffs drop to their lowest, about 100 feet. In the background there is a steep rise of several hundred feet to the Fylingdales moors. By the slipway to the beach are the *Marine Biological Laboratories* of the University of Leeds.

Whitby

Bathing.—A three-mile stretch of gently sloping sands. Pool near Happy Valley.
Distances.—Goathland, 9; Grosmont, 7; Pickering, 21; Ravenscar, 10; Robin Hood's Bay, 7; Scarborough, 21; York, 48; London, 245.
Early Closing.—Wednesday.
Hotels.—*Royal, Metropole, Daneholm, Kirby's, Saxonville, Marvic, Riviera, George, Plough,* *Beach Cliff, Albany,* and many others.
Library.—Station Square.
Museum & Art Gallery.—Pannet Park.
Population. 12,130.
Post Office.—Baxtergate.
Sports.—Sea and freshwater angling, boating, bowls, tennis. *Whitby Golf Club,* Upgang. Putting.

Picturesque Whitby lies on both banks of the *Esk* which, in its lower reaches, becomes the upper and lower harbour. The mouth of the river points due north, with the old town on the East Cliff and the modern town on the West Cliff. Whitby is full of tradition and history and is a highly popular holiday resort.
In the **Old Town,** the thoroughfare known as **Flowergate** is so ancient that Domesday Book refers to "Flore", and its name occurs in a charter granted in the time of Abbot Roger, whose rule was from 1222 to 1224. Flowergate leads to **St. Ann's Staith,** the Marine Parade and the West Pier. The Staith is the starting place of the motor, sailing and rowing boats and leads to the **Fish Market.** The Lighthouses on the East and West pier heads are quite dissimilar. West Pier Lighthouse can be visited, and gives fine views of the harbour and coastline. At

the landward end of the West Pier are the old Coastguard station and the Lifeboat House. Higher up the harbour on the east side, is housed the Motor Lifeboat *Mary Ann Hepworth,* which has a record of courageous and arduous service. Paved slopes give access, at low water, to the excellent sands. Near the top of Church Street are the famous **199 Steps** to the Abbey. The **Caedmon Memorial Cross** stands on a solid base of stone, and rises to a height of about 20 feet. On the front are four carved panels.

St. Mary's Church, a rather ugly ecclesiastical curiosity is Norman in origin. There are many quaint and interesting epitaphs in the churchyard.

Whitby Abbey was probably the third or fourth monastery erected on the site. The ruins comprise only the choir of the church, with its north aisle and transept, and parts of the north aisle and the west front. The prevailing style of the ruins is Early English. During the bombardment of Whitby in 1914, the west front of the Abbey was struck by a shell and badly damaged. Near the crumbling outer wall of the Abbey are the remains of a 15th-century cross.

The **Abbey House,** near the Abbey ruins, is supposed to occupy the site of the Abbot's House, and was formerly the Manor House of the Cholmleys. The Abbey stables are now used as a Youth Hostel.

Excursions and walks from Whitby include—

The **High Lighthouse** *(weekday afternoons)* on the cliff-edge two miles south.

To Sandsend and Mulgrave Woods (3 miles). Bathe with caution. Mulgrave Woods *(free).* The present castle is the seat of the Marquis of Normanby. There is little of the old castle remaining.

To Lythe and Goldsborough (4 miles). **Lythe** is a neat village about a mile from Sandsend. The restored church is of Norman date. **Goldsborough** is a tiny hamlet once the site of Roman signal stations.

To Ruswarp on the *Esk* about a mile above Whitby. The large market here is a collecting and grading centre. **Sneaton Castle** is the centre of an Anglican community. Services in the beautiful chapel are open to visitors.

To Sleights Bridge and Aislaby (3 miles). Via **Briggswath** with views over the moors, or by the Woodlands and Groves Hall.

To Falling Foss, a streamside walk from Sleights. The fall has a drop of 40 feet and has hollowed out a great basin (slippery after rain).

The Esk Valley. Grosmont at the junction of the *Esk* and its principal tributary is a good place for angling and the starting point of several fine walks. **Egton** stands about 500 feet above sea level. St. Hilda's Church was rebuilt in the 19th century but retains its Norman shape. There is good angling at **Glaisdale** and the hunting in the district is famous. The graceful Beggar's Bridge crosses the river near the station. **Lealholm** is very picturesque from which one can explore the peaceful Fryup Dale. **Danby** is the centre of a pleasant district. Danby Moor abounds in tumuli. **Danby Castle** dates from the reign of Edward I. Its kitchen with a massive fireplace is still in good repair. **Danby Beacon** (988 feet) gives fine views. **Castleton** has good fishing and shooting and some fine walks over the moors. The *Robin Hood Inn* here dates from 1671. On **Easby Moor** (1,064 feet) is an obelisk in memory of Captain Cook.

Goathland is situated high up among the moors about nine miles from Whitby in a region of waterfalls, woods, heather, ferns and mosses. There are several hotels and a parish room where social events are held. A footpath to **Mallyan Spout** (an easy 10 minutes' descent) starts from the *Mallyan Spout Hotel,* opposite the church. One can walk upstream to **Nelly Ayre Foss,** though most visitors prefer to go by road.

Midway between Goathland and Grosmont is **Beckhole** a tiny hamlet in the beautiful valley through which the *Murk Esk* winds.

Whitby to Saltburn. The coastline north of Whitby is as interesting as that to the south. At first the cliffs are low, but they gradually rise until at Kettleness they are 375 feet above the sea, the height increasing still further at *Boulby Cliff*, one of the loftiest points on the English coast.

Kettleness, five miles from Whitby, is a small hamlet in a wild windswept spot. A popular walk is round the bay to **Runswick** *(hotel)* perched on the rugged hillside in the most curious and higgledy-piggledy fashion. The "streets" are mere paths leading from one house to another. **Hinderwell** is a large straggling village. The chalice used in the church is dated *c.* 1420 and one of the oldest in England.

Staithes once an important fishing centre though only a few boats remain was the H.Q. of the Staithes Group of artists of whom Dame Laura Knight is the most famous. Captain Cook as a lad once served here in a drapery shop. The tiny bay is shut in on the north-west by the prominent **Nab** its extremity being a sheer precipice.

Saltburn-by-the-Sea *(Alexandra, Zetland, Queen)* is a popular holiday resort 19 miles along the coast from Whitby. The modern town occupies a commanding site on a steep cliff more than 100 feet above the sea. The prominent headland, *Huntcliff,* shuts out the east winds, while other hills protect it from the west. There are some good firm sands for games and bathing, and boating, golf and tennis. There is a miniature railway in Valley Gardens. The Pier is popular with anglers.

Skelton is a typical Cleveland village, two miles south, the site of two churches and a castle, seat of the Whartons.

Upleatham a little west has an ancient church, one of the smallest in England.

Guisborough, the ancient capital of Cleveland, has the ruins of a famous Priory founded early in the 12th century by Robert de Bruce, the second lord of Skelton. All that remains is a 12th-century gatehouse and the east end of the 14th-century church, a magnificent relic. Three miles south-west is **Roseberry Topping** (1,057 feet), the most notable though not the highest of the Cleveland Hills, that distinction belonging to Bottot or Burton Head (1,485 feet). The monument on the neighbouring height of Easby Moor is to Captain Cook. He was born at Marton, six miles west.

Marske occupies the centre of the bay between Saltburn and Redcar where the cliffs begin to descend to the level of the *Tees* estuarine region. The wide coast road here is separated from the beach by sandhills. Considerable residential development is taking place.

Redcar

Amusements. — Dancing in Pier Ballroom. Amusement park.

Beach. — Gently sloping sand. Covered swimming baths.

Distances. — Guisborough, 7; London, 256; Middlesborough, 8; Saltburn, 6; Thirsk, 36; Whitby, 26.

Early Closing. — Wednesday.

Hotels. — *Park, Coatham, Royal, Swan, Red Lion.*

Population. — 38,000.

Post Office. — Cleveland Street.

Races. — Meetings throughout summer.

Sports. — Bowls, golf, tennis. Good sea fishing.

The most northerly resort on the Yorkshire coast, Redcar is a favourite holiday ground for Northerners. It offers colour, music and gaiety to thousands of visitors. Redcar Race Week at the end of July is the most important of some 17 meetings between May and October. The course, noted for its straight mile, is one-and-a-quarter miles from the station. In a building on the promenade is the *Zetland* one of the oldest lifeboats in the world.

The Yorkshire Dales

The Yorkshire Dales, together with the fine centres Harrogate and Ripon, offer wonderful opportunities for an enjoyable holiday. Those in search of the picturesque will find everything to be desired in the way of mountain and valley, moorland and woodland, old-world villages in lovely settings. Those in search of antiquity will find no lack of interest. The strenuous walker will delight in the wind-swept fells. The whole area composes one of Britain's extensive National Parks, and the local inhabitants have for long been jealous to preserve and improve the amenities of their surroundings. The air is pure, healthful and bracing; the tempo of life does not move too swiftly. In this wide and various district there is everything the most demanding holiday-maker could desire.

Harrogate

Distances.—Bradford, 19; Doncaster, 41; Leeds, 16; London, 204; Ripon, 11; Thirsk, 22; York, 22.
Early Closing.—Wednesday.
Entertainments.—Cinemas, Royal Baths Assembly Rooms and Valley Gardens (concerts), Royal Hall (orchestral concerts). Annual Festival. Harrogate Theatre.

Hotels.—*Majestic, Cairn, Granby, Old Swan, St. George, Prospect, Eversfield, Green Park.* Many private hotels and boarding houses.
Population.—62,000.
Post Office.—Cambridge Road.
Sports.—Bowls, tennis. Golf: *Harrogate, Pannal* and *Oakdale* clubs, all 18 holes.

Harrogate stands on a tableland 400 feet above sea level almost midway between the Irish Sea and the North Sea, and is graced with healthful bracing air. In recent years it has become a popular conference and trade fair centre. High Harrogate stands on a plateau with wide views. Low Harrogate, the principal business quarter, is set on the western slope of the hill and in the valley at its foot. **The Stray** is a park-like common of 215 acres. The **Valley Gardens** are noted for their floral displays and there are sports facilities and entertainments. **Harlow Moor** is a large expanse of firs, gorse and heather. The **Royal Baths** building, where medicinal treatment and baths were formerly administered is now a complex of rooms available for functions and entertainment. Harrogate Waters (there are 88 wells within an area of two square miles) possess in various degrees the curative qualities of nearly every known spring in Europe. A valuable constituent of some of the waters is Barium. Another important constituent is Manganese. The former Pump Room now houses a **Museum of Antiquities** *(daily, free)*.

To Ripley. This pretty village lies four miles north of Harrogate. It consists principally of one broad street, prettily shaded with trees and a peaceful square with stocks and a market cross. The church (All Saints') was erected in the 15th century. It contains tombs and monuments of many members of the Ingilby family. In the churchyard is the pedestal of an ancient weeping cross said to date from the 2nd century.

Ripley Castle *(Suns and Bank Hols, June to Sept. Gardens additionally on Sats, fee)* is the seat of the Ingilbys. It is a Tudor building on the site of a feudal fortress, of which the 15th-century gateway and 16th-century tower may yet be seen.

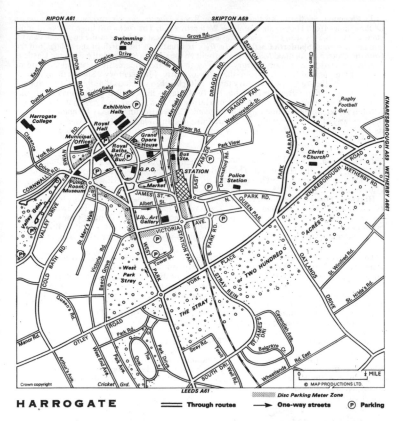

HARROGATE ▓▓▓ *Disc Parking Meter Zone* ▬▬ **Through routes** ➝ **One-way streets** Ⓟ **Parking**

Ripley to Knaresborough. There is a direct road from Ripley to **Knaresborough** (4 miles), passing near the village of **Scotton,** where Guy Fawkes resided in early life. Part of the house in which he lived is still to be seen. Away to the left is the **Scriven Park** portion of the Slingsby Estate. From the back entrance, by the keeper's lodge, are visible the trees and wall of Appleby Carr where fishing and skating are permitted in season.

The road between Ripley Castle and the Church descends to the river, and is continued as a bridle road to **Clint** and Hampsthwaite *(teas)* — a very pleasant walk. Hampsthwaite stands beside the *Nidd*, its church and old bridge close neighbours. Except for the tower, the church was almost entirely rebuilt in 1901, but it still contains some Norman and medieval relics.

To **Little Alms Cliff and Fewston.** Little Alms Cliff is an outcrop of gritstone commanding fine views. Across the moors is **Swinsty Reservoir** (Leeds Waterworks) the lake fringed with graceful trees beyond which are the green hills. On the brink of the reservoir is **Swinsty Hall,** a fine old building dating from the 16th century. **Fewston** is locally known as "the moving village", because at various times it has suffered subsidence. The Church has been twice burnt down, a fact which accounts for the absence of ancient monuments.

To Plumpton, Spofforth, Ribston. Plumpton Rocks *(fee to grounds, refreshments available)* lie three miles from Harrogate along the Wetherby road. The rocks are huge blocks of millstone grit but most visitors are less interested in its geological aspect as in the large lake nearby and pretty scenes. **Spofforth Castle** *(daily, free)* is situated to the north of the village, not far from the Church. A fortified Manor House built on the site of a Saxon Hall *c.* 700; the Castle is usually referred to as a 14th-century building though the undercroft, in excellent state of preservation, probably dates from the 12th or early 13th century. Spofforth village is dominated by the sturdy 14th-century tower of its **church,** a spacious building of Transitional Norman architecture. **Ribston Hall,** built in 1674, stands in beautiful grounds on the banks of the *Nidd* some six miles south-east of Harrogate. It was here in 1709 that the famous Ribston Pippin apple was first raised in England. The return journey may be made (footpath only) by way of Goldsborough and Knaresborough. In **Goldsborough** the chief features are its Early English Church, restored by Sir Gilbert Scott, and its **Hall,** of the period of Elizabeth I.

To Harewood. The name of the village has changed four times: Heraward, Whorewood, Harwood, and finally Harewood. The local people pronounce it "Harewood", whilst others pronounce it "Harwood". The **Church** *(All Saints')* is said to date from the time of Edward III.

Harewood House. *(House and gardens open daily, Easter to Sept. Suns only in Oct. In winter Park and gardens only, on Suns, fee.)* The seat of the Earls of Harewood, Harewood House was built in 1759–67, and is a good specimen of Corinthian architecture. From its elevated position in a park of great beauty (about 1,800 acres), designed by Capability Brown, the house commands a wide view. The pleasure grounds and gardens comprise nearly 150 acres.

To Wetherby and Boston Spa. From the east end of the Stray at Harrogate, Wetherby Road leads by Spofford to **Wetherby** a market town on the Great North Road. It was at one time held by the Knights Templars, and afterwards by the Hospitallers. A picturesque bridge spans the River *Wharfe.* There are several interesting inns including the *Swan and Talbot* both being old coaching halts. Boating is popular on the river. There is also a golf course and a steeplechase course.

Five miles south is **Boston Spa,** a pretty place on the *Wharfe,* which here falls gracefully over a weir. Boston became a spa by virtue of its saline spring. There is some good fishing in the river.

To the south-east of Boston Spa is **Clifford** where the modern church has been built in Norman style.

Two miles north of Boston Spa and three miles west of Wetherby, near the village of Walton, is the **National Lending Library for Science and Technology.** Opened in 1962, the library houses the largest loan collection in the United Kingdom of the world's scientific literature, and provides a postal loan service to U.K. organisations. There is a small reading-room.

To Cowthorpe and Marston Moor. Reached by an eastward turning from the Great North Road about three miles north of Wetherby is **Cowthorpe** where the church is of great interest. Built from the materials of an earlier church, the tower projects on both sides of the west wall with an outside supporting arch. Only one similar construction is known — at Baginton, Warwickshire. East of Cowthorpe is **Tockwith** near which is **Marston Moor,** scene of the famous battle fought July 2, 1644.

Nun Monkton, to the north of the Knaresborough–York road, has a large village green with a Maypole. The beautiful little church is a gem of the Transitional and Early English periods.

To Knaresborough. Knaresborough *(Commercial, Board Inn, Crown)* stands on the summit of a hill overlooking the *Nidd* which at this spot runs through a romantic glen and beneath precipitous rocks. The town is noted for its linen manufacture while visitors are attracted by its natural charms and historical associations.

The **Castle** *(daily, Easter–Oct., fee)* is now only a fragmentary keep and some isolated piles of weatherworn masonry among which are bowling and putting greens. The Church is old and spacious mainly Early English and Perpendicular. In the grounds of Conyngham Hall is the town's zoo.

Ripon

Distances.—Fountains Abbey, 3; Studley, 3; Newby Park, 4; Aldborough, 7; Ripley, 7; Brimham Rocks, 9.
Early Closing.—Wednesday.
Hotels.—*Spa, Unicorn, Black Bull, Studley Royal,*

Station.
Population.—11,110.
Post Office.—Old Market Place.
Racecourse.—York Road.
Sport.—Tennis, bowls and golf.

Ripon is a pleasantly quiet and well-ordered city, occupying a beautiful site, 11 miles north of Harrogate, and 23 north-west of York. It stands 80–100 feet above sea-level close to the spot where the *Skell* and the *Laver* unite with the *Ure*. Ripon resembles other ancient towns in having narrow streets. The oldest portions of the city are probably those forming **Stonebridgegate** and **Allhallowgate**, both having been close to the monastery around which the city grew. The city, locally claimed to be the second oldest in England, was incorporated in the reign of Alfred the Great, 886. The still-existing Wakeman's horn blown each evening at the Market Cross and in front of the Mayor's residence, was presented in token of the charter. The chief magistrate was styled "Wakeman", (Wakeman = Watchman) and associated with him were twelve Aldermen and 36 assistants. The last wakeman, Hugh Ripley, a certain "merchant and mercer", was nominated by the Crown as the first Mayor, who was appointed in 1604, in accordance with the terms of a charter granted by James I.

The Wakeman's House, in the south-west corner of the Market Place, is a very interesting building (13th century) furnished in the 16th-century style. At the rear (entrance through the café) is a small *Folk Museum.*

In the spacious **Market Place** is a 90-foot high Market Cross, erected in 1780.

Ripon Cathedral. The Cathedral is dedicated to SS. Peter and Wilfrid, and is in various styles of architecture, from Saxon to Late Perpendicular. It is constructed of millstone grit, with magnesian limestone dressings, and consists of a nave and choir, with aisles, transepts, with an eastern aisle formerly divided into chantries, a square central tower (or lantern), and two others at the west end, all of the same height (121 feet). An apsidal building, on the south of the choir, serves as a Chapter House and Vestry, and over it is a Lady-loft. There is a Saxon Crypt, under the lantern, and an Undercroft below the Chapter House; the latter was for ages used as a charnel house, but the bones were re-interred in the graveyard in 1865. The Cathedral is 270 feet long internally. The nave is 87 feet wide and over 90 feet high, being exceeded in this direction by Liverpool Cathedral, Westminster Abbey, and York Minster alone.

Historical Note.—The Cathedral originated from the monastery founded by Eata, Abbot of Melrose, in 657. For only four years did the Scottish monks occupy the building erected. About the year 669 Bishop Wilfrid began to erect a new monastery, the foundations being laid some 200 yards from the old building. Of this structure the crypt remains, but otherwise little is known of it except that it was of wrought stone, whereas Eata's was of wood.

A few years later, Wilfrid, having lost the Royal favour, was deposed, and his enormous diocese was divided into three sees of Hexham, York, and Lindsay. Subsequently another diocese was formed, and of this Ripon was made the cathedral town. In 686 a new sovereign recombined the sees of York and Ripon, and made Wilfrid bishop of the reformed diocese. Eleven-and-a-half centuries passed before there was again a Bishop of Ripon. The first was Eadhead (681 to 686), the next was Charles Thomas Longley (1836 to 1856), afterwards Bishop of Durham, then Archbishop of York, and finally Archbishop of Canterbury.

The monastery was destroyed by fire by King Eadred, Athelstan's brother and successor, during his devastation of the North, in consequence of a rebellion aided by the Archbishop of York. It is said to have been rebuilt a few years later either by the Archbishop of Canterbury or the Archbishop of York, and then, in the years that preceded the Norman Conquest, the monastery was converted into a college of secular canons.

Most probably ruin once more fell upon the minster when William laid desolate the land between the *Humber* and the *Tees*, for in Domesday Book "waste" is the description of the site of Ripon.

The facts respecting the earliest restoration of the minster are unknown, but south of the choir is Norman work, which is believed to be due either to the first Norman Archbishop, Thomas of Bayeux (1070–1100), or to Archbishop Thurstan (1114–1141). With the exception of the Saxon crypt and the Norman portion to which reference has just been made, the church was rebuilt by Archbishop Roger de Pont l'Evêque

(1154–1181), and of his work there still remain the two transepts, half the central tower, and portions of the nave and choir.

Passing over the various alterations and additions made during a period of between six and seven centuries, we come to the year 1829, when restorative works were begun under the direction of Blore. From 1862 to 1870 a much more extensive restoration was entrusted to Sir G. Gilbert Scott. In 1956 a major restoration was begun and still continues. In 1836 the diocese of Ripon was re-created out of portions of the sees of York and Chester, and Ripon Minster became the new cathedral.

Also of interest in Ripon are the **Old Deanery** erected about 1625, and now a hotel; **St. Agnes Lodge,** said to date from the time of Henry VII, which claims to have received Mary Queen of Scots, on her way from Bolton Castle to Tutbury, and the remains of **St. Anne's Chapel** in High Saint Agnesgate, dating from the 15th century.

Adjoining the chapel is **Thorpe Prebend House** built at the beginning of the 17th century which contains fine panelling and a noteworthy staircase.

To Brimham Rocks *(daily, fee, Tea House),* situated off the Pateley Bridge road six-and-a-half miles from Ripon. The rocks are huge masses 200, 300, 400 and even 500 tons in weight. They are of every conceivable shape.

To Boroughbridge and Aldborough. Boroughbridge *(Three Arrows, Crown, Three Greyhounds)* is prettily situated on the *Ure,* six miles south-east of Ripon. There is good fishing in the *Ure* and its tributaries, and also boating. **The Devil's Arrows** are three great monoliths in the fields to the west of the town. **Aldborough** was once a town dating from the time of the Britons, who named it *Iseur.* It is a quiet, charming village, with a maypole on a spacious green, pleasant houses and old church. Many excavations have been made disclosing foundations of walls and bastions.

To Newby Hall. The Hall is situated on the north bank of the *Ure,* about four miles south-east of Ripon. **Newby Hall** *(Weds, Thurs, Sats, Suns and Bank Hols, and Tues, Easter–Oct., fee)* is one of the most famous Adam houses in England standing in 40 acres of grounds. The house contains a wealth of beautiful objects including fine classical statuary and Gobelin tapestries.

To Markenfield Hall. This fine 14th-century mansion *(Mons, May–Sept., fee)* lies just off the Harrogate road three miles south of Ripon. The Hall is surrounded by a moat.

To West Tanfield, a picturesque village beside the *Ure,* six miles by road (bus services) north-west of Ripon. The Church, which stands near the scanty remains of the Castle, was originally a Norman structure, but its architectural features are of the Perpendicular style.

To Masham, Jervaulx and Middleham. Masham *(Kings Head)* 10 miles north-west of Ripon is a pleasant little town (golf, fishing). The large Market Place, even larger than that of Ripon, has a venerable cross in the centre. **Jervaulx Abbey** *(daily, fee)* (3 miles): Apart from a few pillar-bases and the lower part of the walls the church is practically non-existent, but there are two altars. The remains of the Chapter House are entered by a doorway flanked by two round-headed windows. There are considerable remains of the domestic buildings.

Middleham Castle *(daily, fee)* was founded in the Norman period by Robert Fitzrandolph, but in the 13th century passed by marriage to the great Neville family. Its destruction was ordered in 1646 by a Parliamentary Committee sitting at York.

Studley and Fountains Abbey. A very beautiful approach to the Abbey is by way of Studley Deer Park to the gates of the Abbey Grounds. From these the path continues via ornamental lakes, temples, statuary, lawns and trees to the Abbey itself. From the lodge gates, around which cluster the few cottages forming the village of **Studley Roger,** the splendid avenue of beautiful limes leads to **Studley Church** about a mile distant and situated on the highest ground in the park. The church was built by the first Marchioness of Ripon in 1871, in memory of her brother killed in Greece.

Fountains Abbey *(standard hours, fee)*, a Cistercian foundation of the early 12th century, is the most extensive monastic ruin in England. The plan of the secular buildings can be clearly traced. The church is Transition Norman and Early English in style with a Perpendicular tower and an additional transept at the east end in which is the beautiful Chapel of Nine Altars. The monastic buildings include the Cloister, Chapter House, Refectory, Buttery, Monks' Warming House, Kitchen and Infirmary.

Fountains Hall *(fee)* is a well-preserved Jacobean mansion.

How Hill lies a mile south of the Abbey. Here the monks had a watch tower and chapel, connected by tunnel to the Abbey.

Upper Nidderdale

About 14 miles from Harrogate is **Pateley Bridge** *(Crown, Harefield Hall)* a popular centre for walking and cycling. "Pateley" derives from "pate" the local term for badger and "ley" a field. The church was built in 1827. Over the bridge over the *Nidd* is **Bridgehousegate,** part of Bewerley parish.

Ravensgill is a beautiful gorge. Interesting near at hand are the **Stump Cross Stalactite Caverns.** The road past the entrance ascends to Hebden where a lane leads to **Hebden Ghyll.** From Hebden to Grassington is less than two miles. Upper Nidderdale comprises Stonebeck Down, Stonebeck Up and Fountains Earth and bears little resemblance to the other dales.

Wath stands near the foot of **Gouthwaite Reservoir;** at its head is **Ramsgill,** birthplace of the murderer Eugene Aram. Near the hamlet of Stean, at the head of How Stean Gorge, are **Blayshaw Bents,** or Crags, which rise to 1,100 feet above sea-level. The **Calder Hills,** in the neighbourhood, are large heaps of slag, the refuse of ironworks which existed in medieval days. Eight miles from Pateley Bridge is **Lofthouse** *(Crown)* from where a steep and narrow road leads over the fells to Masham and on through Wensleydale. Just beyond Lofthouse is **How Stean** *(fee)* a narrow impressive gorge separating the two divisions of Nidderdale.

From Lofthouse a steep and twisting road leads in one mile to picturesque **Middlesmoor.** The head of the vale is surrounded on three sides by lofty mountains, the two most prominent being **Great** and **Little Whernside.** The area contains caves and potholes, such as Manchester Hole and Goyden Pot. Only experienced cavers should attempt exploration as there is a danger of flooding.

Wharfedale

Wharfedale and especially that part of it above Ilkley is the finest of the dales displaying great beauty and variety of scenery.

Otley is an ancient town with busy printing machinery works. Overlooking the town is the steep **Chevin** giving fine views.

Ilkley (Pop.: 22,000. Hotels: *Craiglands, Stoney Lea, Troutbeck,* etc.) stands on wooded slopes on both sides of the *Wharfe.* It is a prosperous holiday centre with clean bracing air. There are attractive walks to **Hebers Ghyll,** the **Cow and Calf Rocks** *(views)*, **Panorama Rocks** and to **Burley-in-Wharfedale.**

Ilkley to Bolton Abbey. Buses run between Ilkley and Bolton Abbey. There is a road on either side of the *Wharfe.* That through Addingham is the busier, and between Addingham and Bolton Bridge there are lovely views across the river of well-wooded country rising to the moors. The road *via* Beamsley is prettier in itself and has some nice glimpses of the river through the trees; but motorists will find it narrow and winding.

Bolton Abbey, or Priory, was founded on its present site in 1151. While most of it is in ruins enough remains to evoke memories of its former glory. The nave is Early English and is in use as the parish church. The Choir now in ruins was originally of late Norman structure. It and the south transept were rebuilt in the 14th century. To the west of the church is **Bolton Hall,** formerly the gateway of the Priory. To the east is the *Wharfe,* here crossed by a footbridge which has superseded the nearby *Stepping Stones,* an ancient causeway. On the opposite side of the river is a high ridge of moorland known as the *Hill of the Standard.*

Bolton Woods *(daily, fee)* are pretty. Beyond the *Cavendish Pavilion* is the **Strid,** a narrow chasm from four to five feet across through which the *Wharfe* rushes violently, and traditionally the site of the death of the "Boy of Egremond" and of the legend of the "White Horse of Wharfedale" said to rise from the river before the occurence of a fatal accident.

At **Bardon Bridge** is Bardon Tower originally one of six square towers occupied by keepers of the once vast forest in this part of Wharfedale. The tower and the old Chapel attached is now a ruin.

Burnsall *(Red Lion, Fell)* is a popular centre for fishing and boating with a noteworthy church with an old Norse font and, in the churchyard, some old stocks. From Burnsall it is but a few miles to—

Grassington *(Wilsons Arms, Devonshire)* a large village on a hillside sloping down to the north-east bank of the *Wharfe.*

Kettlewell *(Race Horses, Blue Bell, King's Head)* is a grey, quiet self-contained village situated in a fine part of Upper Wharfedale at the foot of **Great Whernside** (2,310 feet). From Kettlewell there are good walks to **Middleham** and **Leyburn,** to **Aysgarth, Bainbridge** and **Hawes** and to **Arncliffe** and **Litton.** From Arncliffe there is a hilly walk over the moors to **Malham.**

Skipton and Airedale

Skipton is regarded by many as the gateway to the Dales and the first town in Airedale. It is a busy market town and headquarters of many of the activities of the Dales, including the Craven Pot-holing Club. The Church is famous for its roof, constructed in the time of Richard III, for its beautiful screen, and for the emblazoned tombs of the Earls of Cumberland. **Skipton Castle** *(daily, fee)* stands on a rocky eminence and is a fine example of a fully-roofed massive medieval fortress.

Rylstone is a pretty village on the Grassington road.

Malham is an upland village set among some of the most remarkable rock scenery in Yorkshire. **Malham Cove** is a great limestone amphitheatre with 300-foot walls. **Gordale Scar** is equally impressive especially after rain when the waterfall of Gordale Beck is in full spate. The large lake of **Malham Tarn** is three miles north of the village.

Settle *(Golden Lion, Falcon, Royal Oak)* is picturesquely placed on the *Ribble* and under a limestone scar. The curiously-named town of **Giggleswick** adjoins on the west. Here is a well-known school and to the west the striking *Giggleswick Scar.* The Langcliffe road continues through **Horton-in-Ribblesdale. Clapham** midway between Settle and Ingleton is well-placed at the foot of **Ingleborough** (2,373 feet). In Ingleborough Cave are magnificent stalactite formations.

Wensleydale

The characteristics of the dale are verdure and gracefulness. The valley is that of the *Ure* and the dale takes its name from the little town of Wensley near the foot of the dale; further up are Bainbridge and Aysgarth and at the head, Hawes.

Leyburn *(Bolton Arms, Golden Lion)* is a small town spread out along a steep hill with fine views. The most noticeable feature is *The Shawl* a lofty terrace behind the town.

Wensley, a pretty townlet, is of great antiquity and once an important market centre. The church has many interesting details including a carved screen from Easby Abbey.

Bolton Castle *(fee)* was built in the days of Richard II. The ruins have been partly renovated.

At **Aysgarth** *(George and Dragon)* the river is broken by a series of cataracts well seen from a path by the old bridge. Near the falls is the church with an interesting rood-screen.

Askrigg *(King's Arms)*, five miles west, has an old cross and a bull ring. *Mill Gill Beck* which here joins the *Ure* has two pretty falls.

Bainbridge *(Rose and Crown)* south of the dale is an attractive village around a pleasant green in which are preserved the old stocks. An old custom of sounding a horn at 9 p.m. still prevails.

Hawes *(White Hart, Fountain)* is a quiet grey town 850 feet above sea-level chiefly remarkable for being a market town so far up the head of a dale set amidst the fells. A mile along the Sedbergh road is Hardraw with **Hardraw Force** the highest unbroken fall in Great Britain.

Ingleton *(Ingleborough, Bridge, Wheatsheaf)* is known far and wide for its falls and caves. The falls are situated on the *Twiss* and the *Doe* or Dale Beck which converge here. The **Pecca Falls, Thornton Force** and the **Beezley Falls** are all notable. The limestone of the district is riddled with caves and potholes—caves containing vertical passages and accessible only from above. Weathercote Cave at **Chapel-le-Dale** is open and well worth a visit.

Swaledale

Swaledale is the remotest and wildest of the Yorkshire Dales. The hills on both sides hem it in closely and woods abound. **Catterick** is famous for its military training camp.

Richmond (Pop.: 7,500. Hotels: *King's Head, Fleece, Le Chateau, Richmond*) is one of the most strikingly situated towns in Britain being built on a rock around the base of which the *Swale* forms alternate pool and eddy. With its spacious cobbled Market Place, Norman Church, Castle, Grey Friars Tower, remains of town walls, ancient wynds and alleys it is a picturesque yet busy town. The original **Castle** *(daily, fee)* was built in 1017. The keep is 109 feet high with walls 11 feet thick. **Trinity Church** is notable in having a shop let into the exterior wall. The Parish Church was extensively restored in 1860 by Sir Gilbert Scott. In Friars Wynd is the unique Georgian Theatre dating from 1788.

Down river is **Easby Abbey** *(daily, fee)* founded in 1155 for Praemonstratensian canons. The ruins are more beautiful in their situation than in themselves. The principal remains are of the Refectory and parts of the Infirmary.

Villages of interest in Swaledale are **Grinton, Reeth** at the foot of Arkengarthdale, **Feetham** and **Gunnerside. Muker** *(Farmer's Arms)* is an endearing little stone-built village at the junction of Cliff Beck with the *Swale* which makes some pretty falls.

Keld is a handful of houses in a pocket in the hillside at the meeting-point of Great Skeddale with Swaledale where the *Swale* begins to rush the gorge between *Kisdon* and *Rogan's Seat.* There is a Youth Hostel at Keld Lodge.

Four miles along the Brough road is **Tan Hill** where is one of the highest inns in England. The **Buttertubs Pass** to Hawes provides a glorious view over the head of Swaledale.

The North-East

This section covers the north-eastern counties of Northumberland, Durham, Tyne and Wear and part of Cleveland. Within this area are some of the best-known parts of England.

Durham is most famous for the magnificent cathedral and castle of its county town. It has its coal mines and its industrial regions, but it has also many places of great interest and beauty, not least the valleys of the Tees, the Wear and the Derwent, extending up to the wild moorlands of the Pennines.

Northumberland includes a small part of the coalfield, but apart from this it is one of the least spoilt and most sparsely populated counties. It is well worth visiting for its long, firm sands (the "lordly strand of Northumberland"), its splendid castles, its beautiful valleys, and the lonely mountainous moorlands of the Cheviot Hills, along the Scottish border. The county is crossed from side to side by that unique and fascinating fortification, the great wall of Hadrian.

DARLINGTON TO SUNDERLAND VIA STOCKTON AND HARTLEPOOL

Darlington

Distances.—Barnard Castle, 16; Bishop Auckland, 12; Durham, 19; Hexham, 45; London, 242; York, 48.
Early Closing.—Wednesday.

Hotels.—*King's Head, North Eastern, Imperial.*
Population.—85,890.
Post Office.—Northgate.

Darlington, on the Skerne, a tributary of the Tees, is a busy market and industrial town with large engineering works and many other manufactures. Its industrial growth was initiated by the opening, in 1825, by George Stephenson, of the Stockton & Darlington Railway, the first passenger railway in England. The No. 1 Locomotive, which drew the first train at a speed of up to 13 m.p.h., is displayed at Bank Top Station, south-east of the town centre. The Church of St. Cuthbert is an outstanding example of Early English architecture (1190–1220) with a spire added in the early 14th century, a solid stone rood-screen (unique in a parish church) and many other interesting features.

A167 (the York road) runs south to **Croft,** on the Yorkshire bank of the river Tees. Another road, leading east from the bridge, goes through **Hurworth** and **Neasham,** pretty villages on the Durham bank. It then takes a circuitous course to reach **Middleton St. George** *(Devonport),* with a charming street on a high bank above the river. Farther east is the new airport for Teesside (see below).

A67 leads east from Darlington via **Haughton-le-Skerne** (pronounce *Haw-ton*), which has an attractive village green characteristic of south Durham and a mainly Norman church with good 17th-century woodwork.

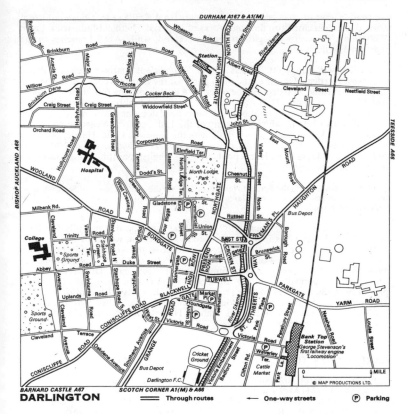

DARLINGTON

Through routes ◀— One-way streets Ⓟ Parking

Stockton-on-Tees *(Queen's, Vane Arms)* now in the new county of Cleveland is situated on the north bank of the tidal *Tees*. It is an industrial town and port that developed after the opening of the railway from Darlington in 1825. The exceptionally wide High Street, which contains the parish church of St. Thomas (1712) and the Town Hall of 1735, has been the scene of a market held regularly since 1310, the largest and oldest open-air market in the North.

A19 (the York road), running south to **Egglescliffe,** on the high bank of the Tees above Yarm (in Yorkshire), passes **Preston Hall** *(weekdays and Suns, Apr.-Sept.)* which contains a museum of arms and armour and of local history, including a section of the original line of the Stockton & Darlington Railway.

A19, to the north, is the main road for Hartlepool and Sunderland. **Norton,** now a suburb of Stockton, retains the nucleus of an 18th-century residential village and an interesting church with a Saxon tower. **Billingham,** to the east of

415

the road farther on, has grown in thirty years from a village to a busy industrial town, dependent chiefly on the huge works of Imperial Chemical Industries. From **Wolviston,** A19 keeps straight on for Sunderland, while A689 branches to the right for Hartlepool.

Hartlepool (Pop.: 97,110. Hotels: *Grand, Staincliffe* at Seaton Carew) combined with **West Hartlepool** is one of the main ports for the Durham coalfield and with a large timber trade. Hartlepool, the older part, dates from the foundation in about 640 of a Saxon convent, of which St. Hilda became abbess in 649. This was destroyed by the Vikings in about 800, but a headstone of that time is preserved in St. Hilda's Church, which is mainly of the 13th century. Near the coast is a section of the 13th-century Town Wall, with the Sandwell Gate. Hartlepool has a long sandy beach. The *Gray Museum and Art Gallery (admission 10 to 5.30, Thurs to 1; Suns 3 to 5),* in West Hartlepool, contains English paintings and collections illustrating local history.

A178 runs south along the shore of Hartlepool Bay, via the bathing resort of Seaton Carew, then returns to Stockton via **Port Clarence,** connected by transporter bridge across the Tees with Middlesbrough.

A1049 from Hartlepool joins A179 from West Hartlepool at the hillside village of **Hart,** which has a Saxon and later church. Farther on, we turn right to rejoin A19, a more attractive route than the coast road, cross the wooded valley of Castle Eden Dene, and keep west of the New Town of **Peterlee** *(Norseman),* founded in 1948 to serve the coal-mining community of south-east Durham. Beyond **Easington,** a hilltop village with a 13th-century church, the road skirts the inland part of **Seaham,** a coal-exporting port laid out in the early 19th century by John Dobson for the Marquess of Londonderry, the landowner. Lord Byron and Miss Milbanke were married in 1815 at Seaham Hall, to the north. A19 continues north to Sunderland.

DARLINGTON TO ALSTON VIA BARNARD CASTLE

From Darlington, the A67 road running west on the north side of the Tees, crosses the A1 (M) Motorway (no junction) to **Piercebridge** *(George)* an attractive village of low whitewashed and red-tiled cottages built round a green on the site of a fort on the Roman road of Dere Street, which ran from York to Corstopitum (near Corbridge). **Gainford,** charmingly situated on the Tees farther on, has a well-restored 13th century church. A67 goes on to Barnard Castle.

Barnard Castle *(King's Head, Montalbo.* Pop.: 5,360) is a delightful old market town with wide streets in a beautiful position on the steep north bank of the Tees, and is a good centre for exploring Teesdale. Charles Dickens stayed at the King's Head in the Market Place while on a visit to investigate conditions in the Yorkshire schools (described in *Nicholas Nickleby*). Below the octagonal Market House of 1747, the main street leads down past the 16th-century Blagroves House (now a restaurant) to the old bridge over the river.

The **Castle** *(daily)* on a high bluff above the Tees, was built by the Baliols after 1093, but was confiscated by the Crown in 1296 after the revolt of John Baliol, King of Scotland, the nominee of Edward I. The chief features are the walls and buildings round the inner ward or courtyard. These include the 12th–13th-century Round Tower, with a curious flat-domed vault, and the Great Chamber, which has a 15th-century window bearing the crest (a boar) of Richard III, who occupied the castle while Duke of Gloucester.

In Newgate, to the east of the town, is the **Bowes Museum** *(daily)* an ornate mansion in the style of a French château, built in 1869–92 for John Bowes and his French wife, the Countess of Montalbo. It now contains period rooms with their outstanding collections of works of art: porcelain, paintings, furniture, textiles, ecclesiastical art, and many other treasures. In the basement are rooms illustrating the rural life of Teesdale.

Two roads ascend the valley of the Tees above Barnard Castle. B6278, on the north (Durham) side, leads to **Eggleston,** from which it continues as a very hilly moorland road to Stanhope, in Weardale, while B6282 goes on up the valley. B6277, on the Yorkshire bank, runs via **Cotherstone,** a typical stone-built village in a pleasant position above the river, and **Romaldkirk,** a charming village scattered round its green, with the interesting mother-church of Teesdale, partly of the 12th century and containing an unusual 18th-century pulpit and reading-desk.

Both roads rejoin at **Middleton-in-Teesdale** *(Heather Brae, Cleveland Arms),* a small agricultural and quarrying town (once a lead-mining centre) on the Durham bank of the river, enclosed by moorlands. B6277 continues on the north bank to the *High Force Hotel,* below which, in a narrow defile, is **High Force,** the most impressive waterfall in England, the foaming Tees throwing itself over a precipitous basalt rock, over 70 feet high, into a charmingly wooded glen.

The road goes on through open moorland to **Langdon Beck,** a hamlet from which a cart-road (on the left) is extended by a footpath for $3\frac{1}{2}$ miles to **Caldron Snout,** the highest waterfall in England, where the Tees descends for some 100 feet by a series of cascades, in a wild ravine, at the junction of Durham, Yorkshire and Westmorland. A reservoir constructed above the fall has drowned many of the rare plants, such as Teesdale violets and spring gentians, for which the valley is noted, a relic of the Arctic tundra which once covered much of the North. B6277, leaving the upper part of Teesdale, ascends the Harwood Beck, among open, breezy moorlands, then crosses the watershed at **Yad Moss** (1,962 feet) before descending the upper region of the remote and secluded South Tyne valley for **Alston,** in Cumberland.

DARLINGTON TO HEXHAM VIA WEST AUCKLAND

From Darlington the A68 road, a useful and interesting cross-country route to upper Tynedale and Scotland, runs north-west, crossing the A1 (M) Motorway, beyond which A6072 branches right via **Shildon,** with collieries and railway-wagon works, to **Bishop Auckland.** A68 keeps on to **West Auckland,** a characteristic village with 17th-century houses round a large green, on the edge of the Durham coalfield.

A68 climbs above the valley of the Gaunless to **High Etherley,** where it is joined by A6073 (from Escomb), then descends over the deep valley of the Wear. On the right is seen **Witton Castle** *(daily, April-October, 10 to 7),* a 15th-century tower house extended in the 18th and 19th centuries, in a fine wooded park which is a favourite picnic area. **Witton-le-Wear,** a village attractively situated above the north bank of the river, has a medieval tower-house remodelled in the 17th century.

Our road climbs again, steeply above the valley, crossing the road from Durham to upper Weardale, into which there is a splendid view. Beyond **Tow Law,** a bleakly exposed market town with iron foundries, the road reaches its highest point (at 1,066 feet), with a wide view over the heather-covered Pennine moorlands to the west. The undulating road goes on to **Castleside,** the immense and unsightly steelworks at Consett standing out to the east. It then descends precipitously into the valley of the Derwent, which forms the boundary between Durham and Northumberland.

Ascending steeply again, A68 crosses, at **Carterway Heads,** the road from Newcastle to the upper Derwent valley, which opens to another lovely view on the left. From **Kilnpit Hill,** the road descends at length into the valley of the Tyne, across which there is a wide prospect to the country of Hadrian's Wall. At **Riding Mill** *(Broomhaugh House)* we turn left on A695, the road along the valley on the south side, join A69, coming across the river from **Corbridge,** of which there is a good view, and keep on the south bank to **Hexham.**

DARLINGTON TO DURHAM AND NEWCASTLE

A167, the former Great North Road, runs north from Darlington to the A1 (M) Motorway, beyond which it is continued by A1 to **Aycliffe,** on the Skerne, which has a Norman and Early English church with remains of Saxon crosses. Further on is the New Town of **Newton Aycliffe,** founded in 1947 and mainly serving a large industrial estate. Beyond **Rushyford** *(Eden Arms)* the road enters the Durham coalfield (whose atmosphere is much cleaner than formerly) and beyond **Croxdale** *(Bridge)* it descends to cross the wooded valley of the Wear.

About a mile farther on, A1050 branches to the right for **Durham,** but A1 keeps on, by-passing the city on the west via **Neville's Cross,** commemorating the battle of 1346 in which the invading Scots were roundly defeated and David II was taken prisoner. At **Framwellgate Moor** the Great North Road is joined by A177, coming from Durham, and the A1 goes on through a colliery district via **Pity Me,** where a road on the right descends over the Wear towards **Finchale Priory** *(daily)* founded in 1196 for Benedictines as a cell of Durham and charmingly situated on the bank of the rocky Wear. The remains, chiefly 13th–14th centuries, include the fine refectory and the prior's house. Farther on the main road keeps to the right to by-pass Chester-le-Street.

Chester-le-Street (Pop.: 19,980. Hotel: *Lambton Arms*) is a market and colliery town on the site of a Roman fort (hence its name). The monks of Lindisfarne (Holy Island), carrying the body of St. Cuthbert, settled here in 883, after eight years of wandering, and here it remained until the see was removed in 995 to Durham. The 13th–14th-century Church has a slender tower and spire, 169 feet high, with an unusual anchorite's cell attached to it. In the north aisle are fourteen effigies of the Lumley family, all but three of them made after 1594 for John, Lord Lumley.

Lumley Castle, to the east beyond the *Wear,* is a characteristic late-14th-century stronghold, with alterations made in 1721 by Sir John Vanbrugh, and is now occupied by Durham University. **Lambton Castle,** on the other bank of the river and north of the Sunderland road (A183), is a picturesque 19th-century mansion, formerly the seat of the Earl of Durham, but now a residential college for adult education.

Beyond Chester-le-Street we rejoin the A1, which goes on through the coal-mining district for **Gateshead** *(Five Bridges, Springfield,* at Low Fell, to the south), a large industrial town on the Tyne, opposite Newcastle, with many engineering and other works. St. Mary's Church, on the steep bank of the river, is partly of the 14th century and has notable 17th-century pews. The Shipley Art Gallery *(weekdays 10 to 6, Sundays 3 to 5),* near the Durham road towards Low Fell, is mainly notable for its British and Dutch marine paintings. The Great North Road crosses the river by the Tyne Bridge for Newcastle.

Durham

Boating.—On the *Wear*.
Distances.—Darlington, 19; Alston, 42; Hartlepool, 18; Hexham, 30; London, 260; Newcastle upon Tyne, 15; Sunderland, 13.
Early Closing.—Wednesday.
Entertainments.—Cinemas, ballroom.
Hotels.—*Royal County, Three Tuns, Neville's Cross,*

Neville's Cross; *Redhill,* Crossgate Moor.
Library.—South Street.
Market Day.—Saturday.
Population.—29,100.
Post Office.—Claypath.
Sports.—Golf, putting, bowls, tennis, ice rink, indoor swimming pool.

Durham is one of the most historic and interesting cities in England, the older part standing on the summit of a high peninsula almost enclosed within a loop of the *Wear*. Above the steep wooded banks rise, side by side, the imposing Norman cathedral and the gaunt castle of the powerful prince-bishops, who held sway over much of the North-East in the Middle Ages. Superb views of cathedral and castle are obtained from the railway station, high above the valley, from the wooded riverside walks known as The Banks, and from Framwellgate Bridge, built by Bishop Skirlaw about 1400, from which Silver Street ascends sharply to the Market Place.

Durham first developed round the cathedral established here in 995, when the bishop's see was transferred from Chester-le-Street. The bishop, as count palatine, held his own courts of law and was master in his own princedom, which extended at times as far as the Scottish Border. From as early as the Norman period Durham had this curiously double aspect: "half church of God, half castle 'gainst the Scot", in the words of the immortal Sir Walter. In 1832, Bishop Van Mildert gave up his princely revenue for the foundation of the University (the oldest in England except for Oxford and Cambridge), which still occupies the castle and houses in the narrow streets on the hilltop.

The **Castle** *(weekdays during first 3 weeks of April and July–Sept.; Mons, Weds and Sats in other weeks)* on the neck of the peninsula above the Market Place was founded by William the Conqueror. Much of the present building is early medieval, the work especially of Bishops Pudsey and Flambard. The most interesting features are the Great Hall (now the dining hall for University College students), the splendid Staircase built in 1662 for Bishop Cosin and ascending to Bishop Tunstall's 16th-century Gallery and Chapel, where a magnificent late-Norman doorway admits to the Bishop's Apartments. Higher up is the Norman Gallery of Bishop Pudsey, and on the ground floor is the remarkable Norman Chapel, the oldest part of the castle, built about 1072 for Pudsey. The medieval Keep, rising from its motte, was largely rebuilt after the castle was taken over by the University.

On the other side of the broad Palace Green soars the noble **Cathedral,** the church also of a Benedictine monastery founded in 1083, mostly built between 1093 and 1133, and the most splendid work of Norman architecture in Britain. The majestic nave was completed for Bishop Flambard; it has immense piers to the arcades, with striking incised ornamentation and zigzag moulding, and the high roof vaults include some of the oldest in England, raised before 1096. Practically the only additions to the Norman cathedral have been the beautiful Galilee Chapel, added in the late 12th century for Bishop Pudsey and the burial-place of the Venerable Bede (who died in 735 at Jarrow), the impressive 13th-century Chapel of the Nine Altars at the east end, and the great central tower, 218 feet high, rebuilt in the second half of the 15th century.

The interior has numerous features of interest. Among these may be mentioned Prior Castell's Clock (in the south transept), made about 1500 and recently well restored; the sumptuous 17th-century stalls of Bishop Cosin, in the choir; the 14th-century bishop's throne, said to be "the highest in Christendom", incorporating the tomb of Bishop Hatfield; and the magnificent stone altar screen made for John, Lord Neville about 1380 and attributed to Henry Yevele, architect of the naves of Westminster Abbey and Canterbury Cathedral. Behind the high altar still lies the body of St. Cuthbert though his shrine was destroyed in 1540. In the Cathedral Library, formerly the monks' dormitory, west of the cloister, are Northumbrian stone crosses, superb illuminated manuscripts, the restored wooden coffin in which St. Cuthbert was brought to Durham in 995, with the Saint's pectoral cross and stole.

DURHAM

Palace Green has some delightful 17th-century buildings, as well as a new Library and halls of residence of the University. The names of **North** and **South Bailey,** to the east, remind us that these were once part of the city's fortifications. Lined by attractive old houses, now mainly occupied by the University, they lead down to the fine **Prebends' Bridge,** over a peaceful reach of the *Wear.* **Elvet Bridge,** built for Bishop Pudsey in the 12th century, crosses the river to the suburb of **Elvet.** On Elvet Hill, farther south, are interesting new buildings for the University, among them the **Gulbenkian Museum** *(daily),* with rich collections of oriental art and archaeology.

The road from Durham to Stockton (A177) crosses the *Wear* to Shincliffe and goes on through **Sedgefield** *(Hardwick AArms),* a pleasant small market town which has a large green and a church of the 13th and 15th centuries containing excellent 17th-century woodwork.

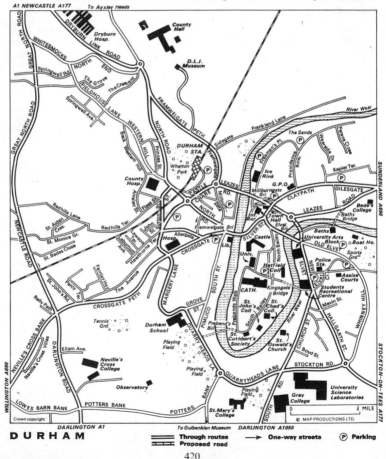

D U R H A M

≡ **Through routes**   ⟶ **One-way streets**   Ⓟ **Parking**
▨ **Proposed road**

420

A new open-air Museum is being established at Aykley Heads, near the road (A177) which ascends to Framwellgate Moor, on the Great North Road.

DURHAM TO SUNDERLAND VIA WASHINGTON

We leave Durham on the east by A690, from which the Hartlepool road (A181) diverges on the right in about a mile, passing **Sherburn Hospital,** which retains the 13th-century gatehouse of a hospital founded about 1181 by Bishop Pudsey. The Sunderland road goes on through a colliery district, passing (on the right) a road to **Pittington,** whose isolated church has a north arcade of about 1175 with unusual carving inspired by Durham Cathedral. Another road (on the left) descends to **Finchale Priory. Houghton-le-Spring** (pronounce *Haw-ton*), on the main road, has a fine 13th–14th-century church containing the tomb of Bernard Gilpin (died 1583), the "Apostle of the North", who was rector here.

An alternative route to Sunderland (A182; to the left), passes west of the prominent **Penshaw Monument,** erected in 1884 in memory of the 1st Earl of Durham, Governor-General of Canada, and crosses the *Wear* to **Washington,** a colliery town built round the nucleus of an old village and itself the centre of a New Town, designated in 1964. The 17th-century **Old Hall** *(daily, except Friday)* embodies parts of an early-medieval house, the home of the Washington family, ancestors of George Washington, and their descendants from 1181 to 1613. Restored in 1955, with American assistance, as a community centre, it contains old furniture and memorials of the first President of the United States.

B1289, turning to the right farther on, reaches the suburbs of Sunderland at **Hylton Castle** *(daily),* consisting of a huge tower-house of about 1400, with the arms of the Washingtons on the front, and a detached 15th-century chapel.

Sunderland (Pop.: 215,650. Hotels: *Grand, Palatine, Ashbrooke Park*), the largest place in Co. Durham, is a seaport and industrial town at the mouth of the *Wear,* famous for its shipbuilding yards and marine-engine works, though it has also glassworks and other important manufactures. A new Civic Centre was begun in 1966 to the designs of Sir Basil Spence. The fine Museum and Art Gallery *(daily),* in the Central Library facing Mowbray Park, contains Saxon glass found at Monkwearmouth, old Sunderland pottery and glass, and interesting ship models. **Monkwearmouth,** on the north side of the river, has a restored church preserving the porch, the tower and part of the nave of a monastic church founded in 674 by Benedict Biscop. The Venerable Bede entered the monastery in 680, at the age of seven, but later transferred to the sister house at Jarrow.

DURHAM TO BARNARD CASTLE VIA BISHOP AUCKLAND

This route follows the Darlington road (A1050, A1) across the *Wear* to Croxdale, then bears right on A6074 through **Spennymoor,** the centre of a colliery district. There is a wide view over the Wear valley to the north before A689 branches right for Bishop Auckland.

Bishop Auckland (Pop.: 34,780. Hotels: *Wear Valley, Castle*) is a market and industrial town at the junction of the *Gaunless* with the *Wear.* The wooded Bishop's Park, entered through a Gothic gatehouse of 1760, is open to the public, and from it there is a view of Auckland Castle, the country seat of the Bishops of Durham since the 12th century. The mansion is mainly of the 16th and 18th centuries, but the Gothic chapel was converted from a hall by Bishop Cosin, who was buried here in 1672.

Just over a mile south, on the Darlington road, is the large Early English church of **St. Andrew Auckland,** containing a Northumbrian cross of about 800 with remarkable carving.

From A688, traversing the main street of Bishop Auckland, A6073, coming from St. Andrew Auckland, goes on westward. In 1½ miles a road on the right descends to **Escomb,** a rebuilt village in the Wear valley, with one of the oldest and most complete Saxon churches in England. Built probably in the 7th century, partly with stones from the Roman fort at Binchester (north of Bishop Auckland), it was finely restored by Sir Albert Richardson, who also provided new furnishings.

A6073 ends on A68, by which we turn left to **West Auckland.** At the west end of the green, we branch right on A688 to pass the deer-park of **Raby Castle** *(Easter and May–Sept., Weds, Sats and Suns, 2 to 5 ; daily except Fris, in August),* one of the finest 14th-century castles in England, with splendid gatehouses and massive corner towers. The seat of the Neville family until 1626 and then of the Vanes, it was partly remodelled inside in the 19th century and has many fine paintings.

Staindrop, farther on, is a pleasant village with a long green shaded by trees. The interesting church, showing work from Saxon times to the 15th century, contains excellent 15th-century and later monuments of the Nevilles. A688 goes on to join A67 before reaching Barnard Castle.

DURHAM TO WEARDALE VIA TOW LAW

The best route from Durham to the beautiful upper valley of the *Wear* leaves the city on A690 to the west, crossing the A1 at Neville's Cross, then recrossing the *Wear* for **Brancepeth,** an attractive village with a massive Castle, the seat before 1569 of the Earls of Westmorland, a branch of the Neville family, but extensively rebuilt in the 19th century. In the grounds *(open)* is the 13th–15th-century church of St. Brandon, well worth visiting for its 14th–16th-century monuments of the Nevilles and its beautiful woodwork made for John Cosin, rector here from 1625 and later Bishop of Durham.

A690 goes to the colliery towns of Willington and Crook, but a more interesting, if hillier, route turns right on an unclassified road beyond Brancepeth, then right again on B6299 to join A68 before reaching **Tow Law.** From here B6297 keeps on to its junction with B6296, which descends sharply into Weardale at **Wolsingham,** a small town with some 16th–18th-century houses, at the beginning of the narrow upper part of the dale.

B6293 goes up Weardale to **Frosterley,** a village once famous for its marble, a black limestone full of fossils which is seen in the fonts of Durham Cathedral and many humbler churches. Farther on is **Stanhope** *(Phoenix),* the capital of Weardale, an old town with a good 13th-century church. A former lead-mining place, it is now the centre of a quarrying district, with cement works.

B6278, crossing the dale here, is an exhilarating but exceptionally hilly road connecting Teesdale at Barnard Castle with the Derwent Valley at Edmundbyers.

B6293 continues up the pastoral dale, among swelling moorlands, to **St. John's Chapel,** an attractive village employed mainly in quarrying, and thence to **Cowshill** *(hotel),* a remote hamlet near the quiet head of Weardale. From here B6293 climbs steeply up to the **Killhope Cross** (2,056 feet), the highest point reached by any main road in England, with extensive views of the Pennine moorlands towards Cross Fell, their highest summit before descending to **Alston,** in Cumberland. B6295, keeping to the right beyond Cowshill, ascends to a point over 1,850 feet up where it leaves County Durham for Northumberland. This road then drops down to **Allenheads,** at the head of East Allendale.

DURHAM TO HEXHAM VIA EBCHESTER

This interesting cross-country route leaves Durham on the north-west by A177 and A691, crossing the Great North Road and ascending the pleasant Browney Valley to **Lanchester,** an attractive village which has an interesting church, mainly of the 12th and 13th centuries, with Roman columns in the north arcade and a Roman altar in the porch. These came from the fort of *Longovicium* (on Dere Street), of which there are some remains near the Weardale road (B6296).

The Hexham road leaves the valley and climbs up to **Leadgate,** on the edge of the ironworking district around Consett. Here B6309 keeps straight on, following the course of the Roman road of Dere Street and descending steeply to **Ebchester,** in the beautifully wooded Derwent Valley, where we cross a road from New-castle. Hence the road ascends to the isolated village of **Whittonstall,** with wide view all round, before going down again west of the attractive valley of the Stocks-field Burn. **Stocksfield** is on the road (A695) along the south side of the Tyne Valley from Newcastle to Hexham, and opposite Bywell. We turn west and join the route from Darlington at **Riding Mill.**

Newcastle upon Tyne

Distances.—Alnwick, 34; Barnard Castle, 39; Dar-lington, 33; Durham, 15; Hexham, 20; Morpeth, 15; Stockton-upon-Tees, 34; Hartlepool, 29; London, 274.
Early Closing.—Wednesday.
Entertainment.—*Theatre Royal, Playhouse, People's Theatre.* Cinemas, dancing, concerts in City Hall.
Hotels.—*Royal Turk's Head, Royal Station, County, Swallow; Imperial, Embassy, Avon, Cairn,*

Northumbria, Sanderson (these six at Jesmond); *Gosforth Park,* and many others.
Post Office.—St. Nicholas Street.
Population.—221,400.
Sports.—Bowls in public parks. Tennis in parks and several clubs. The Northumberland County Tennis Ground is at Osborne Road. Golf at Town Moor and Gosforth. Horse Racing at Gosforth Park.

Newcastle upon Tyne, the principal city of North-East England, is a busy industrial place, famous for the export of coal and for its numerous heavy engineering works. It occupies a strategic position on the steep north bank of the Tyne, about 9 miles from its mouth. Newcastle is connected with Gateshead by several notable bridges over the river, including the **High Level Bridge** (1849) of Robert Stephenson, carrying both road and railway, the **Tyne Bridge** of 1928, which served as a "model" for the famous Sydney Harbour Bridge, and the **Swing Bridge** (1876) on the site of the original Roman bridge.

Newcastle occupies the site of a settlement *(Pons Ælius)* on the line of Hadrian's Wall, but the city owes its foundation to the building of a castle here by Robert Curthose, the eldest son of William of Normandy, while on his way back from an incursion to Scotland in 1080. The town suffered many times from the proximity of the Scots, but in 1644 it held out against them for ten weeks on behalf of Charles I. The centre of Newcastle was well laid out in the early 19th century in a series of fine streets and terraces by Richard Grainger, a speculative builder, with the assistance of John Dobson and other architects.

From the **Central Station,** an impressive building by Dobson (1850), Collingwood Street leads east towards the Tyne Bridge, passing the **Cathedral** (the seat of a bishop since 1882), mainly of the 14th century and formerly one of the largest parish churches in England. Its tower is crowned by a famous lantern spire raised in the 15th century and the earliest of its kind. From the cathedral, St. Nicholas Street leads south to the **Castle,** which consists of a fine 12th-century keep, built for Henry II, and the restored 13th-century Black Gate *(admission to* *both, weekdays 10 to 4 or 5, Mondays from 2),* containing interesting collections of antiquities.

Below the castle is the older part of the city, reached via The Side. Here, in **Sandhill,** are some picturesque houses and opposite is the 17th-century **Guildhall,** given a new front in 1796. On the hill further east is **All Saints' Church,** a classical church of the late 18th century containing the splendid German brass of Roger Thornton, who died in 1429. From The Side, Dean Street climbs steeply to the gracefully curving **Grey Street,** the finest part of the new town laid out by John Dobson.

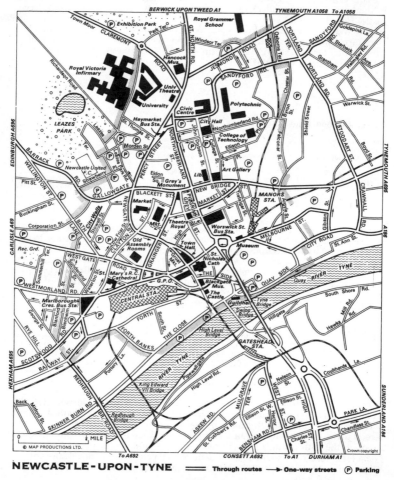

NEWCASTLE-UPON-TYNE ═══ **Through routes** ⟶ **One-way streets** Ⓟ **Parking**

To the north of the town centre are the new **Civic Centre** designed by George Kenyon and completed in 1969, and the buildings of the **University of Newcastle,** established in 1963, which include an excellent Museum of Antiquities, with outstanding Roman and Saxon collections, including finds from Hadrian's Wall. Farther north is the **Hancock Museum** of natural history, beyond which the Great North Road skirts the extensive **Town Moor** (the scene of a great fair in June) and passes the interesting **Museum of Science and Engineering.**

To the north-east, in the outer residential suburbs of the city, is the delightful wooded ravine of **Jesmond Dene,** presented to Newcastle by Lord Armstrong, the engineer.

NEWCASTLE TO SOUTH SHIELDS AND SUNDERLAND

This route lies almost wholly through an industrial region, but takes in some places of interest. It crosses the Tyne Bridge to Gateshead, then branches left on A184 to **Felling,** where the main road to Sunderland keeps straight on. A185, on the left again, goes through the shipbuilding and engineering towns of **Hebburn** and **Jarrow,** on the south bank of the Tyne. Beyond the latter is the parish church of St. Paul, embodying the original nave and an 11th-century tower of the famous monastic church founded in 685 by Benedict Biscop, of which the Venerable Bede was an inmate from the age of twelve until his death in 735, writing his famous *Ecclesiastical History* here. A new road tunnel leads under the Tyne from Jarrow to Howdon, east of Wallsend, while A185 goes on to South Shields.

South Shields (Pop.: 100,220. Hotels: *Sea, New Crown, Seahaven*) is a busy port and an industrial town at the mouth of the Tyne, the estuary of which is enclosed by the long South Pier. It has also a popular seaside resort with extensive sandy beaches and some attractive parks. On The Lawe, the low hill above the river, are the excavated remains of the Roman fort of *Arbeia (daily, Suns in May-Sept. only)*. The Central Museum in the main street contains a model of the first lifeboat, designed here in 1789 by William Woodhave.

A183 runs southward, reaching the shore at **Marsden,** in the bay of which is the precipitous *Marsden Rock,* now a bird sanctuary. The road goes on along the high cliffs via the attractive village of **Whitburn,** then descends to reach the outskirts of Sunderland at **Seaburn** *(hotel)*, which is extended south by **Roker** *(hotel)*. Both are favourite seaside resorts with wide sandy beaches and good bathing.

NEWCASTLE TO BLANCHLAND VIA EBCHESTER

The beginning of this very attractive route starts through the industrial west suburbs of Newcastle by A695, but after crossing the Tyne by Scotswood Bridge it bears left on A694 to ascend the richly wooded valley of the Derwent. On the south side of this, opposite **Rowlands Gill,** are the fine grounds of **Gibside,** a dismantled mansion of the 17th century, partly remodelled in 1805. The charming **Chapel** *(Easter-Sept., daily except Tues., Oct. and Mar. Weds, Sats, Suns, Nov.-Feb., Suns only)* designed in 1760 by James Paine and well restored by the National Trust, is linked by a long avenue with a prominent Column of Liberty, 140 feet high, built in 1757.

A694 continues through the wooded valley to **Ebchester,** whose church stands on the site of the Roman fort of *Vindomora* and contains a Roman altar. At **Shotley Bridge** *(Crown and Crossed Swords)* the Derwent is crossed by A691, climbing to **Carterway Heads,** on the road from Darlington to Hexham. We then descend (on B6278) to recross the Derwent for **Edmundbyers,** a typical moorland village round a large green. B6278 goes on over lofty heather-clad moors to Stanhope, while B6306 bears right, passing a new reservoir that has become a favourite sailing resort. This road crosses the Derwent again to Northumberland and **Blanchland,** an entrancing village built in the 18th century round a square that was once part of a Premonstratensian abbey founded in 1165 and is enclosed by a gatehouse of about 1500. The *Lord Crewe Arms Inn* here was formed out of 13th-century ruins, probably of the abbey guest house, and the parish church preserves the choir and north transept of the abbey church.

B6306, leaving the secluded upper valley of the Derwent, climbs northward across the moors before descending to **Hexham** over the beautiful Devil's Water. Above **Linnolds Bridge** here are the Hexham Levels, the site of a battle in 1464 in which the Lancastrians under Henry VI were severely beaten by the Yorkists under John Neville, later created Earl of Northumberland.

NEWCASTLE TO CARLISLE VIA HEXHAM

This, the main road from Newcastle to Carlisle (A69), keeps to the north side of the Tyne Valley at first, following the line of Hadrian's Wall as far as **Heddon-on-the-Wall,** where the first upstanding lengths of the wall can be seen. A69 goes on direct to Corbridge (*see* below), but a more interesting road descends on the left to **Wylam.** Hence the Tyne is followed upstream to **Ovingham** (pronounced *Ovin-jam*), which has a 13th-century church with a Saxon tower near which is buried Thomas Bewick (*d.* 1828), the famous engraver. **Prudhoe,** on the steep southern side of the river, has a ruined 12th–14th-century castle now under restoration. The riverside road continues to **Bywell,** charmingly situated on the Tyne, a "decayed" village with a 15th-century gatehouse-tower and two churches in adjoining churchyards, both mainly of the 13th century, though one has a fine Saxon tower. The road ascends away from the Tyne to regain A69 before it reaches Corbridge.

Corbridge *(Angel, Radcliffe House),* a pleasant small town on the north bank of the Tyne, was the capital of the Kingdom of Northumbria in the 8th century. In the churchyard is a 14th-century fortified priests' house of a type peculiar to Northumberland, while the church, mainly of the 13th century, has a Saxon tower above the porch at the west end. The tower arch is built with stones from *Corstopitum (daily from 9.30, Suns in winter from 2),* the considerable remains of which lie just to the west of the town. This was a depot for the legions on Hadrian's Wall and the excavations include a huge storehouse, one of the largest Roman buildings in Britain. The museum here contains a good collection of inscribed and sculptured stones, including the 3rd-century "Corbridge lion".

A69 crosses the Tyne by a stout 17th-century bridge and is joined by the road from Durham and Darlington before going over the Devil's Water below the ruins of **Dilston Castle,** once the seat of the Earls of Derwentwater, the last of whom was executed after the Jacobite rising of 1715. It then continues on the south bank to Hexham.

Hexham (Pop.: 9,710. Hotels: *Royal, Beaumont*) is a delightful old market town with a long main street and an unusual Market Hall of 1766. Overlooking this is the 14th-century Moot Hall (now a library), once the tower-house of the bailiff of the Archbishop of York, who was lord of the regality of Hexham. Beyond is the 14th-century Manor Office, the prison of the regality, the only one of its kind in England.

To the west of the Market Place rises the splendid Priory Church, a "text-book of Early English architecture", first built in the 7th century by St. Wilfrid, whose original crypt survives. From the south transept, which contains a Roman monument and a Saxon cross of the 8th century, rise the complete, if well-worn, night stairs which led from the dormitory of the Augustinian canons. In the beautiful choir are the bishop's stone chair of the Saxon cathedral, remarkable 15th-century chantry chapels, and numerous medieval paintings, some on the rood screen. The nave, destroyed by the Scots in 1296, was rebuilt in 1908.

From Hexham the rather secluded route to North Tynedale crosses the river as A6079, then ascends above the east bank of the North Tyne (with beautiful views) to **Wall** *(Hadrian)*, beyond which, on the right, is a stretch of the Roman wall. The road crosses the Military Road to **Chollerton,** whose church has a 12th-century arcade built of Roman columns and a font made out of a Roman altar. An unclassified road on the left here ascends North Tynedale via **Barrasford,** which stands opposite **Haughton Castle** (partly of the 13th and 14th centuries). Beyond **Chipchase Castle,** a mainly 18th-century house added to an earlier tower, we cross the river to **Wark-on-Tyne** *(Battlesteads),* once the capital of the regality of Tynedale (it still has its old motte-hill), and go on up the dale by B6320 for **Bellingham** (pronounced *Bellin-jam*), whose church, partly of the 13th century, has an unusual stone-vaulted nave (probably of the 17th century).

B6320 climbs out over the moors for Otterburn, but an unclassified road continues up North Tynedale, entering the **Border Forest Park,** a large area of remote country, partly of barren moorland but including the largest man-made forest in Britain. At **Lewisburn** is a museum *(Easter-Sept., Sats and Suns, 2 to 5; daily during the last week in July and in Aug.)* depicting the varied wild life of the forest, and at **Kielder** is a village built in 1952 by the Forestry Commission, near the 18th-century *Kielder Castle,* formerly a shooting-lodge of the Duke of Northumberland. Beyond this the road crosses the Border to Liddesdale, in Scotland.

A69 goes on through charming country south of the Tyne. A road on the right in 2 miles leads to **Warden,** which has a Saxon church tower incorporating a Roman arch, near the junction of the North and South Tynes. The main road crosses the South Tyne at the small town of **Haydon Bridge.**

A686, on the left before this, ascends steadily past **Langley Castle** *(May-Sept, Weds, 2 to 7),* an imposing 14th-century tower house, well restored and now a school. A turning on the left farther on, B6295, descends to **Allendale Town** *(Hotspur, Riding, Dale),* a small agricultural town and summer resort above the East Allen. This road ascends the pastoral and wooded dale, among high moorlands, to **Allenheads,** a secluded hamlet near the head of the dale, then climbs over towards the head of Weardale. A868 *(see* above) drops down in great zigzags to the beautifully wooded valley of the Allen below the junction of its two branches. It then goes up a section of West Allendale before climbing out and over the open moors to **Alston,** in Cumberland.

A69 continues westward up South Tynedale to **Bardon Mill** (the nearest point on this road to Housesteads) and thence to **Haltwhistle,** an attractive small market town with a good 13th-century church. At **Greenhead** it is joined by the road along Hadrian's Wall *(see* below), and farther on it crosses the Cumberland boundary on its way to **Carlisle.**

NEWCASTLE TO CARLISLE VIA HADRIAN'S WALL

As far as Greenhead, this road follows the line of **Hadrian's Wall,** the great fortification built between A.D. 122 and 130, under the orders of the Emperor Hadrian, as the frontier in Britain of the Roman Empire. The wall stretched for over 73 miles from Wallsend on the Tyne through Northumberland and Cumberland to Bowness-on-Solway. Here our road (B6318) keeps straight on. There is little to see of the wall for the first few miles, as it was pulled down to provide a foundation for the road, constructed after the Jacobite rising of 1745, when the Hanoverian troops were unable to get across country to come to grips with Bonnie Prince Charlie. On the right, however, can be seen the ditch which followed the wall for much of its course, and on the left is the *Vallum*, a flat-bottomed ditch designed to protect the fortification on the south side. The road runs through high-lying country to **Stagshawbank,** an open common once noted for its large sheep fair, at the point where the Wall was penetrated by Dere Street, leading from Corstopitum into what is now Scotland.

Beyond **St. Oswald's,** a solitary 18th-century chapel marking the spot where Oswald, the Christian King of Northumbria, pitched his camp before the battle of 634 in which he defeated the heathen King Cadwalla, the steep Brunton Bank descends into the valley of the North Tyne. On the left of the Hexham road is a good length of Hadrian's Wall, which stood originally about 15 feet high and measures up to 9 feet thick, together with a fine example of a turret. These were small tower blocks with accommodation for a few soldiers and there were two between each milecastle, the barrack buildings about one Roman mile (1,620 yards) apart, from which the wall was patrolled.

B6318 crosses the North Tyne at **Chollerford** *(George)* and a little beyond is the entrance to *Chesters,* which has a fine park containing the remains of the Roman cavalry fort of *Cilurnum (daily),* one of the seventeen large forts, all of "playing-card" shape, which stood on the Wall. Near the bank of the river is the large bath-house, the best-preserved in Britain, and on the farther bank is the abutment of the bridge which carried the wall and the Roman military road across the river. The museum contains a large and fine collection of antiquities.

Our road climbs west from the valley to **Limestone Corner,** which commands a wide view over North Tynedale to the Cheviot Hills. Beyond the farm of **Carrawburgh** (pronounced *-bruff*) are the earthworks of the fort of *Brocolitia,* outside which is a remarkable Temple of Mithras, of the 3rd century, discovered in 1950. Before the farm of **Sewingshields,** the road, cutting through the Vallum, diverges left from the line of Hadrian's Wall, which climbs along the crest of the Great Whin Sill, a long outcrop of basaltic rock.

The road, continuing through wild and beautiful country, runs about ½-mile south of **Housesteads,** a farm near the remains of the infantry fort of *Vercovicium (daily, 9.30 or 10 to 4.30, 5.30 or 7; Suns from 2 in winter),* the most interesting as well as the finest in situation of all the forts on the Wall. The Wall itself can be followed on foot to the west, where there is an excellent example of a milecastle, on the lip of the basaltic crags, while to the north, among the desolate moorlands stretching away towards the Border, are the small Northumberland Lakes.

B6318 goes on to the *Twice Brewed Inn,* near an information centre of the Northumberland National Park. The road on the right here leads to **Steel Rigg,** where another section of the wall may be walked. To the west rises **Winshields Crag,** the highest point attained by the wall (1,230 feet), with a view extending to the Border Hills, in the north, Cross Fell on the Pennines to the south, and Skiddaw and Saddleback in the Lake District to the south-west. The road goes down to **Greenhead,** on a tributary of the South Tyne, at the junction with the main Newcastle-Carlisle road.

B6318, on the right here, leads to **Gilsland** *(Station),* an angling resort and a former spa in the valley of the Irthing. To the west of it are other fine stretches of Hadrian's Wall, descending to *Willowford Farm,* beyond which can be seen the abutment of the bridge by which the wall crossed the river, while high on the farther bank (in Cumberland) is the farm of *Birdoswald,* adjoining the large fort of *Camboglanna (daily, on application).*

NEWCASTLE TO JEDBURGH VIA OTTERBURN

A696, the beginning of the finest of the roads across the Border into Scotland, runs north-west from Newcastle to **Ponteland,** now the nucleus of a residential area, with an interesting 12th–14th-century church. The road continues through quiet pastoral country to **Belsay,** a small estate village of about 1840 outside the beautiful grounds of Belsay Hall. A696, passing below **Shaftoe Crags,** where the Earl of Derwentwater hid before the Jacobite Rising of 1715, leaves on the right a road to Wallington. The main road passes north of **Capheaton,** with a fine 17th-century hall where Swinburne the poet lived with his grandfather, and **Kirkharle,** the birthplace of "Capability" Brown, the famous 18th-century landscape-gardener.

A696 crosses the Alnwick-Rothbury road to **Kirkwhelpington,** from which it climbs over a fine sweep of moorlands to **Otterburn** *(Percy Arms, Otterburn Tower),* a small village in the broad upland valley of the Rede.

Otterburn is well known for the battle fought here in 1388, when the invading Scots led by the Earl of Douglas defeated the English under Harry Hotspur, an encounter celebrated in the Scottish ballad of "The Battle of Otterbourne" and the English ballad of "Chevy Chase".

B6341, on the right before Otterburn, leads to Rothbury via **Elsdon,** built round a large green, with a fine example of a fortified priest's house, of about 1400, and a 14th-century church with unusual vaulted aisles, perhaps of the 17th century.

Beyond Otterburn, A696 joins A68 (coming from Corbridge), which ascends the wild Redesdale via **Rochester** *(Redesdale Arms),* with some remains of the Roman fort of *Bremenium,* on Dere Street, and **Byrness** a village built by the Forestry Commission on the edge of the Border Forest Park. The road passes the attractive **Catcleugh Reservoir,** then climbs up from the head of the dale to **Carter Bar** (1,370 feet), where it crosses the watershed and passes from England into Scotland, the finest of all the Border crossings. This was the site of the "Raid of the Reidswire", the last of the Border battles (1575), and the splendid view includes the Cheviot Hills, on the Border, and the Lammermuirs, the Eildon Hills and Ettrick Forest, all in Scotland.

A68 winds down into the valley of the Jed Water, on the Scottish side, for **Jedburgh.**

NEWCASTLE TO TYNEMOUTH AND WHITLEY BAY

The best route from Newcastle to the popular seaside resorts of Tynemouth and Whitley Bay is A1058, which avoids Wallsend and other shipbuilding and engineering places on the north bank of the Tyne.

Tynemouth

Distances.—Morpeth, 17; Newcastle upon Tyne, 9; London, 281; South Shields, 9.
Early Closing.—Wednesday.
Entertainments.—Cinemas, operatic and dramatic societies, dancing.

Hotels.—*Grand, Park.*
Population.—68,740.
Post Office.—Saville Street, North Shields.
Sports.—Boating, bowls, tennis, golf, cricket. Indoor and open-air pools.

Tynemouth is a residential town and a sea-bathing and sailing resort with excellent sands and a bracing atmosphere. On a bold headland overlooking the estuary of the river is the *Priory (daily),* refounded in 1090 for Benedictines. The ruins consist mainly of the 12th- and 13th-century church with the vaulted 15th-century Percy Chantry, approached through a 14th-century gatehouse-tower and barbican, part of the so-called Castle.

From **North Shields,** a fishing port adjoining Tynemouth, a car ferry crosses the Tyne to South Shields.

A193 runs north from Tynemouth through **Cullercoats** *(Bay),* once a fishing village, to Whitley Bay.

Whitley Bay

Early Closing.—Wednesday.
Hotels.—*Esplanade, Royal, Rex, Holmedale, Hamilton, Newquay, Station,* and many others.

Population.—37,830.
Sports.—Bathing, sea angling, golf, etc.

Whitley Bay is the most popular seaside resort on the north-east coast, with good sands, a long breezy promenade, colourful gardens, and a fine open greensward, The Links, to the north. At the north end of the bay is **St. Mary's Island,** with its attractive lighthouse, accessible at low tide by a causeway.

A193 continues north along the coast to the port of **Blyth,** passing the small seaside resort of **Seaton Sluice,** which has a disused harbour, cut out of the solid rock by the Delavals in the early 17th century. A190 turns inland beyond this for **Seaton Delaval Hall** *(May-Sept., Weds, Suns and Bank Hols, 2 to 6),* the last masterpiece of Sir John Vanbrugh, built in 1718–29 and restored after a fire in 1822. The fine west wing contains furniture, Oriental porcelain and portraits of the Delavals, and the tiny Norman church close by is also of interest.

NEWCASTLE TO ALNWICK VIA MORPETH

This route follows the Great North Road (A1) through the favoured residential suburb of **Gosforth** and passes **Gosforth Park,** with its racecourse. It leaves the coalfield beyond **Seaton Burn,** where a road (A1068) branches right for Alnwick via Warkworth, and crosses the river Blyth at **Stannington** before reaching Morpeth, which is now being provided with a by-pass.

Morpeth (Pop.: 14,050. Hotels: *Queen's Head, Newcastle House*) is an old market town in the charmingly wooded valley of the Wansbeck. To the south of the river are the fine 14th-century parish church, and the motte and 14th-century gatehouse of the castle. Facing the market place are the 15th-century Curfew Tower and the Town Hall, built in 1714 by Vanbrugh.

Bothal, four miles downstream and reached via the Newbiggin road (A197) is a small model village with a 13th–14th-century church and the fine 14th-century gatehouse-tower of a ruined castle. On B6343, upstream, **Mitford** has a ruined castle and a restored church, both of the 12th and 13th centuries, attractively situated in the wooded glen.

A697, diverging left from the Alnwick road about three miles north of Morpeth (*see* below), is an interesting route to the Border. It crosses the Coquet at **Weldon Bridge** *(Anglers Arms),* where B6344 branches left for Rothbury, passing near **Brinkburn Priory** *(daily),* an Augustinian foundation of which the well-restored 12th-century church survives, hidden away in the depths of the dale.

Climbing on to the heather-covered moors, A697 crosses the Rothbury-Alnwick road and passes east of **Whittingham** (pronounce *Whittin-jam*), a pleasant village on the Aln with a 15th-century tower-house and a church with a Saxon tower. **Callaly Castle** *(June-Sept., Sats, Suns and Bank Hols),* below finely wooded crags to the south, consists of a 15th-century tower-house charmingly added to in the 17th and 18th centuries.

A697 goes on over the Breamish, up whose sequestered valley a by-road runs to **Ingram,** a remote village which has an information centre for the Northumberland National Park. The main road skirts the foothills of the Cheviots before reaching Wooler, on the route from Alnwick to Coldstream.

A1 continues northward from Morpeth, leaving the road to Wooler and Coldstream on the left (*see* above) and crossing the beautiful Coquet at **Felton,** which has an interesting church. It then goes on through upland country, with wide views, to Alnwick.

Alnwick

Distances.—Berwick-upon-Tweed, 29; Edinburgh, 80; Newcastle upon Tyne, 34; London, 308.
Early Closing.—Wednesday.

Hotel.—*White Swan.*
Market Day.—Monday.
Population.—7,570.

Alnwick (pronounced *An-nick*) is a delightful stone-built market town finely placed on a hill above the river Aln. It is entered at the south end by the **Hotspur Gate,** the only relic of the medieval town walls. In the charming Market Place are the 18th-century **Town Hall** and the classical **Northumberland Hall,** an assembly hall of 1826. **St. Michael's,** the interesting parish church, of the 14th and 15th centuries, lies to the north-west, beside the Wooler road.

Alnwick Castle *(May-Sept., Sun. to Thurs., 1 to 5)*, in a beautiful park, is one of the most splendid fortified houses in the country. Since 1309 it has been the principal stronghold of the powerful Percy family, of whom the most famous was Harry Percy, son of the 1st Earl of Northumberland. Celebrated by Shakespeare as "that Hotspur of the North" (in *Henry IV*), he was killed at the battle of Shrewsbury in 1403.

The oldest parts of the castle are the 12th-century walls, strengthened by the 1st Lord Percy in the early 14th century, when the towers were added. An imposing gatehouse of about 1400, defended by a formidable barbican or outer gate, admits to the outer courtyard or bailey, while the inner courtyard is reached from the middle bailey by a mid-14th-century gatehouse. The medieval keep was much restored in about 1764 for the 1st Duke of Northumberland, but the impressive state rooms here were mostly reconstructed in 1854–65 for the 4th Duke, who employed Italian artists to decorate them. The rooms contain Italian and other paintings and ornate 18th-century French furniture. The 14th-century Postern Tower, east of the keep, holds a collection of medieval and other antiquities.

ALNWICK TO HEXHAM VIA ROTHBURY

This quiet cross-country route, linking the Northumbrian coast with upper Tynedale, leaves Alnwick on the south-west by B6341, which ascends on to the heathery uplands of Alnwick Moor, affording a fine distant view of the Cheviot Hills. It crosses the Morpeth-Wooler road and goes on over the moors of Rothbury Forest before descending to Rothbury.

Rothbury (Pop.: 2,500. Hotels: *Newcastle House, Coquet Vale*) is an attractive market town, with a wide green, in a very beautiful part of Coquetdale, facing across the river to the serrated ridge of the Simonside Hills (1,447 feet). The much rebuilt Church contains a font with a stem made from a carved Northumbrian cross of the 9th century and a bowl dated 1664. To the east of the town, reached by the Weldon Bridge road, are the lovely grounds of **Cragside** *(Easter-Sept., daily, 10 to 8)*, remarkable especially for their rhododendrons. The house was built in 1870 by R. Norman Shaw for Lord Armstrong, the engineer.

B6341, crossing the Coquet beyond Flotterton and running through a valley west of the Simonsides, leads to Otterburn via Elsdon.

From Flotterton a charming road ascends the Coquet to **Harbottle,** which has the remains of a 12th-century castle, and **Alwinton,** the highest village in the dale, beyond which it enters a deep and lonely defile in the Cheviot Hills. We skirt the boundary of the large Redesdale Artillery Range as far as the farm of **Fulhope,** near the head of the dale, beyond which the road (closed when the range is in use) climbs out and over the moors for Rochester.

The Hexham road (B6342) runs south from Rothbury, skirting the east side of the heather-covered Simonsides. It goes on through open, little-visited country to **Wallington** *(Apr.-Sept., daily except Tues and Fris)* now in the care of the National Trust, a delightful house of the 17th and 18th centuries, with fine plasterwork done by Italian craftsmen and one of the best collections of porcelain in England. The central hall, built after 1846, has scenes from Northumbrian history painted by John Ruskin, William Bell Scott and others. The grounds are charming.

B6342 reaches the Newcastle-Jedburgh road, from which A6079 continues through quiet moorland country, crossing the line of Dere Street (A68), and **Chollerton,** it is joined by the road up the east side of North Tynedale. Thence to **Hexham.**

ALNWICK TO COLDSTREAM VIA WOOLER

This very attractive road (B6346) from Alnwick crosses the Aln and skirts the large and beautifully-wooded **Hulne Park** *(no cars admitted; permits for walkers from Alnwick Castle estate office).* Near the entrance is a 14th-century gatehouse, the only survival of **Alnwick Abbey,** a Premonstratensian house founded in 1147, and a footpath runs through the park for 1½ miles to the sequestered 13th-century ruins of **Hulne Abbey,** the oldest and best-preserved example of a Carmelite friary in England.

Beyond **Eglingham,** B6346 bears left over the Breamish to the main Morpeth-Wooler road; the unclassified road straight on, east of the river, leads to **Chillingham,** a secluded village with a church containing the elaborate tomb of Sir Ralph Grey *(died* 1443). The Greys lived at **Chillingham Castle,** built in the 14th century but altered since. Beyond the castle, towards the slopes of Ros Castle, a height on the Great Whin Sill, rises the beautiful park *(weekdays, except Tues, 10 to 5; Suns 2 to 5),* in which can be seen the last wild cattle in England, a herd emparked here for over 700 years. The cattle, invariably pure white in colour, are usually peaceable, but must not be approached.

At **Chatton,** to the north of Chillingham, we turn left on B6348, crossing the broad valley of the Till (the lower section of the Breamish) to Wooler.

Wooler (Pop.: 2,000. Hotels: *Tankerville Arms, Black Bull, Ryecroft*) is an old-fashioned market town on a hill above the wide strath of the Till and at the north-east edge of the Cheviot Hills, for which it forms the best touring centre, though few roads penetrate far into the hills, which can be adequately explored only by walkers.

A quiet road, leaving the town on the south, ascends the beautiful valley of the Harthope Burn to **Langleeford,** below the northern flanks of **Hedgehope** (2,348 feet). A cart-road goes on thence to **Langleeford Hope,** the last farm in the glen, and the nearest point for the ascent (steep, hard going) of **The Cheviot** (2,676 feet), the highest summit of the Cheviot Hills, covered by a vast waste of desolate peat hags (good views from the edges only). The descent may be made by the fine ravine of Henhole and the College Valley *(see below).*

From Akeld *(see below),* B6351 goes on through the lovely valley of the Glen, skirting the distinctive hill of **Yeavering Bell** (1,182 feet), below which is the site of a unique 7th-century palace of the Kings of Northumbria. Beyond **Kirknewton,** whose church has unusual 13th-century vaults in the chancel and transept, a by-road branches left up the remote valley of the College Burn, which rises on the west slopes of The Cheviot (*see* above). The road is public only as far as the hamlet of **Hethpool**; beyond that motorists require permits from the Estate Office in Wooler. B6351 continues up the valley of the Bowmont Water for Yetholm, in Scotland.

A697 runs north-west from Wooler, skirting the Cheviot Hills, to **Akeld** (*compare* above), then crosses the Glen and follows the west side of the broad Till Valley.

On the other side of the river (and reached by B6354) is **Ford,** an estate village built after 1859 for the Marchioness of Waterford, who herself painted the murals of Biblical scenes (incorporating villagers) in the school. The church dates mainly from the 13th century, the castle from the 14th century, though much restored. Farther north (by B6354) is **Etal** (pronounce *E-tal*), a charming village of whitewashed houses, with the 18th-century manor house at one end and a ruined 14th-century castle at the other.

Beyond Crookham, an unclassified road on the left leads through **Branxton** to north side of **Flodden Field,** where a monument indicates the site of the battle of 1513 in which an English force led by the Earl of Surrey defeated the invading Scottish army under James IV, who was killed with many of his nobles. The road north from Branxton church regains A697, which joins the Berwick-Coldstream road at **Cornhill.**

ALNWICK TO BERWICK VIA BAMBURGH

This road, a longer but much more interesting alternative to the Great North Road, follows A1068 from Alnwick, crossing the Aln to **Lesbury,** beyond which B1338 turns left for **Alnmouth** *(Schooner, Hope & Anchor),* on the estuary of the Aln, an attractive little seaside resort with good sands and an excellent golf course.

A1068 goes on south to **Warkworth** *(Sun, Warkworth House),* a village beautifully placed on a peninsula almost surrounded by the Coquet, which is crossed by a fortified 14th-century bridge. The fine church, near by, is partly of the 12th and 14th centuries, with a tower and spire of about 1200. From the market place the steep main street ascends to the **Castle** *(daily),* since 1332 a magnificent stronghold of the Percy family, as described by Shakespeare in *Henry IV.* The extensive ruins, mostly of the 13th century, include the imposing gatehouse and the great hall, with the attached Lion Tower, added about 1480. The unusual keep, on the motte to the north, dates from the 15th century. On the north bank of the Coquet, and reached from the castle by boat, is a singular 14th-century Hermitage *(admission as for castle),* hewn out of the sandstone rock.

From Lesbury, B1339 runs north to Longhoughton, beyond which an un-classified road bears right to **Howick,** beautifully secluded in a wooded valley. In the church is a monument to the 2nd Earl Grey, promoter of the Reform Bill of 1832, who lived at **Howick Hall** (1782; *April-Sept., daily, 2 to 7),* which has charming gardens. The road hence goes on north for **Craster,** a fishing village with a small harbour.

A footpath leads along the coast for 1½ miles to **Dunstanburgh Castle** *(daily),* on a basaltic rock which is an outcrop of the Great Whin Sill. Begun in 1313 by Thomas, Earl of Lancaster, to command a small harbour in the cliffs, it comprises an immense open bailey, surrounded by a long wall with towers and reached through an impressive gatehouse-tower, altered about 1380 for John of Gaunt.

The road from Craster runs inland to **Embleton** *(Dunstanburgh Castle)*, which has a 13th-century church and a restored 14th-century priest's house fortified in the Northumbrian manner. B1339, continuing north, joins B1340, which regains the coast at **Beadnell** *(Beadnell Towers, Craster Arms)*, a fishing village and a quiet summer resort, with fine sands and a view across its bay to Dunstanburgh Castle. Farther on is **Seahouses** *(Bamburgh Castle, Dunes, Beach House, Links)*, a popular seaside resort and a fishing village.

The busy harbour is the place of embarkation *(motor-boats daily in summer, tides permitting)* for the **Farne Islands,** the easternmost extremity of the Great Whin Sill, consisting of some thirty small islands and rocks, between 1½ and 5 miles from the shore. The islands are famous as a breeding-place for sea-birds and grey seals, and the best time to see them is late May and early June. St. Cuthbert died in 687 on the Inner Farne, the largest island, which has striking cliffs up to 80 feet high.

B1340 goes on, skirting a long belt of sand dunes, to Bamburgh.
Bamburgh (Hotels: *Lord Crewe Arms, Mizen Head, Victoria, Radcliffe*), a charming village mainly built round a green, was the capital of Northumbria from the 6th to the 8th century. The fine Church, mostly of the 13th century, has an unusual vaulted crypt below the long chancel. In the churchyard is the elaborate tomb of Grace Darling, and in the Memorial Museum opposite *(daily in summer)* is the small boat in which she set out with her father from Longstone, the outermost of the Farnes, to rescue the survivors of the *Forfarshire,* wrecked in 1838.

Above the village, on a huge basaltic rock, rises the dominating **Castle** *(Easter-Sept., daily, 2 to 8)*, a royal stronghold from the Norman period to the time of Henry VI. The splendid keep dates from the 12th century, but the state apartments were rather too well restored in the 18th century and again after 1894 for Lord Armstrong, the engineer.

B1342 runs inland from Bamburgh, skirting the broad sands of Budle Bay, to reach the Great North Road south of **Belford.** Thence to Berwick, *see* below.

ALNWICK TO BERWICK AND THENCE TO COLDSTREAM

The Great North Road (A1), less interesting than the coast road *(see* above), crosses the Aln north of **Alnwick Castle** by the Lion Bridge, built in 1773 by Robert Adam and surmounted by the Percy lion, and runs north through open country (wide views) to **Belford** *(Blue Bell, Black Swan)*, a small market town and once an important coaching stage. A1 goes on, east of the wooded Kyloe Hills, to **West Mains.** Here a road descends on the right to the coast, where a causeway (dry only for about 5 hours at low tide) crosses the broad sands to Holy Island.

Holy Island *(Northumberland Arms, Lindisfarne)*, formerly named Lindisfarne, was the birthplace of Christianity in the North of England. St. Aidan, invited from Iona (in Scotland) by Oswald, the Christian king of Northumbria, established a bishopric in 635. St. Cuthbert, who became bishop in 684, was buried here, but in 875, when the Vikings desecrated the monastery, the monks fled, carrying the saint's body. **Lindisfarne Priory** *(daily, Suns in winter from 2)* was refounded after 1081 for Benedictines; the ruins consist of the 12th-century church, with decoration resembling that in the cathedral at Durham, and the fortified domestic buildings, of the 13th and 14th centuries. Close by is the 12th- and 13th-century church of the village, also called Holy Island. On the other side of the bay rises the restored **Lindisfarne Castle** *(April-Sept., usually daily, except Tues, 2 to 6)*, built about 1550, on a precipitous basaltic rock.

A1 continues from West Mains to **Tweedmouth,** where it crosses the river to Berwick.

Berwick-upon-Tweed

Distances.—Alnwick, 29; Edinburgh, 57; London, 337; Newcastle upon Tyne, 63.
Early Closing.—Thursday.
Fishing.—In the *Tweed* (famous for salmon), from the pier and from boats off river mouth.
Hotels.—*King's Arms, Castle, Tweed View, Castle Vale* and others.

Post Office.—Woolmarket.
Library.—Museum Buildings, Marygate.
Population.—11,300.
Sports.—Golf, bowls, tennis, water sports, speedway.

Berwick is a delightful old port and fishing town and a market town on the north bank of the Tweed, near its mouth. Originally in Scotland, it changed hands no less than thirteen times from 1147 to 1482, when it was finally taken by the English, and it is now part of Northumberland. The narrow 17th-century Old

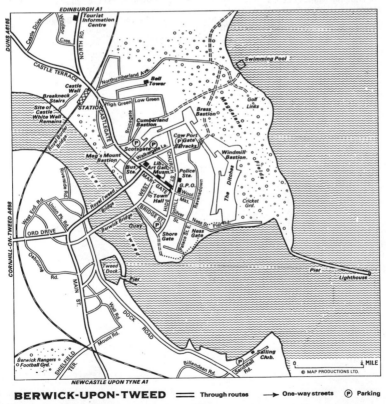

BERWICK-UPON-TWEED ══ Through routes ⟶ One-way streets ℗ Parking

435

Bridge has been supplemented by the Royal Tweed Bridge, a concrete road bridge of 1928, while upstream is the Royal Border Bridge of the railway, built in 1847 by Robert Stephenson. At the foot of Marygate, the main street, is the prominent 18th-century Town Hall, and to the north of this is the classical Parish Church of 1652, one of the very few built in England during the Commonwealth.

Marygate, at its upper end, penetrates the Elizabethan Ramparts, a unique and interesting system of fortifications constructed in 1558–69 as a bastion against the Scots. Of the previous town walls, built during the reign of Edward I, the only surviving section descends the steep slope to the river west of the station, which itself stands on the site of the castle where the king delivered judgement in 1292 in favour of the claim of John Baliol to the Scottish throne.

From Tweedmouth, A698 and B6470 (on the right) ascend the south side of the river for **Norham,** which has a large green and a fine church, partly Norman, where Edward I summoned a convention in 1290 to decide between the rival claims of John Baliol and Robert Bruce to the Scottish throne. The imposing Castle *(daily, from 9.30; Suns from 2),* facing across the Tweed into Scotland, was from 1121 a frontier stronghold of the prince-bishops of Durham. Mainly of the 12th century, it was partly rebuilt after 1513, when it was attacked by James IV on his way to Flodden Field.

A698 goes on across the deep-set Till by the graceful 15th-century **Twizel Bridge,** near the *Tillmouth Park Hotel,* and at **Cornhill** *(Collingwood Arms)* it is joined by the road from Wooler. It then crosses the Tweed to **Coldstream,** in Scotland.

Index

437